ORGANIZATIONAL BEHAVIOR
ITS DATA, FIRST PRINCIPLES, AND APPLICATIONS

ORGANIZATIONAL BEHAVIOR

Its data, first principles, and applications

JOE KELLY
Professor of Management
Concordia University

1980   THIRD EDITION

RICHARD D. IRWIN, INC.   Homewood, Illinois   60430
Irwin-Dorsey Limited   Georgetown, Ontario   L7G 4B3

ISBN 0-256-02284-4
Library of Congress Catalog Card No. 79–90542

Printed in the United States of America

1 2 3 4 5 6 7 8 9 MP 7 6 5 4 3 2 1 0

Preface

The overall objective of this Third Edition is to make this book available to a wider audience of students, while still maintaining a high level of academic probity in the actual writing. An impossible dream? Perhaps. But fortunately I was able to draw on a range of useful advice provided by a number of professors of organizational behavior who had used the Second Edition to teach either undergraduates or graduate classes. In some respects, their advice could be followed in a fairly straightforward way. What these professors argued for and what I have set out to implement is to write a somewhat shorter, better structured, more easily read text which could be used by a wider range of students. Before plunging into the academic objective of the book, I would like to say something about the format of the text which can make or mar the pleasure and ease of reading, irrespective of the academic message.

A somewhat different chapter format is used, which I hope retains the better features of the previous editions but adds something significant which helps the reader to find the way more easily through the dense and sometimes apparently (and occasionally actually) contradictory elements of organizational behavior. This new method which many fine teachers use is called the diagram approach. To get the reader going each chapter begins with an incident, typically a management encounter which sets the tone for the chapter. Next comes the diagram which gives an overview of the chapter, spelling out the main topics and hinting at possible elements and themes. Then follows the actual material organized by topics and supplemented by boxes of research material. The chapter closes with a summary, questions, glossary, and a debate, and where appropriate, incidents and exercises.

The academic objective of this Third Edition of *Organizational Behavior* is to set out in a comprehensive and comprehensible way what we know about this burgeoning field of knowledge, which is now struggling out of its adolescence and is facing an intellectual identity crisis. To understand this crisis it is necessary to begin with the facts, the bare behavioral facts of organizational life. And while there is a surfeit of empirical facts about people in organizations, they do not come to us untrammeled.

To exploit and make the best of this Hawthorne Effect that behavioral facts are always seen through the lens of a particular paradigm or model, organizational behavior is viewed as empirical, interpretive, and revolutionary or consciousness raising.

Its empirical base is well established and continues to grow, perhaps too much like Topsy. In many ways, we have taken in more facts than we can digest. To try to bring this vast factual feast under some degree of control, it is necessary to introduce model building at the earliest possible stage. The structure (the actors), process (the plot of events), values (the magic) model is given further development to bring out its drama and existential elements. Analysis is still needed, but so is synthesis.

Analysis we know about, but synthesis is harder. This is the new problem in OB. How do you put the facts together to make organizational life meaningful? The answer used to be and still is, "It all depends; it's a matter of contingencies." And we went off on a wild-goose chase for contingency theories which were seen as the missing links in The Big Picture. Well, we were wrong-headed. We built contingency theories that at first sight were beautiful behavioral cathedrals which were all light and airy. But as more ugly facts emerged, the contingency cathedral became more rococo until the arches began to sag. We had overreached ourselves.

To begin again we have to have a more modest aim. Certainly we have to begin with the facts. But we have to keep in mind that, "we describe what we see; we see what we describe." Thus it is always a question of interpretation. People want to make life meaningful and they perceive and record accordingly. Hence the immense importance of the discovery that the two hemispheres of the brain do different things—one a rational computer, the other an intuitive Ouija board. Effective executives exercise both hemispheres. But making OB a simultaneous double header requires a certain artistic as well as scientific skill.

All is not lost in this more androgynous approach to OB. It is still necessary to look to the great interpreters of business behavior. It is still necessary to look at classical, human relations, and systems theory. But it is no longer the question of asking whether they are true or false. The object of the exercise is to understand not only what these theories say in terms of propositions and where they came from historically, but also how they can be applied.

Pausing for a moment, thus far we have spoken of the empirical and interpretative aspects of OB. We have still to justify its revolutionary aspects. We shall return to this aspect in a moment. What about the contents of OB?

Part I deals with the three theories of organizations, the classical, human relations, and systems. The classical theory is approached practically as the basis of traditional management, of how to get things on schedule, and the like. Human relations is moving slowly away from Hawthorne towards human resources planning. Systems is all about chunking information, and for me, why are airline pilots fighting with directors of in-flight service? It's all a question of sociotechnical systems.

Part II deals with personality and motivation. A separate chapter deals with executive career development and all its attendant anomalies and achievements. Another new chapter has as its subject the modern executive: male and female. The androgynous argument is gone into in some detail.

Part III deals with group dynamics. Of especial interest is the chapter on leadership. While Fred E. Fiedler and Robert J. House are still there in more modest measures, the aim is to come up with something more practical and relevant.

Part IV has as its focus the organization. We begin with a brief look at the rise and fall of the organization. Next we turn to organizational politics, which is essentially concerned with the struggle between power and authority, organizational Watergates and the Looking Glass War. Next, we turn to "Conspiracies Theories versus Pluralism." Our last chapter in Part IV deals with the organization and its environment.

Part V deals with organizational decision making, conflict, and development. The new approach to decision making tells us the score. There is still material on rational decision making. But how do managers make decisions? We can develop useful models by careful analysis of well-documented decisions such as the Cuban Missile Crisis, leading to Graham T. Allison's three models: rational, process, and political. Inevitably decision making involves conflict management. What's new in conflict management? The answer is that it is now possible to develop a more effective and meaningful structure, process, values model of conflict.

You may say what's so revolutionary about all this? Old wine in new bottles. True, true, but the labeling on the bottles has changed. OB is no longer presented as being based on psychology, sociology, psychiatry and therefore scientific. OB is not a subdivision of management or even business.

Organizational behavior is an optic, a perspective, a process for looking at events, a way of life. It has empirical facts, interested and interesting interpretations, and powerful paradigms. But what's revolutionary and consciousness raising about it? The answer is that you cannot fully understand bounded rationality ("there's more out there than you can think"), autocratic-submissive relations ("I really like my boss"), the distribution of roles in a work group ("I'll play doctor, so you can play patient"), the male-female allocation of abilities ("Me Tarzan, you Jane"), and so on, without beginning to realize that unbeknownst to yourself you have slipped your intellectual anchor. And where will the good space ship called OB come to rest? It won't.

April 1980   Joe Kelly

Contents

ORGANIZATIONAL BEHAVIOR
ITS DATA, FIRST PRINCIPLES, AND APPLICATIONS

DIAGRAM SUMMARY OF CHAPTER 1

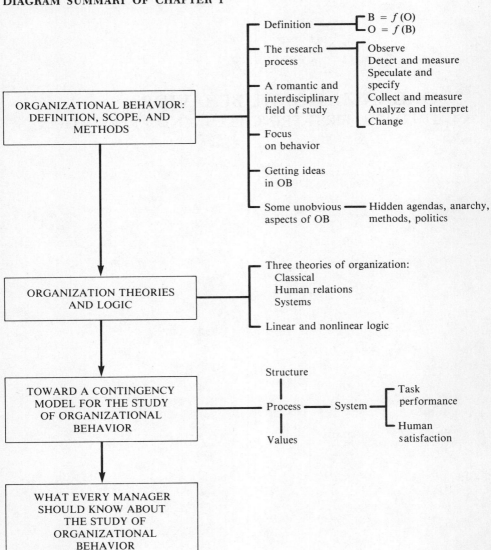

1

Getting into organizational behavior

HOW TO MAKE WORK FUN

Carla has quit a high-paying, esteem-lowering job as a manager of a fast food restaurant of a well-known chain to go back to school to study business. She is visiting Rick, an old friend from her last year of undergraduate school who is also in the business school. Rick is puzzled why she would throw over a good-paying, solid job.

RICK: I know—you got fired.

CARLA: No, I fired them.

RICK: What you want to go and do that for?

CARLA: I knew you would say that.

RICK: Come on. You had it made.

CARLA: I know I'm young, I'm intelligent, I can manage people and facilities. But I'm bored. I'm not going to spend the rest of my life watching a bunch of high school dropouts drool over burgers served up with tender, loving care.

RICK: What do you want? What do you think you are going to get in business school?

CARLA: I don't know. At least I'm not sure. But I believe what Woody Allen said about work. He said that the things that are really pleasurable in life, whether it's work or playing softball or working on your stamp collection, really require no effort.

RICK: What subject in this business school is going to make work fun—an entertaining, amusing, enlightening, movable feast that gets things done? You tell me.

CARLA: I think OB will. It's all about organizations . . . how to put 2 and 2 together to get 5, or to get 3 if your enemies are throwing the dice . . . how to make conflict work for you. . . .

RICK: I can see you've read too many pop-psych books. I'll bet you don't even know what OB is.

3

ORGANIZATIONAL BEHAVIOR IS SIMPLY . . .

You know that strange feeling you get when you do something out of step, like walking into the wrong washroom? Everybody sends you a message, but nothing is actually said. Well, organizational behavior is in somewhat the same position. OB is taught in the business school, though it would probably be more at home in the school of dramatic arts. Sometimes it's straight out of the theater of the absurd: subordinates thank their bosses for firing them. Sometimes it's out of the theater of cruelty; the minority rules the majority by refusing to come on board.

OB uses many methods and a good deal of mathematics. It is not as respectable as psychology but it tries harder (which can be very trying). Sometimes it proves the obvious, like the fact that bosses believe in the organization more than the employees do. Sometimes it is cute—Murphy's law (Anything that can go wrong will), the Peter Principle (People float up to their own level of incompetence), Parkinson's law (Work expands to fill the available time). Sometimes it accomplishes crazy things: Healthy people are sent into mental hospitals to do research, and some of them turn crazy.

OB people also have a strong need to bamboozle, to make the obvious more complex than it really is. They talk about n Ach when they mean the need to achieve. They often hide quite trivial findings in a sea of verbiage.

Nevertheless, OB is a growth industry, mainly because of consumer demand. Managers want a map (any map) and the navigational instruments to negotiate the world of the organization, a terrain as mysterious as the face of the moon.

TOPIC 1
Organizational behavior: Definition, scope, and methods

DEFINITION

$B = f(O)$ and $O = f(B)$

Organizational behavior is essentially concerned with what people do in organizations. Since the subject matter is behavior, it ought to lend itself to a scientific approach. But it is necessary to keep in mind that when people are brought together in organizations they behave differently. To hold this idea in sharp focus it is useful to keep the basic psychological process in mind—perception, emotion, and action. In organizations, people see the world differently than they do as individuals; they experience peculiar feelings; and act or behave in strange ways.

For example, studies of chief executives by Chris Argyris found that they behave in a rather aristocratic manner that places their subordinates in win-lose situations and generates feelings of dependency among them. In such a context subordinates are more likely to agree with the boss. In terms of the psychological process, they perceive the boss as threatening. They feel apprehensive, and they act in a conforming manner. Putting it thematically, B(behavior) = $f(O)$.

While bosses would be the last to admit this autocratic attitude, they are quite expert in winning consent. Perhaps from the superior's point of view the process could be called *consensus formation*. Irrespective of the subtle differences between conformity and consensus, this is what organizations are all about—focusing people's behavior on the task to be achieved. The organization is structuring their space, processing their behavior, and forming their values.

More technically put, an organization develops a structure (a framework of perceptions or roles), a process (a sequence of meaningful events) and values (a set of useful beliefs) for a purpose. Therefore, $O = f(B)$.

Now as the structure, process, and values of an organization develop, the individuals in it are required to join work groups. The formal, or upfront, organization consists of sections, departments, committees, and so on. But every formal organization also creates an informal one. We know from the research of Tom Burns, a sociologist at Edinburgh University, that cliques and cabals inevitably emerge to challenge and make fun of official authority. Such formal and informal groups fall within the domain of organizational behavior.

Thus the OB plot begins to thicken. To follow, you need to know something about not only individual psychology but also group dynamics. The real problem for OB, however, is to push beyond the individual and group levels to get to the organization.

A good working definition: organizational behavior is *the systematic study of the nature of organizations: how they begin, grow, and develop, and their effect on individual members, constituent groups, other organizations, and larger institutions.*

This definition encompasses the elements of earlier efforts to understand the interactions and relations between the organization and individual behavior. It indicates that the subject takes in and goes beyond psychology, group dynamics, organizational psychology, and industrial sociology, as illustrated in Figure 1–1.

To understand how organizational behavior developed, three points must be kept in mind. First, organization theories are culturally bound, that is, they are products of their times. Just as bureaucracy can be understood better if it is seen as an administrative device which the Prussians borrowed from the French to unify Germany, so can "adhocracy" be better understood as a purely American invention of the 20th

FIGURE 1-1
Organizational behavior

FOCUS	SUBJECT MATTER	TYPICAL PROBLEM
Individual	Industrial psychology	The relation between individual productivity and illumination in the work area.
Group	Group dynamics	How the primary working group restricts production and develops a value-norm-reinforcement-sanction system.
Organization	Organizational psychology	How an organization structures perceptions of different work groups.
Society	Industrial sociology	Conflict between organizations, such as unions versus business firms.

century—an instant-build, immediate-destruct system to get to the moon and back.

Second, you get the organization you deserve. For example, mass production developed as the product of the automobile assembly line, with ideas Henry Ford borrowed from the Chicago meat-processing factories, where the slaughtered animals were moved from one work station to another by overhead hook. This peculiarly American triumph is summed up in the industry's tough motto, "Move the iron." But it was the American dream of production in mass, low prices, and first-class wages which enabled Americans to buy what they built.

Third, organization theory is derivative; it derives its concepts, language, and ideas from other disciplines.

THE RESEARCH PROCESS

History has it that industrial psychology, an early precursor of organizational behavior, had its beginnings on December 20, 1901, when a group of Chicago businessmen were given a short talk about psychology's potential uses in advertising. Some eight decades later organizational behavior has become a large, complex, convoluted subject, with numerous fascinating issues. It is not only concerned with business but is also relevant to the study of other organizations, including those in military, religious, and leisure settings, among many others. Organizational behavior researchers are interested not only in developing behavioral experiments, but, also as Marvin Dunnette points out in the *Handbook of Industrial and Organizational Psychology,* "in such intriguing problems as basic strategies in Casino Blackjack, decision processes by baseball batters, and the epidemiology of ski injuries."

This variety has generated a considerable breadth of subject matter which makes the material difficult to summarize and organize. Dunnette nevertheless has devised a six-step plan for utilizing methods of inquiry to bring about organizational change (see Figure 1–2). The steps are:

1. *Observe* behavior of individuals in organizations in their natural settings.
2. *Detect and measure* differences in behavior against a standard criterion.
3. *Speculate and specify* by developing hypotheses which establish causal relations about the variables in consideration.
4. *Collect and measure* data that illuminate the problem under study.
5. *Analyze and interpret* the data and the process of working through this data to develop new hypotheses, models, and theories.
6. *Change* the situation, with a view to improving effectiveness or human satisfaction.

FIGURE 1–2
Steps in planning for change through organizational behavior

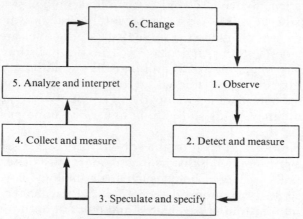

Source: Based on Marvin Dunnette, *Handbook of Industrial and Organizational Psychology* (Chicago: Rand McNally College Publishing Co., 1976), p. 10.

The student of organizational behavior, therefore, must develop considerable skill in theory building. As Kurt Lewin pointed out, nothing is more practical than a good theory. And of course theories represent a level of generalization that goes a step beyond statistical summary of the data. Indeed, many researchers in this field have shown great skill in building theories, although the data are only mildly suggestive of the theoretical direction they have taken. Not only are academics interested in theory building, so also are executives who wish to base their management decisions on empirical foundations and theoretically sound grounds.

As Robert Dubin points out in "Theory Building in Applied Areas":

> A theory is the attempt of man to model some aspect of the empirical world. The underlying motive for this modeling is either (1) that the real world is so complex it needs to be conceptually simplified in order to understand it, or (2) that observation by itself does not reveal ordered relationships among empirically detected entities. A theory tries to make sense out of the observable world by ordering the relationships among elements that constitute the theorist's focus of attention in the real world. The process of building a theory requires hard work and ingenuity.

But organizational behavior is not all hard work. It is, or can be, fun, mainly because so many of the things that happen in organizations are funny. But they don't seem too funny if you approach them strictly from a scientific point of view. This is rare in organizational behavior, in any case. A different approach is required.

A ROMANTIC AND INTERDISCIPLINARY FIELD OF STUDY

Organizational behavior is a rather nebulous field of study, and it is silly to consider it as if it had a specific intellectual jurisdiction. It can be described as romantic in the sense that its principles are difficult to define in scientific terms, and its boundaries are indistinct. Therefore it is necessary to approach OB problems like walking a line in a demarcation dispute. The student of OB must be something of a polymath—a person of encyclopedic learning—with interests in a variety of different fields and willing to act in a number of problem-solving areas.

Is OB multidisciplinary or interdisciplinary? If it is multidisciplinary, the presumption is that its practitioners must have a significant knowledge of a variety of fields, such as psychology, psychoanalysis, transactional analysis, group dynamics, social psychology, industrial sociology, administrative psychiatry, and cultural anthropology. This intellectual point of departure can easily make the OB academic look foolish in the eyes of his or her colleagues.

It is more realistic to think of OB as an interdisciplinary effort in which a number of specialists from different fields get together to work on a particular problem. This line of attack is fruitful when a group made up, for example, of psychiatrists, sociologists, and computer science people get together to solve a particular problem. When people are drawn from so many disciplines, being functionally bilingual, or even trilingual, can be an asset.

But academics who live in the margins of other people's diciplines inevitably begin to show more tolerance than they should. Interfacing with academics in other disciplines can lead to a certain degree of intellectual drift, which can end in romanticism. The acid test for the romantic relates not to the empirical grounds on which a hypothesis rests or its affinity with other well-established hypotheses or theories. The touch of real quality is to be found in an intuitive feeling for the OK–ness of the proposition. This may not be a bad way to proceed, provided the OB practitioner has developed his or her sensitivities with some care and is still capable of recognizing nonsense when it is presented as research.

Most OB people over 40 have at one time or another believed in some interesting propositions which at first sight are difficult to reconcile. These widely held beliefs include the following aphorisms:

1. Flat organizations are more effective than tall ones.
2. The smaller the span of control, the more effective the leader.
3. Horizontal communications are to be preferred to vertical communications.
4. Everybody should know everything instantly.
5. An environment rich in information is best.
6. Hidden agendas are more interesting than public ones.
7. Informal organizations are superior to formal systems.
8. Participation is effective in all circumstances.
9. Managers with a high need to achieve do better than those with a high need for power.
10. Conflict, anxiety, and stress are bad for you.

Organizational behavior as a creative science

These generalizations reflect the creative component in organizational behavior. Even the most rudimentary scientific law represents a generalization beyond the incidents observed. There are always divergent ways of generalizing from the same data. As Nelson Goodman points out in *Ways of Worldmaking:*

> . . . The scientist . . . seeks systems, simplicity, scope; and when satisfied on these scores he tailors the truth to fit. . . . He as much decrees as discovers the laws he sets forth, as much designs as discerns the patterns he delineates.
>
> . . . we must distinguish falsehood and fiction from truth and fact; but we cannot, I am sure, do it on the ground that fiction is fabricated and fact found.

OB people have their own preferences. But they ought to check their theories against some solid criteria. According to Abraham Kaplan in *Conduct of Enquiry,* a good theory meets the following criteria or norms:

Correspondence: It fits the facts.

Coherence: It fits together logically.

Parsimony: It explains the most for the least assumption.

Pragmatism: It predicts further events.

Intuition: It is plausible or aesthetic.

FOCUS ON BEHAVIOR

The distinctive feature of organizational behavior is that it focuses on human behavior, a commodity which can be observed, measured, and objectively analyzed. This is precisely what this book is about— the behavior of people in organizations. But it is important to keep in mind that it is about *structured observation* of behavior. It is observation with a purpose, and that purpose is to establish some general rules that govern organizational behavior.

For example, if you wanted to study executives, you could basically do three things: Ask them what they do—interviewing; look at work records—examination of documents; or study them in action— observation. Let's presume that you follow the third option and decide to make an observational study of executive behavior. How would you

FIGURE 1-3

Steps in preparing an observational study of managers based on Henry Mintzberg,
The Nature of Managerial Work

COMMAND	ACTION	DIFFICULTIES
Define the problem	Observe executive behavior	First find an executive. Then get the executive to agree to allow you to study subordinate managers.
Tease out relevant factors	Look at behavior and communications	How long should the study last? What about private meetings?
Develop appropriate categories	Break behavior into programming, technical, and personnel work	How do you know when a manager is "programming"?
Suggest possible relations	Ask managers before you start what they think they do	They will have no idea. It will be "garbage."
Simplify the problem	Study the managers for five weeks	Academic opponents will challenge your sample.
Make predictions	List your predictions in the form of hypotheses	You usually do this at the end of the study, but put them at the front of the report.
Start again, if necessary	Read Mintzberg's book more carefully Redefine the problem, etc.	It is hard work to read the book carefully and start over.

go about it? A quick look at Henry Mintzberg's *The Nature of Managerial Work,* which is to be found on the desks of most American managers, suggests a particular approach. What counts is the ability to break the problem into analytical bits, or operational units. The sequence shown in Figure 1–3 is based on Mintzberg's ideas.

GETTING IDEAS IN ORGANIZATIONAL BEHAVIOR

Getting ideas and getting going in organizational behavior is a tricky business. It is all a question of being part of the right matrix—with the right people, at the right time, fighting the right battle. Figure 1–4 gives examples of how researchers have implemented the three basic methods of study.

One of the most useful research efforts of my academic life was triggered off by meeting an extremely creative academic at a college in Scotland who wanted to get to the top but had no ready means to get there. His opportunity was afforded when he encountered the work of Sune Carlson at a convention. At the time, in the mid–1950s, there were only several copies of Carlson's book, *Executive Behavior,* in Britain. He brought Carlson to the Western academic world and won his spurs.

I was intrigued with Carlson's work, but I could not just repeat what had been done; I wanted to give it a fresh twist. I had taught work study and thus had heard about random sampling being used to determine how many machines were actually working at a given time. I decided to do observational study of executive behavior at randomly determined times. Fortunately, I had access to a Glacier Metal Company plant and its executives.

None of these connections is made explicit in the research report which appears in a learned journal. But this brief look at the origins of a research exercise has something to say about methods of generating ideas.

Luck or serendipity

The first element to note is luck, or, to give it its scientific name, serendipity. You have a method, such as activity sampling, in your head and you are looking for a target. Thus far, the effort is essentially inductive; you begin with the facts, the actual behavior. In brief, you let the facts speak for themselves. But can they?

Formulating questions

A different approach is suggested by looking at matters deductively. For example, you can look at a theory and see what can be deduced

FIGURE 1–4
Methods of implementing the three basic methods of study in OB: Observation, interviewing, and examination of documents

METHOD	MODE	EXAMPLE	RESEARCHER	INTERESTING FINDING
Observation	Direct	Study the behavior of chief executives	Henry Mintzberg	Executive work is fragmented, disjointed, action oriented and ad hoc
	Indirect	Diary study of chief executives	Rosemary Stewart	The boss's work is constantly being interrupted
Interviewing	Direct	Interview of successful executives in high-powered technological companies	Michael Maccoby	The successful executive is a games player, an existentialist whose life is full of choice and chance
	Indirect	Questionnaire study of executive attitudes in Sears Roebuck	Lyman Porter	Executives love the company, but they don't like being moved about
Examination of documents	Direct	Examination of Pentagon Papers	David Halberstam	The war in Vietnam was settled by bureaucratic politics in Washington
	Indirect	Court transcript of fight between IBM and TELEX	Court record	Good big ones beat good little ones

from it. Carlson was puzzled, after reading some of the standard tomes on management, to find that top managers spend so much of their time planning. The critical question for Carlson became: How would an observer recognize planning as behavior? Or, as Mintzberg put it: How can you recognize a manager who is planning?

To pursue this type of question, it is necessary to look below the surface of organizational behavior at some of its unobvious characteristics.

SOME UNOBVIOUS ASPECTS OF ORGANIZATIONAL BEHAVIOR

There are a number of unobvious characteristics of organizational behavior which help to define the subject and provide useful clues on how experts in this field think.

ORGANIZATIONAL BEHAVIOR
{
Hidden agendas
Anarchical viewpoint
Dramatic and experiential methods
Political orientation
}

Hidden agendas

Organizational behavior people tend to be somewhat suspicious, indeed paranoid of commonsense explanations of events. They tend to regard such explanations as facile, if not simple minded. They believe there is always something going on below the surface which is not obvious to the "untrained" eye.

To understand events, OB people believe, it is necessary to discover the hidden agenda, as opposed to the public agenda. The hidden agenda deals with the covert, sometimes unconscious needs people have but dare not reveal to others.

One of the best examples of a hidden agenda in action was provided by the Nixon presidential press conferences. There was apparently a deep hatred between Nixon and certain members of the media. Both parties worked on the public agenda of defining government policy for public consumption, while the hidden agenda concerned a guerrilla war between Nixon and his "enemies." The excitement came when the hidden agenda jumped up to the surface during these TV encounters. Then the whole game could be given away. The student of OB is rarely an innocent bystander.

Anarchy: The order of the day

Pursuing hidden agendas, of course, works against the interests of good order. It helps to give OB an anarchical flavor which is, in fact, quite appropriate.

The ideal organization, from an OB viewpoint, would be a flat structure (so near the horizontal that it would have zero height), run by shop-floor people who meet in committees or T groups all day, every day, but who come in two hours before 7 A.M. to do the actual work. And if you challenged the OB researcher on this design, the reply might be: "But research shows the average person works productively only 25 percent of the time. What with naturally selected rest periods. . . ." In brief, OB people are against the government and authority and for the shop floor, the underdog, the disabled, and the naive.

They are also for participation, involvement, and nonalienation. If this makes OB look somewhat ridiculous and counterproductive, nothing could be further from the truth.

OB is an alternative life-style which is only taken seriously by successful and highly profitable companies who know how to turn such intelligence to good use. One of the most successful companies in Canada is Steinberg's, a food and department store chain with stores mainly in Quebec and Ontario. A significant element in Steinberg's success has been its ability to mobilize OB for its own purposes. It has always been in the forefront of research in this area; it was first to use the Managerial Grid and job enrichment, and when these were no longer appropriate, they moved into assessment centers. Always, it used top-notch behavioral scientists.

This behavioral science activity helped to give the company a certain mark of distinction which makes the executives look and feel good. They love OB, because it not only removes the capitalist lackey image but also enhances their management skills. Indeed there is a certain hubris attached to OB exercises at Steinberg's which can be quite infectious and very good for the adrenaline. The National Film Board of Canada has made a series of movies about Steinberg's behavioral science efforts which have reached a wide market (see Chapter 17 opening). Most executives who have seen the Steinberg movies cannot believe that management is carried out in such an open manner. Virtual anarchy prevails; hidden agendas explode here and there, and executives say nasty things to the president. Like good drama, it is thrilling, exciting, stirring, and it always has a happy ending.

The symbiotic relationship of OB and management is outlined in Figure 1–5.

Dramatic experiential methods

Students of OB try to gain insights into the drama of executive encounters. Here OB is immensely helped by developments in social psychology, such as role theory. Just as children learn about life by playing games, so executives can learn a great deal by playing out the roles of participants in an encounter.

Many uninitiated observers were astounded at the number of re-

FIGURE 1–5
The cozy love-hate relations of management and
organizational behavior

ORGANIZATIONAL BEHAVIOR	MANAGEMENT
Makes explicit hidden agendas	Sticks to public agendas
Supports anarchy to facilitate participation and creativity	Supports hierarchy in the interests of good order and discipline to get the job done
Believes that organizations are counterintuitive— perhaps unknowable	Argues that the implicit can be made explicit and can be managed
Accepts organizational politics and believes in the conspiracy theory	Denies that there are any politics and believes in pluralism

hearsals Nixon's White House staff went through to practice their lines. But we know this only because politicians like Senator Sam Ervin, who was skilled in the dramatic art of running meetings, showed them up in the Watergate hearings.

The dramatic and experiential nature of OB training is evident in its methods. It focuses on the development of interpersonal skills acquired in T groups and encounters, as recorded on video tape. VTR enables the whole scene to be replayed in a way which makes hidden agendas public and reveals the existence of conspiratorial forces. When such methods are used, a knowledge of organizational politics becomes a must.

Organizational politics

In the midfifties, the idea got around that OB equations were missing a vital variable which in real life was absolutely necessary. It dawned on theorists that power is the decisive factor in most organizational encounters. Soon no OB treatise was complete without an analysis of power: its structural sources (information control), its processes (the power play) and its values (the paranoia of "shoot to kill, not maim").

This next escalation in OB theory, the development of organizational politics, was derived from the emphasis on power. It encompasses the study of the acquisition and distribution of power and its payoffs, and the formation of political parties with special interests.

The conspiracy theory of organization became a reality when the Watergate affair was revealed as a web of cliques and cabals. And the roles of the CIA and the FBI became evident in the Warren Committee's investigation of the assassination of President John F. Kennedy. Many OB theorists came to realize that they had been playing their academic fiddles while Washington burned. The real sources of OB information were the reports of investigative reporters like Dan Rather, rather than the academic articles of management journals.

Organizational behavior utilizes two kinds of logic—linear and nonlinear. Linear logic is concerned with systematic analysis of activities, such as define the problem, spell out the factors determine the problem, list the alternatives, and so on. Nonlinear logic is a different kettle of fish; managers, for example, use metaphors (the organization as a pyramid, a computer, a chessboard, a can of worms) and draw maps (organization charts) to facilitate their thinking. Going from a kettle of fish to a can of worms in one sentence is an example of nonlinear logic, like these metaphors and maps.

TOPIC 2
Organization theories and logic

There is no one philosophy that describes how managers think. At least three different organization theories have been developed, and the particular philosophy a manager develops is to some extent a product of his or her cultural environment. Managers can function better, however, if they share the same broad outlook and strategic visions, the same operating rules and tactical doctrine.

Getting these visions, rules, and doctrines together is what organization theory is all about. It is a mistake to believe that an organization theory need be true in all circumstances; the important thing is that it be shared and understood. Indeed, if you are cynical, you don't have to believe it as long as you understand it.

THREE THEORIES OF ORGANIZATION

In broad terms, three different theories of organization have been identified: the classical, human relations, and systems approaches. (See Figure 1–6.) Each of these theories employs a different metaphor of how the firm acts and different assumptions about human behavior.

Classical theory

The classical theory of organization treats the organization as a machine and assumes that its members are largely guided by rational and economic considerations. The human model employed is that of economic man, a highly abstract individual who acts for analytical purposes only. One is presumed to be guided primarily by considerations of self-gain. In the pursuit of one's own interests, one is led by an

Human relations theory is more realistic than classical theory. The organization is seen as made up of work groups, each with its own values, norms, reinforcements, and sanctions (V, N, R, S), as shown in Figure 1–7. Values define objectives; norms specify means to reach

FIGURE 1–7
Coordinators in a small organization comprised of different work families, each with its own values (V), norms (N), reinforcements (R), and sanctions (S)

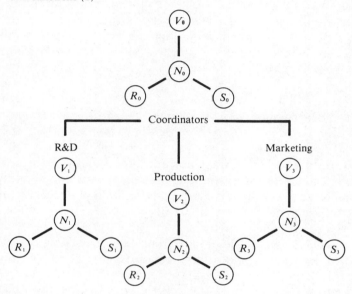

the objectives that are acceptable to the group; reinforcements are the rewards for conforming with these norms; and sanctions are the punishments for failing to conform. From time to time, the group of coordinators is called together to manage the overall effort.

Systems theory

In the third organization theory, systems theory, it is assumed that the organization consists of a set of interrelated parts. It functions like a living creature, in the sense that it is goal seeking and it trades with its environment—importing things, transforming them through a mysterious set of processes, and exporting them into the environment with value added, all for a profit.

The history of systems theory can be traced to developments in weapon systems and aerospace. In systems, the task is always the primary consideration. The German military in 1940 were the first to recognize that combat formations should be designed, trained, and applied to accomplish a particular task and then disbanded. Their success in building task forces of combat engineers, armored infantry, paratroopers, and bombers brought the static fortresses of France and Belgium to a state of ruin. Britain and the United States took up the idea with enthusiasm, and soon task forces—which cut across conventional military structures, processes, and values—were everywhere.

With this concept of the task force, project management was just around the corner. Soon organization analysts were no longer looking at organization charts (which are all about structure and tell you who can speak to whom, who can initiate contacts, who can authorize expenditures, and so on) and were instead plotting and charting information flows (which tell you more about what was said and done, by whom, when, where, and why). In the systems approach information (and access to it) is king, and conventional authority relations go by the board.

In the new technostructure, a new logic emerged. The emphasis was on project management, and a new style of leader emerged who was a facilitator or consultant to a team of resource people of diverse skills who were working on a batch of assignments at any one time.

The aerospace industry, which has problems of rapid obsolescence, was the first to adapt the systems approach. In this adjustment it was greatly facilitated by the U.S. Air Force, which was locked into the systems approach by developments in weapon systems which had to provide target identification, locking-on capacity, and fail-safe capability, all produced by zero-defect programs. The Air Force developed a program of equipment acquisition which set the style for aerospace firms.

The aerospace firms were faced with the problem of high innovativeness, which required systems that could invent, prototype build, and manufacture within tight cost and time schedules.

The RAND (R&D) Corporation, a think tank, was set up, partly with Air Force funding, to provide guidance and counsel in the formulation of future policies. In the new spirit of independence emerging, rationality and imagination were the aces. If organizational problems could be thrown into systems form, dramatic new solutions apparently suggested themselves.

What's the message?

This swift look at these three organization theories suggests three reasons why organization theories are important. They help managers to get things in perspective; to develop the big picture, which they can share with their colleagues; and, above all, to formulate strategies and tactics to deal with new situations.

The answers these theories suggest are not always necessarily the best. But with a common management theory, the debate can go on in

FIGURE 1–8
Application of organization theories to doctor-patient relationships

ORGANIZA-TION THEORY	DOCTOR-PATIENT RELATION	RELATION	CONCEPT OR DISEASE		
			CAUSE	CURE	METAPHOR
Classical	 D | P	Imperialistic	Physiological	Drugs	Complex amoeba
Human relations	D——P	Buddy-buddy	Psychological	Talking	Adaptive talking animal

Systems	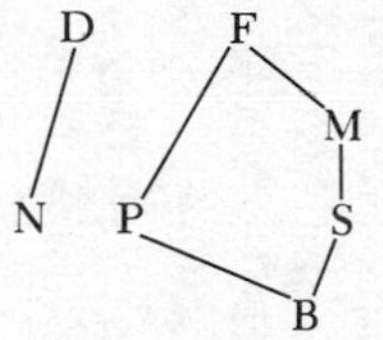 D F—M—S
	  \ / \
	   N—P——B
		Computer talking to computer	Double bind in family system	Redesign system	Computer

Existential	Any of the above: Take your pick	Patient treats doctor	Faulty script, scenario, plot	Select new "movie" for self	Theater of the absurd (or cruelty)

Key: D = doctor; P = patient; F = father; M = mother; S = sister; B = brother; N = nurse.

an ordered, structured, and systematic way. Problems can be considered; a consensus can be reached, and action can be taken. Figure 1–8 illustrates how the various organization theories can be applied to doctor-patient relations, for example.

In the world of systems, the universe is seen as a set of systems interfacing. Inputs are transformed into outputs, but it is not possible to know the whole thing. From the world of the black box (the part of the system that is unknown), it is only a small step into the world of myth, magic, and mysticism.

A surprising number of systems theorists have taken this step, having found their way through the human potentials movement (see Chapter 3). In such a melange of rationality and irrationality, of myth and mathematics, systems theory turns to the relationship between existentialism and systems. They both give primacy to choice, but choice in a world which is never completely explicit, for it cannot be.

LINEAR AND NONLINEAR LOGIC

All managers do not think in the same way. Some proceed in a very systematic, careful manner in problem solving. They rely on analysis; they break up the problem into manageable bits and then deal with each bit systematically. These managers are said to use linear logic. Another type of manager proceeds in a much more chaotic way, jumps all over a problem, and comes up with an intuitive, creative solution that works. They use nonlinear logic.

The physiological basis of linear and nonlinear logic has been provided by neurosurgeons from California who, in experiments with severe epileptics, have been able to demonstrate that the two hemispheres of the brain do different cognitive things (see Figure 1–9). Robert Ornstein, a psychologist, showed that the same basic division of labor applies to normal people. Man has a bifunctional brain.

Managers use the left side of the brain to analyze a problem, but there comes a time when a synergy of the capabilities of the right and left sides is necessary, if they are going to develop creative, imaginative policies. (Of course, there is a danger that these categories, "left brain" and "right brain," will become unwelcome stereotypes.) The message for senior management is clear: They should place a high value on intuition, creativity, and nonlinear logic in subordinates. Their view should be that there is nothing so unequal as the equal treatment of unequals.

Nonlinear logic starts with an idea, the whole. Linear logic develops the whole from an analysis of the parts. As the learning theorist E. L. Thorndike put it some years ago, sometimes it is better to start with the part; sometimes the whole. It all depends on the task and whether it has been done before. Whether linear or nonlinear logic is called for is always a matter of judgment.

FIGURE 1-9
The different functions of the two hemispheres of the brain

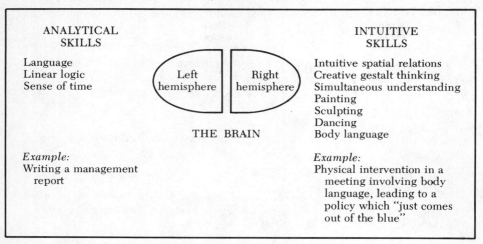

ANALYTICAL
SKILLS

Language
Linear logic
Sense of time

THE BRAIN

INTUITIVE
SKILLS

Intuitive spatial relations
Creative gestalt thinking
Simultaneous understanding
Painting
Sculpting
Dancing
Body language

Example:
Writing a management
  report

Example:
Physical intervention in a
  meeting involving body
  language, leading to a
  policy which "just comes
  out of the blue"

In a brilliant new book called *Spontaneous Apprentices: Children and Language*, George A. Miller, a professor of psychology at Rockefeller University, speaks of "the left hand" of "subjective accidents, odd metaphors, wild guesses, happy hunches, and chance permutations of ideas that come from who knows where," versus "the right hand" of "order and lawfulness, technique and artifice." To get the left side going involves intuitive skill in nonlinear logic. This means some skill in fooling around with models—"what if" models, or contingency theory—is needed.

TOPIC 3
Toward a contingency model for the study of organizational behavior

The contingency model for the study of organizational behavior is based on the idea that no one way of organizing things can be best in all circumstances. A model refers to a relatively simple system which can be used to represent a more complex one. Organization models are dynamic guides which help executives to structure situations. The model to be presented is based on an imaginative integration of structure (the actors and their interrelationships), process (the management of information), and values (both traditional and new). The aim of the model is to help managers get away from managing things in a wholly mechanical fashion.

The model can be applied to organizational problems through the two general processes of analysis and synthesis. Before a management problem can be understood it has to be analyzed into its component parts. But this is only half the battle. The second half consists of synthesizing the various elements, or putting them together in a matrix which shows how they are connected. Analysis uses linear logic; synthesis uses nonlinear logic.

A CONTINGENCY MODEL FOR THE STUDY OF ORGANIZATIONAL BEHAVIOR

Critical dimensions

The three integral dimensions of organizational behavior are structure, process, and values, as shown in Figure 1–10.

FIGURE 1–10
The basic model: Who (the structure of actors) does what, when, and where (the process of events, the plot), and why (the values); what was produced (the task performance); and how you feel (human satisfaction)

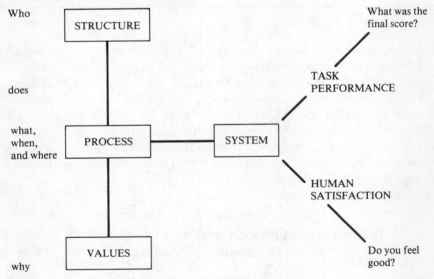

An example: Structure, process, and values of a problem-solving group

R. F. Bales of Harvard, in "Some Uniformities of Behavior in Small Social Systems," has provided an excellent analysis of what happens when a group is given the task of solving a problem. In terms of structure, as shown in Figure 1–11 a task specialist (TS) spends time "zeroing in on the problem," "getting the show on the road," and generally "tying up loose ends." Meanwhile the human relations specialist (HRS) is rushing up with plasma to treat the wounded the task specialist has hit on the way to solving the problem. The eccentric (ECC) is

FIGURE 1-11
Roles in a problem-solving group

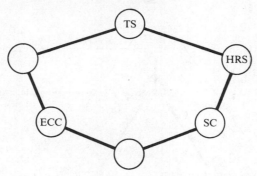

being funny, introducing bizarre but potentially useful ideas. The scapegoat (SC) is picking up the hostility floating around the group. The various roles are welded into a particular structure which allows the group to work on its two problems: work (task) and nonwork (human relations).

As the structure evolves, the group is also working through the process, which in this case consists of:

1. Clarification—What is the problem?
2. Evaluation—How do we feel about it?
3. Decision—What are we going to do about it?

At the same time, a value system is evolving. A useful paradigm for looking at values, norms, reinforcements, and sanctions is shown in Figure 1-12. Here the overriding value is democracy in the group.

As a behavior system, the group can be described in greater detail, but the point is to show how the dimensions of structure, process, and values can be applied to a group. The same kind of analysis can be applied to a football team, an infantry platoon, an assembly-line work group, a cell in the Communist Party, or a family in the Mafia.

End products: Task and human

All living systems are goal oriented. The system achieves (or at least attempts to achieve) its goals by working on a task or set of tasks. In the process of working on the task, the organism experiences a degree of satisfaction or dissatisfaction. In the behavioral sciences, a major effort is made to measure task achievement and human satisfaction and also to ascertain the relations between them.

As shown in Figure 1-13, the task end products are productivity and profitability. The human end product (systems activity) is mea-

FIGURE 1–12
Value system in the group

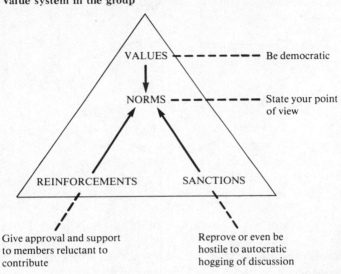

sured in terms of job satisfaction at the individual level, group satisfaction at the group level, and morale at the organizational level. These end products are indicated by such measures as absenteeism, labor turnover, and number of grievances. A major issue in organizational behavior is the relationship between productivity and job satisfaction, which will be considered later.

Research method

In organizational behavior research, the type of research method employed will to some extent determine the research findings and

FIGURE 1–13
Measures of end products

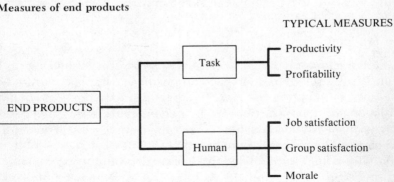

FIGURE 1-14
Research methods

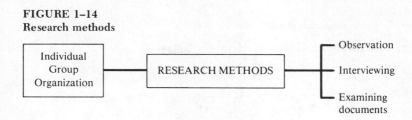

therefore the concepts generated. Figure 1–14 illustrates three principal methods used. Two entirely different pictures of the effective
executive emerge, depending on whether the data are collected by
asking his subordinates for a description or by observing him in
action.

Environment

The kind of setting in which the data are collected will have a
significant effect on the relations being studied. While it is obvious
that there are important differences in environments between a study
conducted in the 1920s in Chicago (to measure the relation between
productivity and group norms) and a similar study conducted in Japan
in the 1970s, some theorists are inclined to gloss over such differences.
Environment is often the societal conceptual level—the relationships
between all of the other factors and the society as a whole.

The contingency model for this text

It is now possible to fit all these different factors together and come
up with a model for this text. Figure 1–15 is the contingency model of a
system for the study of organizational behavior. The items in par-
entheses indicate features (not yet discussed) which will sometimes be
added. The model is intended to be flexible and adaptable to systems
which will not always fit this skeleton in exact details.

The model is described as a contingency model because it is tied to
the view that it is no longer possible to accept the simplistic view that
X causes Y under all conditions; the conditions $(C_1, C_2, \ldots C_n)$ under
which the relation holds have to be specified. The model employed is
meant to direct the reader's attention to the fact, for example, that
structure is a function of technology and that structure in turn significantly affects process (how people communicate), which in turn affects
organizational values. Structure, process, and values, collectively and
individually, affect end products (much depends on how you measure
them). But all this depends on how you found out (the research method
employed).

FIGURE 1–15
Model for the study of organizational behavior

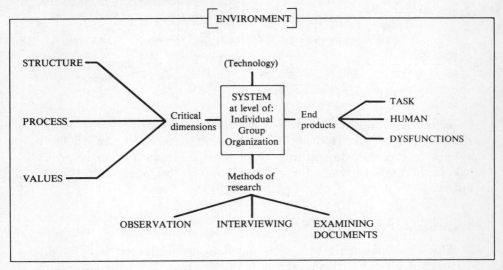

The "it-all-depends" proposition is what the contingency approach is all about. The contingency approach should be clearer when you have reviewed such ideas as the relation between the values of employees and hierarchical levels in Chapter 2, the connection between the norm of restricting production and the social class of workers in Chapter 3, the conditions which favor one leadership style over another in Chapter 12, and so on. Now it is important to consider the relation of the form:

$$X \rightarrow Y \text{ under conditions } C_1, C_2, \ldots, C_n$$

and to suggest which variables constitute the conditions. The contingency model used in the text spells out the set of variables to be considered for organizational relations.

The purpose of introducing the model early in the text is to provide a frame of reference which will help the student of organizational behavior organize the diverse material in this field of inquiry. Each chapter uses the model as a means of integrating and putting together concepts and research findings developed in that chapter. The object of the model is to stimulate the reader to conceptualize in structure, process, and value terms when looking at the behavior of individuals, groups, and organizations, and to try to link these factors to the end products, task and human. The model also highlights the importance of both the environment and the way the system was studied (i.e., the methods of research).

TOPIC 4
What every manager should know about the study of organizational behavior

The most important thing to know is that the object of the study of organizational behavior is to build up a vivid portrait of an isolated land called the organization which, for modern man, can be as fascinating and unique as the face of the moon. Organization theory tries to put together a taste of everything there is in that mysterious, world. The several "mystery plays" written by organization theorists have been gone into briefly: classical theory, human relations theory, and systems theory.

Systems theory treats the organization as a giant amoeba which consumes men, money, material, and energy. How are we going to get at this amoeba? The line of approach is provided by our contingency model, with inputs of structure, process, and values and outputs of two kinds—task and human. Who (the structure, or cast) does what, where, when, how, and how much (the process, or acts, scenes, and lines) and why (the values, or magic, myth, and mystique). The measurements of end products try to explain the notions of suboptimization, including the koan (a paradox to be meditated on): "Don't let the best become an enemy of the good."

Selecting "the facts" according to the paradigm

Organizational behavior deals explicitly with organizational matters. Thomas Kuhn in *The Structure of Scientific Revolutions,* notes that it is a mistake to suppose that we can describe the facts in neutral-observation language. What you see in an organization is a function of your paradigm, which describes the set of assumptions you use to describe a situation.

For the classicaly oriented, an organization is seen in the light of John Dalton's atomic theory, with roles for atoms and organization charts for molecules. To the human relations oriented, the organization is seen in terms of informal groups and hidden agendas. To the systems people, organizations are made up of information flows, connecting and disconnecting situations, filters, amplifiers, suppressors, and equations. To each his own particular paradigm, which in turn directs attention to "the facts" in their proper context.

Characteristics of organizational behavior

Organizational behavior is an interpretive ·science in search of meaning; the aim is to make meaningful "the facts of organizational life." In brief, it is at once empirical, interpretive, and critical (see Figure 1–16).

FIGURE 1–16
Organizational behavior is empirical, interpretive, and critical

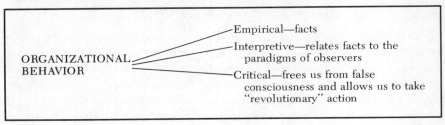

ORGANIZATIONAL
BEHAVIOR

- Empirical—facts
- Interpretive—relates facts to the paradigms of observers
- Critical—frees us from false consciousness and allows us to take "revolutionary" action

The critical knowledge of organizational behavior transcends both empiricism and interpretation, and it produces the emancipating effect of freeing us from false consciousness and eliminating forces beyond our control. The whole point of the critical aspect of organizational behavior is to provide a guide to "revolutionary" action.

The moral of the story is that we still need facts; we still need to be able to interpret these facts in the light of the paradigm of the observer; but above all we need to be able to free ourselves from the confines of our present form of life, to be able to take innovative action. This book is devoted to fathoming the facts, the interpretations, and the critical aspects of organizational behavior.

Thus the contingency model for the study of organizational behavior is based on an imaginative integration of drama, information, and existentialism. The object of the model is to get managers away from the idea of doing things in a wholly mechanical fashion. Hence the emphasis is on drama.

What it amounts to is that the manager must learn to step out of role and respond to the drama of the occasion. But no drama is going to do any good unless the manager has the appropriate information, timely and presented in easily understood fashion. To go forward, the manager has to adopt an essentially existential view of the world.

The new posture toward organizational behavior requires an existential approach, with the emphasis on decision (refusal to choose to act unfree), authenticity (real, not phony, relations must structure the solution), and good faith (maximum information made available to all parties involved). People are accepted as they are and are not prejudged using stereotypes.

Answers are not as important as the process used to reach for them. Problems are not regarded as incapable of solution; a dialectical approach is invoked which assumes that evolving solutions will generate new problems, and so on. The process must be approached in good faith. As Eldridge Cleaver put it, "If you are part of the problem, you have to decide if you want to be part of the solution."

OVERVIEW

Organizational behavior as a field of inquiry and operation is only just beginning. All sorts of interesting problems in such diverse fields as the military, the women's movement, public administration, education, the commune, the church, and the kibbutz await exploration and creative solutions. A whole new field is mushrooming in a way which is going to have traumatic effects—both for the traditional academic psychologist and for the executive who has lived with relative certainty in a world of low technological complexity, complaisant consumers, and no Young Turks bent on playing the systems game. A dramatic intellectual escalation is underway. You will want to be there.

REVIEW AND RESEARCH

1. Explain the sequence: industrial psychology, human relations, organizational behavior.

2. Draw up a continuum of organizations ranging from small groups (e.g., a football team) to large and complex organizations (e.g., universities, large corporations). Make a comparison table based on the headings: Specialization, Coordination.

3. Organizational behavior research and theorizing have developed very rapidly in North America (the United States and Canada). What conditions have favored this rapid growth?

4. Develop a model for an interview showing the different choice points and feedback loops. Develop a strategy for job hunting from this model.

5. Compare and contrast the structure, process, and values of any two of the following: the Catholic Church, an infantry division, the Mafia, a mental hospital.

6. Review the last four issues of the following periodicals: *The Administrative Science Quarterly, The Journal of Management,* and *Management International.* List the various articles that relate to organization theory.

7. What are the characteristics of the systems approach? Develop a systems description of the interaction between a methadone treatment center and the drug pusher's network on the street. Specify structure, process, and values for each subsystem and show how they interact.

8. Describe the experience of being institutionalized in one of the following organizations: the military, the church, a school of business, the scouts, or a large corporation such as IBM.

9. Review the last 12 issues of the *Harvard Business Review* and *Fortune.* Compare and contrast these two journals under the following headings: Editorial point of view, Readability, Focus of interest, Depth of analysis, Relevance, and Omissions. Cite examples to support your judgments.

10. Develop definitions of alienation, anomie, and apathy. To what extent do they apply to your own experience? If they do not, why?

11. What is existentialism? What does it have for you?
     a. What gives your life meaning?
     b. Try to state what your three most fundamental values are.
     c. What are the choices you face today?
     d. What holds you back from making these choices?
     e. Write down the names of two people you understand and two people
         you do not understand. Try to list their respective values, attitudes,
         needs, and expectations.

GLOSSARY OF TERMS

Contingency approach. In organizational behavior, the presumption that a
relationship can only be valid under certain conditions or contingencies.
More specifically;

$$X \xrightarrow{\text{causes}} Y \text{ under conditions } C_1, C_2, \ldots, C_n$$

For example, one-way communication is more effective than two-way
when the task is simple, the group is structured, the status gradient is
clear, and communication is restricted (e.g., by radio).

Existentialism. A new approach in the area of psychology-philosophy-ethics
where the emphasis is on a holistic view of man ("man supersedes the sum
of his parts") in an interpersonal setting. The purpose of existentialism is
to make people more aware of the choices open to them, to stop them from
choosing to act unfree, and to make life more meaningful by the perceptive acceptance of reality as something which is seen through value-
loaded senses.

Linear and nonlinear logic. Linear logic requires a systematic, careful analysis of a problem which breaks the problem up into manageable bits. It is
widely believed that the left hemisphere of the brain is used for linear
logic. Nonlinear logic apparently disregards systematic, careful analysis
and jumps from one alternative to another, until arriving at a solution
which is absolutely right and which appears to come out of the blue. It is
widely believed that nonlinear logic is a function of the right hemisphere
of the brain, which specializes not only in intuitive, spatial relations but in
creative thinking.

   Apparently good executives can get the right hemisphere to come up
with odd metaphors, wild guesses, and happy hunches, while the left
hemisphere keeps their intellectual house in good order and subject to
discipline.

Management theories. 1. The *classical theory of organization* is concerned
with a narrow range of relatively simple tasks and emphasizes a limited
number of variables. In this approach man is thought of as a machine
motivated exclusively by economic considerations. The theory assumes
that an organization, given an overall mission, will be able to identify the
required tasks, allocate and coordinate these tasks by giving jobs to sections, place the sections within units, unite the units within departments,
and coordinate departments under a board, all in the most economic
manner.

2. The *human relations school* argues that an organization should be considered as a social system which has both economic and human dimensions. Effectiveness is achieved by arranging matters so that people feel that they count, that they belong, and that work can be made meaningful.

3. The *systems approach* treats an organization as a sociotechnical system and is concerned with the development of optimal organizations within which the objective and the available resources, both human and technical, determine the activities to be performed and the methods of work to be employed.

Organization. A social system of two or more groups constructed for the purpose of achieving goals.

Organizational behavior. The systematic study of the nature of organizations: how they begin, grow, and develop, and their effect on individual members, constituent groups, other organizations, and larger institutions.

Research process. The Research process has six steps: observe behavior, detect and measure differences, speculate and specify by developing hypotheses, collect and measure data, analyze and interpret data, and change the situation.

Theory. A theory is a simplified interpretation of a complex world that makes sense out of observable facts by ordering the relations among the elements that the theorist studies in the real world. A good theory satisfies the criteria of correspondence (fits the facts), coherence (hangs together), parsimony (explains the most with the least), pragmatism, and prediction (forecasts future events).

DEBATE: The organization man versus the liberated manager

PRO: The organization man

This view sees the manager as the person who *sets objectives; plans* the work; *organizes* the people into tasks according to their age, aptitudes, and abilities; *leads* them in a way which turns work into fun; and *evaluates* performances in a way that ensures correspondence between plan and action. That is, the manager does things through people: plans, organizes, leads, and evaluates the efforts of other people.

Management is a verb, a doing word. But what does managers do? They talk. We know from scientific studies of executive behavior that they spend tremendously long hours working (12–14 hours a day plus "homework"), and most of this is what psychologists call interacting time. The time spent with others is made up of a myriad of fleeting, superficial, often distracting contacts. A lot of these contacts are in meetings, but most are swift touching-base signals which terminate with the manager giving an "OK—carry on" signal.

THE BEFORE PICTURE: THE TRADITIONAL MANAGER

This managerial life-style can be disturbing to outsiders. They are likely to view managers as having sold their services to the highest bidder (usually the image of a bloated capitalist smoking a cigar is invoked) or as a kind of powerbroker who gets people together to do what the manager wants.

One such outsider was W. H. Whyte, an editor of *Fortune* magazine, who wrote a brilliant and widely read book called *The Organization Man.* Managers like to think about themselves as tough guys who go in and do it their way, win the order, get a coronary, are fired—then make it all the way to become chairman of the board. Whyte painted another picture: a guy with a crewcut, in a buttoned-down collar, grey flannel suit, and polished leather shoes, who drove a Buick or an Olds (a Cadillac would have been conspicuous consumption), tutored his wife how to toady up to the boss, and was an all-around conformist.

CON: The liberated manager

THE AFTER PICTURE: MOBICENTRIC, EXISTENTIAL, OR LIBERATED MANAGER

The organization man concept was just emerging as the WASP ethos or value system was going into decline. The organization man was replaced by the mobicentric manager (the executive who likes to travel, to change jobs—movement itself is a narcotic), the existential executive (concerned with chance and choice, doing your own thing; "What I can be, I must be"), and the liberated manager (seeking to liberate organizations from their imperialist, oppressive, autocratic ways through alternative life-styles, unorthodox dress and language, nonlinear logic, TM).

We shall deal with many of these ideas, including self-actualization (how to turn yourself on, through work), the stay-versus-leave choice matrix, and nonlinear logic (How to make $2 + 2 = 5$) in the text. The last chapter, for example, is devoted to the life-styles of the new manager. An obvious question for the student of management is: Where and how do you get that style?

Questions

1. Which of these two types of manager is the more important?
2. Can they work together?

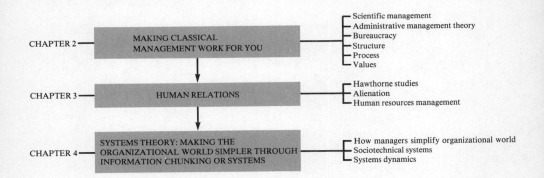

CHAPTER 2 — MAKING CLASSICAL MANAGEMENT WORK FOR YOU
- Scientific management
- Administrative management theory
- Bureaucracy
- Structure
- Process
- Values

CHAPTER 3 — HUMAN RELATIONS
- Hawthorne studies
- Alienation
- Human resources management

CHAPTER 4 — SYSTEMS THEORY: MAKING THE ORGANIZATIONAL WORLD SIMPLER THROUGH INFORMATION CHUNKING OR SYSTEMS
- How managers simplify organizational world
- Sociotechnical systems
- Systems dynamics

part I

ORGANIZATION
THEORY IN ACTION

DIAGRAM SUMMARY OF CHAPTER 2

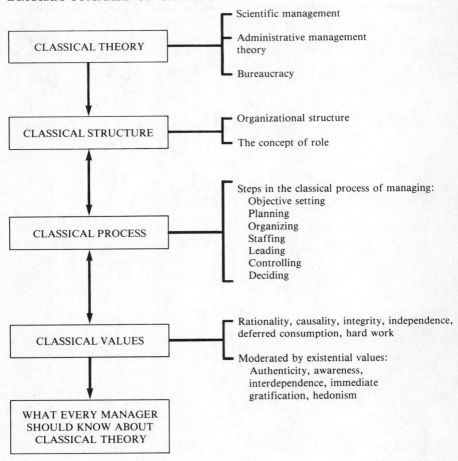

CLASSICAL THEORY
- Scientific management
- Administrative management theory
- Bureaucracy

CLASSICAL STRUCTURE
- Organizational structure
- The concept of role

CLASSICAL PROCESS
- Steps in the classical process of managing:
  - Objective setting
  - Planning
  - Organizing
  - Staffing
  - Leading
  - Controlling
  - Deciding

CLASSICAL VALUES
- Rationality, causality, integrity, independence, deferred consumption, hard work
- Moderated by existential values: Authenticity, awareness, interdependence, immediate gratification, hedonism

WHAT EVERY MANAGER SHOULD KNOW ABOUT CLASSICAL THEORY

2

Making classical
management work for you

CORPORATE CONSENSUS FORMATION

The president enters the meeting room at 3:05 P.M. Present are
Tom, vice president of manufacturing, who is opposed to the new
company reorganization plan; Dick, vice president of personnel, who
will go along; Harry, director of quality control; Paul, director of operations research, who is also opposed; and several plant managers.

PRESIDENT (groaning): Paul, I would like to see you in my office at 9:00 A.M.
  tomorrow morning. OK? OK. (President moves to the top of the table.)
      (with a winning smile): Getting a tan, Tom—golf, I guess. (Pause.)
  Gentlemen, let me call the meeting to order. Hopefully, this won't take
  long. You have read your briefing on the company reorganization plan. You
  were invited to respond *in writing*. The only one responding was Dick,
  who gave a balanced but favorable analysis. (A terse description of the
  plan—objectives, alternatives, criteria for choice, solution, implementation, etc.—follows.) The floor is now open for comment.

DICK: Can I start the ball rolling? Can executives transferred by the plan take
  their secretaries with them?

PRESIDENT: Good thinking, Dick—the answer is yes and no. But, in fact, yes.
  Paul, you look worried.

PAUL: Yes, I am. Tomorrow—I mean—how is this reorganization going to
  affect people like myself who have kids in high school, yet will have to
  move every three years, mandatory?

PRESIDENT: I thought you would bring that up. Check Appendix III B. It has
  the answer.

PAUL: But that doesn't get to the nub of the matter. (The debate continues for a
  time.)

PRESIDENT: Paul, why don't you schedule a meeting with Dick to sort this one out?

A PLANT MANAGER: How will this reorganization affect the scheduling of maintenance? Now its computer planned, except for breakdowns, and, I quote, "local arrangements."

PRESIDENT: Hang on. Let's get the planning and scheduling maintenance manager in here. (Then follows a discussion which effectively cuts away Tom's empire, which is dependent on his control of maintenance. By some sleight of the hand, this is passing into the hands of an assistant in the president's office.)

Is there any further disagreement on the plan? I am going to go round the table—poll you.

TOM: Hmm. Not really.

DICK: I'm for it.

HARRY: Hmm. I don't know.

PRESIDENT: Yes or no, Paul.

PAUL: I'm on board.

PRESIDENT: I'll now ask Tom to summarize what's been agreed.

The president in this case, the expert in getting consensus, seems to believe organizational structure does not exist except in the minds of people. To hold such an abstract concept in the minds of the organization's members, the president must do considerable work to shape

"At our last meeting eight members of the Board disagreed with you and you said they'd be sorry."

Reprinted by permission *The Wall Street Journal*.

their perceptions. As you can see from how the president got every-body on board, this is fairly easy to achieve because most members think the organization is bigger and better than they are (the group mind thesis). The organization meets many of their own personal needs as well as its unique needs, and they are unaware or reluctant to admit that they are against the organization. In any case, they are held in position by a set of double binds which keeps them deferential in attitude and compliant in behavior.

ORGANIZATION THEORY

Academic theorists and successful executives have developed or-ganization theory, its principles and practices. This theory is concerned with the basics governing business in terms of authority, technology, and economics. As we have noted, it has evolved from the stage of classical theory via human relations to the systems approach and is now taking an existential tack. Organization theory encompasses both the formal and the informal organization.

Classical structure

Classical structure is best exemplified in Max Weber's view of the organization. In a bureaucracy, activities and responsibilities are or-ganized according to a hierarchy, by functional specialists, who do things by the book, follow official channels, and are mainly guided by precedence and administrative efficiency. The principles of classical management are listed in Figure 2–1. Bureaucrats, the middle man-

FIGURE 2–1
Principles of classical management

CLASSICAL STRUCTURE
{
Chain of command
Unity of command
Functional organization
Span of control
Clear delegation
Authority matches responsibility
}

agers in classical structures, are selected by examination, promoted by merit, and enjoy tenure. They generally are too frightened to rock the boat. But higher level decisions nevertheless are open to appeal. This works very well on paper, but the whole complex apparatus can come unstuck unless the informal organization agrees to go along for the ride.

Informal organization

The informal organization refers·to the extensive interlocking set of cliques and cabals which lies below the surface of all human systems. These invisible organizations also have to be managed if the system is to succeed.

The structure of authority

The structure of an organization results from the division and grouping of tasks into functions, sections, departments, and divisions. The object in individual terms is to define the authority, responsibilities, and duties of every person in the system and to coordinate their activities toward a common end. Ross A. Webber, in *Management: Basic Elements of Managing Organizations*, notes that there is a variety of levels of delegation (see Figure 2–2).

Structure varies from organization to organization, of course. For

FIGURE 2–2
Levels of delegation

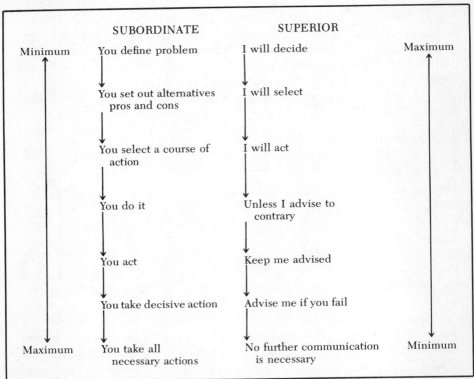

Source: Adapted from Ross A. Webber, *Management: Basic Elements of Managing Organizations* (Homewood, Ill.: Richard D. Irwin, 1975). © 1975 by Richard D. Irwin, Inc.

example, the organization of a chemical manufacturing company is very different from the organization of a department store, which in turn is very different from the organization of a company building experimental aircraft.

TOPIC 1
Classical theory

Classical theory has three strands: scientific management, administrative management theory, and bureaucracy.

SCIENTIFIC MANAGEMENT

Many of the techniques used today by managers, including work study (time and method study) and quality control, have their origins in the scientific management movement. Frederick W. Taylor, the first management consultant, created and developed scientific management. Taylor's concept of the working man was based on the Protestant work ethic, which has the values of achievement, deferment of consumption, rationality, and individualism. Taylor assumed that workers would work flat out to maximize their economic interest and thus ought to welcome scientific management.

Based on his experiences at the Midvale and Bethlehem steel companies and as a consultant to many firms, Taylor formulated specific rules for management:

1. Select the right man for the job.
2. Decide by method study on the one best way to do the job.
3. Develop differential piecework plans that reward effort.
4. Carefully plan the actual work process.
5. Develop line and functional specialization.

Applying these principles, Taylor was able to achieve dramatic increases in productivity (see Box 2–1).

Taylor's ideas had a significant and sustained impact on management, and today his principles are still built into most organizations. Helping him to spread the gospel of scientific management were Frank and Lillian Gilbreth, an engineer and a psychologist, who—to the subsequent delight of many readers—practiced such techniques on their *Cheaper by the Dozen* family.

While Taylor was not an organization theorist, he did provide a number of explicit concepts concerning management. He pointed out the importance of separating planning from operating, from which the modern concept of line and staff work was derived. At the same time, industrial psychologists were investigating hours of work and fatigue and devising selection tests.

Box 2–1: The case of the pigs

When Frederick Winslow Taylor was introducing the principles of scientific management at the Bethlehem Steel Company, he was assigned the task of moving 80,000 tons of pig iron from an open field into the works. Taylor found that the work gang, on the average, was loading about 12½ long tons per man-day, for which the wages were $1.15 a day. After studying the matter Taylor concluded that a first-class pig iron handler ought to be able to handle between 47 and 48 long tons per day, for which he proposed to pay $1.85 a day. The method Taylor used for selecting his first convert to this system is rather interesting.

. . . Finally we selected one from among the four as the most likely man to start with. He was a little Pennsylvania Dutchman who had been observed to trot back home for a mile or so after his work in the evening, about as fresh as he was when he came trotting down to work in the morning. We found that upon wages of $1.15 a day he had succeeded in buying a small plot of ground, and that he was engaged in putting up the walls of a house for himself in the morning before starting work and at night after leaving. He also had the reputation of being exceedingly "close," that is, of placing a very high value on the dollar. As one man whom we talked to about him said, "A penny looks about the size of a cartwheel to him." This man we will call Schmidt.

The task befoe us, then, narrowed itself down to getting Schmidt to handle 47 tons of pig iron per day and making him glad to do it. This was done as follows. Schmidt was called out from among the gang of pig iron handlers and talked to somewhat in this way:

"Schmidt, are you a high-priced man?"

"Vell, I don't know vat you mean."

"Oh yes you do. What I want to know is whether you are a high-priced man or not."

"Vell, I don't know what you mean."

"Oh, come now, you answer my questions. What I want to find out is whether you are a high-priced man or one of these cheap fellows here. What I want to find out is whether you want to earn $1.85 a day or whether you are satisfied with $1.15 just the same as all those cheap fellows are getting."

"Did I vant $1.85 a day? Vas dot a high-priced man? Vell, yes, I vas a high-priced man."

"Oh, you're aggravating me. Of course you want $1.85 a day—everyone wants it! You know perfectly well that has very little to do with your being a high-priced man. For goodness sake answer my questions, and don't waste any more of my time. Now come over here. You see that pile of pig iron?"

"Yes."

Reference: F. W. Taylor, *Principles of Scientific Management* (New York: Harper & Bros., 1947).

ADMINISTRATIVE MANAGEMENT THEORY

While scientific management was essentially concerned with the shop-floor level, administrative management focused on the higher management levels. This theory was developed by Lyndall F. Urwick (born in 1891).

Integral to Urwick's approach is the paradigm of rationality—the idea that logical analysis rather than personalities should determine

"You see that car?"

"Yes."

"Well if you are a high-priced man, you will load that pig iron on that car tomorrow for $1.85. Now do wake up and answer my question. Tell me whether you are a high-priced man or not."

"Vell—did I got $1.85 for loading dot pig iron on dot car tomorrow?"

"Yes, of course you do, and you get $1.85 for loading a pile like that every day right through the year. That is what a high-priced man does and you know it as well as I do."

"Vell, dot's all right. I could load dot pig iron on the car tomorrow for $1.85, and I get it every day don't I?"

"Certainly you do—certainly you do."

"Vell, den, I vas a high-priced man."

"Now, hold on, hold on. You know just as well as I do that a high-priced man has to do exactly as he's told from morning till night. You have seen this man here before, haven't you?"

"No, I never saw him."

"Well, if you are a high-priced man, you will do exactly as this man tells you tomorrow, from morning till night. When he tells you to pick up a pig and walk you pick it up and walk, and when he tells you to sit down and rest, you sit down and rest. You do that right straight through the day. And what's more no back talk. Now a high-priced man does just what he's told to do, and no back talk. Do you understand that? When this man tells you to walk, you walk; when he tells you to sit down you sit down, and you don't talk back to him. Now you come on to work here tomorrow morning and I'll know before night whether you are really a high-priced man or not."

This case illustrates Taylor's misconception in trying to obtain maximum productivity even at the expense of imposing on the worker a burden that would be exhausting to the average man. Several times in Taylor's writing it may be observed that there is some confusion between the normal goal to be reached and the "maximum amount of work which a first-rate man of [each workman's] class can do and thrive." When he turns to the problem of those workers who cannot reach such a standard, Taylor recommends that they be declared redundant, unless they can be found work in another part of the plant. While it is true that Taylorism did bring substantial financial rewards to those workers who eventually were selected, his fundamental mistake was to imagine that these methods could be generally applied. On this point, Taylor was bitterly opposed not only by the trade unions but by independent research workers.

how organizations should be structured. For example, the theory of departmentalization assumes that an organization planner, given a purpose, will be able to identify the required tasks and thus the jobs, to organize the jobs in sections, to place the sections within units, to unite the units within departments, and to coordinate departments under a board—all in the most economical manner. (See Figure 2–3.)

In administrative management terms, efficiency is to be achieved

FIGURE 2–3
Example of an organization chart

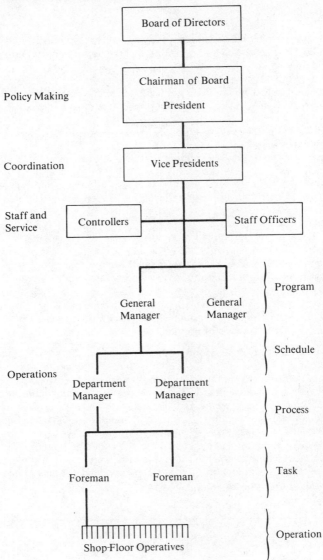

by task specialization. Three kinds of formal relations—line, functional, and staff—are recognized. Line management is responsible for production and includes the general manager, department manager, foremen, and shop-floor or production workers. Functional management includes managers who deal not with a product but with a function, such as planning or programing. Staff managers have neither direct line nor functional responsibilities but derive their purpose from a senior manager for whom they think (by preparing plans) and, on specific occasions, act.

For such matters as routine administration and separation of line and staff, and above all for a definition of what constitutes staff work, the military is not to be surpassed; most textbooks on the management process, even in the 1970s, have reported this source of concept, experience, and practice. The concepts of line, functional, and staff management are almost universally accepted today; and in the past they provided a useful semantic device for conducting discussions to clarify rules, roles, and relations in industrial organizations. But that day has now passed and a different perspective, in which information and process are the aces, is emerging.

Urwick provided managers with a vocabulary which could describe relations in terms of line, function, and staff; he set out the concepts of span of control and unity of command; and he gave management formal guidance on how delegation and coordination should be achieved. Box 2–2 describes a manager who would not delegate.

Box 2–2: Howard Hughes: An American emperor who wore no clothes

The life of Howard Hughes is a terrible example of what happens to the manager who cannot delegate. Hughes, who showed his genius in two typically American triumphs, movies and aviation, operated as a tycoon who could not share power with his subordinates. His need to make every single decision, no matter how trivial, ultimately destroyed him.

Hughes was an only child. His mother took him out of summer camp because of a polio scare, and in time Hughes developed a pathological fear of germs. He became isolated from the real world; contact had to be made through his aides, the "Mormon Mafia." Through the routine carrying out of Hughes's lunatic orders (for example, he once wrote a long memo on how to wash a can), they confirmed him in his madness. In the end Hughes literally became the emperor who wore no clothes. While his aides assured him by their behavior that everything was perfectly normal.

In business Hughes behaved "as if he were missing the gene for corporate success." He nearly ruined two great companies he bought, TWA and RKO. As Lord Acton pointed out, "Power corrupts; absolute power corrupts absolutely."

Reference: Donald L. Barlett and James B. Steele, *Empire: The Life, Legend, and Madness of Howard Hughes* (New York: W. W. Norton & Co., 1979).

BUREAUCRACY

Traditional classical theory (especially as developed by Taylor), which was essentially seen as a development of industrial engineering, had by 1930 lost most of its élan, largely because it lacked any significant theoretical base. Max Weber had developed a sociological theory of organizations which could have provided just such a theoretical base if academics and executives writing in this field had known of his work; but his seminal theorizing did not have much effect in English-speaking countries until the 1940s. There were several reasons for this delay. One was that Weber wrote in a ponderous, legalistic, convoluted style which made it difficult to unscramble and tease out the relevant concepts for organization theory. The other reason was that Weber treated bureaucracy as an ideal type.

Max Weber qualified in law and was on the staff of the University of Berlin. His father, a lawyer, was a member of the Prussian Diet and a National Liberal member of the Reichstag, and his mother was from a Westphalian family of scholars. His home background may explain both his scientific interest in religious phenomena and his passionate interest in the fate of modern nations. In his youth, he met men eminent in political and academic life who apparently spent a good part of their time debating what directions the new industrial states of their day should take. There was one academic who above all was taken seriously, and that was Karl Marx, whose radical views were adopted by German scholars long before they attracted serious attention in either England or America. Though Weber was not a socialist, he was strongly influenced by Marx's analysis of modern society. As Albert Salomon put it, "Max Weber became a sociologist in a long and intense dialogue with the ghost of Karl Marx."

To avoid vagueness, Weber introduced the concept of the ideal type of bureaucracy, to which existing cases could be compared. It was this notion of bureaucracy as an ideal type which turned off many scholars and delayed serious consideration of Weber's ideas. Yet these ideas, as events showed, were to be of tremendous value in integrating organizational thinking and in suggesting useful theoretical frames for important empirical work.

Weber's interest in bureaucracy at first was peripheral, for his first concern was the distinctive features of modern Western capitalism—which, from his historical studies, he realized was only one form of capitalism. He argued that the changes in values resulting from the Reformation provided an ethical, and hence an economic, climate which facilitated the development of modern capitalism. Weber put forward the view that the Protestant environment in England, and later in New England, was the significant reason why these areas underwent industrial development so rapidly. For Weber, Protestantism—with its emphasis on the virtues of hard work, sobriety, and accumulation of material goods, all as signs of God's grace—gave a society the edge in mobilizing human energies to produce goods, not for personal consumption but as a means of getting to heaven.

But modern Western capitalism achieves its excellence through rationally constructed organizations which are strikingly different in character from earlier types of organizations. The Protestant ethic is applied as a motivation for satisfying personal wants and needs.

The key question behind Weber's analysis of organization is: Why do people obey authority? Fundamentally, he argued, there is always a conception of authority, but the basis of that authority is different in different kinds of institutions. In any institution, one person or a small number of individuals give orders and others obey, and what is vital to understand in this context is that the person giving the orders expects to be obeyed. Why? The reason is that both the official and the subordinate share certain beliefs about the rightness of the process; in short, the authority is seen to be legitimate.

The five marks of bureaucracy

Weber's theory of bureaucracy has five characteristics or marks:

1. Tasks are distributed among various members of the group as official duties, usually accompanied with division of labor and specialization of function.
2. Offices or roles are organized into hierarchical structures in which the scope of authority of superordinates over subordinates is clearly defined.
3. A formal set of rules governing behavior is specified which ensures uniformity of organization.
4. Officials are required to assume an impersonal attitude in contacts with both other officials and clients which inevitably produces a considerable measure of psychological distance between superiors and subordinates.
5. Employment in a bureaucracy is usually assumed to be a career for life, and promotion is by merit.

The bureaucrat

The bureaucrats or officials who run the bureaucracies are personally free, but they must act impersonally, according to the rule which defines their specific areas of competence. They are selected according to merit, receive special training for their posts, and enjoy corporate tenure. They are not elected to their posts but are appointed according to their qualifications, usually measured by examination. They are paid a salary, with increases according to age and experience, and receive a pension when they retire. Locked in a web of red tape of their own making, they are unable to cope with the exigencies of a changing situation.

What happens in a bureaucracy is that the mind of the official develops a particular perceptual frame of reference within which going by the book becomes de rigueur. This condition induces a kind of astigmatism which makes the bureaucrat see the real world in such a way that both self-interest (in terms of seniority, tenure, and salary) and administrative convenience (in terms of finding generalized solutions to problems that facilitate record keeping) become paramount.

To fully understand classical management, it is necessary to look more carefully at classical structure, process, and values (see Figure 2–4).

FIGURE 2–4
Classical organization theory structure, process, and values, as moderated by existential values

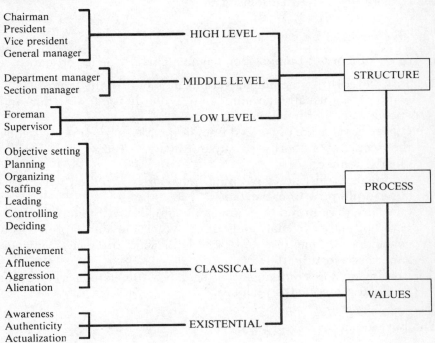

TOPIC 2
Classical structure

Classical theorists describe firms as closed and static systems in which the emphasis is on hierarchical authority, span of control, role definitions, and maximal breakdown of tasks. They try to relate the structural variables to work efficiency as the most important output variable, and they deemphasize the human variable. The object is to generate maximum job performance through the specification of work routines or programs, which are defined by work study, production planning, and budgeting controls. It is assumed that communication will mainly be in the vertical direction, with orders flowing downward and reports flowing upward.

ORGANIZATIONAL STRUCTURE

Regardless of the organizational theory they follow, most managers have come to accept the reality of the structure that permeates business organizations. The structure of the firm defines how the business proceeds in a systematic way, both in the exercise of authority and the coordination of functions. These arrangements of authority and functions are experienced as a structuring of social space by employees.

Early research in the area of structure dealt mainly with such configuration variables as span of control and the number of levels of hierarchy. Based on limited research, many conclusions were drawn. For example, it was widely believed at one time that the span of control at a maximum covered six people. Then research at Sears, Roebuck & Company showed that larger spans of control facilitate opportunities for individual development, improve morale, and lead to higher productivity.

There have been many attempts to relate structural variables such as the number of levels of hierarchy to productivity, effectiveness, and morale. In general such studies tend to show that small companies with less than 5,000 people and flat structures are more effective and satisfying.

In spite of Parkinson's law (which suggests why the number of admirals expanded much faster than the number of aircraft carriers), research studies show that administrative components decrease as organizational functions increase.

THE CONCEPT OF ROLE

The most important thing for the manager to know about the concept of role is that it is intimately connected with the idea of expectations. When you want people to do something, or to actively fill a role, you have to figure out (and perhaps manage) the expectations of the act that they carry in their heads. This involves the sociology of roles, or the relationships among the parts, people take in an organization.

In traditional classical management, individual job descriptions were always prepared with the following subheadings: title, introductory paragraph, list of functions, decisions to be made, method of review, kind of person to fill the role, and salary. Each position was considered separately.

Managers now know that the sociological meaning of roles also has a bearing on role definition. If roles cannot be defined individually, they must be defined in sets. For example, the president and the vice

Box 2-3: The classical management of roles

DEFINING THE IMPOSSIBLE: OBJECTIVES

For the classical manager, everything begins (and all faults can be traced to) the definition of the objectives. In this superrational, cerebral world, logic is out, and a swift definition of objectives is in. Definitions of intention are spelled out as categorical imperatives, with no room left for excuses such as "I was trying my best." Every infantry officer who attended West Point or Sandhurst or the Kiev War Academy knows you don't say "Intention: We will try to knock out the pillbox," but rather "Intention: Knock out the pillbox." In management, too, the program is spelled out in categorical terms: "Intention: Manufacturing the product in the right quantity at the right quality, on a schedule determined by sales, within the company policy."

Once the classical manager has drawn up a list of objectives, they are divided into three categories: vital, important, and nice to have. Classical managers like Peter Drucker's pithy aphorisms, such as "Efficiency is doing things right; effectiveness is doing the right things right."

KEEPING THE OTHER GUY IN PLACE

Classical managers know their place and how to keep the other guy in place. They do this with expressions like, "What you are telling me is that you are unwilling to conform with your job description."

Classical managers also "keep a stiff upper lip" and hate "playing it by ear" unless they "have it in writing": *Nobody* gets carte blanche. Management is the act of getting results through people—not with them, but through them.

THE CLASSICAL ARGOT: GET IT IN WRITING

The peculiar vocabulary of classical management consists of expressions like "Try a little synergy." Synergy is the technique used to defeat ordinary arithmetic, where $2 + 2 = 4$, and replace it with organizational arithmetic, where $2 + 2 = 0, 1, 2, 3 \ldots n$, depending on the technique of corporate adding used.

Winston Churchill used classical management terminology when he told a general in 1940, "Please explain to me in writing why we lost France. Use one side of a foolscap sheet."

Classical managers get everything in writing—applications for promotion and raises, complaints, charges or nepotism. The classical executive might ask that a letter be typed with an original, carbon copies for others, a file copy, and a copy for "the file of last resort." The idea is to have what the English call "belts and braces" so that you won't be caught with your pants down.

Classical managers think in terms of zero-defect programs and fail-safe mechanisms.

presidents can collectively define their roles with a far greater chance of success than bringing in a consultant who would take each one individually.

Preparing role specifications

The preparation of exact role specifications, usually in written form, was introduced during World War I, when staff officers compiled

They admire quality control programs which achieve zero defects with whimsical but effective BAD (Buck-A-Day) programs, which means that every employee has to reduce costs by at least $1 a day or $250 a year. If they fail, they're BAD guys.

Classical managers make up lists of things to do *today.* They occasionally send memos to themselves, in an operation called papering the files, and they dictate memos into their tape recorders in cars and planes. Elliott Richardson, psyching himself up to resign during the Saturday Night Massacre, which forced Archibald Cox out of his job as special Watergate prosecutor, stayed up all night writing notes to himself headed "Why I Must Resign."

Frequently, a written analysis of a problem can be valuable. For example, Bernie Cornfield trained his mutual fund salesmen to close a sale by dividing a blank page into columns headed pro and con and then helping the client to fill in the arguments, with a little selective coaching.

TELL ME WHAT I HAVE SAID

Classical managers, many of whom have been engineers, often utilize an electrical engineer's model of communication. A plant manager might say: "Please repeat back what I've said, so that there can be no uncertainty about what I've proposed."

This penchant for ensuring fidelity in information communicated is particularly valuable in production scheduling and quality control. Accuracy is critical in situations that can be blueprinted, green-lighted, and separated into go–no go decisions.

But, two-way communications are not always preferred. It all depends—on the people involved, the setting, and the nature of the task (structured or unstructured). If there is "an answer at the back of the book, the procedure is specified. If there is no one right answer, you can do what you like.

WEAR A NICE DARK SUIT AND A . . .

The classical manager wears a dark, single-breasted suit with a white shirt and a tie and shined black shoes. A color-coordinated suit, shirt, and tie may be OK, but the classical manager can get upset if subordinates wear far-out clothes or double-knit suits which bag at the knees.

TIME IS OF THE ESSENCE

For the classical manager, time is spelled *money:* "Check with my secretary, who'll try to fit you in." Courses for executives on how to make effective use of time are greatly in demand. They are taught, for example, to call subordinates at 8:45 A.M. when they won't be there but their secretaries will, and then ask the secretaries to take notes.

elaborate tables of organization for the infantry. The new organizational doctrine, which went by the book, spelled out, in writing, who could do what, where, and when, and precisely who was responsible to whom. A participant in that great war of attrition, where everything depended on railway timetables, synchronized watches, and zero hour, was Urwick, who read Taylor's *Scientific Management* as a colonel on his way to a battle on the Somme. When Urwick later founded an international firm of managerial consultants, the administrative management theory he proposed included such novel ideas as unity of command, the role of the staff officer, and departmentalization by purpose, process, person, and place.

Urwick's ideas were taken up with a vengeance in the United States by Luther Gulick, who believed that management should be reduced to "standard nomenclature, measurable elements, and rational concepts." Soon all organizations—hospitals, factories, schools, hotels, churches—were being set up as if they were a cross between an infantry division and General Motors. For a time the notion that logical analysis rather than personalities should determine roles, rules, and relations, worked. Education benefited from set time periods, qualified specialists, and examinations, as did medicine, religion, and even charity.

Box 2–3 gives some notes on how classical managers manage roles. Somewhere along the line, in the midfifties, the relations between roles began to change, however. Children started checking parents, and patients began suing doctors.

TOPIC 3
Classical process

STEPS IN THE CLASSICAL PROCESS OF MANAGING

A widely employed method for getting things done in management is shown in Figure 2–5. This method is based on seven steps: setting the objective, planning, organizing, staffing, leading, controlling, and deciding.

FIGURE 2–5
Seven-step classical management process

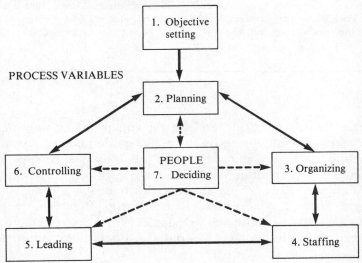

Objective setting

The manager's first step is to decide what he or she is trying to do. This means specifying the objective. Effective management is always management by objectives. The basic proposition is not only that the end determines the means, but also that the means determine the end.

Planning

Once the objectives have been determined, the process of planning can begin. Planning delineates goals and ways of achieving them, not any goals but those that will help the manager reach the objective. Planning essentially consists of action undertaken to meet future needs effectively. It requires an examination of the strengths and weaknesses of the business; the resources available in terms of people, money, material, moxie, and information; and a forecast of future demands and development, a guestimate of what things are going to be like (see Figure 2–6).

FIGURE 2–6

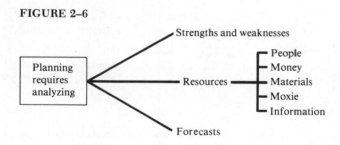

Planning is a disciplined intellectual activity which builds on facts and inspired but controlled guesses (the two are clearly separated). It is a deliberate mental activity which involves the invention of concepts, the manipulation of ideas, the generation of data, and the anticipation of many possible outcomes. It is also contingency oriented: Plan A applies for Contingency 1 (e.g., IBM does not introduce a new model) and Plan B applies for Contingency 2 (e.g., IBM introduces a new model). Figure 2–7 is an example of a plan for research on a new product.

Planning always involves participation. Plans do not always work out, due to the wrong "facts," poor guessing, inaccurate forecasting, or changes in the environment, such as the emergence of OPEC as an influence on the automobile industry. When the right people participate in planning, however, at least they know what is going on, and they can steer the system. And, of course, participation ensures a measure of commitment.

FIGURE 2–7
A plan for research in solar cells

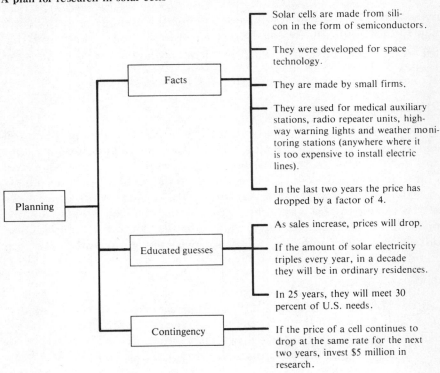

Short-range planning involves specific instruments or activities, such as:

The expenses and revenue forecast. An estimate of future revenues and expenses in dollars and cents terms.

The cash forecast. A probable cash flow statement intended to avoid shortages and exploit surpluses.

The pro forma balance sheet statement. An advance version of the balance sheet based on information contained in sales, material, and labor plans.

The budget. A detailed statement of financial position for a definite period based on estimates of expenditures and proposals for financing.

PERT—Program Evaluation and Review Technique. A planning and control technique developed by the U.S. Navy to get the Polaris submarine built and operational in a tight schedule. PERT identifies short-range steps in long-range jobs and gets them done on time.

Organizing

In organizing, an organization is set up to provide a structure (comprised of divisions, plants, departments, sections, or roles) to put the plan in operation. In Washington, D.C., it is said that Democrats believe that a good man will get the job done even if the structure is a bit sloppy, but Republicans believe that if the structure is right, a second-class tractor salesman will be able to do the job.

While planning is neither well understood nor well structured, organizing has been very carefully researched and is highly structured.

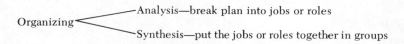

Organizing
    Analysis—break plan into jobs or roles
    Synthesis—put the jobs or roles together in groups

Organizing utilizes job descriptions and organization charts. It is concerned with authority and responsibility, delegation, and centralized, decentralized, and other types of organizational structures.

Staffing

Staffing the organization involves finding people who can fill the roles and grow with them. This text is concerned with the staffing of management jobs, or the hiring and career development of managers. We will also look at the business school graduate, especially the MBA, and at such topics as executive alienation and what happens to managers when they are fired.

The sorts of issues to be encountered in staffing include:

How are executives hired? How are interviews conducted? What does the assessment center (bringing together groups of candidates with selectors for a period of days) accomplish?

What are the different stages of development for an executive?

How much feedback does a young manager need?

What is the best policy for the MBA on a starting-level job: stay or quit?

Is there a firing routine? How can managers cope with it?

Is there much executive alienation in an organization? What causes it, and what can be done about it?

How can executives grow?

Leading

Once the right people are in position, the next issue is how they can be led so that the job gets done.

What kind of leadership is most effective? Is democratic, employee-centered, supportive, and concerned leadership best in all circumstances? Or, is it more important to structure the plan, reduce the number of viable alternatives, selectively control feedback, and firm up deadlines with autocratic leadership? Behavioral scientists have provided useful models to help managers choose the most effective leadership style.

Manipulation and power and authority are other aspects of leadership to be considered.

Controlling

Goals have been specified, plans formulated, organizations set up and staffed, people given leadership. The next step is controlling, the technical name for the process whereby performance is checked against standards. Controlling ensures that organizational objectives are being met.

In brief, controlling means controlling people—putting constraints on their behavior, their choices. But it is not only coercive and reward oriented, it is also normative—people have to believe that the process is rational, productive, and possible.

Controlling is closely related to planning, as their proximity in the circular diagram in Figure 2–5 indicates. It is essentially concerned with checking, regulating, rectifying, and keeping the action within the limits of the plan. It is not only a postmortem activity dealing with events after the fact but also goes on simultaneously with other functions of the management system. By analyzing past and present performance, controlling helps to devise standards and plans for future action.

Deciding, the integrating step

The first step in the classical management process is the selection and definition of an objective. Planning works on the issue, or the objective to be achieved, through organizing, staffing, and leading, while controlling evaluates the effort. At the deciding stage, however, a single objective may no longer be appropriate. In classical decision theory, the notion that a system has multiple objectives is accepted as a point of departure. Objectives may be added or reduced as a result of decision making, the integrating step between planning and controlling (see Figure 2–8).

Deciding, therefore, is the hub of the classical management process shown above in Figure 2–8, and it holds the other steps of the process in place. The circular model of the management process demonstrates

FIGURE 2–8
Decision making as the integrating step between planning and controlling

its essential unity as a set of interlocking steps. Once the circular process has been completed, it may be necessary to go around once again—to make sure every step is firm, tight, and fitting.

In classical theory, organizational decision making goes by certain rules:

1. Organizations are monitored by multiple, changing goals.
2. Organizations make considerable use of programed decisions.
3. Organizations employ rather simple rule-of-thumb decision rules which require the sequential examination of alternatives, and acceptance of the first satisfactory alternative.
4. Organizations engage in directed search; they seek to avoid uncertainty through the use of routine procedures.

Herbert A. Simon, in "Recent Advances in Organization Theory," specifies three stages in the overall process of making a decision:

Diagnosis: Searching the environment for occasions calling for a decision—the intelligence activity (borrowing the military meaning).

Evaluation: Inventing, developing, and analyzing possible courses of action—the design activity.

Implementation: Selecting and implementing a possible course of action—the choice activity.

Essentially, Simon is proposing that a manager *satisfices*, that is, seeks satisfactory alternatives rather than optimal answers, guided by the negative principle that the best must not become the enemy of the good.

TOPIC 4
Classical values

Values are the social glue, the psychological electrostatic field forces, that hold the organization and its members on track. Everybody has values, though other people's may be difficult to recognize because they are different. Managers need moral frames of reference within which to exercise choice and commit themselves.

Values comprise a class of beliefs which are held by members of a society or group concerning what is desirable or "good." These value systems help people make choices between competing human interests in regard to what constitutes desirable ends. Traditional classical organizational values emphasize rationality, causality, integrity, independence, deferred consumption, and hard work. An antithetical value system would underscore authenticity, awareness, interdependence, immediate gratification, and hedonism (pleasure seeking). Existentialism has such a value system.

The white Anglo-Saxon Protestant (WASP) ethos which has dominated our organizational life is generally recognized to be declining. Overachieving and conspicuous consumption are going out of fashion. Existential values could provide the catalyst for the coming change.

Moderation of classical values

Classical values have a certain no-nonsense, let's-get-on-with-the-job quality. They are essentially the underlying beliefs which collectively help to get a job done: rationality, perfectability, work hard–play hard, postpone consumption, save for a rainy day. Classical managers are essentially doers who find it hard to delegate.

But managers have to be distinguished from entrepreneurs, who have quite a different value system. Entrepreneurs play for much bigger stakes in a winner-takes-all context; managers take calculated risks aimed at the achievement of an objective. Entrepreneurs are concerned with the end, managers with the means. Managers see themselves as instruments of the entrepreneurs or owners—they have instrumental values which are concerned with getting on with the job.

Young managers now entering business typically have the attributes of both managers and entrepreneurs. Research has provided abundant data to show that they have not abandoned classical values but rather have added some of the values from the existential sys-

FIGURE 2–9
Classical-existential values of today's managers

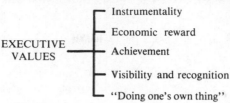

tem (see Figure 2–9). They have strong yearnings for recognition, visibility, and above all for "doing their own thing," but not at the expense of economic advancement or job tenure.

A good example of these changing values is their attitudes toward job transfers involving relocation. Even though accepting the principle of mobility increases the chances of promotion, young executives are resisting this corporate policy. One reason is that their husbands or wives do not want to disrupt their own careers, and another is the value placed on family life.

Thus the classical values of rationality, instrumentality, and achievement are being moderated by existential values. This is a gross simplification, however, because executive values vary along many different dimensions.

Personnel managers, for example, put a great deal of stress on human relations values. Production managers emphasize hands-on skills which reflect strong technological values. Marketing people wear suits, drink wine, and drive cars which reflect the values of their clients. And so on.

Values also vary by organizational level:

TOP MANAGERS:	"I believe in the free enterprise system."
MIDDLE MANAGERS:	"I believe we have to take a tougher line."
SUPERVISORS:	"I believe . . . I don't know, I'm in a bind."
OPERATORS:	"Stand by your friends." "Don't tell *them* anything." "Get the biggest buck for the least effort."

The president, who can see the big picture, can accept the firm's values completely. And since he is frequently isolated from the bad news from below, he can see no reason to think otherwise. Middle managers are usually tougher. They have to be because, contrary to conventional wisdom and Harry S Truman, so many of the bucks stop there.

The traditional shop-floor values of operators are designed to provide a feeling of solidarity and promote the interests of workers. This is an oversimplification, of course, since their values, like others, are a function of religion, race, sex, age, and community. Volkswagen located its American plant in New Stanton, Pennsylvania, because sociologists had found a high index of the traditional work ethic there.

The values of foremen and supervisors are a product of their double bind of being caught in between management and the shop floor. Not paid enough to assimilate the executive ethos, and affected by the camaraderie of the operators, the supervisor ends up as management's man on the firing point.

That's why values are ill defined, so that they can deal with ambiguity and complexity. But if you are a manager, you have to be careful you don't end up without a chair when the music stops. This is what happened in the early sixties when some General Electric managers ended up in jail for colluding on prices with the competition. Somebody misread the signals or somebody changed the rules. The executives involved felt that if the company expected them to follow a particular rule regarding collusion on prices, they should have been brought up before their superiors and told to sign a legal statement that they had read the rule, understood it, and would diligently apply it.

Executives have to understand values and be able to distinguish between the legal and the "legit". And they have to be ready to act as a reasonably prudent man, in the eyes of the law.

TOPIC 5
What every manager should know
about classical theory

In the classical approach, Taylor, Gulick, and Weber set out to study organizations with scientific precepts. Figure 2–10 illustrates how this approach can be evaluated using the elements in the contingency model developed in Chapter 1.

In terms of structure, to the classical theorist the key to precision and effectiveness is a centralized, pyramidal authority structure in which the number of hierarchical levels, spans of control, and line-staff relations are carefully defined. Thus the first thing a classical theorist does when setting up an organization is to draw up an organization chart with line (vertical) and staff (lateral) relations clearly laid out. Then elaborate job specifications setting out authority, responsibilities, functions, rank, and duties are written.

FIGURE 2–10
The classical approach to the study of organizational behavior

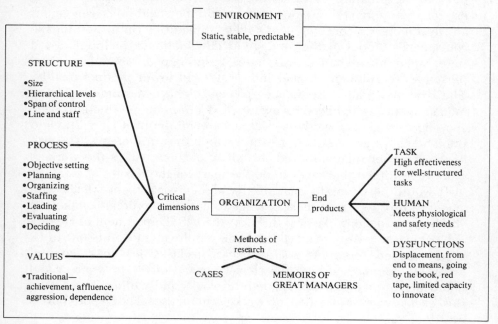

Weber codified the classical system in terms of staffing and structure: efficiency is achieved by arranging offices according to hierarchy and jurisdiction; experts are appointed to these offices who, guided by the book (precedent), deal with clients (the customer); and the bureaucrat comes into the organization by examination, moves through it by merit, and retires from it (he cannot be fired) with a pension.

So much for structure. What about process? The total task of management can be broken into seven elements, to use up dated classical analysis: objective setting, planning, organizing, staffing, leading (command and coordination), controlling, and deciding.

In this essentially bureaucratic approach, it is presumed that the organization man will always act in the best interests of the firm and will behave rationally. The value system is based on four elements; achievement, self-control, independence, and endurance of pain and distress. It would be wrong to presume that the Protestant work ethic is dead in America. For example, a Daniel Yankelovitch survey found that 79 percent of U.S. college students feel a meaningful career is an important element in life.

In terms of end products, the presumption is that increasing productivity or profitability will bring satisfaction in its wake, following the work ethic, "work is joy." But when productivity falls, management puts on the pressure by tightening up controls. Increasing controls, especially through the use of general and impersonal rules, can generate dysfunctional consequences. These difficulties (indicated on the contingency model in Figure 2–10 as *dysfunctions*), include wasted time, higher maintenance costs, figure fudging, poor morale, impaired personnel recruitment, higher unit costs, and lower product quality. The dysfunctional consequences of control have a spiraling effect: management, as it becomes aware of declines in productivity (the shop-floor or factory workers do the bare minimum that will avoid punishment), increases the pressure, which in turn increases the visibility of power relations. And this show of force makes the workers more determined than ever to do the least for the most.

It would be wrong to imagine that the classical theory deals with ancient history. In fact, most businesses and public organizations are still organized along classical lines. As the U.S. Department of Health, Education, and Welfare's task force on employment points out in its report entitled *Work in America,* monotonous tasks and bleak regimentation are common to both the shop floor and office, to workers and managers, to men and women, and to blacks and whites. The cost of this excessive routinization of work is immense. The report points out:

> Characterologically, the hierarchical organization requires workers to follow orders, which calls for submissive traits, while the selection of managers calls for authoritarian and controlling traits. . . .
>
> The more democratic and self-affirmative an individual is, the less he will stand for boring, dehumanized and authoritarian work. Under such conditions, the workers either protest or give in, at some cost to their psychological well-being. Anger that does not erupt may be frozen into schizoid, depressed characters who escape into general alienation, drugs and fantasies.

Not unexpectedly, management and workers have turned to human relations for a way out of this dilemma.

REVIEW AND RESEARCH

1. Why did the theory of bureaucracy develop at the turn of the century in Germany?
2. Select any large-scale organization in business, government, or the military and assess the degree to which it conforms to bureaucratic principles.
3. Why was project management invented? What projects are suitable for project management? List the pros and cons of project management.
4. What is matrix management? What organizational problems are best tackled by matrix management?

5. What is an adhocracy (a coined term which should be decipherable)? Which industries are most suitable to be treated as adhocracies? Why?
6. Describe the personality of the adhocracy man. How does it compare with the organization man of the 1950s?
7. Describe and explain the human reaction to working in the automobile industry.
8. How do conglomerates like ITT manage such diversified interests?

GLOSSARY OF TERMS

Administrative management. A management system which includes such principles as fitting people to the organization structure; need for unity of command; use of special and general staffs; departmentalization by purpose, process, persons, and places; delegation; balancing of authority and responsibility; definition of the span of control.

Bureaucracy. Organization structure possessing some sort of administrative machinery and specialized secretariat to keep the organization working.

Dysfunctions. Unanticipated end results which are not congruent with the original intention of the organizational goal. For example, increased quality control on car manufacture can lead to the dysfunctions of slower production and the concealing of defects.

Effectiveness. The optimal mix of productivity, innovation, and control of inter- and intraorganizational stress.

Formal organization. A hierarchical differentiated system of interrelated groups and roles which has been designed by the chief executive as an efficient system for accomplishing the mission of the organization. The two principal determinants of the behavior of members are the structure and values of organization. Structure specifies communication routes, defines authority, and sets methods of redress of grievance. The network of social relations is defined between individuals and groups. The value system helps to define the goals for which organizational members strive and specifies their ideals.

Informal organization. Informal organization is the inevitable antibody of formal organization and represents the backlash of the organized against the organizers. Patterns of interpersonal and intergroup relations always develop within and parallel to the formal organization. The informal organization inevitably will not have the same aims as the formal organization, and it usually includes cliques and cabals. An informal organization is likely to develop when the formal organization proves to be inefficient or when it fails to meet important human needs of its members.

Scientific management. A management system which includes such principles as selecting the right man for the job, deciding by method study on the one best way to do the job, developing differential piecework processes, careful planning of the actual work process, and developing line and functional specialization.

Social organization. A loosely organized set of interrelated groups which has emerged to achieve a particular purpose (e.g., a political party).

DEBATE: Values and geography

From *The New York Times*, Sunday, February 19, 1978.

> In the East, people ask you where you went to school, in the South, they ask you what family you come from. In the Middle West, the question is, "Where do you work?" In the West, it is: "What do you drive and how much do you make?" If you have a Mercedes and lots of money, you don't have to have anything else.

METHOD OF DEBATE

Divide the class into groups according to geography or value system (classical or existential) and try to define accurately the values that represent your point of view.

DIAGRAM SUMMARY OF CHAPTER 3

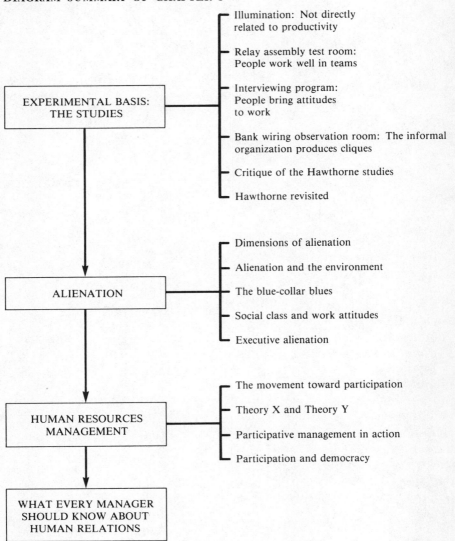

EXPERIMENTAL BASIS: THE STUDIES

- Illumination: Not directly related to productivity
- Relay assembly test room: People work well in teams
- Interviewing program: People bring attitudes to work
- Bank wiring observation room: The informal organization produces cliques
- Critique of the Hawthorne studies
- Hawthorne revisited

ALIENATION

- Dimensions of alienation
- Alienation and the environment
- The blue-collar blues
- Social class and work attitudes
- Executive alienation

HUMAN RESOURCES MANAGEMENT

- The movement toward participation
- Theory X and Theory Y
- Participative management in action
- Participation and democracy

WHAT EVERY MANAGER SHOULD KNOW ABOUT HUMAN RELATIONS

3

Human relations

HUMAN RELATIONS IN ACTION

The first human relations manager I met who had bridged the gap between Dale Carnegie and Andrew Carnegie was my boss at a pharmaceutical company with headquarters in London. Incidentally, this was a pharmaceutical company with a difference; it did not make any profits. Any money left over after doing research and giving the employees very good working conditions was put into a trust to support medical research.

My main duty was helping train new employees to package the product. Two thirds of the 1,500 people worked in packing, and the products were mainly aspirin and laxatives.

The packing workers were all women in white uniforms who sat along an assembly line, counting aspirin with a bat with 50 holes in it, pouring the tablets into a bottle via a filter funnel, banging a label on, and sticking a cork in the neck of the bottle. While I didn't realize it then, this was Adam Smith's celebrated pin factory, with each person performing a different task, one filling, another labeling, and so on. Contrary to the views of a social science student who visited the plant periodically and saw "the terrible alienation of mass production" and what it did to human beings, the women were as happy as larks—chatting to each other, steady and serious at their work. I was told that they would knock themselves out working anytime a world crisis came on: "You should have seen them during the invasion, especially after D-day. . . ."

The method my boss used to get productivity was quite ingenious. The company was an international one with its head office in London and plants in Sydney, Bombay, New York, Rome, Montreal and so on. On the wall along the production line, he had a colored map of the world put up, on which London and our various plants were marked with penny-sized discs. Each day when the women came in, we asked them where they would like to go. If "Three Coins in a Fountain" was playing locally, for example, they were off to Rome. The red band on the map joining London and Rome was broken into eight equal units, each unit representing an hour's output for the whole work group, as scientifically calculated by time study. As each hour of work was completed, a cardboard plane was moved forward one step, and we were one step nearer to la dolce vita.

The work was all done by numbers, through time and motion study. The scientific-looking engineers stood around in white coats, with ramrod backs, clutching to their bosoms boards with stopwatches attached. They never seemed to be speaking to the workers; I suppose they would have had to record such interactions under the heading "personal," those percentages of wasted time that time study people allow when calculating "standard time." Most of these time study people had been recruited from Lyons Tea Houses, which in the fifties were presumed to be models of scientific efficiency. Their cafeteria service was reputedly controlled by a plate whose size was an optical illusion, so that customers filled them with lettuce and cucumbers, which left no room for the more expensive meat.

Despite the intimidation of the time study engineers, this boss knew how to make work fun for the workers. He applied human relations to classical management theory.

HUMAN RELATIONS THEORY

Classical management is the only way to organize. People have to be put in roles; one person has to be put in charge of this, another that; things have to be organized. But, you may say, people are not things. Nevertheless, when scientific principles were applied to people, they had to be treated as things. Management seems to be saying, like Frank Sinatra, "I did it my way." And subordinates seem to be replying, like Nancy Sinatra, "Dem boots are made for walking, and I'm going to walk all over you."

To avoid such conflict between the Franks and the Nancies, it is necessary for classical management to be modified by human relations. The place of human relations in the organization theory framework is shown in Figure 3–1.

The human relations orientation has emerged in a number of forms, including human relations, human resources management, and the human potential movement (see Figure 3–2). The objective of this

FIGURE 3–1
How classical theory is modified by human relations to produce systems theory

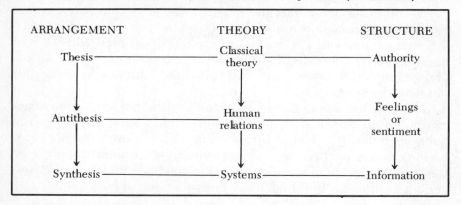

FIGURE 3–2
Three variations in human relations

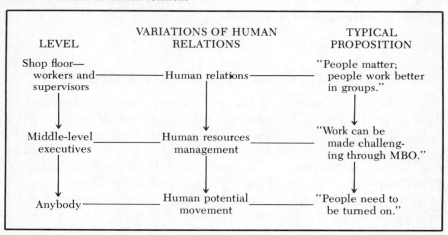

chapter is to present these variations of the human relations theme so that the reader can form a judgment in regard to their relevance, empirical foundation, and utility. (The human potential movement is introduced in the last section of this chapter.) But perhaps it is just as well to keep in mind that behavioral scientists are human and they do err, usually in their own favor.

WINNING AND LOSING THE ORGANIZATIONAL WAR

In the pharmaceutical company described at the beginning of the chapter, the time study men, with their allies, the production planning and control people won the great organizational war. A huge coliseum-like hanger filled with the latest German packing equipment, laid out in great long lines, with extremely wide aisles so that the forklift trucks could work up and down the lines without interfering with production. The walls were tastefully painted and the hall illuminated by concealed lighting, following the direction of an expert in interior decoration who had been brought down from Mayfair to select the scheme.

Each day the women were allocated to different work groups according to production demands. But they didn't seem to be enjoying their scientifically selected surroundings. They were ordering more packing cases than they needed and building walls around their work stations. Driven out of the small rooms which had filled the nooks and crannies of the old buildings, they finally retaliated by leaving.

What was causing this exodus? "What does woman want?" became the cri de coeur of the personnel managers, who had never heard of the Hawthorne experiment of the twenties and the finding that people like to work in small groups in separate rooms.

TOPIC 1
Experimental basis: The Hawthorne studies

The theoretical basis of the human relations school was established through the Hawthorne experiments, which are considered classics by virtue of their scope, significance, and design. The experiments were carried out at the Western Electric Company's Hawthorne Works in Cicero, a suburb of Chicago, and are closely linked with the name of Elton Mayo. As professor of industrial research at the Harvard School of Business Administration, Mayo was the person most responsible for developing these experiments and publicizing their significance.

The Hawthorne studies can be considered under four headings: (1) the experiments on illumination, (2) the relay assembly test room, (3) the interviewing program, and (4) the bank wiring observation room.

THE EXPERIMENTS ON ILLUMINATION

The Hawthorne experiments on illumination provide a classical example of the consequence of applying scientific methods, as used in the physical sciences, to a social problem. The object of the experiment at the outset was to ascertain the relationship between productivity and illumination. To this end, productivity was measured at various levels of illumination. Contrary to expectations, the results showed that output rose and fell without direct relation to the intensity of illumination.

THE RELAY ASSEMBLY TEST ROOM

To find out why, it was decided to isolate a small group of women in a separate room away from the regular working force, where their behavior could be scientifically investigated. The task chosen was the assembly of small telephone relays. The rate of output was then five relays in six minutes (approximately 500 a day), so that even small changes in productivity would be immediately obvious.

The way the team was selected is important. Two operators who were friendly with each other chose three other assemblers and a layout operator. The only other person in the room was a research assistant who kept records of production, rejects, weather, temperature, and a log of hour-by-hour happenings. The chairs, fixtures, and work layout were similar to those in a normal department.

In setting up this experiment, therefore, a small group of operators was isolated. What happened was that they began to think of themselves as an elite in the midst of a sea of mass production. Thus scientific structuring of a social situation turned out not to be as "clinical" as the psychologists had thought.

The relay assembly study started with six questions:

1. Do employees actually get tired out?
2. Are rest pauses desirable?
3. Is a shorter working day desirable?
4. What is the attitude of the employees toward their work and the company?
5. What are the effects of changing the type of work equipment?
6. Why does production fall off in the afternoon?

To answer these questions a number of test conditions were introduced.

Results and conclusions

The most significant result to emerge from this part of the research was that throughout the study the average hourly output of the employees continued to rise. No matter what change was introduced, the output rose until it stabilized at a high level. A number of explanations have been offered for these somewhat unexpected effects.

1. Perhaps not too surprisingly, the women liked to work in the test room; they thought it was "fun." Though each knew that she was producing more than in her regular department, she said it was not due to any conscious effort.

2. A new supervisory relationship developed which apparently enabled the women to work freely without anxiety. Although they were far more thoroughly supervised than before, to their mind the

Box 3–1: A closer look at friendly supervision in action

Alex Carey's Hawthorne critique points out that the whole of the Hawthorne claim that friendly supervision and resulting work-group social relations and satisfactions are overwhelmingly important for work behavior rests on whatever evidence can be extracted from the relay assembly test room (RATR) study, since that is the only study in the series which exhibits even a surface association between the introduction of such factors and increased output. The RATR study began with five women specially selected for being both "thoroughly experienced" and "willing and cooperative," so there was no reason to expect this group to be more than ordinarily cooperative and competent. Yet from very early in the study "the amount of talking indulged in by all the operators" had constituted a "problem," because it "involved a lack of attention to work and a preference for conversing together for considerable periods of time."

The operators, especially 1A and 2A, were threatened with disciplinary action and subjected to continual reprimands. "Almost daily," 2A was "reproved" for her "low output and behavior." The investigators decided 1A and 2A did not have the "right" mental attitude. 1A and 2A were replaced by two workers chosen by the foreman "who were experienced relay assemblers and desirous of participating in the test. These two women (designated Operators 1 and 2) were transferred to the test room on January 25th, 1928. They both immediately produced an output much greater (in total and in rate per hour) than that achieved by any of the original five operators and much above the performance at any time of the two women they replaced.

Operators 1 and 2 had been friends in the main shop. Operator 2 was the only Italian in the group; she was young (21), and her mother died shortly after she joined the test room; after this "Operator 2 earned the larger part of the family income." "From now on the history of the test room revolves around the personality of Operator 2." Operator 2 rapidly (i.e., without any delay during which she might have been affected by the new supervision) adopted and maintained a strong and effective disciplinary role with respect to the rest of the group, and led the way in increased output in every period from her arrival till the end of the study. In this she was closely followed by the other new worker, Operator 1.

Carey summarized the outcome of this study as follows:

1. The dismissed workers were replaced by two women of a special motivation and character who immediately led the rest in a sustained acceleration of output. One, who had a special need for extra money, rapidly adopted and maintained a strong disciplinary role with respect to the rest of the group. The two new operators led the way in increased output from their arrival till the end of the study.

2. Total output per week showed a significant and sustained increase only after the two operators who had the lowest output were dismissed and replaced by selected output leaders. These workers accounted for the major part of the group's increase, both in output rate and in total output, over the next 17 months of the study.

3. After the arrival of the new workers and the associated increase in output, official supervision became friendly and relaxed once more. The investigators, however, provided no evidence that output increased because supervision became more friendly rather than vice versa. In any case, friendly supervision took a very tangible turn by paying the operators for time not worked, so that the piece rate was in effect increased.

Reference: Alex Carey, "The Hawthorne Studies: A Radical Criticism," *American Sociological Review*, Vol. 32 (1967), pp. 403–16.

character and purpose of supervision were different. They regarded the test-room observer as a friendly representative of management and not as a supervisor who "bawls you out."

3.   To their delight, the operators felt that they were a kind of élite and further that they were taking an important part in an interesting experiment which "proved" that management was interested in them.

4.   Over the experimental period there was a strengthening of the group bonds that held the women together; four of them started going out together both in the evenings and on weekends, and they all helped each other at work.

5.   The group developed leadership and a common purpose (increase in output rate).

Alex Carey of the University of New South Wales questions these conclusions in "The Hawthorne Studies: A Radical Criticism." Carey compares Hawthorne conclusions and Hawthorne evidence (see Box 3–1) and challenges the conclusion:

> . . . that social satisfactions arising out of human association in work were more important determinants of work behavior in general and output in particular than were any of the physical and economic aspects of the work situation to which their attention had originally been limited. This conclusion came as "the great *éclaircissement* . . . an illumination quite different from what they had expected from the illumination studies." It is the central and distinctive finding from which the fame and influence of the Hawthorne studies derive.

Carey came up with his own startling conclusion:

> A detailed comparison between the Hawthorne conclusions and the Hawthorne evidence shows these conclusions to be almost wholly unsupported. The evidence reported by the Hawthorne investigators is found to be consistent with the view that material, and especially financial, reward is the principal influence on work morale and behavior. Questions are raised about how it was possible for studies so nearly devoid of scientific merit, and conclusions so little supported by evidence, to gain so influential and respected a place within scientific disciplines and to hold this place for so long.

THE INTERVIEWING PROGRAM

The interviewing program came through criticism of the Hawthorne studies very well. The critical point demonstrated by the interviewing program is central to the human relations movement: If you let people talk about things that are important to them, they may come up with issues that are at first sight unconnected with their work. These issues are how their children are doing at school, how the family is going to manage with all the medical bills, what their friends think of their jobs, and so on. Talking about such matters to a sympathetic listener who does not interpret is therapeutic. This is precisely what happened at Hawthorne, where a nondirective interviewing strategy was adopted. So successful was this strategy that more than 20,000 employees were interviewed.

Above all, the interviewing program showed that the attitudes people bring to their work are as important as those they pick up at work. Nevertheless, a major criticism of the Hawthorne researchers was that they did not pay sufficient heed to what was going on in Cicero at the time of their study. The Chicago area was right in the middle of bootlegging, gangsterism, organized crime, and political corruption, which characterized Prohibition and the Roaring Twenties. It is hard to believe that researchers like Mayo were not aware of this wider social context, which certainly affected workers' attitudes. Not only were the issues staring the man-in-the-street in the face, but sociologists from schools such as the University of Chicago were addressing such matters as social disorganization.

Whatever criticism can be levelled against the researchers for not looking outside the workplace, they did come up with a wealth of data about what was going on inside the plant. They failed to find the Mafia outside, but they did find Mafialike structures inside, in the primary working groups. These informal groups were organized like gangs, with bosses and sidekicks who had built an elaborate social apparatus to ensure that just the right amount was produced. If somebody stepped out of line, he was given "the message" and then "the hammer." This discovery of the informal organization—the elaborate apparatus to control production, with its own convulted rules, its own particular hierarchy of capos and buttonmen—was the critical discovery of the studies. To find out more about how the informal organization operated, the bank wiring room experiment was set up.

THE BANK WIRING OBSERVATION ROOM

The research procedure in the bank wiring observation room experiment was rather similar to the relay assembly test room method, except that it was male operators who were being studied in this case. The workers in this group consisted of nine wiremen, three soldermen, and two inspectors, who were engaged in the assembly of terminal banks for use in telephone exchanges.

The method the men had devised for controlling production is rather interesting. Two techniques were used, one semantic, the other physical; nicknames were given to workers who produced too much, or minor physical punishments were awarded. An example of the latter was the technique of "binging." A bing is a very hard blow applied to the muscles of the upper arm. The person binged has the right to bing back if he wishes.

In the mores or value system of the work group, a central determinant was the need to restrict production. These mores or beliefs can be listed under four headings:

1. Don't be a rate-buster (you should not turn out too much work).
2. Don't be a chiseller (you should not turn out too little work).
3. Don't be a squealer (you should not tell your superiors anything that would harm an associate).
4. Don't act officiously (you must conform to the mandates of the informal group).

These four simple categorical imperatives served as the defense mechanism of the informal social organization, a mechanism the group developed to protect themselves both from within and without.

The development of cliques

An intriguing manifestation of informal organization is the development of cliques. Two cliques were noted in the bank wiring room (Figure 3–3). Clique A consisted of four wiremen, one solderman, and

FIGURE 3–3
Informal organization within the group

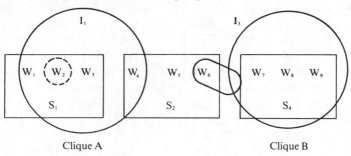

Clique A   Clique B

an inspector; this group usually gambled. Clique B consisted of one solderman and three to five wiremen; this group practiced binging. Job trading was only allowed within cliques. Members of Clique A considered themselves superior to Clique B; they thought their conversation was on a higher plane. Apparently those in Clique B spent a lot of time not only binging, but also quarreling over the opening and shutting of windows. To many, this appears to be a stupid and infantile method of dissipating energy. But it may also be viewed as telling evidence of the reaction to the repressions and frustrations that have been an inevitable part of modern industrial life.

CRITIQUE OF THE HAWTHORNE STUDIES

H. A. Landsberger has presented, in *Hawthorne Revisited*, a brilliant review and assessment of the Hawthorne experiment. The data on the studies were presented by F. J. Roethlisberger and W. J. Dickson in *Management and the Worker*. According to Landsberger, the data:

> . . . are such as to leave the reader with the impression that Western Electric was a thoroughly unpleasant place at which to work during those years and that the authors knew it. . . . Many of those who worked at Hawthorne thought of it as a semi-sweated beehive with individuals at all levels—including lower and middle supervision—transferred arbitrarily from job to job and department to department. Favoritism was not infrequent and serious personal tragedies were often callously ignored.

Landsberger also criticizes the human relations theorist's for emphasis on shop-floor strivings for status and prestige at the expense of their personal desire for power, control, and economic advantage. In passing. Landsberger takes a gentle sideswipe at the Hawthorne researchers for giving advice to managers on how to manipulate subordinates. This how-to-do-it aspect of *Management and the Worker* is regarded as a very dangerous practice.

The human relations school fails ultimately because it does not have a proper frame of reference; it fails to acknowledge the importance of sociological forces; it fails because it does not recognize conflict as a creative force in society. In particular, the idea that conflict is always bad warrants closer examination. Perfect organizational health is not freedom from conflict. Conflict, if properly handled, can lead to more effective and appropriate adjustments.

At the sociological level, the Hawthorne researchers gave inadequate attention to the attitudes that people bring to work. The "us versus them" feeling, the sense of class consciousness that unites shop-floor workers, receives scant attention. This failure on the part of Mayo to analyze the causes of social unrest—coupled with his idea that society is in a state of anomie (i.e., composed of morally confused, isolated people in a society disorganized and full of confusion), where "conflict is a social disease" and cooperation is social health—represents the.main criticism leveled against Mayo.

The scientific status of the Hawthorne studies has been widely challenged, and with good reason. Laboratory psychologists challenge both the experimental design employed and the validity of the findings. The studies can be defended on this count by arguing, as Alan Cubbon does in "The Hawthorne Talk in Context," that the researchers were "contextualists"; that is, they were mapping out the social forces of the primary working group in a particular setting or context rather than carrying out an exact scientific experiment. But this defense leaves them open to the attack of the sociologists, who charge the researchers with failure to place the Hawthorne studies in a wider social context.

HAWTHORNE REVISITED

In 1975 the Western Electric Company and The Harvard Business School marked the 50th anniversary of the Hawthorne studies with a symposium. A critical question: Is Hawthorne worth revisiting? The answer must be in the affirmative. After 50 years, the Hawthorne studies remain the most comprehensive, systematic, and indeed the most exhaustive experiments of shop-floor people actually working.

These experiments have been extensively criticized, mainly by Australian and English researchers. Regardless of its empirical basis, however, the notion that human relations is good not only for people but for productivity gained wide currency. Some of the speakers at the symposium were able to exploit these criticisms to show how the Hawthorne studies favor the contingency theory of management. For example, an article titled "Hawthorne Revisited" by William F. Dowling noted that:

> Paul R. Lawrence, a key speaker at the conference, found in the Hawthorne experiment clues to what he calls the bimodal definition of the meaning of work, the distinction between the three women who appreciated the increased job scope and were productive and involved in their work and the two who were uncooperative and had to be replaced. To put it another way, it's the distinction between people who are turned on by job autonomy and challenge—the majority, says Lawrence—and those nurtured in urban subcultures "that have deeply conditioned them to see work as a simple exchange of time and minimal energy for fair pay and decent conditions. They do not expect to live on the job, only off the job."

In the symposium much was made of the Hawthorne effect—the notion that if special attention is paid to a particular group of workers (e.g., by putting them in a scientific experiment), productivity will rise independently of changes in conditions. In the early days of human relations, the Hawthorne effect led to the notion that participation increases satisfaction, which in turn increases productivity. This is now regarded as a gross oversimplification. It was pointed out in "Hawthorne Revisited" that the enduring message of Hawthorne is different, and it has only recently achieved prominence:

> . . . It was the keynote of the convocation, best captured by Richard Hackman's remark that "The contingency theory of everything is the major theme of the conference." To put it more precisely, the contingency theory maintains that it takes different kinds of people and different kinds of organizations to perform different kinds of tasks. The

function of the behavioral scientist in industry is to assist in the task of matching the person, the organization, and the task.

We think that's what Roethlisberger had in mind when he observed: "I wasn't preaching any model of the way an organization should be. The conceptual scheme of a social system was primarily an investigatory, diagnostic tool." Hawthorne preached no dogmas; held out no hope for panaceas; expounded no universal truths, except the universal that each work situation is different and that we can never assess the appropriateness of any one factor in the work situation except in relation to the totality.

To figure out the significance of this statement that each work situation is different, it is necessary to look at the idea of alienation.

TOPIC 2
Alienation

The concept of alienation is an important one for the student of organizational behavior. Alienation has been defined in psychological terms. Erich Fromm argues that rapid technological and economic changes have estranged human beings from their real nature. In *The Sane Society*, Fromm points out that:

By alienation is meant a mode of experience in which the person experiences himself as alien. He has become, one might say, estranged from himself, he does not experience himself as the creator of his world, as the creator of his own acts—but his acts and their consequences have become his masters, whom he obeys, or whom he may even worship. The alienated person is out of touch with himself as he is out of touch with any other person. He, like the others, is experienced as things are experienced; with the senses and with common senses, but at the same time without being related to oneself and the world outside productively.

THE DIMENSIONS OF ALIENATION

Melvin Seeman has advanced the view that alienation is not a uniform experience but is a concept which can be better understood in terms of experiencing five dimensions: powerlessness, meaninglessness, normlessness, isolation, and self-estrangement.

Using these five dimensions, Robert Blauner has collected data on alienation among American industrial workers. Like most sociologists, Blauner believes that while the working class in the United States is not a potentially revolutionary force, nevertheless Marx's idea of alienation in the work process is valid. In *Alienation and Freedom*, Blauner argues that "Today, most social scientists would says that alienation is not a consequence of capitalism per se but of employment in the large-scale organizations and impersonal bureaucracies that pervade all industrial societies." Having established that alienation does not necessarily follow from the capitalist mode of production, Blauner goes on to argue that it is wrong to assume that the worker must be alienated or nonalienated. The important point is to state the conditions under which alienation will arise. Since there are structural differences within modern industry, it can be assumed that certain conditions are more alienating than others.

Predictably, in the automobile industry Blauner found a higher level of alienation; indeed, for him, the automobile worker is the prototype of the alienated worker. (See box 3–2 for another writer's findings about workers in the automobile industry.) The most satisfied group of workers were the process workers in the oil refinery, who, being highly trained and not engaged in hard physical work, had considerable freedom and discretion, mainly because the production processes were automated. As Blauner points out, while alienation remains a widespread characteristic of factory life, "for most factory workers the picture is probably less black and white than for workers in the automobile and textile industries, where they tend to be highly alienated, and the printing and chemical industries, where freedom and integration are so striking."

ALIENATION AND THE ENVIRONMENT

The environment from which organizational members come has a significant say in how the workers are likely to respond in the work situation. Individuals from a particular environment or community bring a particular set of values and attitudes to their work which significantly affects their behavior in regard to such matters as whether they will observe or reject the production norms of a group and how they will respond to a job enrichment program. Figure 3–4 diagrams alienation as a function of both the task and the environment.

The culture a person brings to work is partly responsible for the values and attitudes displayed there. But what is culture? In the language of the sociologist, it is usually thought of as some kind of vague, complex, inchoate cognitive map which people of a particular com-

FIGURE 3–4
Alienation

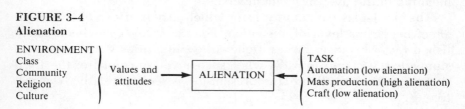

Box 3–2: Auto managers and workers: Likes and dislikes

Studs Terkel has compiled interviews with hundreds of American workers who talk about their jobs and how they feel about them. Some idea from auto managers and workers—the "organizers" and the "organized"—indicate possible sources of alienation.

SHOP–FLOOR WORKERS

PHIL STALLINGS: 27 years old, married, spot welder at Ford Motor Company assembly plant in Chicago.

Likes:
 "I know I could find better places to work. But where could I get the money I'm making?"

Dislikes:
 "Repetition is such that if you were to think about the job itself, you'd go slowly out of your mind."
 "You're nothing more than a machine when you hit this type of thing."

Signs of alienation/stress:
 "They give better care to that machine than they will to you. . . . you get the feeling that the machine is better than you are."
 "When a man becomes a foreman he has to forget about being human, as far as feelings are concerned."
 "When you go into Ford, first thing they try to do is break your spirit."

About boss:
 "How would you like to go up to someone and say ' would like to go to the bath-room?' If the foreman doesn't like you, he'll make you hold it, just ignore you. Should I leave this job to go to the bathroom I risk being fired."
 "When I first went in there, I kind of envied foremen. Now I wouldn't have a foreman's job."

NED WILLIAMS: Married, six children, stock chaser at Ford assembly plant.

Likes:
 "I think of a certain area of proudness. You see them on that highway, you don't look

---

Quotations from Studs Terkel, *Working: People Talk about What They Do All Day and How They Feel about What They Do* (New York: Pantheon Books, 1974).

munity carry around in their heads, albeit unconsciously, and which gives a particular style to everything they do, feel, or think. Culture is synonymous with the learned and shared ways of believing and be-having, which are part of the community's life-style and give social meaning to the lives of its members.

The particular community from which a person comes may well affect her or his level of alienation. For example, it has been estab-lished that job satisfaction is higher in communities with substantial slum areas, since presumably when such a worker compares the alter-native positions available, the present job is seen as relatively attrac-tive.

and see what model it is or whose car it is. I put my labor in it. And somebody just like me put their area of work in it. It's got to be an area of proudness."

Dislikes:

"Sometimes I felt like I was just a robot. You push a button and you go this way. You become a mechanical nut."

Signs of alienation/stress:

"Some of the younger guys . . . got nothin' to lose. They don't show up. . . . Give 'em a week off, they don't care. . . . If I could figure 'em out, I could be a millionaire and just sit on the porch out here."

About boss:

"He (the foreman) was a little shotgun. Go to the washroom, he's looking for you, and right back."

"You can do twenty years of right and one hour of wrong and they'd string you."

"He was pushing. Somebody's pushing him, right?"

WORKERS AND MANAGERS

In the automobile industry, those working on an assembly line generally find their work monotonous and extremely boring. As a result, they try not to think of what they're doing while at work. They generally obey their foremen because they know they *must* obey, not because they agree with or respect them. In fact, most of the foremen are extremely disliked by the workers. The younger workers feel the stress of their situation much more than the older ones, and sometimes have doubts as to their worth as human beings. The older workers have grown to accept plant life and cannot understand why the younger workers are so irresponsible. The one point of agreement among all is that they are well paid, and the benefits are good.

The managers, on the other hand, like their work very much. Aside from the money, they seem to enjoy their positions of authority. By and large, they do not question their bosses, but accept orders without questions. Unlike the workers, the managers interviewed indicated no major dislikes with their positions, and showed no signs of stress.

THE BLUE–COLLAR BLUES

Work is the means whereby the goods and services needed by society are provided. But work does not serve only economic purposes; the workplace is somewhere to meet people, converse, form friendships, and attain social status. Work also contributes to self-esteem; often it is at work that a person makes the grade and finds meaning for life. In Marxist (and in some Americans') terms, the worker sells himself as something useful, that is, he has value.

We have noted the decline of the Protestant ethic of thrift, hard work, and postponement of gratification. The U.S. Department of Health, Education, and Welfare report entitled *Work in America* tabulated the results of a recent survey by the University of Michigan, in

"I find this work truly fulfilling in many ways—there's the exercise, the sense of accomplishment, and, most important, the opportunity to make lots of noise."

Reprinted by permission *The Wall Street Journal*.

which 1,533 American workers of all occupations ranked the following aspects of work in order of importance:

1. Interesting work.
2. Enough help and equipment to get the job done.
3. Enough information to get the job done.

4. Enough authority to get the job done.
5. Good pay.
6. Opportunity to develop special abilities.
7. Job security.
8. Seeing the results of one's work.

The Michigan study indicates that workers want to become masters of their own environments, and this means an end to meaningless work. Surprisingly, 80 to 90 percent of American workers replied in the positive when they were asked by Gallup pollsters, "Is your work satisfying?" Perhaps a more useful question would be "What type of work would you try to get into if you could start all over again?" An indication of intrinsic job satisfaction and the effect of a job on self-esteem can be derived from answers to the question "Would you choose similar work again?" (See Table 3–1).

TABLE 3–1
Percentages of workers in occupational groups who would choose similar work again

Professional and white-collar occupations		*Working-class occupations*	
Urban university professors	93%	Skilled printers	52%
Mathematicians	91	Paper workers	42
Physicists	89	Skilled autoworkers	41
Biologists	89	Skilled steelworkers	41
Chemists	86	Textile workers	31
Firm lawyers	85	Unskilled steelworkers	21
Lawyers	83	Unskilled autoworkers	16
Journalists (Washington correspondents)	82	*Blue-collar workers, cross section*	24
Church university professors	77		
Solo lawyers	75		
White-collar workers, cross section	43		

Source: U.S. Department of Health, Education and Welfare, *Work in America.*

To try to alleviate job dissatisfaction, some managers are treating workers with tender, loving care. Nevertheless, blue-collar blues are still a major problem, both on the job and in the office. And like Archie Bunker, the workers take their frustrations home in the evening. They are becoming increasingly alienated from society.

Television's Archie Bunker is the prototypical blue-collar worker. His alienation was sharpened in comparison to his son-in-law, who was getting an education and was on his way up. Being socially mobile, he was adopting the values of the class he proposed to join.

SOCIAL AND WORK ATTITUDES

Class is an important factor determining work attitudes. Americans base a person's status quotient (SQ) on money, education, and social background, but also on the work the person does.

Richard Coleman and Lee Rainwater have devised a new categorization of social class in *Social Standing in America: New Dimensions*

FIGURE 3–5
Two views of social class

Coleman and Rainwater*		Traditional Sociology	
The old aristocracy		U	UU
The new rich or success elite			LU
Middle Americans	Comfortably off	M	UM
	Just getting along		LM
The lower class: Just surviving		L	UL
The nonworking welfare class			LL

Key: U = upper; M = middle; L = lower.
* Richard P. Coleman and Lee Rainwater, *Social Standing in America: New Dimensions of Class* (New York: Basic Books, 1978).

of Class (see Figure 3–5). Some quotations from the book indicate people's feelings about social class:

"Of course, there's class. Look around you. A man driving a Cadillac feels he can thumb his nose at me because I'm driving an old VW."

"You know there's class when you're in a department store and a well-dressed lady gets treated better."

"Most people look down on the poor like me because you have to live so shabby and can't help yourself."

"I'm a carpenter and I won't fit with doctors and lawyers or in country club society. We have different interests and want to do different things."

"I would suppose social class means where you went to school and how far. Your intelligence. Where you live. The sort of house you live in. Your general background, as far as clubs you belong to, your friends. To some degree the type of profession you're in—in fact, definitely *that*. Where you send your children to school. The hobbies you have. Skiing, for example, is higher than the snowmobile. The clothes you wear . . . all of that. These are the externals. It can't be [*just*] money, because nobody ever knows that about you for sure."

Class identification

A good illustration of how social class affects job behavior is revealed by considering two shop-floor types, restricters and rate-busters. W. F. Whyte pointed out that the social and family backgrounds of the restricters were urban and working class, whereas rate-busters were from farms or lower middle-class families. Melville Dalton argued that while overproducers are likely to hold middle-class aspirations, underproducers do not.

Thus it seems reasonable to argue that a worker's class identification may affect his behavior and attitudes at work. To test this proposition, Milton R. Blood and Charles L. Hulin, in "Alienation, Environmental Characteristics and Worker Responses," developed a construct which can be viewed on a continuum running from integration with middle-class norms to alienation from middle-class norms. At the integrated end of the construct are to be found those workers who are involved and upwardly mobile; at the alienated end are those workers who view their jobs instrumentally, as a means to an end, who want good money for their work but in return for minimal involvement.

Blood and Hulin found that workers living in communities fostering alienation from middle-class norms (i.e., communities with more slum conditions, higher urbanization, greater urban growth) predictably organize their lives differently than workers from communities fostering integration do. Thus alienated workers have norms, but they are not the *middle-class* norms which are presumed to prevail at most places of work.

Not only shop-floor or blue-collar workers are alienated, however. Alienation is also pervasive among executives, particularly at middle-management level.

EXECUTIVE ALIENATION

According to *Work in America*, alienation is a commonplace, not only among blue-collar workers but also among white-collar workers, including managers. The report notes that most American organizations are still organized bureaucratically, with monotonous tasks and bleak regimentation—and the cost of this excessive routinization of work is immense, for workers and managers, men and women, black and white people.

The problem is integral to the nature of bureaucratic organizations, which puts a premium on following orders and doing it by the book. The more democratic and self-affirmative a person is, the less she or he will be able to put up with the dehumanizing aspect of behavior modification as it has been applied to work. The result, is either apathy and moral indifference or open hostility. For the executive who wants to or has to stay in the system, the anger which does not erupt may well be frozen into alienation. Often the only way relief can be found is through alcohol, drugs, debauchery, or withdrawal.

Coping with executive alienation

Coping with executive alienation starts with the acceptance of two fundamental points. One, top management is essentially tough, autocratic, sophisticated, manipulative, and totally demanding. Two, conventional change strategies have failed to get top management to abandon its autocratic ways voluntarily. Thus top management generates problems for subordinates.

To get more information about these problems, I asked senior managers the question "What problems do you generate for those who have to work with you?" and reported the results in "Organizational Development through Structured Sensitivity Training."

While some of the answers dealt with communication difficulties (one of the top executives claimed he did not generate any problems—he regarded the question as an impertinence), most managers answered by saying "The other guy is the problem," the "other guy" in this case being the subordinate. Their comments about subordinate managers have a familiar ring; they included "Have to repeat instructions," "People can't keep up with me—I get ahead of them, at least, I think I do," "Sometimes wish others would try harder." One executive described his problem in this fashion: "Not too approachable in a human relations context, tending to be too scientific."

Yet when I asked such managers to describe the "manager they liked working for best," they used phrases such as "delegated responsibility and authority," "did not oversee closely," "faith in subordinates," "expected good work," "was fair," "left me alone—allows me to work on my own," "lays down guidelines—expresses confidence—gives recognition," "respect for human beings," "took my advice," "provided constant feedback," "his door was always open." In a sentence, their "best boss" was considerate, supportive, trusting, and helping.

Executive bifocals

In trying to reconcile how top managers "look up" and "look down" the hierarchy, an interesting model emerges. Apparently, top managers use bifocals, with human relations lenses to look up hopefully and expectantly to their bosses and task-oriented lenses to look down on their subordinates. This could account for Tom Burns's famous finding in his study of self-recorded behavior by a department manager and his subordinates ("The Directions of Activity and Communications in a Departmental Executive Group"): When the superior recorded "giving orders," his subordi. ate recorded "receiving advice". It also sheds light on F. E. Fiedler's finding that a boss accepts or rejects a subordinate depending on performance, while D. Katz and R. L. Kahn found effective supervisors to be supportive and democratic. As behavior research has shown, in the so-called autocratic shift, if you want to know how your subordinates perceive you, turn through 180 degrees and record how you think about your own boss.

In sum, the executive lives in a schizophrenic world, prefering a nonthreatening boss while threatening subordinates. How is this chain to be broken? One possible answer may involve junior and middle managers more fully in critical decision making. This means human resources management.

TOPIC 3
Human resources management

In the late forties, fifties, and early sixties a new form of human relations began to emerge which was associated with the work of Abraham Maslow, Frederick Herzberg, W. F. Whyte, Chris Argyris, and Rensis Likert. Human resources management is essentially an attempt to apply the basic principles discovered at Hawthorne to the management of people in the workplace. It seeks to use workers and managers effectively to achieve the organization's objectives, while facilitating personal development.

THE MOVEMENT TOWARD PARTICIPATION

Human resources management is based on compatibility between the goals of the individual and the goals of the organization. A dramatic change in the corporate climate in recent years, which recognizes this relationship, is encouraging a move toward employee participation. Pace-setting companies such as IBM, General Motors, Xerox, and Bank of America have experimented with internal ombudsmen, worker participation, and employee privacy codes.

The basis for the movement toward participation is trust. But a major force for these changes has been the threat of legal liability, if the rights of employees are not protected. These include the right to complain about illegal or unethical behavior of superiors (including sexual exploitation). In reviewing such cases, the courts have noted the absence of an "open door" that would allow employees meaningful access to superiors. In the area of employee privacy, there has been a fundamental change in attitudes toward life-styles, dress, and political attitudes.

Many companies are also developing new policies of corporate self-disclosure to make information available about company procedures and policies. A major reason for such a policy of corporate transparency is to make sure that all employees and managers know company policy and follow it. These policies are being devised as a response to a larger movement of ideas, supported by government, management, and unions, which values rights of expression, privacy, participation, and corporate responsibility. Adopting these ideas requires both new organizational designs and new executive styles, which makes the work of Douglas McGregor necessary reading for every manager.

Douglas McGregor has contrasted the traditional management view, which he labels Theory X, with a view which sees workers as human resources, Theory Y.

THEORY X AND THEORY Y

In *The Human Side of Enterprise,* McGregor presents an interesting and insightful picture of how human endeavor can be mobilized more fruitfully through effective human resources management. His participative Theory Y is developed by comparison with the more conventional views of Theory X.

Theory X

McGregor introduces Theory X by listing three fundamental propositions held by conventional management:

1. Management is responsible for organizing the elements of production—money, material, men, and machines—all in the interest of maximizng economic returns.
2. This process requires directing employees' efforts—motivating them and controlling and modifying their behavior to suit the requirements of the organization. The implication is quite clear: People can and must be manipulated.
3. Inherent in Theory X is the proposition that people are passive and even resistant to the needs of the firm unless they are persuaded, punished, or controlled.

Underlying this conventional theory are certain implicit assumptions regarding human nature. Sensitive managers usually acknowledge they have believed some of these at some stage in their personal development.

According to McGregor, management employing the conventional approach has two alternatives: it can take either a hard or a soft line. The hard approach, which requires devising tight controls, has the unfortunate disadvantage that it breeds counterforce, restrictive practices, and antagonism. The soft approach is also unsatisfactory; even though relationships are excellent, morale high, and tensions low, nothing much in a productive way may happen.

McGregor challenges this conventional management wisdom by arguing that it is based on a mistaken notion as to cause and effect. His view is that the assumptions on which Theory X is predicated may be accurate descriptions of employee behavior and attitudes at the moment, but they are not innate; they represent the responses of the individual to organizational forces—behavioral effects of particular managerial attitudes.

Following Abraham Maslow, McGregor assumes that all motivation can be broken into four basic categories: (1) physiological and safety needs, (2) social needs, (3) ego needs, and (4) self-fulfilment needs.

Theory Y

The assumptions of Theory Y include:

1. Management is responsible for organizing production, that is, for the integration of money, materials, men, and machines in the interests of economic objectives.
2. People are not naturally passive or resistant to organizational needs. If they are, it is because of their experience in organizations.
3. Management has the responsibility to exploit the complexity of human motivation, including the need that people have for autonomy—the need to direct their own behavior and to assume some responsibility for their destinies.
4. The principal responsibility of management is to organize matters so that people can meet and achieve their own goals by directing their own efforts towards organizational objectives.

McGregor was not unaware of the difficulties involved in making Theory Y a living and dynamic actuality in contemporary industry. He recognized that it would take some time and would require extensive modification of the attitudes of both management and labor before such revolutionary ideas would become acceptable as a basis for organizational policy. Nevertheless, he was essentially optimistic. In *The Human Side of Enterprise* attention was directed to some innovative ideas which he regarded as consistent with Theory Y, including:

1. Decentralization and delegation.
2. Job enlargement.
3. Performance appraisal.

Theory Y can be illustrated by its approach to the problem of performance appraisal. The individual is held responsible not only for setting targets or objectives for himself but also for a significant part of

the evaluation of his performance. McGregor was quick to point out
that this still leaves an important role in the process of assessment to
the worker's superior. He rightly argued that by this method of self-
targeting, where a subordinate is held responsible for setting his own
standards, the employee is encouraged to take a larger responsibility
for defining and planning his own contribution to business, and in this
way the company is able to exploit his egoistic and self-fulfilment
needs.

McGregor suggests that management ought to reconsider the assumptions of current managerial philosophies and should abandon the
carrot-and-stick theory of motivation. McGregor's message is clear,
"Management must assume that onus of developing conditions of
employment for their people so that they feel free to exploit their
self-fulfilment needs. This is an ambitious and optimistic hope." If
such conditions are not developed, many employees, at all levels, may
well experience the modern disease of alienation. A better answer is
participative management.

PARTICIPATIVE MANAGEMENT IN ACTION

Donnelley Mirrors

A brilliant example of participative management in action is Donnelley Mirrors, Inc., located in Holland, Michigan. DMI, which holds
70 percent of the domestic market in automobile mirrors and is a major
manufacturer of other glass products, saw its sales rise in 1975 from
$3 million to more than $18 million. DMI makes use of many of the
concepts of human resources management.

DMI got into behavioral science experimentation when it made an
effort to apply the Scanlon Plan in 1952. The basic idea behind the
Scanlon Plan is that not only can people be productive, but they want
to be. As John F. Donnelley points out in an interview entitled "Participative Management at Work":

> We are indebted to Rensis Likert of the Institute for Social Research
> at the University of Michigan for the concept of interlocking work teams.
> It has been very useful. To show you how the teams work, let's first
> contrast them with the usual organization setup. Here's a traditional
> organization chart [Figure 3–6A]. You see these groups of men all re-
> sponsible to a single boss. There are many potential teams on this chart,
> but in spite of much management rhetoric, few of these groups operate
> as teams. Even when a group meets with its boss, there is a tendency to
> have a series of one-to-one dialogues with him. Likert found that some
> groups in companies do act as teams and consequently show consistently
> higher performance. There's good teamwork when the head of one team
> is also part of a successfully working team at the next higher level and
> becomes a sort of "linking pin" between the two teams.

FIGURE 3–6

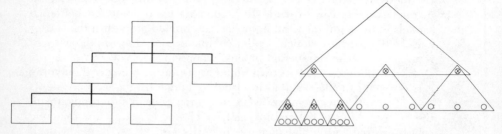

A. Typical organization pattern   B. Concept of interlocking work teams

Source: John F. Donnelley, "Participative Management at Work," *Harvard Business Review*, January–February 1977. Copyright © 1976 by the President and Fellows of Harvard College; all rights reserved.

In the concept of interlocking work teams, Donnelley says,

> . . . The one-to-one lines of reporting are gone [Figure 3–6B]. If the peer members of the team support one another, they can deal more realistically with the boss. He can, in fact must, become a leader to remain effective.
>
> The key to the communication of ideas between work teams is the linking pin person. His presence and influence on the "home team" *and* in the team at the next level provide a steady flow of information and understanding of people's needs and of company policies in both directions. The concept is one of participation. Each person manages his own task with participation in the entire company's concerns through his linking pin.
>
> With this approach, we try to achieve consensus among team members, and very often we do. When a team cannot decide an issue, the team leader, using the members' input, makes the decision. Thus there is no abdication of management responsibility, while there is a maximum of participation by those the decision affects.

Volvo

One of the most successful examples of participative management is the operation of the Volvo assembly lines at Kalmar, Sweden. In designing the Kalmar plant, the management decided to break up the traditional assembly line and develop a more human system of management. Pehr G. Gyllenhammar, managing director, describes the plan in "How Volvo Adapts Work to People":

> The design for Kalmar incorporated pleasant, quiet surroundings, arranged for group working, with each group having its own individual rest and meeting areas. The work itself is organized so that each group is responsible for a particular, identifiable portion of the car—electrical systems, interiors, doors, and so on. Individual cars are built up on self-

propelling "carriers" that run around the factory following a movable conductive tape on the floor. Computers normally direct the carriers, but manual controls can override the taped route. If someone notices a scratch in the paint on a car, he or she can immediately turn the carrier back to the painting station. Under computer control again, the car will return later to the production process wherever it left off.

Each work group has its own buffer areas for incoming and outgoing carriers so it can pace itself as it wishes and organize the work inside its own area so that its members work individually or in subgroups to suit themselves. Most of the employees have chosen to learn more than one small job; the individual increase in skills also gives the team itself added flexibility.

To gain a sense of identification with its work, a group must also take responsibility for its work. The myriad inspection stations with "watchdog" overtones that characterize most factories have been abandoned at Kalmar. Instead, each team does its own inspection. After a car passes about three work group stations, it passes through a special inspection station where people with special training test each car. A computer-based system takes quality information reports from these stations and, if there are any persistent or recurring problems, flashes the results to the proper group station, telling them also how they solved similar problems the last time. The computer also informs the teams when their work has been particularly problem-free.

There have been quite a number of criticisms of the Volvo way of organizing work, however. For example, a number of American auto workers who were sent to Sweden to gain experience at first hand on this type of assembly work came away somewhat disillusioned with the ideas of industrial democracy. They found the work boring, and they felt that the Swedes were too sympathetic to their bosses. They missed the United Auto Workers, especially their own well-tried grievance procedure. Basically, these Detroit auto men preferred the rough and tumble of the traditional U.S. car assembly lines.

At one time Volvo had plans to set up an automobile manufacturing plant in the United States. These plans have now been scrapped, mainly because Volvo cannot keep its costs under control.

PARTICIPATION AND DEMOCRACY

Many organizational theorists start from the proposition that what is desirable in management is maximum feasible participation. The basic idea is that everybody should participate in everything. However, political theorists suggest that this view may be misleading. It is wrong to presume that participation and classical democracy are synonymous. Political theorists such as Gaetano Mosca and Robert Michels argue that in every society and organization an elite must rule, and democracy is mainly involved in the process of selecting the elite. Michels, in his famous iron law of oligarchy, says that an elite must emerge to take control even of a democracy, as happens in democratic trade unions.

The reality is that most people are just not interested in participating in everything. And, contrary to the views of many unrealistic social scientists, this is just as it should be. If everybody were involved in everything, negotiation for action would be tremendously time-consuming and complicated.

Another curious difficulty of democracy is the tyranny of the majority. Democracy is typically defined as government by the majority, taking into consideration the interests of minorities. In modern organizations, however, frequently the vociferous members of the majority take over the command of the organization and may terrorize the minority. When faced with this accusation, the majority denounces the detractors as enemies of democracy.

TOPIC 4
What every manager should know about human relations

Reacting to the rigidities of formal structure and hierarchy and the overspecification of classical organizational theory, human relations theorists focused on the development of job satisfaction and the improvement of worker morale, for the purpose of improving productivity. A significant effort was made to define the interactions and informal structure of the primary work group.

Douglas McGregor developed Theory Y, which requires a democratic participative approach by managers, as an answer to Theory X, which allows managers to behave in an autocratic, domineering (in some sense, imperialistic) way. Chris Argyris has pointed out, in *Personality and Organization,* that Theory Y requires managers who can treat subordinates as mature individuals, who are capable of managing themselves and making intelligent decisions to allow the organization and themselves to function. Unfortunately, Argyris has very little to say about the dysfunctional consequences informal interactions can have for the business.

The theory of human relations should be modified to take into consideration the values and attitudes which people bring to work. Further, it would be wrong to presume that this environmental constraint applies only to shop-floor workers. There is considerable evidence to support the view that organizational level structures the attitude employees take to human relations.

Human relations and organizational level

Human relations as a personal style finds less favor as one ascends the hierarchy of an organization. In simple terms, this means that shop-floor or production workers, foremen, and some junior managers prefer human relations; more senior managers prefer good human resources planning. The typical senior manager prefers to operate in a situation which makes the best use of his resources and stretches him to the limit but ensures that he is properly rewarded for his efforts, *even though,* in the short run, conflict may be produced and considerable anxiety generated. Research findings suggest, on the other hand, that junior managers asked to describe the "manager they liked working for best," describe a personnel-oriented executive who is supportive in personal relations and behaves in a generally considerate way, which usually involves a fair amount of consultation and participation. For top managers, Wilfred Brown's idea of optimal organization, presented in *Exploration in Management,* represents a step beyond good human resources planning. For Brown, optimal organization is a function of the task and the resources available to achieve the task (technical, human, and economic), not a function of personality:

$$\text{Optimal organization} = f(T, R)$$

In summary, it is possible to argue that human relations is best suited for some shop-floor workers, good human resource planning for senior management, and optimal organization for top management.

As yet the experimental evidence is slim for the proposition that as one ascends the hierarchy of a business organization, the need for human relations diminishes. Nevertheless, behavioral scientists recognize that top management seems more capable of describing business behavior in objective terms; appears to be less involved in emotional terms; and seems to be capable of more dispassionate analysis of organizational problems, spanning a longer period of time.

Demise and resurrection

Academics, have been writing the obituary of human relations since its birth as a management philosophy in the 1930s. Ridiculed by unions as a form of "cow sociology" which turned factories into unthinking places of comfort; scorned by hard-headed managers who saw human relations as the soft option which destroyed the challenge of creative conflict (which, to their way of thinking, got things done even if a little angst was generated on the way); hammered into the ground by tough-minded behavioral scientists who defined the effective executive as a psychologically distant task specialist who rejected subordinates for poor performance—human relations always seemed to be about to die.

The human potential movement

Yet in some curious, little-understood way, it has managed to survive. Rejected as a science, it has reemerged as a "religion" in the form of the human potential movement. The human potential movement is a newly emerging, quasi-scientific value system which began attracting support among the middle classes of North America in the 1970s. It is a burgeoning movement which is largely leaderless, inchoate, and ill-defined but which uses such methods as sensitivity training, T groups, and encounter groups. It has been described as "therapy for normals" and "the acidless trip."

The human potential movement represents a reaction to the alienation of affluence and to the mobile, ambitious ethos that was presumed to be a requisite of industrial society. One of the consequences of a highly mobile society dedicated to high achievement and affluence was a breakdown of intimacy between people, facilitated by the contraction of the extended family into the nuclear family and, lately, the disintegration of the nuclear family.

It is generally recognized that good human relations are sorely needed; this organizational approach could help to restore man's dignity. If it failed, it is because the economic mandates of the organization do not permit executives to support good human relations in times of trial, when the chips are down.

Human relations was right for the time it appeared, when it represented a necessary correction to the excesses of classical theory. By treating organizations as human systems, it argued for participation, creativity, and commitment, all to the good. The basic criticism of

FIGURE 3–7
Human relations as a system

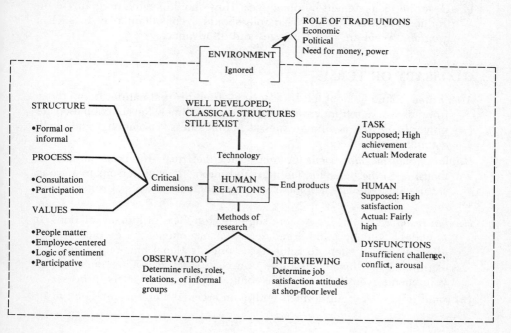

human relations is that the model of the organization employed leaves out important variables and makes assumptions about causality that have turned out to be simpllstic (see Figure 3–7). Human relations is insufficient and provides too narrow a perspective; but it was a necessary step in the evolution of organization theory, for it paved the way for the systems approach.

REVIEW AND RESEARCH

1. Describe the strategy of a person who has very effective human relations skills.
2. Why do managers prefer human resources planning to human relations?
3. Describe a situation where you have deliberately restricted production. Why did you do so? List your answers under the headings: the primary working group's (a) values, (b) norms, (c) reinforcements, (d) sanctions.
4. Why was human relations right for its time?
5. In what ways has human relations as a management philosophy failed, and what are the reasons?
6. Compare and contrast the value systems inside the Hawthorne plant with the value systems outside, in the immediate environs of the plant. In your opinion, why did the Hawthorne researchers choose to ignore the attitudes people brought to their work?
7. Why do most North Americans still prefer human relations as a statement of their personal style, in spite of its clash with the realities of the world?
8. Compare and contrast human relations as a personal style, as a management philosophy, and as a value system.
9. Describe management by objectives. How should such a program be introduced to a company? What role should a consultant play in such a program? What are its advantages and disadvantages?

GLOSSARY OF TERMS

Alienation. Estrangement felt by a person—from his real nature, from others, from his work, or from groups or society. The dimensions of alienation are powerlessness, meaninglessness, normlessness, isolation, and self-estrangement.

Human potential movement. A quasi-scientific, quasi-religious movement focusing on the behavior, feelings, and interactions of persons in a group setting, with the intent of increasing sensitivity, awareness, insight, and so on.

Human resource planning. A more sophisticated view of human relations. It is widely held by middle and senior management; the emphasis is on effective use of talent to achieve the organizational mission through the exploitation of human resources in a way which facilitates personal development, even if considerable conflict is developed in the process.

Informal group. A group formed within an organization but unrelated to its formal structure; typically, in business organizations, an interaction of lower level workers to promote their common interests. The informal group represents the reaction of the organized against the organizers.

Meaningful work. That type of work which enables an individual to identify himself with his work and to derive a feeling of worth from his work role.

Needs. McGregor's Theory X and Theory Y presuppose four basic categories of needs (developed from Maslow's motivation theory): (1) physiological and safety needs, (2) social needs, (3) ego needs, and (4) self-actualizing needs.

Theory X. Embodies classical, traditional views, approaches, and behavior. It may be summarized as task oriented and quite rigid.

Theory Y. Embodies concepts of better management approaches, including not only the organization of production but attempts to meet human needs such as autonomy and self-fulfilment. It may be summarized as more human relations oriented and flexible.

DEBATE: The pros and cons of human resources management

PRO: The case for HRM

Using the example of job enrichment, Chris Argyris makes the case for human resources management in "Personality vs. Organization," as follows:

> Let me quote from just two of the voluminous research studies that demonstrate the efficiency of job enrichment. The first is the ambitious and significant attempt by the Gaines dog food division of General Foods to design an entire plant using horizontal and vertical enlargement of work. The key features of the design are the following:
>
> 1. Autonomous work groups that develop their own production schedules, manage production problems, screen and select new members, maintain self-policing activities, and decide questions such as who gets time off and who fills which work station.
> 2. Integrated support functions. Each work team performs its own maintenance, quality control, and industrial engineering functions—plus challenging job assignments.
> 3. Job mobility and rewards for learning. People are paid not on the basis of the job they are doing, but on the basis of the number of jobs that they are prepared to do.
> 4. Self-goernment for the plant community.
>
> A second significant experiment in job enlargement is taking place at Volvo's new auto assembly plant in Kalmar, Sweden. Volvo faced serious problems—wildcat strikes, absenteeism, and turnover that were getting out of hand. Turnover in the old car assembly plant was over 40 percent annually. Absenteeism was running 20 to 25 percent. Now, assembly has

been divided among teams of 15 to 25 workers, who will decide how to distribute the job of car assembly among themselves. Each team determines its own work pace, subject to meeting production standards that are set for them. Each team selects its own boss, and deselects him if it's unhappy with him.

The new plant cost approximately 10 percent more than it would have if it had been constructed along traditional lines. Will the benefits justify the e:.tra expense? Time alone will tell—the plant has been on stream for only a matter of months—but Pehr Gyllenhammar, the managing director of Volvo, hopes that it will realize both his economic and social objectives: "A way must be found to create a workplace that meets the needs of the modern working man for a sense of purpose and satisfaction in his daily work. A way must be found of attaining this goal without an adverse effect on productivity."

CON: The case against HRM

One reason HRM has been criticized as inappropriate is that managers not only prefer a manipulative approach to the direction of subordinates, but they also accept being manipulated themselves, if it gets the job done and they share in the payoffs. Another reason is that HRM apparently works only in particular show plants, and even there it does not work without considerable dysfunctions.

Most U.S. shop-floor workers seem to share the views of the group of Detroit auto workers who, after sampling democratic auto assembly systems in Sweden, opted for the traditional Detroit way of doing things. At least if you are not getting a fair share you can complain to management, follow the grievance procedure, or strike.

Most managers also do not have sufficient time to apply HRM effectively. As Walter R. Nord and Douglas Durand point out in "What's Wrong with the Human Resources Approach to Management":

> Recent research on the nature of managerial work has shown that managers operate under severe time restraints. Their work is characterized by brevity, fragmentation, and an open-ended character. Their workload substantially reduces the time they have to devote to any one problem, approach, or system. These pressures are accentuated by rapidly changing environments. An approach that requires greater commitments must show disproportionate or offsetting benefits, and HRM approaches, even though they may save time in the long run, are very time-consuming at first.
>
> Our studies at Manchester Manufacturing Company revealed that HRM programs, such as participative management, management by objectives, and the Managerial Grid®, absorbed substantial time and energy from all participants in the organization. When time was short, even the strong philosophical commitment of Manchester's top management to HRM strategies was not enough to overcome the urge to centralize decisions. Thus even managers who find the HRM viewpoint

attractive and are willing to equalize power differentials may find the HRM approach impractical because of the costs in time and energy. A number of management experts have commented on the limitations time places on the feasibility of such innovations as MBO.

EXECUTIVE ATTITUDES TO HUMAN RELATIONS

There is apparently a widespread feeling among executives against HRM as a soft-hearted aspect of human relations. As a board chairman pointed out in a letter to the *Harvard Business Review* (May–June 1978) following a piece on TM (transcendental meditation):

> . . . In general we have too much time out from work now—coffee breaks, loafing, and so on. Our Creator determined we must work and work hard—at least after eating from the Tree of Knowledge. Stress, from fear of enemies, human animals, nature, cannot, should not, be avoided. It is the strengthening, evolutionary process for body and mind, part and parcel of man's development and better everyday living.
>
> From childhood on, our efforts should be directed to building up this inner strength, to later writing out and determining to live by a philosophy of life. We could then meet any circumstances without flinching.
>
> For our nation to compete and survive, its work force must consist of those who can and will work, who need no crutch, no support from coddling processes.

This chairman is not alone in his view. In another letter in this issue a company president who had driven himself too hard and had developed cardiovascular problems pointed out:

> I imagine that many of the American corporate decision makers are still the hard-driven, motivated "doers" rather than the contemplative "thinkers" who can understand and appreciate the necessity to relax. I would guess that most executives who read the article might dismiss it as giving too much opportunity to employees to "take another break." I hope this is not true.

The point being argued is that U.S. executives have a mania not only to succeed, but also to get ahead of others. Human relations get in the way.

Question

Can the pros and cons of HRM be reconciled? How?

DIAGRAM SUMMARY OF CHAPTER 4

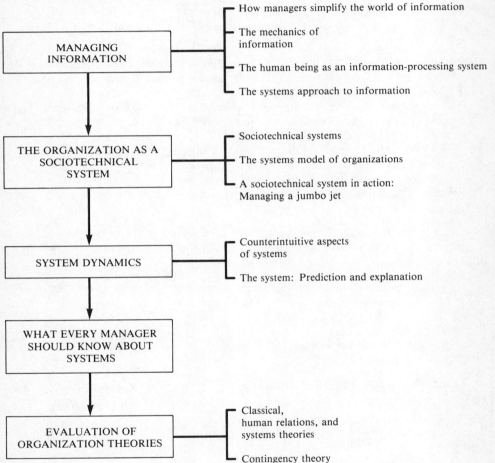

4

Systems theory: Making the organizational world simpler through information chunking or systems

THE PALACE GUARD: AN INFORMATION COSA NOSTRA

The Watergate affair was a contemporary exercise of information Machiavellianism (see Chapter 15). Under the direction of Robert Haldeman and John Ehrlichman, who had earned their livings in the world of Madison Avenue where manipulating public opinion is the daily diet, the White House machine became an instrument of revenge and fear. They saw the White House as under a state of siege from Communists and other real and imagined enemies. In this atmosphere of paranoia, the intelligence-gathering operations of the plumbers were seen as necessary and proper.

Douglas Hallett worked on Charles Colson's staff in the Nixon White House from June 1971 to September 1972. (He then became a student at Harvard Law School.) Hallett comments, in an article in *The New York Times Magazine:*

> John Ehrlichman's shop was in many ways the most image-oriented. Because Big John could gesticulate with his eyebrows, play up-to-the-net tennis and think up great catch-phrases ("This is a credit-card Congress," was my favorite), he was able to con the press into believing his Domestic Council was some kind of fulcrum for creative thinking. For the most part, it was not. Bud Krogh did accomplish a great deal in his areas of D.C. government, drugs and crime control, when he was not running the "plumbers" operation; many of Ehrlichman's people seemed to me to spend as much time on dreaming up new ways to spend the huge "administrative budget" he had somehow won for them as on

anything else. Every time I talked to one of them, it seemed, they were asking whether I thought a royal-blue or an emerald-green carpet would look better on their office floor.

Though himself a lawyer, Ehrlichman seemed to favor business-school graduates and former advance-men in hiring his staff. They, in turn, were biased toward technocratic management studies and reorganization plans in lieu of policy-making. The substantive programs that received the Administration's strongest support—the SST, the Lockheed loan guarantee, the ABM—were invariably technological. The one major substantive program for which the Administration was able to work up enough enthusiasm to win legislative backing—revenue-sharing—is really just another technocratic innovtion, directed at changing by whom and not for what Federal money is spent.

In *Palace Guard*, Dan Rather, CBS White House correspondent, and Gary Paul Gates, a writer at CBS, say that the key man on Nixon's staff was H. R. (Bob) Haldeman, who turned the executive branch into a kind of bureaucratic Cosa Nostra in which he was consigliori ("Even Mitchell has to go through me"). Haldeman came back to Nixon only after the assassination of Robert F. Kennedy, when he was sure he was backing a winner in the Nixon campaign. It was Haldeman, seen as the evil genius, who did in-depth marketing surveys of Nixon's chances and came up with CREEP (Committee to Re-elect the President). According to Rather and Gates, Haldeman used his power without scruple, spreading calculated leaks and sleazy rumors about opponents' drinking and sex habits.

The supreme irony is that it was the Palace Guard who earned their spurs as information managers. They knew that people live by the image, not the reality of things, and set out to restructure people's (including the president's) perceptions. By feeding the president pre-digested news, so that he saw no ordinary TV or newspaper news accounts, they created the ultimate credibility gap. The illusion makers abbreviated, destroyed, recycled, disseminated, denied, leaked, withdrew, interrupted, discharged, stored, mailed to themselves, filtered, cut, edited, ate, digested, regurgitated, refurbished, analyzed, . . . information—until everyone had it up to the eyeballs.

THE INFORMATION EXPLOSION

It has been estimated that the amount of information on record doubles every seven years. People can only absorb 40 bits (binary digits, the basic units of information) per second; this rate has not changed since the Stone Age. To survive in modern society, more sophisticated ways of processing information, such as those provided by improvements in computer technology, are needed. And people must have a means to filter out essential information from the massive amounts they are constantly exposed to.

TOPIC 1
Managing information

HOW MANAGERS SIMPLIFY THE WORLD OF INFORMATION

The process managers use to simplify the world of information is to break it down into manageable portions, or chunks. By chunking, for example, a rear gunner in a bomber can split world space into the face of a clock and identify targets with such terms as "Bandits, eight-o'clock high."

One way chunking makes information more manageable is by restricting choice. Henry Ford simplified the marketing of automobiles by offering the Model T in any color, provided it was black. McDonald's uses the same formula to structure the choices of its customers, and restaurants achieve the same effect by offering daily specials. The basic idea is always to chunk the information into categories the information receiver can digest.

Chunking is the process of breaking down the information coming into the system into digestible parts. Normally, systems automatically key themselves to the critical information variables in the environment, and they adjust their internal dynamics accordingly. If they don't, they are dead. A good example of chunking in action is provided by Chrysler's fight for its survival in 1979.

Top management at Chrysler had to simplify its world into two key variables: lack of cash flow (external variable) and surplus of unsold cars (internal variable) which was generating huge daily interest charges in millions of dollars. Focusing on these two variables forced Chrysler to do two things: reduce the price of its cars and secure a loan guarantee from the government. Chrysler was chunking the world into its basic essentials of two critical decision variables, which tied its internal dynamics to the external environment input.

In information processing, the amount of information in a message is defined in such a way that the nature of the information is irrelevant. Information theorists have developed a system of bits (a contraction for *binary digits*) to measure the amount of information a message contains. As George A. Miller points out, "A message that reduces the number of possibilities a great deal gives a large amount of information. The convention has been adopted that every time the number of alternatives is reduced to half, one unit of information is gained. This unit has been called one bit of information."

Put another way, a bit is the amount of information communicated by selecting between two alternatives: yes or no, 0 or 1 (the two binary digits usually used), right or wrong. The capacity of an information channel is measured in bits. Box 4–1 describes information as a measure of freedom of choice in selecting among alternatives.

Box 4–1: Information as a measure of freedom of choice

The existential approach to organizational behavior recognizes information as a measure of how free the manager is to choose between alternatives in decision making, since the choice is based on the information available. A necessary step in finding the freedom the existentialist seeks is to discover the rules governing information. This is precisely what Warren Weaver did in *The Mathematical Theory of Communication*.

THE LOGARITHM OF BITS

If 1848 was the year of political revolutions, 1948 was the year of information revolutions. For it was in 1948 that Norbert Wiener's *Cybernetics* and Claude Shannon's famous papers on the mathematics of communication were published. And soon after, Warren Weaver linked information and uncertainty in a famous formula. For Weaver,

. . . information is a measure of one's freedom of choice when one selects a message. If one is confronted with a very elementary situation where he has to choose one of two alternative messages, then it is arbitrarily said that the information, associated with this situation, is unity. . . . The concept of information applies not to the individual messages (as the concept of meaning would), but rather to the situation as a whole. . . . To be somewhat more definite, the amount of information is defined, in the simplest cases, to be measured by the logarithm of the number of available choice.

Reference: Claude Shannon and Warren Weaver, *The Mathematical Theory of Communication* (Urbana: University of Illinois Press, 1949).

Effective chunking uses selective aggregation. An airline might not want to know the load factor (percentage of seats filled) for each flight, but a daily record between gateway cities (New York and Chicago, e.g.) might be useful. It all depends on what the firm wants to find out.

The basic problem in chunking information is whether to play a hunch and specify the chunks with limited information processing, or to go by the manual and search the situation systematically. For example, a plane has come down in Alaska and you have some flight data. But you know there are two valleys where planes usually are found. What do you do: Follow your hunch as to where the plane might be, or analyze the flight data?

THE MECHANICS OF INFORMATION

The compressors

While it is necessary for management to select and digest information, it can become distorted in the boiling down process. Sophisticated information is simplified as it is distilled and abbreviated for easy reading by managers. The men at the top of large corporations and governments read only intelligence digests which concentrate voluminous reports and computer printouts in a few pithy paragraphs of basic intelligence, stripped of subtleties. These compact summaries form the data base for critical decisions and actions.

The information compressors, therefore, are powerful. David Halberstam's *The Best and the Brightest* is fascinating because it reveals the true nature of the fire fights, not in Vietnam but among the information mechanics and processors in Washington who compressed the compacted (and on occasion invented) data to keep a light at the end of the tunnel.

The cue seekers

Effective information seekers pick up information selectively, collecting data on the basis of clues or cues. The editing of data begins by deciding on the rules of the game. Professors may talk a lot, in an interesting, even exciting way, but how do you know what is relevant—and relevant for what? There is one set of answers for the semester exam, and another for real life.

An article in the London Sunday *Times* for May 7, 1978 described a study at Edinburgh University which identified three types of students:

> First, there were the "cue-seekers" who made a point of finding out the names of the examiners, discovering their hobby-horses and reading their books. They even sought out the staff over coffee and button-holed them about the exam papers. Surprisingly often, they got useful information. And these students did better than average in the exams. The average performers were the "cue-conscious", who just listened for the hints about exam topics—"it might be worth your while looking at this"—that university tutors tend to drop. Finally, there were the "cue-deaf," who tried to revise the whole syllabus. They did worse than average in the exams.

Managers, like students, have to determine the critical success factors in their information needs (see Box 4–2).

The interpreters

While information plays a critical part in all organizations, its importance is most evident during wartime. In World War II the Allies developed a method of breaking the German ciphers. ULTRA was the name given to the operation which had, as its mission, the reconstruction of the Enigma machine the Germans used to code their strategic messages. It was successful and provided the Allies with vast amounts of information about enemy intentions and capabilities. Thus in many respects, the war was fought in a game theory context in which each

Box 4–2: Critical success factors in information needs

Executives are being swamped by information. When John T. Rockart interviewed a number of executives on their data needs, one chief executive said: "The first thing about information systems that strikes me is that one gets too much information. The information explosion crosses and criss-crosses executive desks with a great deal of data. Much of this is only partly digested and much of it is irrelevant."

The problem is defining exactly what data the chief executive needs. For example, many apparently pay very little attention to formal reports and computer printouts but rely rather on informal oral communication. Rockart quotes Henry Mintzberg in "Planning on the Left Side and Managing on the Right Side":

" . . . it is interesting to look at the content of managers' information, and at what they do with it. The evidence here is that a great deal of the manager's inputs are soft and speculative—impressions and feelings about other people, hearsay, gossip, and so on. Furthermore, the very analytical inputs—reports, documents, and hard data in general—seem to be of relatively little importance to many managers. (After a steady diet of soft information, one chief executive came across the first piece of hard data he had seen all week—an accounting report—and put it aside with the comment, "I never look at this.")"

To overcome these difficulties Rockart made a conceptual breakthrough coming up with the notion of critical success factors (CSF) to determine the information actually needed by managers. Rockart's ideas were developed from the work of D. Ronald Daniel, now managing director of McKinsey and Company. In introducing the concept in "Management Information Crisis," Daniel cited three examples of major corporations whose information systems produced an extensive amount of information, although very little of it was useful in assisting managers to perform their jobs. Rockart notes:

To draw attention to the type of information actually needed to support managerial activities, Daniel turned to the concept of critical success factors. He stated,

" . . . a company's information system must be discriminating and selective. It should focus on 'success factors.' In most industries there are usually three to six factors that determine success; these key jobs must be done exceedingly well for a company to be successful. Here are some examples from several major industries:

In the automobile industry, styling, an efficient dealer organization, and tight control of manufacturing cost are paramount.

In food processing, new product development, good distribution, and effective advertising are the major success factors.

In life insurance, the development of agency management personnel, effective control of clerical personnel, and innovation in creating new types of policies spell the difference."

The conclusion is that traditional financial accounting systems rarely provide the data needed. Using the concept of CSF, the data processing department can provide the chief executive officer with the critical information needed to make the organization effective.

Reference: John F. Rockart, "Chief Executives Define Their Own Data Needs," *Harvard Business Review,* March–April 1979, pp. 81–93.

side had almost perfect knowledge of the other's intentions and strengths.

But information, no matter how prompt, prolific, and accurate, is necessarily neutral. Its interpretation by the managers involved is always of critical importance.

THE HUMAN BEING AS AN INFORMATION-PROCESSING SYSTEM

The computer analogy

The first fully modern electronic computer, designed by the American mathematician John von Neumann, was introduced in 1940. The computer, which promised (or threatened, depending on your point of view) to transform our world more than any other technological advance, has reached into nearly every realm of human development; and in the process it has transformed not only the shape of society but also the way man thinks. A new state of mind has emerged—an outlook which takes the view that man and the computer are two species of a more abstract genus called the information-processing system.

Six subsystems

The information-processing aspect of the computer has a general analogy in the biological field. Every organism has the following subsystems:

1. A *sensor* subsystem, which is concerned with the reception and recognition of information.
2. A *data processing* subsystem, which is concerned with breaking down this information into terms and categories which are meaningful and relevant to the organism.
3. A *decision* subsystem, in which decisions are made. Decisions may involve:
   a.   Self-regulatory of homeostatic processes.
   b.   Adaptive or learning processes.
   c.   Integrative processes.
4. A *processing* subsystem, which integrates information, energy, people, and materials to implement the decisions, accomplish tasks, and produce output.
5. A *control* subsystem, which ties the whole system together by a set of feedback loops. These loops incorporate the equations of the critical decision variables which, if not respected, lead to lack of growth and the eventual demise of the organism.
6. A *memory* subsystem, which is concerned with the storage and retrieval of information.

The subsystems in a living system are paralleled in the computer, as shown in Figure 4–1. But because the computer can only deal with input information that has been encoded in mathematical terms and in rigorously defined ways, its users must review carefully the quality of the information they work with.

FIGURE 4–1
Basic computer process modules

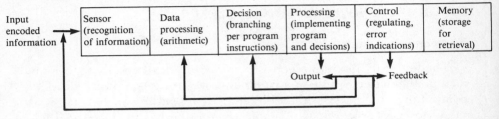

THE SYSTEMS APPROACH TO INFORMATION

The currency of organizational behavior is information. And information is infinite in quantity; is expensive to collect; must be treated selectively; can only be picked up with a taxonomy (classification) based on yesterday's experience (and thus is to some extent irrelevant); causes surprise (which is how we measure it); and is fraught with uncertainty. The best way to deal with information is to use the systems approach shown in Figure 4–2. The uncertainty cannot be removed, but it can be reduced.

Using the systems approach, the organizational analysts ideally

FIGURE 4–2
The information-processing system

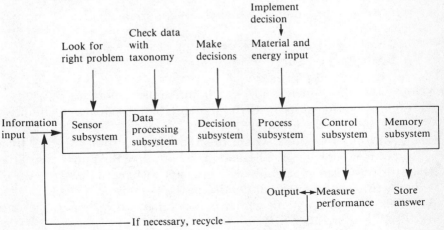

keep cool and allow the problem to run over them, hoping to pick up the right problem, and so on. Dilemmas include:

1. The right problem may be hard to even visualize, while the wrong problem is easily capable of analysis and solution.
2. The taxonomy may be known, but some of the facts won't fit it.
3. Perhaps a decision should be made at once; perhaps it should be postponed.
4. Tight control is desirable, but it may stifle innovation.
5. The memory subsystem may be storing aging information, when what is needed is an entirely new framework.
6. The system may be recycling the old problem when it should instead be used to try a new problem.

It was with the appearance of H. A. Simon's seminal papers and books on organizations that the true dimensions of organizational behavior, the scope of its concern, the multiplicity of its source disciplines, and its potential payoff became apparent. Reading Simon after reading the human relations literature of the 1940s and the industrial psychology papers of the 1920s was like acquiring stereoscopic vision and the ability to see a full range of colors after staring for decades at a blurred black-and-white image. The world had suddenly become larger, as organizational behavior slipped its moorings to the group and sailed into the sea of organizations in societies. Its final port of call may never be reached, but it traverses an infinitely more interesting world where all sorts of people come together to study organizations as sociotechnical systems.

TOPIC 2
The organization as a sociotechnical system

SOCIOTECHNICAL SYSTEMS

Increasing disenchantment with both the classical theory and the human relations approach led theorists in the late 1950s to search for a different optic, a new perspective. A dramatic new approach was needed which would enable organization theory to move forward and escape from the sharply defined claustrophobia of classical theory without falling into the marshmallow of human relations. Open systems theory, which required treating the organization as an organism which trades with its environment—importing inputs, transforming them, and exporting a product (person, thing, idea, or energy) to the environment—was the approach to which behavioral scientists turned in the hope of making a fresh beginning in organization theory.

Open systems theory draws its inspiration from the biological sciences, which have replaced the physical sciences as a main source of metaphor for the social sciences. We can look at the organization-as-organism metaphor from three aspects. The first aspect focuses attention on the interaction between the organization and its environment and sees the essential task of management as the managing of the boundary conditions, that is, the interchange between the external realities and the internal processes. This first aspect focuses on the concept of openness. The second aspect turns on the word *system* and argues the idea of interrelatedness—that everything that does or can occur is dependent on everything else that does or can occur. All organizational events are interlocked. The third aspect follows from the second and is essentially negative. It represents a rejection of linear causal trains as a means of explaining organizational phenomena; the concept of simple cause and effect is discarded.

A definition of system

First of all: What is a system? In the 1956 edition of *General Systems, the Yearbook of the Society for General Systems Research*, A. D. Hall and R. E. Fagen define a system as a set of objects together with relationships between the objects and between their attributes.

This definition, though it emphasizes relationships and implies the holistic (hanging together) aspects of systems, is too terse for our purpose. If we define a system as an entity which consists of interdependent parts, we must qualify it. There are two basic types of systems, closed and open. Living systems are open systems, that is, open to matter-energy-information exchanges with an environment. Human organizations are living systems and can be analyzed accordingly.

THE SYSTEMS MODEL OF ORGANIZATIONS

In systems theory, organizations are viewed as open or sociotechnical systems which trade with their environment. They import information, material, and energies, do something with or to them, and export them to another system. The advantage of the systems approach is that it reveals organizations as social institutions which somehow or other beat the second law of thermodynamics, by which the amount of entropy (or disorganization) in the system is said to tend to maximize. Organizations achieve effectiveness by reducing entropy or disorganization.

When information is received, uncertainty is reduced. Information can be measured by the amount of surprise it induces in the receiver, and organizations help to bring the degree of surprise under control.

Systems principles are based in part on the following concepts:

1. The whole is more than the sum of its parts. A related principle is synergy, or the effectiveness of combined action.

2. Organizations are goal seeking.
3. The cybernetic ideas of feedback and equilibrium affect system operation.
4. Systems are arranged hierarchically.
5. A system can achieve the same state from a variety of beginning states—the principle of equifinality: "There's more than one way to skin a cat."

The organization as a system of information flows

In systems theory, organizations are seen as systems of information flows—as sets of black (unknown-content) boxes connected by a series of inputs, transformation, and outputs. Information is the organizational currency, and it has to be searched for, bought, processed, and sold to some other system. The contemporary executive is a serial processer of information who needs to bring sensory data about the environment down to an optimal level where it can be handled. When the executive suffers overload or is placed in an environment of sensory deprivation, bizarre behavior may result. (See Box 4–3 for a solution to the problem of information overload.)

It is possible to develop a theory of organization in which everything, including role, status, and power, can be defined in informational terms.

The significant input for the organization is intelligence, which describes the process of collecting, condensing, filtering, analyzing, interpreting, and transmitting the technological and ideological information needed in the decision-making process. Behavioral scientists, concerned with the problem of how intelligence shapes organizational actions, believe that managers ought to act on the best information available. H. L. Wilensky, in *Organizational Intelligence, Knowledge, and Policy in Government and Industry,* describes "high-quality intelligence as:

> . . . *clear, timely, reliable, valid* (the tests include logical consistency, successful prediction, congruence with established knowledge or independent sources), *adequate* because the account is full (the context of the act, event, or life of the person or group is described), and *wide-ranging* because the major policy alternatives promising a high probability of attaining organizational goals are posed or new goals suggested.

The commodity of the systems approach is not capital, land, or people, but information. Information—in the form of intelligence, better ideas, knowledge, call it what you like—is the critical input. And the skill at a premium is the management of information.

Robert McNamara typified the new breed of information manager (see Box 4–4). He earned his spurs in the military during World War II,

Box 4–3: The parable of the spindle

What is a system in the business sense? Elias Porter has provided a parable from the restaurant industry which has implications for an answer to that question.

Once upon a time the president of a large chain of short-order restaurants invited a team of consultants—a sociologist, a psychologist, and an anthropologist—to contribute to the solution of the human relations problems in the restaurants.

The first to report was the sociologist. In his report he said:

It is during the rush hours that your human relations problems arise. We can see one thing which, sociologically speaking, doesn't seem right. The manager has the highest status in the restaurant. The cook has the next highest status. The waitresses . . . have the lowest status and yet they give orders to the cook.

It doesn't seem right for a lower status person to give orders to a higher status person. We've got to find a way to break up the face-to-face relationship between the waitresses and the cook. Now my idea is to put a spindle on the order counter. The wheel on the spindle has clips on it so the girls can simply put their orders on the wheel rather than calling out orders to the cook.

The psychologist was next to return, and in his report he said:
It is during the rush hours that your human relation problems arise.
Psychologically speaking, we can see that the manager is the father figure, the cook is the son, and the waitress is the daughter. Now we know that in our culture you can't have daughters giving orders to the sons. It louses up their ego structure.

The psychologist then offered the same solution of the spindle wheel.

In the anthropologist's diagnosis of the situation he reported that:

It is during the rush hours that your human relations problems arise.
Man behaves according to his value system. Now, the manager holds as a central value the continued growth and development of the restaurant organization. The cooks tend to share this central value system, for as the organization prospers, so do they. But the waitresses, they couldn't care less whether the organization thrives or not as long as it's a decent place to work. Now, you can't have a noncentral value system giving orders to a central value system.

The anthropologist then offered the same spindle-wheel solution as the other two scientists.

Let us observe the functions the spindle fulfills. First, the spindle acts as a memory device as well as a buffering device for the cook. Second, it acts as a queuing device, as it

working with a team of operations research (OR) specialists who gave early signs of their collective genius by deciding to leave the military as an ongoing team. Offering their services to the highest bidder in terms of challenge, prestige, and reward, they went to the Ford Motor Company and, with Henry Ford II, staged Ford's great postwar comeback. When McNamara, who became president of Ford, was called to Washington to serve as secretary of defense, rapid assimilation of systems theory by government departments and their clients in private industry was ensured.

provides proper waiting time and does all the standing in line for the waitresses. Third, the spindle permits a visual display of all the orders waiting to be filled. The cook, having random access to all orders, is able to organize the work around several orders simultaneously. The last function of the spindle is to provide feedback to both waitresses and cook regarding errors. The spindle markedly alters the emotional relationship and redirects the learning process.

It is significant that in this parable the three scientists each discovered that human relations problems arose mostly during the rush hours, in the period of "information overload." How a system responds to conditions of overload depends on how the system is designed.

One of the most common adjustments that a system makes to an excess input load is to increase the number of channels for handling the information. Restaurants put more waitresses and cooks on the job to handle rush-hour loads. But there comes a time when just increasing the number of channels is not enough. Then we see another common adjustment process, that of queuing or forming a waiting line. We have already seen that the spindle makes it unnecessary for the waitresses to queue to give orders.

The hostess can make another adjustment by keeping a list of waiting customers; by jotting down the size of the group, she can selectively pull groups out of the queue according to the size of the table last vacated.

A system can be so designed as to permit omissions, a simple rejection or nonacceptance of an input. In restaurants, when waiting lines get too long, customers will turn away. Also when people are in the queue, they are not spending money. One solution is to install a bar. This permits the customers to spend while waiting.

Another big time-saver in the restaurant system is the use of the chunking process. Big chunks of information can be predetermined by special arrangements. You may find a menu so printed that it asks you to order by number.

A rather unusual adjustment process that a system can adopt to cope with overload is to accept an increase in the number of errors made. It's better to make mistakes than not to deal with the input.

This article looks at organizations as systems which process information—transforming the information from one form into another—and which are or are not designed to cope with the conditions of overload that may be imposed on them. This frame of reference is expressed as an interest in how the structure or design of an organization dynamically influences the operating characteristics and the capacities of the system to handle various conditions of information overload.

The most dramatic success of systems organization was the Apollo Project to put a man on the moon. This effort utilized project management, defined as "doing what we say we are going to do." The conventional loyalties of the NASA people and the technicians from the aerospace firms broke down as the task became the focal point of their lives.

The systems approach has spread to other industries, facilitated by the widespread use of computers, which make information a key raw material.

Box 4–4: McNamara—always on schedule

Robert McNamara's brilliance was evident in the way he applied statistical techniques and rationality to intimidate others. David Halberstam describes McNamara as "a remarkable man in a remarkable era":

> He was Bob, Bob McNamara, taut, controlled, driving—climbing mountains, harnessing generals—the hair slicked down in a way that made him look like a Grant Wood subject. The look was part of the drive: a fat McNamara was as hard to imagine as an uncertain one. The glasses straight and rimless, imposing; you looked at the glasses and kept your distance. He was a man of force, moving, pushing, getting things done, *Bob got things done,* the can-do man in the can-do society, in the can-do era. No one would ever mistake Bob McNamara for a European; he was American through and through, with the American drive, the American certitude and conviction. He pushed everyone, particularly himself, to new limits, long hours, working breakfasts, early bedtimes, moderate drinking, no cocktail parties. He was always rational, always the puritan but not a prude.

Halberstam describes McNamara as always on schedule. He required subordinates to speak quickly and be gone; he did not allow anyone to abuse his time. As Halberstam points out, he was well equipped to handle the military:

> Those who wasted his time—except of course those above him—would feel his cold stare, and this included almost everyone, even General Maxwell Taylor. The first time Taylor went over to see McNamara at the start of the Kennedy years, Taylor arrived a little early. He stood outside the Secretary's office while McNamara waited for the exact moment of their appointment. When it came, Taylor was held up on the phone for a few minutes because the White House had called him. So McNamara waited for Taylor and finally Taylor waited for McNamara a bit more, and then he went in and was given one of the icier treatments of his life.

To McNamara, time was not just money; it was even more important: it was action, decision, cost effectiveness, and power.

Reference: David Halberstam, *The Best and the Brightest* (New York: Random House, 1969). © 1969 by Random House, Inc.

Systems theory and cybernetics

System theorists have been greatly influenced by cybernetics, defined by Norbert Wiener as "the science of control and communication in animals and machines." In the cybernetic approach, it is assumed that the system to some extent must be self-regulating, which would presume a feedback of information. But these systems have become so complex that it is improbable that all the facts and relations will ever be known.

To meet this particular difficulty, operations researchers have introduced the idea of the black box. This "unscientific" term refers to a unit of a system whose mechanisms are unknown. It can be thought of as a way of relating input variables to output variables, so that when the input data are manipulated, it is possible to first record and then predict output data without really knowing what is going on within the unit.

The organization as an organism

The organization can be thought of as an organism in the computer analogy sense discussed above. To distinguish innovative organizations from mechanistic organizations, which have more rigid structures and control systems, Tom Burns, a sociologist at Edinburgh University, has suggested the idea of organic organizations. In these organizations, where roles have been left unfrozen and people interact, a structure with survival value in a changing technological environment evolves.

In this approach an enterprise is thought of as being influenced by its environment, its political climate, its markets, and government policy. Management (as the brain of the organism) must make decisions which will help the organism solve the problems of a changing environment; this presumes that a business organization should be treated as an open system, as a sociotechnical system.

A SOCIOTECHNICAL SYSTEM IN ACTION: MANAGING A JUMBO JET

A good example of a sociotechnical system concerns the operation of a modern airliner (see Figure 4–3). The system can be broken down into three subsystems: air crew, cabin staff, and passengers.

FIGURE 4–3
Three subsystems on an airliner

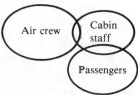

In a jumbo jet like the 747 there are typically three pilots: a captain, a second officer, and a third officer. From a technical point of view, the roles are highly prescribed; jobs are arranged according to checklists, and pilots are only allowed to fly together as a crew for approximately a month at a time. The object of this formality is to inhibit the development of informal groups and behavior which encourages idiosyncratic and personalized work styles. This could prove fatal if one pilot drops out or is replaced.

This formality makes good technical sense. It is easy for military-trained pilots, who comprise most of the captains, to accept. Second officers may resent this overstructuring of behavior, especially in regard to interactions with the cabin staff, who have their own problems in a sociotechnical sense.

The giant planes, such as the 747 with its 350 passengers, have turned the stewardess job into that of a glorified waitress-in-the-sky. Further, the introduction of male flight attendants has changed the definition as well as the nature of the work. The large number of attendants on each plane, organized under a director of in-flight services, has helped to provide a social support system. Strong trade unions have developed to represent the interests of the attendants.

The passengers' various life-styles are reflected in the characteristics of the third subsystem.

Conflict in the sky

A running conflict between the cabin staff and the pilots is not unusual. To understand this conflict it is necessary to understand the background of the subsystems.

When airliners were first introduced, they carried quite a large crew which included pilots, a navigator, a radio operator, and frequently an engineer, as well as a cabin staff of one or two stewardesses. Over the years the role membership of these two groups has significantly changed. Because of technological changes, the navigator, engineer, and radio operator have been exchanged for the three pilots on the flight deck.

The cabin staff now can include up to 13 flight attendants. In the beginning the one or two stewardesses on a plane were mainly recruited from the nursing profession. After a while there was a need for linguists. Soon the airline companies had developed a tight role specification for stewardesses which required them to be of a particular height and weight, and unmarried. Occasionally they were fired because they got married (their job-life expectation at this time was between 12 and 18 months) or had put on weight.

Given their respective career histories, it can come as no surprise that the real conflict is between the plane's captain ("This is my ship. What I say goes, and I will tolerate no nonsense from anyone while I am in charge.") and the director of in-flight services ("I am in charge of the back end of the plane. What happens in there is my business. This is not a damned boat.") Figure 4–4 illustrates this situation.

An example is the director of inflight services on a Canadian airliner

FIGURE 4–4
Intergroup conflict between air crew and cabin staff on an airliner

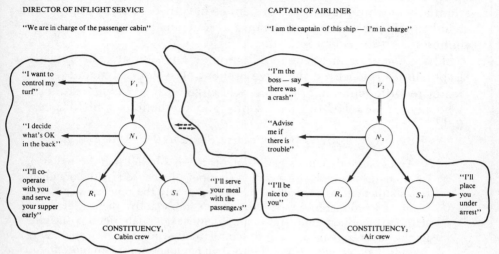

Key: V = values; N = norms; R = reinforcements; S = sanctions.

confronting the captain soon after takeoff from Charles de Gaulle Airport in Paris and saying: "Land the plane; I have flown my hours according to the management-union agreement." The captain placed him under close arrest and locked him in the washroom until the plane got to Montreal. Subsequently there was an investigation by the company, and the captain was suspended for a month.

An effective way of dealing with this conflict is to put a group of pilots in one room and in-flight services directors in another and have each group develop a description of their own role and those of the other group. The process is recorded on videotape, and the groups are then brought together and both sets of perceptions are presented.

The important point is that once the various subsystems (in this case, the air crew and cabin staff) are specified, a sociotechnical approach must be used. Each group represents an imbedded amalgam of technical skills and social values. To unravel the technical and social dimensions of the matrix is quite a complex process, touching not only on operational considerations but also revealing underlying psychological forces.

TOPIC 3
Systems dynamics

In systems dynamics, the principles of feedback control are applied to organizational problems to get a better conceptual picture of how organizations operate. Systems dynamics, which is largely a result of military research and development, makes extensive use of computer simulation techniques. These principles have been widely applied in wind tunnels and ship-towing tanks as a means of verifying theories before their full-scale application.

J. W. Forrester, head of the Computer Division at MIT Lincoln Laboratories, pioneered the development of systems dynamics. Forrester recruited a number of electrical engineering graduate students who helped develop the philosophy and methodology of this new field.

As Edward B. Roberts points out in *Systems Dynamics:*

> The system dynamics philosophy rests on a belief that the behavior (or time history) of an organization is principally caused by the organization's structure. The structure includes not only the physical aspects of plant and production process but, more importantly, the policies and traditions, both tangible and intangible, that dominate decision-making in the organization. Such a structural framework contains sources of amplification, time lags, and information feedback similar to those found in complex engineering systems. Engineering and management systems containing these characteristics display complicated response patterns to relatively simple system or input changes. The analysis of large non-linear systems of this sort is a major challenge to even the most experienced control systems engineer; effective and reliable redesign of such a system is still more difficult. The subtleties and complexities in the management area make these problems even more severe. Here the structural orientation of system dynamics provides a beginning for replacing confusion with order.

The MIT group developed an original computer simulation program called DYNAMO which can be used to solve organizational problems. DYNAMO is a system of equations—linear and nonlinear, algebraic and differential, which can contain several thousand variables. Because organizational systems are complex, they can contain as many as 100 variables, and therefore they are suitable for the DYNAMO program. Using this model, managers can develop a better causal picture of what is happening in their organizations, and "what if" situations can be explored. Further sensitivity analysis of the model reveals the areas of genuine debate. Causal-loop diagrams can be developed to explain how organizations are in fact operating.

COUNTERINTUITIVE ASPECTS OF SYSTEMS DYNAMICS

One of the interesting findings to emerge from systems theory is the fact that systems do not behave in the way they ought to, at least in commonsensical terms. This is mainly because organizations as social systems are multiloop, nonlinear feedback systems. Forrester has developed the concept of industrial dynamics as a means of getting at this complex idea.

A good example of the counterintuitive nature of social systems is provided by a quick look at a problem faced by airlines flying the North Atlantic. Until recently, predicting that market was made easy by an international arrangement that all airlines would charge essentially the same fare. Then, that unorthodox genius Freddie Laker proposed walk-on, no-reservation, no-service flights across the Atlantic for very low fares. After engaging in a legal contest with the airline establishment, Laker was able to put his Sky Train, as he called his transatlantic service, in effect. Soon he was swamped with business.

To counter this, airlines like Pan American, British Airways, and Lufthansa got together and worked out a formula to calculate how many spare seats they had available on the North Atlantic run. Each airline was then given a quota of seats that could be sold at "Laker prices" on a standby basis. Almost immediately the airlines began to experience the internal conflict that inevitably arose when the passenger who was paying the full fare discovered that a companion was only paying one third of that. At first, the airlines responded to the problem by offering some sort of personalized service for full-fare passengers (usually business executives). But they were unable to resolve this problem, which could only be recognized in retrospect. This situation was also compounded by the conflict between the air crew and cabin staff discussed above.

Systems dynamics computer models are very different from classical and human relations models of organizations. A computer model is derived from statistical time series data, which represent a statement of the essence of the structure of the organization it presumes to represent. Forrester cites as an example, in *Urban Dynamics,* the problems faced by large U.S. cities (like New York, Boston, or Chicago) from too much cheap housing occupied by poor people on welfare. When a great number of poor people move into a building which formerly supported a smaller number of rich people, the net effect is to create additional demands on the social systems of the community, without providing additional productive resources. Forrester provides many other illustrations in *World Dynamics,* and Dennis Meadows and his coauthors, who came up with the doomsday prediction in *The Limits to Growth,* were trained by Forrester.

Systems design people argue that there are no shortcuts in solving complex organizational problems. In the process of suboptimization, the best may become the enemy of the good. As Forrester points out, there are no utopias in organizational systems. There are no sustainable modes of behavior which are free of stress.

We shall return later to the application of the Forrester systems design model, DYNAMO, to analyze the life processes of a particular company. It produced findings wholly at variance with common sense.

THE SYSTEM: PREDICTION AND EXPLANATION

There is a relation between organization theories and larger historical events. Just as the success of the New Deal helped to establish human relations as a school of management, so did its failures create a demand for the systems approach. In the sixties, serious doubts developed about whether the country could afford human relations management and whether it was working. This heightened the importance of the planning, programming, budgeting system (PPBS) which McNamara brought with him from the Ford Motor Company. Another example of the systems approach in action is zero-based budgeting, which Jimmy Carter, as governor of Georgia, showed could be applied to the management of a state budget.

Perhaps the most dramatic application of the systems approach to the solving of practical problems was Jay Forrester's computer model of organizations. Forrester developed a set of equations which could interact to describe the functions of a system as they influence one another.

This model could be applied at a number of levels. At the macro end of the scale it was used by Dennis Meadows et al. to show, in *The Limits to Growth,* how Spaceship Earth was heading for a disaster, burying itself in its own ecological debris. While Meadows's doomsday view is not wholly convincing, the problem is not in the model but in its assumptions.

Forrester's model can be used to show that the problems of cities like New York and Detroit can be predicted or "explained" in a relatively small number of equations. One major factor that goes a long way to predict the decline of such cities is the fact that the tax base in the center of these cities is declining. But it is one thing to predict in behavioral science; it is another thing to explain. Fleshing out this prediction about the relationship between the number of taxable dollars and the quality of life reveals the true value of the systems approach. The sequence goes something like this: A city like New York is alive and vibrant in the fifties. But it attracts a variety of people of all social classes and ethnic backgrounds. School desegregation is ordered by the Supreme Court, and the affluent move out of the area. As unemployment and welfare rolls increase in the central city, so does crime. The next level of affluence moves out, and the poor flow in to fill the void. Social services, including schools, police, and medical services, cannot be sustained. Businesses begin to leave the area. The system is in the process of adjusting itself to the environment. This systems model could also be applied to business organizations.

TOPIC 4
What every manager should know about systems

What has this brief review of systems theory to tell us that is relevant to the study of organizational behavior? First, that information, which is becoming the critical input in industry and pushing capital into second place as a factor of production, is something which can be measured. And information is measured by the amount of surprise that it elicits. When information is received, uncertainty is reduced.

Management, because it needs to control its level of uncertainty, has a sustained and growing interest in information systems. This is precisely what the computer analogy is all about: Open systems can also be thought of as information-processing systems. If you understand how any information-processing system operates and works, it will provide a good guide for the study of the individual, the group, and the organization as information processors. A diagram of an information system according to the contingency model developed in Chapter 1 is shown in Figure 4–5.

FIGURE 4–5
Systems approach to information

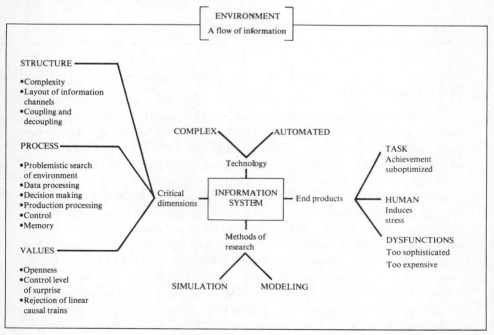

TOPIC 5
Evaluation of organization theories

CLASSICAL, HUMAN RELATIONS, AND SYSTEMS THEORIES

The three organization theories considered in Part I—classical, human relations, and systems—have unique characteristics, as has been pointed out in Chapters 2, 3, and 4. The structure and process of each theory can be defined by its approach to differentiation (how jobs are broken down) and integration (how jobs are held together or coordinated). Figure 4–6 illustrates this distinction. The value system of the theory can be summed up in its approach to this basic issue.

FIGURE 4–6
How organization theories approach differentiation and integration

ORGANIZA-TION THEORY	METHOD OF DIFFERENTIATION	METHOD OF INTEGRATION
Classical	Narrow work-role definitions and hierarchy	Objective setting, planning, and control
Human relations	Facilitation, taking up social roles	Participation
Systems	Connection and disconnection of informational systems	Creation of new liaison subsystems

Value assimilation

Classical organizations had little difficulty absorbing the human relations value system spawned by the Hawthorne studies. Human relations values stress the superiority of feeling over thinking and promote an expanded interpersonal consciousness and a spirit of openness.

While organizations seem to be able to assimilate human relations values fairly easily, more difficulty has been experienced in trying to incorporate the values of the systems approach, which are largely derived from the concepts of information theory. Information theory has its own particular mystique, as this chapter has indicated.

In recent years there has been a backlash against the computer, against systems, and against organizations in general. The motives of overachieving, conspicuous consumption, and overdefinition and specification as moral frames of reference have had some setbacks. Increasingly managers are seeking a world in which there can be a

Box 4–5: An introduction to existentialism

"God is dead." (signed) Nietzsche

Managers have turned away from traditional approaches to organizational behavior and moved toward existentialism basically because they believe life is too short to fool around with. They want to be committed to something; they are seeking "engagement," or commitment. But commitment to what? Existentialists come in all sizes and shapes: some are existential atheists like Jean-Paul Sartre; others are existential communists; some are even existential Catholics.

It is important first to realize that existentialism is a highly subjective philosophy, like a philosophical Rorschach inkblot onto which people can project all sorts of belief systems. For the outsider, it is extremely difficult to understand. Unlike traditional philosophies, it does not deal with such notions as the first-cause–uncaused argument about the existence of both God and the universe. Rather it describes an attitude, an optic, a perspective, a posture, and a process.

A useful way of getting into existentialism is to accept that inside every fat man there is a thin one trying to break out. In the same way, inside every human being there is an artist trying to find the way out in order to express the terrible yearnings, hurts, and insights floating around inside. When the artist-genie escapes, dramatic and terrible things can happen which can only partially be accounted for by poetic license. Human beings would have to be strangled by organization before the whisper of the artist would be completely muffled. For those who can listen to the supplicating artist within, it is but a short step to the terrifying conclusion, "I am God."

In more technical terms, to grasp the meaning of existentialism it is necessary to discriminate between essence and existence. Essence is the ultimate nature of a thing or entity which can be observed and known; existence, which refers to having a place in a dangerous and dynamic world, is what really matters. A self-aware individual is not only conscious on reflection of his own existence as a free agent in the world, he is also terribly aware not only of his self-awareness but also of a self, suffused with angst, anxiety, and aspiration. It is a self which is desperately trying to make life meaningful by giving his destiny purpose and plan.

"Nietzsche is dead." (signed) God

People cannot come to terms with destiny lying in their beds, gazing at the ceiling, seeking inspiration through meditation, important as that may be. It is necessary to become involved and to try for commitment—to develop a frame of belief that can be tested against action. The ultimate personal fact contained in the universal fact, "All men must die," relates to the essence of man but has the existential correlate, "I, too, must die."

In coming to terms with reality, the existentialist readily recognizes the necessity to give up the ideas of a world of complete objectivity and theoretical detachment. Above all, there are no innocent bystanders. The best point of departure for the existentialist is the idea of perception. What human beings see out there is a function of their values, attitudes, needs, and expectations (VANE). They describe what they see; they see what they describe. Only the individual involved in the incident is involved; only the involved have significance; to the completely uninvolved, life is meaningless because it has become a closed system. And a closed system is a machine, a mechanical thing subject to the second law of thermodynamics and therefore dead or dying.

Thus, the existentialist cannot escape into the cozy corridors of rational thought, away from the rough and hard, to contemplate the realities of life, never mind structure. All the uncertainties of life cannot be plotted, measured, and insured against. To meet life head on or tangentially, or even to watch it slipping and sliding past in all its glory, it is necessary to be brave. Unfortunately, if you were brave yesterday, there is no guarantee you will be brave today.

happy marriage of affluence and technology which does not exclude joy and spontaneity. These new managers are seeking an efficient organizational society which will not only underscore effectiveness but also allow for the existential values of authenticity, awareness, and interdependence. Box 4–5 is an introduction to the topic of existentialism.

CONTINGENCY THEORY

A theory of organizations is needed in which the classical organizational values of achievement and affluence can be coupled with the existential values of authenticity and awareness. The contingency model introduced in Chapter 1, which recognizes that conditions dif-

FIGURE 4–7
Comparison of the structure, process, and values of organization theories

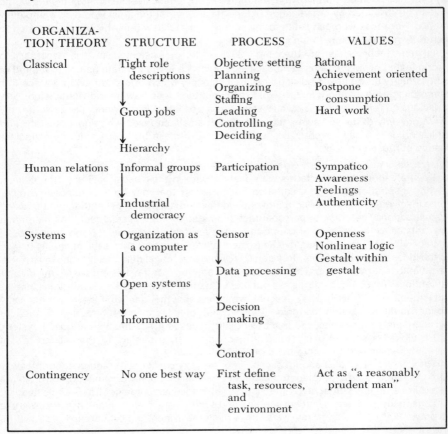

ORGANIZA-TION THEORY	STRUCTURE	PROCESS	VALUES
Classical	Tight role descriptions ↓ Group jobs ↓ Hierarchy	Objective setting Planning Organizing Staffing Leading Controlling Deciding	Rational Achievement oriented Postpone consumption Hard work
Human relations	Informal groups ↓ Industrial democracy	Participation	Sympatico Awareness Feelings Authenticity
Systems	Organization as a computer ↓ Open systems ↓ Information	Sensor ↓ Data processing ↓ Decision making ↓ Control	Openness Nonlinear logic Gestalt within gestalt
Contingency	No one best way	First define task, resources, and environment	Act as "a reasonably prudent man"

ferentially affect outcomes, and it is not possible to provide for all contingencies, represents this theory. Figure 4–7 compares the structure, process, and values of all four theories: classical, human relations, systems, and contingency.

As tentative new organizational forms (such as democratic or participative management) emerge, contingency theory makes it possible to identify the conditions that are likely to lead to effective management.

REVIEW AND RESEARCH

1. Describe the main subsystems of any system. Consider the organization of a hospital or a police force and identify the organizational elements that correspond to each of these subsystems. How is performance monitored?

2. What is the computer analogy? Compare and contrast the organization, the group, and the individual as information-processing systems.

3. Using the systems model, describe the structure, process, and values of any organization that you are familiar with. How are end products measured? What dysfunctions are generated?

4. How are the traditional concepts of management related to the systems concept?

5. The Planning, programming, budgeting system (PPBS) has been widely used in government. Does PPBS have equal applicability in business? If not, why not?

6. How would you use the systems approach to describe the following types of organizations? Use a process flowchart to identify the critical choices and decision variables.
   a. An air defense system (subsystems include radar, data-plotting room, command group of officers, fighter aircraft and missiles, ground control of aircraft, statistical evaluations group).
   b. A manufacturing company (subsystems include market research, R&D, production planning and control, management decision groups, production shops, quality control and inspection, and accounting).

7. The problem is to relate planning to systems analysis. Select an organization with which you are familiar. List the different kinds of plans that are developed according to level (company, plant, department, section, squad, individual) and function (production, technical, and personnel). Use the systems approach to draw a diagram to integrate the plans. Can they be integrated? How much integration is needed? How should it be achieved?

8. Compare the classical, human relations, systems, and contingency theories of organization under the following headings: structure, process, values, level of analysis, measurement of end products, impact of the environment, and dysfunctions.

GLOSSARY OF TERMS

Black box. Term used by systems analysts to denote that part of a particular system whose internal mechanism is unknown. The analyst knows the input-output relationship pertaining to the black box but does not know how the input is transformed into the output.

Communication. In a broad sense, all of the procedures by which one mind may affect another. The three levels of communication are the technical, the semantic, and the effectiveness levels. All organizations are communication systems.

Computer analogy. The concept that human beings or organizations and computers are two species of a more abstract genus called the information-processing system.

Control. Methods used by an organization to police performance and monitor the behaviors and attitudes of its members; the feedback subsystem.

Cybernetics. Term coined by Wiener and derived from a Greek word meaning steersman to describe the science of feedback mechanisms. It may also be viewed as a study which attempts to explain how systems achieve a balance while pursuing a mission.

Existentialism. Approach in the area of psychology-philosophy-ethics which emphasizes holistic view of human beings in an interpersonal setting. The purpose of existentialism is to make people more aware of the choices open to them, to discourage them from choosing to act unfree, and to make life more meaningful by the acceptance of reality as a value-loaded perception.

Information process. The process by which a system collects information, processes it, stores it, and takes action and formulates plans based on it. All systems may be thought of as information processors; for all, information is the key input and its management a critical process.

Open system. A system which trades with its environment and has the following main characteristics: (1) interrelation among component objects, attributes, and events; (2) holism; (3) goal seeking; (4) input, transformation, and output; (5) negative entropy; (6) information processing; (7) regulation; (8) differentiation; and (9) equifinality.

Organizational effectiveness. The achievement of goals, measured against the following criteria: (1) organizational productivity, (2) the ability of the organization to innovate, and (3) the control of inter- and intraorganizational stress.

Organizational objectives. The multiple set of hierarchical goals or ends which the organization tries to achieve, recognizing that the ascription of a single simple objective to an enterprise is no longer appropriate.

System. Any entity which consists of interdependent parts, qualified as to whether it is an open or closed system and is organic, mechanistic, human, and so on.

System subsystems. Systems have the following subsystems: (1) sensor, (2) data processing, (3) decision, (4) processing, (5) control, and (6) memory.

DEBATE: Bureaucracy versus democratic participation

A basic assumption of this book is that today's managers espouse a variety of management theories. Which theory a manager holds is a consequence of whether the position is line, staff, or function; at what level the manager is in the organization; how much and what kind of education the manager has had, and so on. In spite of this diversity, by and large the most widely espoused approach is the classical theory— and not only among line managers.

BUREAUCRACY IS STILL WITH US, GOING STRONG

In spite of Max Weber's idea that bureaucratic management is an inevitable outgrowth of the technical revolution in industry, many management theorists in the sixties forecast the demise of the classical theory. For example, Warren Bennis, a well-known behavioral scientist who established an important reputation at M.I.T., achieved fame for his theory of organic populism, a theory of management in which the key words are smallness, temporariness, and participation. In this theory, changing organizations are made up of temporary, ad hoc groups, governed by democratic means with a rotating leadership. In "Beyond Bureaucracy," which appeared in 1965, Bennis predicted a much less rigid, less permanent type of structure than is the norm in classical theory:

> . . . there will be adaptive, rapidly changing *temporary systems*. These will be "task forces" organized around problems to be solved. The problems will be solved by groups of relative strangers who represent a set of diverse professional skills. The groups will be arranged on organic rather than mechanical models: they will evolve in response to a problem rather than to programmed role expectations. . . . This is the organizational form that will gradually replace bureaucracy as we know it.

Now Bennis, older and wiser, and having switched from professor to administrator (as university president), takes a different view. William F. Dowling, editor of *Organizational Dynamics*, in an interview with Bennis published in the Winter, 1974 issue, catches the essence of this change:

DOWLING: Dr. Bennis, several years ago you wrote frequently about the fact that bureaucracy was on the way out, that democracy was inevitable, and that over a period of time—the time scale wasn't too clear—bureaucracy was going to wither away, to be replaced by temporary systems made up of diverse teams of specialists. Now, if I read you correctly, you've undergone a complete change of heart. You feel that bureaucracy is the inevitable form of organization in a large-scale enterprise, be it public or private.

BENNIS: Yes, I think that's true. I began changing my mind about the democratic tendencies because the original hypothesis was so sweeping that it wouldn't have validity for every kind of situation. In fact, when I first wrote about the demise of bureaucracy I did talk about certain conditions that had to obtain if bureaucracy was to disappear, although critics never understood them fully, because they were easy to overlook. Actually, it's very difficult to do too much damage to the hypothesis for one reason: The time scale was between 25 to 50 years, which is kind of laughable, because it doesn't leave too many people around to see whether it's going to be true or not.

BORN AND BRED TO BUREAUCRACY

People in postindustrial society have been born and bred to the ideas of chain of command, line-staff relations, and span of control. They basically expect things to be managed classically, and this makes them easier to be managed classically. This is the message emerging from the U.S. Department of Health, Education, and Welfare report *Work in America*. Work is still organized bureaucratically, bosses are mainly autocratic, few efforts are made to enrich jobs, and many people suffer from stress and alienation brought about by their work.

It will not be easy to change this situation. As Fred E. Emery points out in "Bureaucracy and Beyond":

> Admittedly, it will be hard to debureaucratize the industrial corporations and administrative structures of societies that are very heterogeneous in their national origins and hence their values, such as that of the United States, or deeply rooted in a feudal past, such as those of France and Germany. Despite these difficulties, I think Western societies will successfully re-integrate their productive and administrative structures with their traditional cultural values. My optimism is based not only on what has happened in the Sixties—at Volvo, for example—but on the fact that a willingness to look at the technological requirements of a productive system as closely as Taylor did has, in my experience, always yielded a "democratic" design solution at least as productive as a design based on the bureaucratic concept of redundant parts.

THE NEED TO RECONCILE CONTRADICTIONS

Putting the bureaucratic and democratic approaches together in an organization inevitably involves the need to reconcile contradictions. As Emery points out:

> The efficiency of an organization can only be *reduced* if its various parts or aspects are designed according to contradictory design principles. There must be interfaces between such aspects or parts, and at these interfaces the conflict in principles would undermine coordination. In discussing how the U.S. aerospace industry was forced by environmental pressures toward the second design principle in R&D work but [was], overall, hung up on the first principle, Donald R. Kingdon

observes in his study *Matrix Organization:* "Of course, these two principles, or organizational purposes, may not always be in accord with each other. In fact, it is more nearly the case that the two are in conflict with one another and that conflict resolution is a necessary part of the matrix organizational form."

The target that men will increasingly set for themselves is not just de-bureaucratization but the positive target of redesigning their work organizations on the second principle, that is, of democratizing work.

Questions

1. Can democracy ever replace bureaucracy in North America?
2. Or are North Americans too far gone on materialism, individuality, achievement, and aggression to function in democratic work groups?

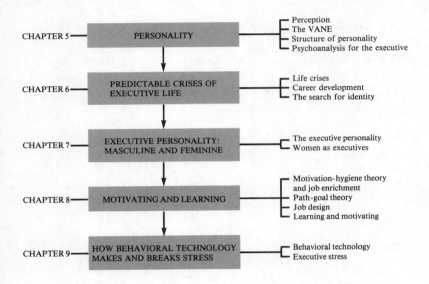

CHAPTER 5 — PERSONALITY
- Perception
- The VANE
- Structure of personality
- Psychoanalysis for the executive

CHAPTER 6 — PREDICTABLE CRISES OF EXECUTIVE LIFE
- Life crises
- Career development
- The search for identity

CHAPTER 7 — EXECUTIVE PERSONALITY: MASCULINE AND FEMININE
- The executive personality
- Women as executives

CHAPTER 8 — MOTIVATING AND LEARNING
- Motivation-hygiene theory and job enrichment
- Path-goal theory
- Job design
- Learning and motivating

CHAPTER 9 — HOW BEHAVIORAL TECHNOLOGY MAKES AND BREAKS STRESS
- Behavioral technology
- Executive stress

part **II**

PEOPLE MOVING
THROUGH
ORGANIZATIONS

DIAGRAM SUMMARY OF CHAPTER 5

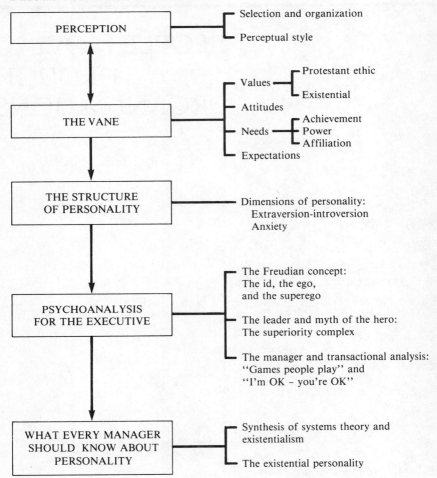

5

Personality

HOW THE EXISTENTIALISTS INVADED MODERN CONSCIOUSNESS

The cabalistic code of the ad men has been broken, revealing a devilishly clever attempt to write an up-to-date *Lives of the Saints*. The copywriter has almost accomplished the impossible: giving the new saint, that phantom, the existentialist, an eerie reality. The goal is to powerhouse you right out of your seat and down to the nearest store to buy some of the things the existentialist eats, drinks, dreams, flies, or otherwise uses.

The copywriters have emerged as the impresarios who produced the idea of the existentialist out of the WASP cornucopia. Laced with the truth, the near truth, and what one day may become the truth, their ads insidiously create in the minds of the people a hazy picture of the existentialist and the vague outline of a map with instructions on how to get to Shangri-La, that land to the west of California where existentialists live.

The copywriters' work of fiction is being serialized in ads which can serve as a sort of summary of what existential man is about. Advertising people once had an affair with the great WASP, who lived next door to the Jones in a male chauvinistic, calvinistic America. Unfortunately, they lived in a cage of experience that ultimately limited their capacity to consume. Their motivation limited them to steak, booze, and bigger, more expensive automobiles. A new consumer with a wider range of needs was needed to purchase all the things the system was producing. This consumer must need the new low tars; want to drive and pay for any car with more mpg; be likely to fly to London for the theater and pub crawling, to Acapulco for swimming, and to Aspen for skiing; eat only nature foods; and be willing to pay $45 for sneakers.

The ads which are designed to keep people consuming, however, have emerged as a means of undoing the American Dream by getting people in touch with the multifaceted personality of the existentialist—more complex, cool, tortured, sensate, sensuous, sexy, liberated, and liberating; more mysteriously, magically mythological. The existentialist has tried and rejected encounter, bioenergetics, Gestalt-guided fantasy, primal scream, neo-Reichian touch, Rolfing, Lowen expressive therapy, marathon groups, psychodrama, Synanon, cooperative help, couples' groups, family therapy, network therapy, and spontaneous groups. "I'm OK—You're OK" is not OK.

In the forties, during the classical period of organization theory, the ad men sold toothpaste by telling you it preserved your health by saving your gums. In the fifties, when they discovered human relations, they sold it to help you avoid bad breath, which hindered your interactions with others. But in the seventies and eighties, they raised the existential question, "If he kissed you once, will he kiss you again?"

PULLING YOURSELF TOGETHER

It is impossible to give a full and comprehensive account of executive behavior without raising questions of why they behave as they do. For example: Why do effective executives spend so much time on personnel matters? Why don't they concentrate their efforts on production? When we ask such questions regarding executive behavior, we are trying to explore questions of motivation. Motivation is concerned with the study of the direction and persistence of action. Personality is the organizing center around which people's motives form a unified and integrated system.

The aim of this chapter is to present an organized summary of some of the contemporary theories of personality that may be of interest to the executive, indicating their possible relevance for the study of organizational behavior.

Gordon W. Allport, in *Personality: A Psychological Interpretation*, examines a mass of different definitions and then gives the neatest, most penetrating, and most frequently cited definition: "Personality is the dynamic organization within an individual of those psychophysical systems that determine his unique adjustments to his environment."

For Allport, personality is dynamic and describes something which is always in the process of becoming. Personality is seen as an expanding system seeking new and better levels of order and transaction. Thus his definition emphasizes the idea of organization, of how people pull themselves together by trying to integrate their values, attitudes, needs, expectations, and abilities to give their lives meaning. Implicit in his definition is the belief that a person achieves this integration by a particular life-style which is unique to the person. This personal style is stamped on everything that comes in contact with people and thus determines the form of their adjustment. The idea of adjustment to the environment is included in the definition, for personality has the functional value of facilitating survival and the evolution of behavior. Environment describes the field of forces, the culture, the roles, and the interaction set—the situational context in which people find themselves.

Allport sees personality as an open system which is engaged in an extensive transactional commerce with its environment. Information in the form of stimuli is absorbed and transformed, and responses are generated. This is known as the S-R model. Personality stands between the stimulus and the response and tries to achieve some "good order and military discipline" between the input of the stimulus and the output of the response. This good order is not a static framework but an evolving one which, in the case of the healthy person, over time can handle more complexity by becoming not only more differentiated but also more integrated. Thus personality as an open system has to achieve not only stability but growth.

The study of personality stresses a cognitive approach in which information and meaning are key concepts. How the individual deals with the problem of reducing uncertainty through coding inputs has become the natural point of departure for studying personality. What is being studied here is how perception, or the process of coding, structures the stimulus so that the person sees the world in terms which are meaningful. Thus the student of personality begins by inquiring what effect values, attitudes, needs, and expectations (the VANE) have on perception; and, following Allport's idea of becoming, how the environment (the stimuli outside and inside the person) affects the VANE.

THE VANE MODEL

The stimulus-organism-response (S-O-R) model improves on the stimulus-response (S-R) model by adding the organism to the picture. The organism—the person—has values, attitudes, needs, and expectations, which are symbolized as the person's VANE. The VANE affects how people feel, perceive, and behave (as indicated in Figure 5–1).

A telling illustration of how a person's VANE affects his perception of the world is revealed by reports of flying saucers being "seen" all over the globe. Although the U.S. Air Force, after examining 12,618 sightings over a period of 22 years, gave up, people still saw UFOs (unidentified flying objects) of all kinds, formed organized percep-

FIGURE 5–1
Personality as the transformation process

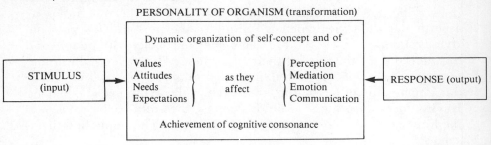

tions about them, and claimed to have met their occupants and taken jaunts in them. The *New York Times* of June 25, 1972, reported:

> Even though the thousands of reports in the files of the Aerial Phenomenon Research Organization have not been thoroughly analyzed, a pattern of sorts can be established by reading them. Reports of U.F.O.'s that have been examined from close range say they have portholes or windows in the outer rim of the ring. This rim spins when the disk moves, the portholes giving the impression that the U.F.O. is surrounded by a ring of spinning lights. When the U.F.O. lifts, bright white light streams from grids on the bottom of the craft.

Which goes to show that even unworldly things are seen in worldly terms. The example highlights the relationships between perception and attitudes; whatever it is that people see in the sky, they tend to interpret it in terms of their social, interpersonal, political, and cosmic attitudes.

Every marketing man is a keen student of perception and attitudes; and anyone who ever took a course in consumer psychology has heard of subliminal perception—which suggests that moviegoers will buy more popcorn if "eat popcorn" messages are periodically flashed, extremely briefly, on the screen, although they are not consciously aware of being exposed to the message. Perception research of this genre was begun during World War II to train antiaircraft gunners in aircraft identification. Using a tachistoscope, which allows a picture to be thrown on a screen for an extremely brief period (so brief that few subjects consciously see it), an instructor would first present a series of pictures of aircraft silhouettes. The gunners were asked to note down the types of aircraft shown. On the first showing, the response was poor. Then a second series would be shown which included a subliminal "pinup girl." This series inevitably brought forth catcalls, hoots, and whistles; thus sexual stimulation was used to initiate the gunners' perceptual modification. Although use of this technique has run into difficulties, it is a dramatic example of what behavioral technology may hold in store.

TOPIC 1
Perception

Perception describes the process whereby people become aware of the outside world and themselves. It is necessary to begin by putting aside the commonsense view that perception simply registers what is "out there." A fundamental assumption of the psychology of perception is that an individual distorts his perceptions of the outside world to make it congruent with his set of beliefs and attitudes.

The commonsense view of perception (that the eye is a camera and the mind a film which can completely and minutely examine itself) presumes that all the information gathered by our senses actually reaches the mind. Common sense argues that reality is mirrored in the mind. But new ideas of perception—structuralism, as it has been called—have produced the insight that knowledge about the world enters the mind not as raw data but in already highly abstracted form—structures. The structure is known in psychology as a gestalt, which is the German word for configuration or shape. In the preconscious process of converting raw data into structures, information is inevitably lost. The creation of structures—the establishment of gestalts—is nothing less than the selective destruction of information to facilitate the recognition of patterns which have meaning for the perceiver. (The idea of selective information was introduced in Chapter 4.) Therefore, without all the raw data, "the mirror of reality" thesis of perception fails. Instead, for the perceiver reality is a set of structural transformations of primary data taken from the world.

This view of perception was pioneered by Jerome S. Bruner of Harvard, who argues that perception involves an act of categorization. Bruner is saying that when we perceive something we try to fit it into a classification system or frame of reference, and a trading process goes on between the perceived qualities of the thing and the hole in the classification system where we think it should fit. In the process, some

FIGURE 5–2
Stimulus and perception by the organism

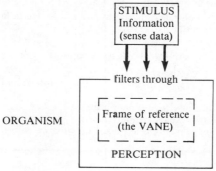

of the qualities of the object are derived from the classification system and tried on the object for size. Perceptual readiness refers to the relative accessibility of the category system to the kinds of stimulus information being inputted. The frame of reference includes values, attitudes, needs, and expectations. Figure 5–2 illustrates this transactional classification as the organism responding to the stimulus by filtering sense data though the frame of reference.

SELECTION AND ORGANIZATION

In this approach to perception it is presumed that each person behaves in a way consistent with his or her perceptual field, the somewhat fluid and dynamic organization of personal meanings carried around in a person's head. This "little world" in which a person lives has also been called the psychological field, life space, or phenomenonal field. (The last term is derived from the Greek *phainesthai,* which means "to appear.") Thus for the perceiver, reality lies not in the event but in the phenomenon, or his perception of the event. If a person is reacting to something as real, then that phenomenon is real for that person.

Since a person is constantly bombarded by sensory stimulation, there must be processes of selection and organization to make this glut of data meaningful. Perception is, first of all, a selective or screening process which ensures that some information is processed and some is not. This selective process requires categorizing stimuli into two

FIGURE 5–3
Rules the interviewer applies to organize perceptions

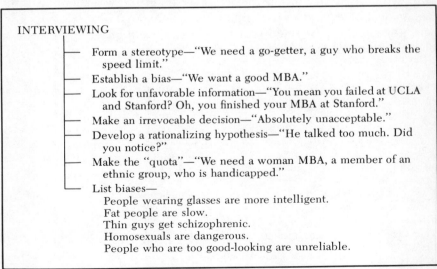

INTERVIEWING
- Form a stereotype—"We need a go-getter, a guy who breaks the speed limit."
- Establish a bias—"We want a good MBA."
- Look for unfavorable information—"You mean you failed at UCLA and Stanford? Oh, you finished your MBA at Stanford."
- Make an irrevocable decision—"Absolutely unacceptable."
- Develop a rationalizing hypothesis—"He talked too much. Did you notice?"
- Make the "quota"—"We need a woman MBA, a member of an ethnic group, who is handicapped."
- List biases—
  People wearing glasses are more intelligent.
  Fat people are slow.
  Thin guys get schizophrenic.
  Homosexuals are dangerous.
  People who are too good-looking are unreliable.

kinds: those of which a person is aware and can recognize fairly readily after selection, and those which may be below the threshold of awareness.

The second component of perception is organization. A person "sees" his environment in such a way that it has personal meaning for him. The sensory data that is processed must be ordered or classified in some way that allows him to ascribe meaning to the stimulus data. An individual does not rest content with a mass of unorganized data but devises and perceives a good gestalt, or meaningful and satisfying shape or form. Thus the perceptual world is organized in ways that are mandated not only by the construction of the central nervous system but also in accordance with the values, attitudes, needs, expectations, and self-concept which each person brings to his perception of "reality." (See Figure 5–3 for a list of "rules" employed by interviewers, for example.)

PERCEPTUAL STYLE

Many factors which affect what a person perceives have been identified. The first is response disposition: A person tends to perceive familiar stimuli more readily than unfamiliar ones. Second, an individual more quickly perceives things about which he has strong rather than neutral feelings. Third, there is the factor of response salience, which refers to the structuring effect of motivation on perception.

Box 5–1 suggests how the study of perception affects marketing. Perceptual style is also related to personality.

Box 5–1: Fooling around with perceptions

Fooling around with perceptions is a major marketing occupation. For example, how would you steal a chunk of the lightbulb market from General Electric, who has the franchise, so to speak, in that area.

The answer lies in finding the answer to the question: What has the average person who goes shopping for lightbulbs got on his or her mind? According to the marketing people at Westinghouse, who want a share of the game, the answer is: "Nothing, lightbulbs don't turn me on." The firm questioned 900 women, many of whom reported hostile feelings: "The bulbs keep blowing out."

Westinghouse's answer is a new type of bulb called Turtle-lite, which has longer filaments to guarantee longevity. But to beat out the opposition, the pursuit of perceptions is necessary. The real battle is for minds and hearts, and it can be won by pushing shape, packaging, and display.

Market research has shown that the usual angular, flat-topped configuration for bulbs works best, but the new bulb borrows the clean, sharp image of contemporary car bodies. By the game of the name, "Turtle-lite" was chosen to project an image of long-lived, slow-but-steady service.

For Westinghouse, a lightbulb is not just a lightbulb. For the student of organization behavior, X is never just X.

Perceiving people

The stability of our personal perceptions makes us feel more comfortable and allows us to make predictions about future behavioral events. (Figure 5–4 suggests some of the problems of perception.) The term *stereotyping* is widely used to describe bias in perceiving others,

FIGURE 5–4
Some problems of perception

Stereotyping: "I expected him to act like that because he is one of those people."

Halo effect: "I like her independence. I like her a lot. She is a winner. I rate her high on all qualities."

Expectancy: "We were expecting a whiz kid, and we got one."

Projection: "You are the one who is aggressive. You haven't spoken since we met."

Selective organization: "Did you hear the way he said 'Commie'? He is a fascist."

Defensive: "I don't wanta know."

FIGURE 5–5
Rating scale showing the halo effect

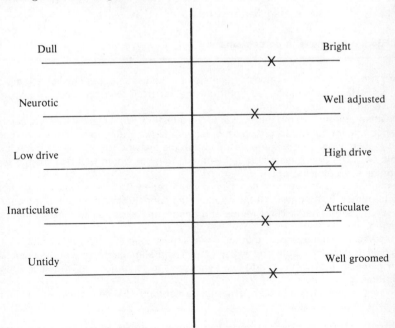

Box 5–2: Stereotype of the WASP manager

The stereotype of the WASP manager has him arriving early and leaving late (the WASP manager is, of course, a man). He is clean limbed and neatly button-down collared, smiles a lot but rarely laughs, and keeps a tidy desk, with a photograph of his wife and kids and, often, a plaque with THINK in capital letters. He uses expressions like "What can I do for you?" and "That's not on my agenda," and "I would like to spend a lot of time with you, but—" His telephone style is revealing: "Jones speaking. Run that before me again. On whose authorization? Did you keep a record of all expenses? I want a complete and detailed account, in writing, of what happened on my desk tomorrow morning. My opinion of the propriety of the matter? I cannot comment as I do not have all the facts. In any case, this matter is now sub judice."

He likes to be described as having "nerves of steel", being unflappable", staying cool under pressure, revealing no emotions, with ice cubes for blood. His enemies say he has a brain like a steel trap which feeds on facts. His friends say he has a charismatic aloofness, indeed a cool manner. To his superiors he has an infinite capacity for hard work, for sticking to tight schedules. His subordinates know that he places a high value on achievement, self-control, and capacity to endure pain and distress. He is sufficiently skilled in dissimulation to give out the public view that he believes that "politicking is basically bad."

He sees communication as exclusively vertical: Orders flow down; reports flow up. He believes in top management omniscience, omnicompetence, and omnipresence— "somebody at the top" (and only him) knows the whole score. His attitude to uncertainty can be summed up in the statement, "When in doubt, carry out instructions and complain afterwards." When subordinates start to give trouble, he arranges off-the-record meetings for bitching.

His committee meeting style is a dead giveaway. He prefers the two-man attack once he has roughed them up: "Every boss needs an SOB, and I'm his." He defines policy by long lists of functions and duties. He likes to be charged with writing minutes of meetings, and, of course, he keeps a complete file of meetings going back to World War II. You can recognize him because he raises his right hand to get permission to speak. He thinks it is an insult to describe someone as "a good committee man."

The WASP manager is against unions, especially shop stewards, who he thinks have a direct line to Moscow. He votes Republican, carries *The Wall Street Journal,* buys *Business Week,* and is on the office circulation list for the *Harvard Business Review* and *Fortune.* What he in fact reads, aside from business reports and computer printouts, is the *Reader's Digest* and the Book of the Month. He believes that Nixon made a terrible mistake—not burning the tapes. He believes Britain is going down the drain because the workers put down their tools at the drop of a hat, either to have a wildcat strike, or, worse still, to make tea. The country he admires most is Japan, where people are still prepared to work for a living. Germany is still OK—"at least they have some discipline, and they are clean."

His preferred religion is Presbyterian, Baptist, or Lutheran. Christian Science is OK; even Catholicism may be OK if it is not made too much of. The main thing is to follow the Protestant ethic of hard work.

particularly people of other ethnic groups. (See Box 5–2 on the WASP stereotype.)

Another example of perceptual constancy or unity is the halo effect, whereby an assessor of another person judges others by himself and rates him highly not only on one personality trait which is like his own but on a whole spectrum of traits. Figure 5–5 illustrates how a manager may unconsciously be affected by the halo effect in making an assessment of a subordinate.

In judging other people we commonly use ourselves as the norm, and the better we know and accept ourselves the more accurate will be our perceptions of the other. If you are status-conscious yourself, you are more likely to interpret the other man's behavior in terms of keeping up with the Joneses. Organizational neophytes are frequently disturbed by the paranoid outbursts of organizational veterans, who see in small nuances (such as who was invited to a particular meeting) some strong signal of power mania.

The perceiver is limited in his ability to judge others by his own values, attitudes, needs, and expectations; and it is as well for practical purposes to accept that accuracy in perceiving others is not a single skill.

TOPIC 2
The VANE

A major problem in organizational behavior is to try to get a handle on the dimensions of the person's VANE (values, attitudes, needs, and expectations). Values, attitudes, and needs are discussed below; expectations are considered in Chapter 8.

VALUES

The value system of classical, traditional organization theory represents an individualistic, rational approach to life which sets the highest values on achievement, aggression, and affluence. Historically derived from Calvinism, this Protestant ethic system presumes that a man is predestined to either heaven or hell and that the ticket is made out according to how well he manages his stewardship of the worldly goods that come his way. Hard work and thrift are intrinsic goods; good works which benefit the less fortunate are to be practiced in moderation.

This pervasive value system seeped into every aspect of life, defining attitudes toward everything, particularly anything that smacked of enjoyment (payday was on Friday, which was favored as a drinking night for the working classes because it provided the least chance of upsetting the work week). Even the name *Protestant ethic* is misleading, for the value system pervaded every religious and ethnic culture to some extent. The past tense is also misleading; though under attack, it has not vanished.

If the traditional value system no longer pervades, there is no one replacement. Contemporary society exhibits a melange of value systems, "new" coexisting with "old." This is in a world which took Sigmund Freud seriously; where children were fed on demand, according to Dr. Benjamin Spock; where the taboo was taken out of sex by the pill; where consumption had to exceed productivity to keep the gross national product growing. It was also a world where democratic leadership was a must (to be enforced at gunpoint, if necessary); where pushbutton nuclear war nearly eliminated the need for infantrymen; where instant communications via TV satellites landed us in the global village after supper in our dining rooms. No human being could devise a system that would let everybody work at once, and the women's movement turned the nuclear family inside out. With the notion that God was dead came the realization that most people were only half alive. As the membership of the traditional religions of the West began to decline, increasing numbers of people turned to the newly "discovered" religions of the East and to instantly invented religion in such forms as the human potential movement. What the "new" religion promised was mysticism, mystery, and the magic of transcendental experiences to give meaning to a life robbed of time by time study, reduced to a few simple therbligs by method study, and consumed with anxiety and guilt in the rat race of career trajectories.

Curiously, management was an accomplice in the search for a new value system. It encouraged the development of T groups, democratic leadership styles, job enlargement, management by objectives, and Theory Y managerial styles. Business helped to set the scene for the rejection of traditional work roles; inevitably, the crunch came first in traditional industries like railways, shipyards, public utilities (including the police, garbage collectors, and teachers), and the automobile industry. Though money is an issue, it is the basic indignity of having to do the same thing day in and day out for 40 years that cannot be forgotten and forgiven. Hence the success of Alvin Toffler's *Future Shock* (the future cannot be faced), Charles Reich's *The Greening of America* (there is no hope of structural change; consciousness raising is the only way forward), and Mario Puzo's *The Godfather* ("I'll make him an offer he can't refuse"). The dialogue has broken down; the legitimacy of authority relations, which depends on a moral consensus, has gone, to be replaced by power relations.

To establish a new dialogue based on awareness and authenticity, an existential approach is required which would encourage people to stop talking at each other and begin to act in good faith, recognising the basic validity of the other person's optic. Such a dialogue would try to reach, not compromises that reflect the extant power situation, but rather a meeting of minds that would lead to a good society where people can find dignity again.

ATTITUDES

Attitude may be defined as the predisposition or tendency of a person to evaluate some symbol, person, place, or thing in a favorable or unfavorable manner. The person's opinion constitutes the verbal expression of an attitude. In essence, an attitude is a state of mind which people carry around in their heads, through which they focus on particular objects in the environment, such as foreigners, Communists, pornography, the unions, men or women, students or professors.

Attitudes are made up of three elements: (1) cognitive, (2) affective, and (3) conative. The dimensions of an attitude are presumed to follow a sequence such as (1) cognition ("I see the Communists as a threat to the stability of the free world"), (2) emotion ("I feel strongly about the Red threat"), and (3) behavior ("I would rather be dead than Red"). This sequence, or train of cognition, emotion, and behavior, may be followed in some circumstances but not in all; the three elements interlock and interact. For example, by changing people's behavior it is possible to change their attitudes also.

NEEDS

Measuring needs

A useful way of gaining insight into personality is with a projection test, in which a person projects meaning while perceiving something. The method involves presenting an unstructured, incomplete, or ambiguous stimulus such as an inkblot or a picture and asking the person what he sees. Presented with a stimulus which has no definite, fixed, or correct meaning, he may attempt to infer the nature of the object from the category systems which structure his perceptions and thus reveal, at least in part, something of his values, attitudes, needs, and expectations.

Almost any kind of stimulus material may be the basis for a projection test. H. A. Murray devised an extremely useful projection test called the Thematic Apperception Test (TAT), which consists of 20 pictures presented to a subject, one at a time. The person is asked to tell a story which can explain the events in the picture. Using the TAT, Murray identified about 20 basic needs, including the need for achievement, the need for affiliation, and the need for power. Both David McClelland and J. W. Atkinson have built on Murray's work, refining and intensively investigating these three needs.

Atkinson argues that a particular motive—whether it be achievement, affiliation, or power—is actually a label for a class of incentives which, when they are activated, produce essentially the same result.

When they are activated you experience a sense of satisfaction and pride in accomplishment, or a sense of belonging, or a feeling of being in command, which correspond respectively to n Ach, n Aff, and n Pow.

The need for achievement

The need for achievement may be defined as the need to master or overcome difficulties. The need is presumed not to operate as a motive until it is brought on or aroused by certain situational cues or incentives which signal the individual that certain behaviors will lead to feelings of achievement.

Since achievement motivation is learned, it should be possible to specify the conditions of development which lead to its establishment. McClelland describes persons high in achievement as "independent in action as well as thought; their independence appears almost to be a consistent 'way of life' which either originates or is reflected in their relationship to their parents." Box 5–3 summarizes more of his achievement theory. McClelland argues that the general level of achievement motivation in a given society is connected with economic growth. After careful examination of a wide variety of evidence, he concludes that a relationship exists between the general level of achievement motivation and cycles of increased productivity and industrialization.

An executive who spends a great deal of time thinking about the job and how to achieve excellence and thus advance his or her career has a high need for achievement. Some of the elements of this need have been revealed by study of this kind of executive. Achieving executives actively seek to take responsibility for finding solutions to problems. They get a charge, not from the payoff, but from managing the situations that generate the payoff. Research findings suggest that they are not interested in gambling games, where the outcome is mainly determined by chance. They welcome decision making which involves risk if their efforts are a significant factor in determining the outcome. But in setting the level of risk, they set moderate goals and take calculated risks.

Once achieving executives have set their goals, they are capable of evolving a set of alternatives which will let them reach their goals. They are then able to evaluate each of these alternatives against a set of criteria and make an intelligent selection. Having selected an alternative, they can spot blockages impeding their intention and develop tactics to circumvent or remove them. They have a strong need for feedback to monitor their efforts and to give them satisfaction as they move toward their goal.

Box 5–3: The need to achieve

David C. McClelland, chairman of the Department of Social Relations at Harvard, has developed one of the most interesting modern theories on motivation. This theory states that a person's desire to do things better is due to a very specific motive: the need for achievement, or *n Ach* motive, which is acquired rather than genetic.

McClelland describes persons who exhibit the following characteristics as possessing the *n Ach* motive:

1. They "set moderately difficult, but potentially achievable goals for themselves."
2. They "prefer to work at a problem rather than leave the outcome to chance or to others." That is, "they are concerned with personal achievement rather than with the rewards for success per se."
3. They have "a strong preference for work situations in which they get concrete feedback on how well they are doing."

The strength of the *n Ach* motive is measured by "taking samples of a man's spontaneous thought [such as making up a story about a picture he has been shown] and counting the frequency with which he mentions doing things better."

Research has shown that not all people who are considered great achievers score high in *n Ach,* because success in the various professions depends on other motives as well as personality characteristics. It has been found, however, that business executives tend to score high in *n Ach* and that companies which have a significant number of executives high in *n Ach* tend to grow faster.

Analysis of the evidence also indicates that the *n Ach* motive can be acquired through training, by teaching a person to think and behave in *n Ach* terms. Such training has been given to American, Mexican, and Indian business executives and to underachieving high school boys. "In every instance save one [the Mexican case], it was possible to demonstrate statistically, some two years later, that the men who took the course had done better [made more money, got promoted faster, expanded their businesses faster] than comparable men who did not take the course or who took some other management course." In the group of high school boys it was found that "the boys from the middle class improved steadily in grades in school over a two-year period, but boys from the lower class showed an improvement after the first year followed by a drop back to their beginning low grade average." This result may indicate that the environment in which a person lives helps to encourage the expression of the motive.

McClelland is somewhat cautious about his findings but nonetheless optimistic, and he takes the view that this approach to the motivation to work could be very useful in helping underdeveloped groups and countries to help themselves.

Reference: D. C. McClelland, "That Urge to Achieve," *Think* (published by IBM), vol. 32 (November–December, 1966), pp. 19–23.

The need for power

The executive who spends time thinking about how to influence, control, and manipulate others as an end in itself has, of course, a strong need for power. The power-hungry executive desires to possess people, to punish them, to bend them to her or his will, and to make them give way in argument. Bedevilled by a compulsive need to influence others, those with a high power need are frequently fans of both Dale Carnegie and Niccolo Machiavelli.

This need to dominate others often manifests itself in an argumentative, polemical, verbally fluent life-style. Typically others see power needers as forceful and outspoken, but also hard-headed and demanding; others feel they have to respond to them.

From an occupational optic, people with a strong need for power enjoy persuasion, cajoling, and seduction as means of influencing others, and they are strongly attracted to roles such as teaching and public speaking. Motivation studies of managers reveal that while entrepreneurs and managers have significant needs for achievement, the man who makes it to the top in business is usually strongly motivated by the need for power.

But the need for power does not guarantee a place at the top of the pecking hierarchy, and even when n Pow executives arrive, what they do is influenced by other needs. ·

The need for affiliation

The person who spends days and nights thinking about how to get other people to love them have a strong need for affiliation. Such n Aff people are more alert to the feelings and needs of colleagues, and they seek roles which offer opportunities for friendly interactions. In corporate affairs, they are attracted to the human relations type of personnel appointments. The curious thing is that the need for affiliation does not seem to be important for effective executive effort and performance and may even be detrimental. But it is widely believed, at least by psychoanalytically inspired organizational psychologists, that superior executive performance requires a basic affiliative attitude. At least, executives who are short on n Aff can be made to feel guilty unless they achieve considerable interpersonal competence.

This idea appears naive and has little contact with reality. There is a wealth of examples of high-powered corporate officials who got to the top by delivering the goods and who in the process were not overly scrupulous or careful about whose toes they stepped on. Such high performers frequently are more complex mentally than their colleagues, and attempts by the less able to interpret their behavior are often misleading. The high performer might argue that less complex systems cannot control or understand more complex systems, as every budding student of operations research knows. The less powerful may not have a counterargument—but they can make the others feel guilty.

TOPIC 3
The structure of personality

In empirical-based behavioral science, a major effort has been made to describe personality structure in terms of its principal dimensions and to measure these dimensions. To develop these dimensions,

psychologists began by drawing up lists of traits. A trait is any enduring characteristic which gives to behavioral acts their typical color or
quality; trait names are adjectives which describe behavior (mature,
timid, loyal, and so on). The trouble with traits, as Allport soon discovered, is that there are too many of them. Allport searched the dictionary and found over 3,000 trait words for describing personality.

DIMENSIONS OF PERSONALITY

The two broad personality scales that are most widely accepted by
psychologists as descriptive of personality structure are the large,
ubiquitous, and virtually unavoidable dimensions of extraversion and
anxiety. Trait patterns related to neurotic anxiety and extraversion are
illustrated in Figure 5–6.

FIGURE 5–6
Trait patterns related to combinations of levels of neuroticism
and extraversion

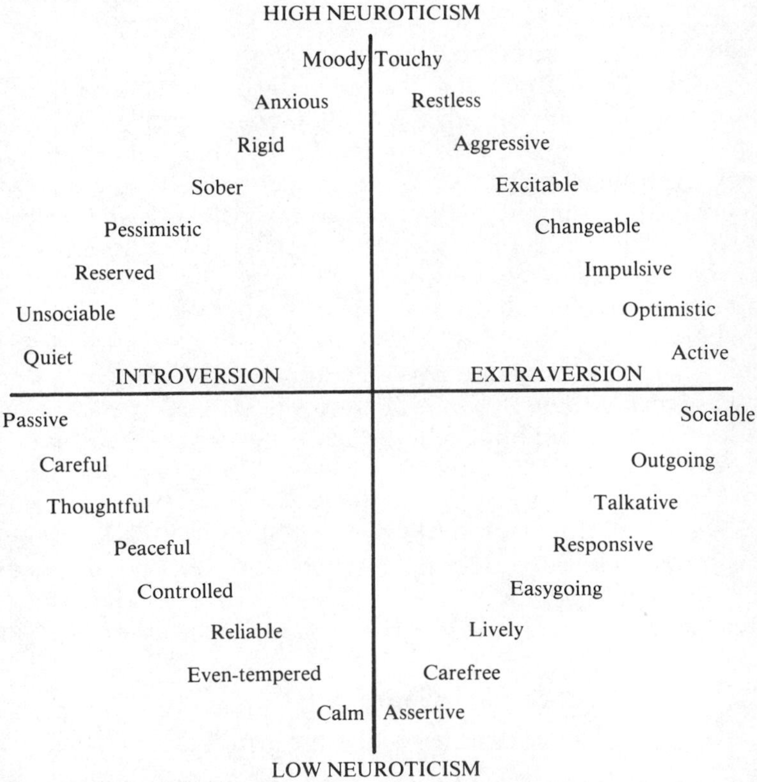

HIGH NEUROTICISM

Moody | Touchy

Anxious   Restless

Rigid   Aggressive

Sober   Excitable

Pessimistic   Changeable

Reserved   Impulsive

Unsociable   Optimistic

Quiet   Active
INTROVERSION   EXTRAVERSION

Passive   Sociable

Careful   Outgoing

Thoughtful   Talkative

Peaceful   Responsive

Controlled   Easygoing

Reliable   Lively

Even-tempered   Carefree

Calm | Assertive

LOW NEUROTICISM

Source: Adapted from H. J. Eysenck, *Eysenck on Extraversion* (New York: John
Wiley & Sons, 1973), p. 27.

Extraversion

The extravert is oriented toward the outside world. He is characteristically outgoing and spontaneously more concerned with restructuring his environment than with analyzing its effects on his "inner being." The extravert seems to have the capacity to suppress negative feedback or criticism. He is strong in drive and zestfully involved in accomplishing things. He is sometimes described by psychologists as a sociophile, that is, he prefers to be with people. He is assertive— even, on occasion, aggressive.

The introvert, the obverse of the extravert, is oriented toward the inner world of the psyche; he tends to be shy, withdrawn, and inhibited in social affairs. The introvert is usually introspective and as such is more interested in the world of ideas than practical affairs. There is a strong correlation between neuroticism and introversion.

Figure 5–7 illustrates the distribution of the extraversion-introversion trait. Modern research findings support the view that the

FIGURE 5–7
Distribution of the extraversion-introversion trait

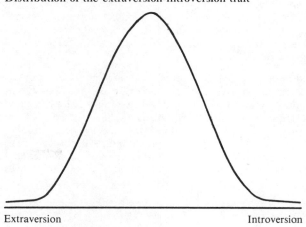

Extraversion   Introversion

extraversion-introversion dichotomy is a far from simple dimension of personality and is in fact made up of a number of components which are organized within the framework of a type. (Box 5–4 explains why extraverts get bored with work.)

Anxiety

Few executives, if any, apparently escape the anxiety which seems to be the dominant emotion of modern life. A great number of people, including many executives, suffer from a kind of cosmic hypochondria,

Box 5–4: How extraverts get bored with work

How personality factors affect employees' response to the formal demands made on them by the organization is obviously of some interest to the student of organizational behavior. In an attempt to add some empirical knowledge to this rather neglected area, Robert Cooper and Roy Payne, social psychologists at the University of Aston, England, focused on the personality factor of extraversion as conceived by H. J. Eysenck of London University. Cooper and Payne chose extraversion because it has been shown in laboratory studies that, compared to introverts, extraverts (1) get bored quickly with tasks of a routine nature, and (2) are less disciplined in their general behavior. Generalizing from the laboratory results, Cooper and Payne hypothesized from (1) that in routine industrial jobs extraverted workers, because of extreme feelings of boredom, will seek more varied forms of activity, and this will lead them to have higher rates of absenteeism and labor turnover; and from (2) that extraverted workers will be less well adjusted to their jobs in general.

To test these hypotheses, the investigators gave the Eysenck Personality Inventory to a large group of female workers engaged in repetitive, machine-paced work in the packing department of a tobacco factory. They then related the workers' extraversion scores obtained on the personality inventory to such features of worker behavior as labor turnover, absenteeism, and job adjustment. The results were in general accord with the hypotheses:

The more extraverted workers had shorter periods of service to their credit than the less extraverted (more introverted). The investigators regarded this as evidence that extraverted workers will withdraw permanently from work of a routine nature.

The more extraverted workers also tended to take more non-permitted absences (but this did not hold for permitted absences, e.g., certified sickness).

The more extraverted workers also tended to be less well adjusted to their jobs in general.

An interesting feature of this study was the investigators' prediction that the more extraverted workers would have a higher turnover rate over the 12-month period following the administration of the personality test. When the group of operators who had left the company in this period were compared with their colleagues who had remained, it was found that the former group was significantly higher on extraversion.

This study, therefore, suggests that extraverted individuals will react against narrowly defined work roles and that this reaction will represent a dysfunctional contribution to the organization's general aims of motivating its members to work effectively and to remain as members.

Reference: Robert Cooper and Roy Payne, "Extraversion and Some Aspects of Work Behavior," *Personnel Psychology*, vol. 20, no. 1 (1967), pp. 45–57.

marked by a diffuse anxiety neurosis and frequently coupled with a vague sense of futility.

Anxiety is characterized by diffusion of emotion in the sense that the cause may be difficult to specify and the choice of focus open. Psychologists are inclined to treat individuals as if they have a "free floating pool of anxiety" which is continually searching for a focus. In *The Meaning of Anxiety*, Rollo May defines anxiety as "the apprehension cued off by a threat to some value which the individual holds essential to his existence as a personality."

Although at one time it was customary for clinical psychologists to view any form of anxiety as unhealthy, the contemporary attitude is a little different and is based on the notion that a low level of anxiety may have some utility. However, it is usual to treat neurotic anxiety as irrational, in the sense that even a logical explanation of a subject's anxieties may not necessarily lead to their alleviation. (See Box 5–5 for a description of real anxiety.)

Box 5–5: Real anxiety: Coming under fire in Vietnam

Michael Herr, a war correspondent of the Vietnam war, writes about coming under fire:

Once it was actually going on, things were different. You were just like everyone else, you could no more blink than spit. It came back the same way every time, dreaded and welcome . . . your senses working like strobes, free-falling all the way down to the essences and then flying out again in a rush to focus, like the first strong twinge of tripping after an infusion of psilocybin, reaching in at the point of calm and springing all the joy and all the dread ever known, *ever* known by *everyone* who *ever* lived, unutterable in its speeding brilliance, touching all the edges and then passing, as though it had all been controlled from outside, by a god or by the moon. And every time you were so weary afterward, so empty of everything but being alive that you couldn't recall any of it, except to know it was like something else you had felt once before. It remained obscure for a long time, but after enough times the memory took shape and substance and finally revealed itself one afternoon during the breaking off of a firefight. It was the feeling you'd had when you were much, much younger and undressing a girl for the first time.

Source: *Dispatches,* by Michael Herr (New York: Alfred A. Knopf, Inc., 1977).

TOPIC 4
Psychoanalysis for the executive

THE FREUDIAN CONCEPT

Sigmund Freud is widely recognized as the founder of psychoanalysis, the oldest and most influential personality theory. His most dramatic and significant innovation was mapping out the role and function of the unconscious. People often find themselves doing things again and again for reasons of which they are either totally or partially unaware. Freud introduced the idea of the unconscious as the repository for ideas of this type, which cause people to behave in odd ways which they cannot justify or whose justification makes them wonder what is going on. Freud gives many examples of this sort of apparently contradictory behavior, such as a normally grumpy and discourteous middle-aged father surprising everybody by leaping up to hold a chair for an attractive young girl taking her place at the table. (The interest of psychoanalysis for executives is explored in Box 5–6).

Box 5–6: Psychoanalysis is for the executive who is YAVIS and W

Since the forties, executives have become increasingly interested in psychoanalysis, not so much as a therapy but rather as a general explanatory model of behavior. Many executives realize that psychoanalysis can do little for the seriously ill, such as the schizophrenic, and that many neurotics can only expect their hysterical misery to be transformed into common unhappiness. We know from observational studies of executives that they spend up to 80 percent of their time talking. Their interest in psychoanalysis is logical, since psychoanalysis is sometimes described as Freudian talk therapy.

As a recent article in *Time* magazine pointed out, the question may be raised as to how effective psychoanalysis is. Psychoanalysts usually cite the one-third rule of thumb: of all patients, one third are "cured", one third are helped to some extent, and one third are not helped at all. In essence, psychoanalysis has an elitist image; most patients are of the middle and upper classes. Psychoanalysis works best for the YAVIS (young, adaptable, verbal, intellectual, and successful). It is also useful to be W (wealthy). Executives are interested in it not only for therapeutic reasons but also because it provides the intellectual point of departure for many interesting management concepts, including transactional analysis, T groups, and counseling.

Reference: "Psychiatry on the Couch," *Time,* April 2, 1979.

Freud was his own best publicist. By his brilliant, extremely witty, and urbane writing he did much to awaken the generations of the 1920s and 1930s to the implications of the unconscious, especially to the notion that it is the apparently hidden source of man's animal nature. Freud's final view was that man is driven by two basic or fundamental instincts, Eros (sexual or life instinct) and Thanatos (aggression or death instinct). The conflicts between them can be expressed as sex versus aggression, love versus hate, life versus death, and so on.

Figure 5–8 may help to explain Freud's concept of the unconscious. Complex I, which is troubling the patient, could be repressed during hypnosis, but the unconscious would find a method of returning I to consciousness. Freud thought that real emotional problems are deeply embedded in the unconscious, and he developed techniques such as dream analysis and free association to locate them.

FIGURE 5–8
Freudian concept of the unconscious

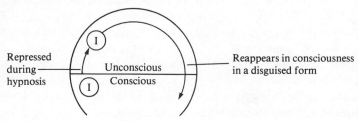

Freud developed a model of personality based on three psychic systems, the id, ego, and superego. The id is the source of energy for both the libido and the ego (libido being the biological drives, the "instincts" seeking gratification). Freud characterized the basic drives as being sexual, but he included much more in the term *sexual* than other theorists did.

The id can be thought of as what the person wants and goes after; it is in closer touch with the body and its processes than with the external world. It operates on the principle of maximizing pleasure and minimizing pain. The id is the foundation on which the personality is built. It is infantile and recognizes nothing external to itself.

The ego may be briefly described as consciousness, or how the person goes about getting what he (the id) wants. The ego is in contact with reality; it has to mediate between the desires of the id, the strictures of the superego, and reality.

The superego is basically a censor mechanism. When it is conscious, it represents conscience. The identifications upon which the superego is based are those of idealized and omnipotent parents. As the ego sets out to get what the id wants, the superego dictates what the permissible methods and strategies are. While it represents the moral values of parents, authority figures, and society, the superego should be recognized as internalized—it is the person's own value system, what he has taken in and made his own, even if in part unconsciously.

THE LEADER AND THE MYTH OF THE HERO

Of particular interest to managers is the unusual relation which exists between the leader and the led. Psychoanalysts have compared the leader-follower relation to the hypnotist-subject relation and have argued that the *Führerprinzip* flourishes in an environment of frustration and hysteria. Psychoanalysts have had a great deal to say about leaders, and through their behavior they furnish some of the best insights into how leaders function. (Box 5–7 gives an example of a Freudian follower's thought in action.)

Freud's writings, for example, have much to say about leaders, and so do his own personality and style of leadership. When Freud was first tentatively explaining his new ideas on the nature of hysteria, he formed a circle of devotees, some of whom eventually considered psychoanalysis to be too demeaning to the role and character of women. Freud has been described as the original male chauvinist. His apparent indifference, if not hostility, to women was not only a direct outcome of his theories but also an expression of his early life. Because he had been a victim of an Oedipus complex himself (Freud was the adoring child of a young mother nearer in age to her son than to her husband), he greatly exaggerated its importanct to others.

Box 5–7: Four types of executive

Adapting the ideas of Carl Jung, Roy Rowan describes four types of executives in a recent article:

A consulting firm specializing in personal-chemistry repair work is run by Dr. Paul Mok, a Harvard-trained psychologist. Mok began what he calls CST— Communicating Styles Technology—with Drake-Beam & Associates in New York. Borrowing heavily from the Swiss psychiatrist Carl Jung, he divided all businessmen into four types, each characterized by a distinct communicating style: (1) *Intuitor*—Wordy but impersonal. Writes in abstract terms. Wears mixed, unpredictable clothing. Likes futuristic office furnishings. (2) *Thinker*—Precise and businesslike speech. Writes in well-structured specifics. Dresses conservatively. Prefers a plain, distraction-free workplace. (3) *Feeler*—Speech is warm and humorous. Writes personalized letters and memos. Clothes are colorful and informal. Adorns office with mementos and snapshots. (4) *Sensor*—Abrupt but to the point. Writes brief, urgent notes. Wears functional, unfancy clothes. Too busy to be neat, his office is often cluttered. Mok believes that most executives are essentially sensors, though nobody is all one type or another.

His main effort is concentrated on helping businessmen to identify their own communicating style, using a self-administered multiple-choice test about work habits, success expectations, behavior under pressure, and personal deficiencies. He then tries to teach them how to divine the communicating style of the bosses, underlings, and clients they must deal with. "Almost anybody," says Mok, "can adapt to the communicating style of an adversary for short periods of time, enabling the chemistry between them to improve."

Now in business for himself in Dallas (appropriately on a street named Lovers Lane, since Mok classifies himself as a feeler), he counts Alcoa, Caterpillar Tractor, Exxon, I.B.M., and U.S. Steel among his clients. He found that one company he works with suffered from a surplus of thinkers on top. "I urged them to recognize the sensors and feelers in middle management who were being underutilized," he says, adding: "The only trouble is, most companies don't call me in until the personal-chemistry problem is so acute it may be curtailing sales."

As an example, Mok cites the difficulty that Dallas-based Electronic Data Systems, Inc., was having in signing up banks as clients—until he taught E.D.S. salesmen the gentle art of "style flexing," or getting on the other guy's wavelength. According to Mok, most of the salesmen were supersensors, while the bankers were largely thinkers. He urged the salesmen to improve their precall planning, slow down their sales pitch, and leave a more detailed presentation for the bankers to mull over. Business improved markedly.

Source: Roy Rowan, "Watch Out for Chemical Reactions at the Top," *Fortune,* September 25, 1978.

The Oedipus complex, concerned with the sexual attraction a child feels for the parent of the opposite sex, is a central concept in Freudianism. Some of his own unresolved Oedipal forces Freud expressed through his dominance of the Viennia Psychoanalysis Society, which he founded in 1903. In 1911 the Viennese psychoanalyst Alfred Adler, together with another member of Freud's original group, Carl Gustav Jung, broke with "the master" over the relative importance of the sexual libido in personality development.

Adler's system of psychoanalysis is based on the concept of compensation, or a drive for power in an attempt to overcome the inferiority complex. Failure or disappointment produces an inferiority complex which may well be overcome through compensation, including the will to dominate others. Leadership thus may become a form of overcompensation. The small man (Hitler, Napoleon, Stalin and Mussolini were all short in stature) may become tremendously self-assertive and dominant and may seek to be the hero of an adopted country (Napoleon was an Italian; Hitler an Austrian; Stalin a Georgian). Adler is having a healthy revival now in the form of the I'm OK, you're OK idea. (See Box 5–8 for an explanation of superior performance.)

Jung broke with Freud for a different reason, which has great significance for the social psychology of leadership. Jung attached much importance to the existence of a collective unconscious as the reposi-

Box 5–8: Superiority comes from coping with an inferiority complex: Alfred Adler

The man who first introduced the idea that people are not OK and that they devote their lives to trying to make themselves OK is Alfred Adler. This is the Viennese eye doctor and psychoanalyst who brought us such brilliant and truly useful ideas as the inferiority complex, neurosis as a compensation or a drive for power to overcome inferiority feelings, and the child's fear of the parent.

When Adler received a postcard in the fall of 1902 asking him to join a small group that "meets Wednesday to discuss problems of neurosis," he came under the influence of the original parent of modern times, old Papa Freud. It is little wonder that Adler invented the inferiority complex after what he went through with Freud, whom he once asked: "Do you think that it is such a great pleasure for me to stand in your shadow for the whole of my life?" Adler was the first major defector from the master.

Adler invented the system of Individual Psychology that Eric Berne and Thomas Harris were later to find so useful. Individual Psychology gave preeminence to the idea that the individual represents a unified and self-consistent whole striving toward a goal which is floating "out there." For Adler the drama was everything, and life could only be understood in terms of the finale. The individual was seen as a novelist who wrote his own script in terms of his "style of life."

For Adler, people's style of life is mainly determined by how they overcome their inferiorities. An individual with a superiority complex is only reacting to a feeling of inferiority. A good example of this phenomenon is the short man who walks tall.

In this view, life-style is a series of compensations. These compensations are most obvious in the case of individuals suffering from some organ inferiority such as a defect in vision, speech, or physique (Beethoven's congenital ear disease or Winston Churchill's speech defect). A popular example is men who compensate for their feelings of inadequacy by presenting themselves as superjocks. Adler labeled the search for ways to overcome inferiorities the masculine protest.

In Freud's eyes, Adler went too far when he not only rejected the idea that everything is determined by sex, as Freud said, but with the masculine protest he suggested that "the child" really wants to be "the man." The masculine protest describes the strategy and life-style a person adopts in the struggle to control his or her feelings of inferiority, rather than any sexual attraction. The masculine protest of modern times is best expressed in the John Wayne syndrome.

tory of ancient modes of thought, which he called archetypes. These archetypes include vague primitive notions of birth and death, magic and heroes.

Another of Freud's disciples, Otto Rank, developed the myth of the hero even further. Rank was described by Havelock Ellis as "perhaps the most brilliant and clairvoyant of Freud's many pupils and associates." Nevertheless, in 1925 he broke out of the inner circle of loyal analysts. When his *The Trauma of Birth* was published, Freud and Rank parted company. Freud, who had considered naming Rank as the guardian of his children, now declared, "I have forgiven him for the last time."

Rank was interested in the social aspect of psychotherapy. His well-received book *The Myth of the Birth of the Hero* has been ranked alongside Sir J. G. Frazer's *The Golden Bough* for its elucidation of the interactions among myth, religion, politics, and the theater. Rank developed a new anthropology of the myth of the changeling which is central to an understanding of theater, history, and politics.

THE MANAGER AND TRANSACTIONAL ANALYSIS

Eric Berne and games people play

Following Alfred Adler in several ways, Eric Berne, a psychiatrist from San Francisco, also was rejected by traditional psychoanalysts; when he applied for membership in a psychoanalytical society he was not accepted. His revenge was inventing transactional analysis, or TA. Berne had his own weekly meeting (on Tuesday) of TA analysts which began at 8:30 in the evening (if you rang the bell at 8:20, according to one of his colleagues, the door remained shut) and finished at 10:00.

The experience of psychoanalysts seems to suggest that people function best in small groups of dedicated individuals. When the group members, who usually go through some form of baptism to gain admission, know enough, they go elsewhere to spread the word. This is good for the populace, who get a choice in terms of therapies, but bad for prophets and psychoanalysts.

Transactional analysis is a system of individual and social psychiatry which is concerned with the psychology of human relationships. In *Games People Play* Berne describes 36 scripts people have devised to govern their transactions—the rules they play by. A typical game is "Courtroom," in which the husband says to a third person something like, "What do you think she has done now? She did. . . ." And the innocent bystander pleads neutrality as the wife opens up with "This is the way it really was . . ."

In presenting the idea that people tend to spin out their lives by engaging in certain games, Berne strips the surface innocence of conventional relations and reveals what is simmering just below the surface in most human encounters. His penetrating and stimulating analysis takes as its starting point the idea of stimulus hunger—which he summarizes by noting, "If you are not stroked, your spinal cord will shrivel up." He uses this term, *stroke*, to describe a social stimulus such as "Hello," and he defines a transaction as an exchange of strokes.

The repertoire of ego states: The parent, the adult, the child

To explain games, Berne makes use of the idea that each individual has a limited repertoire of ego states (see Figure 5–9). There are three principal kinds:

1. Ego states similar to those of the parental figure.
2. Ego states which are concerned with the objective appraisal of reality.
3. Ego states which are fixated in early childhood.

FIGURE 5–9
Berne's repertoire of ego states

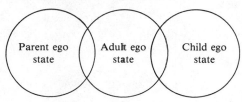

In talking about the Child ego state, Berne is careful to avoid the words *childish* and *immature*. In the Child are to be found intuition, creativity, and spontaneous drive and enjoyment. The Adult is essential for survival because of its reality-testing function, which enables it to process and analyze data and compute probabilities. The Parent has two functions: It enables an individual to assume the role of parent, and it automates many decisions. According to Berne, these three aspects of personality are necessary for survival.

Salespeople are professional games players, as the following example provided by Berne illustrates:

SALESMAN: This one is better, but you can't afford it.
HOUSEWIFE: That's the one I'll take.

An analysis of this transaction is shown in Figure 5–10. At the conscious, ostensible, social level, the salesman (Adult ego) is stating two objective facts: "This one is better" and "You can't afford it." At the Adult level, the housewife should reply, "Right, both times." However, an ulterior or psychological vector was aimed at the housewife's

FIGURE 5–10
Transaction between salesman and housewife

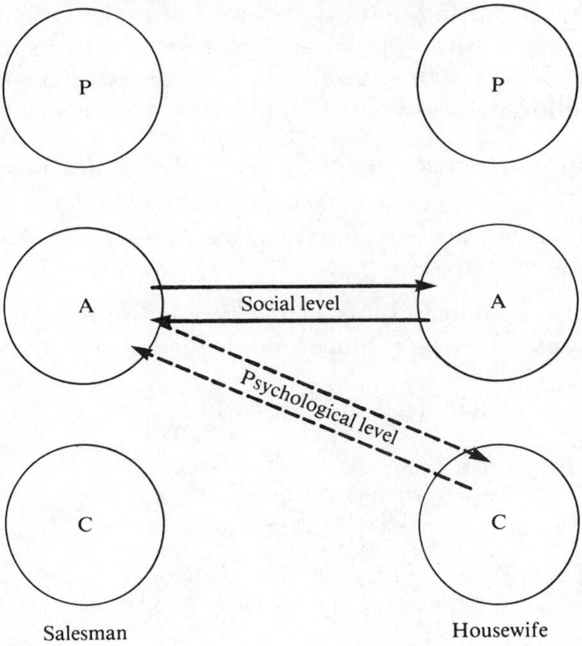

Salesman   Housewife

An angular transaction

Child. The validity of the salesman's judgment is vindicated by the Child's response, which in effect is "Irrespective of cost, I'll show you that I'm as good as anybody."

Berne's theory of games has considerable relevance for the student of organizational behavior. For a start, Berne's idea of stroking certainly has relevance to the way in which salutations are exchanged by executives.

Although Berne's theory lacks theoretical consistency and has no considerable body of empirical data to lend it validity, it has considerable pragmatic relevance. A psychiatrist who refers a troubled patient to the works of Freud, Jung, or Adler runs the risk of adding mental confusion to the patient's other problems, but a copy of *Games People Play* may give the patient a valuable insight into her or his own personality dynamics. As a tool for analyzing organizational behavior, it has considerable potential, to say nothing of the fun it is to use.

Thomas Harris and I'm OK—you're OK

Dr. Thomas A. Harris, a psychiatrist, developed Berne's ideas into a teaching and learning device which is of great interest to executives because of its simplicity and ease of understanding and the extent of its application to organizational problems. The device is transactional analysis (TA), the central thesis of which is that most people suffer from a vague sense of inferiority (they feel that they're "not OK").

Differing balances among these ego states result in four basic life positions:

1. I'm not OK—you're OK (the anxious, dependent position).
2. I'm not OK—you're not OK (the "give-up" position).
3. I'm OK—you're not OK (the thug position).
4. I'm OK—you're OK (the balanced, Adult position).

Transactional analysis can be taught to executives and other employees—and in spite of its simplifications, it is useful. For example, in the American Airlines training school for flight attendants, trainees spend a fair amount of time learning about ego states. On the basis of the Berne gospel that people are divided into three types—the Parent, domineering and scolding; the Adult, reasoning and reasonable with; and the Child, creative and innovative but also likely to throw a tantrum or to sulk—the trainees are encouraged to covertly categorize their passengers and react accordingly. Having been introduced to the mysteries of Berne and Harris, they move on to learn TACT—transactional analysis and customer treatment.

TOPIC 5
What every manager should know about personality

We began this chapter by saying that an understanding of personality is necessary for an understanding of organizational behavior. Figure 5–11, modeling personality as a system, summarizes many of the concepts about personality we have discussed.

SYNTHESIS OF SYSTEMS THEORY AND EXISTENTIALISM

An extremely fruitful approach to personality theory is provided by a synthesis of systems theory and existentialism. In formulating such a theory, certain guidelines can be identified:

1. Personality is seen as an open system trading with its environment.
2. Perception, which involves an act of categorization, requires searching the environment for information.
   a. Each person has an optimal capacity for handling information, arousal, novelty, and conflict.
   b. Some of the characteristics of the stimulus are inferred from the category system.

FIGURE 5–11
Personality as a system

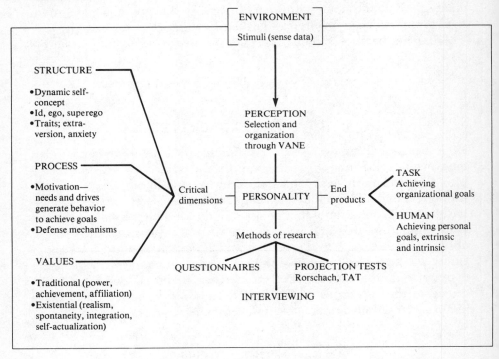

c.   The category system (or set) is greatly influenced by the individual's VANE.

d.   People strive for perceptual simplicity—they see "things" as a gestalt.

3.   Decision making is central to existentialism. To act unfree continually is to run the risk of becoming neurotic.

4.   In terms of behavior, individuals struggle to be authentic, to give their lives meaning, to achieve some kind of identity.

5.   The personality process is unknowable, which leads to the use of the black box concept as a means of controlling and limiting our need to control and to understand.

6.   The systems approach by itself is insufficient because the system of personality has the unique characteristic of being self-conscious (i.e., aware of itself). This procedure echo systems which interact with the originating system.

7.   Man represents the fusion of two great trends, both present in animal evolution from the lowest to the highest forms, which have reached their fullest development in humans. These two trends are:

a.   A decrease in the instinctive determination of behavior.

b.   An increase in the size and complexity of the brain (humans are capable of symbol formation and language) and an increase in self-awareness and self-control.

THE EXISTENTIAL PERSONALITY

A picture of existential man (and woman) can be drawn from the work of Carl Rogers and A. H. Maslow, two American psychologists who have made a significant and sustained effort to introduce existential psychology to American academics. Rogers, who regards the self as a nuclear concept in his theory of personality, has developed from his many years as a practicing clinician some ideas of what it means to be a fully functioning person. Maslow's unique contribution emerges from his preoccupation with healthy people rather than neurotic ones. Maslow felt that too much effort in psychology had been directed at the study of man's frailty and not enough towards his strength. He developed a psychology that recognizes man's need for love, compassion, gaiety, zest, and excitement and made a study of what makes healthy people healthy and great people great. Out of this research emerged a description of what self-actualizing people are like. The composite picture of the existential personality that emerges from the work of Rogers and Maslow has the characteristics discussed below.

Existential man is intentional; he places high value on choice, particularly in regard to his own identity. Like Ibsen, he is constantly trying to ascertain where his destiny is. "What I can be, I must be" is a directing principle which helps him to achieve self-actualization—a movement from the self he is not, towards the self that he really is.

In formulating his ethical position, existential man somehow allows the "is propositions" to interact with the "ought propositions"—to facilitate the marriage of the behavioral and ethical sciences. The naturalism of John Steinbeck, Ernest Hemingway, and John Updike seems natural to him. He is essentially inner directed and suits himself, with minimal disregard of the interests of others. He views himself as a person in the process of becoming. Life is a process rather than a striving for an end state. He wants to live joyously and has the capacity "to stand in awe again and again of the basic goods of life, a sunset, a flower, a baby, a melody, a person." He has frequent "mystic" or "oceanic" experiences, not necessarily religious in character. He has intimate relations with a few specially chosen people.

Existential man has a full life trying to understand his self, coming to terms with it, keeping his perceptions of reality accurate, and trying to divine his own destiny and understand the other fellow on the same terms. He is searching for an image of himself that is accurate enough to be workable yet acceptable to him and that will allow him to live his life with joy and zest.

REVIEW AND RESEARCH

1. What is perception? What are the factors which determine how people are perceived?
2. List the main subsystems of any system and show how they can be applied to human personality.
3. Make a list of defense mechanisms and give examples of each from your own experience.
4. Why are executives attracted to Freud's theory of personality?
5. Compare and contrast the extravert and introvert personality types. What occupations are suitable for each type?
6. Why is an optimal level of anxiety necessary for survival and growth?
7. Why is the theory of achievement motivation so attractive in North America? Outline a training program to develop the individual's need to achieve.
8. Why are managers more highly motivated at work than shop-floor operatives?
9. Define your VANE (1) before you came to business school and (2) now.
10. How does a manager identify the VANE of subordinates? What problems may arise from the actions taken to identify these factors? How can the manager use this knowledge profitably?

GLOSSARY OF TERMS

Achievement motive. The need to master or overcome difficulties. The motive is presumed not to operate until it is brought on or aroused by certain situational cues or incentives which signal the individual that certain behaviors will lead to feelings of achievement.

Anxiety. The apprehension caused by a threat to some value which the individual holds essential to his existence as a personality (Rollo May). Anxiety is characterized by diffusion of emotion in the sense that the cause may be difficult to specify and the choice of focus open.

Ego. That part of personality whereby the individual becomes aware of external reality and himself (i.e., consciousness and self-concept). In psychoanalysis, the part of the psyche which is an outcome of reality testing and which mediates among the id, superego, and reality.

Extravert. Person oriented toward the outside world, characteristically outgoing and spontaneously more concerned with restructuring his environment than analyzing its effects on his "inner being." The extravert seems to have the capacity to suppress negative feedback or criticism. He is strong in drive and is zestfully involved in accomplishing things.

Id. The source of psychic energy; principally the person's pleasure-oriented drives striving for gratification or release. The function of the id is to provide for the immediate discharge of energy or tension.

Identification. The process whereby a person assumes the characteristics, attitudes, mannerisms, or eccentricities of another person.

Introvert. The obverse of the extravert; a person oriented toward the inner world of the psyche. Such a person tends to be shy, withdrawn, inhibited in social affairs, and more interested in the world of ideas than practical affairs.

Perception. The process whereby an individual becomes aware of the outside world and himself. Sense data are filtered by a frame of reference, and a trading process goes on between the perceived qualities of the thing and the individual's classification system.

Perceptual readiness. The relative accessibility of the category system to the kinds of stimulus information being input. The frame of reference includes subjective elements such as values, attitudes, needs, and expectations.

Personality. The organizing center around which people's motives form a unified and integrated system. "Personality is the dynamic organization within an individual of those psychophysical systems that determine his unique adjustments to his environment" (Allport).

Projection. The ascription of one's defect or motive to another when one will not admit it in one's self.

Rationalization. The development of plausible motives for behavior to avoid recognizing the true motives.

Reaction formation. Producing, because of repression and anxiety, behavior directly opposite to what might be expected.

Regression. Relapsing into an earlier stage of psychosexual genesis as a consequence of frustration.

Repression. The process whereby an individual's frustrated motives and anxieties are subjected to forces which make them less accessible to consciousness.

Self-actualization. The need to realize who one is; need for self-fulfilment.

Sensitivity. The capacity to predict what an individual will feel, say, and do. Sensitivity is not a single and global trait but is made up of a number of relatively independent components.

Sublimation. The channeling of sexual energy into a socially acceptable direction. Often used loosely of any substitution of a higher satisfaction for a lower one.

Superego. A censor mechanism reflecting values inculcated by parents and authority figures. When it is conscious, it represents conscience.

Unconscious. That part of the mind which holds ideas and feelings which are not readily recalled and which require a special technique to facilitate recall. The preconscious is that part of the mind from which ideas can be summoned more readily than from the unconscious.

EXERCISE

THE PLOT

Plot *I* (how you perceive yourself) with a •
Plot *Me* (how you perceive others perceive you) with a 0
Invite someone to plot *Him* (how he or she perceives you) with an X

involved	cool
closed	open
bright	stupid
dying	alive
becoming	being
obsessional	flamboyant
attacked	attacker
long, thin ——————musclely——————	small, fat
gourmand	gourmet
driving others insane	driving yourself insane
insensitive	guilt ridden
beautiful	ugly
sexless	sexy
heterosexual	homosexual
anal ——————genital——————	oral
coronary ——————ulcer——————	cancer
bad lover	good lover
a straight line	a circle
indifferent	apologetic
not OK	OK

DEBATE: Where are the three-dimensional people?

A revolution in sexual values has changed in a profound way how men and women perceive each other in the workplace. In many respects the advantage has passed to young, educated women. This shift has forced men, particularly white, middle-class, educated ones, to reexamine their own position. Many of the assumptions they have held about themselves are being challenged.

People's assumptions about themselves and others are based on culturally determined stereotypes, or mental pictures of what they expect from members of a class or group. A widely held masculine stereotype, which is supported by behavioral science research, is that men tend to run away from emotional confrontations. The male, therefore, is two dimensional—concerned only with analytical bite and task orientation. Where are the three-dimensional men?

The missing dimension is related to concern for people, gut reactions, sensitivity, risk taking, creativity. The feminine stereotype is that women have this dimension, but they are lacking in the two others that men are acknowledged to possess. Where are the three-dimensional women?

Question

In terms of personality, are women more likely than men to develop their missing dimensions?

DIAGRAM SUMMARY OF CHAPTER 6

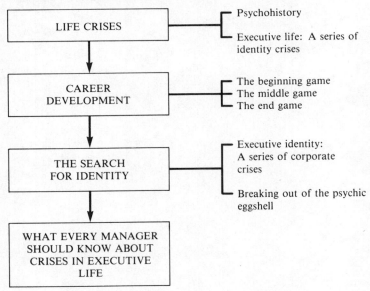

6

Predictable crises of executive life

SOMETHING HAPPENED

Robert Slocum, the central figure in Joseph Heller's novel *Something Happened*, is a well-groomed, sourly witty middle-level executive who works in the communication business. He is restless and bored, spinning in the wind. A comparison can be made with the Syrian-American Yossarian, the madly sane bombardier of *Catch 22*, whose attitude was described by Heller in the following terms: "It was a vile and muddy war, and Yossarian could have lived without it—lived forever, perhaps." And now you know what happened when he tried to live forever.

Slocum is the man in the grey flannel suit 20 years later. What happened to the young lions, what happened to the men on the bridge of the U.S.S. *Caine?*

Slocum is a husband and the father of three children. He is beset by domestic problems with an aging mother in an institution and a retarded son at home. His daughter quarrels with him constantly, and his other son is slipping away from him.

Slocum wishes it would all go away and leave him alone. At his work, he is an operator who defers to his superiors and is cavalierish to his subordinates.

Slocum is bored and anxious, but on the whole he feels more at home at his office. Like a great number of executives he finds vacations a drag and close relationships "suffocating." He suffers from a vague sense of inferiority: "Something did happen to me somewhere that robbed me of confidence and courage." He is beset by feelings of apathy, anxiety, alienation, and anomie.

Combatting this Cassandra complex, which predicts doom and misfortune, is the challenge management faces today. How can this generally felt sense of despair, this loss of direction, be overcome? Most middle-aged executives find it hard to accept the total pessimism of *Something Happened*. But the unrelieved boredom, the daily doses of death dished out at the office, touch nerve centers of pain.

TOPIC 1
Life crises

Many executives, like Robert Slocum, experience, without warning, a loss of nerve in the middle of their thirties. When it happens they wonder what has hit them. Midlife inevitably brings intimations of our own mortality. It is one stage in the life cycle which ranges from birth to death.

Erik Erikson proposed the idea of a life cycle with eight sequential stages of psychosocial development in *Childhood and Society*, published in 1950. Erikson himself had an identity crisis. The son of a Jewish mother and a father who abandoned his family before his son's birth, Erik rejected the name of his German Jewish stepfather. He invented his own name, Erik, son of Erik.

Each stage in Erikson's life cycle is characterized by a crisis. But for Erikson a crisis is not a catastrophe but a turning point in an individual's psychohistory.

PSYCHOHISTORY

Psychohistory is a new interdisciplinary concept which combines the insights of psychoanalysis with the events of history. It is of particular interest to executives because its study illuminates the personality and motivation of leaders and offers important clues to the kinds of problems they encounter in their own personal development. Freud initiated this method in his study of Leonardo Da Vinci. Erikson, a student of Freud, produced two pioneer psychobiographies, *Young Man Luther* and *Ghandi's Truth*.

Psychobiographies show how distinguished people coped with the crises in their lives as they moved from stage to stage. These crises produce feelings of guilt and self-doubt which have to be overcome if people are to make their way, successfully. In *Thrice Born*, a psychohistory of President Jimmy Carter, Bruce Mazlish and Edwin Diamond point out that:

> The middle-aged Carter obviously solved his psychosocial crisis of generativity—on many levels. Jimmy and Rosalynn Carter had their fourth child in October of 1967, some 15 years after the birth of their

third child. He won the governorship the next time out in 1970, surrounding himself with a small band of loyal workers in their twenties and thirties.

Still it wouldn't be very good psychohistory to believe that the 1966 political defeat is enough by itself to explain Carter's "new life." Our hunch, pending more work, is that Jimmy Carter's rebirth in 1966–67 was actually a third birth. There was, of course, his actual "first" birth in 1924. Then, there was a kind of "second" birth at the time of his father's death in 1953. Only later, in the conversion experience of 1966–67, as we have described it, did the "third" birth occur.

EXECUTIVE LIFE: A SERIES OF IDENTITY CRISES

As executives enter new stages of the career trajectory, they experience sensations of being reborn and beginning a new life. Any change is a disruptive process which can result in feelings of self-doubt and anxiety. Somehow or other executives must overcome these feelings in order to make it through to the next stage.

Self-conscious personal growth requires a person to be able to jump from one stage to another when the moment is ripe. To achieve this trajectory of growth, it is necessary to have some kind of ground plan. Sigmund Freud, like Erikson, described the stages of development which cover the life span, though Freud's were largely limited to the transition from infancy through adolescence. Freudian psychoanalysis traces out the ground plan as the child moves through the oral phase, then the anal, phallic, and latency phases, and finally through the stage of puberty into adult life.

The problems of adolescence are especially important for the study of organizational behavior. The student struggles through role confusion to find an occupational career path. The problem of the executive at 40 and 50, working through middle age, is whether the right path was chosen, and whether further struggle would be fruitful. On such problems of personal growth and identity, Erikson has provided some guidelines in *Identity: Youth and Crisis.* What happens in the inbetween period, when people are in transition between one stage and another? People "in between" ask for and need a moratorium. Erikson is particularly helpful in his definition of a moratorium—how society allows people a substantial respite while they change identities to meet changes in their careers.

TOPIC 2
Career development

The term *career* has for many executives an aura of adventure, as something that is moved through, the swifter the better. Donald E.

Super and Douglas T. Hall, in "Career Development," trace the term to its Latin origin, *caruss,* meaning a cart or a chariot. And perhaps executives are right to think of a career as a chariot race which has much in common with the rat race of contemporary society. Executives "pursue" careers, just as they "engage" in occupations, "get" jobs, and "occupy" positions.

Super and Hall define a career as a sequence of positions occupied by a person during the course of a lifetime. Implicit in this approach is the recognition of life stages and their relationship to the developmental tasks of growth, exploration, establishment, maintenance, and decline.

Box 6–1: The first years as a manager

Bruce Buchanan II, assistant professor of government at the University of Texas at Austin, reports a study of executive commitment based on a questionnaire survey of 279 business and government managers. Eight organizations participated in the study. Five were domestic agencies of the federal government located in Washington, D.C. Three were Fortune 500 manufacturing concerns located in the northeastern United States. All were among the largest bureaucratic work organizations in American society and were chosen to exemplify such organizations.

THE FIRST YEAR

In the first year, Stage 1, management recruits undergo basic training and initiation.

Most who find themselves in the early stages of management development programs in large organizations are young persons who have recently decided on management careers and who are questioning whether the reality of that career is congruent with their inner sense of self. . . . the primary concern of those at this career stage is safety: getting established with and accepted by the organization. Certainly such people are intensely anxious to prove themselves by showing that they can learn and adjust to the demands of the new environment.

Initially, the most influential are experiences which attune the recruit to what is expected of him. His mild anxiety over his ability to live up to expectations activates the affiliative tendency and prompts him to identify and attach himself to significant others who can furnish guidance and reassurance. The creation of this initial reference group is a profoundly important experience. By gratifying first needs for guidance and reassurance and ultimately for respect and affection, such groups probably exert a lasting influence over individual attitudes toward the organization. Moreover, interaction with veteran managers is the principal means by which recruits absorb the subtleties of organizational culture and climate.

Of decisive importance is the quality of the initial work assignment:

If it is challenging and stimulating, such that it bolsters the self-image and gratifies the achievement needs of the individual, it will affect the commitment attitude positively. If, on the other hand, the job seems trivial or unimportant to the organization, the opposite effect can be expected.

Reference: Bruce Buchanan II, "Building Organizational Commitment: The Socialization of Managers in Work Organizations," *Administrative Science Quarterly,* December 1974.

Adapting Erikson's terms for the life stages, Super and Hall developed a composite model of adult career stages. In Stage 1, *identity*, young people in the teens and early twenties face a period of trial jobs, getting established, settling down, and identity problems. In Stage 2, *intimacy*, the young manager of 25 to 35 cuts away the connective tissue with mentors and begins the process of establishment in the organization. Stage 3, *generativity*, covers the 35–60 age category, the period of greatest possible advancement, which can result in growth, maintenance, or stagnation. Stage 4, *integrity*, completes the identity search for managers after 60, as they begin to prepare for withdrawal from the organization.

What about loyalty conflicts?

. . . many recruits are torn between learning and surrender to the new environment on the one hand and suspicion and mistrust of it on the other. Thus, an early concern of many will be to sense whether the organization is trying to dominate them and subvert their individuality through a substitution of organizational for personal values. Research has consistently demonstrated that challenges to, or attempts to change, ego-related attitudes will encounter defensiveness, resistance, and even solidification of the threatened attitude. To the extent that recruits feel threatened or compromised, commitment will probably be undermined.

THE SECOND THROUGH FOURTH YEARS

Stage 2, the performance stage, signals a shift in emphasis from safety and security to a concern with achievement, the making of a mark by carrying out an assignment with real responsibilities.

Most influential will be those that reinforce the fledgling manager's sense that he is making a real contribution, carrying his own weight. This class of experience is labeled personal significance reinforcement or personal importance. Managers who believe themselves to be making significant contributions and who sense that their contributions are appreciated are likely to develop commitment.

Another characteristic . . . will be uncertainty regarding the suitability of the career choice. Thus, experiences which reinforce the occupational self-image may well contribute to the growth or organizational commitment. These might include interaction with a supportive peer group which anchors favorable attitudes toward the organization or reassurances from superiors. Romanticization of the organization and its aims might also bolster identification and assuage self-doubt. Such experiences are called self-image reinforcement . . .

Another potentially influential experience is fear of failure. . . .

If they perceive that loyalty is expected of successful managers in their organizations, they will be motivated to adopt such an attitude.

THE BEGINNING GAME

A scenario of the executive game has been designed by Bruce Buchanan. In "Building Organizational Commitment," Buchanan views early stages as influence-susceptibility stages, rather than career stages, subject to:

> a law of primacy which holds that the earlier an experience, the more potent its effect, since it influences how later experiences will be interpreted. . . . This plasticity, role-readiness, and a special motivation to conform during this period is at its peak during the first few years and may diminish rapidly thereafter . . . [that] new managers are *tabula rasa* insofar as the organization is concerned suggests that enduring attitudes toward the organization are formed during this period.

Stage 1 is the first few years of work, usually as a management trainee (see Box 6–1 for further details).

THE MIDDLE GAME

In broad terms, the middle game covers the time from assuming the office of departmental manager to becoming a vice president of a medium-sized company or the direction of a major function such as sales, production, research, or personnel in a larger company. In the seventies the middle game marked a shift from $15,000–20,000 to $40,000–100,000 a year, from a Mustang II or a Triumph sports car to a Buick Electra or an Oldsmobile 88. On the domestic front, probably a family of three was growing up. As the oldest child went into high school there was a greater motivation to stay in one place. Some of these socioeconomic characteristics are likely to change in the eighties.

For the young executive who has put in the first five corporate years, the middle game is a period of mixed hazard and opportunity. Unjustified complacency is a major drawback. There is usually a constant nagging anxiety about sticking to a particular role too long, as complacency is challenged by the emergence of the mobicentric manager who has made it, the attractive offers of computer firms, the mushrooming of consultancy, the slowing down of the aerospace and electronics industries, the managerial advantages accorded ethnics and women, the pleasures of the existential culture, and a multitude of other social and corporate factors.

Middle game obsolescence

The U.S. Department of Health, Education, and Welfare report *Work in America* cites evidence that increasing numbers of America's

4 to 5 million middle managers (plant foremen up to top management) are seeking midcareer changes. A general feeling of obsolescence seems to overtake managers when they reach their late thirties. This is a critical problem for their bosses, the presidents and vice presidents who face the choice of either trying to save these early flameouts by reinvigorating them, or firing them. (See Box 6–2 for an example.)

Box 6–2: R. B., a workaholic

A typical workaholic is described in a study published in *Business Horizons:*

. . . R. B. was a rising executive in his mid-thirties. Married, with three children, he lived in one of the wealthier New York suburbs and was active in civic and church groups. Already director of marketing in a large consumer products company, it appeared that R. B. was destined for a much higher position. At this stage, R. B. and his family appeared to be the epitome of the American dream. Closer scrutiny, unfortunately, would have revealed overextended financial commitments, inability to manage mundane daily affairs, and a lack of communication with the family. These conditions existed because R. B. had no time for his family except in those activities which complemented his drive towards the top of his organization.

When a wrong decision by R. B. resulted in the loss of several accounts, he became erratic in his business dealings. Younger men within the company started challenging him, though he was but 38. Under increasing pressure, R. B. began to lose confidence. He was no longer able to charm upper management nor effectively consummate deals with clients. Finally, he was relieved of his job. By this time, he was in severe financial trouble and it seemed that no amount of hard work could extricate him from his plight. Unable to withstand further pressure and lacking support at home, R. B. committed suicide by asphyxiation.

Source: Albert Porter, Arthur F. Menton, and Seymour Halpern, "Hopkins' Syndrome: A Study of Compulsion to Work," *Business Horizons,* vol. 13 (June 1970), p. 92.

Research on executive careers suggests that early flameouts go through a midlife crisis by the age of 35. With "too old at forty" just five years away, many have floated to their level of incompetence. They are tempted into depression, drugs, debauchery, or drink and finally peter out.

In existential terms, the executive has become colonized. As Marcus G. Raskin, a founder of the Institute for Policy Studies in Washington, argues in *Being and Doing,* the new industrial state colonizes executives and turns them into dependent and subjugated persons:

In the pyramidal structure even if the individual has great latitude in his life style and the appearance of choice (freedom for lust), he lives according to forces external to the relationships which he might otherwise freely seek. As the individual grows older, he comes to represent those forces in his life relationships.

Work in America says:

> Characteristically, middle managers perceive that they lack influence on organization decision-making, yet they must implement company policy—and often without sufficient authority or resources to effectively carry it out.
>
> A general feeling of obsolescence appears to overtake middle managers when they reach their late thirties. Their careers appear to have reached a plateau, and they realize that life from here on will be a long and inevitable decline. There is a marked increase in the death rate between the age of 35 to 40 for employed men, apparently as a result of this sudden "mid-life" crisis.

In any case, the executive approaching the menopause or, in males, the climacteric) may well be in an excrutiating position. Confronted with inner anxieties about the original career choice, reduced physical and sexual vigor, outward signs of aging, salary prospects which are plateauing out, the executive has to decide again whether to continue to work for the greater glory of the organization.

For most executives, the decision means finding a new job either within the organization or outside it. For those who have to move out the experience can be somewhat traumatic, for they have not been prepared for it. For the executive on the way out, the signs of the need to switch, apart from a vague sense of anxiety, are not all clear. But the manager who is slipping gives certain recognizable signs, such as working excessive hours, including weekends; being unwilling to go on vacation (which he sees as an opportunity for superiors and competitors to get together to plot his demise, a paranoia which is frequently justified); and excessive control systems for checking on everything from customer complaints to subordinates' expense accounts, to photocopying costs, and so on, right down to the number of paper clips being used.

THE END GAME

The making of a modern Medici prince: The career trajectory of Lee Iacocca

The career of Lee A. Iacocca, described as the toughest and shrewdest salesman in Detroit, illustrates many of the structures, processes, and values of the managerial career. Iacocca, who was later to become the beleaguered president of Chrysler Corporation, brought the Ford Motor Company such innovations as the Mustang, the Mark III, the Maverick, and the Econoline truck. Eventually, he became president of Ford.

Iacocca started at the bottom of the professional and executive ladder in Ford's Dearborn, Michigan, headquarters after completing a BS degree in industrial engineering at Lehigh University. He started in a Stage 1 job as an executive trainee but short-circuited a number of stages by persuading the company to grant him a leave of absence to accept a Wallace Memorial Fellowship at Princeton University. In 1946 he received a master's degree in mechanical engineering, after submitting a thesis on torque converters. Then, back at Dearborn, he completed the training program he had dropped out of in 9 months instead of 18.

He was assigned as a transmission engineer to Ford's Edgewater, New Jersey, plant. This was not what he wanted, and when the company would not give him a sales assignment, he quit. And after being rejected by Ford's New York office, he managed to get rehired by Charles Beacham, the Eastern District manager located in Cherber, Pennsylvania, near Philadelphia.

In spite of the usual exhaustive executive stint, working long hours and dreaming up gimmicks to sell Ford automobiles, Iacocca went unnoticed until he came up with the campaign slogan, "56 for 56," which promised buyers in 1956 a new Ford for $56 a month. This successful sales ploy came to the notice of Robert S. McNamara, then general manager of the Ford Division, who adopted the campaign nationwide. It helped to sell 72,000 extra cars, and Iacocca was called to Dearborn. By the age of 35 he had been successively truck marketing manager and head of car and truck sales for the Ford Division. Though in Stage 3 in terms of career, he was still in Stage 2 according to chronological age.

Now Iacocca, like many other ambitious executives, had set his sights on becoming a vice president by 35, apparently a magic number for executives and professionals. Young executives are fond of saying, "As long as I earn my age, OK, but I want to be a VP by 35." The same phenomenon is noticeable among academics; many professors set their sights on being a dean by 35. Why 35? Probably because 40 is too near 45, which to the popular mind signals the beginning of the end. By 45, managers feel they have "run out of gas," unless, of course, they have "made it." Making it is a major American pastime which means being comfortably ahead of schedule in terms of one's correct career trajectory. Those who do not make it are losers.

To his own way of thinking, Iacocca at 35 was a loser, though he was a winner is anyone else's ballpark. His sense of disappointment was shortlived, however. Eighteen days after his 36th birthday, he was named vice president and general manager of the Ford Division, the heartland of the Ford empire. He had arrived at the edge of the end game at the early age of 36. It was 1960.

To understand how Lee A. Iacocca became president of Ford, it is necessary to go back to 1956 and consider a basic polarity of the automobile industry, safety versus speed. McNamara, who was on the side of safety, introduced that lackluster but functional automobile, the Falcon. Iacocca was for speed: "You sell on Monday what you race on Sunday." While he only managed to get bucket seats in the Falcon, he found a vehicle for his youthful philosophy in the Mustang, which became one of the most successful cars in Detroit history.

The Mustang, the poor man's Thunderbird, was planned like D-day, with careful but sophisticated body design. After meticulous market research, it was introduced at the New York's World Fair in April 1964. It cost only $2,368 for the basic model and was to propel Iacocca into the position of executive vice president of Ford's North American automotive operations.

The next crisis in Iacocca's career came when Arjay Miller, one of the original McNamara team, was appointed vice chairman of the board in 1968. Henry Ford II bypassed Iacocca and brought in Semon

FIGURE 6–1
Stages of executive career development and problems faced

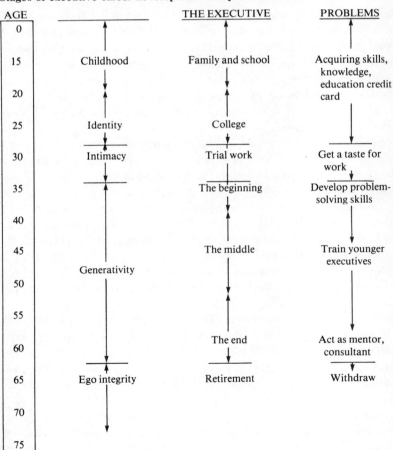

E. (Bunkie) Knudsen, a long-time executive of General Motors. Iacocca's point in his career trajectory graph was out of line with his point on his personal development and growth (PDG) graph, which is to a significant extent a factor of age. (Figure 6–1 shows the age-related stages of executive career development.) Knudsen became president of the company, and Iacocca was appointed a vice president of a large Ford fiefdom.

The scene was set for a classic war. Iacocca, sovereign in his own corporate city-state, waged war against the ex–General Motors man, who was ultimately fired by Ford himself in 1969. For Ford's money, though, Iacocca was still not ready. But even with the Ford empire split into three large fiefs, Iacocca was the de facto president, and he became the de jure president on December 10, 1970.

Lee A. Iacocca made it, all the way. Like General George Marshall, he knew the value of loyalty and brought his team with him from his days in Pennsylvania. (We shall return to Lee A. Iacocca's career in Chapter 18, on conflict in organizations.)

But Iacocca was to face yet another crisis when, in the late seventies, Henry Ford fired him from the presidency because he had become too powerful. Iacocca moved to Chrysler, which was itself going through a massive crisis. Soon he became chairman of the board and led Chrysler's fight for corporate survival.

TOPIC 3
The search for identity

To the executive, *Oedipus Rex* is the myth of identity, and Sophocles' theme is a quest for self-knowledge. Since the interpretation of the Oedipus theme is a function of the interpreter and the times, Freud's interpretation has meaning as a reflection of Victorian morality in a Viennese middle-class setting. As noted in Chapter 5, he devised the Oedipus complex to describe the attraction a child has for the parent of the opposite sex. The successful resolution of this Oedipal conflict is a positive identification with the same-sex parent and the emergence of a well-differentiated superego. This struggle was expressed differently by Alfred Adler as the masculine protest.

The executive is interested in the issue of identity, of defining who he or she is. Like Oedipus, the executive is faced with three questions: Who am I? Where am I going? Why? Sophocles' play is concerned with Oedipus' search for self-knowledge and the gamut of existence, repression, and projection which has to be gone through to find the truth about oneself. When Oedipus learns the truth (he is married to his mother and has had children by her), he cuts out his eyes. Rollo May points out that it is important that he is not castrated but instead cuts out his eyes, the source of his vision of the world and himself. It is this terrible process, fraught with guilt and anxiety, of coming to terms with oneself that is so devastating.

EXECUTIVE IDENTITY: A SERIES OF CORPORATE CRISES

A peculiar paradox is generated by the encounter of the executive with the organization. Not only do they have different needs, expectations, and resources, but there is also a corporate conundrum: The organization is "the executive writ large," and the executive becomes "the organization writ small." To get these two scripts together requires consideration of the technical, but real, concept of organizational socialization.

The basic managerial problem in an organizational context is to tie executives into corporate structures so that they become effective functioning units. This means commitment. It is not sufficient for executives to absorb goals, adopt preferred means, assume basic responsibilities, and exhibit OK role behavior. Beyond going through the motions processwise, the executive has to show initiative, display commitment, and, in effect, become the organization. This requires a deep, pervasive, and powerful personal commitment.

Commitment is a partisan attachment to the values, processes, and structures (in that order) of an organization. The organization is more than brick and mortar or even a stepping stone in one's career, and belonging to it is far more than earning one's bread and butter.

From the executive side of the paradox, things look different. Increasingly, today, organizations are seen as a means to an end. To understand how this has come about, it is necessary to look again at the executive career trajectory, which can usefully be considered under two headings: prework experiences and corporate career structure.

What are managers like before they become managers? While we are far from having a complete picture, there are certain clues from research. Larry Cummings' study of MBA students at Indiana University provides some interesting clues. In a fairly well-controlled study, Cummings divided the MBAs into "high academic achievers," who were serious minded, security conscious, and busy building up academic credits, and "leaders," who were mainly concerned with getting into "influence positions," were good at public speaking, had been exposed to a high-achievement-oriented peer group, and came from families in which they were allowed a great deal of independence. The leaders were also less interested in other people's motives, which suggests a extroverted personality, and preoccupied with the process of influence. Many of them had been exposed to relatively poor health as children; the ability to overcome illness or disabilities and even exploit them occurs again and again in the biographies of leaders.

The cognitive style of managers is another variable (see Figure 6–2). Liam Hudson, in *Cult of the Fact*, distinguishes between convergers ("unemotional and objective engineers who like working with things and who work towards the answers at the back of the book") and

FIGURE 6–2
Differences in executives' cognitive style

STYLE	EXAMPLE
Accommodators	Executives
Assimilators	Physical scientists
Convergers	Engineers
Divergers	Social scientists

divergers ("dreamy wide-ranging social scientists" who keep moving "up the funnel," creating more issues and questions and less answers). Two other categories, the assimilators ("hard-headed physical scientists" and "economists" who like making theoretical models) and the accommodators ("tough-minded business students" who like concrete experience and active experimentation) were added by D. A. Kolb, I. M. Rubin, and J. M. McIntyre in *Organizational Psychology.*

These differences in cognitive styles produce some interesting problems in university business schools, because the faculty are mainly divergers and the students accommodators, at least potentially.

In the executive value system, the executive is an instrument of somebody else. Knowing this can make problems for the manager who tries to square his independence with other forces which push him in the direction of dependence and interdependence. The pursuit of an executive identity, therefore, inevitably involves a series of corporate crises. At each different stage, the executive becomes trapped in a psychic eggshell of his own construction.

BREAKING OUT OF THE PSYCHIC EGGSHELL

Ever since Freud, it has been conventional to regard people in terms of mechanisms. Too many adult problems are summarily explained by reference to the Oedipus complex, for example. The existential argument is that instead of trying to understand the person in terms of the mechanism, we should be trying to understand the mechanism in terms of the person.

Psychoanalysis is too deterministic and closes off choice too completely to be acceptable to existentialists. Analysis consists of identifying and mapping out the unconscious complexes which structure the individual's choice. The existentialist argues that as a person becomes aware of such unconscious forces, he becomes engaged in some kind of choice, even though in many cases his freedom of choice may be circumscribed. When you become aware of a need to comply with authority, which you recognize as a kind of Oedipal echo of some early scene with your father, for example, you still have choices. You can comply or, alternatively, you can be prepared to pay the psychic cost and learn to live free.

Picking up the tab, psychic or otherwise, is difficult, but doing so is central to the existential approach. Will and decision represent the core of the existential concept of personality. The existentialists take from Arthur Schopenhauer the notion of will and from Henri Bergson the idea of "élan vital." Again and again, the existentialist comes back to the central proposition that, no matter the forces structuring your choices, you still have choices. Writers like Albert Camus and Jean-Paul Sartre proclaimed this courageous "vision of freedom" as members of the Resistance in Occupied France. Daily they stood the chance of having the validity of their philosophy of "will to meaning" tested—not in the relative comfort of a psychology laboratory, but in the torture chambers of the Nazis.

Executives in contemporary organizations face choices which are nearly as agonizing. Through the appraisal system, they can be confronted with stereotypes of themselves. This can become an occasion for self-transcendence, a process which Allen Wheelis, a San Francisco analyst, says originates in one's heart and expands outwards. The real choice they have to make is whether they are going to carry on with the caricatures of themselves they are presented with, or if they are prepared to make a bid for freedom and break out of their roles. A fairly common example is the case of the professional accountant who so fully assimilates his professional role that he is unable to behave like a real, live person. He has chosen nonfreedom by enveloping himself so completely in his work role that he is unable to function properly as a person.

This overcompensation is identified by existentialists as neurosis: The individual preserves his center by deviating from his own personality to conform with what he thinks a person should be. There are many examples of this adjustment in North America, where members of minorities may overassimilate their work role as a means of shrinking, if not denying, their ethnic or racial heritage. In existential terms, a neurosis represents an adjustment whereby a person achieves centerness, but in the process also accepts nonbeing.

To break out of the psychic eggshell called neurosis and get back to yourself may take a tremendous act of will. As we have noted, this is a neglected factor in modern psychology. The trouble is, as Wheelis points out, that "knowledgeable moderns put their back to the couch, and in doing so may fail to put their shoulder to the wheel."

People have to stop alibiing, as Catfish Hunter did. An article in *The New York Times* for July 16, 1978, pointed out this characteristic:

> Consider George Scott's comments about Catfish Hunter, which The Times reported on July 3: "That man [Catfish] don't have nothing to be ashamed of, no matter how he goes out. He went out and challenged peoples. He went out and beat peoples. He battle your tail. The man coulda alibied lots of times, 'cause he was pitching hurt, but I never heard him alibi once, 'cause he ain't that type. I'd give him the ball in a big game before I'd give it to anyone. He pitched his 300 innings and won his 20 games for years. He's a Hall of Famer, jack!"
>
> George Scott of the Red Sox and Catfish Hunter of the Yankees are eminently human beings; their humanity is vital and apparent.

"Something happened—I can sense it."

Reprinted by permission *The Wall Street Journal*.

TOPIC 4
What every manager should know about
the crises of executive life

The ancients compared the plot of a drama to the tying and untying of a knot. Executive life has become a knot, and existentialism offers a way of untying that knot. The contingency-model factors in the executive career are outlined in Figure 6–3.

THE EXECUTIVE CAREER TRAJECTORY

The executive career begins when the neophyte is spotted and earmarked by the system, and then selected by an idolized tyrant.

FIGURE 6–3
The executive career

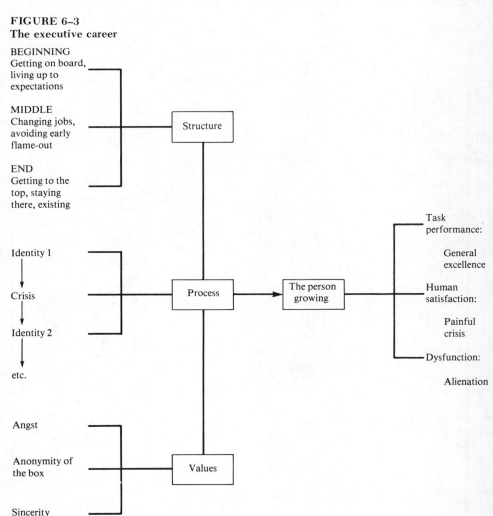

Before he can learn the ropes, loop the loop, work his passage, he must be found. The search is a stereotype in search of a victim. Unscientific selection systems, including group selection procedures, do not select; they socialize.

The executive career can be divided into three major stages: the

Box 6–3: "Get thee to a box"

Existentialists are often to be found in the Garden of Gethsemane, enjoying the self-inflicted wound of being the distorted mirror of society. They don't mind feeling oppressed and alienated because it stirs in them the possibility of a fresh identity. The existentialist sheds his identity with pleasure and joy. He likes conventions because he doesn't know many people so he can experiment with new personas, new people, new ploys. Hence the popularity of masks and disguises and the existential advantage of the moustache. The first step in becoming an existentialist is to find a disguise, a new companion, a new style, a new me, and a different you. And what is the best disguise? A box.

The man who has brought us the box is Kobo Abé, Japan's foremost fiction writer, who knows more about alienation, existentialism, and identity than any Western writer. He sees Japan as one vast "rubber room" full of Zen followers and Samurai who wear straitjackets with sleeves to practice their martial arts and who can't get out of training into the real thing because of historical events which climaxed in 1945.

In his latest book, *The Box Man,* Abé has captured this idea of anonymity as a necessary prerequisite to change. He argues:

As soon as they put the box over their heads, they become no one. Being no one means at the same time that one can be anyone.

All you need to become a Box Man is a large, empty carton. You remove its bottom, cut out a peep hole, get yourself some toilet articles, and hang them all up inside. Get inside, and you are a Box Man. The soft darkness of your new abode will immediately relax you. It will shelter you not only from the rain and cold but from the piercing stares of the hostile world, while permitting you to stare back at people through the hole. Now stand up, and just walk away from it all—from the worries and cares of your Compulsory Life.

Plenty of Box Men wander about the world, subsisting from trash cans, sleeping within their Boxes, holding no jobs, ID's, credit cards, addresses, friends, or families. Most people just ignore the existence of this tribe, but there are some people who grow extremely hostile or downright violent. They are Potential Box Men themselves, desperately fighting their unconscious longings.

Kobo's theme, "the box man cometh," is particularly pertinent for the Western executive, who is trapped in a box in the organization chart or tree, bound by a blueprint of double-entry bookkeeping, in which so much authority is pumped in to match so much productivity pumped out. The contemporary executive wants to drop out of that tree, for it does not bear much good fruit. But the more directly he indicates he wants to go, the harder it is to get away. The catch is that the more reasonable he becomes, the more unreasonable becomes the tree; the more sane he is, the more insane the tree is. He has to be ready to meet insanity with insanity, complexity with complexity, meaninglessness with meaninglessness. A disguise (a box perhaps) may help. Of course, it is dangerous. But, as Abé says, "Without the threat of punishment, there is no joy in flight." The existentialist manager must be ready to go underground.

Reference: Kobo Abé, *The Box Man,* trans. E. Dale Saunders. New York: Alfred A. Knopp, Inc., 1974.

beginning, middle, and end games. In the beginning game the neophyte pays the price of admission. After initiation into the ranks as one of the lowest of the low, the management trainee; there follows a spell as a section manager.

The middle game takes the executive from departmental manager status to one short of vice presidency, like director of a function such as marketing. The middle-aged executive struggles with the crisis of forming a new identity. Erik H. Erikson's ideas on identity, crisis, and moratorium (or in-between periods) suggest the idea of disguises to hide behind while changing.

The end game focused on the career of Lee A. Iacocca, who went all the way at Ford. This chapter closes with Box 6–3, "Get Thee to a Box," which introduces Kobo Abé. His ideas can help the executive develop the right zip and Zen, chutzpah and cheek, moxie and manner to take what's coming.

REVIEW AND RESEARCH

1. Define role both sociologically and managerially. Why are roles always defined in sets? Describe either the professor-subordinate role nexus or the doctor-patient nexus. Which other roles need to be considered?

2. Draw up an interview schedule to enable you to define an executive role. Make and execute a plan to interview an executive in a local firm. (Hints: use a tape recorder; prepare your interview schedule; make sure you look the part—clothes, hair style, manner, etc.)

3. Does role playing always involve acting? What are the cues? Where do you find the scripts? Do you know any good lines?

4. How and why are executives socialized?

5. Describe in broad outline the three stages of the executive career. Use the headings: tasks, problems, conflicts, rewards.

6. Why do young executives need point-blank feedback?

7. Do executives go through a midlife career crisis? Why? What can be done about it?

8. Do you agree that adolescence is a growth stage particularly liable to the identity crisis? Describe the dilemmas of this stage.

9. Why do individuals fear personal growth?

10. Write a short review of the book *Work in America.*

11. What are the most important points to be drawn from the study of the career of Lee A. Iacocca? Your answer should include an explanation of the phrase "Lee is like a Medici prince."

12. When we think of traditional executive values, words like *instrumentality, achievement, upward mobility* and "getting things done through people" spring to mind. Why? What are the new values? Can they be reconciled with the old? How?

GLOSSARY OF TERMS

Box man. The individual in the process of change who needs to hide away from the world in order to catch up or find personal growth and development.

Career. Sequence of positions occupied by a person during the course of a lifetime. Executive careers can be divided into three stages: the beginning, the middle, and the end.

Cassandra complex. The web of alienation and anxiety which the modern manager experiences, arising mainly from bureaucratic boredom and banality.

Executive identity. A series of corporate crises the manager faces in moving through the organization, assimilating its rules, roles, and relations. To meet these crises, the manager must make his role meaningful, i.e. his executive identity.

Persona. The mask Greek actors used to wear when appearing on stage. The persona represents the public part of personality which an individual presents to the world.

Psychohistory. An interdisciplinary field, drawing on psychoanalysis and history, which is being developed to study the individual's personal growth and development.

Workaholic. A person who has a compulsive and obsessive need to work excessive hours and who inverts a normal relationship between home and the office. Only at the office is the workaholic at home.

DEBATE: "Get thee to a box" is good advice for the midlife manager, versus Young Jacks and Jills need the box, too.

Divide the class into two groups according to age.

PRO: Reread both the material on Robert Slocum at the beginning of the chapter and Box 6–3, "Get thee to a box."

CON: Reread Box 6–1, "The first years as a manager."

Question

Who faces the bigger problem, the younger manager or the middle-aged executive?

INCIDENT

Harold Evans is an affable, well-turned-out, fair-haired man who is manager of customer complaints of a pharmaceutical company in New York. At the beginning of the year, Harold had had a nervous incident at work because of the tremendous pressures of his job. His physician prescribed a major tranquilizer. But unfortunately, while the drug was effective in removing the symptoms of anxiety, by the middle of the summer Harold had developed the twitching mouth movements and mincing step of tardive dyskinesia. This disease derives its name, late-appearing movement disorders, from *tardive*, which is related to the word *tardy*, and *dyskinesia*, which comes from the Greek work *kinesi*, meaning to move. It does not develop until the patient has been taking the drug for many months or even years.

Harold was so affected by this condition that he had trouble dealing with people on the telephone, and the more he tried, the worse his speech became. A number of customers had called in and spoken to Harold's superior about it. The personnel manager, therefore, called Harold's superior and the company physician to a meeting to decide what was to be done.

The company doctor advised the group that the word *tranquilizer* was confusing, because it is used for two entirely different kinds of drugs. The minor tranquilizers, which include Valium, Librium, Miltown, and Equanil, are basically antianxiety drugs and do not cause tardive dyskinesia. The major tranquilizers, on the other hand, which include Thorazine and Mellaril, are essentially antipsychotic drugs and can cause the disease.

What are the choices open to this group, and what action should they take?

DIAGRAM SUMMARY OF CHAPTER 7

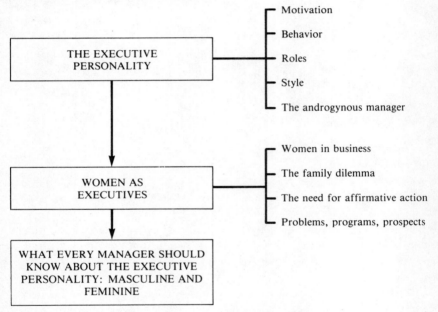

7

The executive personality:
Masculine and feminine

THE WOMAN WASP

"I want a career, to be independent. But I don't want to stop being treated like a woman.

"I'm planning to join the Chesapeake and Ohio Railway, Head Office Sales. I know I can sell, but I wonder how I'm going to be able to handle relations at work.

"Yes, I think I may try too hard. At business school, very few guys dated me, maybe because all I wanted to talk about was the courses.

"I would like to get away from home for a bit, get away from my folks.

"I don't want to be just somebody's housewife; I want to have my own identity. But I do want to get married. Most guys are not aggressive enough, though—I want one who is competitive."

The picture that emerges from talking to this young woman executive is one of confusion, conflict, and care. She wants a personally fulfilling life-style, neither dominated nor dominating. And she wants to show she can make her way in a world of organizations in which she is the exception rather than the rule. Stereotypically, woman is not expected to demonstrate the characteristics which ensure success in classical organizational terms. As these values are modified by existentialist concepts, however, and as it becomes recognized that there is no typically male or female manager, the difficulties should disappear.

When we review what is known about the executive personality, inevitably a portrait of the male executive emerges. Female executives are members of a small but rapidly increasing group which is too new to have been studied much. But descriptions of the effective executive are increasingly using the word *androgynous,* to represent both masculine and feminine characteristics.

TOPIC 1
The executive personality

What we know about managers has been derived from studies of the behavior of executives. The executive personality can be described in terms of motivation, behavior, roles, and style.

MOTIVATION

Managers have more powerful achievement imagery than non-managers, as measured by the TAT. Managers have a fixation about achieving. They rate "having an interesting job" higher, and score higher on initiative tests, than the general population. Not unexpectedly, they have a significant need for power, and they often obtain exceedingly high scores on scales measuring persuasiveness. (See Box 7–1 for further details on the needs of executives.)

Edwin E. Ghiselli conducted a large-scale survey entitled "Some Motivational Factors in the Success of Managers," which showed these differences in needs or motives among managers:

1. Middle managers (in comparison to workers in general) have a lower desire for security and for financial reward, and a higher desire for self-actualization.
2. Successful middle managers have less desire for security and financial reward than those who are unsuccessful. They also place more value on self-actualization than their less successful counterparts.

Ghiselli also argues:

As with the other managerial traits, as one proceeds from the lower occupational levels to the higher ones there is a greater and greater amount of self-assurance manifested by the personnel at those various levels. There is a substantial distinction between lower and middle management, but also between middle and upper management. Highly placed executives are outstanding in the confidence they have in themselves.

It would be wrong to assume that the same characteristics hold for all managers. For example, Japanese executive decision processes are so different from those of North America that it would be idle to expect similar executive profiles in the two areas. Areas of specialization also affect managerial motivation. Personnel managers tend to have interest profiles similar to those of other people-oriented professionals, such

Box 7-1: A scientific snapshot of the executive

Using such techniques in questionnaires, interviews, and projective instruments, J. P. Campbell and his colleagues at the University of Minnesota have compiled research data on the needs of managers. The result is a scientific snapshot of the executive which has a distinct, black-and-white outline.

Managers have distinctive motives and needs. They rate such factors as achievement, power, and status, together with income and advancement, as important; have higher achievement imagery; and consider "having an interesting job" more important than the general population does. They achieve higher scores on initiative than members of most other occupational groups and score high on directing people and on the initiation of activities. Studies of managers in different functional areas found that personnel managers tend to show higher humanitarian interests, and sales managers show high interest in social factors.

Successful managers tend to exhibit a lifetime pattern of high achievement, power, and economic motivations. They are more dominant and interested in directing others, and they prefer independent activities with some risk. Observational studies show that they enjoy interpersonal contact and reject regimentation. Research evidence indicates that candidates seek out managerial jobs because of their high achievement motivation characteristics; they do not acquire achievement motivation merely by holding a management job.

Other research studies have reported variances in expressed needs and motives according to hierarchical level. Higher level managers place much more importance on self-actualization and autonomy needs. They define success in terms of pride in personal accomplishment and the esteem of others. Thus, there is a self-actualization factor which keeps the top dog barking and growling for more bones.

However, there are other studies which contradict this picture of the overachieving "happy warrior." In the Achieving Society, D. C. McClelland found that the men at the top seem to express less of an achievement need. Nevertheless, the major findings in this area suggest that expressed motives do not, in general, change a great deal as an individual rises in the hierarchy of an organization.

Research studies on preferences among rewards indicate that professional people in the United States value job security, opportunities for advancement, and interesting work, while managers prefer hypothetical jobs which would provide low security and high pay. Managers indicate a strong preference for straight salary and litle interest in pensions, insurance, or vacations. Middle managers, when compared to the general population, are low on preference for job security and high on self-actualization.

Campbell and his group included in their report a list of the 12 adjectives judged most and least descriptive of "successful" executives.

Most descriptive of successful key executives	Least descriptive of successful key executives
Decisive	Amiable
Aggressive	Conforming
Self-starting	Neat
Productive	Reserved
Well-informed	Agreeable
Determined	Conservative
Energetic	Kindly
Creative	Mannerly
Intelligent	Cheerful
Responsible	Formal
Enterprising	Courteous
Clear-thinking	Modest

What these two lists add up to, apparently, is "Good guys come last," and "Tough wins again."

Source: J. P. Campbell, E. E. Lawler, and Karl E. Weick, *Managerial Behavior, Performance, and Effectiveness"* (New York: McGraw-Hill Book Co., 1970).

as YMCA secretaries and social science teachers, who all score high in humanitarian interests. And presidents of companies are unique, quite different from other occupational groups.

It is also possible to separate the effective from the ineffective executive. The effective executive:

1. Has a lifetime pattern of high achievement, power, and economic motivations.
2. Is more dominant.
3. Scores higher on the political and economic scales of such personality measurement instruments as the Allport-Vernon Study of Values.
4. Is more interested in directing others, prefers independent activities, enjoys a measured risk, rejects regimentation, and enjoys interactions.
5. Had a high need to achieve before becoming a manager, not the other way around.

Higher level managers place greater emphasis on self-actualization and autonomy needs and opportunities for personal growth and a high value on participation in goal setting.

BEHAVIOR

Behavioral studies of executives indicate beyond all reasonable doubt that managers feel compelled to work excessive hours at an unrelenting pace, with few opportunities for breaks or recreation. This critical executive fetish becomes more pronounced at higher levels in the hierarchy and must be regarded as a function of the kicks, rewards, and challenges senior executives get out of their jobs. The manager's life is suffused with brief contacts and fleeting interactions; it is highly fragmented, with a fair level of noise. Managers appear to operate at several levels simultaneously, or at least in rapid succession.

Managers apparently spend most of their time communicating, mostly by the spoken word and mostly at meetings. For most, writing letters is not a major activity. Managers have a preference for the immediate, the concrete, and specific problems which they immediately simplify through some model. The scheduled meeting is the mainstay of their days.

The manager's job: Fact and fiction

In the classical view, the manager organizes, coordinates, plans, and controls. We know from observational studies of executive behavior, however, that managers are not in fact reflective, regulated workers who are kept informed by sophisticated systems. Their life is much

Box 7-2: Keeping the executive clock from running out

An executive's time apparently belongs to everybody but the executive. As Parkinson's law points out, work expands to fill the time available for its completion. An 80/20 rule applies to the use of executive time: the most trivial 20 percent of an executive's tasks consumes 80 percent of the time available.

Why do executives permit such a poor return on their own time? Roy Rowan suggests some reasons:

> While many executives are overworked, they are also, in the view of the time-management consulting crowd, under-organized. And as is their way, the consultants have compiled a vast dictionary to describe these organizing ills. It includes terms such as "Procrastination Quotients" (a high PQ indicates a tendency to dally on tough decisions), "Stacked Desk Syndrome" (enables an executive to say to himself: "Look how busy I am"), "Open Door Myth" (invites interruptions), "Fat Paper Philosophy" (induced by memoitis and spread by Xerox machines and magnetic-tape typewriters), "Analysis Paralysis" (immobility caused by substituting study for courage), and "Planning Paradox" (failure to plan because it takes time). . . .
>
> William Oncken, chairman of a Texas consulting firm, warns of what he calls "reverse delegation." He cites the example of a boss passing a subordinate in the office corridor. "Good morning," says the subordinate. "By the way, boss, we've got a problem." As Oncken explains, the boss knows enough to get involved, but not enough to make an on-the-spot decision. "So glad you brought this up," responds the boss politely. Right away, says Oncken, the monkey has been transferred from the subordinate's back to the boss's back. The care and feeding of monkeys, Oncken warns, is one of the biggest time-killers. His advice is to avoid becoming "your subordinate's subordinate." . . .
>
> "Priorities" had always been the byword of Donald Rumsfeld when he was a Navy pilot, Congressman, and NATO ambassador. As Gerald Ford's White House chief of staff, he wrote the following reminder to himself: "Control your own time. Don't let it be done for you. If you are working off the in-box that is fed to you, you are probably working on the priority of others." Later Secretary of Defense and now president and c.e.o. of G. D. Searle & Co., Rumsfeld admits that "life is never what one plans. But you've got to look backwards and forwards and see how you're spending it."

The problem is to work smarter, not harder. Rowan gives the results of a *Fortune* survey of more than 50 presidents, vice presidents, and chairmen which asked them to rank the ten worst time wasters. The weighted order of finish was:

1. *Telephone.* "Answering all of those irrelevant questions courteously wears me down."
2. *Mail.* "Monday is deluge day."
3. *Meetings.* "Often an ego trip for the people who call them."
4. *Public Relations.* "The company name ought to speak for itself."
5. *Paperwork.* "The blizzard never ends."
6. *Commuting.* "A big waste."
7. *Business Lunches.* "The conversations are often indigestible."
8. *Civic Duties.* "Long and boring."
9. *Incompetents.* "The worst are those who violate company policy."
10. *Family Demands.* No comment.

Other major time-wasters mentioned by the executives: Coping with government regulations, the rumor mill (who's getting ahead and how), drop-ins with suggestions on ways to improve the company, and bottlenecks created by the boss. One executive simply sent his regrets: "I don't have time to think about it."

Reference: Roy Rowan, "Keeping the Clock from Running Out," *Fortune,* November 6, 1978.

more of a jumble of intertwined interpersonal, informational, and decisional rules. (See Box 7–2.)

Henry Mintzberg, in "The Manager's Job," describes four myths about the manager's job which do not hold up to careful scrutiny.

1. *Folklore: The manager is a reflective, systematic planner.* The evidence on this issue is overwhelming, but not a shred of it supports this statement.

    Fact: Study after study has shown that managers work at an unrelenting pace, that their activities are characterized by brevity, variety, and discontinuity, and that they are strongly oriented to action and dislike reflective activities.

2. *Folklore: The effective manager has no regular duties to perform.* Managers are constantly being told to spend more time planning and delegating, and less time seeing customers and engaging in negotiations. These are not, after all, the true tasks of the manager. To use the popular analogy, the good manager, like the good conductor, carefully orchestrates everything in advance, then sits back to enjoy the fruits of his labor, responding occasionally to an unforeseeable exception.

    But here again the pleasant abstraction just does not seem to hold up. We had better take a closer look at those activities managers feel compelled to engage in before we arbitrarily define them away.

    Fact: In addition to handling exceptions, managerial work involves performing a number of regular duties, including ritual and ceremony, negotiations, and processing of soft information that links the organization with its environment.

3. *Folklore: The senior manager needs aggregated information, which a formal management information system best provides.* Not too long ago, the words total information system were everywhere in the management literature. In keeping with the classical view of the manager as that individual perched on the apex of a regulated, hierarchical system, the literature's manager was to receive all his important information from a giant, comprehensive MIS.

    Fact: Managers strongly favor the verbal media—namely, telephone calls and meetings.

4. *Folklore: Management is, or at least is quickly becoming, a science and a profession.* By almost any definitions of *science* and *profession,* this statement is false. Brief observation of any manager will quickly lay to rest the notion that managers practice a science. A science involves the enaction of systematic, analytically determined procedures or programs. If we do not even know what procedures managers use, how can we prescribe them by scientific analysis? And how can we call management a profession if we cannot specify what managers are to learn? For after all, a profession involves "knowledge of some department of learning or science" (*Random House Dictionary*).

*Fact: The managers' programs—to schedule time, process informa-
tion, make decisions, and so on—remain locked deep inside their
brains.* Thus, to describe these programs, we rely on words like
judgment and *intuition,* seldom stopping to realize that they are
merely labels for our ignorance.

ROLES

Based on a sustained and thorough review of the literature,
Mintzberg came up with the idea of ten working roles in these roles
are interrelated and are performed by all managers.

Interpersonal roles:
  Figurehead—symbol
  Leader—defines interpersonal relations
  Liaison—makes external contacts
Informational roles:
  Monitor—searches out information
  Disseminator—transmits information
  Spokesman—represents firm
Decisional roles:
  Entrepreneur—initiates
  Disturbance handler—manages conflict
  Resource allocator—controls
  Negotiator—sorts out

STYLE

We do not know factually what style is appropriate in which circumstances. It seems safe to assume that the effective supervisor is
concerned with both getting tasks accomplished and with human relations, and that the workers provide both productivity and satisfaction.
Workers apparently have a strong need for a human relations approach,
although this is not true for all work groups studied. Robert J. House's
work with middle managers and professionals suggests that effective
managers must be concerned about task effectiveness, but their human
relations skills do not affect productivity or satisfaction. Can it be that
middle managers prefer good human resource planning, even if a little
anxiety is generated in the process? Top managers live in an entirely
different world, if we are to believe a philosopher-king like Wilfred
Brown, who argues in *Exploration in Management* that optimal organization is not a function of personality.

The "odd couple" leadership style

A good example of executive leadership style is provided by a
quick look at the National Broadcasting Company brass, particularly

Box 7–3: "NBC's Mrs. Clean"

Time gives this portrait of a woman at the top:

She is known variously as "the Ayatullah," "St. Jane" and "Attila the Nun," a reference to the six months she once spent in a Berkeley, Calif., convent. As those sour nicknames show, the rise of Jane Cahill Pfeiffer, 46, chairman of NBC, has produced a predictable mix of envy, admiration, fear and resentment, laced with a dollop of old-fashioned male chauvinism.

Not that anyone doubts Pfeiffer's ability to hold her own in the rough-and-tumble of network politics. She is not just attractive and intelligent. Thomas J. Watson Jr., her boss and mentor at IBM, calls her "brilliant and practical." A West Coast producer, less admiringly, terms her "conservative, moralistic, businesslike and hard." A liberal arts major at the University of Maryland, the Washington, D.C.–born Pfeiffer joined IBM soon after leaving the convent at the age of 23. In her two decades there, she rose from a trainee job to a vice presidency, with a reputation for quick decisions and no false moves.

On leave from IBM, she became a White House Fellow, worked for Housing and Urban Development Secretary Robert Weaver, and began to collect powerful friends in Washington. Pfeiffer left IBM in 1976, after marrying fellow V.P. Ralph Pfeiffer Jr., the divorced father of ten children. She turned down several job offers, including one from President Carter, who wanted to make her Secretary of Commerce. Her reasons: she needed time to recuperate from a thyroid cancer operation, and she was reluctant to spend so much time away from her husband. Pfeiffer then worked as a top-drawer consultant to several major companies, including NBC. Last fall, in a surprise move, she became the $225,000-a-year (plus up to $200,000 a year in bonuses) chairman of NBC, responsible to the network's new president, Fred Silverman.

As an administrator, Pfeiffer is reluctant to delegate authority. Her style runs more to mastering all the minutiae herself and plunging into an array of meetings to keep on top of the corporate scene. Instead of long memos, she scratches out terse notes to staffers on file cards, many of them dashed off during her commute from Greenwich; Conn., in her chauffeur-driven $46,000 gray Cadillac.

Much of the current gallows humor at NBC eddies around the relationship of Silverman and Pfeiffer, a.k.a. "the Odd Couple" and "Mr. Tough and Mrs. Clean." By most standards, the two top executives are indeed mismatched. Silverman is rumpled and raffish, a volatile high roller, known for his seat-of-the-pants decisions on programming. Pfeiffer is formal and controlled, a superb administrator, known for her idealism and belief in "high programming standards." Where Silverman's language is direct and often unprintable, Pfeiffer's fluctuates between girls' school ("Oh gosh, gee whiz") and "high IBM" ("I am on a steep learning curve").

One of Pfeiffer's problems could be her idealism. According to a friend, "She always believed in making a better world. Corruption is totally alien to Jane, and she wants to clean it up right away. She's a nun." Says another source: "I have the feeling that she thinks television is a dirty business, period, and she has to save us from ourselves by cleaning house." Another opinion is that her IBM training will be of limited use at NBC. Says a former executive at a TV production company: "Jane Pfeiffer is a virgin who comes out of the structured school. I'm not sure the structured school works in the entertainment business."

So far the critics do not seem to have ruffled Pfeiffer. "The pressure doesn't get to me," she insists. Somewhat defensively, she also says of her role in handling the unit managers' scandal, "I'm not the avenging angel. I'm not Joan of Arc." Her edgy employees would probably accept those statements. Trouble is, they are not quite sure yet just who she is.

Source: *Time* magazine, May 14, 1979, p. 88.

the chairman and the president, who work on the sixth floor of the RCA Building in Manhattan. This is known to subordinates as "the court of the Borgias" because political paranoia has been running high for NBC, which has been last in the TV ratings game.

Fred Silverman, the president of NBC, was brought in to give the network back its place in the sun. Silverman's second in command is chairman Jane Cahill Pfeiffer, a former IBM vice president who has stepped on toes trying to sort out the network's tangled organization structure. It is widely assumed that she has a clear line to RCA chairman Edward H. Griffiths. *Time* magazine describes her as Mrs. Clean (see Box 7–3).

The organizational relation of Pfeiffer and Silverman can be diagrammed as follows:

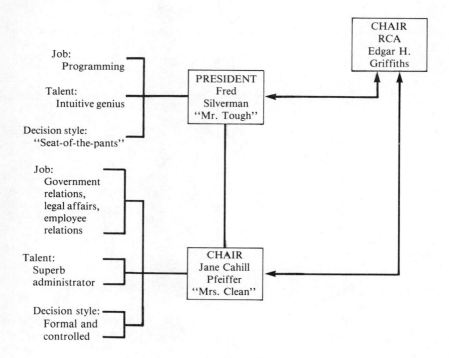

THE ANDROGYNOUS MANAGER

In American society, numerous traits are identified stereotypically as being either masculine or feminine. The tendency has been to create a dichotomy of male and female types, although there are many differences among individuals of the same sex and many similarities between individuals of the two sexes. Research findings, for example, have indicated that male top managers have higher verbal skills (supposedly a feminine trait) and are less masculine than male engineers are.

Psychologists engaged in the study of sex-role stereotypes are concluding that neither the traditional male nor the traditional female role is sufficient alone. The argument for androgyny applies particularly to executives. It is difficult to act out the strictly masculine, or classical organizational, leadership role today, due largely to contradictions in expectations brought on by cultural changes. In contemporary society much is expected of men and women alike, in terms of both task achievement and self-fulfillment.

The most effective managers, apparently, would exhibit both characteristics which have been called masculine and those which have been called feminine (see Figure 7–1). Creative architects, for

FIGURE 7–1
How stereotypical male and female traits are combined in the androgynous manager

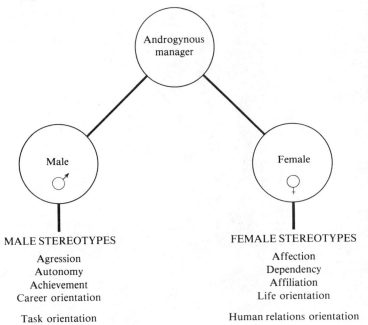

example, were found to have higher scores than others on feminine tendencies but not to have correspondingly lower scores on masculine tendencies.

Initial research results on androgyny have shown that androgynous people are likely to fare best today. Sandra Lipsitz Bem, in "Androgyny vs. the Tight Little Lives of Fluffy Women and Chesty Men," found androgynous people have the most stable identities and are less likely to be patients in psychiatric clinics. In one study, androgynous college men described both parents as affectionate, and androgynous college women described both parents as being encouraging, intellectual, and achievement oriented.

The contingency model of the androgynous executive personality as a system is diagrammed in Figure 7–2.

FIGURE 7–2
The executive personality as a system

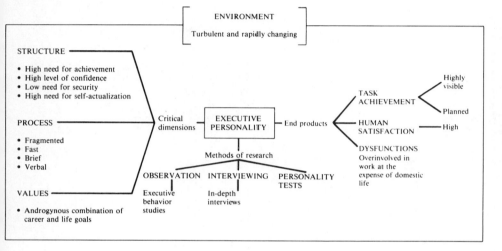

TOPIC 2
Women as executives

WOMEN IN BUSINESS

The entry of women into the U.S. labor force is one of the most outstanding phenomena of our century. In 1890 only about 18 percent of all working-age females had a job or said they wanted one. Today, women represent 40 percent of the entire labor force, up from 30 percent in 1950 (see Figure 7–3). All indications suggest that the style of the traditional nuclear family (father, mother, children), with the husband working and the wife taking care of the family and the household, is on its way out.

As opportunities for women open up in the world of work, women are finding that a job offers the promise of a more self-fulfilling role in life than that of helpmate to a man-with-a-career. In any case, inflationary pressures on family incomes are making it necessary for more and more women to find work. Most jobs available to women are at the lowest organizational levels. Nevertheless, there are openings for

FIGURE 7–3
Proportion of U.S. labor force comprised of women

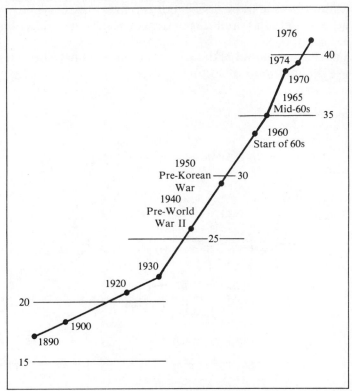

Source: *The New York Times*, September 12, 1976. © 1976 by The New York Times Company. Data from U.S. Department of Labor.

women who have the educational background to enter the managerial hierarchy.

Equal social and professional status for women in business would affect the very nature of how hierarchical organizations function. While some successful working women do not regard themselves as feminists because they believe that this battle has been fought and won, the women's movement has had only limited success in increasing opportunities for women in business. For example, in the 1,200 biggest U.S. companies there are about 150 female directors, versus 20 five years ago. In the traditional industries such as steel, automobiles, oil, and railroads, few women have made it to the vice-presidential level. In newer fields such as computers, communication, and finance, more women have made it to the top, though they tend to be in personnel and corporate relations positions. Many women are becoming sales representatives; for example, 12 percent of Xerox's traveling sales force and 7 percent of Levy Strauss's are women.

To prepare for business careers, increasing numbers of women are entering business schools. For example, in 1979, women comprised between 24 to 33 percent of the graduating classes in the business schools at Wharton, Stanford, and Columbia. As *Time* Magazine (January 5, 1976) pointed out, however, a business degree does not guarantee success or equality:

> Carol McLaughlin, a graduate student at Wharton, has surveyed Wharton graduates from 1945 to 1974. Among her findings: after being out of Wharton for 7½ years, men were earning an average salary of $23,000 a year *v.* $17,000 for women. On the average, the men had a staff of 30 people reporting to them; women averaged two or three. Observes McLaughlin: "The staff size is really startling. It shows that women are kind of doing things, but they are not really managing." From the comments on her questionnaires, McLaughlin has determined that "there

Reprinted by permission *The Wall Street Journal.*

are an awful lot of discouraged women out there." One Wharton alumna wrote, "I work twice as hard as a man just to prove I am not a dumb woman." Anti-female prejudice leaves a mark even on the most success-ful women. Virtually all harbor memories of slights and obstacles that were—or are—put in their paths.

The environment and the input and output variables of the con-tingency model of the woman executive considered as a system are diagrammed in Figure 7–4.

FIGURE 7–4
The woman executive as a system

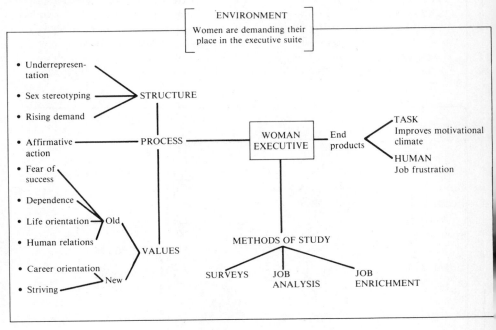

THE FAMILY DILEMMA

Married women, particularly those who are mothers with small children, often must not only find rewarding work for themselves but also must make acceptable arrangements for the care of their family. In effect, women who work outside the home automatically have two full-time jobs; they do not give up their traditional responsibility for domestic logistics when they pursue a career.

American attitudes toward marriage and family have changed sig-nificantly since World War II, however. For the first time in American history the average household consists of fewer than three persons. Marriages are decreasing and divorce rates are increasing; women are choosing to stay single longer, and when they marry they are having fewer children.

In marriage, husbands and wives are working out new arrangements to give the wife more opportunities to follow her own occupational destiny. Some couples have reversed the traditional roles; the husband stays home and minds the house and child, while the wife goes out to bring home the bacon. But such arrangements require great care if the family is going to continue as a functioning unit, as *Time* magazine (January 5, 1976) noted:

> Carla Hills [formerly secretary of the Department of Housing and Urban Development] and her husband Roderick, chairman of the Securities and Exchange Commission, get up about 6 a.m. Before leaving at 7:15, she tries to spend some time with at least a couple of their four children—braiding a daughter's hair, playing with another for a few minutes. She keeps a kitchen bulletin board, telling who will be home for dinner (one of the parents always tries to make it), listing each child's chores and times for piano lessons. Both Carla and Rod bring home work at night, but they often pore over it in the living room in order to sit with the children. Says she: "I often feel like a piece of salami, with a slice here for one and a slice there for another, and there isn't enough to go around."

Despite sex stereotyping, apparently a lot of men are enjoying the change and are discovering that women's liberation from exclusively household concerns can be to their benefit.

What happens to men as more and more women take on a bigger role at work? The basic idea of the nuclear family, with the husband as the breadwinner and the wife as the homemaker, is increasingly being challenged. There is abundant evidence that the financial independence of women has contributed to a rising divorce rate. And, as the pressure for the man to be the breadwinner declines, men increasingly are opting for shorter work hours in preference to higher salaries. Men with working wives also are less likely to accept job transfers from city to city. And they are more frequently in and out of the labor force, rather than staying in a job, if possible, until retirement.

THE NEED FOR AFFIRMATIVE ACTION

In a male-dominated profession such as business management, and in a society which devalues women and socializes them to devalue themselves, judgments about female executive competence are necessarily patriarchial. A survey of 46 male and 33 female psychotherapists, reported by Inge Broverman et al. in "Sex-Role Stereotypes and Clinical Judgments of Mental Health," revealed a picture of the mentally healthy woman which differed from the picture of the mentally healthy man by being

" . . . more submissive, less independent, less adventurous, more easily influenced, less aggressive, less competitive, more excitable in minor crises, more easily hurt, more emotional, more conceited about appearance, less objective, and less interested in math and science."

The feminist thesis is that women have been painted into a corner by men as unfit for executive posts.

It is increasingly being argued that the conventional ideas of masculine and feminine behavior can be changed. No longer is the idea acceptable that characteristic behaviors of men and women are immutably set by genes at birth. As medical psychologist John Money, from Johns Hopkins University, spells it out in *Man and Woman, Boy and Girl,* there are only four imperative differences between men and women: women menstruate, gestate, and lactate; men impregnate.

Despite the evidence coming forward in regard to the greater importance of the environment than heredity in structuring sex roles, there seems little hope for any immediate breakdown of sex-role stereotypes. One way women can hasten the process is by exerting considerable effort to take up their proper roles in business and society. The 32 million employed women in the United States constitute a powerful force.

Irrefutable evidence of the unequal status accorded women at work

Box 7–4: Women in Levi Strauss and Company

The position of women in the organizational structure of a large manufacturer is described in an article in *Time* magazine:

BUNCHED LOW

The company, which employs 18,000 people in 35 plants, began to study a year ago how its women were treated. It found that most women were bunched into the lowest-paying jobs as secretaries, patternmakers, stencilers. Most men were in the better paid posts as salesmen or cloth cutters. Though 85% of the company's employees were women, only 9% of the 572 managers were women. Says Sharon Weiner, who heads Levi Strauss's "Affirmative Action Program for Women": "When a woman came to the door for a job, she was told only about those that had historically been held by women. Nobody ever sat down and thought what it was like to be a woman in the company."

One of the new program's immediate goals is to lift more women into jobs that once were monopolized by men. The first woman recently completed the management-training program; she is now a product manager. All together, 13 other women have been promoted to management positions after on-the-job training.

The chiefs of all the company's manufacturing divisions are under orders to appoint women to the next two management posts that open in their personnel departments. Personnel Boss Thomas Borrelli rejects the notion that women are bad management risks because they are more likely to leave than men. Says he: "The tendency has been to compare the turnover of managers with the turnover of sec-

Source: *Time* magazine, March 20, 1972.

is the fact that women generally receive about 60 percent of the pay that men receive, and, further, the percentage is falling. Only 1.1 percent of all women working receive $15,000 or more, comparrd to 13.5 percent of men. Since 1963, when the equal-pay law was passed, followed by the Civil Rights Act of 1964, there has been a significant body of legislation which makes it illegal to discriminate against an employee on the basis of sex.

While most executives would agree that equal work merits equal pay, little has been done in fact to remedy the inequality. Increasingly, women have sought remedy in the courts. Revised Order No. 4 of the Office of Federal Contract Compliance Programs, requiring federal contractors to have affirmative action programs, with goals and timetables, to remedy sex discrimination in employment, was issued in 1972. That year 10,400 people (comparad to 5,800 in 1971) filed charges of sex discrimination before the Equal Employment Opportunity Commission. A number of consultancy firms have appeared to help firms comply with such regulations.

In their fight for their rightful place at work, women have a powerful ally in the federal government. Under the threat of contract cancellation, it can compel corporations which do substantial business with the government to hire women and to remedy the underutilization of their women employees. Many firms have conformed to such man-

---

retaries. But if you look at the turnover of women managers, it is probably less than men."

SECRETARIES OUT

For the first time, Levi Strauss is moving women into its field sales force; two are already working, one is in training, and orders are out to hire at least seven more before September. Some retailers warned that women in selling would have trouble with lecherous buyers. Haas rejects that argument. A more serious concern is that married saleswomen with children could face problems at home if they were forced to put in three-day or four-day stretches on the road. "We let the woman decide if she can handle it," says Borrelli.

Levi Strauss is also working to upgrade some office jobs that are now held by women. In the past year, 15 secretaries have been raised to administrative assistants—and not in name only. They allocate department budgets, make periodic changes in the size of salesmen's territories and investigate the causes of canceled orders. Indeed, top management reasons that many executives can do without secretaries; some are being phased out by promotion or attrition. The company has also liberalized its maternity-leave policy. In the past, women who left had no guarantee that they would get their jobs back. Now they can take up to 60 days' leave and be assured that their old posts will be waiting for them; Borrelli says that most women find this arrangement adequate.

dates by giving secretaries of chief executives imposing titles such as assistant vice president, while they keep "the girls" working as secretaries.

One company which has recognized the critical role secretaries play as personal assistants to executives is San Francisco's Levi Strauss, producers of denim Levis. The chairman of Levi Strauss, Walter Haas, Jr., perhaps prodded by government but also responding to the young customers who buy the gear the firm manufactures, undertook an extensive Affirmative Action Program for Women (see Box 7–4).

PROBLEMS, PROGRAMS, PROSPECTS

Achievement motivation in women

The early research on achievement motivation led psychologists to a conceptual distinction between fear of failure and hope for success. Matina Horner, in some original research for a 1968 Ph.D. thesis entitled Sex Differences in Achievement Motivation and Performance in Competitive and Non-Competitive Situations, discovered a fear of success (FOS) in women. Now research suggests that males relate a higher percentage of FOS stories when subjects are asked to respond to unstructured cues. What researchers are trying to decide is whether FOS is an intrapsychic phenomenon in women or a sex-type role stereotype shared with some men. Some women, holding the more traditional sex-role stereotypes, thus may react more to success in the traditional male way. Part of the problem in challenging Horner's original results is that history has moved on, and women have in fact changed.

The women's movement

The idea of women's liberation has evolved into a full-fledged social movement, as Janet Saltzman Chafetz notes in Masculine, Feminine, or Human? The women's movement is involved in attempts to bring about a wide variety of specific legal and institutional changes. But it goes further, Chafetz says, "to question some of the core values of society and its definition of appropriate behavior for both sexes." The National Organization for Women (NOW), formed in 1966, is oriented to both normative changes and such bread-and-butter issues as helping women achieve equality in organizations.

Programs and prospects

Many large companies have begun programs to increase the number of females in executive ranks. IBM for example, established a program to improve the status of women in 1970. Two posts, those of vice president of communications and director of executive resources, have been filled by women who report to the chairman.

Company programs to raise the status of women usually include the following steps:

1. A comparison of women's salaries with men's.
2. Analysis of the work force to define the female human resources available for training and promotion.
3. Fresh job analysis to ensure that jobs are defined in realistic terms.
4. Attitude surveys among women employees to determine their needs and aspirations.
5. Use of sensitivity training sessions to make men aware of emerging women's needs.
6. Use of job enrichment programs to make clerical jobs more interesting.

If women are to achieve equality in society, they must make a conscious effort to participate in institutions which have traditionally put them down. As Phyllis Chesler notes in *Women and Madness:*

> The centuries of female spiritual, political and sexual sacrifice will be better redeemed by the female entry into humanity and public institutions than by rejecting them because they are not perfect—or because the efforts to integrate them are difficult and heartbreaking—or because they have traditionally been based on the oppression of women. For example, science, religion, language and psychoanalysis have . . . been used against women. This does not mean that these modes and institutions . . . must necessarily be sacrificed or discarded as hopelessly tainted . . .
>
> Women's ego-identity must somehow shift and be moored upon what is necessary for her own survival as a strong individual . . . Such a shift in ego-focus is extremely difficult, and very frightening. It grates and screeches against the gain of all "feminine" nerves and feelings, and implies retribution. Some women go "mad" when they make such a shift in focus.

The benefits women can realize by taking their rightful role in organizations are not only psychological but tangible in economic terms. They make it well worth the effort to shift and change their ego identity as a necessary prerequisite for participating in this traditionally male institution.

Not only will the female ego have to undergo changes as women take their place in organizations, but the male ego must change to accommodate them. And ultimately, the women's movement is likely to have effects on organizational behavior as significant as those brought on by the emergence of the trade union movement, years ago.

TOPIC 3
What every manager should know about the
executive personality: Masculine and feminine

The most important things to know about managers' personalities is that they are highly motivated, they have a fixation about achieving, and they seek challenge in their work. As managers ascend the hierarchy, they display more self-confidence and pay less attention to security.

In terms of behavior, they work excessive hours at a relentless pace, in activities which are characterized by brevity, variety, and discontinuity. They seek action and avoid writing, while favoring verbal media such as telephone calls and meetings. Priorities and schedules are what their lives are all about; their goal is to work smarter, not harder.

In terms of style, they tend to be highly task oriented but somehow or other are able to manage the human dimension simultaneously. This means they typically develop an androgynous style, representing an optimal mixture of masculine and feminine characteristics. In short, the really effective managers are able to put together aggression, autonomy, achievement, and career orientation (typically considered masculine qualities) with affection, dependence, affiliation, and life orientation (typically considered feminine qualities) to develop an effective managerial style.

REVIEW AND RESEARCH

1. Write a brief essay defining managerial motivation.
2. Compare and contrast "effective" and "less effective" managers. See Box 7-1.
3. What has Henry Mintzberg to tell us about the reality of managerial behavior?
4. How can you avoid reverse delegation? See Box 7-2.
5. Why are so many women entering the work force?
6. What difficulties face women aspiring to be executives?
7. What is sex stereotyping?
8. How does affirmative action work?
9. Do women have a fear of success?

GLOSSARY OF TERMS

Androgynous. Having the characteristics of both male and female. Androgynous managers stereotypical combine male characteristics such as aggression with stereotypical female characteristics such as interpersonal sensitivity.

Affirmative action programs. Corporate plans to give women and other members of minorities a better chance to take their rightful place at work.

Executive behavior. Made up of a great number of brief encounters.

Managerial motivation. Characterized by a high need to succeed, to take charge, and to be rewarded not only by money but also by more challenging work.

DEBATE: Androgynous managers make better managers, versus males are better equipped for the job

In the current drive to place more women in managerial positions, the key questions posed have been: What traits characterize the successful manager? Are women likely to possess the characteristics, attitudes, and temperaments necessary for success in business?

PRO: Androgynous managers are better

The report of a recent study by Sandra Lipsitz Bem entitled "Androgyny vs. the Tight Little Lives of Fluffy Women and Chesty Men" indicates that androgynous (from *andro*, male, and *gyno*, female) people are more flexible in meeting new situations and less restricted in what they can do and how they can express themselves. Those who are not burdened by rigid sex roles can adapt more comfortably to the diverse situations encountered today by executives. Bem says 35 percent of the population is considered to be androgynous, as compared to 50 percent who adhere to "appropriate" sex roles and 15 percent who are cross-sex-typed.

The experiment was conducted by first classifying the sample into three sex roles (masculine, feminine, and androgynous) and then testing their reactions to various situations. Sex roles were defined by measuring the attitudes of the subjects on a list of 60 personality characteristics categorized as traditionally masculine (ambitious, independent, assertive), traditionally feminine (affectionate, understanding), and neutral (truthful, friendly).

It was hypothesized that sex-typed men and women would do well only in situations where the behavior is traditionally considered appropriate for his or her sex. Those who were androgynous would do well regardless of the sex-role stereotype attached to the particular action.

A series of five experiments showed this hypothesis to be correct. A subsequent experiment proved that masculine men and feminine women would consistently avoid an activity that was inappropriate for their sex, even if it paid more!

CON: The male managerial stereotype is preferred

A 1973 experiment by Virginia Ellen Schein has shown that male middle managers perceive successful middle managers as possessing characteristics, attitudes, and temperaments more commonly ascribed to men in general than to women in general. A follow-up study conducted in 1974 showed that female middle managers perceived the same characteristics. That is to say, they too felt that the male stereotype possesses the predominant requisite characteristics of successful managers.

For the later study, reported in "Relationships between Sex-Role Stereotypes and Requisite Management Characteristics among Female Managers," a sample composed of 167 female managers was drawn from 12 insurance companies in the United States. The type of department, type of company, position level, and age were all similar to those of the male sample investigated by Schein in 1973.

A list of 92 words was rated in terms of how characteristic they are of women in general, men in general, or successful middle managers. Ratings were on a five-point scale. There was a large and significant resemblance between the ratings of men and managers ($r = .54$, $p < .01$). There was also a resemblance between the ratings of women and managers ($r = .30$, $p < .01$), but the degree of resemblance was significantly less than that between men and managers. Age did not moderate the relationships.

This association between sex-role stereotypes and requisite management characteristics may foster a view of women as being less qualified than men for managerial positions. To the extent this is true, the results imply that female managers are as likely as male managers to make *selection, promotion, and placement decisions in favor of men.*

Conclusions

For females (and, for that matter, males) to be placed in a position of management, they must demonstrate to the person responsible for selection, attitudes, and temperaments which are generally characterized by the male stereotype. And yet, if they wish to be successful managers in a fluid environment, their attitudes (once in the management position) must be flexible. Only a blend of both sex roles can ensure this flexibility.

INCIDENT

How to stop feeling guilty when you think you're right

Penny, a senior nurse in a well-known San Francisco hospital, has asked to see her supervisor, Sharon.

PENNY: I give up. I'm leaving.

SHARON: What happened to the bright young thing who was going to save the world?

PENNY: I wish I knew. This morning was the last straw. In the OR the surgeon held out his hand and I handed him a clamp. I thought that's what he needed. He threw it on the floor and started bawling me out. I *apologized*, for heaven's sake.

SHARON: Don't worry about that. That's par for the course. Surgeons are prima donnas. You have to stop saying "Yes Doctor" when your brain or your feelings tell you to say "No."

PENNY: Do you really believe I can get away with that? Forget it. I hate the doctors, resent the patients. . . .

SHARON: Hang on, Penny. Don't go overboard.

PENNY: I think I'll take a course in electrocardiography.

SHARON: No, that's not what you need. You need a course in assertiveness training.

Question

What would Penny gain by taking a course in assertiveness?

DIAGRAM SUMMARY OF CHAPTER 8

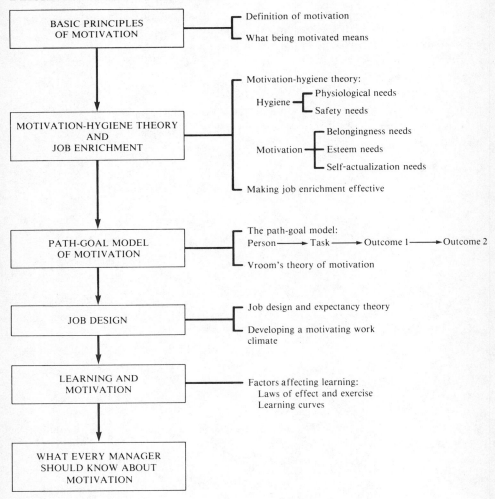

8

Motivating and learning

JERRY SANDERS'S CREDO: EVERY COMPANY HAS ITS OWN PARTICULAR MOTIVATIONAL STRENGTH

The management of an organization must be able to identify and build on its strengths. For example, in the booming semiconductor industry each company may score well on one dimension of effectiveness but not so well on the others. Intel Corporation is outstanding in the field of circuit design, Texas Instruments has the best management, and National Semi-conductor has the best manufacturing capabilities.

Another company in this rapidly expanding field is Advanced Micro Devices, which is trying to build its strength on microcomputers. AMD, as the company is known in "Silicon Valley," California, has been playing the follow-the-technology-leader game for the past ten years. It has become one of the fastest growing, most aggressive companies in the industry and is in the process of moving into the microcomputer business. When Jerry Sanders, the chief executive of AMD, was interviewed by Peter Schuyten for an article in *The New York Times* for February 25, 1979, he said of the technological leap his company was about to make: "I can't really say we excelled during this first decade, that we broke out of the pack. Ah, but our second 10 years, that is going to be our divine decade. We are going to become more of a technology leader, and more of a factor in the business. That is going to be our excelsior decade."

When Sanders decided to expand the company he read up on management theory to find out how to run it more effectively. He discovered Peter Drucker's *Managing for Results*, which he refers to as the Mein Kampf of Advanced Micro Devices: "As I started to get into it, I realized that you had to focus on big opportunities to understand what your resources were." Sanders therefore decided to bypass the development of proprietary technology and circuit design. Instead AMD would replicate, or "second source," standard products made by others. Because AMD was not a leader in process technology, Sanders decided to concentrate on reliability; integrated circuits frequently failed to perform up to the specified electrical characteristics.

Nevertheless, Sanders seems to have a knack for spotting new technologies and markets. AMD has continued to follow its established practice of second sourcing in terms of microprocesses, but has also developed peripherals for these products.

In 1977, West Germany's Siemens AG was looking to acquire a U.S. company with established experience in the microprocessor field. Instead of selling out, Sanders struck a deal with Siemens. With this new money, AMD was in a position to expand.

"We are making our thrust into the filet of the multi-billion-dollar data processing market," Sanders said in the *New York Times* interview. "Up until now we have participated and benefited from the existing universe of products that other people created. In our second decade we are going to create our own universe of products."

In describing his own motivation, Sanders said: "I care only about being rich, and the success of Advanced Micro Devices, in that order."

As the interview noted, "his lifestyle is more suited to that of a Hollywood film mogul than an electronics executive. He and his wife Linda and their three daughters live in the wealthy San Francisco suburb of Atherton, and there is a beach house in Malibu for weekends. She drives either a Mercedes or an Excalibur, he a Rolls Royce Corniche or a sleek white 308 GTS Ferrari."

"I still want to be rich," he says. "I wonder if I'll ever be rich enough that I don't say that? I doubt it."

Jerry Sanders cares about being rich. Money turns him on. But he wonders if he will be ever rich enough. To become rich he created AMD, which he piloted through all sorts of difficulties to make the company a great success. To be successful, Jerry realized that he had to focus on his opportunities and understand his resources. Jerry Sanders was motivated to succeed.

This brief look at Jerry Sanders and AMD illustrates the basic principles of motivation.

TOPIC 1
Basic principles of motivation

DEFINITION OF MOTIVATION

If personality describes the structure or anatomy of the person, motivation sets out the process of what makes the person do things. In motivation, both heredity and environment are relevant. Both physiological needs (such as hunger, thirst, and sex), which are largely determined by innate factors, and psychogenic needs (such as self-actualization), which are greatly influenced by the nature of the social environment, have to be considered.

Motivation is essentially concerned with attributing causes to and reasons for behavior. Its study is designed to reveal the intentions embedded in actions. Motivation is concerned with both impulsive and deliberate behavior and with relating a person's internal dynamics to external circumstances.

The basic principles of motivation are proposed by G. Litwin and R. Stringer in *Motivational and Organizational Climate:*

1. All reasonably healthy adults have a considerable reservoir of potential energy.
2. All adults have a number of basic motives or needs which can be mobilized to channel and regulate the flow of this energy.
3. Motives can be arranged in hierarchies which reflect different levels of readiness to engage in particular actions.
4. Whether a motive is actualized depends on the situation.
5. Different motives have different trigger mechanisms.
6. Motives lead to different patterns of behavior.
7. It is possible to orchestrate the different motives that are aroused or actualized.

WHAT BEING MOTIVATED MEANS

Motivation has to do with the forces that maintain and alter the direction, quality, and intensity of behavior. The motivation of a person has three aspects:

1. The direction of behavior—what the person chooses to do when presented with a number of options.
2. The intensity, amplitude, or strength of response once the choice has been made.
3. The persistence of the behavior—how long the person is able to maintain an effort.

What does it mean when you say you are motivated? It may mean that you are all set to go. There is something you are going to do, or at least going to have a good go at. You know what's in it for you if you do, or perhaps if you don't. You are mobilized. You may wonder if you'll run out of adrenalin before getting started. You may even wonder, "Why in the world am I doing this? There must be easier ways of doing things." Then you think, "I'm not backing off. I'm going through with it. Luckily, the perceptual astigmatism of motivation comes into play, and you get tunnel vision about what you are going to do. The alternatives are out of the way—rightly or wrongly, you're off.

Afterward, you may feel somewhat tired. It possibly didn't turn out quite as you expected. Motivation seems to work like a Gestalt completion test; a bit of a circle is missing and you feel you can pull a task, T, together:

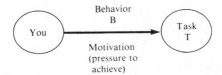

Put another way, your motivation causes you to behave (B) in a way that will achieve the task and get the payoff, P, which can be extrinsic (salary, promotion) or intrinsic (satisfaction of a job well done):

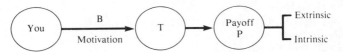

This may work for you, but how do you motivate or energize the people who work with you? What are their values, attitudes, needs, and expectations that you can stimulate (manipulate)?

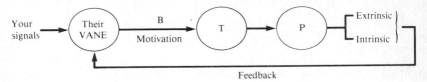

TOPIC 2
Motivation-hygiene theory and job enrichment

Modern managers have found the concept of motivation a natural and fruitful starting point for looking at business behavior. Inherent in this approach is the notion that personality can be thought of as a system of organized drives and that the parts of personality hold together because a change in one part of personality produces a change in other parts.

Central to the concept of personality is the idea of motivation (i.e., behavior instigated by needs and directed toward the goals that can

FIGURE 8–1

cause	generate	to reach	lead to

NEEDS ➝ DRIVES ➝ BEHAVIOR ➝ GOALS ➝ REDUCTION OR RELEASE OF TENSION

satisfy these needs). Figure 8–1 illustrates the motivation sequence. It is widely believed that when people are motivated, they are in a state of tension, and this generates energy. They feel impelled to take some kind of action. Motivation selectively organizes an individual's perception so that learning is structured in a certain direction.

Basically there are two categories of needs:

1. *Physiological needs,* associated with hunger, thirst, warmth, cold, sleep, sex, pain. It is generally assumed that the body regulates its activities in some cybernetic manner to achieve some kind of homeostasis or stable condition wherein action can be taken to correct any imbalance of physiological needs (e.g., a person who is deprived of salt and then is offered a choice of two foods will automatically opt for the food with the greater amount of salt).
2. *Psychogenic needs,* learned by the individual through association with other people. They include: (*a*) the need for affiliation (the need to belong), (*b*) the need for achievement, and (*c*) the need for power (the need to control and dominate others).

A. H. Maslow, in *Motivation and Personality,* classifies human needs into five categories:

1. Physiological needs (e.g., thirst, hunger, sex).
2. Safety needs (e.g., security, order).
3. The need to belong (e.g., identification, love).
4. Esteem needs (e.g., success, self-respect).
5. The need for self-actualization (i.e., need for identity, self-fulfilment).

Maslow's theory is the most widely taught view of motivation in business schools and provides the theoretical framework for much organization theory. He takes the view that a "lower need must be filled before the next higher need can emerge." Once the lower need has been met, it occupies a less important role.

THE MOTIVATION-HYGIENE THEORY

Frederick Herzberg produced in the 1960s a new and exciting theory of motivation which builds on Maslow's work. In his widely read *Work and the Nature of Man,* Herzberg sets out his concept of man's basic needs in his now famous motivation-hygiene (M-H) theory. The two basic propositions of M-H theory are:

1. The factors producing job satisfaction are separate and distinct from those that lead to job dissatisfaction.
2. *a.* The factors that lead to job satisfaction (the motivators) are achievement, recognition, work itself, responsibility, and advancement.
    b. The dissatisfiers (hygiene factors), such as company policy and administration, supervision, interpersonal relations, working conditions, and salary, contribute very little to job satisfaction.

In brief, according to Herzberg, employees feel good about their work when it provides the opportunity for psychological growth within which they can find the fulfilment of self-actualizing needs. A "hygienic" environment, on the other hand, reduces or prevents discontent. As Herzberg points out in *Work and the Nature of Man:*

> To reiterate, mankind has two sets of needs. Think about man twice: once about events that cause him pain, and, secondly, about events that make him happy. Those who seek only to gratify the needs of their animal natures are doomed to live in dreadful anticipation of pain and suffering. This is the fate of those human beings who want to satisfy only their biological needs. But some men have become aware of the advantage humans have over their animal brothers. In addition to the compulsion to avoid pain, the human being has been blessed with the potentiality to achieve happiness. And, as I hope I have demonstrated, man can be happy only by seeking to satisfy both his animal need to avoid pain and his human need to grow psychologically.

Table 8–1 shows how Herzberg's factors can be compared to those of Maslow and to Douglas McGregor's Theory X and Theory Y (see Chapter 3).

TABLE 8–1

Maslow	Herzberg	McGregor
Physiological needs Safety needs	Hygiene factors	Theory X
The need to belong Esteem needs The need for self-actualization	Motivators	Theory Y

Herzberg's research method

Herzberg's research technique is based on the critical-incident technique and uses interviewing as its method. Subjects interviewed were asked what job events had occurred in their work that had led to their extreme satisfaction or extreme dissatisfaction. The findings are graphed in Figure 8–2.

FIGURE 8–2
Comparison of satisfiers and dissatisfiers

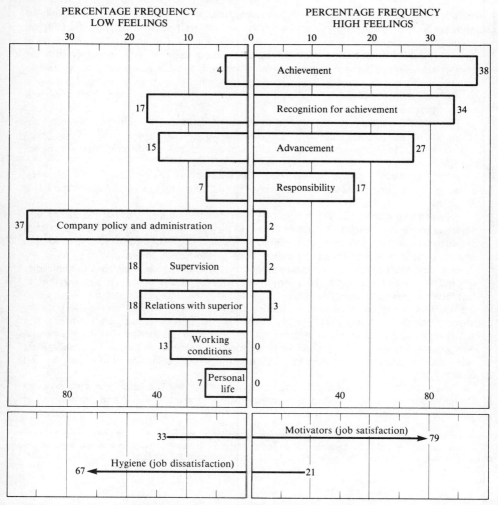

Source: Data on a survey of Pittsburgh accountants from Frederick Herzberg, Bernard Mausner, and Barbara Snyderman, *The Motivation to Work* (New York: John Wiley & Sons, 1959).

Both the research technique and M-H theory as a whole have been severely criticized (see Box 8–1). The concept of self-actualization is not an entirely happy one; for the shop-floor operative it is almost meaningless, and for top management it is almost an act of faith. It is as well to bear in mind that academics, who place considerable value on autonomy and inner direction, have an obsession about making work meaningful. The notion that it is possible for human beings to realize

Box 8–1: The facade of the dual-factor theory

Robert J. House and Lawrence A. Wigdor have reviewed the evidence on the validity of Herzberg's dual-factor theory of job satisfaction and motivation. The approximately 40 studies they reviewed criticize the theory on four grounds. The first is that the theory is methodologically bound. The critical-incident method used by Herzberg recounts extremely satisfying and dissatisfying job events. When things are going well people tend to take the credit, but they protect their self-images when things go poorly by blaming failures on the environment. Whenever the critical-incident method is employed, the results will be an artifact of the method.

The second criticism is also related to research methodology. The respondents' descriptions of their previous behavior was evaluated by a rater, which required an uncontrolled evaluation. Rater contamination of the dimensions derived could easily have occurred.

A third criticism is that no measure of overall satisfaction was employed in the research on which the theory is based. A person may dislike a part of a job yet still think the job is acceptable.

A fourth major criticism which might be leveled is the inconsistency of the theory with previous research. Situational variables seem to play an important role in any relationship between satisfaction and productivity. Further research is needed to be able to predict in what situations worker satisfaction will produce greater productivity.

In a secondary analysis of Herzberg's data, House and Wigdor show results contradictory to the results presented by Herzberg in *Work and the Nature of Man*. It is shown that, in fact, achievement and recognition are more frequently identified as dissatisfiers than working conditions and relations with a superior. Studies directly testing the Herzberg theory are summarized, and they yield results that for the most part fail to support the theory. The voluminous studies cited show that one factor can cause job satisfaction for one person and job dissatisfaction for another. This result can occur even in the same sample. Also, these studies show that intrinsic job factors are more important to both satisfying and dissatisfying job events.

These results led House and Wigdor to conclude that the two-factor theory is an oversimplification of the relationship between motivation and satisfaction and the sources of job satisfaction and dissatisfaction.

Reference: R. J. House (with Lawrence A. Wigdor), "Herzberg's Dual-Factor Theory of Job Satisfaction and Motivation: A Review of the Evidence and a Criticism," *Personnel Psychology,* vol. 20 (Winter 1967), pp. 369–89.

their true nature through creative work which is its own reward is an exceedingly attractive proposition. Herzberg's scale indicates, however, that management is much more highly motivated in the growth, recognition, and achievement sense than are supervisors, who, in turn, are more highly motivated than shop-floor operatives.

The idea of self-actualization implies that it is possible to design jobs and organizations that are not only compatible with the human personality but which by their very design will allow the complete flowering of individual talent. Herzberg describes the search for such designs as job enrichment.

MAKING JOB ENRICHMENT EFFECTIVE

Behavioral and social scientists and personnel specialists today are excited about the development of new strategies for job enrichment. Behavioral scientists are developing sets of diagnostic techniques for existing jobs and maps for translating the diagnostic results into specific actions to be taken to bring about change.

One such team, made up of J. Richard Hackman, Greg Oldham, Robert Janson, and Kenneth Purdy, has come up with a realistic plan of action for effective job enrichment. In "A New Strategy for Job Enrichment" they asked what makes people get "turned on" to their work. They found that workers who really get a kick out of their jobs consider work to be a lot like play. Three things matter to workers: first, they must see their work as meaningful or worthwhile; second, they must believe they are personally responsible for the outcome of their efforts; third, they must have knowledge of results. When these three conditions are present, employees feel good about themselves when they perform well.

Hackman and his colleagues point to recent research which has identified five core characteristics of jobs which elicit a sense of meaningfulness, awareness of responsibility, and knowledge of results.

1. *Skill variety.* The degree to which the job requires the worker to challenge skills and abilities.
2. *Task identity.* The degree to which the job requires the completion of a whole and identifiable piece of work.
3. *Task significance.* The degree to which the job has a salient impact on the lives of other people.
4. *Autonomy.* The degree to which the job gives the worker freedom, independence, and choice in scheduling work and determining how to carry it out.
5. *Feedback.* The degree to which a worker, in doing a job, gets information about the effectiveness of efforts.

Hackman's team developed a motivating potential score (MPS) as a summary index to measure the amount of motivation in a particular job. Unfortunately, however, everyone is not able to become internally motivated in work, even when the job has very high MPS ratings.

They also developed a diagnostic procedure in the form of a package of instruments to measure, not only the MPS characteristics of jobs, but also the current levels of motivation, satisfaction, and work performance of employees. This strategy of job enrichment was tried out on a project conducted at the Travellers Insurance Companies. One of the experimental work groups was a set of 98 keypunch operators and verifiers for whom rates of output were inadequate, error rates were high, and absenteeism was higher than average. The work was reorganized to make the operators responsible for certain accounts, give them several channels of direct contact with clients, and provide feedback on performance. The operators were allowed to set their own schedules and plan their daily work.

The results were dramatic. Productivity increased, error rates decreased, absenteeism fell off, and worker satisfaction increased. Supervisors were able to change their jobs to spearhead the enrichment effort, since many of the routine supervisory chores were being performed by employees. The actual savings in one year amounted to more than $64,000.

Job enrichment is not always the answer, however, as Box 8–2 shows.

Box 8–2: Identifying unenriched jobs

David Whitsett argues that job enrichment has mistakenly been used as a strategy for solving problems within some organizations when, in fact, it cannot be applied everywhere all of the time. The most common symptoms the job enrichment remedy has been designed to cure are evidence of employee unrest or dissatisfaction in the form of low morale, high turnover, excessive absenteeism, poor productivity, or unacceptable production quality. The application of job enrichment techniques to these problem areas has met with success in many organizations and led to "many enrichment failures and much misdirected activity" in others.

A fundamental condition must exist before enrichment can make meaningful contributions: The organizational structure must provide an opportunity to redesign the job. Also, managers must realize that people can be dissatisfied for many reasons: they can be underpaid, poorly supervised, work in unacceptable conditions, or be bored or uninterested with their assignments. "Since job enrichment is a process for making work more interesting," Whitsett says, "it can help only when the last mentioned reason is the cause of the symptoms."

Whitsett lists three characteristics of a well-designed job. The first relates to the nature of the job; it should be a complete piece of work so that the person performing the task can tell where it begins and where it ends. There should be a receiver or "customer" of the work—a known group affected directly by the task. Second, the jobholder may decide what procedures to use, priorities to take, and methods to use for problem solving. If prescribed methods must be followed and unusual situations turned over to superiors, then the assignment is poorly designed for enrichment. Finally, in a well-designed job, the worker should receive frequent and direct nonsupervisory feedback on performance. This feedback should specify individual contributions as opposed to group praise.

By examining organization charts, work-flow diagrams, training manuals, and job titles, you can discover which jobs cannot be characterized as well designed. However, Whitsett cautions that there must be significant deviation from the criteria in order to make the job eligible for meaningful enrichment. He suggests several conditions in an organization which are clues that the opportunity for enrichment exists: communication units or jobs, "super gurus", overspecialization, and dual reporting relationships.

The presence of special units to handle communication indicates that this function has

Reference: David A. Whitsett, "Where Are Your Unenriched Jobs?" *Harvard Business Review*, January–February 1975.

Possible disadvantages

Job enrichment programs to improve the quality of working life can be surprisingly difficult to implement. For example, Steinberg, a Canadian department store chain, has been introducing changes to allow workers to make more decisions about their work, in order to make their jobs more meaningful, "not ones that could be performed as efficiently by a robot or trained monkey."

These objectives are achieved through union-management committees which define the boundaries of the exercise and monitor its progress. Primary working groups of shop-floor workers, aided by a consultant, set up semiautonomous groups for each cycle of the work. But each worker is responsible for the whole task, not just one part of the job.

---

probably been removed from line jobs. Segregating the communication function of work processors to avoid interrupted work eliminates feedback and gives communicators feedback for work they did not perform. Similarly, quality control functions remove this responsibility from the line worker. The same is true for troubleshooters or expediters; hot-line expediters are not responsible for the initial error promoting complaints, yet they receive feedback on matters over which they have no control. Hence, two poorly designed jobs result.

The existence of super gurus ("Go ask Charlie—he'll tell you how to handle it") within an organization probably indicates that an important part of the decision-making process is lacking for junior members. This clue, Whitsett states, is substantiated by statements reflecting the length of time necessary to "become competent" in a department. If a manager maintains that it takes eight years to become a competent technician, and if in fact one can become a surgeon in that time, the position is not properly defined.

Overspecialization of functions can create an excessive number of job titles. The work may be so fractionalized that employees never experience the sense of accomplishment that comes from finishing a task satisfactorily.

In dual reporting relationships, C, who reports to both A and B, may shift some responsibilities downward to D, E, F, or G, and so on throughout the organization. Unclear divisions of responsibility or overcomplicated work flows may result in duplication of functions or deviation from a worker's defined job. These factors suggest job enrichment is necessary.

The strength of Whitsett's article lies in his belief that every organization afflicted by employee unrest or lack of interest should not undertake job enrichment programs. If there are jobs to be enriched he offers hints as to their discovery, but he cautions that job enrichment is not a cure-all. The enriching changes must be acceptable to the persons involved. Managers must realize that some workers actually prefer highly repetitive tasks. Finally, the environment of the organization must lend itself to enrichment programs. The company may be experiencing a stable environment, or it might be undergoing major changes which would yield opportunities for job redesign. In either case, a key element in job enrichment success is the commitment of management in developing the newly designed work.

Somehow or other, management, the workers, and the unions have to be brought on board. The path-goal theory of motivation can resolve many of the difficulties job enrichment has encountered.

TOPIC 3
The path-goal model of motivation

THE PATH-GOAL MODEL

The more hard-headed organizational psychologists, who believe that behavioral scientists should engage in theoretically relevant empirical research, have come up with the extremely important path-goal (P-G) model. The underlying idea is that people can make choices that reflect their preferences in terms of their utilities.

The P-G concept received its initial thrust from the work of Victor Vroom, an organizational psychologist at Yale. Vroom argues that performance is a multiplicative function of motivation (M) and ability (A):

$$\text{Performance} = f(\text{M,A})$$

Motivation to perform a task can be assumed to vary with (1) the utilities of outcomes associated with the performance of that particular task and (2) the instrumentality (belief that performance and outcome are linked) of performance for the achievement or avoidance of particular outcomes.

In *Work and Motivation,* Vroom defines motivation as "a process governing choices, made by persons or lower organisms, among alternative forms of voluntary activity." This concept of motivation is complex and difficult to grasp. Basically, it is a hypothesis about decision making which is essentially outward looking. The presumption is that people can make intelligent and rational estimates about the consequences of particular choices and how such consequences will affect their own interests. Thus the path-goal model presupposes that people can estimate expectancies (in terms of probabilities that range from 0 to 1) in regard to both whether they can carry through particular tasks and the likelihood that their efforts will be noticed and rewarded accordingly. It is further assumed that they can arrange their preferences in a hierarchy of particular outcomes; that is, each person has a set of utilities on which to base choices. Employees, both superiors and subordinates, are assumed to be aware, at least intuitively, of the logical train presented in Figure 8–3.

Why is this concept so important? Perhaps the best answer is that it avoids the general error of the human relations approach, which puts the cart before the horse by arguing that enhancing human satisfaction always leads to improved task performance. The P-G model gets the horse and cart in the right order by arguing that getting the task right

FIGURE 8–3
The path-goal sequence

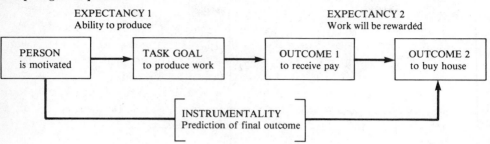

determines human satisfaction. This point can be illustrated by considering some of the advantages of the P-G model in terms of its ability to explain findings which had previously seemed contradictory.

For example, the P-G model can explain why job enrichment programs are not uniformly successful. In "Job Enlargement, Individual Differences, and Worker Responses," Charles Hulin and M. R. Blood found that many city workers have a preference for work which is routine and nonchallenging but is well paid; they do not want to become overinvolved in work. And they believe that overproducing will disassociate them from other members of their work group. Workers from small towns, on the other hand, respond well to job enrichment; they appear to welcome challenging work which promises better pay and the prospect of promotion. This reflects their value identification with the middle classes and presumably with their bosses. What these empirical facts show is that these two groups of workers have different concepts of instrumentality and utility. These same concepts affect attitudes towards pay and performance among managers and professionals, many of whom apparently believe that rewards are unrelated to effort and largely reflect academic qualification and salary at the time of joining the organization.

If such empirical findings are true, management is compelled to adopt a different strategy from that suggested by the human relations approach. In the application of P-G theory, the emphasis must be on carefully investigating what employees' expectancies, utilities, and instrumentalities are; and then, presumably, setting out to change the structure of the situation to provide what management and the workers want.

VROOM'S THEORY OF MOTIVATION

Vroom's theory of motivation, which is much more difficult to grasp then Herzberg's, has scientific validity and has generated a considerable amount of empirical activity since it was published in 1964.

Vroom has taken up the idea of the path-goal hypothesis, which maintains that for a person to be motivated, the task must evoke some of his needs, and the successful completion of the task must be instrumental in reaching his goals, and developed it into a full-blown expectancy theory of motivation. In *Work and Motivation,* he defines motivation as "A process governing choices, made by persons or lower organisms, among alternative forms of voluntary activity."

Implicit in Vroom's theory is the perception of behavior as instrumental for the achievement of some outcomes and the evaluation of the outcomes. In Figure 8–4, the expectancies are the probabilities the person sees, first, of accomplishing the task goal, and, second, of being rewarded for this achievement. Task accomplishment may be high, medium, or low productivity. The first (reward) level of outcomes includes such things as pay, promotion, good working conditions, and job security. The second-level outcomes are the individual's needs,

Box 8–3: An empirical test of Vroom's model

In a 1969 article, J. G. Hunt and J. W. Hill review research on Vroom's model:

Vroom has already shown how his model can integrate many of the empirical findings in the literature on motivation in organizations. However, because it is a relatively recent development, empirical tests of the model itself are just beginning to appear. Here we shall consider one such investigation

[The study by Jay Galbraith and L. L. Cummings, entitled "An Empirical Investigation of the Motivational Determinants of Task Performance,"] utilizes the model to predict the productivity of operative workers. Graphic rating scales were used to measure the instrumentality of performance for five goals—money, fringe benefits, promotion, supervisor's support, and group acceptance. Similar ratings were used for measuring the desirability of each of the goals for the worker. The authors anticipated that a worker's expectation that he could produce at a high level would have a probability of one because the jobs were independent and productivity was a function of the worker's own effort independent of other human or machine pacing. [The accompanying diagram] outlines the research design.

Multiple regression analysis showed that productivity was significantly related positively to the instrumentality-goal interactions for supervisor support and money, and there was an almost significant ($p < .10$) relationship with group acceptance. The other factors did not approach significance and the authors explain this lack of significance in terms of the situational context. That is, fringe benefits were dependent not so much on productivity as on a union/management contract, and promotion was based primarily on seniority. Thus the instrumentality of productivity for the attainment of these goals was low and the model would predict no relationship. The Galbraith and Cummings study thus supports Vroom's contention that motivation is related to productivity in those situations where the acquisition of desired goals is dependent upon the individual's production and not when desired outcomes are contingent on other factors.

Source: J. G. Hunt and J. W. Hill, "The New Look in Motivational Theory for Organizational Research," *Human Organization,* vol. 28 (Summer 1969), pp. 100–109.

FIGURE 8–4
Vroom's model of motivation

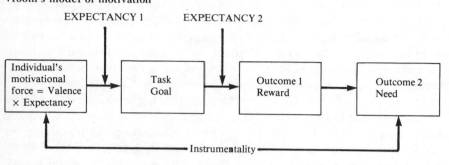

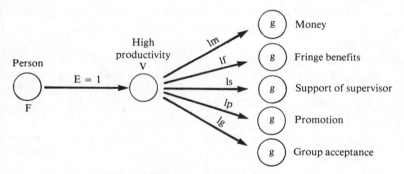

g = Desirability of a particular outcome (rating)
I = Instrumentality of production for particular outcomes (rating of relationship)
E = Expectancy (=1 here because worker sets own pace and is assumed to be capable of high productivity)
V = (Valence) the sum of the cross products of instrumentality and g
F = (Force) expectancy times the valence of productivity
Productivity = Objective measures of amount of production in relation to the production standard

More work must be done before we can make any statements concerning the overall validity of Vroom's model. But the vigor of his formulation, the relative ease of making the concepts operational, and the model's emphasis on individual differences show considerable promise. We are also encouraged by the results of relatively sophisticated studies testing the theory. We believe it is time for those interested in organizational behavior to take a more thoroughly scientific look at this very complex subject of industrial motivation, and Vroom's model seems a big step in that direction.

physical (food, shelter), ego (status, fulfilment), and so on. Vroom's model uses two unusual concepts, valence and instrumentality.

The valence is the strength of an individual's preference for a particular outcome and is related to his concept of utility—how he values a particular outcome. The instrumentality is the individual's perception of the relationship between first-level outcomes (rewards or incentives) and second-level outcomes (needs). He has the second-level outcome in mind (predicts it) from the outset. For example, a highly productive worker may see high productivity as a means of increasing her income (first-level outcome), which in turn is instrumental in achieving improved status (second-level outcome), perhaps by facilitating home improvements. Another worker may be quite happy with his pay and see medium productivity as leading to a first-level outcome of group acceptance, which meets his need to belong, a second-level outcome.

Valence is measured by asking workers to rate important personal goals, such as promotion, pay, and pleasant working conditions, in the order of their desirability. Instrumentality is measured by asking employees to state the relation and direction between a first-level outcome (e.g., pay) and a second-level outcome (e.g., acceptance by the work group).

According to Vroom, instrumentality, like the coefficient of correlation, varies between $+1$ and -1. This means that when the instrumentality is $+1$, a first-level outcome is seen as always leading to a particular second-level outcome, and when the instrumentality is -1, it is seen as never leading to a particular second-level outcome. Vroom, in *Work and Motivation*, defines the valence of the first-level outcome as: "A montonically increasing function of an algebraic sum of the products of the valences of all [second-level] outcomes and his conceptions of its instrumentality for the attainment of the [second-level] outcomes."

The expectancy aspect of Vroom's theory is based on the notion that people have expectations concerning the outcomes that are likely to arise as a result of what they do. Expectancy can vary between 0 (no expectation of relation) and 1 (expectation is certain). Expectancy can thus be expressed as a subjective probability ranging from 0 to 1 (note that it is the subject's perception of probability that is used, not the objective probability). (See Box 8–3.)

In this theory of motivation, it is useful to distinguish between two types of expectancies. The first (Expectancy 1 in Figure 8–4 above) measures the subjective probability of an employee accomplishing a particular task goal. Basically, it reflects an employee's assessment of his own skills in regard to the task in hand. Expectancy 2 describes an employee's expectation as to whether the accomplishment of a particular goal will lead to a particular first-level goal. In his theory of motivation, Vroom ties valence and expectations together by arguing that the force on an individual (his motivation) to exert a given amount of effort is a monotonically increasing function of the algebraic sum of the products of the valence of all first-level outcomes and the strength of his expectancies that each level of performance will be attained by that amount of effort.

TOPIC 4
Job design

JOB DESIGN AND EXPECTANCY THEORY

As one way to motivate employees to more effective performance, changing job design through techniques such as job enlargement or enrichment has often been advocated. Edward E. Lawler has made use of expectancy theory to analyze the effects of such changes and the conditions which determine how they should be applied.

Lawler contends, in "Job Design and Employee Motivation," that job design mainly affects the instrumentality of good performance by clarifying and increasing the rewards. It is less relevant in changing workers' expectancy concerning the amount of effort required to achieve "good" performance. The most powerfully motivating rewards are those that are internally mediated and thus are available immediately when workers feel that their performance has been good. These rewards appeal to high-order needs such as self-esteem, self-actualization, and the use of valued abilities. Externally mediated rewards, such as recognition or pay, require that achievement be noticed and evaluated by other people, and there is generally some perceptual distortion that makes workers feel a discrepancy between achievement and outcome.

The content of the job determines the extent to which employees are able to derive feelings of accomplishment from good performance. Lawler lists three critical characteristics:

1. Employees must be provided with meaningful feedback on their performance.
2. Valued abilities must be utilized in performing the job effectively.
3. Employees must feel they have a high degree of control over the setting of goals and the paths to their attainment.

In designing jobs to incorporate these characteristics, consideration must be given to both their horizontal and vertical dimensions. The horizontal dimension includes the number and variety of the operations an individual performs on the job. The vertical dimension includes the degree to which the jobholder controls the planning and execution of the job and participates in the setting of organization policies. Horizontal enlargement is desirable mainly to provide the worker with feedback through the production of something approximating a finished product, while vertical enlargement provides some control over the work environment. However, this control is most effective if it relates directly to the work process rather than to general company goals. Neither vertical nor horizontal enlargement ensures that employees will be able to utilize valued abilities. This and the possession of high-order needs are variables which may be quite different in any given situation.

Lawler points out that since the motivational effects of job enlargement are largely based on intrinsic factors, it is reasonable to expect that the worker's increased effort will be mainly directed toward achieving higher quality production. It may also be necessary to reduce the division of labor and the degree to which machinery can be utilized. It is not surprising, then, that heightened motivation is manifested not in greater quantity of output but rather in better quality and increased job satisfaction.

DEVELOPING A MOTIVATING WORK CLIMATE

Human relations research focuses on the identification of the factors that generate a motivating work climate. A motivating work climate is a work situation in which important rewards are perceived to be tied to work performance.

At one time managers, following the lead of behavioral scientists, widely believed that all employees are motivated by a desire for achievement and growth. Now they recognize that increases in pay, especially through incentives, can have dysfunctional effects. Employees beat the bonus system, for example, by goldbricking or reporting false data. As Lawler points out in his article "Developing a Motivating Work Climate," "Satisfaction, like motivation, can be influenced by rewards, but in a different way; basically, the more employees value their rewards, the more satisfied they are likely to be."

Managers must begin again the business of designing jobs in a way that ensures that there is a necessary relation between job design and reward systems. Because human needs are a personal matter, reward systems should be designed to suit the particular needs of each individual. For this reason many high-technology companies, such as the systems group of TRW, are experimenting with cafeteria-style fringe benefits, whereby employees can choose the particular rewards they value most. New employees need realistic job previews so they do not feel they were misled by a too-optimistic job description.

In the systems approach, no one way of job design is always correct. Lawler says, in the article cited above:

. . . An interesting example of how this can be done is provided by the approach used at an electronics plant where management learned that many workers did not like their jobs and were not motivated by assembly-line work. The company offered employees the option of remaining on the line or switching to an enriched job that involved assembling the entire product. About 50 percent switched, and the company ended up building its products on both an assembly-line and individual-build basis.

To some, this decision may appear to be silly because "obviously" one approach must be best and therefore should be used by all. From a motivational point of view, however, neither approach was best for all, and it made sense to that management to use both.

The conclusion is that there is no simple relation between job satisfaction and performance (see Box 8–4).

ox 8–4: The satisfaction causes performance issue

A widely held belief of human relations theory is that improving job satisfaction directly improves performance. Or, to put it another way, improving employee morale cuts down turnover and absenteeism and increases production. The Hawthorne studies are frequently cited as evidence in support of this proposition.

The current view is that satisfaction is not related to performance or, if it is, the correlation is very small. Some statistically oriented psychologists, for example, believe that a low but consistent relationship exists. The question is why job satisfaction is such an important variable. Probably the most important reason is that there is evidence to suggest that high job satisfaction reduces absenteeism and turnover.

In path-goal theory terms, it can be argued that the satisfied individual is motivated to work where her or his important personal needs are met. Edward Lawler and Lyman Porter say, in "The Effect of Performance on Job Satisfaction":

> It well may be that a high general level of satisfaction of needs like self-actualization may be a sign of organization effectiveness. Such a level of satisfaction would indicate, for instance, that most employees have interesting and involving jobs and that they probably are performing them well. One of the obvious advantages of providing employees with intrinsically interesting jobs is that good performance is rewarding in and of itself. Furthermore, being rewarded for good performance is likely to encourage further good performance.

TOPIC 5
Learning and motivation

All theories of motivation exploit or depend on the basic principles of human learning. Learning is such a common phenomenon that most executives take it for granted. In the broadest terms, learning refers to the development and modification of behavior to get somewhere or do something.

In most basic learning situations the learning process can be considered in terms of the linking of a particular stimulus to a particular response (see Chapter 9). The stimulus-response model popularized in behavioral technology by B. F. Skinner traced this concept back to Ivan Pavlov's Nobel Prize studies on the conditioned reflex. Pavlov showed that a dog which would salivate when food was presented and a bell was rung would become conditioned to salivate upon hearing the bell, though no food was presented. Pavlov also introduced the concept of reinforcement, which concerns the reward or punishment which follows a particular response. Positive reinforcement refers to rewarding, and negative reinforcement to punishing, conditions. A reinforcer may be thought of as any object or event that has the effect of increasing the strength of the response.

FACTORS AFFECTING LEARNING

The law of effect and the law of exercise

It is widely assumed that learning does not take place in the absence of motivation. Many experiments in the psychology of learning are being directed at determining the effects of different motives on the degree, rate, or amount of learning. Skinner coined the term *operant conditioning* to refer to the process of how the organism operates on the environment in order to get a reward. The word *operant* emphasizes the idea that the behavior operates on the environment to produce consequences.

The law of effect states that rewarded behavior is retained and punished behavior is dropped. This idea is widely used in explaining human learning. People who are striving to modify their behavior, and who make what is regarded as a positive adjustment, are given positive feedback, or a reinforcement, which facilitates learning. Those who make a negative adjustment may be denied positive feedback and may well receive some form of negative sanction which inhibits further performance of a maladjustive act.

Knowledge of results is an important factor in the learning process, and the timing of the feedback of information is extremely important if the learning is to be effective. For example, an infantryman learning to shoot has to know immediately after he fires where his shot fell in the target area. Given this kind of feedback data, he is in a better position to modify his behavior accordingly.

Knowledge of results also plays an important part in social learning. E. E. Smith and S. S. Knight, in "Effects of Feedback on Insight and Problem-Solving Efficiency in Training Groups," report that management trainees who met on a daily basis in small syndicates and reviewed one another's managerial styles showed a greater increase in self-insight regarding their roles as leaders, and they also apparently improved in problem solving. Knowledge of results is the most common, probably the most important, single source of reinforcement for the learner.

Closely linked to the law of effect is the law of exercise, which argues that the more frequently one is placed in a learning situation, the more effective the learning will be.

Relative economy

Relative economy in learning is concerned with the best procedures for developing efficiency. For example, how should effort in learning be distributed? Should people practice steadily until they have mastered a skill, or should they distribute the practice period, taking breaks in between? The research evidence suggests that over a wide range of situations, distributed practice is more effective than massed practice.

Whole versus part

A great deal of work has been done in the psychology of learning to decide whether learning a whole job is superior to breaking the job into parts and learning the parts. In parts learning, the individual is not only required to learn each individual part but must be able to combine the separate parts so that the whole performance can be accomplished. No overall conclusion has been reached in this field.

Learning curves

An extremely useful learning concept which is valid for a wide range of situations is the learning curve, a diagrammatic presentation of the amount learned in relation to time. A typical learning curve will show on the y-axis the amount learned and on the x-axis the passage of time. Figure 8–5 represents a generalized learning curve, which shows the extent to which the rate of learning increases or decreases with practice.

Initial spurt

There are certain general characteristics of learning curves. For example, at the beginning the rate of learning frequently shows a spurt. Usually the graph levels off at some stage, indicating that maximum performance has been achieved. Apparently at the beginning of the learning process, the subject is very highly motivated and seems to exhibit a significant surge of effort. Many experienced trainers exploit

FIGURE 8–5
Diagram of a generalized learning curve

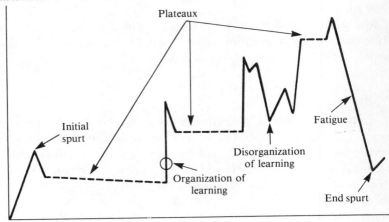

Amount learned

Plateaux

Initial spurt

Fatigue

Disorganization of learning

Organization of learning

End spurt

Time

this initial spurt by selecting the most important items to be communicated and presenting them as a package to the students at the beginning of the training unit. In many ways it is possible to exemplify the initial spurt with the aphorism "The first step is the best step."

Learning plateau

A common characteristic of the learning curve is the learning plateau. At some point in the learning process there is usually a flattening off in terms of improvement, a plateau. Frequently the process of learning is marked by discontinuities and involves escalating from one plateau to another. Most learners are only too aware of the experience of finding themselves on a plateau, which manifests itself in the feeling that they are never going to get anywhere.

Jumping from one plateau to another is called organization of learning. Organization of learning is achieved when the learner discovers a new and more effective method of performing particular tasks. For example, in learning to drive—the escalation is achieved when the trainee discovers it is possible to locate the gearshift lever by kinesthetic feedback, rather than by visually searching for the stick. Much the same escalation takes place with more academic subjects—for example, in mathematics, the student learns to apply calculus in dealing with the problems of business.

Disorganization of learning is an actual falloff in performance. This falloff or disorganization frequently arises when the subject has to choose (though frequently not consciously aware of the choice) between alternative methods of tackling a task.

End spurt

Another aspect of the generalized learning curve is the factor of fatigue. In the end spurt, when the subject knows the training session is coming to an end there appears to be a brief resurgence of interest and effort. After-dinner speakers may exploit this by prefacing the last quarter of an address with the remark "finally" followed by "to sum up," then "lastly," followed by "my penultimate point is . . . ," and then "before I sit down. . . ."

The new training technology

A revolution in educational methods can be expected as college campuses absorb new technologies such as programmed learning (PL), computer-assisted learning (CAL), and video-tape recording (VTR). The Carnegie Commission on Higher Education estimates that within the next three decades between 10 and 20 percent of campus instruction and 50 percent of off-campus education will be carried out by television, PL, CAL, and the use of cassettes and other electronic devices. This projected use of electronic resources for education has been termed "the fourth revolution."

TOPIC 6
What every manager should know about motivation

WHAT MAKES PEOPLE GO?

The most important thing a manager should know about motivation is that at the bottom of every problem are people. And you cannot get things done unless you have some idea of what makes people go. The contingency model of motivation as a system is shown in Figure 8–6.

The S-R model and behavior modification

The first thing a manager ought to keep in mind is that people are extremely good at adaptive behavior and at learning things that increase their chances of survival. This means having an insight both into what behaviors are desirable and what reinforcements will facilitate their emergence; knowing something about the work of B. F. Skinner and his ideas on behavior modification is helpful in this respect (see Chapter 9). Behavior modification as a means of engineering

FIGURE 8–6
Motivation as a system

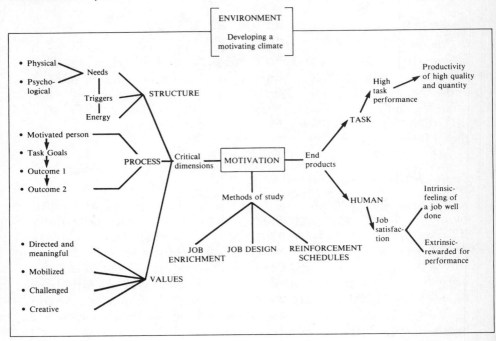

behavior to improve performance in business situations is being tried by a number of American firms, including AT&T, Ford, and United Airlines. When used by the "wrong" people to produce "wrong" kinds of behaviors, behavior modification can be dangerous. Nevertheless, the S-R concept is useful and can provide an important conceptual base for improving performance at work.

The S-O-R model, perception, and the VANE

A more attractive model for most executives is the S-O-R model, which emphasizes the idea of "feelingful awareness." This means that a person's perception is influenced by his or her VANE: values, attitudes, needs, and expectations (see Chapter 5). Gestalt psychologists have set out the laws of perception:

1. The whole is more than the sum of the parts.
2. Perception is in fact organized according to certain principles, (a) proximity, (b) similarity, and (c) "good fit".
3. What a person perceives is influenced by his values, attitudes, needs, and expectations.

A. H. Maslow has developed a hierarchy of needs which, going from the lower to the higher, moves from physiological, safety, love, esteem, and ego, to self-actualization. Frederick Herzberg, building on Maslow's work, has developed a motivation-hygiene theory which is based on the proposition that it is necessary to look twice at motivation. The first look is to find out what is causing the dissatisfaction so it can be remedied by working on the hygiene aspects, as by providing improved working conditions, job security, or salary increases. The second look is to improve job satisfaction by introducing the factors of motivation, for example, achievement, advancement, and recognition. Although Herzberg's theory has been widely criticized by academics, it is widely used as a means of job enrichment.

The P-G model and performance

The path-goal model is widely used by academics, and to a lesser extent by executives, as a conceptual frame of reference. In this approach, the executive's job is to specify the path-goals of subordinates, spelling out expectancies, utilities, and instrumentalities. Using path-goal theory, E. E. Lawler has shown that all people do not respond in the same way to job enrichment, and that individuals differ not only in their goal orientations but in the abilities and attitudes they bring to work.

The findings on motivation of managers can be summarized as follows:

1. Motivation is highest among top managers.
2. Highly motivated managers prefer open-minded, approachable bosses.
3. Money provides positive motivation for managers.
4. Executives overestimate the pay of their subordinates, underestimate the pay of their bosses, and generally feel underpaid.
5. Managers are more dominant than others, interested in directing others, and prefers independent activities.
6. All managers do not have the same utility function.
7. Managers score higher on initiative tests than the general population.
8. Managers place a high value on self-actualization and autonomy needs and opportunities for personal growth.

Existentialism and a healthy personality

The existential concept has turned out to be an extremely useful notion of personality for the executive because it recognizes two contending forces, intractability and potentiality. Existentialism directs the executive to discover a potential for personal growth and development and focuses on the notion of will. To the existentialist will and decision represent the core elements of personality. No matter the forces structuring the choices, the individual still has choices. Ultimately, these choices involve issues of identity. When the crunch comes, as the cliché says, the executive faces the choice of carrying on with the caricature of self or breaking out of a frozen role.

In the existential approach, a person is seen as an open system, trading with the environment. Identity and self-evaluation are critical considerations.

REVIEW AND RESEARCH

1. Define motivation. What are the basic principles of motivation?
2. Explain the motivation-hygiene theory. Critically evaluate this theory. (See Box 8–1.)
3. How can job enrichment be made effective?
4. Describe the path-goal model of motivation.
5. How can job design be improved using expectancy theory?
6. List with examples the principles of learning.
7. Draw from memory the learning curve.
8. Compare and contrast the S-R, S-O-R, P-G, and existentialist models.
9. How can you motivate subordinates effectively?
10. How can you motivate superiors effectively?
11. *a.* What can be learned about organizational growth in high-technology industries from the brief look at the rapid development of Advanced Micro Devices at the beginning of the chapter?
    b. What comments can you make about the personal motivation of Jerry Sanders?

GLOSSARY OF TERMS

Expectancy theory. Motivation model based on the notion that individuals have expectations concerning the outcomes likely to occur as the result of what they do and that they have preferences among outcomes. Vroom's model incorporates expectancies (probabilities of outcomes), valence (strength of preference for a particular outcome), and instrumentality (prediction that "reward" outcomes will lead to "need-fulfilling" outcomes).

Law of effect. The principle that rewarded behavior is retained and punished behavior is dropped.

Law of exercise. The principle that the more frequently one is placed in a learning situation, the more effective the learning will be.

Learning. The development and modification of the tendencies that govern psychological functions. In its simplest form it is the development of the ability to link a particular stimulus to a particular response.

Learning curve. A diagrammatic presentation of the amount learned in relation to time. A typical learning curve will show on the y-axis the amount learned and on the x-axis the passage of time.

Motivation. Process whereby needs instigate behavior directed toward the goals that can satisfy those needs. Motivation has three aspects: (*a*) direction of behavior (choice among options); (*b*) intensity, amplitude, or strength of response; and (*c*) persistence of the behavior.

Motivation-hygiene (M-H) theory. The two basic and fundamental propositions are:

1. The factors producing job satisfaction are separate and distinct from those that lead to job dissatisfaction.

2. (*a*) The factors that lead to job satisfaction (the motivators) are achievement, recognition, work itself, responsibility, and advancement. (*b*) The dissatisfiers (hygiene factors), such as company policy and administration, supervision, interpersonal relations, working conditions, and salary, contribute very little to job satisfaction.

Needs. Maslow's hierarchy of needs classifies human needs into five categories:

1. Physiological needs; e.g., thirst, hunger, sex.
2. Safety needs; e.g., security and order.
3. The need to belong; e.g., identification and love.
4. Esteem needs; e.g., success, self-respect.
5. Need for self-actualization; i.e., need for identity and self-fulfilment.

DEBATE: Is there a work ethic crisis?

There is a continuing debate in the United States on the issues of whether people in fact really want to work and really find work satisfying. Studs Terkel begins his book *Working* by noting that work by its nature inevitably involves violence—not only industrial accidents and shouting matches, but nervous breakdowns and kicking dogs. Merely surviving is in some cases a major achievement.

Yes, there is

J. Richard Hackman, in "The Design of Work in the 1980s," summarizes the evidence and supports the proposal that there is a work ethic crisis.

Considerable evidence can be marshaled in support of this contention. Perhaps most widely publicized is a project sponsored by the Ford Foundation to test how satisfied U.S. automobile workers would be working on highly "enriched" team assembly jobs in a Swedish automo-

bile plant. Six Detroit auto workers were flown to Sweden and spent a
month working as engine assemblers in a Saab plant. At the end of the
month, five of the six workers reported that they preferred the traditional
U.S. assembly line. As one put it: "If I've got to bust my ass to be
meaningful, forget it; I'd rather be monotonous." Arthur Weinberg, a
Cornell labor relations expert who accompanied the six workers to Sweden, summarized their negative reactions:

" . . . They felt it was a deprivation of their freedom and it was a
more burdenosme task which required more effort which was more tedi-
ous and stressful. They preferred the freedom the assembly line allowed
them, the ability to think their own thoughts, to talk to other workers, sing
or dance on the assembly line, which you can't do at Saab. There is a
freedom allowed on the assembly line not possible in more complex
work. The simplified task allows a different kind of freedom. The American workers generally reacted negatively to doing more than one task.
They were not accustomed to it and they didn't like it."

No, there isn't

According to a 1978 Conference Board Report, however, most
Americans were happy with their jobs. The greatest satisfaction was
reported among white-collar workers between the ages of 25 and 44,
and job dissatisfaction was most marked among people under 25 and in
blue-collar occupations. The study of 5,000 U.S. families found 59
percent were "satisfied" with their jobs and 28 percent were "very
satisfied". Only 10 percent said they were "dissatisfied," and 3 percent
"very dissatisfied".

"Critics stressing the dull, impersonal nature of much modern work
may have some valid points, but latest survey findings suggest that
their views are considerably overstated," said Fabian Linden, director
of consumer research at the Conference Board. "Besides money, there
are obviously many compensatory benefits in today's work environment." Strong community spirit, scope for fooling around at work,
involvement, pleasant physical working conditions, and good pay
scales make Americans content with their jobs, and job dissatisfaction
lessens with age.

A PESSIMISTIC ANSWER

Hackman argues that there are persuasive arguments on both sides
of the question. He identifies two conclusions:

Conclusion One: Many individuals are presently underutilized and
underchallenged at work.
Conclusion Two: People are much more adaptable than we often
assume.

Hackman says there are two choices for the 1980s. Route one to
managing people is to fit jobs to people; Route two is to fit people to

the jobs. Hackman concludes, pessimistically, that we will continue down Route two. One reason is that modern technology is so good that machines will be made "people proof" (that is, work will be designed so that people cannot screw it up). Second, personnel psychologists will extend their considerable skills in selecting the right person for the job.

Hackman maintains that where job enrichment has been a success in a pilot project, the idea has not percolated into other parts of the organization. He points out that "there are very few instances in which even a highly successful program has been diffused throughout the larger organization in which it was developed—let alone from organization to organization—with the same success." His final conclusion is:

> As should be apparent from my remarks, I am in favor of the ideas and aspirations of Route One. But as may also be apparent, I suspect that the pessimistic outlook may have validity, that it may be too late to change directions, and that my description of Route Two will turn out to be a good characterization of what work will be like in the 1980s and beyond.

Question

Do you believe there is a work ethic crisis?

INCIDENT

The new workers*

Three young workers, aged twenty and twenty-one, were hired to clean offices at night. One evening the foreman caught one of the young janitors (who went to school during the day) doing his homework; another was reading the paper and the third was asleep with his feet up on a desk. The foreman exploded and gave them a written warning. The workers filed a grievance protesting the warnings: "We cleaned all the offices in five hours by really hustling and who the hell should get upset because we then did our own thing." One young worker said, "At school during study period I get my studies done in less than the hour and no one bugs me when I do other things for the rest of the time. We cleaned all those offices in five hours instead of eight. What more do they want?"

The union steward said he tried hard to understand what they were saying: "But the company has the right to expect eight hours work for eight hours pay. I finally got the kids to understand by taking them outside and telling them that if they got the work finished in five hours, then the company would either give them more work, or get rid of one

---

* Reprinted from John Haynes, "The New Workers: A Report," *New Generation*, vol. 52 (Fall 1972).

of them. They're spacing it out nicely now and everyone's happy," he said, satisfied to have settled the grievance within the understood rules.

Question

    If you were the personnel manager in this particular organization and you were asked to counsel the foreman, what guidance would you give him?

DIAGRAM SUMMARY OF CHAPTER 9

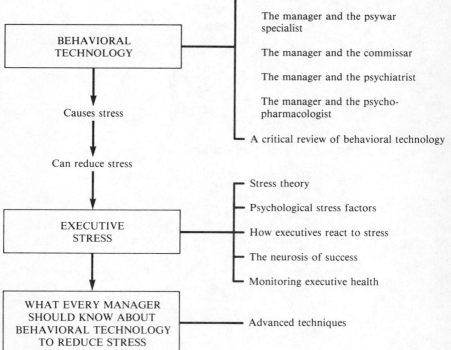

BEHAVIORAL
TECHNOLOGY

The manager and the S-R
technologist: B. F. Skinner

Behavioral technologists at work:

The manager and the psywar
specialist

The manager and the commissar

The manager and the psychiatrist

The manager and the psycho-
pharmacologist

A critical review of behavioral technology

Causes stress

Can reduce stress

EXECUTIVE
STRESS

Stress theory

Psychological stress factors

How executives react to stress

The neurosis of success

Monitoring executive health

WHAT EVERY MANAGER
SHOULD KNOW ABOUT
BEHAVIORAL TECHNOLOGY
TO REDUCE STRESS

Advanced techniques

9

How behavioral technology makes and breaks stress

POSITIVE REINFORCEMENT AT EMERY AIR FREIGHT

Emery Air Freight has made extensive use of positive reinforcement as a means of improving business efficiency. By encouraging employees to increase the use of containers, Emery has realized an annual savings of $650,000. The company also has been criticized for manipulating its employees, however. Edward J. Feeney, Vice President, Systems, counters this criticism in an interview published in *Organizational Dynamics* (Winter 1973):

> Actually, the charge that you're manipulating people when you use positive reinforcement—I prefer myself to say that you're shaping their behavior—is a hollow one to start with. People in business manipulate their employees all the time—otherwise they would go bankrupt. The only questions are, how effective are you as a manipulator and what ends do you further with your manipulation? Our end is improved performance, and we've been damned effective in getting it.

Emery has made selective use of positive reinforcement (PR), but before it is applied, a company audit ascertains where the best potential for profit payoff exists. At Emery, PR is fully operative in three areas: sales and sales training, operations, and containerized shipments.

The technique emphasizes praise and recognition and avoids censure. The article notes:

> Of all forms of praise, the most effective, according to Feeney, is praise for the job well done—expressed in quantitative terms. Not "Keep up the fair work, Murray," as shown on TV, or even "Great going, Joe—

keep it up," but "Joe, I liked the ingenuity you showed just now getting those crates into that container. You're running pretty consistently at 98 percent of standard. And after watching you, I can understand why."

In bestowing praise Emery follows B. F. Skinner fairly closely. For example,

> Feeney tells a story that illustrates both the necessity for continuous feedback and the way in which previous consequences determine present behavior. Emery requires any employee who receives a package damaged during shipment from an airline to fill out a fairly time-consuming form. At a certain installation, he pointed out to the boss that without feedback and P.R. the employees wouldn't bother—the reinforcements they got from filling out the form were all negative. The paperwork was time-consuming and boring, they were likely to get some flack from airline representatives who would in their own good time find ways of hitting back, they were taking time from their number one priority—getting the shipment delivered on time. A check revealed that no damage forms were turned in. However, a physical check of cartons received showed several damaged, one with a hole punched in the side, another that looked as if a hand had reached into the top and taken something out, etc. Feeney feels that his colleague, at this point, got the message. The only way around the problem of getting the damage slips filled out was to (1) specify the desired behavior—i.e., set the standard; (2) require the employee to provide continuous feedback—keep daily records on how many cartons were damaged and submit them to his supervisor; and (3) whenever feasible, positively reinforce the behavior—when the feedback showed that it was justified.

Emery's use of PR behavior modification has improved performance. But it is necessary to treat the experiment with some reservations because Emery's undeniably successful method cannot be applied to all companies. Emery has been particularly careful not to set individuals or groups competing against one another.

A few other companies, including Michigan Bell Telephone and Ford Motor Company, have experimented with positive feedback. A company considering PR ought to consider it with other alternatives for improving productivity, such as job enrichment and job enlargement, organizational development, the Scanlon Plan, and so on.

Despite the reputation it has with businessmen because of its association with Skinner's behavior modification techniques, PR has much to recommend it. As the editor of *Organizational Dynamics* points out:

> Feeney is probably correct: A lot of managers practice positive reinforcement without knowing it. He cites, for example, Vince Lombardi, who provided endless feedback on performance to his players and who after a really bad defeat never uttered a word of criticism in the locker room. True, but until more organizations consciously and systematically

apply positive reinforcement, it will never get the recognition that it appears to deserve.

BEHAVIORAL TECHNOLOGY: MAKING PEOPLE BEHAVE

How can you get people to believe, feel, and act as you want them to? One answer is through behavioral technology, the applied science of behavior control. It is based on the research of psychologists, pharmacologists, psychiatrists, and sociologists, fleshed out by the experiences of corporate officials, the practical expertise of the interrogator who uses brainwashing techniques, and the insights of the new wave of organizational development (OD) consultants.

Quite rightly, many people have negative ideas about behavioral technology; often it is seen as Faustian, the behavioral scientist's soul having been sold to the devil in exchange for the power to manipulate people's minds. The modern Machiavellis of the behavioral sciences have developed techniques which go well beyond such well-established methods in brainwashing and hypnosis; their exciting new repertoire includes genetic engineering and electrical and chemical stimulation of the brain (ESB and CSB, respectively). Some behavioral scientists—influenced by the superior performance of drugs over any other form of psychotherapy in dramatically shortening the average stay in mental hospitals in the 1960s—are looking for a "peace pill" to control the aggression of corporate and political leaders.

Figure 9–1 provides an overview of the various levels of behavioral technology—the ways in which behavioral scientists try to affect people, and the concept or model they have in mind as they do so.

One of the many methods of control utilizing the S-R concept we will look at in this chapter is behavioral modification, which regulates behavior through the use of rewards and punishments. It is possible, for example, to modify deviant sexual behavior such as fetishism, homosexuality, and transvestism through the contiguous pairing of a primary aversive stimulus (such as an electric shock) with a stimulus eliciting the undesirable response or symptom. Behavior modification can be used effectively with groups as well as individuals; it has been used in the form of a token economy to regulate the behavior of an entire ward of psychiatric patients. Patients who take care of their personal needs, attend scheduled activities, and help in the ward are rewarded with tokens which can be used to get cigarettes, money, and passes for watching television; patients who do not are punished with fines (removal of tokens).

Behavioral modification may sound like the ordinary work situation, where you get paid for doing what the boss wants. In fact, a great deal of the experimentation carried out in the behavioral sciences uses a paradigm which in effect creates an employment relation between the

FIGURE 9–1
Levels of behavioral technology and models of man

	TECHNOLOGY	MODEL
Individuals	Genetic engineering	A person is a complex of DNA molecules
	Electrical and chemical stimulation of the brain (ESB, CSB)	A person is a cluster of neurons
	Stimulus-response (S-R)	A person is a vending machine
	Stimulus-organism-response (S-O-R)	A person is a dynamic integration of values, attitudes, needs, expectations, self-concept, and perception
	Path-goal (P-G)	An internal cognitive map helps the person measure utility and probability of paths (means) and goals (ends)
Groups	T groups	The world is a microcosm of the group, and vice versa
Organizations	Organizational development (OD)	The person is an element in the system
	Organizational gestalt	Fusion of the system and existential man

experimenter and the subjects. In "Some Unintended Consequences of Rigorous Research," Chris Argyris argues that a good deal of behavioral research creates a Theory X (master-servant) relationship between the researcher and the subject, with predictable consequences for the latter's behavior.

A surprising number of both American and European senior corporate managers are familiar with basic behavioral science ideas. The success of magazines such as *Psychology Today* and *New Society* is to a large extent a reflection of this interest. Other magazines such as *Time, Newsweek,* and *Playboy* devote a significant amount of space to behavior. Many books and movies also reflect this interest. An excellent example of a film of this genre is *A Clockwork Orange,* directed by Stanley Kubrick of *Dr. Strangelove* fame. ("How I learned to stop worrying and love the bomb"). Based on Anthony Burgess's book, *Clockwork Orange* portrays a young punk (Alex) who is given to a sadistic satyriasis which is triggered by the music of Beethoven. He lands in jail, the behavioral technologists do their thing, and Alex is cured both of his violent excesses and his love of Beethoven, but in the process he is turned into a robot. Although his slavishly conditioned aversion to violence renders him unfit to survive in the chilling society Burgess sees just over the horizon, he is "saved" when he returns to his previous savage self. What interests the executive in such movies is the ability of behavioral technology to dramatically transform behavior and attitudes.

STRESS DEFINED AND REFINED

Behavioral technology can also create or mitigate stress. The subject of stress has become a major focus of research for behavioral scientists, one of whom, Joseph E. McGrath, came up with this interesting definition in *Social and Psychological Factors in Stress:* "Stress is defined as the anticipation of inability to respond adequately (or at a reasonable cost) to perceived demand, accompanied by anticipation of negative consequences for inadequate response."

Figure 9–2 shows some stress factors from a stimulus-organism-

FIGURE 9–2
Input-output model of stress

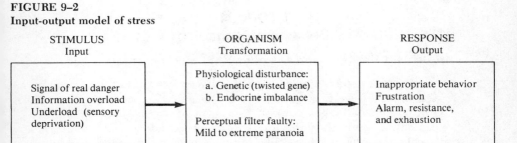

STIMULUS Input	ORGANISM Transformation	RESPONSE Output
Signal of real danger Information overload Underload (sensory deprivation)	Physiological disturbance: a. Genetic (twisted gene) b. Endocrine imbalance Perceptual filter faulty: Mild to extreme paranoia	Inappropriate behavior Frustration Alarm, resistance, and exhaustion

response (S-O-R) view, according to input, transformation, and output. Stress may arise, of course, from the perception of real danger in the environment. Stress may also be generated by information overload or underload. The personality may process information through a faulty perceptual filter which transforms a neutral environment into a hostile one; or it may suffer from a physiological disturbance created by a faulty gene or an endocrine imbalance. The behavior elicited may be inappropriate. Frustration is highly likely. Hans Seyle points out, in *The Stress of Life,* that when responses to stress are required too often and in increasing quantities, the probable result is alarm, resistance, and eventually exhaustion.

One of the curious things about stress is that, in small quantities, stress improves performance. But as the stress increases, performance degradation in terms of psychomotor skills sets in. To measure the effect of stress on performance, speed, accuracy, number of errors, and error tolerance are measured.

The subject of stress has been a major area of inquiry since the shell-shocked casualties of World War I startled the military into studying the problem. During World War II, with battle fatigue affecting 1 soldier in 10, the investments in stress research increased rapidly, especially in regard to the problems of combat pilots who faced a three-dimensional form of high-speed stress that had never been seen before. During World War II, Allied flight surgeons developed rules of thumb which took into consideration information about personality, separation anxiety, and guilt processes, as well as such physical factors as weight loss, fatigue, and so on. Such personal factors were weighed against the importance of the mission and the chances of survival.

Stress is best thought of as a state of the total organism under difficult or extenuating circumstances. Capacity to withstand stress is a function of (1) the individual, (2) the situation, and (3) the social context.

TOPIC 1
Behavioral technology

In *Beyond Freedom and Dignity*, B. F. Skinner argues:

> What we need is a technology of behavior. We could solve our problems quickly enough if we could adjust the growth of the world's population as precisely as we adjust the course of a spaceship, or improve agriculture and industry with some of the confidence with which we accelerate high-energy particles, or move toward a peaceful world with something like the steady progress with which physics has approached absolute zero (even though both remain presumably out of reach). But a behavioral technology comparable in power and precision to physical and biological technology is lacking, and those who do not find the very possibility ridiculous are more likely to be frightened by it than reassured. That is how far we are from "understanding human issues" in the sense in which physics and biology understand their fields, and how far we are from preventing the catastrophe toward which the world seems to be inexorably moving.

Skinner is suggesting the application of the science of behavior to a design for society. Managers have made considerable progress in exploiting behavioral technology as a means of controlling what is happening at the workplace.

The classical theory of management employs an S-R model which is the basis both of aversion therapy and behavior modification. Aversion therapy changes behavior through the use of unpleasant or aversive stimuli. Skinner has developed an S-R technology which has been applied in various areas: in education, to develop teaching machines which program learning, and in mental hospitals, to get patients to make their beds, dress themselves properly, and attend and take an interest in lectures.

THE MANAGER AND THE S-R TECHNOLOGIST: B. F. SKINNER

Stimulus-response technology is a science of control that aims to change human behavior by applying principles discovered in the psychology laboratory to real-life situations. The major exponent of this point of view is Burrhus Frederic Skinner, professor of psychology at Harvard and one of the most influential of living American psychologists. Central to his approach is a technique of conditioning which has been used with great success in training laboratory animals, particularly rats and pigeons. Skinner believes that the same techniques can be applied to humans. In his famous didactic novel, *Walden Two*, Skinner describes a utopia where control of the environment enables human behavior to be predicted and shaped exactly as if it were a chemical reaction.

Such a proposition is of great interest to both managers and organization theorists; if such a model is possible, organizational control is within their grasp. Even if few managers believe this, many behavioral psychologists do, and it is in the interest of managers to understand the intellectual infrastructure of the scientists who may study them and their organizations, and whose hypotheses may affect organizational behavior.

Skinner's presumption is that behavior is determined not from within but from without. The basic argument is that by arranging effective rewards, such as feeding a pigeon only if it turns clockwise, behavior can be directed. In brief, rewards or sanctions determine whether a particular behavior becomes habitual. For Skinner the reward contingency system is the way. Reinforcing the right responses and punishing the wrong ones eventually produces what society wants. What society wants is another argument—which leaves Skinner open to the charge of being undemocratic. Behavior control (if not thought control) has been established through the conditioning process which emerged from Skinner's work with pigeons, which have been taught such bizarre behaviors as walking figure eights, dancing with each other, and even playing Ping-Pong.

Even though "pigeons aren't people," Skinner's ideas have been applied in various settings, such as schools and mental hospitals, and in business firms, to reward "good" behavior with compliments, in addition to the usual organizational reward system which provides pay incentives, status, and opportunities for self-actualization. Behavior control through strategies of contingent reinforcement have been codified in the school of psychology known as behaviorism.

Behaviorism

Behaviorism, or S-R psychology, concentrates on the study of the linkage between the stimulus and the response elicited. The goal is the control and prediction of behavior. Skinner says in *Walden Two:*

> I've had only one idea in my life—a true *idée fixe*. To put it as bluntly as possible—the idea of having my own way. "Control" expresses it. The control of human behavior. In my early experimental days it was a frenzied, selfish desire to dominate. I remember the rage I used to feel when a prediction went awry. I could have shouted at the subjects of my experiments, "Behave, damn you! Behave as you ought!"

By experimenting with positive and negative reinforcements on animals, particularly pigeons, Skinner learned to predict and control their behavior. To achieve control, he developed an operant conditioning apparatus (the Skinner box) which contains a food dispenser activated by a lever. Animals in this apparatus gradually learn to control their environment by pressing the lever and thus receiving a pellet of food. Over the years, more complex equipment has enabled him to teach rats, pigeons, and monkeys fairly complex skills.

Central to Skinner's approach is his belief that human behavior can be predicted exactly as if it were a chemical reaction, because behavior is determined from without rather than from within. Thus the control of the environment is the critical factor in determining what people will do and become.

The ratomorphic fallacy

Behavior therapy has been criticized both because it lacks an underlying theory to explain human personality and because it treats human beings as objects. Skinner answers such criticism by arguing that freedom and free will are illusions. Skinner has been accused by Arthur Koestler of a "ratomorphic" fallacy—attributing to humans processes that have been demonstrated only in lower animals.

Behavior modification

In spite of the criticisms of behaviorism, there is a growing interest among social scientists (and to a lesser extent among executives) in developments in behavior modification or behavior therapy, in the hope that this new approach may provide a practical tool for shaping, improving, and directing the behavior and attitudes of organizational members. In addition to its established usage in schools and mental hospitals, the application of behavior modification to other populations, but in a training context and for actual operating situations, is being considered by behavioral scientists.

Behavior modification, in its simplest form, aims to change the individual's responses by changing the environment, essentially by changing the reinforcement contingencies. The actual process requires systematic reinforcement of positive behavior and ignoring undesired behavior or exercising negative reinforcements (punishments or sanctions). Therefore this technique focuses on overt behavior and not on the underlying causes. During the 1960s there were tremendous developments in behavior modification programs, which have now spread far beyond their original use into broader settings such as industry and the military.

W. C. and E. P. Hamner, in "Behavior Modification on the Bottom Line," refer to the use of applied reinforcement theory at the Weyerhaeuser Company, which has a Human Resource Research Center. The director of the research center describes this company's positive reinforcement program as follows:

> The purpose of our positive reinforcement program is threefold: (1) To teach managers to embrace the philosophy that "the glass is half full rather than half empty." In other words, our objective is to teach managers to minimize criticism (which is often self-defeating since it can fixate the employee's attention on ineffective job behavior and thus reinforce it) and to maximize praise and hence fixate both their and the employee's attention on effective job behavior. (2) To teach managers that praise by itself may increase job satisfaction, but that it will have little or no effect on productivity unless it is made contingent upon specified job behaviors. Telling an employee that he is doing a good job in no way conveys to him what he is doing correctly. Such blanket praise can inadvertently reinforce the very things that the employee is doing in a mediocre way. (3) To teach managers to determine the optimum schedule for administering a reinforcer—be it praise, a smile, or money in the employee's pocket.

Albert Bandura has described how behavior modification can be applied to the training situation. But applying this technique to training problems requires a very rigorous definition of the training objectives, in terms of both the specific desired behaviors and the specific behavior variables that are open to manipulation and change. After the behavior has been modified, the whole personality system must be made self-regulating through some process of integrating the new behavior with the old.

This synthesis of the old and new behaviors is usually achieved in fact by some process other than conditioning, such as appealing to the subject's imagination, some form of exhortation, or supplying the subject with suitable rationalizations for the proposed change in his cognitive map. In spite of the behaviorist's search for a simple and automatic theory of behavior, the S-R model is ultimately focused on only one element of the human condition. Useful change strategies recognize that people are full of values, attitudes, needs, and expectations; that they carry cognitive maps around in their heads; and that they act as members of a wider social community.

BEHAVIORAL TECHNOLOGY AT WORK

As new developments in behavioral technology appear, are tested, and are reported, possibilities open up for their application to business and management. Managers may find new ideas in the behavioral modification experiences of psywar specialists, interrogators, psychiatrists, and psychopharmacologists. In any case they suggest the wide-ranging possibilities of the technique.

The manager and the psywar specialist

Psychologists have made a great number of contributions to military efforts, some of which are useful and relevant in a civilian context. Psychological torture, for example, was practiced on IRA prisoners in the recent "troubles" in Ulster, as Peter Watson reports in *War on the Mind:*

> Irish prisoners became totally psychotic. "The symptoms were loss of the sense of time, perceptual disturbance leading to hallucinations, profound apprehension and depression, and delusional beliefs. . . . One man is said to have heard and seen a choir conducted by the Protestant leader, Ian Paisley; another could not stop himself from urinating in his trousers and on his mattress; a number had suicidal fantasies."

Watson says organizational psychologists can learn much from the military, from:

> . . . the cell structure of underground insurgencies to the psychological effects of weapons, from the selection of men to work behind enemy lines to the ways to induce defection, from the way to stop men chickening out of battle to how to avoid being brainwashed, from tests to select code-breakers to the use of ghosts to harry tribal peasants. . . .

He cites more than 1,000 studies revealing a strong alliance between the military and the behavioral scientist.

According to Watson, Vietnam was the most psychological war ever waged. From the beginning the Kennedy administration was extremely interested in the psychology of guerrilla warfare; the object of the exercise was "to win hearts and minds." As Watson points out, "psychology and politics are converging."

Thus "psywar," "psyops," and even "psy-warriors" have arrived. Psychologists are helping to develop psychotechnology, which, as one U.S. general put it, helps to interlock perception of electronic data to targeting the missile, tying the "beep" to the "boom." Watson refers to a study which showed that an infantryman is a combination of 41 essential skills, 13 of which could be improved by training. Military psychology helps not only to put the weapons and bionics together, but also to plot "good" organizational politics.

The manager and the interrogator

Modern-day interrogation techniques are another example of behavioral technology at work. Consider for example the techniques used on suspects held in isolation at a police station—"helping the police with their inquiries" before they are charged.

The usual police setup involves an interrogation area, ideally consisting of two rooms—a reception room and the interrogation room proper, which can only be reached through the reception room. The area is selected for its remoteness in the building, usually the basement. When suspects are taken there the most roundabout route possible is used, to increase the sense that they will be tucked away miles from anywhere.

The suspect is taken to the interrogation area by uniformed policemen, who then immediately disappear in order to build the impression that this is not a normal police matter. The suspect is passed through the reception room, where a secretary takes notes on the tape recording of the interrogation. Contrary to a widely held belief, the suspect is not left for ages to "sweat it out." The interrogator is already in the room when the suspect arrives. The room has no windows and is completely soundproofed but otherwise is designed to resemble a regular business office. The interrogator is not a shirt-sleeved cop sucking a cheroot but looks like a well-dressed (grey suit, white shirt, dark tie, black shoes) businessman. The suspect will be told to sit in a particular chair—straight-backed, with no armrests, probably fixed to the floor, and just far enough away from the desk so he cannot rest his elbows on its edge. The interrogator is comfortably seated in a well-padded, mobile armchair in which he will continually move about, to emphasize his freedom.

The interrogation is craftily organized in three stages. First comes the "friendly interviewer" stage; this is used to get basic information about the suspect and his movements, and also to establish in his mind that the interrogator is no ordinary policeman from the local station (although he may well be), nor does he have the normal police attitude to criminals. The purpose is to get across the personality of the interrogator, his professionalism and humanitarianism. But then the situation is deliberately and dramatically turned upside down.

In the second stage, the attitude of the interrogator may suddenly alter. Under his desk he may have a hidden buzzer connected to the reception room (there is a code for various messages). Suddenly, unannounced, someone may enter with papers that the interrogator studies but doesn't allow the suspect to see. After this, the interrogator stops being friendly and acts as if the case is solved—an eyewitness has been found, or one of the accomplices has talked. If neither of these is likely, the interrogator may be called away and replaced with a verbal bully.

If none of these tactics work, the third phase begins. Here, interrogators make use of some findings from prison research on the behavior of criminals. Most people have what is called by psychiatrists a body buffer zone, an area around us into which we do not let others come—usually a circle with a radius of about two feet. Criminals, curiously enough, often have different shaped zones. They might be able to stand someone coming quite close to them from the front but not from behind; sitting, but not standing, and so on. So, rather than the conventional eyeball-to-eyeball interrogation, the interrogator asks many questions sitting or standing behind the suspect, out of sight. Thus the behavioral technologist engineers consent and monitors the actual behavior.

The manager and the psychiatrist

Dealing with a dangerous psychopath

Behavioral scientists have developed the impressive abilities to make and break conflict at will, to get experimental subjects to give others severe electric shocks, to persuade people to live in sensory-deprived environments for up to seven days at a time, and to get subjects to sleep with electronic gear on their bodies which will deny them the opportunity to dream. They are even able to persuade workers to "participate" their way to higher production. The behavioral technologist is seen as a modern Machiavelli preoccupied with regulating human psychosocial evolution.

The preferred treatment of skyjackers, for instance, stresses that they are not normal people who can be dealt with like ordinary criminals. A Dallas psychiatrist, David Hubbard, the only U.S. psychiatrist who has studied the skyjacking phenomenon (supported by a $200,000 grant from a private Dallas foundation), has taped hundreds of hours of interviews with 50 imprisoned skyjackers. He worked with airline crews to develop techniques for handling piracy and outlined his ideas in a 1971 book called *The Skyjacker: His Flights of Fantasy*.

Those who find themselves the victims of air piracy, Hubbard recommends, should treat skyjackers like frightened animals. Passengers and crew should move slowly and deliberately and show courtesy, warmth, and understanding in order not to trigger their latent violence by making them feel cornered or attacked. Passengers should stay aloof; women flight attendants should avoid seductiveness, if the skyjacker is a man, and everyone should avoid trickery, which is alarming to paranoids.

At the same time, however, those not directly involved should be ready to take advantage of promising situations. For example, when an AWOL sailor hijacked a Braniff 707 to Buenos Aires, Dr. Hubbard was able to use outside forces to good effect. While waiting for the skyjacker to get physiologically low, Hubbard counseled against actions that might cause his adrenaline to flow. He had demanded a DC–8 for a flight to Algeria, but the plane was kept out of sight. A radio operator whose voice, after 17 hours, had come to sound familiar and comforting to the skyjacker was replaced. After letting him stew in isolation for two and one-half hours, Hubbard injected a note of anxiety by having airline officials notify the crews that they were no longer physically fit to fly. Hearing this, the skyjacker let two crew members leave the plane, and five hours later he gave himself up.

The behavioral technology aspects of the treatment of skyjackers can perhaps best be seen in the recommendations for deterrence. The greatest deterrent, according to Hubbard, would be an international agreement to send air pirates back to the countries where they committed their crimes. Another deterrent, which takes into account the possible motives of the skyjacker, would be to eliminate the death penalty so that skyjacking cannot become a form of suicide. Hubbard also favors stressing the skyjacker's sexual problems, where applicable, to make piracy seem humiliating rather than heroic.

The manager and the psychopharmacologist

Like behavioral technologists, biologists are exploring genetic engineering as a means of determining human behavior. Scientists have progressed well beyond the early students of psychology, who associated crime with various bumps on the head. The ideas of the late 19th-century Italian criminologist Cesare Lombroso, who claimed that criminals could be recognized by such physical stigmata as lobeless and small ears, receding chins, foreheads "villainously low," and crooked noses, are now just as passé as the view that physical build determines personality and even the form of insanity. Psychology and criminology texts at one time would have been incomplete without the life histories of two infamous families, the Jukes and the Kallikaks, who between them had an army of offspring with a myriad of disabilities and criminal characteristics. More recently, a possible link between the XYY chromosome and individual and criminal behavior has been suggested. Genetic engineering would set out to eliminate such XYY individuals.

CSB and ESB

Psychopharmacologists, greatly encouraged by the success of chemotherapy in controlling not only anxiety and tension but also in alleviating major psychoses, are being urged to develop a peace pill to monitor the aggressions of national leaders. The basic proposition is that the brain can be influenced by chemical or electrical stimulation—CSB or ESB.

The most celebrated student of ESB is Jose Delgado, who has used electrical power to control an aggressive bull in the bullring. After surgically implanting electrodes in the brain of a bull, Delgado could halt the charging animal and bring it to a screeching stop by pressing a button on a radio transmitter whose signal activated the electrode. After several stimulations, the bull's naturally aggressive behavior disappeared, and it became completely placid. A similar device has been implanted in the brain of a man given to uncontrollable bursts of rage. When he feels such an attack coming on, he presses a button on his battery pack and remains peaceable. Much of Delgado's work has a science-fiction ring to it, and his accounts of transforming reserved and poised personalities into warm, spontaneous, affectionate, grateful people are amazing.

In CSB, instead of wires, scientists implant fine tubes in the brain through which various chemicals are dripped to produce changes in emotions. But the most practical method for treating a large number of people is the familiar pill. Today there are drugs that produce euphoria and drugs that heighten sensory awareness. There are drugs that perk up a depressed mind and tranquilize a case of jittery nerves. There is even a drug that tones down the extravagant thoughts and actions of a manic person.

A CRITICAL REVIEW OF BEHAVIORAL TECHNOLOGY

Some achievements

What can behavioral technology do to affect organizational behavior? Almost everything, including motivate. Almost 30 years ago Ernst Dichter showed what a knowledge of motivation research could do when applied to the marketing of automobile. In "The World Customer" he showed that men regard cars not only as a means of transportation but also as status, power, and sex objects: "Hit my car, hit me." The car is an extension of the driver's personality, and the connection between the foot and the gas pedal is an extension of the person's being. With these not unreasonable assumptions, it is easy to believe that some male drivers see convertibles (especially the red variety) as the steed struggling at the bit to take them to their mistresses, real or imaginary. Thus the powerful, low-slung convertible

(Cougar, Dart, XK–140) is put in the window of the showroom to lure the family man in to buy the standard sedan.

This is not a very telling example, compared with the modern techniques of motivation modeling, which can turn insipid, boring, lackluster executives into go-getter tigers who will hustle to get the job done on schedule.

Behavioral technologists believe, correctly in my opinion, that there are myriad ways in which people's behavior can be controlled. The techniques vary widely, from the relatively simple operant conditioning through which children learn multiplication tables to the complex strategies of the T-group trainer and the military brainwasher, who can get people to tell all, to let it all hang out, and to experience conversion. Newer and more dramatic techniques are constantly being developed. Delgado's ESB techniques described above have been used with human beings, for example to help patients suffering from epilepsy. The implications of such research are indeed awesome.

Behavioral technology has had a "bad press," as C. R. Rogers and B. F. Skinner note in "Some Issues Concerning the Control of Human Behavior": "Those who have explicitly avowed an interest in control have been roughly treated by history. Machiavelli is the great prototype. As Macaulay said of him, 'Out of his surname they coined an epithet for a knave and out of his Christian name a synonym for the devil.'"

The measure of the potency of behavioral technology for the manager, however, is the degree to which it can reduce stress.

TOPIC 2
Executive stress

STRESS THEORY

Stress research as a distinct field of inquiry has had an independent existence for only about 20 years. The pioneer investigator into the implications of stress, Dr. Hans Selye of the University of Montreal, defines stress as the nonspecific response of the body to any demand made upon it. Selye was the first to assemble a unified catalog of the neuroendocrine consequences of physical and perceptual overload, reactions to demanding, unexpected stimuli. Sociology and biology are brought together in the new concept of sociobiology (Box 9–1).

One of Selye's most dramatic breakthroughs was his discovery that he could take two similar groups of rats and dispose one group to heart disease by injecting an excess of sodium chloride and certain hormones. When both groups of rats were subjected to stress, none of the control group suffered, but all of the predisposed group died. Selye drew the conclusion that the endocrine glands, particularly the adren-

Box 9–1: Sociobiology

Sociobiology has presented an interesting new point of view in regard to the biological basis for the social behavior of both animals and human beings. Edward O. Wilson, a Harvard professor and world authority on insects, has suggested that human social behavior may in part be genetically controlled.

In *Sociobiology: The New Synthesis,* Wilson describes how organizations emerge among Central American ants, recognizing four pinnacles of social evolution among social insects. They develop organizations centered on single queens; an elaborate caste of workers, drones, and soldiers; communal homes; and young-rearing systems. It is a highly regimented society in which the ordinary insect is as nothing. Wilson describes what happens when the ants search for food:

The chains and clusters break up and tumble down into a churning mass on the ground. As the pressure builds, the mass flows outward in all directions. Then a raiding column emerges along the path of least resistance. No leaders take command. As the workers run onto new ground they lay down small quantities of chemical trail substance, guiding others forward. A loose organization emerges in the column, based on behavioral differences among the castes. . . . The smaller and medium-sized workers race along the chemical trails and extend them, while the larger clumsier soldiers travel for the most part on either side. At the height of the raid the workers spread out in a fan-shaped swarm with a broad front. Columns like braided ropes extend from the swarm back to the bivouac site where the queen and immature forms remain in safety.

The moving front of workers flushes a great harvest of prey: tarantulas, scorpions, beetles, roaches, grasshoppers, wasps, ants and many others. Most are pulled down, stung to death, cut into pieces and quickly transported to the rear. Even some snakes, lizards and nestling birds may fall victim.

In considering human sociobiology, Wilson suggests the possibility that a propensity for warfare and genocide is built into human genes. Male dominance, the territorial imperative, the tendency to form tribal groups, maternal care for children, and play all may be genetically determined, Wilson says. Both sociologists and biologists have reacted strongly to such a genetic view of human behavior.

Reference: Edward O. Wilson, *Sociobiology: The New Synthesis* (Cambridge, Mass.: Belknap Press of Harvard University Press, 1975).

als, were the body's prime reactors to stress. Selye found that the adrenal glands were the only body organs not to shrink under stress.

Figure 9–3 illustrates some of Selye's theory from a systems view. Many external conditions, all defined as stressors, are seen as affecting the brain, which in turn signals the adrenal and pituitary glands. These glands produce the hormones ACTH, cortisone, and cortisol, which stimulate protective bodily reactions. Selye defined the initial reactions to short-term stressors as the *alarm reaction* and the *local adaptation syndrome* (LAS), both of which have survival value and relevance in regard to immediate stressors. The LAS facilitates short-term homeostatic regulation of the body process; but in cases of extreme or prolonged stress, the body progressively brings in more subsystems of

FIGURE 9–3
Schematic flow of influence and feedback

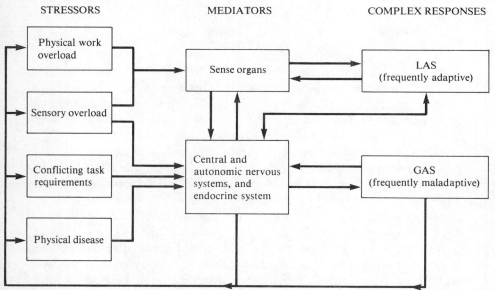

Reprinted by permission from Jan Berkhout, "Psychological Stress," in Kenyon B. DeGreene (ed.), *Systems Psychology* (New York: McGraw-Hill Book Co., 1970).

the body until the whole human system is mobilized. The end point of this tendency is the *general adaptation syndrome* (GAS), which may exacerbate or mask the symptoms of almost any medical problem. This stage is characterized by the features of chronic endocrine imbalance and deteriorated psychomotor performance. This condition of adrenal exhaustion indicates that the person, because the neuroendocrine system has been overmobilized for too long a time, is no longer capable of responding to new environmental conditions.

The initial reaction to stress is alarm, which is followed by a rallying of the body's defenses. The sequence begins as mental stresses are transmitted from the cerebral cortex of the brain to the hypothalamus. The body seems to react to all threats, even purely semantic threats, as if it were dealing with a physical attack. Signals are sent through the sympathetic and parasympathetic nervous systems, and adrenaline floods the blood stream. The endocrine orchestra comes into action, which causes tensing of the muscles, dilation of the pupils of the eyes, constriction of the skin vessels, paling, deeper breathing, pounding heart, and pressure on the bladder. If the stressor is countered, stability returns. But if the attack is prolonged, the defense system gradually wears down, and Selye's GAS ensues.

Walter McQuade, writing on "What Stress Can Do to You," brilliantly summarizes the impressive evidence that the chronic ailments afflicting middle-aged Americans are at least partly due to organizational stress and tension.

PSYCHOLOGICAL STRESS FACTORS

Genuine danger is the most obvious stress factor, but there are many others, both physical and mental. Monotony is a psychological stressor which has particular significance for automobile assembly plant operations. General Motors has redesigned work assignments to find "larger" jobs for production workers.

Sensory deprivation and perceptual isolation also constitute stress factors. There is considerable disagreement among scientists studying sensory deprivation as to how long a person need be isolated to produce measurable stress responses. Military intelligence has been experimenting with such techniques as a means of breaking down prisoners' defenses.

Another factor increasing stress which is of great interest to executives is the disruption of circadian periodicity, the 24-hour cycle of night and day which is the most compelling organization factor of human life. Disruption of this cycle—as everyone who has ever stepped off a transatlantic jet knows—constitutes a stress factor which can adversely affect not only psychomotor performance but also personal stability and executive judgment. Among airline staffs, this disturbance of the circadian cycle is recognized as a distinct stress factor. Reported shifts in eating and sleeping habits and changes in the endocrine balance are obviously interconnected. Box 9–2 describes how biorhythms may be useful in predicting performance.

Sleep deprivation, currently a major field of psychological enquiry,

Box 9–2: Can biorhythms predict performance peaks and lows?

Are you having a "good day"? Have you had a "bad day" recently? Increasingly, scientific evidence is becoming available to suggest that everyone has both good and bad days.

Biorhythm charts have been devised to explain where a person is in physical, emotional, and intellectual terms. The basic biorhythm idea is that the human being is influenced by three internal cycles: a physical cycle lasting 23 days, an emotional cycle lasting 29 days, and an intellectual cycle lasting 33 days. Using these charts, it is possible to identify critical days when individual performance, in terms of judgment, coordination and sensitivity, is likely to be impaired.

Athletes are guided by these charts, as are airlines in decisions as to who flies with whom in the cockpit. Japanese taxi drivers dangle color-coded origami (folded paper) cranes in their cabs to signal other drivers that they are having critical days.

The scientific validity of biorhythms has certainly not been established at this time. Nevertheless, biorhythmic signals can usefully be employed to help predict when people should undertake or avoid critical activities.

causes a steady deterioration in performance of psychomotor tasks. Sleep is a complex, many-faceted process with many stages, each apparently serving distinct physiological and psychological functions. Research psychologists are paying a great deal of attention to rapid eye movement (REM) sleep, which is clearly associated with dreaming and whose suppression is conducive to bizarre behavior patterns. Denial of REM sleep offers considerable potential for brainwashing and getting confessions from prisoners who, because of the stress induced, may well be willing to go along with their captors.

HOW EXECUTIVES REACT TO STRESS

Many behavioral scientists, as well as physicians, believe that cardiac disabilities may be as much a function of stress as of cholesterol level, blood pressure, smoking, glucose level, and the like. This is not a contradiction of the importance of these physical symptoms. What appears to happen is that stress aggravates the level of cholesterol or blood pressure and promotes such unhealthy activities as smoking and overeating. McQuade's article, "What Stress Can Do to You," notes that management jobs carry higher risks than most.

> . . . In a detailed study done for NASA at the Goddard Space Flight Center, the investigators from Ann Arbor found that administrators were much more subject to stress than engineers or scientists. Responsibility for people, French explains, always causes more stress than responsibilities for things—equipment, budgets, etc. The rise in serum cholesterol, blood sugar, and blood pressure among ground managers is much greater during manned space flights than during flights of unmanned satellites. Whatever their assignment, the administrators at Goddard, as a group, had higher pulse rates and blood pressure, and smoked more, than the engineers or scientists. Medical records revealed that administrators also had suffered almost three times as many heart attacks as either the scientists or the engineers.

Box 9–3 illustrates, from the same article, some of the ways in which different personalities respond to stress.

Many organizational problems seem to generate executive stress by creating role ambiguity, work overload, job insecurity, lack of feeling of participation, and worry over difficult bosses or subordinates. For example, air traffic controllers, who play a critical role in directing the increasing numbers of planes stacked up over congested airports, are exposed to considerable stress over long periods. Such high information levels and the attendant decisions—any one of which may lead to a calamity—induce a level of stress which is unremitting and which has serious consequences for their digestive tracts. A study of the Academy of Air Traffic Control Medicine in St. Charles, Illinois, showed that the incidence of ulcers among control-tower personnel is

Box 9-3: Which executive type are you?

Walter McQuade reports some interesting research on executive types. Cardiologists Meyer Friedman and Ray H. Rosenman of the Harold Brunn Institute of Mount Zion Hospital in San Francisco maintain that behavior patterns and stress are the principal culprits in the high incidence of coronary heart disease among middle-aged Americans—and that personality differences are of vital importance.

In studying reactions to stress, Friedman and Rosenman have come to the conviction that people can be divided into two major types, which they designate A and B. Type A, the coronary-prone type, is characterized by:

Intense drive

Aggressiveness

Ambition

Competitiveness

Pressure to get things done

Habitually pitting self against the clock

Visible restlessness

An existential miasma of hostility which makes others nervous

Type B characteristics are:

A more easygoing manner

Seldom becomes impatient

Takes more time to enjoy leisure

Does not feel driven by the clock

Not preoccupied with social achievement

Less competitive

Speaks in a more modulated style

The extreme Type A is a tremendously hard worker, a perfectionist, filled with brisk self-confidence, decisiveness, resolution. This executive type never evades. While waiting in the office of a cardiologist or dentist, he or she may be making business phone calls.

Type As speak in a staccato manner and have a tendency to end sentences in a rush. They frequently sigh faintly between words, but never in anxiety, because that state is unknown. They are seldom out sick and rarely go to doctors, almost never to psychiatrists. They are unlikely to get ulcers. They are rarely interested in money except as a token of the game, but the higher they climb, the more they consider themselves underpaid.

On the debit side, they are often a little hard to get along with. They do not drive people who work under them as hard as they drive themselves, but they have little time to waste with them. They want their respect, not their affection. Yet in some ways they are more

Reference: Walter McQuade, "What Stress Can Do to You," *Fortune,* January 1972.

alarmingly high. One group of air controllers was examined by Dr. R. Grayson, who found that three quarters of the members required further tests. These tests revealed that almost a third had ulcers. The incidence of ulcers for American physicians is between 2.5 and 4 percent; even for alcoholics the rate is only 9 percent. The cause among air traffic controllers may be unremitting stress, generated partly by information and decision overload. Box 9–4 suggests one remedy.

sensitive than the milder Type B. They hate to fire anyone and will go to great lengths to avoid it.

Type A, surprisingly, probably goes to bed earlier most nights than Type B, who will get interested in something irrelevant to their careers and sit up late, or simply socialize. Type A is precisely on time for appointments and expects the same from other people. They smoke cigarettes, never pipes. Headwaiters learn not to keep them waiting for a table reservation; waiters like Type As because they don't linger over their meals and don't complain about quality. They usually salt the meal before they taste it and they never send a bottle of wine back. Driving a car, Type As are not reckless but do reveal anger when a slower driver ahead delays them.

Type As are not much for exercise; they claim they have too little time for it. When they do play golf, it is fast-paced. They never return late from vacation. Their desktops are clean when they leave the office at the end of each day.

But in the competition for the top jobs in their companies, As often lose out to Bs. They lose because they are too competitive. They are so obsessed with the office that they have attention for nothing else, including their families. They make decisions too fast—in minutes, rather than days—and so may make serious business mistakes.

Type Bs differ little in background or ability from As; they may be quietly urgent but they are more reasonable men. Unlike Type As, Type Bs are hard to needle into anger Friedman says, "A's have no respect for B's, but the smart B uses an A. The great salesmen are A's. The corporation presidents are usually B's."

What is most tragic in this picture of hopeful, driving, distorting energy is that the Type As are from two to three times more likely than the Type Bs to get coronary heat disease in middle age.

The test program that Friedman and Rosenman offer as their strongest body of evidence was undertaken in 1960 with substantial backing from the National Institute of Health. A total of 3,500 male subjects, aged 39 to 59, with no known history of heart disease, were interviewed and classified as Type A or Type B. Then came complete physical examinations, which are still being performed on a regular basis as the program continues to accumulate data. At one point 257 of the test group—roughly half As and half Bs—had developed coronary heart disease, and 70 percent of the victims of coronary attacks were Type As.

One pointed criticism that opponents make of the Friedman-Rosenman studies is that their method of classifying individuals into Type A or Type B is subjective, relying heavily on signs of tension as observed by the interviewer. The two cardiologists do not deny this but point out that a good deal of all medical analysis is subjective. Says Rosenman, "A migraine is subjective too."

As cardiologists trace heart disease to unrelenting competitiveness, a wave of concern over stress is likely. There is nothing more fascinating to the layman than folklore finally validated by reputable scientists.

THE NEUROSIS OF SUCCESS

One of the most interesting lines of stress research has been the study of the relationships between life's events and illness. A life event is any change in a person's circumstances to which he or she must adapt. This research work was initiated by Harold Wolff and Lawrence Hinkle, who investigated the health records of American employees of the Bell Telephone Company and were surprised to

Box 9-4: A suggested remedy: Sound people out instead of seeing them off

Some ethologists believe that animals have a better time of it than human beings do. Joan McIntyre's book entitled *Mind in the Waters* describes cetaceans as lovely, intelligent underwater creatures with a delightful society: "The cohesion of the group does not allow the dislocation of arguments or grudges. . . . There seems to be little reason to fight. There are no objects to accrue or own. There is constant sexual play, enough to allow everyone the satisfying contact with friends and mates and lovers. There is enough food." These creatures are able to escape human limitations and achieve incredible subtlety and wholeness of perception and expression through their eerie sonar radar, which allows them to see each other's internal body states.

Whales and dolphins are the existential fish, partly because they are doomed to extinction (like all existentialists), partly because they spend so much time sounding each other out, a strictly existential pastime, instead of seeing each other off, as ordinary humans do. Whales and dolphins enjoy a kind of T-group emotional honesty in a complex interpersonal matrix, communicating with each other and humans. These mystical, mysterious animal submariners seem to be genuinely interested in us, and they have arranged for "Project Jonah" to save their ancient cetacean civilization from our new antisubmarine technology which makes harvesting whales an assembly-line, flow process operation. Like Skinner's rats, they'll probably train the psychologist to feed them on demand.

Reference: Joan McIntyre, *Mind in the Waters: A Book to Celebrate the Consciousness of Whales and Dolphins* (Toronto: McLelland & Stewart, 1974).

discover that episodes of illness were not distributed at random, but each employee tended to have a set annual amount of illness. Instead of illness being randomly distributed, a quarter of the employees suffered one half of the total illness, and 1 in 20 experienced very little. Further, those employees with the most episodes of illness not only had a greater variety of illnesses but also had more serious physical and psychiatric illnesses. Wolff and Hinkle showed a clear link relating clusters of illness to periods during which the individual considered his life situation threatening or unsatisfying.

In this human ecology approach to medicine, Hinkle argues that disease may not be the result of any single specific virus but a consequence of many factors, including the effect of change itself. A colleague of Wolff's, T. H. Holmes of the University of Washington School of Medicine, developed a life-change units scale to measure how much change an individual has experienced in a given span of time. Holmes's brilliant insight was that the significance of the change lay not in its threatening or difficult characteristic but in the actual need to adapt to change, whether it was pleasant or unpleasant. Pleasurable and satisfying change takes its toll as well—a kind of neurosis of success. According to Holmes, the amount of stress (whatever its emotional concomitants) and the ability to adjust to it are the two elements in the equation of change whose lack of balance determines illness.

Arguing that different kinds of life changes strike people with different force, Holmes set out to list as many changes as he could and then try to assess the stress value of each. Holmes and R. H. Rahe, in "The Social Readjustment Rating Scale," report the results of a survey of 394 adults who were asked to rate 42 common life events (a divorce, a marriage, a move to a new home, etc.) according to their subjective estimate of the degree of life change and the readjustment each would need. Which changes required a great deal of coping? Which a minor degree? To establish a standard, the event "marriage" was given an arbitrary value, and the subjects were invited to answer, "Does this event involve more or less adjustment than marriage? Would the readjustment take a longer or shorter period?" To Holmes's surprise, it turned out that there was a consensus among people questioned— irrespective of age, race, sex, education, marital status, social class, ethnic origin, and religion—as to which changes in their lives would require major adaptations and which minor adaptations.

Thus it seems reasonable to argue that stress affects health. Like money in the bank, stress, once it has been deposited, appears to bear interest in malice for the subject. The most striking confirmation of this "sleeper" aspect of stress has been derived from studies of military life, where it is reckoned that one year of campaigning ages a man as much as three years in barracks.

Many executives are not puzzled by such findings, for they seem to fit their own experiences and their observations of other executives and go some way to explain the phenomenon of the executive who drops dead the day after he has been given a clean bill of health following a detailed medical examination. The examining physician might have improved his diagnosis if he had gotten the patient to complete Holmes's schedule of recent experiences; it might have been more revealing than his cholesterol level.

MONITORING EXECUTIVE HEALTH

Reading the early literature on executive health gives the clear impression that psychosomatic illness is a very common response to managerial stress. Despite a small but growing body of evidence to the contrary, a widely held myth is that demands made on executives are more stressful than those made on nonexecutives. While we have seen that stress factors do link up with hazards like coronary disease and ulcers, the question is whether executives in general are as subject to stress, as, say, air traffic controllers.

According to Hinkle, the executive's liability to coronary attacks is not as bad as some of the earlier writers in this field would have had us believe. Understandably, a topic of vital interest to executives is the incidence of coronary thrombosis in the management group. The major finding of modern research in the field of executive health is that executives enjoy pretty much the same standard of health as other members of the socioeconomic class of which they are members. Not only is their objective health record good but, compared with less well-off social groups, a higher proportion of the executives report that they enjoy good health; and apparently factors such as stress play a relatively insignificant part. It is now generally accepted that the incidence of coronary disease is closely related to obesity, lack of exercise, and cigarette smoking.

Occupational health is a significant focus of research. For example, D. Morris and a group at the Social Medicine Research Unit in London found in a study of transit workers that the less active bus driver has a much higher rate of myocardial infarction and death from this condition than the more active conductor, whose survival is attributed to the repeated climbing of steps in double-decker buses. A similar discovery was also made in regard to postmen, who had a better health record than more sedentary colleagues such as letter sorters and telephone operators. Aside from cigarette smoking, the two factors of greatest interest are related to the need to avoid obesity and physical exercise.

It is now generally accepted by insurance companies that obesity is associated with an increased liability to death from degenerative diseases. Executives, perhaps in response to C. P. Snow's denunciation of the expense-account lunch, are well placed to take advantage of the necessary dietary requirements of the new regime. Diet, especially protein intake, appears to be a function of socioeconomic class. But obesity only develops when energy from food exceeds energy utilization. Some medical authorities have argued that the obese eat no more (in some cases less) than the slim, but they exercise less.

It is as well to remember that the relations between weight, diet, and exercise have not been settled in a final and conclusive way by scientific standards. But most doctors who have seriously considered the matter have agreed that a regular program of exercise is not only good but necessary for executive well-being. Apparently the best exercise is walking, then jogging, then running.

Many organizations, realizing the importance of their investment in their executive group, have instituted medical examinations as a regular procedure for their top-management group. As with pilots in the airline business, periodic medical reviews for executives evoke an ambivalent response. Many company physicians take the opportunity presented by these examinations to counsel top management on health considerations. Apparently quite a few executives report stress symptoms—including hysterical heart conditions—some of which, at least, must be iatrogenic (induced by the physician) in origin.

Such hysterical cardiac symptoms are not easy to allay even after an

EKG has been prepared. The afflicted male executive studies his skin pallor carefully, keeps a close check on his weight, watches his diet, nags his wife for being indifferent to his fate, keeps feeling his heart and pulse, is an avid reader of any medical literature on cholesterol levels and arteriosclerotic disorders, and has such "an advanced knowledge of biochemistry and physiology" that many overworked doctors express the wish that the *Reader's Digest* would abandon the field of medical education.

TOPIC 3
What every manager should know about behavioral technology to reduce stress

Even a brief glance at the evidence from behavioral science, ethology, and medicine should be sufficient to convince most reasonable people that there are links between aggression, social ecology, and stress. Figure 9–4, modeling stress as a system, indicates the probable role of aggression as a physiological or psychological stress factor. The processes for dealing with stress—the adaptation syndromes—are difficult to detail; it is obvious that society in general (and North American society in particular) has not developed enough ways either to prevent or to deal with the causes and results of stress.

FIGURE 9–4
Stress as a system

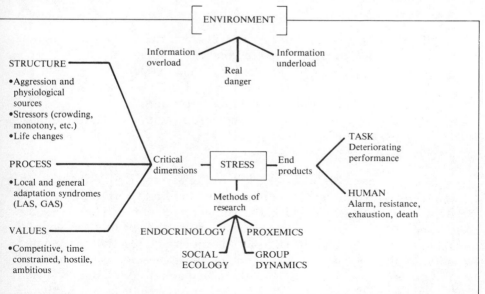

ADVANCED TECHNIQUES

To devise ways to deal with stress, executives are investigating new developments in behavioral technology, and even such ideas as sleep research are being considered to see what light they can throw on executive effectiveness. At the first Canadian International Sleep Symposium, which was organized to study the psychiatric implications of sleep, a recent investigation was reported which showed that the nightly REM time for long sleepers, who normally sleep nine or more hours per night, is approximately double that of short sleepers, who normally get less than six hours of sleep. The long sleepers also had more frequent and longer REM periods. They tended to be more creative, introspective people, less conformist in their general view of life, somewhat inhibited in their sexual functioning and in self-assertion. They tended to be anxious, shy, and mildly depressed, and several had minor somatic complaints. The short sleepers, on the other hand, scored higher on the scale reflecting social presence, sociability, and flexibility. They tended to be more conformist and establishment oriented, and except, for compulsive traits in some, they tended to be relatively healthier. Their life-style involved an action-oriented avoidance of psychological problems, with heavy use of denail and avoidance as defense mechanisms.

Behavioral scientists are conducting biofeedback research to learn how to utilize brain wave control to help executives function more effectively. The brain gives off faint electrical impulses that can be measured by electrodes attached to the scalp which are connected to any electroencephalograph (EEG). Four basic categories of waves have been identified:

1. Beta—14 to 40 cycles per second, characterized by the eyes-open, awake state, in which people generally operate.
2. Alpha—7 to 13 cycles per second, characterized by a state of relaxed awareness of yoga and zen or light sleep and daydream, usually reached through biofeedback training.
3. Theat—4 to 7 cycles a second, associated with sleep and the most creative, problem-solving level.
4. Delta—0 to 4 cycles a second.

Experiments with biofeedback learning as a technique for alleviating tension involve recording brain waves and transforming them into light or sound signals which the subject can follow. There is some evidence that subjects can be trained to monitor their brain waves and achieve the desired alpha state. While much of the activity associated with "alpha machines" is commercial, has little scientific foundation, and plays on the weakness of the disturbed and disabled, real research is going on in this area which may well turn out to be as productive as the studies of REM dreaming.

Visceral learning is based on the belief that human beings can assume responsibility for becoming aware of and controlling such physiological processes as heart rate, blood pressure, and temperature. Techniques are being evolved to get cardiac patients to monitor and regulate their hearts by mental discipline alone, for example.

Staying alive

In both biofeedback and visceral learning, the object is for people to stay healthy through self-control, self-awareness, and body mastering. Intelligent self-control is central to the attack on coronaries. The scientific evidence is overwhelming that men have more and earlier heart attacks than women and that coronaries are more likely in people who have high levels of cholesterol, high blood pressure, diabetes, and electrocardiogram irregularities, who smoke cigarettes, and who have ancestors with heart problems. The likelihood can be lessened by a change in life-style: prudent diets, more exercise, no cigarette smoking, and the elimination of as much stress, tension, and deadline-associated activity as possible. This means a major change not only in life-style but in the demands of society.

Sufficient evidence is available to make it clear that the way organizational life is arranged and the kind of occcupation cause disease. For example, clergymen, scientists, and teachers live longer than the average; Supreme Court justices often live beyond 80. Such life expectations seem to be a function of regular hours and a minimum of pressure and tension.

Corporate executives are conditioned by competition, responsibility, and decision making. Society has built up their needs to achieve and to win power through the exercise of bureaucratic realpolitik, leaving them in many cases with an existential miasma of hostility which makes them likely candidates for coronaries—or so some medical and behavioral scientists seem to imagine the executive life.

Organizational life works out a little differently, however; the corporate executive does not in fact fit the picture of the corporate coronary case, hassled and harassed all day long. Corporate executives live longer than their subordinates, as any good book of actuarial statistics would tell you. In effect, they have transformed many organizations into monastic institutions where they begin the day with the matins of reading from the great teachers of our times in the *New York Times,* follow with prayer meetings to sing the praises of their corporate betters, and, after returning the telephone calls of the favored few, repair to the club for a frugal lunch of filet of sole and white wine. They return to the postprandial relaxation of a boring meeting. And so the day wears on, as they turn the hustle and bustle of corporate life into a daily routine in which there are few unexpected challenges to bring on stress.

To find out more about how executives handle their lives, it is necessary to shift the conceptual basis of the discussion of organizational behavior and move from the individual to the group. This is what Part III is all about.

REVIEW AND RESEARCH

1. Why are executives attracted to behavioral technology?
2. What is behaviorism? What are the arguments for and against this approach to human behavior?
3. How can behavior modification be used in industry?
4. What generates executive stress?
5. What is the neurosis of success?
6. How would you set about changing your life-style? How would you measure achievement?
7. There must be something good to life if it ends with death" and "Death must have something going for it, if they save it for the end" represent two typical death-wish statements. Construct an existential life-style for MBA students that would keep them slim, trim, noncigarette-smoking, full of pep, zip, and panache, and yet ready to go at a moment's notice.

GLOSSARY OF TERMS

Adaptation to stress. Ways of coping with stressors. According to Selye, stressors affect the brain, which signals the adrenal and pituitary glands. Reactions to short-term stressors are (1) alarm, and (2) the local adaptation syndrome (LAS), which facilitates short-term homeostatic regulation of body processes. Under long-run stress, more subsystems are activated until the entire body is mobilized; the end point of this process is the general adaptation syndrome (GAS), characterized by chronic endocrine imbalance, deteriorating psychomotor performance, and adrenal exhaustion; finally, the person is unable to respond to environmental conditions.

Aggression. In a narrow biological sense, patterns of behavior associated with attacking another individual, or an "attack posture"; in a wider organizational context, includes competitiveness and self-assertiveness.

Behavioral technology. An emerging science of control that aims to change human behavior by applying principles discovered through behavioral science research to real-life situations.

Behaviorism. The school of psychology which defines psychology as the positive science of behavior. Behaviorism, which uses S-R psychology, concentrates on the study of the linkage between the stimulus and the response elicited.

Behavior modification. A form of training developed by psychologists who follow Skinner's approach and who set out to change behavior systematically by regulating the use of rewards and punishments as reinforcements. Behavior modification, which exploits S-R psychology, aims to change individual responses by changing the subject's environment.

Biorhythms. The idea that the individual is influenced by three internal cycles: physical, emotional, and intellectual. Biorhythms are studied with the purpose of exploiting biorhythmic peaks, when all three cycles are on the upward trend, and avoiding biorhythmic troughs, the opposite.

Conditioned response. A response that has been imprinted through repeated presentation of a stimulus reinforcement.

ESB and CSB. Electrical and chemical stimulation of the brain as a means of controlling behavior. These techniques have been used with both animals and humans and are likely to be a major area of future development in organizational behavior.

Operant conditioning. A term coined by Skinner which refers to the process of the organism operating on its environment in order to get a reward.

Ratomorphic fallacy. The fallacy of attributing to humans the processes that have been demonstrated only in lower animals.

Reinforcement. Strengthening behavioral conditioning through the reward or punishment following a particular response.

Sociobiology. An interdisciplinary area which deals with the biological basis of social behavior and presupposes that behavior is genetically controlled.

Stress. The anticipation of inability to respond adequately (or at a reasonable cost) to perceived demand, accompanied by anticipation of negative consequences for inadequate response.

DEBATE: Are executives prime candidates for coronaries?

No, they are not

According to Lawrence Hinkle's research in the Bell System throughout the United States, executives are less likely to suffer from heart attacks than are their subordinates. The basic assumption is that executives, being members of the middle class, have better genes, better diets, better medical care, longer vacations, lighter work, and better working conditions and are therefore less vulnerable. The real causes of coronaries according to research are a genetic disposition, high cholesterol levels, smoking, obesity, and lack of exercise.

Oh, yes, they are

Executives are more likely to get coronaries because their work is more stressful. Executive work by its very nature attracts the Type A personality, which is represented by people who are efficient, energetic, and ambitious, who work hard and keep busy, and who are sure of themselves, decisive, and satisfied. Type A executives who get heart attacks are the ones who are stuck in the middle of the hierarchy. The demands of corporate life are so great that executives are exposed to massive pressure, which causes them to overeat, smoke too much, and fail to get enough exercise. The result is a heart attack.

Question

Which side of the argument do you support?

INCIDENT

The "burn-out" case

Behavioral research suggests that the number of burn-out cases, who feel they are locked into narrow job routines, is increasing. Teachers, counselors, and social workers, particularly, are falling victims to stress and are ending up as burn-out cases.

Many teachers in New York City, for example, are experiencing teaching as a stressful activity. Their classrooms are overflowing with kids who need special attention, and they are locked into schools with low staff morale. New York teachers are five times more likely to be the targets of student violence than students are. Many of them are subject to neuroses with associated high blood pressure and insomnia.

People working in the helping professions, such as teachers and counselors, are turning to industrial psychologists to get guidance on how to overcome this problem.

Question

How can the burn-out case be helped?

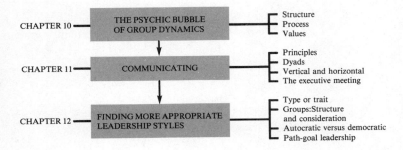

CHAPTER 10 —— THE PSYCHIC BUBBLE
OF GROUP DYNAMICS

— Structure
— Process
— Values

CHAPTER 11 —— COMMUNICATING

— Principles
— Dyads
— Vertical and horizontal
— The executive meeting

CHAPTER 12 —— FINDING MORE APPROPRIATE
LEADERSHIP STYLES

— Type or trait
— Groups:Structure
  and consideration
— Autocratic versus democratic
— Path-goal leadership

part **III**

GROUP DYNAMICS
AND LEADING

DIAGRAM SUMMARY OF CHAPTER 10

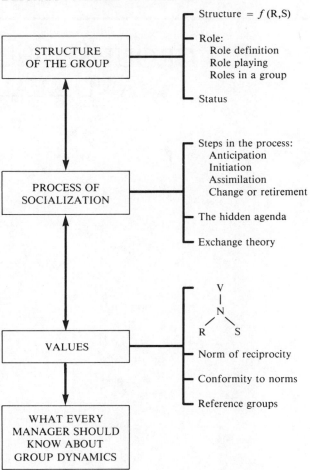

10

The psychic bubble of group dynamics

THE MAKING AND BREAKING OF A PSYCHIC BUBBLE

In the old Hollywood movies, the guy clinching with the gal might say something like, "Let's not fight it, baby. This is bigger than both of us". That's what a group is, something bigger than any individual which has a separate life of its own—and which captures and controls its members. The big question is, who controls the group?

To find an answer to this question, it is necessary to go beyond common sense and consider the technicalities of group dynamics. Technically, a group consists of two or more people who are bounded by a perceptual periphery. Figure 10–1 represents the types of groups comprised of two or three associated persons.

For example, you board a plane and find yourself sitting next to one of the beautiful people, and you hope you will get to know one another. Suddenly the plane hits an air pocket and your companion grabs your hand. You are in a dyadic group! Nobody can burst your little psychic bubble or break into your biosphere.

You begin to work at making a group—creating pseudotasks on which you can both work (your career, your companion's career), identifying common values, establishing new norms of behavior, offering rewards (winning smile for right answers) and sanctions (funny long faces for wrong ones). The values, norms, rewards, and sanctions of this encounter are illustrated in Figure 10–2.

As the plane begins its descent, the bubble starts to deflate: Someone will be waiting at the gate. Making and breaking such groups is what group dynamics is all about.

FIGURE 10–1
Types of groups of two or three persons

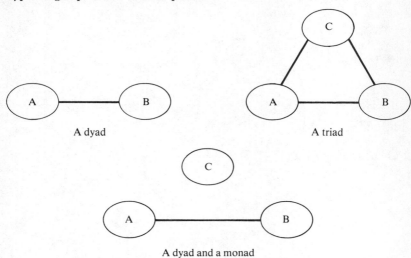

A dyad   A triad

A dyad and a monad

GROUPS AND GROUP DYNAMICS

Group dynamics is concerned with gaining knowledge about the nature of groups, how they develop, and their effects on individual members, other groups, and larger institutions. A group consists of two or more people who bear an explicit psychological relationship to one another. Integral to this concept is the idea that groups are bounded by the perceptual periphery of their members. The implication of this idea of a boundary is that members of a group act as if they believe some cocoon envelops them and separates them from other parts of social environment. The cocoon can be compared to a field of force similar in character to the field generated by a magnet or gravitation.

FIGURE 10–2

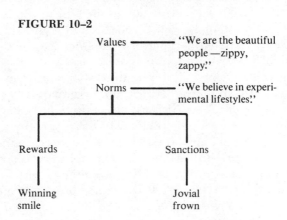

Values ———— "We are the beautiful people —zippy, zappy."

Norms ———— "We believe in experimental lifestyles."

Rewards   Sanctions

Winning   Jovial
smile   frown

This analogy makes it easy to understand why people refer to the feelings of being attracted to one group and repelled by another group. When tension is generated in a group, it is not uncommon to say that the atmosphere could be cut with a knife.

This concept of a group is illustrated in Figure 10–3, a diagram of the social forces in a group. The lines of rejection point out of the

FIGURE 10–3
Lines of social force in a group

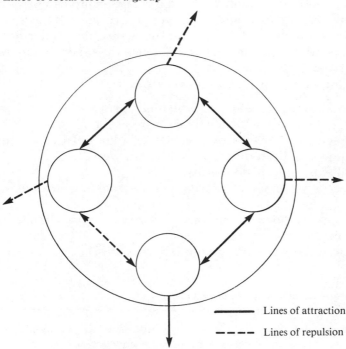

Lines of attraction
Lines of repulsion

group, indicating that it is fairly stable and cohesive. Only one member is shown in the diagram as having a positive force pulling out of the group; the same person is also shown as being involved in a measure of internal conflict. It is a fairly well-integrated group with a relatively low level of internal friction or conflict.

Group theory suggests that people live and work in a microcosm composed of groups, and in a group the members are both captives of the structure and captors in so far as they create and maintain its structure. It is useful to think of a group as a network of relations within which roles for the members emerge.

Groups consist of two or more people who meet the requirements of interdependence and also share an ideology. The members are interdependent; each person's behavior influences the behavior of the other members of the group. Inevitably, on account of their interdependence (which after a time becomes institutionalized), the members develop an ideology based on a common set of values, beliefs, and norms which regulates their behavior and attitudes. This group ideology is developed as the group works on particular tasks and may become peculiar to the group; when a group's values, nouns, reinforcements, and sanctions have been assimilated by its members, it is called a reference group. In this sense leadership can be defined as the ability to influence others in the group; everyone in the group has a degree of leadership. The amount of influence the leader has on the group depends on the amount of influence the other members of the group have on the leader.

People join groups for various reasons:

1. For something to belong to which is bigger and better than themselves alone and which can take care of them.
2. For security: "When they invited me, I knew I had arrived."
3. For power: "United we stand, divided we fall."
4. For identity: "I made the first team."
5. For accomplishment: "We worked as a team to get through, like in "The Paper Chase."
6. For opportunities to interact: "It gives you a chance to meet people."
7. Because they want to huddle (see Box 10–1).

Box 10–1: Informal executive behavior—huddling

Because of the way bureaucracies work, executives make use of informal get-togethers called huddles. These are intimate task-oriented encounters of executives trying to get something done.

V. Dallas Merrell, in *Huddling: The Informal Way to Management Success,* argues that huddling enables executives to deal with emerging matters and to minimize the amount of surprise. It also serves to reduce red tape by cutting through hierarchical channels of communication and minimizing misunderstandings. Because organization charts represent real duties, huddling can compensate for a lack of leadership by taking collective and unofficial responsibility for getting things done.

Of course, huddles, by their very nature, are obscure. They are not documented, and no minutes are kept. Huddlers typically introduce their issues with questions like "Gotta minute?" or "Which way ya walking?"

Huddles are basically intrastructural or interstitial; that is, they are tucked in among official events. Huddling enables managers to touch base or get a reading on matters of great concern.

Reference: V. Dallas Merrell, *Huddling: The Informal Way to Management Success* (New York: American Management Association, 1979).

There are basically two ways groups can be recognized and identified: by asking and by observing. Asking people, in technical terms, is usually described as investigating perceptions and cognitions of individuals. Ultimately this comes down to asking people questions such as, "Who would like to work with whom?" Observing requires actual behavioristic studies. One might, for example, study people in an informal situation, observing how they group themselves for lunch.

Group dynamics refers to adjustive changes in the group structure as a whole produced by changes in any part of the group. In general terms these changes tend to be self-distributive (analogous to the electric charge in a field producing a variation throughout the whole field); any change goes through the whole group. There is a tendency for any action to be balanced by a counterreaction. These two general principles, self-distribution and reaction, mean that the change in groups is relatively slow.

How do groups—in particular, work groups—operate? To get a better insight into why some groups are more productive, why some resist change, and why some disintegrate under pressure, it is necessary to look at the structure, process, and value system of the group.

TOPIC 1
Structure of the group

Group structure $= f(\mathbf{R}, \mathbf{S})$

One characteristic we want to know about a group is its size. It must have at least two people, and theoretically there is no upper limit. The smallest group consists of just two people—doctor and patient, husband and wife. When the group increases in size, its potential complexity rises rapidly. If two people have two relationships going (A's to B and B's to A), a triad has six. A group of four has 12 relationships, and so on according to the $n(n-1)$ formula; so that a group of ten people has 90 interpersonal balls juggling.

In practice, when a group gets above a certain size, it tends to splinter into subgroups. This breaking up is usually anticipated by the formation of cliques which are nearer to the optimum size for the particular group's psychological economy. This is also potentially very complex; even a triad can arrange itself into five different groupings competing for roles, status, and payoffs.

The relations and interactions of a group build up, in time, a web of expectations. If this web becomes too rigid, overwhelming, and unresponsive to changes in the environment, the members may be unable to meet either their own or the group's needs. They may even be destroyed, to no more purpose than the World War II Japanese kamikaze pilot attacking a technologically sophisticated task force. But usually a compromise is worked out between the web of expectations and reality (in the form of goals); even the Japanese suicide pilots were sometimes picked up from the sea "unconsciously" swimming.

Group structure can also be described as the network along which information flows to influence the perceptions, emotions, and behavior of members. In this sense a group is an information-processing system (see Chapter 4).

Group structure essentially describes the complex of roles in a group and how they are fitted together. Structure is a function (f) of role (R) and status (S):

$$\text{Group structure} = f(\text{R, S})$$

When role and status have been defined, the group structure or communication pattern has been defined.

ROLES IN THE GROUP

Definition

A role can be defined as a set or litany of behaviors or attitudes appropriate to a particular position in an organization, irrespective of who occupies it. The word *litany* used to imply that role behaviors have a "sacred" or "holy" aspect; it is not uncommon to find that when one assumes a role, especially for the first time, some kind of quasireligious procedure is prescribed. Doctors take the Hippocratic oath, British officers swear allegiance to the Queen, and U.S. presidents are sworn in. It is not sufficient to describe a role as a set of duties or obligations with a corresponding set of privileges. A role not only encompasses duties and privileges but takes on a mystique which both diminishes and enriches personality.

An organization may be thought of as a giant molecule with roles for atoms. The interlocking complex of roles achieves functional specialization by being populated with people who are expected to behave in particular ways which are functional for the organization. Since the system is interlocked, the roles are connected by a set of rules (which make behaviors legitimate) and relations (which hold the roles in their correct psychological spatial coordinates). The three Rs—roles, rules, and relations—are also held together by the principle of complementarity (reciprocity).

Personality shapes and is shaped by role. As an individual takes up her or his role, his personality moves into a role configuration which structures his perception of the world, moves his self-concept towards his stereotype of the role, and attenuates his behavioral choices as he responds to the signal of the role senders in his group. Figure 10–4

FIGURE 10–4
A role set

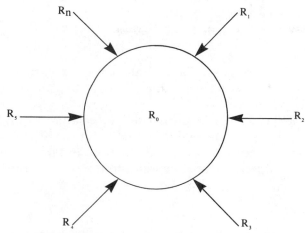

diagrams a role set where R_0 is trying to restructure the person's VANE, perceptions, and dynamic self-concept to fit his group role. R_1 through R_n are role senders—the other members of the group, who want to monitor R_0's behavior to fit the group's values and norms through the use of reinforcements and sanctions. The role senders commonly try to influence the focal person by sending him signals (arrows in Figure 10–4) containing their expectations. The integration of the role senders' expectations will significantly affect the focal person's stereotype of his role, so we can say that role is a function of these expectations (E):

$$\text{Role} = f(E)$$

The role conspiracy

The principle of complementarity states that pairs of roles tend to be grouped around a set of complementary rights and duties. This is, of course, an aspect of the norm of reciprocity. Complementarity means essentially that a role cannot be defined in isolation—it can be only defined in terms of other roles.

For example, consider the doctor-patient relation. Suppose a man has been on the town the night before and comes to in the morning feeling a little off. His wife decides to call a physician, but when the man gets to the doctor's office he feels bright and breezy. The conversation might go like this:

MAN: Hi, Doc!
M.D.: Hello.

MAN: Nice day, Doc.

M.D.: Open the top of your shirt.

MAN: Doc, my wife. . . .

M.D.: Put this in your mouth.

MAN: Uh, uh. . . .

In other words, the doctor-patient relationship represents a conspiracy in which the man has to play patient so that the physician can play doctor, and vice versa.

Complementarity can be illustrated in relation to organizational life. A manager who has been duly initiated into a particular role, with appropriate title, status, access to information, and privileges, will also gain a set of obligations corresponding to the set of rights.

Role playing

A person who takes up a role is acting, albeit in most cases unconsciously. In *The Years of MacArthur,* D. Clayton James predicts that the reader will alternately love and hate General Douglas MacArthur:

> You will find him engaged in acts of rare courage, yet at other times refusing to visit combat areas. . . . He will decide and act on strategic moves with brilliance and boldness on some occasions, yet display inexplicable hesitancy at other times. He will shrewdly bypass enemy strong points, but later demand their seizure despite their uselessness. . . . He will show intense concern over keeping his forces' casualties as low as possible, yet will relentlessly compel his field commanders to assault some objectives which could have been enveloped. . . .

These contradictions in MacArthur's character, James says, were compounded by "his supreme skill at role-playing. . . . An accomplished actor, he could play many parts, and no one has yet finally determined which reflected the real MacArthur. . . . He seemed no more able to refrain from role-playing than [President] Roosevelt, and either man . . . would have rivaled John Barrymore as an actor."

Roles in a group

Figure 10–5 diagrams a typical work group and the kinds of roles likely to emerge in it. The figure indicates that the group aims to accomplish tasks and reach goals. However, it is important to keep in mind that a group is composed of individuals. The people in the group have their own purposes and needs, and the group will not satisfy its aims unless it fulfills theirs. These needs of the individual also influence and shape the kind of role each person takes up.

The task specialist (T) focuses on the group task by attempting to structure the perceptions of members, mobilize their anxieties, and

FIGURE 10–5
Diagram of a group showing roles and relations

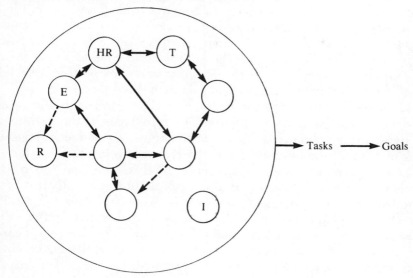

Tasks ────────▶ Goals

direct them. Task specialists are preoccupied with productivity, profitability, and performance. They have a high need for power and try to monitor the behavior of groups by ensuring that a good deal of the verbal communication is channeled through them. To locate the task specialist, look for the person who uses such phrases as "Let's zero in on the problem," and "Let's bear down on the subject." Task specialists, who do not hesitate to exploit the others' needs for achievement or affiliation, inevitably do quite a bit of psychic damage. They get away with it because they are more feared than loved, and because the next member is usually rushing up with some psychic plasma to repair the behavioral wounds.

This is the human relations specialist (HR in Figure 10–5), who tries to spread balm and relieve anxiety and tension. These specialists are essentially concerned with people and usually have a strong need for affiliation. Their verbal style is placatory: "How do all of you feel about this?" "This is kinda interesting, isn't it?" To function properly, the group needs a coalition of the task specialist and the human relations specialist—a formidable combination. In the family, great feats of socialization are achieved when father and mother combine these roles against, but in the interests of the children. It is difficult to combine the two in the same person (which is what behavioral science has often demanded of the executive); but common sense and common experience suggest that groups can work out effective kinds of role specialization.

The eccentric (E in Figure 10–5) is the group member who is allowed and encouraged to break group norms. It is a curious fact that while most members are required to obey the rules, a few are required to break them. Some nonconforming behavior is encouraged, because it gives the group important options when it wishes. Eccentrics have their uses; if they did not exist, the group would have to invent them. The group neophyte may be in hot water for attacking this "odd fellow," for the eccentric usually has friends in high places.

Then, there is the scapegoat or rejectee (R), the person in the group who becomes the focus of hostility. Groups balance the emotional economy by selecting individuals for this role. Whom does the group pick on? Who's the fall guy? Does the rejectee welcome the role?

There are many other roles. Figure 10–5 includes an isolate (I), someone who is technically part of the group but is not really involved in it. Isolates may be simply loners or may like the role of scientifically detached spectator. Other roles might be called father figure, arbitrator, and so on. There are several roles that are concerned with communication between groups—go-between (see Box 10–2), external representative, gatekeeper. The gatekeeper is often of critical impor-

Box 10–2: The go-between

The world of the executive has counterparts in the demimonde of crime. Ever since Edwin Sutherland's landmark portrait, *The Professional Thief,* we have been waiting for the next instalment. Now we have it in the form of the research of Carl B. Klockars, who has produced a definitive study of the go-between, the man who connects the criminal and the consumer, or the professional fence.

In *The Professional Fence,* Klockars, who is an assistant professor of sociology at the University of Pennsylvania and practically unknown in the field of criminology, has painted a brilliant picture of the fence. Klockars grasped the shill of this go-between from the following description a fence gave of his MO:

Maybe this guy [the thief] is trying to set me up, or maybe he's got a tail on him. You never want to let him know where you got the swag. So you set up a drop. There's a lot of ways to do it but if there's trouble I'll just let him leave it on the pavement. Say its's a driver and I think he might have a tail on him. I'll just tell him I'll meet him at such and such a corner in my truck. When he gets there I'll tell him to just keep driving until I blow my horn. When I do, he stops and puts the cartons on the pavement right there and takes off. Then I park my car and watch the load for 10 minutes. Maybe I'll go in and have coffee somewhere, I dunno what I'll do. So after 10 minutes if nobody stops and I see he ain't being tailed, out I go and pick up the stuff.

He is a tough boss when he deals with thieves: "I made him take all the wrappings off before he brought it in my store. And I made him throw 'em away, too. You don't want all those post office numbers around. . . . [Then] he can walk in and sell it to you with the F.B.I. standin' right there. . . ."

Reference: Carl B. Klockars, *The Professional Fence* (New York: Free Press, 1974).

tance; the person in this role selects, edits, routes, recycles, and evaluates information coming into the group.

The gatekeeper

The gatekeeper's role is on the boundary of the group, where information about what is going on in the external world that is of possible interest to the group can be collected. In research and development (R&D) groups, the gatekeeper plays an especially critical part. Frequently a firm's success in innovation is crucially dependent on its gatekeepers.

The creative effort in a business usually involves a three-step process; idea development (the generation of a new concept), problem solving (technical and research effort to show that the idea can in fact work), and implementation (pilot production and transferring the concept into production systems). The gatekeeper plays a critical role in getting the information moving from test tube to production. (see Figure 10–6). It takes particular skills to move across these group boundaries, and gatekeepers have an aptitude for living in the margin between groups. Individuals filling the gatekeeper's role are skilled at dealing with the impediments to communication among groups.

FIGURE 10–6
Three steps in the creative effort presided over by the gatekeeper figure

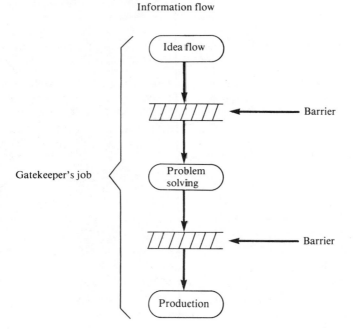

Information flow

Box 10–3: Interpersonal attraction

Interpersonal attraction refers to a positive relationship between two people. Three elements describing close relations between a young man and a young woman; for example, are: favorable attitude ("I adore her/him"), behavioral involvement ("I look at her/him constantly"), and joint belongingness ("We are united together").

Attraction between adults can be based on first impressions, superficial encounters, or sustained involvement. The presumption is that attraction is usually based on finding someone who manifests opposite, complementary or antidote behavior.

A good initial impression may stimulate the perceiver and influence the search for more information. Physical appearance is important, but good looks depend more on a gestalt than on a single feature. If a number of "judges" label a person attractive, then the person is considered to be attractive. Individuals who are rated physically attractive are usually also seen as warm and responsive, interesting, poised, sociable, and so on.

Basically, people like people with whom they are compatible. To like and to be alike have the same root in English.

Ted Huston and George Levinger found that when selecting a game partner, a date, a companion, or a work partner we hope that the one we choose will reciprocate our choice. A major factor in receiving a favorable rating is our own acceptability. All individuals do not respond to every encounter, however; the one we choose has to see the situation as significant.

A good part of interpersonal life consists of brief encounters. Psychiatrists have been developing an arousal model of interpersonal intimacy. M. Argyle and J. Dean, in "Eye Contact, Distance, and Affiliation," suggest the idea of an equilibrium hypothesis which argues that one tends to meet threatening increases in eye contact by moving away or turning one's body to a less direct angle in order to maintain psychological space. Research on eye contact, an important index of nonverbal communication, indicates that it promotes intimacy in females but reticence in males. Body orientation is another important factor.

One of the basic issues in this field is whether attraction leads to self-disclosure. The research answer is in the affirmative. But does disclosure lead to attraction? The answer is, it depends upon the situation. For example, if desirable information is disclosed, then intimacy is enhanced. Does self-disclosure lead to reciprocity? Basically the answer again is yes, but overdisclosure seems to give rise to suspicion rather than trust.

Another vital question in this area is what makes a friend a friend. Friends are persons with whom one has shared experiences, interests, and activities, with whom one feels comfortable. Females make greater distinctions between levels of friendship than males do. Most people distinguish between good friends and casual acquaintances.

Reference: Ted L. Huston and George Levinger, "Interpersonal Attraction and Relationships," *Annual Review of Psychology,* vol. 29 (1978).

Managers in charge of creative groups should actively encourage such boundary roles and reward gatekeepers for maintaining external contacts. The gatekeeper must be encouraged to scan information from external areas.

An important influence on the gatekeeper's role in managing creative change is interpersonal attraction (see Box 10–3)

GROUP STATUS

Status is the rank held by a person and the value of that individual as measured by a group or class of persons. This estimate of rank is based ultimately on the extent to which the person's traits or attributes are seen as contributing to the commonly held needs and values of the group or class. Status is usually legitimated through certain value propositions which provide criteria of status achievement. Inevitably the search for value measures is so demanding that they tend to be applied in a somewhat relentless manner; this, of course, underscores the need people have to achieve some kind of status definition. Not only aristocrats require a *Who's Who;* everybody requires some definition of rank that is visible, uniform, acceptable, useful, and if possible, reasonable. This need produces such criteria as "publish or perish" for university professors.

Some companies claim they have no status systems and manage by pursuing a policy of conspicuous democracy. Where this apparent absence of status holds, however, there is a tendency for senior executives to achieve some kind of isolation or executive apartheid by, for example, timing their lunch to an hour when the mass of the workers has already eaten.

Conscious and explicit recognition of the function of status in regard to the proper discharge of the executive role is necessary. Refusal to recognize the need for a status gradient with appropriate symbols usually leads to covert activities involving devious arrangements and conspiracies which are resented, time-consuming, and expensive.

TOPIC 2
The process of socialization

One of the major reasons people have for joining groups is to define their performance, function, status, and role with regard to their fellows, especially those whose judgment they value. This need to establish consensual validation helps the individual to work through the phases of group socialization and it helps the group to establish itself as a functioning unit.

STEPS IN THE PROCESS

Organizations process not only material, energy, and information but also people. The "new boy" entering the organization has to be taught the ropes before acquiring the three Rs (rules, roles, and relations) of the game. To achieve this personal transformation, the rookie—the trainee, the cadet, the new patient—has to be socalized. Figure 10–7 is an overview of this process.

FIGURE 10–7
Socialization

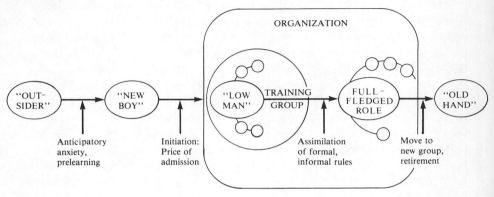

Anticipation

The process of socialization is the assimilation of the values and behaviors required to survive and propser in the organization. It begins even before the person to be processed encounters the organization. Crack institutions such as the Harvard Business School, the Marines, IBM, the Mayo Clinic, and Sing Sing have a distinct reputation which gives off an ambience, a cultural essence which alerts and preconditions initiates for what lies ahead—"It's going to be tough." Nobody can really tell them what lies ahead, not even others who have been through the hoop. Sometimes the process is so dramatic (something like electroshock therapy, which has been compared to facing the patient with the crisis of simulated death) that amnesia is introduced, and the destruction of one identity is achieved and another created. At the very least, anxiety is generated.

As one preliminary, the candidate has to be sold the organization. This may be involuntary (as with imprisonment), but ideally it is a free choice, and candidates value and esteem what lies ahead. They see themselves as members of an élite which has a coveted, distinctive status. For a pilot's wings or a company president's eight-foot desk, there must be a price of admission which only a few can pay.

The prelearning process makes some effort to break down and replace previous reference groups. At the extreme—in a mental hospital, a religious order, a prison, or an officer training school—the old self is symbolically destroyed by a process of stripping which may include removal of clothes, previous status symbols, reference to previous achievements, and even, in some circumstances, hair. New names and titles, such as cadet and management trainee, are conferred. This process of purification prepares acolytes by altering their previous roles and status.

Initiation: The price of admission

The "new boy" becomes the "low man" on the group totem pole. Initiates form a training squad or work group in which the process of role assimilation begins. At this stage the group is assigned problems (cases to handle, floors to polish, litter to pick up, technical information to acquire) which are well beyond their individual capabilities. Considerable anxiety is generated; fear of failure and the possibility of rejection are always there. The squad bosses (professors, psychiatrists, training managers) become the focus of a love-hate relation. To survive, the group forms informal structures, processes, and values, and this peer group takes over the job of indoctrinating other initiates. Such primary groups typically begin with a high level of tension which reaches a maximum just before the midpoint of the training period. Just when the "new man" is weighing the advantages of quitting, there is usually a slight letting up to let him get through to the second half. From then on in, it's cheaper to stay in than quit.

Assimilation

The assimilation of the new role, identity, and value system is developed further by taking the neophyte into the first operational assignment. From a socialization point of view, the object of this part of the exercise is to introduce the neophyte to the complexities and dilemmas of a sector of the organization where the cozy feeling of being inside the training group, with its peer support, is somewhat diminished. The first assignment introduces a world of work families, each with its own territory, mandate, values, and norms—all operative, but mostly hazy and somewhat difficult to pick up. The humiliations of initiation, the learning of new passwords and prayers, must be endured again, until the neophyte eventually is absorbed into the apparatus.

The critical first assignment is apparently designed to make or break the new member. Much depends on the accidents of technology; the assignment may be solvable or not, depending on management or the support of peers, who may also be going through this trial by fire. In any case, the structure of a career path slowly reveals its clues. Of the neophytes, a few will be nudged to the exits; most will be sent to relatively routine assignments and the gradual career escalator; a few will be directed to the fast escalator, with accelerated challenges, status, and rewards built in.

As the new member is freed of the neophyte status and moves into the heartland of the institution, it is necessary to learn new roles and styles. Only the right kind of exposure and visibility will ensure this. Much depends on the sort of assignments members pick up and the people they associate with.

Frequently the organization cannot provide sufficient experience to ensure accelerated growth, and elaborate training rituals in the form of T groups, and other simulated problem-solving exercises have to be gone through. The contemporary acceleration of change makes continual demands for further role developments. In the future, changes in the external environment are likely to outpace and defeat the strategy of concentrating on assimilation of an organization's specific roles. The emergence of the mobile manager, the rapid development of computer firms, the mushrooming of consultancy, the slowing down of the aerospace and electronics business, human liberation in terms of the existential culture, and a multitude of other factors may make single-role assimilation a distinct hazard.

Change or retirement

In any case, as the corporate official enters middle age, he or she may well be in a real crisis. Beset by anxieties as to whether the right career choice was made, fearful of reduced vigor and an aging appearance, and with career and salary leveling off, they in effect enter another adolescence. The principal response has been to succumb to apathy and anomie and, like the old soldier, just fade away. Yet many persons have provided clues to another choice: second (or third) careers, development into new life-styles, and ways of making the term *golden age* more than a mockery. Increasing mobility and personal freedom may contribute. Certainly those who experiment with many roles rather than putting all their eggs in one basket are in a better position to move on—or out—with self-confidence.

THE HIDDEN AGENDA

Group processes are the rituals and rubrics the group develops for handling different behavioral phenomena. In initiation and assimilation, the price of admission is levied, and the neophyte is taught the ropes. A major activity is processing people into conformity—engineering their behavior through group influence. As the group develops, it creates a matrix of values, norms, reinforcements, and sanctions, which we will discuss in the following section on values. Stages of development in groups are outlined in Box 10–4.

Influence by rewards and sanctions is a process. In dealing with processes, it is important to remember that groups have two sets of them, a public agenda and a hidden agenda. The public agenda is the visible, stated set of tasks and goals. The hidden agenda deals with all the undercover processes and is apparently perverse, pathological, and irrational (but only at first sight). Its purpose is to deal with the irra-

Box 10–4: Stages of development in groups

Groups go through definite stages of development.

Stage I: Uncertainty

1. The group seeks orientation. A power and authority structure develops.
2. Conflict breaks out; e.g., hawks versus doves.
3. Cohesion may develop: "Now we are getting somewhere."

Stage II: Developing interpersonal relations

1. Feelings of dissatisfaction with the new structure set in.
2. People are disillusioned: "We are not working right."
3. A crisis of acceptance develops. The question is, to be or not to be. Most groups fail at this point.

Stage III: Group maturity

1. People are accepted for what they are.
2. Conflict is exploited usefully.
3. Decisions are made rationally, but allowing dissent.
4. Members know the score and can live with the consequences.

tional emotions which are inevitably present. It processes such emotions, giving group members their due or their come-uppance, putting people in their places. It involves complex calculations of effectiveness and equity. The Watergate scandal provided an excellent illustration as the group's dynamics were laid bare in televised hearings—a case study of a hidden agenda in terms of not only illicit activities but undercurrents of emotion and relationship among group members.

A theory with considerable explanatory value for both the public and private—or the formal and informal—processes of groups is exchange theory.

EXCHANGE THEORY

Exchange theory sets out to explain group behavior in terms of rewards exchanged and costs incurred in the interaction. Four concepts are fundamental to exchange theory: reward, cost, outcome, and comparison level. Rewards are the payoffs which emerge from the interaction; any behavior that adds to the gratification of a person's needs constitutes a reward as far as that person is concerned. Similarly the term *cost* is a very broad concept and encompasses not only factors such as fatigue, anxiety, loss of status, and punishment, but also the value of rewards which the members miss by not participating in other exchanges. An outcome is defined as rewards minus costs; if positive, the interaction is said to yield a profit; if negative, a loss. The fact that a person profits from an interaction does not necessarily mean that he likes his partner in the interaction. For attraction to develop, it is necessary for the outcome to exceed some minimal level of expectation. Level of comparison describes the process whereby a person evaluates the outcome of a particular interaction against the profit which is forgone elsewhere.

Exchange theory explains why individuals with certain idiosyncrasies receive more than their proportionate share of choices and why one person distinguished by a particular trait selects others with different traits. For example, an effective executive is capable of widening the field of participation for colleagues by structuring relations and activities. For example, if a lunch is arranged to introduce a visiting dignitary, the executive arranges to have associates introduced, initiates topics of conversation which allow them to participate in a rewarding manner, and generally fosters a feeling of tolerance among them.

Effective executives are also able to manage their own emotional economy in such a way as to minimize the cost to their fellows, by monitoring their moods so that they do not inflict their anxieties and depressions on others. In essence, effective group members possess traits that increase the rewards and minimize the costs to their fellows. Those who are rejected are those who raise the costs to their fellows by being hostile, domineering, and inconsiderate.

TOPIC 3
Values: Learning to love your group

VALUES, NORMS, REWARDS, AND SANCTIONS

As a group develops, its own particular ideology or complex of values, expressed in a set of norms or standards for group behavior, emerges. Conformity to the norm is rewarded (reinforcements), and nonconformity is punished (sanctions).

Since values vary according to the group, it is impossible to specify them beyond some basic norms. They are indicated and can be observed by studying groups in terms of such measures as member satisfaction and morale.

An illustration of a shop-floor matrix of values, norms, reinforcements, and sanctions demonstrates how this system operates. Suppose a group of workers (perhaps goaded by a traditional classical management structure) comes up with an overriding value such as "Management is the enemy; they're trying to screw us and we'll show 'em they can't get away with it." The value may be emotional and somewhat unclear, but it produces a precisely defined, specific norm: Production will be restricted to a fixed number of units within a time period. The group then develops a set of rules to maintain the norm (the value), with the reinforcement of group approval and such sanctions as intimidation or spoiling excess production. Communication may be by jokes and double-edged statements, or it may be explicit. The group often employs one person, usually an older, nonthreatening type, to break in new members. This member helps the neophyte with the work and explains the norm until the value is inculcated. If this effort fails, a younger and tougher worker may begin to intimidate the new worker with sanctions, or perhaps the group eccentric is brought into play. The techniques do not always work; a rate-buster who has a different, strong value (and perhaps a low need for affiliation) will break the norm.

THE NORM OF RECIPROCITY

One norm which is basic to all groups is reciprocity, the common idea of equity expressed in such clichés as "tit for tat" or "You scratch my back and I'll scratch yours." This norm expresses the value judgment that when A exercises a right at some cost to B, A thereby incurs the obligation to allow B to exercise a right at some cost to A. The norm of reciprocity binds the group together in a mutuality of rights, obligations, and gratifications.

Alvin Gouldner, in "The Norm of Reciprocity," argues that this norm is universal, in the form of "(1) people should help those who help them and (2) people should not injure those who have helped them." This group dynamics version of the Golden Rule regulates exchange patterns and thus gives the group its stability. The process is always incomplete; the balance of rights and obligations is never perfect. This lack of perfection (something is always owed), coupled with the goodwill of previous exchanges and possible future transactions, keeps the group going (sometimes, as "old boy" class and regimental reunions illustrate, long after the original group functions have been completed).

The establishment of bonds of reciprocity is never unconditional but depends on the principle of comparative advantage—which is the essence of exchange theory.

CONFORMITY TO NORMS

A subject of consuming interest to executives is conformity—the influence the group exerts on individuals to get them into roles, keep them there, and make them follow group norms and in general meet the group's expectations. Groups cannot survive if most of their expectations are not realized. A sufficient number of role holders defaulting on their payments, in terms of meeting expectations, would lead to a breakdown of the basic processes of the group.

What the member must conform to is the group's norms—the specifications of its values. A norm may be defined as a verbal statement that many members believe is a valuable guide to behavior. A norm is thus a behavioral rule accepted by several (usually a majority of) members of the group. Once norms have been specified and codified, group life becomes easier, since recourse to either power or ingratiation will diminish because of lack of necessity. Norms are thus behavioral inventions to facilitate group life.

Why do group members conform? For starters, conformity to group norms is rewarded with reinforcements, and lack of conformity is punished with sanctions. Reinforcements include approval, acceptance, recognition, and positive feedback. Sanctions include denial of membership, rejection, isolation, and negative feedback. Conformity thus offers an inducement to the individual. Higher status also influences members to make their attitudes and behavior conform to the norms of the group. For example, army officers have greater faith in the avowed aims of the army than enlisted men do.

Complete conformity indicates that a member depends entirely on the norms of the group. As Figure 10–8 indicates, utter conformity is not as healthy a situation for the individual as a measure of nonconformity, which allows some options. The anticonformist does the exact opposite of what group norms demand and thus is as much a slave to the situation as the conformist is.

FIGURE 10–8
Axes of conformity and nonconformity

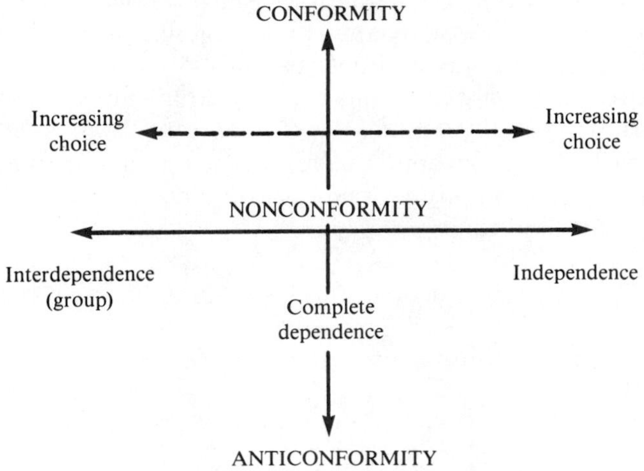

Compliance, identification, and internalization

People may conform overtly without accepting the party line. For example, many POWs in North Korea went through the motions of ideological conversion to communism to survive, without in fact privately changing their political beliefs. Herbert C. Kelman was puzzled by this problem of public conformity without private acceptance. In exploring this problem further in "Compliance, Identification, and Internalization," Kelman distinguished these three processes of social influence.

Compliance occurs when an individual accepts influence from another, hoping to achieve a favorable response from the other person. "Making the right noises," saying and doing the right things to stay in somebody's good books, constitutes compliance. Compliance lacks conviction and manifests itself only when the person is under observation.

Identification occurs when a person adopts the behavior or attitudes of another for the purpose of keeping in good standing with the other person. An example would be a male executive imitating his boss in terms of accent, dress, style, and so on. Identification is similar to compliance in the sense that the conforming person is under the influence of another; it differs in the sense that the individual acts voluntarily, out of admiration rather than compulsion (unlike compliance, when the person does not behave differently in private).

Internalization occurs when an individual is not merely influenced by another's (the group's) values but incorporates them into his or her own value system. The three processes indicate an increasing level of conformity, from behavior that is only an appearance to a restructuring of attitudes within the self-concept.

Engineering conformity

One of the most widely established findings in group dynamics is the fact that opinions converge when individuals become members of a group. The classical research in engineering conformity was conducted by Musafer Sherif, who set his subjects the task of estimating the extent of movement of a single point of light in a completely dark room. The light, though stationary, will be seen to move; and further, the movements are perceived as being erratic. This phenomenon is known as the autokinetic effect. In "Experiments on Group Conflict and Cooperation," Sherif compared individual judgments made in private with estimates made by the same individual as a member of a group. The effect of convening the group was to make the estimates converge.

On matters of this type, where there is no objective actuality, consensus may be essential because consensus is the only reality. Hence the executive's expression "validity by consensus."

Apparently group members experience considerable pressure to conform with peer estimates, even when such estimates clearly run contrary to the facts. This proposition was demonstrated in an extremely influential series of experiments by S. E. Asch. In "Studies of Independence and Conformity," Asch reported experiments in matching the length of a vertical line with three other lines. A subject, after hearing phony "evidence" which contradicts the evidence of his senses, will go along with the phony consensus. The importance of communication in avoiding this sort of pluralistic ignorance is obvious.

Given the social psychologist's ability to engineer consensus, management training, and sensitivity training in particular, is a cinch. By carefully selecting group members and organizing "experiences"— both their nature and sequence—it is apparently possible to get managers to agree to anything.

Group pressures to uniformity are substantial and are based on such considerations as:

1. If uniformity of opinion is held to be important for the group, the group will try to bring this state about to maintain its reality. For example, in management training, "We are here for a week; let's give it a try—let's not pack everything in the first hour of the first day."
2. Groups have a variety of rewards which they can give for conformity—especially indications of esteem and acceptance.
3. Groups usually can exercise sanctions for failure to conform.

REFERENCE GROUPS

It has been suggested that one reason some people do not conform is that they are "marching to a different drum." Nonconformists march to the tune of their own reference groups.

A reference group is any group, real or imaginary, which has significantly affected a person's expectations of life by planting its values, norms, reinforcements, and sanctions in her or his consciousness. It may be a group in the person's past, present, or future. Figure 10–9 designates important potential reference groups.

Aware of the importance of reference groups, some organizations (such as prisons and other total institutions) seek to remove all evidence of their existence by purification rituals. Other organizations deliberately seek out members with compatible reference groups. For example, the English military and foreign service prefer candidates

FIGURE 10–9
Important potential reference groups

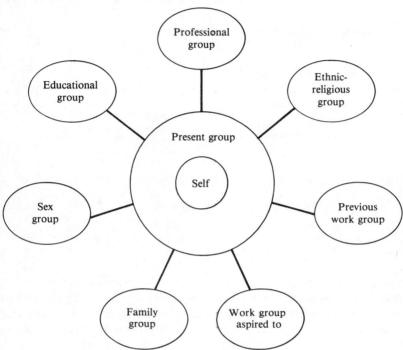

from public (private) schools and Oxbridge, mainly because reference group congruence makes organizational life so much more predictable (if somewhat boring) and eliminates the danger of upstarts who have innovative ideas. In the United States, similar arrangements prevail between top business schools (Harvard, MIT, Stanford) and top corporations (IBM, ITT, Ford), to maintain congruence of reference groups. Not a bad arrangement, in the main—and fortunately, the system is sufficiently inefficient to produce a Ralph Nader from time to time.

Cosmopolitan and local roles

The concept of reference group provides a useful way to consider the difference between two interesting roles: the cosmopolitan and the local. Alvin Gouldner points out in "Cosmopolitans and Locals" that cosmopolitans are mobile, sophisticated experts who take their reference from their professional groups. Locals are organization men who take their reference from their present organizations:

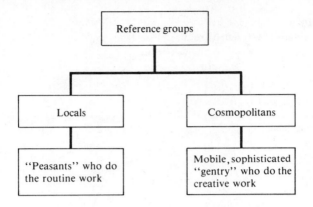

Cosmopolitans and locals can be compared in terms of:

	Loyalty to work group	Professional skill	Reference group
Cosmopolitan	Low	High	Outside work group
Locals	High	Low	Inside work group

A commonly cited example is university departments. Cosmopolitans are copious authors who derive their reference from academic peers in their specialty elsewhere and pay scant heed to what is going on in their own departments. Locals keep the department going—teaching, administering, and maintaining community relations—and are frequently uncertain as to what is happening at the frontiers of knowledge in their discipline. In most universities, cosmopolitans have the highest prestige and salaries while rendering the least service to undergraduate students.

In business, cosmopolitans were traditionally found among the staff experts in personnel, finance, and engineering and locals were in line managers. But now, as management achieves the status of a profession, a new breed of cosmopolitan managers is emerging.

Trading values across groups

One of the most interesting, least studied, yet most crucial aspects of value systems is the trading process that goes on between interacting groups. An excellent illustration of this value overlap was provided by Albert J. Reiss, Jr., a sociologist from Yale University. In *The Police and the Public,* Reiss reported on a study by a team of researchers who investigated how the police operated in 5,360 meetings between 579 policemen and 11,255 citizens.

This study destroys a number of myths. The most important finding was—contrary to the widely held belief that corruption is confined to a "few rotten apples"—that in fact 1 in 5 of the policemen observed was in criminal violation of the law. Corrupt practices included taking money and property from deviants, stealing from previously burglarized premises, not giving traffic tickets in exchange for bribes, accepting both money and goods from merchants, and accepting money to alter sworn testimony. Drinking on duty, ridiculing citizens, and acting in an authoritarian manner were not uncommon.

The reason for this corruption can be found in the fact that police officers as a group are caught between their own values and those of many other groups who have a high influence on them, as shown in Figure 10–10. While they are charged with fighting crime, their efforts

FIGURE 10–10
How other group values impinge on police values

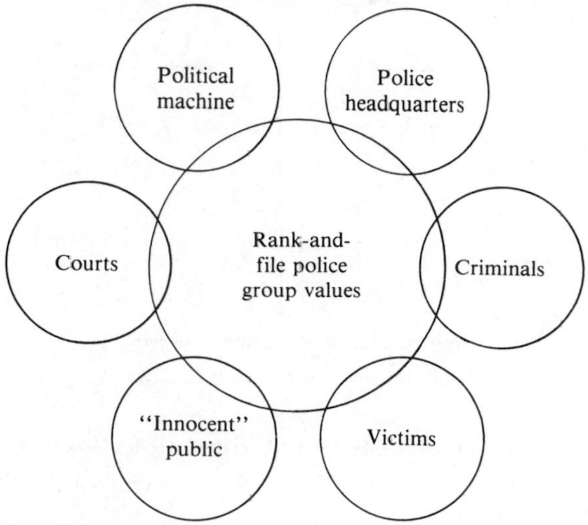

are undermined by other forces in our society. Reiss says, in *The Police and the Public*:

> The judgments of the police and others in the legal system are intricately balanced in a commitment to justice. If, on the average, the officer's sense of justice is not confirmed, or his moral commitments are not sustained by others, he loses his own moral commitment to the system. Where moral commitment is lost, subcultural practices take over.

Techniques like plea bargaining, the condescending manner of judges and prosecutors, punitive treatment handed out by superiors, political interference, and public apathy all serve to force the police officer into role conflict. The point is not whether "going on the take" is justified; the point is understanding that a group, like an individual, needs reinforcement and support from other groups. A web of conflicting and confusing expectations can threaten its very survival.

TOPIC 4
What every manager should know
about group dynamics

A group has a separate life of its own.

1. It has a perceptual periphery—within this skin members view the world differently. A group is a gestalt, a whole, a thing, an entity:

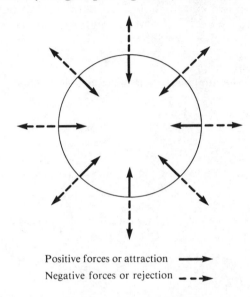

Positive forces or attraction ⟶
Negative forces or rejection ⟶

2. A group has a survival system. It is difficult to destroy or break up.
3. A group cannot survive unless its members value their membership in it.

A group has a structure of rules, roles, and relations.

1. Roles include the task specialist, human relations specialist, eccentric, father figure, exemplar, isolate, observer, scapegoat, holy man, buffoon, neophyte, and many more (there are so many because a group can do so many things).
2. Rules are called norms which cannot be made fully explicit. If you understand why they cannot be made fully explicit, you have made a real beginning in group dynamics.
3. Relations can be categorized as attraction, repulsion or indifference.

There are various types of groups:

1. A primary working group refers to a set of individuals who work in a close, face-to-face relationship over a relatively long period of time.

2.   A reference group is a set of people to which you belong (or wish to) which monitors your values, attitudes, needs, and expectations.

Groups assimilate new members through socialization.

Stages of socialization in organizations include:

> Screening
> Initiation
> Assimilation
> Stripping and purification
> Threat of rejection
> First task
> Make-or-break assignment
> Getting down to work
> :
> :
> :
> Rejection
> Rehabilitation

The process of socialization assimilates the new member into the primary group, which may be defined as a group in which every member interacts directly, and frequently with every other member, usually on a face-to-face basis.

The primary group

The primary group, with its face-to-face interaction, is the nucleus of all organizations and represents the molecular structure (with roles for atoms) from which all social structure is built. The peer group represents an organized but informal group which protects the organized from the organizers. Of necessity, peer groups must be factional. At one time they were regarded as pathological, perverse, and dysfunctional; now they are regarded as a sine qua non of healthy organization.

Functions of primary work groups include:

Providing emotional support for group members.

Facilitating horizontal communication.

Defining standards of performance.

Allowing role specialization.

Creating value systems (i.e., generating a calculus of aims which members more or less accept).

Specifying acceptable norms (i.e., limiting and defining the means which are acceptable to group members).

Specifying sanctions for breaches of conformity.

Exhibiting functional autonomy (i.e., after the original reason for the creation of the group has passed, the group will create new needs to exploit the social capital that the membership has generated).

FIGURE 10–11
The contingency model of the group as a system

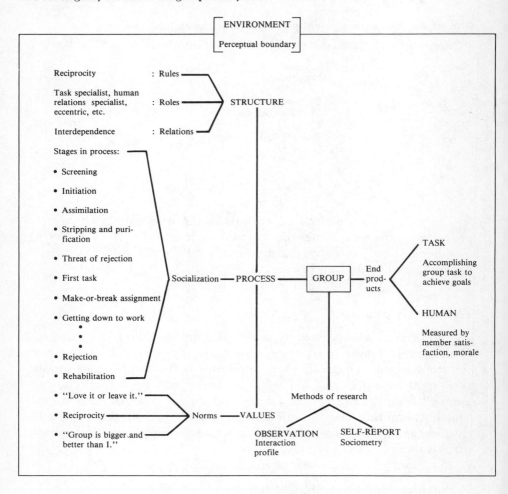

A group goes through certain processes in its development:

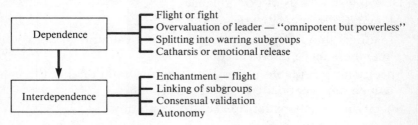

A group is governed by values, norms, reinforcements, and sanctions:

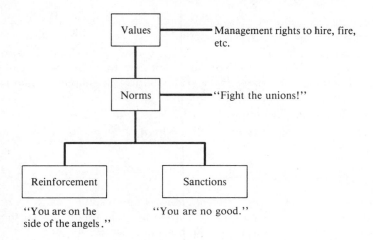

Many of the key concepts of group dynamics can also be reviewed with the contingency model (see Figure 10–11). There are too many kinds of groups to specify particular values or end products, except to point out in a general way what should be looked at and measured in studying a particular group. Fundamentally, there are two methods for studying group behavior: self-report and observational methods, or asking and observing.

REVIEW AND RESEARCH

1. Select a group known to you through experience and:
   a. Define its structure. Include samples of behavior to specify particular roles.
   b. Describe the process of how the group developed. List the different stages of development.
   c. Specify the values, norms, reinforcements, and sanctions of the group.
   d. Decide (setting out the evidence) whether your group was high or low in cohesion.
2. Define the terms *group* and *dynamics*. Work out the analogy between group dynamics and electrolytic action.
3. Compare and contrast a group, a social organization (such as a political party), and a formal organization.
4. How do small groups link the individual to the organization?
5. Why is the concept of role critical in linking social psychology and sociology?
6. "Status symbols are inevitable in any organization." Argue the case for this proposition. How should status symbols be controlled in an organization?
7. Define status and role and show how they are linked.
8. Define the role of a dean in a business school. Describe the role set. Give

examples of role and personality conflict as applied to the office of the dean.

9. How are roles learned? To develop your answer, consider some episode in your life such as your experience in the military, at work, or in some leisure group. Alternatively, consider how your learned a family role (e.g., father, son, daughter, brother).

10. Why do all effective groups have initiation rites?

11. If humans are basically conflictive, why do they cooperate in groups?

GLOSSARY OF TERMS

Clarification. First of three phases of group problem solving (also *evaluation* and *decision;* see Chapter 1). Definition by group members of the facts about the problem and the assumptions needed to solve it.

Compliance. Acceptance of influence in which the individual gives the appearance of conforming while being observed, but in fact lacks inner conviction and behaves differently in private. (See also *identification, internalization.*)

Conformity. Adherence to the norms and expected behavior of the group. Conformity may range from partial to complete dependence on group standards; anticonformity (invariably acting against group standards) also indicates dependence.

Decision. Third phase of group problem solving (after clarification and evaluation); specification of solutions and structuring behavior of the group to choose and carry out the best alternative.

Evaluation. Second phase of group problems solving; attempt by members of the group to establish a consensus of value judgments, spelling out their feelings about the facts and assumptions produced by clarification before proceeding to the decision phase.

Exchange theory. Explanation of organizational behavior in terms of rewards exchanged, costs incurred, outcomes (rewards minus costs, yielding positive or negative result), and level of comparison (evaluating the outcome of a particular exchange in comparison to other possible exchanges).

Group. Assembly of two or more people who bear an explicit psychological relationship to one another; who are interdependent and interact to produce a common ideology; and who form a network of communication and of expectations in order to influence the behavior of group members.

Group dynamics. Adjustive changes in the group structure produced by changes in any part of the group. The study of group dynamics is concerned with learning the nature of groups, how they develop, and their effect on individual members, other groups, and larger institutions.

Human relations specialist. The group role whose holder is primarily concerned with the feelings of persons, trying to placate, relieve anxieties, and release tensions; this role is complementary to that of the task specialist.

Identification. Acceptance of influence in which the individual adopts the behavior and attitudes of another because of admiration for the other person; differs from compliance in that the influenced person does not behave differently in private; differs from internalization in that the person imitates behavior without adopting internally the values from which it springs.

Internalization. Acceptance of influence in which the individual makes the influencing values, attitudes, and behavior his own, incorporating them into his self-concept.

Member satisfaction. An indication of group values in terms of status consensus, perception of progress towards group goals, and perceived freedom to participate.

Morale. An indication of group values in terms of cohesiveness, ability to resolve conflict, community of goals, positive attitudes, mutual goodwill, and so on.

Nonconformity. Independence from group influence which ranges from rejection of the group to acceptance of interdependence within the group. The group accepts nonconformity within limits, because it provides the options necessary for change and growth; it accepts individual nonconformists because of proven ability and the healthy contributions they are perceived to offer.

Reciprocity. A universal norm in groups which embodies the ideas of equity, give and take, rights and obligations. The fact that the balance of favors is never perfect gives the group stability.

Reference group. The group (real or imaginary) an individual uses as a standard for evaluating the standards and behaviors of other groups; usually a crucial group in the person's development, such as family or school.

Role conflict. Anxiety generated in a role holder in one or two ways: intrarole conflict arising from the perception of contradictory expectations by various role senders; or interrole conflict arising from the occupancy of multiple roles.

Roles. The functions group members serve; the parts group actors play. In addition to the two most basic and important roles of task specialist and human relations specialist, common roles include the eccentric, the scapegoat, the isolate, the detached observer, the gatekeeper, the cosmopolitan, the local, and so on.

Socialization. The process by which a new person entering a group or organization is initiated and assimilated so that she or he acquires the values and behavior patterns of the group.

Status. The rank held by a group member, indicating the value the group places on the member's contributions and achievements; usually made visible by status symbols.

Task specialist. The group role whose holder concentrates on achieving group tasks, chiefly through mobilizing the anxieties of members and directing them; this role is complementary to that of the human relations specialist.

DEBATE: Huddling makes management, like football, an exclusively male pastime, versus men huddle because they muddle the formal arrangements

Hints:

1. Reread Box 10–1 on huddling.
2. Review the formal versus the informal group concept. See the section on the hidden agenda.
3. How do women learn to work and play in groups? Are their experiences different from men's? Need they be different?

EXERCISE

A sales training program

You are the senior administrative staff member of a pharmaceutical company employing 1,000 people engaged in the manufacture and sales of drugs. The company employs 50 representatives who are supervised by five regional sales managers. You have been instructed by the president to set up a sales training program for the marketing division. You are to consider the main difficulties the scheme will have to overcome to get started and the subjects to be included in the course. You will not appoint a chairman. You will not appoint a secretary.

INCIDENT

W. Clay Hammer and Dennis W. Organ, in *Organizational Behavior,* say that women going to West Point find it very hard to accept the socialization of new cadets. They quote Gay Gray, who was one of the first 20 women to drop out:

> I think every girl that was there had been brought up independently. That was the hardest thing to do—to learn how to work as a unit. Everyone was just used to doing their part of the job, and all of a sudden we had to do it all together. One of our squad's biggest problems was getting ready for anything on time. We were never ready on time. We had some guys—they were perfectionists or something—and they wouldn't leave their rooms and be ready on time, and the whole squad would get in trouble. . . .
>
> The women didn't really need each other. We needed the squad, the total unit. Everyone seemed capable of handling their own load except for just a few, and I hear it's not just the women who couldn't handle the load. . . .
>
> It was the initiation period [that upset me]. It was necessary because you had to learn to react, to be able to function under stress. I realize

that. That's why I went through it this summer. I didn't do too well. I cried a lot. . . . The haircut really got to me at first. I think it got to a lot of girls at first. I think you have to be able to—like they said, don't let them get that little part inside of you. Just let them have everything they want, give them all they can take except that little part that is you. I guess I felt threatened. I felt like either I was going to have to give my whole self to stay there or leave before they got that part of me. ("The Corps Demands All," *National Observer*, September 25, 1976, pp. 1, 18. Reprinted with permission of Dow Jones & Co., Inc. © Dow Jones, 1976. All rights reserved.)

Question

What advice would you give to a young woman entering a traditionally male-dominated institution?

DIAGRAM SUMMARY OF CHAPTER 11

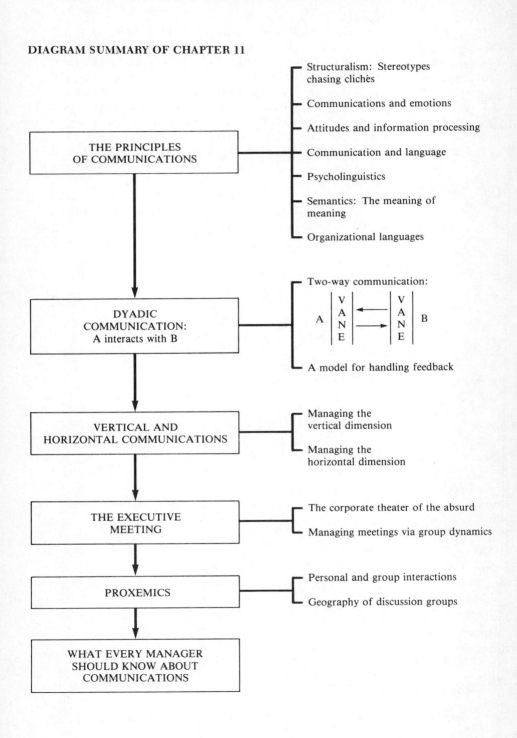

11

Communications

EDWARD CARLSON COMMUNICATES*

Edward Carlson is the man who turned around United Airlines. A major feat! When he took over as chief executive officer in December of 1970 the company had just suffered a $46 million loss, the biggest in its history. Its market share was shrinking, its employees were demoralized and discouraged. A vast centralized bureaucracy was strangling in its own red tape.

How did he accomplish the turnaround? Obviously, neither this brief introduction nor the conversation that follows will provide a definitive answer. We believe however, that Carlson's management philosophy, together with the system he devised for implementing that philosophy, provides a large part of the answer. The philosophy Carlson himself ascribes to the late Henry Kaiser: "Find the smartest people you can, pay them well, give them lots of autonomy and they will make you look good." Wise words, but only part of Carlson's corporate wisdom.

The system Carlson installed at United Airlines was based on a number of complementary and interlocking elements. First, it was decentralized around a number of profit centers, with the top executives in these profit centers competing for bonuses based on the profits that could be attributed to their efforts. Moreover, decentralization extended to the 1,700 individual station managers, each of whom

---

* Reprinted from *Organizational Dynamics*, Spring 1979. © 1979, AMACOM, a division of American Management Associations.

headed profit centers and who competed for recognition, raises, and promotions based on the success of their efforts.

As Professor Richard Pascale of the Stanford Business School has written of Carlson in his paper "Three Chief Executives: How Style Effects Results," "Carlson's system centers on initiative, forever pushing responsibility and accountability out to those closest to the problem and the information relevant to it." This downward diffusion of responsibility and accountability, in turn, rests on his conviction, forged during a working lifetime spent in the hotel business, that wholehearted support rests on participation, and that the difference between confidence and wholehearted support in a service business makes a tremendous difference in both performance and the bottom line.

Other key elements in Carlson's system include what he calls "visible management"—traveling constantly throughout U.A.L., tapping the ideas and listening to the grievances of employees at every level, and urging his senior executives to emulate his example and to do their own "base touching." Carlson also realizes that "visible management" is hollow unless it is accompanied by equally visible feedback. Someone in authority *always* follows up to the employee with a report on the action contemplated as a result of his or her suggestion or complaint.

There's more—lots more to the system—but for the rest, we will let Carlson speak for himself.

EDWARD CARLSON: The other day I picked up some information and passed it on to one of our senior people. He said, "Ed, it's amazing. You've been out of the day-to-day operation for two and a half years. You've got unbelievable sources." And I said, "people feel free to talk with me because I pass it on, and it gets into the mainstream." I always get back to them and say something like, "I enjoyed visiting with you on the plane the other day. Here's what I've done. I've passed your comment on to so-and-so, and you'll hear from him."

WILLIAM F. DOWLING (editor): That's the sure way of keeping your sources of information flowing. If the word got around that talking to Carlson didn't make any difference, your sources of information would dry up. People would feel, "Why stick your neck out—nothing's going to happen anyway?"

CARLSON: Another consideration, as I said before, is that you need to create a climate where people feel free to communicate with you, and not fear that they're going to be discharged because they went over their boss's head. I'm a realist. Often when something has come to me and then gone back down to the supervisor, he has said to his subordinate, "What are you trying to do, make yourself look good? If you were unhappy, why didn't you tell me?" Usually, the person says, "I told you and you didn't do anything about it." It might be little things, like painting a washroom, but it didn't seem so little to the person with the gripe.

DOWLING: By and large, the people who would complain to you, probably do it out of a sense of frustration because the normal channels of communication haven't worked out.

You mentioned something about encouraging your top people to disagree without being disagreeable. You were fearful of what I would call "initial unanimity"—in discussing any important issue—so much so that you sometimes resorted to playing devil's advocate. How strongly do you feel about the virtue of playing devil's advocate?

CARLSON: I don't feel strongly about the specific virtue of playing devil's advocate. In any large company you have a policymaking group, and the success of that group is heavily influenced by the chemistry of the individuals in it. They should feel very comfortable, regardless of who might be sitting around the table, to say, "I don't agree with you," and to initiate a strong discussion.

During my early days with United, these people really didn't know me very well, so it was desirable for me to put an item on the table and to solicit views from highly professional people who had been with the company for many years, before I expressed my views. Why? For two reasons, first, I wasn't sure that I knew enough about the business. Second, in those early days, if I said what I felt too soon, other people inevitably would think "He's already made up his mind and I might as well go along with him."

DOWLING: In effect, it was a form of closure for you to comment early in the discussion.

CARLSON: And another method, which I guess comes with age, is putting an idea on the table. We always had position papers on any major issue before a meeting. I had a pretty good idea of what I thought should be done. I'd start the discussion, and if someone across the table said, "You know, I think this is what we ought to do," I would say, "I haven't thought of it, but you're dead right." Let the other fellow get the credit for the idea, even if the same solution had already occurred to you. I didn't need to get any more credit. I had made my mark in the company and in the business world. Let the people, when they leave that table, say, "I came up with an idea, and the policy committee endorsed it." Some chief executive officers with whom I'm familiar are scared to death to let anyone else feel that they've had a new idea. They reserve new ideas for themselves.

DOWLING: I see your point. When you get to be chief executive officer, the need to hog credit no longer exists. In fact, it's the reverse. You make the organization more effective by stressing the contributions made by other members of top management.

CARLSON: When you run a major company, people constantly stroke your ego. And unless you're careful, you can begin to believe them—at times it can be pretty heady. This is why I prefer Mr. Kaiser's method. Let your subordinates get the credit. Don't be afraid of being challenged by someone who may be smarter than you.

COMMUNICATING

For Edward Carlson, communication means the sharing of information between at least two people. The term *information* is used in this context on the assumption that it is possible to communicate not only facts but also sentiments and attitudes. It is important to realize that most communicators have a particular audience in mind, and communication is seldom random. It is well known that organizations are heavily dependent for their survival and growth on an effective communications system. A business organization, like United Airlines, cannot function properly without decision making; decision making is impossible without communication; and, of course, communication is required to implement the decisions reached.

Studies of executive behavior have found that executives, like Edward Carlson, spend a large proportion of their time transmitting and receiving not only information but also ideas and feelings, as well as issuing and receiving instructions. Only naive managers would summarize the communication process by saying that instructions and directives flow downward in the organization, and reports flow upward. Such managers believe that effective communication requires only that the information to be transmitted be precise and relevant, and the instructions be firm, clear, and unambiguous. Research findings do not support this unsophisticated view.

Good communications do four things: (1) provide information, (2) command and instruct, (3) influence and persuade, and (4) integrate (see Figure 11–1).

FIGURE 11–1
Functions of good communications

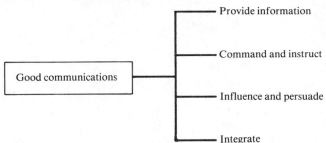

Source: Adapted from Lee Thayer, *Communication and Communication Systems* (Homewood, Ill.: Richard D. Irwin, 1968). © 1968 by Richard D. Irwin, Inc.

TOPIC 1
The principles of communication

Before attempting to communicate about managerial communications, we should put the subject of communications in its proper perspective. The most important things to know about communication are that the process is concerned with the *transmission* of information, ideas, and feelings, and that communication is concerned with the structure, content, and method of transferring messages. Communication does not tell you much in a direct way about how to think up the messages. Rather, it suggests how to encode them and to send them, along with ways and means of figuring out how the receiver decodes them.

Contrary to what many managers believe, communication does not solve all organizational problems. Clear, accurate, even persuasive communications do not eliminate all problems of conflict or always serve to motivate people. Simplistic statements, such as "Two-way communication is always superior to one-way communication," are simply untrue. Nevertheless, behavioral scientists have much to say about communications that is important, relevant, and helpful to managers.

Communication is a function of the rules governing the formation of perceptions. What a person will perceive in a given stimulus situation depends on many physiological and psychological factors. This relation between perception and communication is reflected in the existential idea that "You describe what you see, and you see what you describe." Perception involves a transaction between the perceiver and the sense data.

STRUCTURALISM: STEREOTYPES CHASING CLICHÉS

This view of perception, called structuralism, rejects the common-sense idea of the mind as a camera which simply registers and records everything "out there." It argues that information enters the mind not as raw data but as gestalts or structures. When we perceive things, therefore, we try to fit them into categories, and perception can be viewed as a relation between the "hole" in the category system and the "thing" out there.

In this basically existential view, some of the qualities of the "thing" do not exist but are really part of the category "hole." All visions, therefore, can ultimately be said to be made up of stereotypes chasing clichés, or fallacies fleeing from facts. But both stereotypes and fallacies can be useful as means of sorting data. The laws governing the formation of stereotypes, or the formal structure of the objects of awareness, can be studied in phenomenology. The word *phenomenon* comes from the Greek and means "to appear." In this sense, reality lies not in the event but in the phenomenon.

The laws of phenomenology are:

1. "Things" are seen in a meaningful way.
2. People see things that matter to them.

3. Salience is different for different people.
4. Some people (passive, submissive, low self-esteem, afraid, anxious) are field or stimulus dependent, and others (independent, less threatened though they themselves are hostile, creative, and original) are field independent.

This link between communications and emotions warrants further examination.

COMMUNICATIONS AND EMOTIONS

Forty-odd years ago, in 1938, thousands of Americans were transfixed when they heard a radio announcer say: "We interrupt our program of dance music to bring you a special bulletin from the Intercontinental Radio News. At 20 minutes before 8, central time, Prof. Farrell of the Mount Jennings Observatory, Chicago, Ill., reports observing several explosions of incandescent gas occurring at regular intervals on the planet Mars." As the landing of alien enemies from outer space was reported, listeners panicked.

As we now know, it was only Orson Welles dramatizing the H. G. Wells fantasy, *The War of the Worlds.* Then, however, thousands of Americans from coast to coast acted as if the Martians had really landed, despite several notices that the broadcast was only a dramatization.

The mass hysteria was prompted by the fact that the broadcast came one month after the pre-World War II Munich agreement, a period in which radio programs were frequently interrupted to report developments. People were ready for the worst, and their paranoia was freed by Welles's original presentation, which he offered because he felt people would be bored at hearing "a tale so improbable."

What people perceive is a function of their emotional condition at the time of the event. Therefore, in communication it is important not only to get the timing right but to take into consideration the people receiving the message. When the U.S. government delayed announcing in January 1977 that a Soviet satellite had gone out of orbit and was

Box 11-1: Effective communication is like good advertising

1. The straight story, smoothly told, sells best.
2. It is wrong to lie, but it is permissible to omit information.
3. Testimonials work wonders.
4. Repeat the point.
5. Have a confident, attractive, sincere, respectable-looking person present the message.
6. Don't overdo humor.

heading toward the earth, it was observing one of the principles of communication (see Box 11–1).

ATTITUDES AND INFORMATION PROCESSING

People's attitudes also affect the way they send and receive information. Information processing has offered a new way of looking at attitude-influencing attempts such as persuasion. Like most forms of influence, persuasion arises in a complex informational context.

When an executive such as Edward Carlson presents a view, the message itself is the primary source of information, but it is not the only one. Much depends on the communicator's personality and the audience's identity and reactions. Recipients decide to accept or reject a message on the basis of whether or not the embedded beliefs are in agreement with their own. They compare their attitudes to the attitudes expressed in the message. In effect, those receiving the message try to form some sort of causal framework that will explain the essence of the message. Curiously, unexpected communications are especially persuasive.

The recipient's belief in and acceptance of the message is a function of the communicator's credibility, and credibility in turn is a function of speed of speaking, verbal and nonverbal marks of confidence, vocabulary ideational fluency, and "listenability." Sometimes there is presumed to be a sleeper effect, whereby an opinion change is accepted from a low-credibility source after a time lapse.

Persuasive messages are an important topic of research. One subtle way of inducing belief change employs what is known as the Socratic effect. The communicator presents a syllogistic form of argument which becomes more internally consistent the second time it is presented. The way the case is argued is also important. Another factor is whether the communicator is heckled when making the presentation. Heckling normally lowers the credibility of a communicator, but it will be enhanced if the communicator reacts in a calm manner. Skilled politicians can handle hecklers; allowing them a brief period on the platform to state their positions can be effective.

Sometimes a message induces dissonance, or a feeling of inconsistency or discord, in the recipient. Recipients respond more positively when they have chosen to receive a message voluntarily. Forewarning also increases the chances of acceptance, and the message should not be too intellectually complex.

COMMUNICATION AND LANGUAGE

The complexity and growth capability of language distinguishes Man from the great apes by enabling them to communicate meaning and to share experiences with their fellows. It is largely through language that society is able to create and transmit a culture.

In addition to numerous native or national languages, people speaking a single tongue also use different languages to convey different ideas. Linguistics is the field of inquiry which is concerned with describing the different languages people use, depending on the occasion. For example, in the language of advertising, negatives are forbidden, the past tense and the passive voice are rarely used, and verbs are minimized except in the imperative form (go, get, buy, win). Analysis of the language of advertising suggests that it is only on the surface that advertisements appeal to our rational and observational faculties; at a deeper level they seek to keep these functions dormant and operate, in fact, on our emotions.

Words can be used in three different ways: as symbols, attributes of objects, or objects. A word may be thought of as a symbol insofar as it stands for something other than itself. The ability to use words as symbols or objects is usually a mark of cultural sophistication. The mistaken assumption that there must always be a connection between a word and the object which it represents can cause trouble.

PSYCHOLINGUISTICS

Behavioral scientists interested in problems of language and communication have developed a new field of study called psycholinguistics. It made its first appearance in the early 1950s and draws on the subjects of information theory, psychology of learning, and contemporary linguistics. Jerome Bruner has argued that the structure of a language and its lexical unity influence in a significant way what one notices in the world. Understanding language requires knowing something about the subject of semantics, or the meaning of meaning.

The human mind needs certain principles which, in some way that is not understood, precede experience and can knock data into shapes that are meaningful. Noam Chomsky, through his own work in linguistics which involved studying the form of language and how people speak, arrived at the idea that people are born with a built-in genetic grammar. This in-built ability enables speakers to utter and listeners to grasp countless sentences they have never heard before. Such a genetic grammar supersedes and in a way renders naive the notion of behavior as a series of stimulus-response interactions. The computer programs which have been devised to do translations (*disambigulations* is the computer term) from one language to another must grasp linguistic regularities as well as waywardness (statistically unusual words or idioms).

SEMANTICS

Semantics is the field of inquiry concerned with exploring the correspondence between the symbols used in language and the reality being communicated about. A semantic definition of communication is the interchange of meanings between persons. Many contemporary psychologists are deeply concerned with questions of meaning, which may be defined as the total disposition to exploit or react to a linguistic form.

There are two kinds of meaning, denotative and connotative. The denotative meaning of a word refers to that to which the word points and argues an explicit definition of the referent. The language of mathematics and logic is denotative, or if you like, a "thing language" where a word means only one thing. Connotations are the constellation or complex of ideas, sentiments, and action tendencies which are associated with a particular word and the implicit and attitudinal dimensions of meaning. *Democracy, profitability, them, us,* and *insane* are all words of wide connotation.

It is easy to befog an argument by using terms with a wide range of connotative meanings, and (although this is frowned upon in academic circles) this technique may also be thought of as a way to influence others. Politicians are expert at using terms of wide connotation which have appeal both for the duke and the dustman.

ORGANIZATIONAL LANGUAGES

All organizations develop particular languages that are peculiarly their own. The Watergate scandal supplied a whole new vocabulary with numerous bromides such as "at that point in time" and "in that time frame." Executives seem to have the knack of enveloping a subject in a nebulous cocoon, using such rules as "Never use a word when a sentence will do," "Quote several conflicting sources," and "Obscure, don't clarify."

In developing these new organizational argots, executives make extensive use of the language of computers, the military, and football. "Zero-defect system" is used for perfection. "Here's another input for the hopper" precedes the giving of an opinion. "Preemptive strikes" (hit the other guy first) are backed up by "second-strike capability" (reserve position). And former attorney general (and football coach) John Mitchell called up "When the going gets tough, the tough get going."

Watergate produced a lexicon straight out of *Alice in Wonderland.* "Breaking and entering" was disguised as "intelligence-gathering operations." Papers were not deliberately lost; they were "deep-sixed."

"White House horrors" became a euphemism to make palatable "government-sponsored crimes." Basically, the White House aides were on the side of Humpty Dumpty, who said to Alice, "When *I* use a word . . . it means just what I choose it to mean." There is a good deal of *Alice* around, and not only in the White House. George Orwell could have had organizations in mind when he pointed out that not only does thought corrupt language, but language can also corrupt thought.

Executives have a particularly poor reputation for expressing themselves. Business today is regarded by many sophisticated people in the professions as being a major source of *gobbledygook*, a term widely used by President Franklin Roosevelt to describe polysyllabic, ugly-sounding words held together by tortuous syntax. Examples of gobbledygook include *overkill, cost effective*, and *explicate*. Many executives also have a penchant for vogue words, such as *systems capability, relevance, charismatic, dialogue*, and *parameters*, which they work to death. (See Box 11–2 for some examples of organizational language.)

Box 11–2: Examples of organizational language

1. *The 10–T technique*

    "I wonder if any of you know the 10–T system of instruction. You don't? Well in the 10–T system . . . " (Write on a flip chart):

    TTTT—Tell them what you are going to tell them.
      TT—Tell them.
    TTTT—Tell them what you have told them.

    "Now what I am going to do is. . . . "

2. *Telephone twatter*

    Answer your telephone with "hello." Your callers have a high probability of figuring out who you are; they're trying to reach you. It isn't necessary to say something like "Circle 3472, John Jones speaking"—even to your best friend.

    When initiating a call, it is sufficient to say "This is Bob Jones," you don't have to give name, number, and rank.

3. *Making supportive noises*

    "Uh, hu."
    "Uh hu."
    "Ah haa ah."
    "Really."
    "What happened next?"
    "Woooow."

TOPIC 2
Dyadic communication—A interacts with B

TWO-WAY COMMUNICATION

To be minimally human is to use symbols, both verbal and nonverbal, when engaged in face-to-face interaction. "No man is an island" means that to be fully human a person must have personal involvements with others.

What happens when two people interact, when A interacts with B? At the simplest level, there is stimulus and response:

When A communicates with B, B communicates with A. Typically B's response to A elicits some surprise in A, and A may well wonder whether the message has gotten through to B. A may guess that he

---

4. *A one-sided argument*

   "What I like about your idea is. . . ."
   "Perhaps I can restate your argument in my terms. . . ."
   "You've got to accentuate the positive, minimize the negative."
   "I shall summarize your views, then mine and ask Michael (the man in his pocket) to judge between them."
   "This is not an argument. Just a discussion."
   "I always say there are three basic L's, listening, learning, loving."
   "With all due respect. . . ."
   "Can I take that question under advisement?"
   "Can I get back to you later on this afternoon on that,—oh, you only want to know the time!"

5. *Hogging the conversation*

   "Would you like me to address the subject of _____ ?"
   "Four points are worth noting: (a) This is something in your area, Bill. . . . Hang on a minute. I would like to go right through (b) . . . ."
   "You'll love this."
   "Did I ever tell you the one about. . . ?"

6. *Creative talk*

   "I'm only talking off the top of my head, but let's see if this idea goes into orbit."
   "Just an Aunt Sally to be shot down."
   "Let's run it up the flagpole and see who salutes it."
   "You feel it hasn't got enough pizazz."
   "You want to put that one in a stacking orbit. Round Chicago and then New York."

is not transmitting on B's frequency; if he is of an analytical turn of mind, he might ask B to elaborate on his reaction. If both A and B use a VANE model, some progress may be made:

$$A\ \begin{vmatrix} V \\ A \\ N \\ E \end{vmatrix} \rightleftarrows \begin{vmatrix} V \\ A \\ N \\ E \end{vmatrix}\ B$$

If A and B are to communicate effectively they will both need to know something of each other's values, attitudes, needs, and expectations. This implies that the person's perceptions are influenced by the frame of reference used to evaluate incoming information, which in turn is largely determined by the person's VANE (values, attitudes, needs, and expectations; see Chapter 5).

As A interacts with B, the hope is that both will develop the ability to see things from the other person's point of view. Taking the role of the other is an essentially human characteristic. The capacity for empathy—to get into the psychological processes of the other, to anticipate the other person's possible actions and responses vis-à-vis one's own action and responses—is integral to the whole subject of human relations. Communication thus involves emotion and cognition, as well as perception through the VANE:

COMMUNICATION

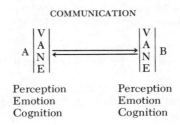

One interesting conclusion which emerges from this model, and which has been confirmed by research, is that the prospect of increased interaction makes A and B like each other more. If A and B are to communicate, then there must be some degree of value consonance. If they wish to communicate, they must tune their value systems (like the variable condensers in radios) in to each other to reduce any value dissonance.

A good illustration of this principle of value tuning is the prisoner who learns to like the interrogator. What happens in interactions is that A rewards B for adjustive value tuning, and B rewards A for the attempt to tune in. Many of the Dale Carnegie subroutines are based in part on this principle, that you imply with smiles and a show of good-will that you appreciate the other person. What is really needed is a meeting of minds. This is precisely what is implied in the concept of good faith—you do not prejudge issues and other people's values. The black-white dialogue in the United States has evolved many subroutines to make white administrators realize this principle. For example, the administrator who says, "I know exactly how you feel . . . ," can expect to be cut off in midstream with "How could you possibly know how I feel? You're white." The liberated female–male chauvinist dialogue uses a similar routine. If good faith is present, such routines may lead to a true communication process in which the dissonance is lowered. Unfortunately, too often what is actually going on is a double monologue (with no one listening), instead of a real dialogue.

An effective communicator has to be capable of value tuning to communicate with a large number of different people. Individuals with very strong, highly structured value systems find it difficult to tune in to people who do not share their systems. Management has to make a special effort to "hear" employees (see Box 11–3).

Box 11–3: Listening to employee gripes

Many companies today are making a major effort to find out what their employees really want. Company communication systems are being redesigned to encourage management-employee communications, which can range all the way from face-to-face to computerized reports.

One experiment is with telephone hot lines. An employee can pick up a telephone, dial a number, and check out rumors:—"What is this I hear about a walkout?" IBM uses a relatively simple letter-writing program which enables employees to clarify policies and procedures.

The effort to find out what concerns employees is spreading, as *The New York Times* notes in an October 16, 1977, article entitled "Management Tunes in on Employee Gripes":

. . . In America it is called "Speak Up"; Parliamone Insieme" (Let's Talk It Over) in Italy; "I Digalo" (Tell It) in Spain; and "Wat Heeft U Op Uw Hart?" (What Have You In Your Heart?) in the Netherlands. Last year the "Speak Up" input was 13,000 letters. Letters were answered within 24 hours or, if more time was needed, individuals were so informed and a deadline was set by the management person charged with handling the inquiry.

The manager of one location, for instance, received the following letter: "At Christmas time this year a department gave its manager a gift. This department has the same manager as I have. I feel that this department has an advantage over me in the coming year. Also, I thought it was against "company policy." The company's answer: "It is not condoned and this will be communicated immediately to all managers on the site."

A MODEL FOR HANDLING FEEDBACK

Dyadic communication relies on the principle of feedback; when A communicates to B, B responds to A. The message is often sent back in order to control and evaluate what is sent out.

A useful model for dealing with feedback is the VANE model given earlier. Since the model takes into account the values, attitudes, needs, and expectations of both parties, the rating tells something about the rater as well as the ratee.

Frequently it appears that the one giving the feedback is acting on the assumption that the ratee is simple and uncomplex, whereas the rater is complex and interesting. A model which avoids this trap is shown in Figure 11–2; it takes a systems approach, recognizing several interacting factors. This model was suggested by work done by John Anderson at the Procter & Gamble Company.

FIGURE 11–2
Model for giving and receiving feedback

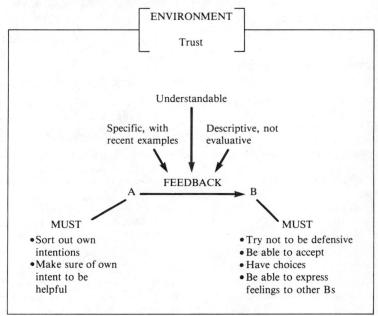

TOPIC 3
Vertical and horizontal communications

As Figure 11–3 shows, executive communication is a three-dimensional experience, with upward, downward, and sideways movement.

FIGURE 11–3
Three-directional flow of executive communications

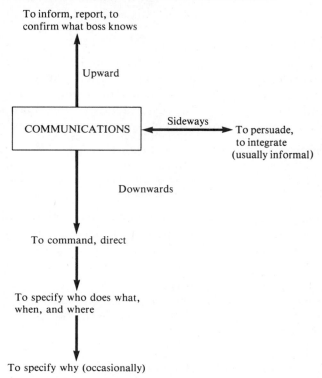

MANAGING THE VERTICAL DIMENSION

A decisive reason why most American prisoners held in North Vietnam were able to stand up to both physical and psychological torture was the fact that a fixed command structure was set up to control the flow of information among the captives. The senior officer according to rank assumed command, and everybody else fell into place. Tying information channels to a hierarchy converted what normally would have been an informal apparatus into an instrument which wielded tremendous power and saved the prisoners from the degradation which was the fate of so many U.S. prisoners during the Korean War.

The same argument for structuring communication applies to business organizations. The issue is not whether structuring is good or bad, but rather how much, where, and when.

Research on path-goal motivation (see Chapter 8) has indicated that structuring reduces ambiguity and facilitates effort, but only in certain circumstances. Further, it has been found that supervisors who initiate structure are more productive not only of task output but also of grievances. Thus structure can generate noise and dysfunctions. But research seems to support the view that initiating structure is sufficient to generate both productivity and satisfaction at higher levels in the hierarchy.

An intriguing and revealing insight into the relation between structure and language has been provided by Lena L. Lucietto of the University of Chicago in a research report entitled "Speech Patterns of Administrators." She found that, first, school principals high in initiating structure use fewer "self" words. But when they do use words like *I* or *me*, they employ them in direct, specific, and forceful contexts:

> *I* want to know why you would reject it.
> Now this is *my* responsibility.
> Let's get your reaction to some of the statements *I've* made.
> Remember what *I* said to you, though.

On the other hand, principals perceived by the teachers under them as low in initiating structure use more "self" words and use them in contexts of cooperation and agreement:

> *I* kind of thought you were.
> It's all right with *me*, in a way.
> *I* agree with you that the other would be top priority.
> *I'm* not trying to be—I don't want to be dictatorial here.
> And *I* do too, you know.
> No, *I'd* agree with you.

Principals high in initiating structure were distinguished from those perceived as low by their use of "attempt" words, like *try, pursue,* and *effort*. Principals perceived as low in initiating structure use similar words, but in a less direct way. The sense of strength which might have been conveyed by the "attempt" word is attenuated by the word *think* preceding it:

> *I think* that if you *try* something like that, I think along those lines, you may have some success with John.

MANAGING THE HORIZONTAL DIMENSION

Lateral transactions are seldom shown on the classical organization chart, but horizontal interactions are often as important as vertical ones. When an organization faces a uniform task, communications can be vertical. But when the tasks vary among departments, horizontal communications, often of an informal nature, are also needed.

Richard E. Walton and John M. Dutton have suggested, in "The Management of Interdepartmental Conflict," that there are two basic ways of handling the external relation among departments or groups, the integrative process (problem solving, information exchange, conscientious accuracy in transmitting information, flexibility, and trust) and the distributive process (bargaining, careful rationing, information distortions, rigidity, and hostility).

The lateral interface

Research findings have underlined the importance of managing the lateral interface. The greater the degree of differentiation among departments, the more complex must be the interface management techniques. Paul Lawrence and J. W. Lorsch reported that the most differentiated firm in their study, "Differentiation and Integration in Complex Organizations," even had a separate integrative department. According to Lawrence and Lorsch, such integrating units must have respected staff members who are organized according to a structure intermediate to the units to be coordinated and who can help managers to confront rather than smooth over conflict.

The structuring of lateral interactions is far trickier than structuring vertical communications. In any case, subunits which fail to sort themselves out are frequently reorganized. Close examination of organiza-

"The motion has been made and seconded that we obey the law."

Reprinted by permission *The Wall Street Journal.*

tional design for lateral communication suggests how particular pitfalls can be overcome. Figure 11–4 models lateral interaction as a system; such models can help to develop sophisticated designs which can respond to different contingencies.

FIGURE 11–4
Tactics of lateral interaction

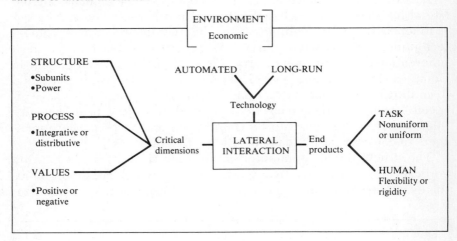

TOPIC 4
The executive meeting

THE CORPORATE THEATER OF THE ABSURD

Running a meeting is exciting as an activity, but as a scientific discipline it is a bore, regulated by long lists of do's and don'ts. From the viewpoint of the manager who has to run the meeting, there is a great need for myth, magic and meaning. Producing and directing meetings is concerned with transforming inputs into outputs, with value added. This $2 + 2 = 5$ aspect of meetings demands a certain savoir faire which owes much more to theater than to science. (See Box 11–4 for some useful advice.)

To come up with an explanation of meetings which feels right to practicing managers, I set out to examine the nexus formed by discussion leading, the theater, and existentialism. Some managers are realizing that the executive meeting, when it is not a black tragedy, can be a gloriously funny comedy if seen from the right perspective. This approach to meetings is essentially model oriented, and the model adopted here assumes an integration of structure (the cast, dramatis personnae), process (sequencing of events), and values (myth, magic,

Box 11–4: The chairperson's job

The committee chairperson's role has been examined by Anthony Jay:

> Let's say that you have just been appointed chairman of the committee. You tell everyone that it is a bore or a chore. You also tell them that you have been appointed "for my sins." But the point is that you tell them. There is no getting away from it: some sort of honor or glory attaches to the chairman's role. Almost everyone is in some way pleased and proud to be made chairman of something. And that is three quarters of the trouble.
>
> MASTER OR SERVANT?
>
> Their appointment as committee chairman takes people in different ways. Some seize the opportunity to impose their will on a group that they see themselves licensed to dominate. Their chairmanship is a harangue, interspersed with demands for group agreement.
>
> Others are more like scoutmasters, for whom the collective activity of the group is satisfaction enough, with no need for achievement. Their chairmanship is more like the endless stoking and fueling of a campfire that is not cooking anything.
>
> And there are the insecure or lazy chairmen who look to the meeting for reassurance and support in their ineffectiveness and inactivity, so that they can spread the responsibility for their indecisiveness among the whole group. They seize on every expression of disagreement or doubt as a justification for avoiding decision or action.
>
> But even the large majority who do not go to those extremes still feel a certain pleasurable tumescence of the ego when they take their place at the head of the table for the first time. The feeling is no sin: the sin is to indulge it or to assume that the pleasure is shared by the other members of the meeting.
>
> It is the chairman's self-indulgence that is the greatest single barrier to the success of a meeting. His first duty, then, is to be aware of the temptation and of the dangers of yielding to it. The clearest of the danger signals is hearing himself talking a lot during a discussion.
>
> One of the best chairmen I have ever served under makes it a rule to restrict her interventions to a single sentence, or at most two. She forbids herself ever to contribute a paragraph to a meeting she is chairing. It is a harsh rule, but you would be hard put to find a regular attender of her meetings (or anyone else's) who thought it was a bad one.
>
> There is, in fact, only one legitimate source of pleasure in chairmanship, and that

Source: Anthony Jay, "How to Run a Meeting," *Harvard Business Review*, March–April, 1976, pp. 51–53.

and meaning). (See Figure 11–5.) The meeting becomes a theater of action—sometimes theater of the absurd and sometimes theater of cruelty. This characteristic of corporate meetings has driven some executives to recognize the "I'm insane—You're insane dimension of interpersonal life.

Regardless of the mystique of meetings, however, group problem-solving efforts should have a logical pattern made up of the following steps:

Box 11–4 (continued)

is pleasure in the achievements of the meeting—and to be legitimate, it must be shared by all those present. Meetings are *necessary* for all sorts of basic and primitive human reasons, but they are *useful* only if they are seen by all present to be getting somewhere—and somewhere they know they could not have gotten to individually.

If the chairman is to make sure that the meeting achieves valuable objectives, he will be more effective seeing himself as the servant of the group rather than as its master. His role then becomes that of assisting the group toward the best conclusion or decision in the most efficient manner possible: to interpret and clarify; to move the discussion forward; and to bring it to a resolution that everyone understands and accepts as being the will of the meeting, even if the individuals do not necessarily agree with it.

His true source of authority with the members is the strength of his perceived commitment to their combined objective and his skill and efficiency in helping and guiding them to its achievement. Control and discipline then become not the act of imposing his will on the group but of imposing the group's will on any individual who is in danger of diverting or delaying the progress of the discussion and so from realizing the objective.

Once the members realize that the leader is impelled by his commitment to their common objective, it does not take great force of personality for him to control the meeting. Indeed, a sense of urgency and a clear desire to reach the best conclusion as quickly as possible are a much more effective disciplinary instrument than a big gavel. The effective chairman can then hold the discussion to the point by indicating that there is no time to pursue a particular idea now, that there is no time for long speeches, that the group has to get through this item and on to the next one, rather than by resorting to pulling rank.

There are many polite ways the chairman can indicate a slight impatience even when someone else is speaking—by leaning forward, fixing his eyes on the speaker, tensing his muscles, raising his eyebrows, or nodding briefly to show the point is taken. And when replying or commenting, the chairman can indicate by the speed, brevity, and finality of his intonation that "we have to move on." Conversely, he can reward the sort of contribution he is seeking by the opposite expressions and intonations, showing that there is plenty of time for that sort of idea, and encouraging the speaker to develop the point.

After a few meetings, all present readily understand this nonverbal language of

1. Identify the problem.
2. Specify its causes.
3. Define its effects.
4. Develop alternatives.

and so on. But this is only the public agenda; the group must also deal with the hidden agenda. Simmering below the surface of the problem-solving efforts are the issues of who loves who or, more important still, who hates who, most.

chairmanship. It is the chairman's chief instrument of educating the group into the general type of "meeting behavior" that he is looking for. He is still the servant of the group, but like a hired mountain guide, he is the one who knows the destination, the route, the weather signs, and the time the journey will take. So if he suggests that the members walk a bit faster, they take his advice.

This role of servant rather than master is often obscured in large organizations by the fact that the chairman is frequently the line manager of the members: this does not, however, change the reality of the role of chairman. The point is easier to see in, say, a neighborhood action group. The question in that case is, simply, "Through which person's chairmanship do we collectively have the best chance of getting the children's playground built?"

However, one special problem is posed by this definition of the chairman's role, and it has an extremely interesting answer. The question is: How can the chairman combine his role with the role of a member advocating one side of an argument?

The answer comes from some interesting studies by researchers who sat in on hundreds of meetings to find out how they work. Their consensus finding is that most of the effective discussions have, in fact, two leaders: one they call a "team," or "social," leader; the other a "task," or "project," leader.

Regardless of whether leadership is in fact a single or a dual function, for our purposes it is enough to say that the chairman's best role is that of social leader. If he wants a particular point to be strongly advocated, he ensures that it is someone else who leads off the task discussion, and he holds back until much later in the argument. He might indeed change or modify his view through hearing the discussion, but even if he does not it is much easier for him to show support for someone else's point later in the discussion, after listening to the arguments. Then, he can summarize in favor of the one he prefers.

The task advocate might regularly be the chairman's second-in-command, or a different person might advocate for different items on the agenda. On some subjects, the chairman might well be the task advocate himself, especially if they do not involve conflict within the group. The important point is that the chairman has to keep his "social leadership" even if it means sacrificing his "task leadership." However, if the designated task advocate persists in championing a cause through two or three meetings, he risks building up quite a head of antagonism to him among the other members. Even so, this antagonism harms the group less by being directed as the "task leader" than at the "social leader."

MANAGING MEETINGS VIA GROUP DYNAMICS

Time wasting

Behavioral studies have found that managers spend up to 80 percent of their time talking, and a fair proportion of this interaction time is with more than one other person. "The manager is in conference and cannot be disturbed" seems to be the message coming through. The implicit, often stated argument is that the manager spends too much

FIGURE 11–5
Structure, process, and values diagram for a discussion group

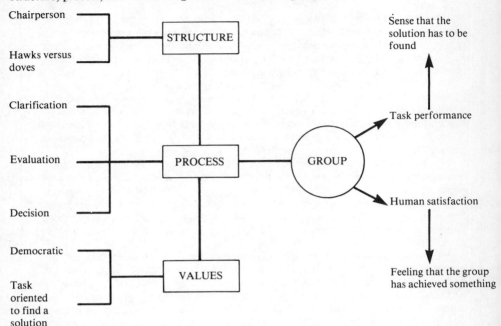

time in conference. Critics of the conference idea have suggested variously that a committee is a meeting called together to design a racehorse which ends up producing a camel; minutes are kept and hours are thrown away; the ideal number is three, with two in absentia; and meetings should be held only at 5:00 P.M. in a room with no table or chairs.

Risk taking

One of the interesting but paradoxical findings to emerge from group dynamics research was the idea that groups take riskier decisions than individuals do. While this may be true as a research finding, experience suggests that managers act in a directly opposite manner. Executive groups apparently are less willing to endorse innovative ideas than individuals are.

An MBA syndrome seems to have emerged which is characterized by supercautious, no-nonsense, no-risk management. Managers with this syndrome are unwilling to support anything other than a sure-fire success. This results in a crisis in risk taking which makes it difficult for research engineers and scientists to get their ideas past management committees. In these committees the iron law seems to be that anyone can veto an innovation," especially in large companies, they have had a positive genius for blocking off ideas. The dearth of innovation is particularly noticeable in the automobile industry, where designers have been playing with the same deck of cards for the last three decades. What they call new models are just products of a reshuffle. American know-how has not been able to cope with the conservatism of such committees.

One way of getting past them would be to figure out how they work and who calls the shots in the deliberations. A key person to get in touch with in such a committee is the gatekeeper described above, who controls the flow of new ideas from the outside world through reading and attending conventions. These gatekeepers know their opposite numbers in competing companies and often know the status of new technology. In getting ideas past management committees it is useful to know whether and when a competing product is likely to come on the market.

Executive debating

Occasionally in meetings the discussion is elevated to the level of a debate. Executive debates not only have a certain entertainment value, they sometimes help to clarify a situation. The goal is to give a good performance. Because executives are frequently skilled in debating techniques and have considerable verbal dexterity, they can usually be counted on for a display of verbal pyrotechnics.

The aim of the debating game is not to be right but to sound convincing. Each party tries to make the other look ridiculous and to denigrate opponents in a cool and elegant manner. In taking one's opponent down, body language is always effective; letting an amusing smile play about the lips while an opponent delivers an argument can often be more telling than an intellectual rejoinder. In the "Kennedy versus Nixon" debates of the sixties, for example, Kennedy freely scored points off his opponent by adopting a patrician aloofness which somehow made Nixon look as if he had been caught with his hand in the till. The really effective executive debater has this nasty knack of making opponents look gauche.

Perhaps the most important thing to keep in mind about executive verbal encounters is that the scene shifts quickly. No guarantee can be given that problem-solving session will not degenerate into a discussion group which can occasionally be elevated into a debate. In the debate, wit is everything, and logic and loyalty are temporarily set aside. It is all a question of proxemics, of who is near whom.

TOPIC 5
Proxemics, or social ecology

Proxemics studies the spatial needs of people and their interaction with the space in their environment. One aspect of proxemics is the systematic study of spatial arrangements, which has an effect on individual and group communications. Who takes the lead in discussions is to some extent a factor of location.

PERSONAL AND GROUP INTERACTIONS

How can you tell whether a person you have just met will be hostile or friendly? Behavioral scientists say that the answer lies not only in spoken words but also in the tone of voice, facial expressions, and body postures that emerge during the initial conversation. The nonverbal element is a message, according to Michael Argyle, a social psychologist from Oxford University, that carries more weight than the actual words.

For example, a committee member has a way of signaling an intent to claim the floor. People can instantly assert their position in the pecking hierarchy by the exchange of a single glance.

The ways people look at each other reveal more than most people realize. The right amount of eye contact can determine who is going to be dominant in an exchange.

M. Argyle and J. Dean reported in "Eye-Contact, Distance, and Affiliation" on experiments using dark glasses and cardboard shields to find out what happens in a conversation when the other person's eyes or face cannot be seen. They discovered that seeing the other person's eyes is necessary to know when he or she intends to start or stop; with shielding, synchronization of the conversation becomes difficult. Shielding the other person's face creates further difficulties because her or his emotional reactions cannot be gauged. Experiments in eye contact have shown that:

1. People who can see better dominate the conversation.
2. Women need and make more use of visual feedback.
3. People make more eye contact when listening.
4. People tend to look away when talking, especially if they are going over their "allotted time."
5. Eye contact promotes good relations only when associated with a friendly facial expression.
6. Different ethnic groups use eye expressions in different ways.
7. In discussion groups, members direct more comments to people opposite than people adjacent; but when a strong leader is present, members direct their comments to adjacent seats rather than to those opposite.

Three factors that significantly affect the quality of relations are eye contact, posture, and distance. Researchers have identified what are called "correct conversational zones":

Conversational level	Distance	Classification
Soft whisper	3–6 inches	Top secret
Louder whisper	8–12 inches	Highly confidential
Soft voice	12–20 inches	Confidential
Low volume	20–36 inches	Personal subject
Normal voice	5 feet	Nonpersonal information

Posture is also important; a person can establish dominance by throwing the head back and speaking in a loud voice. People being addressed who put their hands behind their backs may well be seen as taking a subordinate role.

THE GEOGRAPHY OF DISCUSSION GROUPS

Research has shown that certain places at a table are preferred to others. As shown in Figure 11–6, when two people want to converse,

FIGURE 11–6

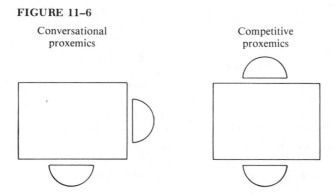

Conversational proxemics

Competitive proxemics

they will sit at right angles to each other across a corner of the table. If they wish to compete, they sit opposite each other.

This well-established principle of proxemics is frequently used by executives who shift from formal to informal seating arrangements, depending on the intentions of the owner of the office. In addition to the informal arrangement shown in Figure 11–7, the visitor may be placed at the side of the desk, away from the desk in an armchair setting, or (a current form of status symbol) the desk may have been concealed or banished from the office completely.

In discussion groups, more autocratic leaders often sit at the head of

FIGURE 11–7

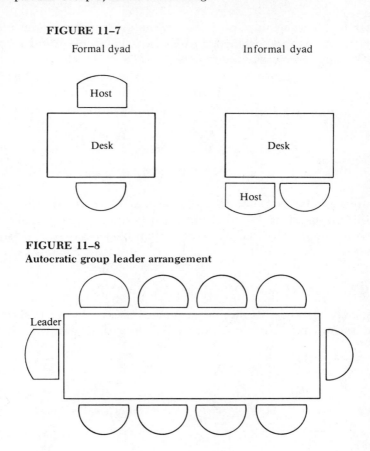

Formal dyad   Informal dyad

FIGURE 11–8
Autocratic group leader arrangement

a table (Figure 11–8). This enables them to structure the situation by putting hostile persons they want to ignore close to them and putting their anchor men at or near the other end of the table, where easy eye contact is possible. More democratic leaders tend to sit in the middle of the group, as in Figure 11–9.

FIGURE 11–9
Democratic group leader arrangement

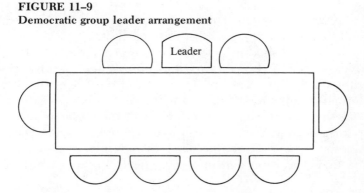

It would be wrong to conclude that mere location is the critical factor determining the role an individual will take up in a discussion. It seems much more plausible to believe that dominant individuals select locations for reasons of tradition, or because this choice advertises the role they are going to take up.

Proxemics can be of great importance in diplomacy, and matters of "who sits where" can create international incidents. For example, when the Vietnam peace talks were being arranged in Paris in 1968, the actual shape of the table to be used led to prolonged, acrimonious discussion which delayed the beginning of the negotiations for several weeks.

The design of a debating chamber can significantly affect the quality of debates. The British House of Commons is a relatively small room with insufficient seating for all members of Parliament; but its smallness facilitates a debate which would be quite impossible in the more formal layout of the U.S. House of Representatives.

The actual "scene of the crime" can be of critical importance, as witness the fact that the Germans in 1940 insisted on bringing out the famous railroad car used at Compiègne for the 1918 armistice, to humiliate the French generals who were to sign the formal defeat of the French army.

TOPIC 6
What every manager should know about communications

RESEARCH FINDINGS

Organizational researchers are coming to regard communication as an important but underresearched topic. Communication was a hot subject in the fifties, receiving a lot of attention which produced interesting findings. At some point, researchers decided that additional effort in this area would not generate new theories or produce insights. Now organizational psychologists are finding communication an area rich in "contingent interactive effects," although a clarifying perspective or theory to explain communication is still not available.

As every executive knows, communication is not only important, it is also pervasive and indeed permeates every aspect of the organization. The subject of communication attracts so many researchers from diverse fields that it is difficult to formulate a conclusive definition. Communication is sometimes defined as social interaction, often as transfer of not only information but of feelings from A to B. But since Marshall McLuhan first said it, researchers have increasingly recognized that there is no message except the meaning people put into it. Figure 11–10 summarizes some of the principal findings about communications.

FIGURE 11-10
Communications research summary

INDIVIDUALS

Type	Conditions	Effectiveness
One way	*Task*—easy to structure Human—power unequal	• Suited to simple tasks • Time-consuming

Two way	Task—unstructured
	Human—power equalized
	Feedback: • Objective
	         • Immediate
	         • Provides
	           reinforcement
		• Suited to complex tasks
		• Preferable when
		  feedback is needed
		• Superior, often not
		  subjective
		• Usually through
		  ritualistic channels
		• Difficult to disassociate
		  from monetary rewards
		  or lack of them

GROUPS: SUPERIOR TO THE SUM OF INDIVIDUALS IN THE GROUP

Type	Conditions	Effectiveness

Committees	Task—not task oriented,
	        uncertain
	Human—emotional, chance to
	        express opinion
		• Can be unrealistic and
		  irresponsible
		• Makes decisions
		  acceptable to group
		• Feeling of corporate
		  responsibility

Command
   meetings
	Task—concentration on job,
	        statements of policy
	Human—power unequal,
	        manager instructs
	        subordinates
		• Assists coordination
		  and exchanges of
		  information
		• Blocks innovation

Brainstorming	Task—unstructured
	Human—supportive, uncritical,
	        hitchhiking
	        environment
		• Outlandish
		• Emphasis on quantity,
		  not quality
		• Freewheeling,
		  synergetic

GUIDELINES

Figure 11-11 is the contingency model of communication as a system. Some guidelines for effective communication are given below, to flesh out the process section.

1.   Before communicating, a person should analyze the problem in as great detail as possible in order to determine exactly what is to be communicated. As is often the case in business, the person may not be able to clarify the issue completely unless the problem is very simple. But any effort in this direction will bear handsome dividends.

FIGURE 11–11
Contingency model of communication as a system

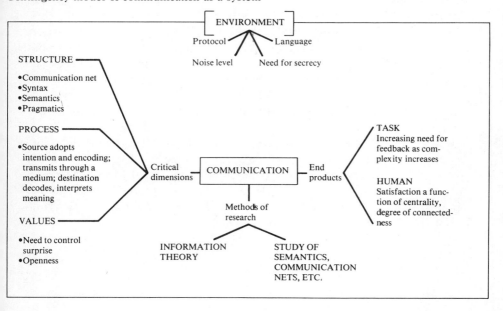

2.   The purpose of the communication should be defined. The intention should be specified, and then the aim defined.

3.   The physical and human environment should be considered (i.e., timing, location, social setting, and previous experience). It is worth repeating that communication is not exclusively verbal.

4.   Others should be consulted if this is thought necessary. Often authority to communicate must be sought before a message is sent, or someone must be put in the picture in regard to the action to be taken. It is useful to remember the headings "For Action" and "For Information," when communications are being planned.

5.   Objectivity is not necessarily a criterion of good communication in every circumstance; sometimes two-sided messages are useful. Communications frequently contain peripheral elements; and nuances of meaning conveyed by the timbre of the voice or the choice of language may turn out to be the significant stimulus. Use of words with a limited range of connotations is often recommended, but often words with wide connotations are best for producing attitude changes in members of work groups.

6.   The communicator should try to influence the person with whom he or she is communicating and to see things from the other's point of view. Different people have different perceptual slants.

7.   The effectiveness of the communication should be assessed if possible. This is usually done by encouraging feedback.

8.   The type of communication process best suited to the purpose should be chosen. For example, in military practice it is useful to give a warning order, then an executive order. This approach may be relevant in a civilian context. Politicians sometimes communicate their plans to the public by the calculated leak; reaction to the leak helps them to decide whether to introduce an intended change. Excessive use of calculated leaks may produce a credibility gap between what politicians say and the public believes.

9.   Many executives seem to believe that it is possible to manage by exclusively vertical forms of communications, but research reveals that a great deal of communication is lateral. If the situation is inchoate or ill-defined, superiors cannot give precise positive instructions that cover all contingencies, and so subordinates must get together to decide what is possible and in the best interests of the organization. Though lacking in hierarchical logic, such horizontal communication has its own organizational logic.

REVIEW AND RESEARCH

1.   Why is the term *communication* so widely used in executive discussions? Why is it wrong to think that most organization problems are problems in communication? Why do so many managers attribute their problems to communication difficulties?

2.   How are perception and communication linked?

3.   Develop a semantic differential scale for measuring people's perceptions of black and white managers. Invite ten of your associates to complete the scale. Collate the data on one scale. What conclusions can you draw from this pilot investigation?

4.   Why are top managers cut off from knowing what is happening in the lower levels of their organizations? How do effective managers overcome this difficulty?

5.   Why is oral usually preferable to written communication? In which circumstances is written communication superior? Why?

6.   Why have committee meetings come under so much fire recently? How can the conduct of such meetings be improved?

7.   What is a command meeting? What problems should be tackled through a command meeting?

8.   Develop a set of rules for brainstorming. Use brainstorming with a group of your colleagues to develop a list of problems suitable for brainstorming.

9.   Why is the structuring of communications essential in business?

10.   When are two-sided messages appropriate?

11.   Discuss the relationship between serial communication and the spread of a rumor.

12. Devise and execute an experiment to study how people group themselves in a leisure area such as the cafeteria. Make a comparative study of people grouping in the library.

13. Design two layouts for discussion groups: (a) for a democratic and (b) for an autocratic group. Discuss the role of eye contact in discussion groups.

GLOSSARY OF TERMS

Adaptation. The process or action of becoming more effectively adjusted to the environmental conditions pertaining to work or learning.

Brainstorming. A technique for generating ideas by means of highly intensive group interaction in which no ideas are criticized, freewheeling is encouraged, and the emphasis is on quantity of diverse ideas.

Cognitive dissonance. The mental state of holding irreconcilable beliefs. Cognitive dissonance arises when a person is exposed to a communication which differs from his own opinion; he may change to a position closer to the communication or derogate both the communication and the communicator.

Command meeting. A meeting between a manager and subordinates in order to facilitate an interchange of information; the manager dominates the meeting (it is not democratic).

Communication. The field of inquiry concerned with the systematic use of symbols to achieve common or shared information about an object or event. The communication process can be thought of as a chain with at least three links: the sender, the medium, and the receiver. The sender encodes the message and transmits it through the chosen medium, and it is then decoded by the receiver.

Feedback. The response to a communication, in which B not only gives a reaction to A's message but also may control and correct further signals, thus making A and B truly interacting members of a communication system.

Noise. The elements of communications which are irrelevant or interfere with the transmission of the message.

Proxemics. The ways in which people consciously or unconsciously structure their microspace.

Semantics. The relations between the symbols and the "reality" to which they refer.

Serial reproduction. Transmission of information from one person to another who, in turn, passes this message to a third person, and so on.

Social ecology. The ecology of human behavior, or the nature of the mutual interaction between man and his environment, including factors such as spatial layouts, territoriality, and body language.

Syntax. The systematic analysis of the grammar of the process of communication.

DEBATE: Groups make better decisions than individuals do

PRO: How to run an effective meeting

While referring a matter to a committee can dilute authority, diffuse responsibility, and delay decisions, meetings do fulfill a deep human need. So argues Anthony Jay in "How to Run a Meeting." Jay feels that a meeting has six main functions that make it superior to more recent communication devices:

1. In the simplest and most basic way, a meeting, defines the team, the group, or the unit. Those present belong to it; those absent do not. Everyone is able to look around and perceive the whole group and sense the collective identity of which he or she forms a part.

2. A meeting is the place where the group revises, updates, and adds to what it knows *as a group*. Every group creates its own pool of shared knowledge, experience, judgment, and folklore. But the pool consists only of what the individuals have experienced or discussed as a group— i.e., those things which every individual knows that all the others know, too. This pool not only helps all members to do their jobs more intelligently, but it also greatly increases the speed and efficiency of all communications among them. The group knows that all special nuances and wider implications in a brief statement will be immediately clear to its members. An enormous amount of material can be left unsaid that would have to be made explicit to an outsider.

3. A meeting helps every individual understand both the collective aim of the group and the way in which his and everyone else's work can contribute to the group's success.

4. A meeting creates in all present a commitment to the decisions it makes and the objectives it pursues. Once something has been decided, even if you originally argued against it, your membership in the group entails an obligation to accept the decision. The alternative is to leave the group, but in practice this is very rarely a dilemma of significance.

5. In the world of management, a meeting is very often the only occasion where the team or group actually exists and works as a group, and the only time when the supervisor, manager, or executive is actually perceived as the leader of the team, rather than as the official to whom individuals report.

6. A meeting is a status arena. It is no good to pretend that people are not or should not be concerned with their status relative to the other members in a group. It is just another part of human nature that we have to live with. It is a not insignificant fact that the word *order* means (a) hierarchy or pecking order; (b) an instruction or command; and (c) stability and the way things ought to be, as in "put your affairs in order," or "law and order." All three definitions are aspects of the same idea, which is indivisible.

Jay argues that the most important question concerns what a meeting is intended to achieve. It is necessary to begin by defining the objective. Jay says that every item on the agenda can be placed in one of four categories:

1. *Informative-digestive*, which includes such things as progress reports and review of completed projects.
2. *Constructive-originative*, or "What shall we do?" function.
3. *Executive responsibilities*, or "How shall we do it?" function.
4. *Legislative framework*, which refers to a system of rules, routines, and procedures within and through which all activity takes place.

CON: Death to groupthink

Irving Janis, in *Victims of Groupthink*, points out that ineffective decisions are often produced by highly competent and intelligent people working in a group decision context. Janis defines groupthink as

> A mode of thinking that people engage in when they are deeply involved in a cohesive in-group, when the members' striving for unanimity override their motivation to realistically appraise alternative courses of action. . . . Groupthink refers to a deterioration of mental efficiency, reality testing, and moral judgment that results from in-group pressures.*

Apparently, in such a group, the members develop an illusion of invulnerability. They become skilled at rationalizing away warnings which in other circumstances they would take seriously, and, they tend to underestimate the group's inherent morality. This leads to the development of stereotypical views of their opponents, whom they tend to underestimate. In such a context individuals who oppose the group's consensus are ridiculed. The net effect is to create a sense of unanimity about the views of the majority.

Some suggestions by Janis for overcoming groupthink:

> 1. The leader of a policy-forming group should assign the role of critical evaluator to each member, encouraging the group to give high priority to airing objections and doubts.
> 2. The leaders in an organization's hierarchy, when assigning a policy-planning mission to a group, should be impartial instead of stating preferences and expectations at the outset.
> 3. Each member of the policy-making group should discuss periodically the group's deliberations with trusted associates in his own unit of the organization and report back their reactions.
> 4. At every meeting devoted to evaluating policy alternatives, at least one member should be assigned the role of devil's advocate.
> 5. After reaching a preliminary consensus about what seems to be the best policy alternative, the policy-making group should hold a "sec-

---

* From *Victims of Groupthink* by Irving L. Janis. Copyright © 1972 by Houghton Mifflin Company. Reprinted with the permission of the publisher.

ond chance" meeting at which every member is expected to express as vividly as he can all his residual doubts and to rethink the entire issue before making a definitive choice.*

Question

How can these two points of view about the efficiency of group meetings be reconciled?

INCIDENT

How Firestone ignored its radial tire crisis

In 1978 Firestone was forced to recall more than 10 million radial tires, although the company had learned of the problem six years earlier. Early in 1972, a Firestone quality control executive who had been described by a company executive as "a guy who does our worrying for us" reported some damaging information from Goodyear. Apparently Goodyear had tested one of Firestone's steel-belted radials, and found a problem with the adhesion of the skin (a rubber compound) to the wire in the belt. Basically the problem was a moisture buildup in the skin and on the steel cord. To solve this problem, Firestone scrambled for years to develop a "dry technology" to prevent the moisture buildup. Meanwhile they were producing defective radials by the truckload.

The National Highway Traffic Safety Administration (NHTSA) finally forced Firestone to recall the radials. According to the NHTSA investigation, the company had had numerous early warnings from its development people that they had a real problem on their hands, because the radial 500 had shown a rising number of tread separations. Eventually, after steadfastly denying to the public that there was something wrong with the tires, the company had to make a "voluntary" recall.

What is interesting from an organizational behavior point of view is that even though the company inspectors and engineers were brutally frank among themselves about the tire failures, there is no documentary evidence that the top management ever weighed the implications of the problem.

Question

How could such an expensive failure of communication take place?

---

* From *Victims of Groupthink* by Irving L. Janis. Copyright © 1972 by Houghton Mifflin Company. Reprinted with the permission of the publisher.

DIAGRAM SUMMARY OF CHAPTER 12

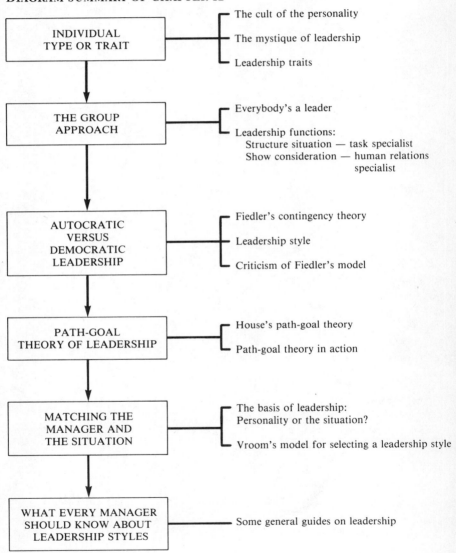

12

Finding more appropriate leadership styles

MACGREGOR*

By Arthur Elliott Carlisle

No question about it—some managers are better organized than others, but how often have you run into a really well organized manager—I mean *really* well organized?

MacGregor, who at the time was manager of one of the largest refineries in the country, was the last of more than 100 managers I interviewed in the course of the study. Although the interview had been scheduled in advance, the exact time had been left open; I was to call MacGregor at his office early in the week that I would be in the vicinity and set up a specific date and time.

Here's how that phone call went: The switchboard operator answered with the name of the refinery. When I asked for MacGregor's office, a male voice almost instantly said, "Hello." I then asked for MacGregor, whereupon the voice responded, "This is he." I should have recognized at once that this was no ordinary manager; he answered his own phone instantly, as though he had been waiting for it to ring. To my question about when it would be convenient for me to come see him, he replied, "Anytime." I said, "Would today be all right?" His response was, "Today, tomorrow, or Wednesday, would be O.K.; or you could come Thursday, except don't come between 10:00

A.M. and noon; or you could come Friday or next week—anytime." I replied feebly, "I just want to fit in with your plans." Then he said, "You are just not getting the message; it makes no difference to me when you come. I have nothing on the books except to play golf and see you. Come in anytime—I don't have to be notified in advance, so I'll be seeing you one of these days," and he then hung up. I was dumbfounded. Here was a highly placed executive with apparently nothing to do except play golf and talk to visitors.

I took MacGregor at his word and drove over immediately to see him without any further announcement of my visit.

MacGregor's modus operandi

"Do you hold regular meetings with your subordinates?" I asked.

"Yes, I do," he replied.

"How often?" I asked.

"Once a week, on Thursdays, between 10:00 A.M. and noon; that's why I couldn't see you then," was his response.

"What sorts of things do you discuss?" I queried, following my interview guide.

"My subordinates tell me about the decisions they've made during the past week," he explained.

"Then you believe in participative decision making," I commented.

"No—as a matter of fact, I don't," said MacGregor.

"Then why hold the meetings?" I asked. "Why not just tell your people about the operating decisions you've made and let them know how to carry them out?"

"Oh, I don't make their decisions for them and I just don't believe in participating in the decisions they should be making, either; we hold the weekly meeting so that I can keep informed on what they're doing and how. The meeting also gives me a chance to appraise their technical and managerial abilities," he explained. "I used to make all the operating decisions myself; but I quit doing that a few years ago when I discovered my golf game was going to hell because I didn't have enough time to practice. Now that I've quit making other people's decisions, my game is back where it should be."

"You don't make operating decisions any more?" I asked in astonishment.

"No," he replied. Sensing my incredulity, he added, "Obviously you don't believe me. Why not ask one of my subordinates? Which one do you want to talk to?"

Subordinates' views of MacGregor

I walked over to Johnson's unit and found him to be in his early thirties. After a couple of minutes of casual conversation, I discovered that MacGregor and all eight of his subordinates were chemical engineers. Johnson said, "I suppose MacGregor gave you that bit about his not making decisions, didn't he? That man is a gas."

"It isn't true though, is it? He does make decisions, doesn't he?" I asked.

"No, he doesn't; everything he told you is true. He simply decided not to get involved in decisions that his subordinates are being paid to make. So he stopped making them, and they tell me he plays a lot of golf in the time he saves," said Johnson.

Then I asked Johnson whether he tried to get MacGregor to make a decision and his response was:

"Only once I had been on the job for only about a week when I ran into an operating problem I couldn't solve, so I phoned MacGregor. He answered the phone with that sleepy 'Hello' of his. I told him who I was and that I had a problem. His response was instantaneous: 'Good, that's what you're being paid to do, solve problems,' and then he hung up. I was dumbfounded. I didn't really know any of the people I was working with, so because I didn't think I had any other alternative, I called him back, got the same sleepy 'Hello,' and again identified myself. He replied sharply, 'I thought I told you that you were paid to solve problems. Do you think that I should do your job as well as my own?' When I insisted on seeing him about my problem, he answered, 'I don't know how you expect me to help you. You have a technical problem and I don't go into the refinery any more; I used to, but my shirts kept getting dirty from the visits and my wife doesn't like washing all the grime out of them, so I pretty much stick in my office. Ask one of the older men. They're all in touch with what goes on out there.'

"I didn't know which one to consult, so I insisted again on seeing him. He finally agreed—grudgingly—to see me right away, so I went over to his office and there he was in his characteristic looking-out-the-window posture. When I sat down, he started the dirty-shirt routine—but when he saw that I was determined to involve him in my problems, he sat down on the sofa in front of his coffee table and, pen in hand, prepared to write on a pad of paper. He asked me to state precisely what the problem was and he wrote down exactly what I said. Then he asked what the conditions for its solution were. I replied that I didn't know what he meant by that question. His response was, 'If you don't know what conditions have to be satisfied for a solution to be reached, how do you know when you've solved the problem?' I told him I'd never thought of approaching a problem that way and he replied, 'Then you'd better start. I'll work through this one with you *this* time, but don't expect me to do your problem solving for you because that's *your* job, not mine.'

"I stumbled through the conditions that would have to be satisfied by the solution. Then he asked me what alternative approaches I could think of. I gave him the first one I could think of—let's call it X—and he wrote it down and asked me what would happen if I did X. I replied with my answer—let's call it A. Then he asked me how A compared with the conditions I had established for the solution of the problem. I replied that it did not meet them. MacGregor told me that I'd have to think of another. I came up with Y, which I said would yield result B, and this still fell short of the solution conditions. After more prodding from MacGregor, I came up with Z, which I said would have C as a result; although this clearly came a lot closer to the conditions I had established for the solution than any of the others I'd suggested, it still did not satisfy all of them. MacGregor then asked me if I could combine any of the approaches I'd suggested. I replied I could do X and Z and then saw that the resultant A plus C would indeed satisfy all the solution conditions I had set up previously. When I thanked MacGregor, he replied, 'What for? Get the hell out of my office; you could have done that bit of problem solving perfectly well without wasting my time. Next time you really can't solve a problem on your own, ask the Thursday man and tell me about it at the Thursday meeting.'"

I asked Johnson about Mr. MacGregor's reference to the Thursday man.

"He's the guy who runs the Thursday meeting when MacGregor is away from the plant. I'm the Thursday man now. My predecessor left here about two months ago."

"Where did he go? Did he quit the company?" I asked.

"God, no. He got a refinery of his own."

Head-office assessment of MacGregor

By the time I had finished with Johnson and Peterson, it was time for lunch. I decided I'd go downtown and stop in at the head office to try to find out their assessment of MacGregor and his operation. I visited the operations chief for the corporation. I had wanted to thank him for his willingness to go along with my study, anyway. When I told him I had met MacGregor, his immediate response was, "Isn't he a gas?" I muttered something about having heard that comment before and asked him about the efficiency of MacGregor's operation in comparison with that of other refineries in the corporation. His response was instantaneous, "Oh, MacGregor has by far the most efficient producing unit."

"Is that because he has the newest equipment?" I asked.

"No. As a matter of fact he has the oldest in the corporation. His was the first refinery we built."

"Does MacGregor have a lot of turnover among his subordinates?"

"A great deal," he replied.

Thinking I had found a chink in the MacGregory armor, I asked, "What happens to them; can't they take his system?"

"On the contrary," said the operations chief. "Most of them go on to assignments as refinery managers. After all, under MacGregor's method of supervision, they are used to working on their own."

Perspective on MacGregor's use of time

. . . In his informational role, MacGregor monitored the output of the management information system he had devised, but he did so after the same information had been reviewed by his subordinates. The dissemination function was partly achieved by the management information system and partly through the joint review of managerial decisions conducted at the Thursday morning meetings. As spokesman for his unit, he was easily accessible to individuals inside and outside the corporation.

What sets MacGregor apart from other managers is that he had consciously thought out his role as an upper-level administrator. He did not blindly adopt the methods of his predecessor; neither did he merely adapt the *modus operandi* he had previously found reasonably successful to the greater demands of running a larger unit. Rather, MacGregor reflected on what the key responsibilities of the executive in charge of a large operating facility really are and concluded that they involve being well informed on changes occurring in the environment that might have an impact on his operation and determining how best to adjust operations to benefit from these changes. At the same time, MacGregor recognized that profitable operations must be carried out in the here-and-now and that a supply of qualified subordinates must be developed for the future.

THE STARTING POINT

As the story of MacGregor suggests, the natural starting point for looking at leadership is the leader. The individual approach essentially begins by asking whether leadership is best understood as referring to a particular type (Charles de Gaulle, Joseph Stalin, Winston Churchill, Napoleon, Adolph Hitler, Franklin Roosevelt, Dwight Eisenhower—what do they all have in common?) or a list of traits (able, active, adept, affected, agreeable, aggressive, amiable, ardent, asinine, attractive, august, average, awesome—to list some of the traits that begin with the first letter of the alphabet). While most executives have their own pet lists of traits or a particular historical, political, or military figure in mind when they talk about leadership, science is not on their side. Increasingly, behavioral scientists are focusing on the systems of rules, roles, and relations that characterize the microsocial world of the group rather than researching the leader's attributes and actions.

The group approach to leadership is concerned with mapping out the *roles* in the group which the leaders can fill; the *relations* that facilitate the exercise of initiative and influence; the *rules* in terms of subroutines and rituals; and the values and norms which are a sine qua non of group life.

What is leadership style? Edwin P. Hollander, professor of psychology at the State University of New York at Buffalo and long-time theoretician and researcher in the field of leadership, catches the subtlety of style when he notes, in "Conformity, Status and Idiosyncrasy Credit," "In a broader sense, style may involve the interactive characteristics of the leader's personality, which stamp his relationships with followers, particularly in terms of the role expectancies which they hold." Box 12–1 suggests a rule governing how much leaders, such as MacGregor, can get away with.

Box 12–1: Idiosyncratic credit pays off, but only when it is paid up

How creative or original (or in some cases deviant or devious) organizational leaders can be depends on the kind of status credit card they carry. To put it more technically, the extent to which managers can deviate from norms is a function of their idiosyncratic credit, which reflects how much they have achieved vis-à-vis their peers.

A manager like Harold Geneen, ex-chairman of ITT, can impose tremendous demands on subordinates, not only to improve performance but also to generate the data needed as evidence of performance. A manager with less of a track record for turning companies around would have a lower idiosyncratic credit. Geneen had the reputation and status needed to impose a complicated control system on the entire ITT organization. This system allowed the company to increase its return on the ordinary dividend for 25 quarters in a row—an incredible feat made possible by one manager's idiosyncratic credit.

The situational approach to leadership maintains that style, structure, and setting are interlocking variables. This optic introduces an element of behavioral science relativity with the view that there are no absolute leaders. Rather, leadership is seen by effective executives such as MacGregor as a process which can by its very nature require different group members to take command at different times. Only then can the group achieve the diversity of goals that normally makes groups superior to individuals in performance.

TOPIC 1
Individual type or trait

THE CULT OF THE PERSONALITY

The cult of the personality, the term Nikita Khrushchev used to denounce Joseph Stalin at the 20th Communist Party Congress, describes the unity and devotion a strong leader can inspire among followers. The rejection of the Man of Iron style of Stalin for the more liberal, less centralized style of Khruschev represents the antithesis of two basic leadership concepts: "Weak people need strong leadership" versus "Strong people don't need leadership." Box 12–2 describes two basically different leadership styles.

Box 12–2: Transactional versus transforming leadership

James MacGregor Burns divides leadership into two types, transactional and transforming. In transactional leadership the leader makes a practical deal with the followers, and in transforming leadership the leader helps subordinates to help themselves in self-actualizing terms. Burns cites Charles De Gaulle as an example of a leader who had the ability to both control and inspire others.

The central message is that the leader has to avoid "narrow, egocentric self-actualization" and must try to create an environment in which subordinates can grow and develop. Executives would be wise to examine their own leadership styles to ascertain to what extent they are transactional or transforming.

Reference: James MacGregor Burns, *Leadership* (New York: Harper & Row, 1978).

A scenario of how strong leadership required by a situation emerges, operates, and is then rejected helps to flesh out the story line of such changes in leadership favor as the replacement of the New Frontier fervor of John F. Kennedy with the stolid, low-profile style of Richard Nixon or the switch of allegiance from the dramatic, lion-roaring, epoch-making style of Winston Churchill to the systematic, low-key consensus management of Clement Attlee.

Charles de Gaulle, the charismatic genius, with his frosty independence and detached historical perspective, was able to bring France in 1958 from the brink of civil war to social and economic stability. His extraordinary achievement was ending the fraticidal crisis in Algeria with the ambiguous reassurance to the French settlers in Algeria that "I have understood you." They thought he was going to support them against the rebels—and he did not. As De Gaulle points out in *Memoirs of Hope, Renewal and Endeavor:* "I tossed them the words, seemingly spontaneous but in reality carefully calculated, which I hoped would fire their enthusiasm without committing me further than I was willing to go." It was a brilliant calculated stroke. But in the end the French people tired of his magnetic leadership, and he was followed by Georges Pompidou, who is described by James McGregor Burns, in *Leadership,* as a master of "low profile, behind the scenes, urbane, consensus management."

THE MYSTIQUE OF LEADERSHIP

De Gaulle's type of leadership is a nonoptional extra: You don't need it until you haven't got it. Leadership begins with a vision of success, the potentiality of snatching victory from disaster. Existentially, a leader frequently has been rejected by both peers and the masses and makes a big comeback. Roosevelt and Churchill made it back, one from infantile paralysis, the other from the disaster of the Dardanelles, and both were strengthened immeasurably by adversity. Leaders have a vision of the future, a sense of impending apocalypse, and the courage to ride the coattails of history. They are not too far out front, where no one can see and follow, and not too far back, where there would be a vacuum at the front.

Leaders must also have a sharp sense of the ridiculous. For example, it is said that when Winston Churchill was recording his famous 1940 speech, "We shall not flag or fail, we shall go on to the end. We shall fight in France, we shall fight on the seas and oceans, we shall fight on the beaches, we shall fight on the landing grounds, we shall fight in the fields and in the streets, we shall fight on the hills, we shall never surrender," he put his hand over the microphone and said to those present, "and we will hit them over the heads with beer bottles, which is all we really have." When the British people, as Churchill himself said, wanted to roar, he roared for them.

In Churchill we can see an ultimate institution, a nonoptional extra whom history seized and magnified to god size and who in turn manipulated history in favor of the gods. Stalin, the Man of Iron, was the messianic free choice who arose from a framework of Marxian and Hegelian determinism to play the crucial role in World War II, as no substitute could have done.

Thus leaders must serve time in the wilderness, must await the call of history, then reemerge through a combination of shrewdness, savvy, style, and charisma and focus on the infinite meaning of finite things. If they can set the world (or a part of it) alight with their vision, they can become saints in the process. But if they live long enough, their canonization may overlap with their denunciation.

A good example of this type of leader is the Ayatollah Khomeini, the spiritual leader who in 1979 returned from exile to become the master of Iran. Khomeini sought to manage a precarious and unstable situation by pursuing a very high-risk strategy—focusing the people's hostilities on the United States.

LEADERSHIP TRAITS

Many studies have been undertaken to ascertain the personality traits of the leader. For example, it has been reported that the leader tends to be bigger and brighter than the rest of a group, but only marginally so. Whatever social psychologists think of such studies, most managers, including many personnel managers, believe they have the ability to select managers or leaders on the basis of a brief interview. This optimistic, if somewhat naive, attitude springs from the belief that a manager is a person who has some of the following characteristics (which ones and how many depend upon the prejudices of the individual making the selection): analytical, intelligent, not too bright, keen, enthusiastic, aggressive, capable of maintaining smooth interpersonal relationships, persuasive, dominant, personally acceptable, tactful, extraverted, well balanced, needing to succeed, ambitious. Different selectors evaluate such traits in their own ways, according to their own biases.

One method which has been used to identify leadership potential is the assessment center, an organizational arrangement in which line managers or supervisors consider candidates for managerial positions and attempt to determine their management prospects and career development needs. Figure 12–1 outlines this process, which is based on the identification of traits and skills.

The trait approach to defining leadership has generally failed, however. One reason is that neither personality nor personality traits are

FIGURE 12–1
The assessment center process

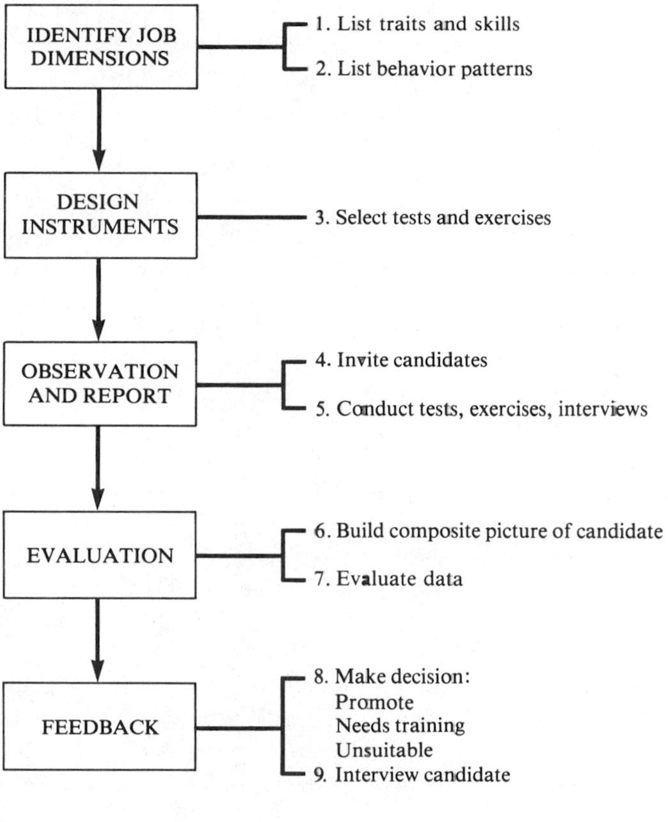

| IDENTIFY JOB DIMENSIONS | 1. List traits and skills |
| | 2. List behavior patterns |

| DESIGN INSTRUMENTS | 3. Select tests and exercises |

| OBSERVATION AND REPORT | 4. Invite candidates |
| | 5. Conduct tests, exercises, interviews |

| EVALUATION | 6. Build composite picture of candidate |
| | 7. Evaluate data |

| FEEDBACK | 8. Make decision: Promote Needs training Unsuitable |
| | 9. Interview candidate |

clearly understood or capable of accurate measurement. Efforts to isolate traits that would distinguish leaders from others have proved dis-
appointing and full of contradictory results. Many social psychologists
hold the view that leadership traits may exist, but if they do, they have
not been recognized.

Research findings have instead pointed to the idea that leadership
is situational. In general, results have indicated that while certain
minimal abilities are required of all leaders, these traits are also distributed among other members of the group according to a normal
distribution curve. A more fruitful line of inquiry might therefore be
based on the theory that there are various leader roles in the group. In
essence, research results have indicated that an approach based on the
individual should be replaced by the group approach to the problem
of leadership.

TOPIC 2
The group approach

EVERYBODY'S A LEADER

In the group approach, the social psychologist is not concerned with
identifying invariant leader traits but takes the wider view that leadership is the performance of acts which assist the group in achieving
certain ends. In these circumstances, leadership may be performed by
one or many members of the group; leadership is regarded as a quantitative variable, not as something which is found in some people and
not in others.

An extremely useful definition of leadership identifies it as the ability to influence others in a group. The virtue of this apparently simple
definition is that it allows for the possibility that all group members
may exhibit a degree of leadership; the leader in the conventional
sense is the one whose influence predominates. In this context leadership is regarded as an interpersonal behavioral event; this means, for
example, that followers can influence leaders by communicating to
them their fears, anxieties, and so on (see Box 12–3). Indeed, the official leader of a group may have no influence; formal leadership need
not coincide with informal.

Inevitably, whenever two or more people get together, one will
dominate, and leadership emerges. The form of leadership in a group
depends on the group members, the task, and the group ideology.
Complex tasks require a hierarchy of leaders, as is the case in modern
business organizations, but in crises a simpler form of leadership is
required. In moments of high drama and tension, choice is made not
logically but on the basis of charismatic qualities attributed to the
leader (e.g., Churchill during the Battle of Britain). Leaders emerge

Box 12–3: Passing it on

One of the incisive portraits of American managers Studs Terkel has provided has as its subject Larry Ross, a former conglomerate president who became a consultant, describing himself as "an adviser to top management in a corporation."

Likes:
"In my climb, . . . money was secondary. . . . It's the power, the status, the prestige. Frankly, its delightful to be on top. . . . "

Dislikes:
"I was always subject to the board of directors, who had pressure from the stockholders. I owned a portion of the business, but I wasn't in control. I don't know of any situation in the corporate world where an executive is completely free and sure of his job from moment to moment."

"Fear is always prevalent in the corporate structure. . . . There's always the insecurity. . . . You're always fearful of the big mistake."

Signs of alienation/stress:
"The executive is a lonely animal in the jungle who doesn't have a friend."

"We always saw signs of physical afflictions because of the stress and strain. Ulcers, violent headaches."

"There's one corporation chief I had. . . . His whole life was his business. . . . He was lonesome when he wasn't involved with his business."

"The most stupid phrase anybody can use in business is loyalty. . . . The schnook is the loyal guy, because he can't get a job anyplace else."

"But the warm personal touch *never* existed in corporations. . . . In the last analysis, you've got to make a profit."

About boss:
"You have men working for you and you have a boss above. You're caught in a squeeze. . . . You have the guys working for you that are shooting for your job. The guy you're working for is scared stiff you're gonna shove him out of his job."

"Even if you're a top man, even if you're hard, . . . by the slight flick of a finger, your boss can fire you."

Quotations from Studs Terkel, *Working: People Talk About What They Do All Day and How They Feel About What They Do* (New York: Pantheon Books, 1972). © 1972 Pantheon Books, a Division of Random House, Inc.

more easily in unstable situations, precisely because the structure of the group is loosened due to some change in one of the major constraints—a change in the nature of the task, a new person joining the group, a powerful person leaving, or a change in the ideological climate.

LEADERSHIP FUNCTIONS

Several research studies have found it useful to analyze leaders' behavior according to two dimensions, initiating structure, and consideration. Leaders high in initiating structure make sure not only that their role is understood by the group but also that official procedures are followed; they try out new ideas on members. This type of structuring leadership is of special value when the group faces a task problem. Leaders who are high in consideration are group oriented; they reward good work and invite participation in the setting of group goals.

There are two related types of group functions: the first, the task function, is concerned with the achievement of some specific goal; the second, the human function, is concerned with the maintenance or strengthening of the group itself. Examples of task functions in a group are stressing the importance of the object of the exercise, focusing attention on production, and reviewing the quality of the work done. Examples of human relations functions in a group are keeping the group happy, settling disputes, providing encouragement, and giving the minority a chance to be heard.

Figure 12–2 relates leadership behavior to group functions. An Ohio

FIGURE 12–2
Leadership behaviors and results

BEHAVIOR DIMENSION	LEADER'S BEHAVIOR	RESULTS
High on initiating structure	Task function: Make specific work assignments; emphasize deadlines; evaluate quality; define work patterns	Superiors satisfied. High productivity, low costs and scrap. High turnover and grievances. Subordinates dissatisfied.
High on consideration	Human function: Consider subordinates' needs; be understanding, warm, supportive, friendly.	Superiors dissatisfied. Productivity low. Intragroup cooperation. Low turnover and grievances. Subordinates satisfied.
Both	Combination	Superiors satisfied. High productivity, low costs and scrap. Low turnover and grievances. Subordinates satisfied.

State University leadership group led by A. W. Halpin and B. J. Winer reported in "A Factorial Study of the Leader Behavior Descriptions" that leaders high on initiating structure (i.e., those who make specific work assignments, spell out deadlines, evaluate the quality of work, and establish well-defined work patterns and procedure) were highly rated by their superiors and generated high performance in terms of productivity, and avoidance of scrap and cost. Researchers at the University of Southern California reported, using a similar scale which measured advance planning and organizing skill, reported that high scores on this scale were described by their subordinates as well organized and by their bosses as highly productive. But, perhaps not too surprisingly, there was some evidence to support the proposition that high-production supervisors (high in initiating structure) had higher rates of grievance and labor turnover than low-scoring colleagues. The Ohio State leadership group also found that supervisors scoring high on consideration (i.e., those who were supportive, willing to explain their actions, warm, and friendly) had more satisfied subordinates who displayed more intragroup harmony and lower levels of grievance and turnover.

Apparently, therefore, superiors and subordinates view the leadership behavior of supervisors from different perspectives. Superiors evidently prefer supervisors who are structuring and thus effective from a task point of view, whereas shop-floor employees (or line workers) prefer supervisors who are considerate and not overly concerned with production. And research has found that production supervisors high on both dimensions can get the production out without increasing either the rate of grievances or labor turnover.

TOPIC 3
Autocratic versus democratic leadership

FIEDLER'S CONTINGENCY THEORY

The research work of F. E. Fiedler, of the University of Washington, is of great interest to executives, such as MacGregor, because it developed a contingency model to facilitate the analysis of leadership effectiveness. Fiedler's findings put him on the side of those who believe in reality-centered leadership. His seminal work, *A Theory of Leadership Effectiveness*, represents an attempt to deal with "the critical, directive, autocratic, task-oriented versus the democratic, permissive, considerate, person-oriented type of leadership."

With a considerable body of empirical evidence behind him, Fiedler developed a theoretical model which set out to define the conditions under which each kind of leadership is more effective. Fiedler's empirical works rely on the measurement of psychological distance. In one study, Fiedler invited leaders to rank (on eight-point bipolar adjective scales) the person they liked working with best and the person with whom they could work least well. The strength of Fiedler's work rests on its diversity, accuracy, and extent. Some notion of the extent of his work may be gained from the fact that he experimented with this measure of psychological distance in studies of high school basketball teams, civil engineering teams, smelter foremen, and managers of cooperatives.

The difficulties he encountered trying to reconcile some of his findings led Fiedler to develop a more complex model. He started with
the rather simple proposition that leadership is essentially concerned
with the problem of exercising influence and power. To facilitate his
analysis, he postulates three important dimensions of the total situation
which structure the leader's role:

1. *Leader-member relations.* The extent to which the leader enjoys
   the confidence and loyalty of others and is regarded as personally
   attractive by them. This aspect is usually measured by a sociometric index.
2. *Task structure.* The extent to which the task represents an order
   from above. The presumption is that a foreman who issues a direct
   order to a subordinate, say, to wear safety glasses, can expect the
   support of the departmental leader if the operator is unwilling to
   comply. Task structure can be operationally defined by:
   a.   The extent to which the decision is capable of being verified.
   b.   The extent of goal clarity (i.e., the degree to which the task
          requirements are known to members of the group).
   c.   The multiplicity of goal paths—the variety of means available

FIGURE 12–3
Fiedler's prediction of leadership styles

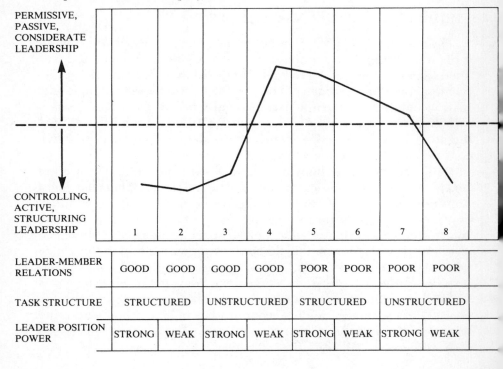

LEADER-MEMBER RELATIONS	GOOD	GOOD	GOOD	GOOD	POOR	POOR	POOR	POOR	
TASK STRUCTURE	STRUCTURED		UNSTRUCTURED		STRUCTURED		UNSTRUCTURED		
LEADER POSITION POWER	STRONG	WEAK	STRONG	WEAK	STRONG	WEAK	STRONG	WEAK	

(whether there are many or few procedures for solving the task).

d. The solution specificity—whether there are one or a large number of correct solutions.

3. *Position power.* The power inherent in the position of the leader, including the rewards and punishments traditionally at his disposal, his official authority, and the organizational support on which he can depend.

Fiedler has classified groups on the basis of these three dimensions. Predicted leadership styles in eight sample groups based on their ratings in these dimensions are shown in Figure 12–3.

LEADERSHIP STYLE

In evaluating leadership style in his contingency model, Fiedler uses as a predictor measure the least preferred co-worker (LPC) score. To obtain this score, individuals are asked to think of all the co-workers they have ever had. They are then asked to describe on a semantic differential scale the one person they have been least able to work with. The assessment is made by rating that person on eight-point bipolar adjective scales like these:

friendly : —— : —— : —— : —— : —— : —— : —— : —— : unfriendly
           8   7   6   5   4   3   2   1

cooperative : —— : —— : —— : —— : —— : —— : —— : —— : uncooperative
           8   7   6   5   4   3   2   1

The LPC scale usually contains 16 to 24 such items. The LPC score is obtained by averaging the item values of 1 to 8. Thus, a high score (Fiedler suggests an average item value of 5 on the eight-point scale) indicates that the person taking the test views her or his least preferred co-worker in relatively favorable terms. A low score (say, an average of 2) means that the least preferred co-worker is described in a very negative, rejecting manner.

The LPC score is somewhat difficult to interpret. At first Fiedler interpreted it as meaning that lower scores indicated a greater task orientation and higher scores a greater human relations orientation, but he came to regard this interpretation as somewhat misleading. According to Fiedler, the low-scoring person describes his least preferred co-worker in a uniform and thus undifferentiated or stereotyped manner, whereas the high scorer spreads his scores on different items over a wider part of the scale (greater item variance). The argument is that the labels "relationship-oriented" versus "task-oriented" for high versus low scores are only valid in situations characterized by anxiety and stress, where the leader has little control. T. R. Mitchell, in "Leader Complexity and Leadership Style," reports some evidence in support of the proposition that leaders with high LPC scores tend to be more cognitively complex in their manner of thinking about groups, while low scorers tend to be more stereotyped in their thinking. But precisely what the LPC scale measures is impossible to say, and this has turned out to be a major difficulty of Fiedler's theory.

Leader styles and the work situation

Using his three-dimensional model, Fiedler examined his earlier empirical work on leadership and presented, in "The Contingency Model," a more sophisticated and convincing explanation of the nature of effective leadership:

> Considerate, permissive, accepting leaders obtain optimal group performance under situations intermediate in favorableness. These are situations in which (a) the task is structured, but the leader is disliked and must, therefore, be diplomatic; (b) the liked leader has an abiguous, unstructured task and must, therefore, draw upon the creativity and cooperation of his members. Here we obtain positive correlations between L.P.C. and group performance scores. Where the task is highly structured and the leader is well-liked, non-directive behavior or permissive attitude (such as asking how the group ought to proceed with a missile countdown) is neither appropriate nor beneficial. Where the situation is quite unfavorable, e.g., where the disliked chairman of a volunteer group faces an ambiguous task, the leader might as well be autocratic and directive since a positive, non-directive leadership style under these conditions might result in complete inactivity on the part of the group. This model, thus, tends to shed some light on the apparent inconsistencies in our own data as well as in data obtained by other investigators.

Fiedler's contingency model, mainly on account of its flexibility, represents an improvement over much of the earlier, more naive work in the leadership field and provides a useful theoretical framework for further research. For the executive the vital point to emerge from Fiedler's work is the realistic view that business can utilize a fairly broad spectrum of individuals in executive positions. One of the most difficult questions raised about any previous theoretical description of a leader was: "How many executives do you know who are like that or operate in that manner?"

As many managers know, the real problem falls in the area of placement and training. The nub of the matter is that executives have to be taught both to recognize their own styles and to accept assignments in work areas where their particular styles are relevant.

Fiedler's view of the effectiveness of manager training

Fiedler has not only generated a very complex but interesting theory, he also has adapted the theory as a means of testing the effectiveness of supervisory training. The results of this part of his research are interesting if somewhat contradictory, since Fiedler earlier spoke of "engineering the job to fit the man." Fiedler now takes a more optimistic view (subject to reservations) in regard to the effectiveness of managerial training.

A negative finding is that training tends to be dysfunctional for task-motivated leaders with poor leader-member relations, and "low" LPC leaders (at a rough approximation, leaders with good human relation skills) with good leader-member relations perform no better with training than without it. Why then should task-oriented managers be introduced in management training sessions to the mysteries of flexible leadership styles and human relations? The answer is that it won't help; it will only make the manager feel guilty in a normal work situation. Another negative finding also seems to confirm the obvious: People who have high human relations skills and already have good relations with their colleagues have nothing to gain from management training.

Fiedler's results do support the proposition that the task which seems to be unstructured to the untrained leader seems structured to the trained leader. In other words, management training helps executives take complex, unstructured situations and turn them into well-defined, clearly structured, and presumably solvable problems.

In "The Leadership Game," Fiedler summarizes his views on leadership training:

> In summary, my own position is that we must train people differentially—not everyone should be trained to behave in the same way or to adopt the same attitudes. In fact, we will be better served by training our leaders in how to change their leadership situations than in how to change their personalities. Leadership effectiveness requires a proper match of person and situation, and trying to change personality is the hard way of achieving this balance. It is an effort with uncertain success that requires years, not weeks. Our recent studies of contingency model training show that leaders can recognize the situations in which they tend to be most successful, and they can modify their situations so that they perform more effectively. We have reason to believe that this approach holds considerable promise for the future of leadership training.

CRITICISM OF FIEDLER'S MODEL

Fiedler has revealed his genius twice; first, in devising the model, which stands like calculus to arithmetic compared with previous leadership models, and second, in his ability to integrate new findings into his model. Nevertheless, Fiedler has been criticized for employing rather small samples; most of the studies reported used sample sizes under ten. Further, few of the studies investigated the full range of the situational types simultaneously.

Box 12–4: Executive relations as interpersonal chemistry

Relationships between executives are of critical importance in determining outcomes. These intangible considerations can make the difference between excellent and indifferent performance.

How do you measure the relation between the vibes one executive gives off and another receives? This interpersonal chemistry reflects a congruence or divergence of the two executives' styles and values—in short, their gut reaction, one to another.

Current U.S. management is an amalgam of authoritarianism and participation, encapsulated in the aphorism: "I'm OK—you're OK. But I am still the boss." As Roy Rowan points out:

> The boss's autocratic hand has been relaxed, power has been decentralized. The new spirit that management is trying to foster is individual resourcefulness, not lockstep compliance. If the laws of thermodynamics applied to business, opening up the system should dissipate the heat and friction. What sometimes seems to be happening instead is that the ego clashes that were once vertical between boss and subordinate have become horizontal.

But sometimes relations do not work out. For example, Rowan says,

> When a combination doesn't mesh, somebody has to go. Instances of top-rung pairings where the chemistry evidently didn't work turn up all the time. William R. Roesch did a bang-up job at Kaiser Industries, but departed when his abrasive style bumped against Edgar Kaiser's gentlemanly manner. A year ago Grant Simmons Jr., chairman of his family's mattress company, fired the heir-apparent, President Robert Tyler Jr., because of what Simmons termed "a difference in management style." Then this summer his own board deposed Simmons as c.e.o.

Finding and hiring their No. 1 and 2 managers can be tricky for chief executive officers:

> Carl Menk, president of Boyden Associates, one of the largest international executive-search firms, claims that 20 percent of the decision whether or not to recommend a person for a job hinges on the first ten minutes of meeting. . . . After nine years in the business, Menk concludes that there are basically only three [management styles]: the style epitomized by the turnaround guy ("the hard-nosed individual," says Menk, "who is not too concerned with personal niceties, but who loves problem solving, particularly bailing out companies verging on Chapter Ten or Eleven"); the style demonstrated by the growth-oriented boss ("comfortable with a hefty advertising budget designed to bring in new markets"); and the so-called maintenance management style ("satisfied with proven techniques, 2 to 3 percent annual growth in a company which has a history of success"). Adds Menk: "There are very few executives whose personal chemistry will allow them to adapt to all three situations."

There is also the question of the T-M balance, the mixture of technical and managerial skills. The important point is that managers must be able to criticize each other constructively without blowing up the corporate ship.

Reference: Roy Rowan, "Watch Out for Chemical Reactions at the Top," *Fortune,* September 25, 1978.

Fiedler's model has also been criticized on theoretical grounds. For example, A. K. Korman has criticized the model as being static and ignoring the long-range influence of the situation on the leader and the group. Ahmed Ashour has suggested that the contingency model be revised and, to facilitate this revision, that new directions be pursued to provide data that will help in devising an improved model. In the first instance, larger samples should be used to clarify the problem of statistical significance. More data should be collected on leader and group behavior using the critical-incident technique. More information, especially of a cognitive and motivational character, is needed in regard to what the LPC score actually measures. More variables, such as size and homogeneity of the group, must be introduced to define the situational characteristic more fully. Longitudinal studies also are required to see how the different variables interact over a period of time.

The major criticism of Fiedler's model from executives is that the model is essentially academic, and no significant effort has been made to apply the findings to actual management operations as a means of improving organizational or group performance. Its application to management training was noted above, however. (Box 12–4 gives some practical advice from a different point of view.)

By this measure Fiedler is compared unfavorably to R. R. Blake and J. S. Mouton, who in the late 1950s and early 1960s took the findings of group dynamics of those days, synthesized them into the managerial grid, and, using T-group technology, trained a generation of managers. Perhaps the crucial difference is that Blake and Mouton used a two-dimensional model, which raised the level of discussion of managers by a quantum leap; whereas Fiedler's contingency model is basically a three-dimensional model, with all sorts of complexities built in.

TOPIC 4
Path-goal theory of leadership

HOUSE'S PATH-GOAL THEORY

Puzzled by a number of contradictory findings in leadership research, Robert J. House of the University of Toronto's business school came forward with an exciting new theory of leadership. His theory is based on Victor Vroom's theory of motivation, with its concepts of expectancy, outcomes, utilities, and instrumentalities (see Chapter 8).

What started House off was the fact that research in the 1950s—dealing with first-line supervisors and measuring the factors of initiating structure and consideration—revealed that leaders who initiate structure for subordinates generally get higher performance ratings from superiors and have more productive work groups, while leaders who are considerate of subordinates have more satisfied subordinates. But there was other evidence that initiating structure for unskilled and semiskilled workers causes dissatisfaction, and that employees in large groups apparently either prefer initiating structure more or dislike it less than employees in small groups. From his own more recent research work on roles at a different occupational level, House found that with high-level employees, initiating structure causes a reduction in role conflict and ambiguity and is preferred.

To explain these apparent contradictions in research findings, House developed a path-goal theory of leadership which has attracted considerable attention among both academics and executives. This theory suggests a way to reconcile these apparently conflicting results.

With revisions and extensions, the theory includes both environmental variables and individual-difference variables. House's basic thesis is that a critical function of the executive is to enrich and enhance the psychological status of subordinates in order to increase motivation to perform (task effectiveness) and satisfaction (human factor). The path-goal theory of leadership focuses the efforts of the executive on the following elements:

1. Recognizing and mobilizing group members' needs for outcomes over which the leader has some control.
2. Making a more active effort to link personal payoffs for subordinates with actual work-goal achievement.
3. Making a detailed and careful analysis of the paths to these payoffs, and making it easier for subordinates to travel these paths by coaching and direction.
4. Interacting with team members to help them to clarify their expectancies, so that they will have a better grasp of the probabilities of particular relations and outcomes. ("If I do this and get there, what are the chances that you (a) will recognize it? (b) reward it?")
5. Reducing frustrating barriers; for example, making sure executives are not held up by lack of computer resources or secretarial assistance.
6. Increasing the opportunities for personal satisfaction, contingent on effective performance.

In stating his theory this way, House links in a dramatic, and clear way how performance and payoffs (extrinsic and intrinsic) are locked in a subtle web of subjective probabilities or expectancies which the executive can be taught how to monitor. House takes the subject of executive leadership out of the age of Aquarius into the age of cost/ benefit analysis, where utility and probability are the aces. The executive has to be able to figure out the networks of utilities and probabilities and come up with the necessary coaching and guidance for the problem, but only when appropriate. As a leader accomplishes these functions, leader behavior increases the motivation of subordinates.

House recognizes that individual differences among subordinates will affect their perception and interpretation of leader behavior. For example, subordinates with high need for affiliation obviously prefer leaders high on consideration; while those with high needs for achievement prefer more structured leadership styles that clarify path-goal relations, generate goal-oriented feedback, and generally facilitate goal achievement. Subordinates with high needs for extrinsic rewards obviously prefer leader behavior that helps them gain recognition, promotion, and salary increases. Another individual factor is subordinates' perceptions of their own ability with respect to the assigned tasks. This recognition of the factor of individual difference clearly ties House's work into established valence-instrumentality-expectation motivation theory.

PATH-GOAL LEADERSHIP THEORY IN ACTION

House has developed his path-goal theory into a contingency theory of leadership. While the state of theorizing about contingency leadership in terms of subordinates' paths and goals is still in its infancy, the early empirical findings provide useful guidelines for managers. The argument is that leadership will be effective by making rewards available for subordinates and making these rewards contingent on the subordinates' accomplishment of organizational goals. The first proposition of path-goal theory is that subordinates see behavior as acceptable, either as an immediate source of satisfaction or instrumental in future satisfaction.

Four kinds of leadership behavior—directive, supportive, participative, and achievement oriented—are identified by House and Terence R. Mitchell in "Path-Goal Theory of Leadership":

> *Leader directiveness.* Leader directiveness has a positive correlation with satisfaction and expectancies of subordinates who are engaged in ambiguous tasks and has a negative correlation with satisfaction and expectancies of subordinates engaged in clear tasks.
>
> *Supportive leadership.* The theory hypothesizes that supportive leadership will have its most positive effect on subordinate satisfaction for subordinates who work on stressful, frustrating or dissatisfying tasks.
>
> *Participative leadership.* In theorizing about the effects of participative leadership it is necessary to ask about the specific characteristics of both the subordinates and their situation that would cause participative leadership to be viewed as satisfying and instrumental to effective performance.
>
> *Achievement-oriented leadership.* The theory hypothesizes that achievement-oriented leadership will cause subordinates to strive for

higher standards of performance and to have more confidence in the ability to meet challenging goals.

In path-goal theory, the role of the leader is to help subordinates by providing coaching, guidance, and the rewards necessary for satisfaction and effective performance in a way that clarifies the paths to the goals and the desirability of the goals. One major finding of this theory is rather old-fashioned; it suggests that consideration leads to higher subordinate satisfaction and that structuring behavior frequently annoys subordinates, especially when consideration is low. The theory argues that consideration is most effective in structured situations and that structure will lead to greater satisfaction in ambiguous or stressful situations.

Path-goal leadership theory has stimulated much research, but more work needs to be done to flesh out the model empirically.

TOPIC 5
Matching the manager and the situation

THE BASIS OF LEADERSHIP: PERSONALITY OR THE SITUATION?

Few problems in organizational behavior are as relevant to executives as the study of leadership. The significance of leadership, described above as the nonoptional extra that is always needed to make things happen, cannot be underplayed. As we have noted, the popular presumption of leadership as a unidimensional personality trait which is distributed throughout the general population does not receive much support. Nevertheless, many people believe that leaders are different, and it is necessary to respond to them accordingly. In fact, there are a number of traits that distinguish leaders from nonleaders. Leaders are slightly taller and heavier; they score higher on tests of intelligence, extraversion, adjustment dominance, and self-confidence. These differences are usually small in magnitude, however.

The critical factors determining effective leadership are only marginally a function of personality considerations; rather, to a large extent, they are a function of the situation. The most powerful research in this area tried to establish a relationship between psychological distance and effectiveness, but the development of a complex contingency model failed to support this relation.

Leadership as a personality characteristic is a basic oversimplification. A more interesting way to approach leadership is to regard it as a group phenomenon; everyone in a group has a chance to lead, depending on circumstances. Within this context the effective leader is one who can generate both productivity and job satisfaction and who exhibits both structure and consideration. But as Rensis Likert points out, leadership skills are always relative to the situation. In *New Patterns of Management,* Likert says:

> Supervision is, therefore, always a relative process. To be effective and to communicate as intended, a leader must always adapt his behavior to take into account the expectations, values and interpersonal skills of those with whom he is interacting. . . . There can be no specific rules of supervision which will work well in all situations. Broad principles can be applied to the process of supervision and furnish valuable guides to behavior. These principles, however, must be applied always in a manner that takes fully into account the characteristics of the specific situation, and of the people involved.

VROOM'S MODEL FOR SELECTING A LEADERSHIP STYLE

Victor Vroom has devised a sophisticated model of leadership which takes into consideration the two basic group functions: achievement of goals and tasks, and maintenance and strengthening of the human relations infrastructure of the group. The basic argument of Vroom's model, based on participation and decision making, is that the amount of participation varies from one situation to another.

Vroom's goal was to develop a normative model which would be helpful to managers in selecting a leadership style according to the situation. He argues for a taxonomy of leadership style which ranges from AI, where the leader makes all decisions, to GII, where groups generate alternatives and develop solutions (see Box 12–5). Managers decisions as to which style is most appropriate in certain circumstances depend on how much information they have, how much time is at their disposal, and how participative their subordinates are likely to be.

Seven rules for choosing among alternative leadership styles

Vroom has developed seven rules to help managers choose among these alternative leadership styles. The rules are:

1. The information rule (Does the manager know enough?).
2. The goal congruence rule (Do subordinates have such different values that maximum participation must be excluded?).
3. The unstructured-problem rule (The problem is so complex that subordinates have to be brought in.).
4. The acceptance rule (The new people have to be taken on board.).
5. The conflict rule (Conflict has to be avoided at all costs.).
6. The fairness rule (Quality of decision is unimportant, but acceptance is critical.).

Box 12–5: Leadership and decision making

Victor Vroom and P. W. Yelton describe one approach to dealing with what they call "one of the most persistent and controversial issues in the study of management"—the participation of subordinates in decision making:

. . . A normative model is developed which is consistent with existing empirical evidence concerning the consequences of participation; it purports to specify a set of rules which *should* be followed in determining the form and amount of participation in decision-making by subordinates to be used in different classes of situations.

The model serves to regulate choices among alternative processes for translating problems into solutions. The alternative processes are defined in terms of amount and form of participation by subordinates and are shown in [the following table].

TABLE
Decision Methods for Group Problems

AI   You solve problem or make decision yourself using information available to you at that time.

AII   You obtain necessary information from subordinate(s), then decide on solution to problem yourself. You may or may not tell subordinates what the problem is in getting the information from them. The role played by your subordinates in making the decision is clearly one of providing the necessary information to you, rather than generating or evaluating alternative solutions.

CI   You share the problem with relevant subordinates individually; getting their ideas and suggestions without bringing them together as a group. Then *you* make the decision which may or may not reflect your subordinates' influence.

CII   You share the problem with your subordinates as a group, collectively obtaining their ideas and suggestions. Then, you make the decision which may or may not reflect your subordinates' influence.

GII   You share problem with your subordinates as a group. Together you generate and evaluate alternatives and attempt to reach agreement (consensus) on a solution.

CONCEPTUAL AND EMPIRICAL BASIS OF THE MODEL

A model designed to regulate, in some rational way, choices among the leadership styles shown in [the table] should be based on sound empirical evidence concerning the likely consequences of the styles. . . . we will restrict ourselves to presentation of a model concerned only with group problems. A comparable model for individual problems has been developed but will not be presented here.

To aid in understanding the conceptual basis of the model, it is important to distinguish three aspects of the ultimate effectiveness of decisions:

1. The quality or rationality of the decision.
2. The acceptance or commitment on the part of subordinates to execute the decision effectively.
3. The amount of time required to make the decision.

Source: V. H. Vroom and P. W. Yetton, *Leadership and Decision-making* (Pittsburgh, Pa.: University of Pittsburgh Press, 1973).

One of us has reviewed the evidence regarding the effects of participation on each of these aspects and concluded:

> The results suggest that allocating problem-solving and decision-making tasks to entire groups, as compared with the leader or manager in charge of the groups, requires a greater investment of man-hours but produces higher acceptance of decisions and a higher probability that the decision will be executed efficiently. Differences between these two methods in quality of decisions and in elapsed time are inconclusive and probably highly variable . . . The critics and proponents of participative management would do well to direct their efforts toward identifying the properties of situations in which different decision-making approaches are effective rather than wholesale condemnation or deification of one approach.

Stemming from this review, an attempt has been made to identify these properties of the situation or problem which will be the basic elements in the model. These problem attributes are of two types: (1) those which specify the importance for a particular problem of quality and acceptance (see A and E below); and (2) those which, on the basis of available evidence, have a high probability of moderating the effects of participation on each of these outcomes (see B, C, D, F, G and H below). The following are the problem attributes used in the present form of the model:

A. The importance of the quality of the decision.
B. The extent to which the leader possesses sufficient information/expertise to make a high quality decision by himself.
C. The extent to which subordinates collectively have the necessary information to generate a high quality decision.
D. The extent to which the problem is structured.
E. The extent to which acceptance or commitment on the part of subordinates is critical to the effective implementation of the decision.
F. The prior probability that the leader's autocratic decision will receive acceptance by subordinates.
G. The extent to which subordinates are motivated to attain the organizational goals as represented in the objectives explicit in the statement of the problem.
H. The extent to which subordinates are likely to be in conflict over preferred solutions.

[The accompanying flowchart] shows the normative model for group problems expressed in the form of a decision tree. The problem attributes are arranged along the top of the figure expressed in less technical language and in Yes-No form. To apply the model to a particular problem one starts at the left-hand side and works toward the right, asking oneself the question immediately above any box encountered. When a terminal node is reached, the prescribed decision-making process from [the above table] (AI, AII, CI, CII and GII) is specified.

Flowchart for Box 12–5

DECISION PROCESS FLOW CHART

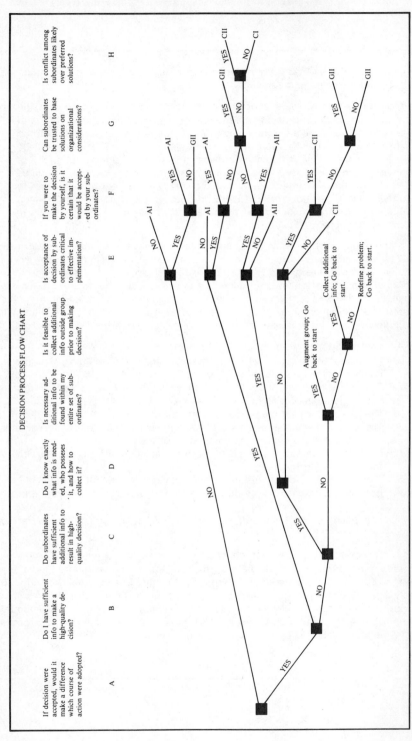

Source: Adapted from V. H. Vroom and P. W. Yetton, *Leadership and Decision-making* (Pittsburgh, Pa.: University of Pittsburgh Press, 1973).

7.   The acceptance priority rule (The only decision that will work is the one reached by maximum feasible participation.).

In training managers in decision making, the Vroom model shows them how to examine their leadership styles. The program exposes executives to a standardized set of cases and allows them to make a choice among the spectrum of leadership responses. The responses are processed by computer, which generates a detailed analysis of leadership styles. Executives are given printouts showing how democratic they are compared to other participants in the program. They are also able to form pictures of the extent to which they vary their styles.

This technique has interesting possibilities because it allows managers to plot not only their own styles but those of their superiors. No long-term evaluations of the effectiveness of the Vroom model have been undertaken, but initial results appear quite promising.

TOPIC 6
What every manager should know
about leadership styles

SOME GENERAL GUIDES ON LEADERSHIP

Terence R. Mitchell provides some guidelines for the study of leadership in "Organizational Behavior":

1.   The performance of a group   motivational structure.
     is a function of the leader's   control and influence
                                      in the situation.
2.   The leader's role is to provide subordinates with coaching, guidance, and rewards, with a view to clarifying paths to goals that achieve satisfaction or effectiveness. Consideration on the leader's part is more effective in structured situations.
3.   People low in authoritarianism like participative leadership, and vice versa. But much depends upon the style of the leader's leader.
4.   Considerate leadership is more successful when the group faces an external threat; structuring leadership works best when the group faces internal conflict.
5.   Charismatic leaders who display confidence, dominance, and purpose help to articulate goals, which has the effect of developing devotion and unquestioning support among followers.
6.   Leadership is transactional, an exchange process between the leader and the follower, involving a psychological contact.

Thus there is no such thing as the *right* way for a manager to operate or behave. There are only ways that are appropriate for specific tasks of specific enterprises under specific conditions, faced by managers of specific temperaments and styles. Therefore, implicit in the careful examination that surrounds the selection of managers is the recognition that there is more to being an effective manager than can be discerned from an impressive track record. Figure 12–4, the contingency model for the study of organizational behavior, provides an analysis of leadership as a system.

FIGURE 12–4
Organizational leadership as a system

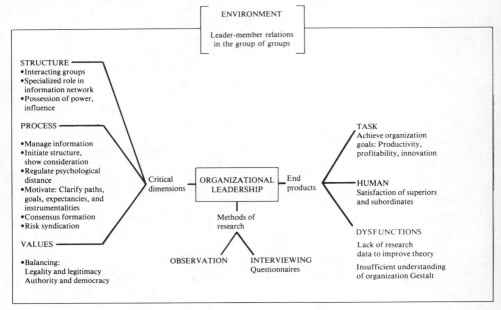

REVIEW AND RESEARCH

1. Why has the trait approach to leadership failed? Why, then, do most managers still believe in the trait approach?
2. What are the leadership functions that have to be exercised in a work group?
3. What are the problems associated with making the informal group leader the appointed leader?
4. Define influence. Why does the boss whom subordinates can influence have considerable influence himself?
5. Describe Fiedler's contingency theory of leadership.
6. How does "Catch 22" work in a business setting?
7. Devise an experiment to test the path-goal theory of leadership.
8. Consider a restaurant where the highest priced meal costs $5, with seating accommodation for 50, and design a work team which sets out the

rules, roles, and relations that govern the executive and the supervisory group.

9. Explain why initiating structure as a leadership strategy produces effectiveness and satisfaction for middle-level executives but ineffectiveness and dissatisfaction for shop-floor workers. Try to tie in your answers with the expectations of (a) shop-floor workers for human relations and (b) managers for good human resource planning.

10. Develop a contingency theory of leadership that integrates Fiedler's and House's work.

11. Explain MacGregor's leadership style.

GLOSSARY OF TERMS

Assessment center. A place in which candidates for leadership positions are gathered, tested, and evaluated in an attempt to prejudge their abilities and potential; the group selection procedure used is a presocialization device.

Consideration. The quality exhibited by a leader in showing respect for subordinates' ideas, concern for their feelings, concern for group rapport and communication, and all human relations (nontask) functions. Leaders with high consideration are likely to satisfy subordinates, less likely to satisfy superiors because they are not as concerned or productive in the task area.

Cult of the personality. The belief that the major source of influence in producing change is the individual rather than the collective or group.

Initiating structure. The quality exhibited by leaders in concentrating on task functions such as planning, scheduling, and production, principally by structuring their own role and those of subordinates toward goal attainment. Leaders high in initiating structure are likely to satisfy superiors, less likely to satisfy subordinates because they are impersonal and maintains psychological distance.

Leader. A person who is willing or eager to accept publicly the responsibility for her or his own and other people's behavior and attitudes; the person who has the most influence in a given situation.

Leadership. In a simple sense, the ability to influence others; in fact a complex social skill requiring flexibility and adaptibility to varying circumstances. Reality-centered leadership is the ability to select the most appropriate pattern for organizational behavior at any given time in any existential situation.

Leadership style. The stamp of the leader's personality on relationships with followers in group interactions, particularly in terms of role expectancies.

Leader-member relations. Interactions of group members, especially the extent to which the leader enjoys the confidence and loyalty of followers and is regarded as personally attractive (usually measured by a sociometric index).

Least preferred co-worker (LPC) score. A measure used by Fiedler to predict and evaluate leadership style, employing bipolar trait ratings of the subject's co-workers; the rating gives some indication of leaders' cognitive complexity and task orientation, but its usefulness and validity remain unclear.

Path-goal leadership theory. The theory developed by House incorporating Vroom's path-goal model of man. The leader uses the concepts of expectancies and instrumentality in motivating followers by clarifying the paths to rewards, structuring roles to avoid ambiguity, reducing roadblocks in the way of goal achievement, helping associates relate their positive valences and needs to organization goals, and in general both making clear the paths that are needed and making the paths easier and more attractive to follow.

Position power. The power inherent in the leader's position, including such traditional manifestations as official authority, ability to reward and punish, and so on; more importantly, the leader's ability to manage and control information flows and to structure role, path-goal, and task perceptions.

Psychological distance. The manner in which the executive varies relationships with others in order to keep task and role functions predominant in dealing with subordinates and to achieve considerable freedom from superiors. The psychologically distant manager sees himself as a professional administrator, in contrast to the psychologically close manager who gives prime importance to human relationships and close informal group interactions.

Semantic differential. C. E. Osgood's concept of the semantic differential is that some of the significant components of the multidimensional meaning of a concept can be measured by inviting subjects to rate the concept on a number of bipolar adjectival scales. Using factor analysis, Osgood has defined three dimensions of meaning—evaluation, potency, and activity.

Sociometry. The study of the dynamic interrelationships of individuals within a social group. Sociometric tests, which are essentially action tests, measure the feelings individuals have toward others in the group; to be effective, the criteria of the test must have explicit meaning for the individual and offer specific opportunities to give information which can be of help in restructuring his social situation.

Task structure. The manner in which organization tasks are defined by leaders to their subordinates, in which it is important that decisions are verifiable (and supported by higher echelons), requirements for reaching goals are made clear, possible goal paths (procedures) are outlined, and solutions specificity (whether there can be only one or many correct solutions) is defined.

Trait. An individual characteristic or adjectival description of personality such as *authoritarian, persuasive, aggressive.* The approach of assessing potential leaders by such (usually intuitive) descriptions has little empirical support but is still used by many "seat of the pants" managers.

Transactional leadership. Describes a relationship between managers and subordinates which is based on the syndication of risks and payoffs.

Transforming leadership. Describes a relationship in which the manager puts the greatest emphasis on achieving personal growth and development for subordinates.

DEBATE: To be effective in management, it is necessary to be other directed rather than inner directed

The concept of role refers to the behavior and attitude that is expected of anyone in a particular position, regardless of the individual filling the role. In David Riesman's writing the extent to which cultural demands shape a person's role is spelled out. In *The Lonely Crowd*, Riesman identifies two different types of roles:

1. *Inner directed.* The control is directed by the individual's family—the person conforms to social norms. He is directed by his inner convictions.

2. *Other directed.* The individual's behavior is monitored to a large extent by the behavior of superiors and the group to which they all belong; the person is no longer a part of a tight family unit. Approval by peers is "almost the only equivocal good in this situation; one makes good when one is approved of." Thus all power is in the hands of the reference group. Other-directed societies emerge when "business, government, the professions become heavily bureaucratized." Success depends on "how competent one is in manipulating others and being oneself manipulated." The social product demanded by society is the right personality.

An example of other-directed leadership is President Jimmy Carter's "I am listening to you" speech spelling out his energy program in the summer of 1979. An example of inner-directed leadership is the style of Senator Edward Kennedy.

Question

Which is the more appropriate style for a manager?

INCIDENT

Can leaders be matched with situations?

F. E. Fiedler's theory develops tools for accurately diagnosing and classifying leadership situations. The object is to help managers to select the most appropriate leaders for particular situations. Fiedler says low-LPC leaders are more effective in situations of high and low control, while high-LPC leaders are more effective in situations of moderate control. Since the leader does not always determine leadership style in a situation, it is necessary to match the right leader to the right situation.

Academics are finding a number of serious inadequacies in Fiedler's leadership-match approach. In the process of moving from research to practice, Fiedler has proposed a number of specific proposals to guide managers in their choices. But his theory has been criticized because he has provided no clear, unambiguous concept of the meaning of LPC, and the LPC score is not necessarily stable in terms of test-retest reliability. His measure of situational favorableness has also been criticized.

Fundamental questions have been raised about the basic validity of the contingency theory in terms of predictability. Perhaps even more questionable is Fiedler's assumption that leadership more than any other single variable determines organizational success. Indeed, we know from research in executive behavior that managers do a lot of things other than leading, including coordinating, following up on work in progress, and making sure that work is flowing through a particular section.

Dian Hosking and Chester Schriesheim, in reviewing Fiedler's work with M. M. Chemers and L. Mahan entitled *Improving Leadership Effectiveness: The Leader Match Concept,* concluded:

> The book is troubled with many of the problems which have plagued Fiedler's Contingency Theory almost from its start, and it has even further compounded some of these problems. Also, despite the publisher's claims that the model and leader match have been "thoroughly validated," this is clearly nonsense. Given the severe problems noted in this review such a claim would almost be amusing, if it were not for the fact that some leaders may be injured by the application of leader match. Researchers ought to be wary about using this book's new Contingency Theory concepts and measures, since they have not been fully articulated, justified, or supported. Readers in general should be doubly wary of implementing leader match or taking the concept too seriously. Perhaps a label should be affixed to all copies of this book: "Caution: Use of Leader Match *May* be Dangerous to your Leadership Effectiveness."

Questions

1. Is leadership the decisive factor determining organizational outcomes? What about technology, structure, power, owning an oil field, etc.?
2. Have organizational psychologists focused too narrowly on the leader and ignored factors like organizational climate?
3. Are leaders bad for us?

CHAPTER 13 — MANAGING THE ORGANIZATION FOR EFFECTIVENESS
- Organization's growth and development
- Study of an organization
- The rise and fall of an organization
- Organizational effectiveness

CHAPTER 14 — ORGANIZATIONAL POLITICS
- Authority
- Power
- The Machiavellian

CHAPTER 15 — THE CONSPIRACY THEORY
- The political technostructure
- The conspiracy of organized medicine
- The Mafia

CHAPTER 16 — THE ORGANIZATION AND ITS ENVIRONMENT
- Economic environment
- Technology
- Environment as a flow of information
- Managing the environment
- Organizational climate

part IV

THE ORGANIZATION: ITS POLITICAL ECONOMY

DIAGRAM SUMMARY OF CHAPTER 13

```
                                              Birth
                                                │ ──── Crisis
                                              Youth
┌─────────────────────────┐                     │ ──── Crisis
│   ORGANIZATIONAL GROWTH  │──────              Maturity
│     AND DEVELOPMENT      │                     │ ──── Crisis
└─────────────────────────┘                    Decline
             │                                   │ ──── Crisis
             │                                  Death
             ▼
┌─────────────────────────┐                  ── Structure
│ STUDY OF AN ORGANIZATION:│──────
│        McDONALD'S        │                  ── Process
└─────────────────────────┘
             │                                ── Values
             │
             ▼
┌─────────────────────────┐                  ── The systems dynamics model
│     THE RISE AND         │
│     FALL OF AN           │──────
│   ORGANIZATION:          │
│   THE SATURDAY           │
│   EVENING POST           │                  ── Why did The Saturday Evening Post fail?
└─────────────────────────┘
             │
             │
             ▼
┌─────────────────────────┐                  ── Definition of effectiveness:
│     ORGANIZATIONAL       │                       Human relations
│     EFFECTIVENESS        │──────                 Adaptation
└─────────────────────────┘                        Intelligence
             │
             │                                ── Defining success:
             ▼                                   A contingency approach
┌─────────────────────────┐
│   WHAT EVERY MANAGER     │
│   SHOULD KNOW ABOUT      │
│ MANAGING THE ORGANIZATION│
│    FOR EFFECTIVENESS     │
└─────────────────────────┘
```

13

Managing the organization
for effectiveness

IS BIG BAD?

That there must be some relationship between organizational size and effectiveness seems obvious, but what this relationship is, is not clear. The popular cry is that big is ugly and small is beautiful. While there is some evidence to support this conclusion, it is not conclusive.

A good example of "big-is-bad" is the U.S. Department of Health, Education, and Welfare. To most organizational observers HEW is rapidly growing out of control. This agency, which employs 1,125,000 bureaucrats, provides essential services to 15 million Americans. While HEW had a modest beginning in 1953, after Medicare and Medicaid it grew so rapidly that organizational chaos soon emerged. An article on the organization of HEW in *Time* magazine for June 12, 1978 placed much of the blame for programs that misfire on the bureaucracy itself.

> . . . In their commendable determination to enforce the letter of the law, officials become too addicted to formulas, too oblivious of ends in their concentration on means. Says Carl Coleman, a public affairs officer in HEW's regional office in Denver: "HEW gets the social engineers, the people they call do-gooders. They're committed, and they make a lot of mistakes because of their ardor." His favorite example: the West Coast bureaucrat who tried to ban father-son school banquets on the ground that they discriminated against women.

The problem is that HEW starts programs too quickly without giving sufficient attention to planning or staffing. As one critic of HEW pointed out, "The people at HEW's management level want statistics showing that large numbers of claims have been processed so they can impress Congress with what a good job they are doing. They don't care anything about quality; all they want is quantity." Perhaps the basic problem is just the sheer size of HEW.

Many executives believe that big is bad and small means profitable, and there is abundant evidence to support the proposition that big business is not necessarily efficient business. For example, a 1978 European Economic Commission report concluded that "the largest firms are hardly ever the most profitable, nor, usually, among the most efficient."

IS SMALL BEAUTIFUL?

Ernst F. Schumacher argues in *Small Is Beautiful* that countries should select technology that is related to their resources and supply of skilled labor. The principle of small-scale, diversified work groups has been applied to work, in automobile assembly plants at Volvo and Saab, and in General Foods.

Over all, employees seem to be demanding more from jobs as well as from life. New sociotechnical designs are required to facilitate greater participation and industrial democracy. But, unfortunately, these rising expectations are emerging at a time when our organizations have to cope with particularly high levels of turbulence. Thus, managers are forced to cope with uncertainty not only in the external internal dynamics of organizations. To understand what is happening, it is necessary to start at the beginning, with the birth of the organization.

MANAGEMENT STYLE AND ORGANIZATIONAL DEVELOPMENT

Organizations are dreamt of, born, develop, mature, achieve distinction, begin to go stale, decline, and disappear. Managers must be perceptive to the growth characteristics of their firms; they must know what stages of development their firms have reached if they are to be able to plan, direct, and control. And if their plans are going to have any relevance, they must change their management style according to the organization's stage of growth.

Like human beings, an organization has an anatomy (structure), a physiology (processes), and a nervous system (a communication network of telephones, telex, Xerox machines, computers). Organizations have relationships; they even have morals. They trade with their environment, importing things such as people, matter, energy, and information, and exporting a product with value added.

Health or effectiveness is measured by the organization's ability to mobilize, develop, and operationalize the right structures, processes, and values to generate enough productivity and satisfaction. But production of what and satisfaction for whom? The answers vary from technology to technology, minute to minute. Effectiveness calls for innovation and adaptation.

Innovation means responding to the mandates of technology and the whip of the marketplace. Innovation means living dangerously, which is always invoked to justify incentive payments to organizations in the form of profits. Guaranteeing profits means fixing the "fix": control of suppliers and manipulation of the market. To stay healthy, the corporate organism does not, in fact, need to grow.

TOPIC 1
Organizational growth and development

Organizations, like human beings, get sick, suffer from growing pains, and sometimes grow obese. They get overweight and have to be trimmed down by consultants or organization doctors.

They have slick names like ITT, IBM, and AT&T, which can usually be read off as defining their territory and task. Organizations have nicknames like ICI, Nobels Division, which used to manufacture explosives and was playfully known by the workers as The Dynamite because of its nasty habit of blowing up.

The organization—the syndicate, the Big House, the corporation, the system, the machine, the organization, the place—has all sorts of interesting, bizarre, indeed human qualities. Morals are necessary both for morale and to avoid an identity crisis.

Most big organizations are fairly straightlaced. This is safer—it keeps the inmates on the straight and narrow and lets the enemy know what to expect.

THE ORGANIZATIONAL CRISIS

The most striking point about organizational growth is that as an organization moves from stage to stage it experiences sharp crises (see Box 13–1 for an example). Organizations, like human beings, have life cycles: they are born, find a name, stake out a territory and a function; they grow up a bit, go through the crisis of puberty as they fight to establish their stability and win a reputation for themselves; next they struggle for uniqueness and adaptability; only to be cast into the menopause, from which they emerge with the serenity of resignation to try to figure out their debt to society and what sort of contribution they can make.

Box 13–1: Evolving organization structures in the restaurant industry

William Foote Whyte, professor of industrial and labor relations and sociology at Cornell University and a man of interdisciplinary inclinations, carried out intensive studies of human relations in 12 restaurants. Data were gathered entirely through interviewing and observation.

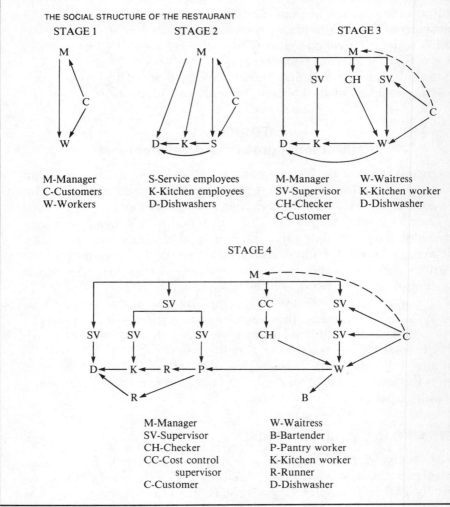

THE SOCIAL STRUCTURE OF THE RESTAURANT

STAGE 1

M-Manager
C-Customers
W-Workers

STAGE 2

S-Service employees
K-Kitchen employees
D-Dishwashers

STAGE 3

M-Manager   W-Waitress
SV-Supervisor   K-Kitchen worker
CH-Checker   D-Dishwasher
C-Customer

STAGE 4

M-Manager   W-Waitress
SV-Supervisor   B-Bartender
CH-Checker   P-Pantry worker
CC-Cost control   K-Kitchen worker
   supervisor   R-Runner
C-Customer   D-Dishwasher

Source: W. F. Whyte, "The Social Structure of the Restaurant," *American Journal of Sociology*, vol. 5 (1949), pp. 302–10.

Gordon L. Lippitt and Warren H. Schmidt, in "Crisis in a Developing Organization," set out to study the crises which organizations go through. In their scheme of organizational growth (shown in Figure 13–1), the critical issue in changing organizations is the management of crisis.

In this study of the restaurant, Whyte describes how someone might start a restaurant with a small short-order business.

The boss has two employees—but no specialization; all work together as cook, counterman, and dishwasher (stage 1). Business booms and our man moves to a new site and expands. Some division of labor takes place. As the business grows, further specialization takes place. At stage 4, the cooks no longer pass the food directly to the waitresses; runners are introduced. Our man has come a way, and is now a manager who dishes out orders instead of food. The particular problem of the large restaurant is to tie together its line of authority with the relations that arise along the flow of work. In the first instance, this involves the customer relationship, for here is where the flow of work begins. The handling of the customer relationship is crucial for the adjustment of the restaurant personnel, and a large part of that problem can be stated in strictly quantitative interaction terms: Who originates action for whom and how often? In a large and busy restaurant a waitress may take orders from fifty to one hundred customers a day (and perhaps several times for each meal) in addition to the orders (much less frequent) she receives from her supervisor. When we add to this the problem of adjusting to service pantry workers, bartenders, and perhaps checkers, we can readily see the possibilities of emotional tension—and, in our study, we did see a number of girls break down and cry under the strain.

While in the rush hour the waitress works under a good deal of tension at best, the supervisor can either add to or relieve it. Here again we can speak in quantitative terms. In one restaurant we observed a change in dining-room management when a supervisor who was skillful in originating action for customers (thus taking pressure off waitresses) and who responded frequently to the initiation of waitresses was replaced by a supervisor who had less skill in controlling customers and who originated for the girls much more frequently and seldom responded to them. (Of the new supervisor, the waitresses would say, "She's always finding something to criticize"; "She's never around when we need her"; "She's always telling you; she doesn't care what you have to say"; etc.) This change was followed by evidences of increased nervous tension, especially among the less experienced waitresses, and finally by a series of waitress resignations.

Here we see that the customer-waitress, waitress-supervisor, waitress-service-pantry-worker relationships are interdependent parts of a social system. Changes in one part of the system will necessarily lead to changes in other parts.

Whyte makes an interesting point about status: "The highly paid and skilled woman in charge of fish preparation strongly resented being called 'the fish woman' and was upset when other workers went by her station holding their noses. She insisted that she be referred to as the 'seafood station supervisor.' "

PHASES OF GROWTH

In the midst of the current preoccupation with interpersonal relationships, personal growth, and self-actualization, it is important to remember that the overall organization structure may still be the most significant factor in determining the success of the enterprise. A. D. Chandler was the first to outline the importance of correlating organi-

FIGURE 13–1
Stages of organizational development

DEVELOP-MENTAL STAGE	CRITICAL CONCERN	KEY ISSUES	CONSEQUENCES IF CONCERN IS NOT MET
Birth	1. To create a new organization	What to risk	Frustration and inaction
	2. To survive as a viable system	What to sacrifice	Death of organization Further subsidy by "faith" capital
Youth	3. To gain stability	How to organize	Reactive, crisis-dominated organization Opportunistic rather than self-directing attitudes and policies
	4. To gain reputation and develop pride	How to review and evaluate	Difficulty in attracting good personnel and clients Inappropriate, overly aggressive, and distorted image building
Maturity	5. To achieve uniqueness and adaptability	Whether and how to change	Unnecessarily defensive or competitive attitudes; diffusion of energy Loss of most creative personnel
	6. To contribute to society	Whether and how to share	Possible lack of public respect and appreciation Bankruptcy or profit loss

zation structure with the business strategy of the firm. Larry Greiner, building on the base established by Chandler, has advanced the intriguing view that organizational change is necessitated by an inevitable reaction to the historical structure of the firm. Unlike Chandler, Greiner does not feel that change is necessarily a planned concomitant of variations in business strategy which result from alterations in the economic and social environment of the firm. Rather it comes as a result of the stresses that business growth places on every kind of management structure.

In "Evolution and Revolution as Organizations Grow," Greiner describes five phases in the history of an organization's management practices—each one an outgrowth of problems which developed in the previous phase. The periods of turmoil when these problems come to a peak are described as revolution, while the intervening periods of relatively long duration and peaceful growth are called evolution. The frequency of revolutionary change is felt to increase with the size of the organization and the growth rate of the industry in which it operates. Older organizations may have institutionalized practices which inhibit change, and high profits may defer the need for new structures. However, continued growth of the firm appears to lead inexorably to a need for changes in management practice. (See Figure 13–2.) If these are not effected, decline and bankruptcy are predicted.

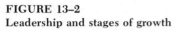

FIGURE 13–2
Leadership and stages of growth

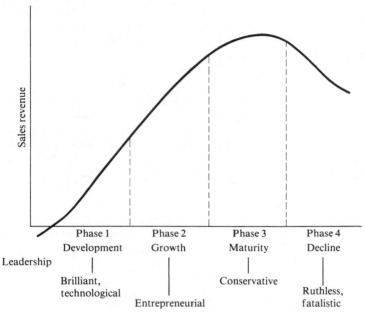

An understanding of these stages of development will help managers to cope more effectively. But to cope with change, management has to focus on the rapidly changing quality of the environment. Change arising from computer technology and electronic technology (e.g., evaluating the opportunities and hazards of the hybrid domestic computer–copying machine–videotape recorder expected in the 1980s), the proliferation of rapid transit systems, the development of new managerial technologies, the growth of international trade, and the demand for ethnic and sexual equality are turning organizations upside down, shaking them all about. More sophisticated managements are not prepared to wait it out and let such changes dominate them, but are entering into the spirit of the times and trying to exploit these change options.

In "Patterns of Organizational Change," Greiner has reviewed the common approaches to change along a "power distribution" continuum ranging from unilateral action (by decree, by replacement, by structure) to power sharing (group decision making and problem solving) to delegated authority (by case discussion, by T-group sessions). Greiner sets out the success pattern for organizational change, which essentially assumes that (1) top management comes under considerable pressure as performance falls off, (2) a new top executive or a consultant is brought in and the agonizing reappraisal begins, (3) top management backs this person in getting everybody involved in fact-finding problem solving, and (4) slowly the change ethos spreads throughout the system. To facilitate such changes, behavioral scientists have invented powerful change strategies, known collectively as organizational development (OD), which utilize T-group technology to facilitate change (see Chapter 19).

TOPIC 2
Study of an organization: McDonald's

McDonald's Corporation provides an interesting example of an organization as an entity reacting to, changing, and surviving in a complex environment (see Figure 13–3). In examining the structure, pro-

FIGURE 13–3

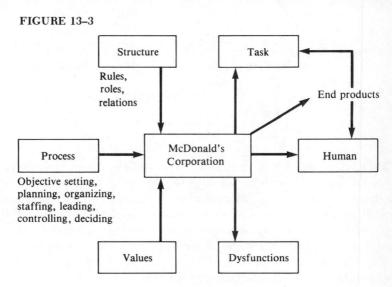

cess, and values of McDonald's Corporation, the process study is divided into seven sections: objectives, planning, organizing, staffing and leading, controlling, and deciding. Each of these sections will look at the company as a whole but within the realm of a specific function.

McDonald's Corporation is one of the most successful, most rapidly expanding, and most managerially accomplished firms in the United

States. The company's growth, both at home and abroad, continues to establish new levels of achievement in sales, income, and return on investment. Total assets exceeded the $1 billion mark for the first time in 1975. A familiar American institution, the hamburger joint, has been transformed into a totaly different, though still essentially American, operation. Using a computerized, standardized, premeasured, super-

Box 13–2: A rare hamburger headquarters

McDonald's corporate headquarters were described in a 1972 article in *Time* magazine:

It is probably the tallest office building in the world built in the profits from hamburgers. But that is not all. When the executives of McDonald's Corp. abandoned their Chicago Loop offices for a new eight-story building in suburban Oak Brook, they also left behind their traditional concepts of office layout. As a result, McDonald's Oak Brook headquarters, opened last March, has a minimum of interior doors and walls, no offices in the usual sense, and what may well be the only waterbed in the world of big business.

On each of the three top floors occupied by the company, there are large open spaces divided into "work stations" by tall green plants, file cabinets and movable pieces of mahogany furniture called TRMs (Task Response Modules). Each TRM contains a closet, a chest of drawers, a bookcase and a built-in desk. In the larger work areas allotted to executives there are such traditional extras as upholstered chairs and round or square oaken tables.

"At first it was horrible," admits Executive Vice President and Project Supervisor John Cooke. "We had people drifting in and out; whole families of curious sightseers came to visit the building." There were also complaints about fellow workers who unknowingly trespassed on the work space of others.

But most of McDonald's headquarters employees, 400 in all, adjusted quickly to the wide-open spaces. Now, says Market Research Coordinator Judy Stezowski, "You always know what's going on. You hear everything." The turnover rate among secretaries and clerical help has dropped in some departments from 100% each year at the old Loop offices to about 25% at the new Oak Brook base. Executives also feel that productivity is up.

By far the most distinctive feature of the building is the "think tank," a sealed-off area on the seventh floor that is available to any employee, male or female, who reserves tank time far enough in advance. President Fred Turner had the idea, after deciding that some employees might want a taste of privacy now and then. The tank has two sections: one soundproofed workroom equipped with dimmable lights, a hassock, a beanbag chair, a desk that can be adjusted from sitting to standing height and walls, floor and ceiling covered in beige pseudo suede.

Rich thoughts. A few steps away is the circular "meditation room," its walls covered with suedelike material and concealing loudspeakers hooked to record-playing equipment. The floor consists of a giant waterbed, 9 ft. in diameter, on which workers recline to think deep and presumably profit-making thoughts. So far, however, no big ideas have emerged, but several recliners have noted that lying on the bed is like lying on a giant hamburger.

That is as close to the real thing as McDonald's employees can get during working hours. Because of local zoning laws, the nearest McDonald's hamburger stand is more than a mile away.

Source: *Time,* February 28, 1972.

clean producing machine, McDonald's has developed a restaurant system that has conquered the fast-food market. Executives at the world headquarters in Oak Brook, Illinois (see Box 13–2), have increased sales to more than 14 times the 1965 figure, to reach a total of $2.5 billion in 1975.

With 130,000 employees in nine countries, from Western Europe to Japan and Australia, McDonald's Corporation, has expanded an uniquely American idea into a truly global operation. The 1975 Annual general report noted 3,706 McDonald's restaurants were in operation, including 182 in Canada and 172 in 19 other international markets, with newly opened outlets in Hong Kong and the Bahamas. Of the nearly 3,500 McDonald's restaurants in the United States, approximately 75 percent were licensed to independent operators. These aggressive, locally involved franchise holders are essential elements in McDonald's' success. All franchise holders must attend McDonald's Hamburger University in Illinois, where the game of doing it the McDonald's way begins. After graduating, the franchise holder's performance, in everything from the cleanliness of the floors to the quality of the hamburgers and the temperature of the frying fat, is relentlessly watched by roving inspectors.

Given its scale of operations, rate of expansion, and tidy financial, training, and merchandizing routines, McDonald's has enough clout through mass buying power to line up steady supplies at stable prices (it purchases 1 percent of all U.S. wholesale beef). Thus is the environment controlled for McDonald's. It gives a virtual license to print money to its franchise holders, who are required to "do it the McDonald way."

THE STRUCTURE

In McDonald's franchise system, which encompasses three quarters of the outlets, each restaurant is a center for production, quality control, retail sales, marketing, and consumption. It differs from other franchise systems, such as A & W, Ponderosa, and Colonel Sanders, in the way it manages the fast-food business.

In the McDonald's organization, every idea, every decision, emerges from the head office in Chicago. Everything is thought of in advance, before questions or difficulties can arise. Rules are set up by the head office which are designed to ensure the attainment of corporate goals and adherence to the firm's values. These rules, regulations and standards have to be followed by both franchisees and company stores, who make up the other quarter of the firm's outlets. As long as the managers go along with the all-powerful Chicago office, the payoff is good: Profits are high in McDonald's.

Buildings and land must be leased from McDonald's Corporation, though equipment for the restaurants may be purchased from independent suppliers. The products may also be purchased locally, as long as they are prepared to specification by the local purveyors. McDonald's has a unique advertising program, OPNAD, the Operators' National Advertising fund, a voluntary cooperative through which a percentage of member restaurants' sales goes for national advertising.

McDonald's is in the management business

McDonald's Corporation is in the management business; its phenomenal success is the result of scientific management of the fast-food business. In order to efficiently market a rigidly controlled product through thousands of McDonald's outlets, the decisions have had to be in the hands of only a few people. These managers have the responsibility of setting up effective methods to reach organizational goals and must make sure that these methods will be applied the same way in all the restaurants. This centralized decision-making process gives the other members of the organization the role of executor, with precise though limited responsibilities.

THE PROCESS

Objective setting

McDonald's overall objective is to maintain its growth by increasing its share of the fast-food market, revenues, profitability in terms of net income, and net income per share. McDonald's was able to increase its net income in 1975 by 32 percent over its performance the year before, for example. Net income was over $86 million, which meant a net income per share of $2.17

Using new packaging, selective menu additions, and innovative marketing approaches and techniques, the company has been able to maintain a continuing record of growth and acceptance. To achieve this record growth, McDonald's is constantly introducing restaurants to serve customers not only in North America, but in Europe and Japan as well. Total assets exceed $1 billion.

Planning: "Know the customer"

One of the fundamental principles of McDonald's is to know its customers and be responsive to their needs. This is basic premise for any firm which hopes to be successful, and it is of the utmost importance to McDonald's and its marketing plans.

McDonald's planning is projected three years in advance in terms of expansion and location. Its flexibility and adaptability can nowhere be better seen than in its expansion plans. McDonald's is not restricted by concrete expansion formulas; if it plans three new restaurants planned for Butte, Montana, which cannot be built, they can just as easily be built in Salt Lake City. This flexibility is considered one of its strongest corporate points, it is pushed as a major selling point to potential investors.

When McDonald's first entered Canada and began building restaurants, its basic requirement was to know where the Colonel Sanders outlets were situated; the plan was to build as near to the fried chicken restaurants as possible. This scheme has only recently been abandoned. A master location chart of McDonald's in Montreal in the early seventies would show every site either front to front or side by side with an established Colonel Sanders outlet. The strategy behind the expansion design of McDonald's is highlighted by its forethought, marketing expertise, and, surprisingly enough, its success.

Organizing

Figure 13–4 illustrates a McDonald's organization tree for a typical store. There is one manager-owner with two assistants, one of whom must be present in the restaurant at all times. The crew chief is responsible for all food preparation. This employee reports directly to

FIGURE 13–4
McDonald's organization tree

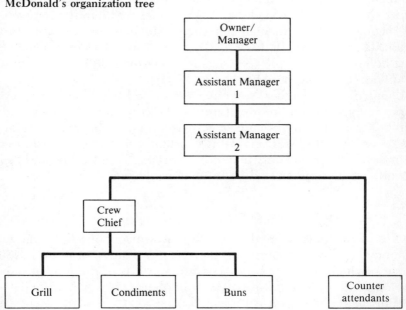

the manager on duty, as do the counter attendants who take customer orders.

The atmosphere is casual but well structured. Jobs are rotated to provide flexibility among the staff. Every employee in the store has been fully versed in McDonald's standards, and anyone who consistently deviates from the norm very quickly becomes an ex-employee.

Staffing

An outlet's staff is a key factor in its success. The grill operator and counter attendants are paid minimum wages. They are expected to work unusual and irregular shifts and to meet standards which would be deemed archaic in other enterprises. Men must keep their hair cropped, their shirts pressed, and their shoes highly polished. Women must wear dark, low shoes, hairnets, and only very light makeup. Both wear uniforms.

As could be expected, McDonald's has a very high employee turnover rate. It is not unusual for a restaurant to turn over 100 employees in a six-month period.

The other side to the high turnover rate is that employees who work hard can move up quickly. Proof of this is the corporation president, Fred Turner, whose first job in McDonald's in 1956 was frying hamburgers. It is not unknown for an employee who does well to be promoted to managing a store. The generally conceded make-or-break point is seven months. If you last that long, you will be there a while.

Anyone who is granted a franchise must become a "McDonald's man". Because of the high return, an average profit of $80,000 before taxes, McDonald's has thousands of applications for franchises every year. The acceptance rate is a mere 10 percent. Licensees are varied: athletes, doctors, lawyers, comptrollers, and others are all McDonald's owners. Half the financial outlay, $225,000, must be in cash. Each McDonald's owner controls 51 percent of the shares and must be a full-time manager (these practices have been recently instituted.)

A factor in weeding out applicants to McDonald's is that the applicant is put through a rigorous set of interviews. At no time between interviews, no matter what promises are made during an interview, will McDonald's contact the applicant. The onus is always on the applicant to contact McDonald's.

Leading

Maintenance of the high standards McDonald's sets for itself is very important. The key position in the organization is the store manager; the key man in the organization is owner Ray Kroc. Each store manager is trained in his image. Every store manager knows the restaurant and what is expected.

Increased sales at McDonald's are largely due to a rapid delivery of a uniform, high-quality mix of prepared foods in an environment of obvious cleanliness, order, and cheerful courtesy. This objective requires well-motivated, well-trained employees, and managers who are willing to work long hours to train and motivate them. This is especially difficult in view of the high turnover rate.

Controlling

Evaluation and control are built into the system, which is in effect an information-processing system. When there is a rush of orders, to handle excess input load the manager increases the number of channels for handling information by hiring more waitresses and cooks. But if a time comes when there are not enough channels and increasing channels is not the answer, queuing is used, and customers line up to wait to place orders. To make the business flow better, McDonald's restaurants chunk information—break orders into chunks. For example, burgers come in three sizes only: a hamburger, a Quarter Pounder, and a Big Mac.

McDonald's achieves efficiency by turning the short-order business into a cybernetic hamburger delivery system. It's all a question of values.

VALUES

"If it is not right, don't serve it!" This is one of Kroc's credos, and it typifies the type of values he has set for McDonald's.

The inherent values of McDonald's Corporation have been structured and manipulated to conform to the basic value system of North American society. As a whole this value system has emphasized the importance of honesty, loyalty, quality, convenience, competitiveness, mechanization, and ecology. McDonald's has accommodated this set of values by establishing a chain of fast-food restaurants that are highly mechanized, quality oriented, and friendly. McDonald's phenomenal success over the past ten years has perhaps to a large extent been due to its adherence to its motto: "Quality, service, and cleanliness." It particularly values friendliness and a "Thank you, come again" attitude.

McDonald's highly mechanized and standardized approach to customer service has been criticized for undermining American culture. Sociologist Vance Packard has said, in reference to McDonald's slick restaurant operation: "This is what our country is all about—blandness and standardization."

TOPIC 3
The rise and fall of an organization:
The *Saturday Evening Post*

Organizations not only are conceived, born, grow, develop, and achieve maturity, they also occasionally die. Both social scientists and executives have an interest in any theory which will explain the rise and fall of an organization.

One of the most interesting pieces of research about the demise of organizations was done by Roger I. Hall, a professor of administration at the University of Manitoba, who reported his results in "A System Pathology of an Organization." What got Hall started on his research were the peculiar circumstances surrounding the demise of mass circulation magazines such as *Life, Look,* and *Saturday Evening Post.* When these magazines went into a state of crisis, each was reporting its highest circulation and largest revenues. What puzzled Hall was how these leading magazines were being simultaneously mismanaged. The fact that they had continued to grow, in spite of tough competition, until they reached a critical point in their history suggests the complexity of organizational pathology.

THE SYSTEMS DYNAMICS MODEL

To explain the failure of these mazagines, Hall applied the method of systems dynamics. Using a simulation of the *Saturday Evening Post* organization in the Curtis Publishing Company, he was able to get an insight into how the magazine, as a system, reacted to changes in control variables such as subscription and advertising rates.

In terms of economics, the revenues for a magazine come from two different but related sources, advertising and circulation. Since these two variables are interlocked, the best way to tackle the study of such an organization is with an industrial dynamics model. Hall exploited the Dynamo model as a means of simulating the complex dynamic feedback systems of the *Saturday Evening Post.* A flow diagram showing a causal chain that gives an insight into the structure and processes of the magazine is shown in Figure 13–5.

The diagram shows the magazine publishing firm as having four corporate building blocks: (1) accounting information flows, (2) measures of performance, (3) managed variables, and (4) relations of the firm with its environment. The Dynamo program language provides insight into the flow diagram of causality in the organization. Once modeled, the organization can be analyzed as if it were a wiring diagram of a self-controlling electronic device which splays out all the basic feedback loops of the system.

Hall made an attempt to base his model on statistically treated

FIGURE 13–5
Basic structure of the model of a magazine publishing firm

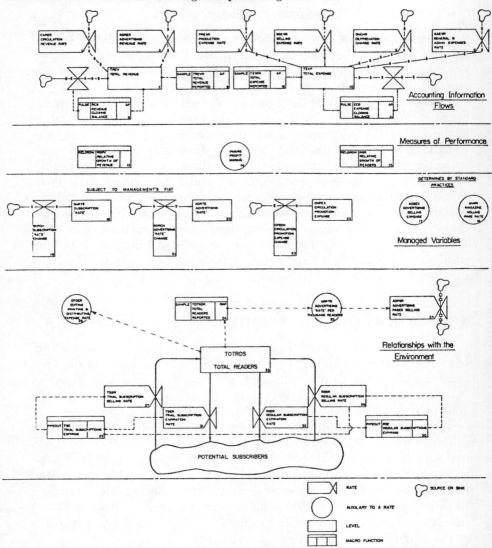

Source: Roger I. Hall, "A System Pathology of an Organization: The Rise and Fall of the Old *Saturday Evening Post, Administrative Science Quarterly*, June 1976.

empirical data which covered a 20-year period of the operations of the old *Saturday Evening Post*. His analysis indicated that the major influence on subscription sales was expenditures on promotion. One finding to emerge was that from 1957 on, the technical revolution caused by new techniques of mass mailing increased the efficiency of promot-

Box 13-3: The rise and fall of the old *Saturday Evening Post*

Through an analysis of management's most significant decisions, Roger Hall has identified four distinct periods of the developmental history of the *Saturday Evening Post* between the years of 1940 and 1960.

Phase 1: 1940–1944

During this period, when the company was inhibited by paper rationing, the management raised the annual subscription rate of approximately $3 to $4.80 in constant dollars, presumably as a device for simultaneously rationing the magazine and compensating for the loss of wartime advertising revenue.

Phase 2: 1945–1947

This period was one of almost unrestrained growth, as readership rose from 3.4 to almost 4 million and revenues grew from $115 to $162 million in constant dollars. But the magazine's profit margin fell from 14 percent in 1944 to 7 percent in 1946. Management's action to counteract the drop in profit margin was to increase the subscription rate substantially, from an annual average of $4.79 in 1944 to over $6.00 in constant dollars per subscriber.

Phase 3: 1948–1950

Hall describes this phase as a period of stagnation. Despite increasing expenditures on circulation promotion, the readership scarcely grew at all. The company was faced with a significant increase in promotional effort just to keep its readership steady.

Phase 4: 1951–1960

The fourth phase was a period of forced growth, as management acted on the proposition that readership was the key to future growth. This was achieved by reducing the subscription rate and increasing the promotional effort.

The accompanying figure from Hall's article on the *Post* shows what happened to readership after the circulation war began in 1952. During this period the magazine's readership grew from 4 to 6 million and the annual revenue grew from $170 to $225 million in constant dollars, but the profit margin fell from 8 percent of revenue to a loss position in

---

Review of Roger I. Hall, "A System Pathology of an Organization: The Rise and Fall of the Old *Saturday Evening Post*," *Administrative Science Quarterly*, June 1976.

ing the magazine. Another surprising finding was that the editorial policy or its quality had no effect on the subscription renewal behavior of readers. Apparently, readers become regular subscribers who renew their subscriptions more or less indefinitely, until they become dissatisfied with the raising of the subscription rate. By 1960 the company was in dire financial straits. (See Box 13–3 for the details of how this disaster came about.)

WHY DID THE SATURDAY EVENING POST FAIL?

Hall's systems analysis of the operations of the *Saturday Evening Post* makes it possible to contrast the underlying chain of cause and effect at work in the system with the symptoms generated by actual problems.

Box 13–3 (continued)

COMPARISON OF MAGAZINE READERSHIP

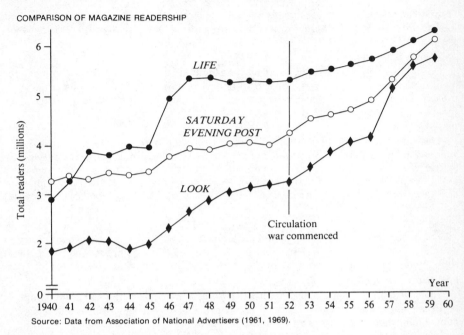

Source: Data from Association of National Advertisers (1961, 1969).

1958–59. As Hall points out, "The company was on the brink of bankruptcy and never really recovered from this policy *cul-de-sac* of too high a subscription rate, too high an advertising "rate," a declining annual volume, and a too high promotional expenditure to solicit trial readers to replace the defecting readership."

. . . For example, the various leaders of the Curtis Publishing Company were, to a large extent, the products of the situations that brought them into power. President Walter Fuller turned the company in the 30s and 40s into an integrated printing and publishing empire and his protegé, Robert A. MacNeal, pursued this vertical empire building philosophy by purchasing a paper company for $20-million in 1950. The model suggests that the symptom was rising production costs and the underlying cause was the magazine volume getting out of control. President Matthew Culligan, a man from the advertising industry, was hired to retrieve the sagging advertising sales (1962–1964) but, as we have seen the root cause was the high advertising "rate" driven up by the need to finance the promotion of subscriptions in the circulation war. President MacClifford (an expert cost-cutter with the nickname Mac-the-knife) was hired to perform the unpleasant surgical operation on the company's excess capacity (1964–1968), which stemmed from a loss of advertising pages and hence, through the advertising-editorial formula, a loss of editorial pages also. It would seem that the owners, by treating the

The death throes

In the final phase of the magazine's history, reduction of the number of pages published necessitated reduction of the firm's printing plant capacity, which led to a disastrous strike. The magazine editors, presumably threatened by the change to biweekly and then to monthly issues, revolted and approached the board of directors, which caused the president of the company to resign. The editors then exploited sensationalism as a means of attracting and holding readers, which backfired when the company was sued for libel and had to pay heavy damages.

According to Hall, however,

. . . the root cause of the sagging profit margin lies in the positive feedback loop relating the number of pages in the magazine, and hence its cost, to the number of readers: (1) as the readership increases, (2) the price of advertising decreases stimulating advertising sales, (3) the increased number of advertising pages leads to the addition of more pages of editorial content, (4) the increased volume of pages attracts more trial subscribers to convert to regular readership, which leads to accelerated readership growth and a feeding back of the outcome to further reducing the price of advertising, and so on, until (5) a feedback effect results in which costs rise more rapidly than the revenues and the profit margin is reduced.

If the management were aware of this process, then one might expect it to prevent the production costs from running away by controlling the number of pages in the magazine. Obviously some relationship between advertising and editorial content must be maintained, otherwise the magazine will become all advertising as the readership grows and the price of advertising declines. An obvious way out of this dilemma is to fix the amount of advertising by controlling the price of advertising. Keeping the advertising "rate" per thousand readers constant will achieve this.

symptoms of the problems that arose, rather than fathoming the real causes, possibly hired leaders with managerial skills that did not necessarily match the needs of the time, thereby compounding the problem.

Hall suggests that the magazine industry can be viewed as a subculture in which pecking hierarchies are established. This arrangement can become intense and sometimes counterproductive. For example, *Look* passed the *Post* in circulation in 1961. *Look* then became preoccupied with being No. 1 but had to pay a high price to try to stay there. Apparently the corporate ego gets involved, and the company takes hasty actions that can have catastrophic results.

Simulation models of the industrial dynamics type provide useful information about not only how organizations develop but also how they die. Using an intelligent simulation model with appropriate empirical data, management should be in a better position to make more effective choices.

Could this disaster have been avoided? Karl E. Weick, discussing the problem in "Organization Design," points out one way to break the pattern which led to it.

> The demise of the *Saturday Evening Post* is a perfect example of pouring money into a defective system and merely reinforcing the defects. For years the *Saturday Evening Post* used the rule of thumb in the publishing industry that the number of editorial pages should match the number of advertising pages. The tight coupling between these two elements means that when advertising shrinks, the magazine's editorial coverage also shrinks. A thinner magazine that attracts fewer readers is generated making advertisers even more reluctant to purchase ads. Eventually profits vanish. But when the ads and editorial pages increase, printing expenses also increase. In fact, the costs of the enlarged magazine rise faster than the revenues, and profits again disappear. Whether publishers try to cope with this vicious circle by increasing promotional expenditures, cutting advertising costs, or buying more high-priced, sensational articles, the outcome is the same.
>
> One way to break this pattern and to insert a *qualitative* change is by controlling the number of pages in the magazine. And one way to accomplish this, of course, is to control the price of advertising. In the old days, advertising was priced on a per-page basis. When the readership increased, the advertiser got more people for the same price. Consequently, the cost per reader went down for him. Changing this pricing method so that the advertising rate per 1,000 readers is kept constant removes the lethal linkage and publishing becomes more stable.
>
> The important point is that the *Saturday Evening Post* could have returned to prosperity not from a quantitative change, not from doing more of the same, not from putting more money in or directing the money to different places, but by acting in a different way.

The *Saturday Evening Post*, in effect, could have avoided disaster if its management had had a better understanding of the nature of organizational effectiveness.

TOPIC 4
Organizational effectiveness

DEFINITION OF EFFECTIVENESS

There is a vast variety of literature which attempts to define useful criteria for measuring organizational effectiveness. A useful way of getting at the complexity of this subject is to break these measures into four categories:

ORGANIZATIONAL EFFECTIVENESS

- Task effectiveness
- Human relations effectiveness
- Adaptation effectiveness
- Intelligence effectiveness

Task effectiveness

The first type of criterion is related to task measures of performance. Typical task measures are productivity and profitability.

Human relations effectiveness

The second criterion is in the area of human relations. At an individual level one such criterion would be job satisfaction, which is measured by the extent to which employees perceive that they are being equitably rewarded in terms of their jobs. An example at the organizational level would be morale.

Until recently the presumption has been that a low index of labor turnover (i.e., few employees leaving) should be equated with a high level of effectiveness. But in reality, high labor turnover is often linked to high levels of effectiveness. This holds true in the life insurance business, for example, where an agent's successes (and perhaps only successes) are in selling policies to relatives and friends, which may indeed be a once-and-only effort. The fact that many of these policies are allowed to lapse may very well be in the financial interest of the insurance company. Thus a rapidly changing force of agents is a good thing. This means conflict and calls for adaptation.

Adaptation effectiveness

If a firm is to be effective it has to be able to adapt to situations and change its procedures accordingly. A critical dimension of effectiveness, therefore, is the organization's capacity to deal with conflict. The main problem is to figure out when changes in the environment are too great to allow the firm to continue with its policies. Ineffectiveness in such a context would be a mismatch between the forces in the environment and the internal dynamics of the firm.

A telling example of this kind of ineffectiveness is the Ford Motor Company's situation in 1977, which was experiencing great difficulty because it did not begin the process of downsizing its cars quickly enough in response to the oil crisis and the ecology environment. This was compounded by the fact that Ford was going through a crisis of leadership as Henry Ford II prepared to make his corporate exit and turn over leadership not to one person, but to a cabinet. This ineffectiveness is generated in a more subtle way by the matching of major internal changes with gigantic external changes.

Intelligence effectiveness

Problems of adaptation, flexibility, and conflict lead to the fourth criterion of effectiveness, related to corporate intelligence. This criterion is made up of a number of subfactors, including managerial analytical skills, organizational information processing, the internalization of organizational values, training and development emphasis, and human resource planning.

DEFINING SUCCESS: A CONTINGENCY APPROACH

An issue of critical importance in organizational effectiveness is how to define success. Success in dealing with any issue depends on the criteria used to evaluate it.

An example is the issue of desegregation in U.S. schools. Robert R. Mayer, dean of Bryn Mawr College's Graduate School of Social Work, studied desegregation in the public schools in Goldsboro, North Carolina. Mayer's three sons attended school in Chapel Hill, N.C., and he had seen on them "the bumps, bruises and fears" that are among the results of desegregation for the children involved. Mayer raises the question as to what is successful desegregation and comes up with a contingency answer, as Darrell Sifford points out in a review entitled "U.S. Desegregation":

> It depends. Mayer says, on your vantage point. "From an administrator's view, success can be getting through a year with reasonable law and order. There's animosity in the halls, but the school is not burned down. That's a short-term idea of success."
>
> And long-term success?
>
> "Elimination of barriers to racial relationships is the goal of the long-term plan and I know of nobody who has yet reached that," Mayer says. "Maybe they're starting to come close now in Little Rock—after all these years. They seem to be fairly harmonious and they're getting back to education.
>
> "But anybody who expects this to happen in a year or two is going to be disappointed. No matter what (desegregation) plan you have, you're in for two, three years of turmoil. Chapel Hill is perhaps the most liberal community in the south and it had a progressive (desegregation) plan early. But four years later my kids were in school and complaining of pushing, hassling and harassment."
>
> Mayer says he agrees with what he views as the two ultimate goals of school desegregation:
>
> The first is equal education for all students. "This is the basis for job equality, income equality, everything. This is where it all starts and it's possible only when children begin their education on a relatively equal footing."
>
> The second goal, he said, is social integration. "If we're ever going to eliminate urban riots, much of our crime, then we have to have social integration," and school desegregation is a primary step in that direction, Mayer said. Social integration is necessary because "I question if a democratic society can survive unless all groups feel an equal stake in it."
>
> Why have some school systems fared better than others when desegregation plans were implemented?

The answer, says Mayer, is that harmony is greatest—or at least disharmony is minimized—in school systems in which "both groups (blacks and whites) are treated equally, in which any discomfort is shared, in which everybody participates and nobody feels he has all of the burden."

According to Mayer, therefore, success from an administrator's point of view can be mere survival without any big blowups. From a teacher's point of view, success can be getting children to learn academic subjects. From a citizen's point of view, success can be defined in terms of social integration. Success cannot be defined until the criteria for judging it have been defined.

TOPIC 5
What every manager should know about managing the organization for effectiveness

In the contingency model for the study of organization behavior, the organization as a system is seen as in Figure 13–6. The most important thing a manager should know about managing organizational perfor-

FIGURE 13–6
The organization as a system

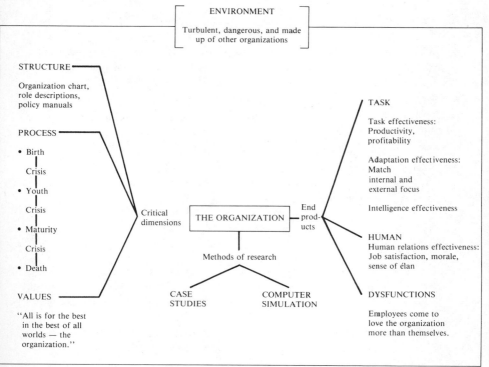

mance is that organizations, like human beings, go through different stages of growth. As the organization grows it moves away from the control of the client and develops its own logic.

As the firm moves from stage to stage it encounters crises. Business organizations usually begin as one-man shows. As they expand more people are brought in, and some kind of management develops. Leadership is basically entrepreneurial. The old guard is less and less able to keep up, and a more professional type of management has to be brought in. A new climate is needed that allows these professional managers to function properly. Larger and more complex bureaucracies have to be created.

As the organization develops new technologies have to be acquired, which in turn require appropriate organizational structures. Speaking in broad terms mature industries (such as shipbuilding) use essentially mechanistic structures (i.e., they are hierarchically arranged). Three types of technology have been identified: long-linked (e.g., car assembly plant), mediating (e.g., bank) and intensive (e.g., aerospace industry). Three types of technologies are defined further in Chapter 16.

REVIEW AND RESEARCH

1. In what way has the organization of HEW become a national scandal? Why? How can it be put right?
2. Describe the different stages of growth an organization goes through in its development.
3. Why must organizations go through crises in order to achieve change?
4. Write an essay setting out the principal reasons for the success of McDonald's.
5. Explain why the *Saturday Evening Post* died.
6. Why do different organizations have different measures or organizational effectiveness?
7. How would you measure the success of desegregation in a specific city or area?
8. From a managerial point of view, it often seems to be true that small is beautiful. Explain why small organizations are often more effective.

GLOSSARY OF TERMS

Change success pattern. This has four steps: (1) Top management comes under pressure, and (2) new manager arrives, (3) "Everybody" is brought into problem-solving process, (4) change ethos spreads throughout the organization.

Effectiveness. Measured by the ability to mobilize the right structures, processes, and values to generate an optimal level of profitability, productivity, and satisfaction.

Organizational crisis. Refers to the necessary moment of truth that the manager must face so that the organization can move to the next stage.

Organizational pathology. Concerned with the inevitable decline and fall of an organization.

DEBATE: The business corporations versus the new class

One of the reasons business organizations are interesting is that 1,000 giant corporations produce about half of all the private product in the United States. According to John Kenneth Galbraith, these huge corporations have shown a highly visible ability to manage the market by raising and cutting prices according to their own best interests. They exercise not only influence in the United States but also in many other parts of the world. The "foreign policies" of the oil companies, ITT, and Lockheed directly affect the State Department.

PRO: Business must dominate

Contrary to expectations, giant corporations such as General Motors, Exxon, and IBM do not behave like microcosms of the larger universe. In reality the modern corporation transcends its market by careful planning. Given the massive investments required to design a 747 or build the Alaskan oil pipeline, it would be insane to act otherwise.

As these large corporations plan their development, they take the power away from the owners or capitalists and place it firmly and irrevocably with the management. These executives argue that government cannot govern without the consent of business; and business cannot function without the cooperation of government. According to Charles E. Lindblom in *Politics and Markets:*

> . . . a market-oriented system may require for its success so great a disproportion of business influence . . . that even modest challenges to it are disruptive to economic stability and growth. Union power may be "too much" for the survival of business enterprise long before it is great enough to match the privileged position of business. Similarly, welfare state demands may be "too much" long before they manifest a political equality in electoral and interest-group activities.

But Lindblom ends his argument on a somewhat hopeful note. "The longer historical story has been one of repeated invalidation of predictions of the impossibility of democracy. . . . Men learn."

The "faceless executives" speak the "official truth" prepared by public relations people. They are exceptionally privileged and highly rewarded for their corporate efforts. In spite of their reluctance to express themselves, they give the corporation considerable political power.

CON: Society must dominate

According to Irving Kristol, in *Two Cheers for Capitalism,* the opponents of the corporation are a group he labels the new class, made up of professors, journalists, and assorted pundits. (Galbraith says the new class is interested in giant business organizations because they make up the dominant force in our society.)

Kristol says the new class is made up of "some millions of people whom liberal capitalism had sent to college in order to help manage its affluent, highly technological, mildly paternalistic 'post-industrial' society". Many of these educated managers find careers in the expanding public sector rather than the private one, which they oppose. While they speak of progressive reform, Kristol says, "in actuality they are acting upon a hidden agenda: to propel the nation from that modified version of capitalism we call 'the welfare state' toward an economic system so stringently regulated in detail as to fulfill many of the traditional anti-capitalist aspirations of the Left."

EXAMPLE

Executive incentive and corporate growth

A good illustration of the problems of organizational effectiveness is provided by a quick look at how a company motivates managers to maximize short-term results at the expense of long-term growth. As Alfred Rappaport points out in an article in the *Harvard Business Review* for July–August 1978, the decline in capital investment and research and development expenditures is a direct result of top management's preoccupation with short-term profit results measured by earnings per share (EPS) growth. EPS has many shortcomings as a measure of business efficiency, not the least of which is that well-conceived decisions to improve medium- and long-term profitability can result in *lower* current EPS. The problem is that managers' bonuses are frequently a function of profit performance. Further, investors and analysts use the stock market price as a measure of top management's ability.

All this short-term optimizing has the effect of circumscribing the manager's motivational time horizon. To overcome this difficulty, it is necessary to develop an extended performance evaluation system in which executive incentive plans are based on criteria which extend five years into the future. This trade-off between long-term and short-term profitability will not be overcome until boards of directors give priority to considering executive compensation plans.

Question

Devise a plan of action to overcome this problem.

DIAGRAM SUMMARY OF CHAPTER 14

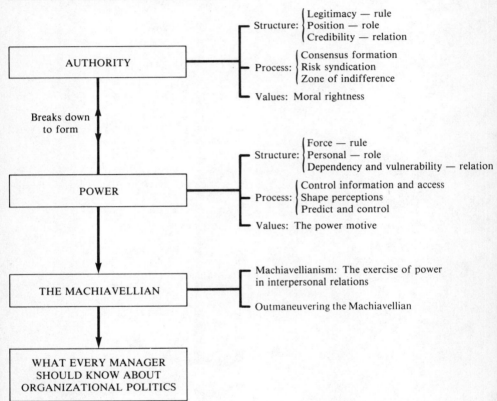

AUTHORITY

Structure:
- Legitimacy — rule
- Position — role
- Credibility — relation

Process:
- Consensus formation
- Risk syndication
- Zone of indifference

Values: Moral rightness

Breaks down to form

POWER

Structure:
- Force — rule
- Personal — role
- Dependency and vulnerability — relation

Process:
- Control information and access
- Shape perceptions
- Predict and control

Values: The power motive

THE MACHIAVELLIAN

- Machiavellianism: The exercise of power in interpersonal relations
- Outmaneuvering the Machiavellian

WHAT EVERY MANAGER SHOULD KNOW ABOUT ORGANIZATIONAL POLITICS

14

Organizational politics:
Authority versus power

MANAGING WITH A PENCIL

"Put him on the line. . . . What? You've got to be kidding. . . . Did you fire the clown? Why not? Why *not?* . . .

"You're telling me that buffoon Jones, the crazy plant manager, has been crediting TV sets into warehouse that haven't been made yet? How did he manage that? Oh, he entered production for the first three days of February for the last three days of January. January owed December . . . Whaat! . . .

"You should have . . . he has written orders. . . . There's more . . . Who needs this? The dispatch manager is shipping out empty boxes with no TVs. That idiot should be here in New York. . . . Look. Get to work on the dispatch guy; make him give you his private records. Get the goods on that ding-a-ling Jones. I'm going to have his head served up on a platter."

$\cdot \qquad \cdot \qquad \cdot \qquad \cdot$

"You think we should take Jones out? . . . You do, eh. Come on, you're itching for blood. I can see your nostrils flaring. . . . Yeh. Well we ain't. Jones can do things for me, for us. He's grateful. He needs a let-off. He really needs a real vicious kick in the teeth which will be transmitted right down the line. I've instructed him to fire his PA, that MBA in charge of control, with a computer for a brain. And a memo is being printed up tonight, reading the riot act. What the old man really objects to is not the production screwups, but the fixing of the books."

POWER AND AUTHORITY

The telephone conversation fragments that open this chapter show how executives make deals and engage in organizational politics. If organizational politics is viewed as the ideological framework determining the distribution, allocation, and maintenance of power, privilege, and patronage, then an analysis of power is a central problem for both executives and management theorists.

To understand power, it is necessary to place it in juxtaposition with authority. Authority is legitimate power; power is more than legitimate authority—it has a corona which conceals a core of action (see Topics 1 and 2). The balance of power breaks down when overt power is used too freely.

WHAT DOES IT TAKE TO SUCCEED IN MANAGEMENT?

Is succeeding in management just a matter of competence, hard work, a few lucky breaks? Or is something else needed? Today's managers are increasingly recognizing that sheer ability and hard work are not sufficient to produce superior performance which will get the right kind of visibility and somehow or other propel the manager to the top. Success depends on more than transforming inputs into outputs with value added, as Figure 14–1, the simplified contingency model for the organization as a system, shows.

FIGURE 14–1

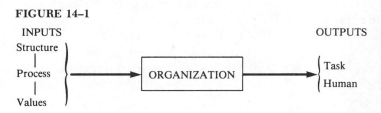

As John Kenneth Galbraith has shrewdly pointed out, the corporate officials who run organizations are the decisive game players in contemporary society. The technostructure which is made up of these corporate oligarchs is concerned with one thing above all: the advancement of the corporate officials. Of course, that they have to pay off all the other parties: the shareholders, the customers, hierarchs of the trade union, officials of regulatory agencies, tax collectors and creditors. Galbraith has demonstrated how the dismal science of economics is hopelessly interwoven with the black art of politics.

It is well to keep in mind that Adam Smith was an 18th-century professor of political economy at Glasgow University. Smith's absorption in economics led him to interview businessmen and visit workshops, and he opened *The Wealth of Nations* with a detailed description of a pin factory which is still mandatory reading for business students. As Smith saw the firm, it was in business to earn a profit, but profits served as a device to transform people's selfish interests into useful service. He took as his point of departure the notion that people act out of their own self-interest.

DEFINITION OF ORGANIZATIONAL POLITICS

The notion of enlightened self-interest is the central concept in organizational politics, which has emerged as an essential topic for the student of management. Organizational politics may be defined as the ideological framework determining the distribution, allocation, and maintenance of power, privilege, and patronage. It is essentially concerned with who gets what, when and how. The focus varies according to the level of analysis, from the individual to society (see Figure 14–2).

FIGURE 14–2
Organizational politics varies with level of analysis

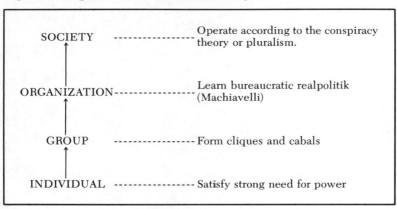

Social scientists studying management have broken away from the sterility of treating politics as a study of formal government institutions and the analysis of voting patterns. And political scientists have become increasingly interested in the analysis of the objectives and composition of interest groups within organizations. They are particularly interested in the studies of cliques and cabals whose members seek to act in concert in the competitive struggle for political power within the organization. Organizational politics is mainly a struggle over scarce values and resources to achieve particular objectives. A basic assumption of corporate politics is that every firm is an organizational power.

What are managers trying to achieve through this political maneuvering? Different answers have been given to this basic question. It is not sufficient to say that they are trying to advance their careers or enhance their self-interests. At least on some occasions, they are engaging in political activity to increase their psychic income, to show who counts, and even on occasion to indulge some of their aggressive fantasies.

In a more positive sense, political maneuvering is always concerned with the management of conflict. The ability to handle conflict successfully is a critical executive skill. All this maneuvering means moving in political circles, however (see Figure 14–3). To travel the organizational circle, it is necessary to understand how authority and power are interlocked.

FIGURE 14–3
Moving in political circles

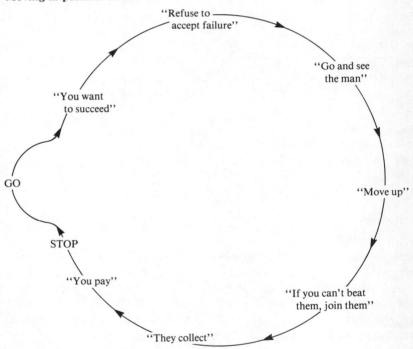

TOPIC 1
Authority

To try to achieve conceptual clarity about how the term *authority* is used, it is useful to look at it from the three perspectives of the contingency model for the study of organizational behavior: structure (rules, roles, and relations), process (how authority is exercised), and values (underlying beliefs and expectations that transcend the particular judgments involved).

THE STRUCTURE OF AUTHORITY

The structural optic is essentially an exercise in moral geometry. It looks at authority through the prism of formal position, legitimacy, and the rewards and sanctions inherent in the office. In this context, authority refers to the vertical status relationships between incumbents in formal positions. The bases of structural authority are: the rule (legitimacy), the role (the position or office), and the relation (credibility).

Rule: Legitimacy

Legitimacy, or ethical sanctification, is the rule for authority. Legitimacy is the presumption that the relation is right and proper in a moral sense. In its most explicit form, legitimacy takes a legal form when those in authority have the right to demand obedience and those subject to authority have the duty to obey.

When a relation is perceived as legitimate, there is a suspension of the critical faculties of the subordinate. This suspension is especially important when it is difficult or impossible to justify in a rational way the adequacy of a course of action by the mandates of the situation; here assent may be achieved, not by rational persuasion, but by appealing to values, attitudes, needs, and expectations that transcend the particular situation.

Role: Position

A useful, if not always true, aphorism is that authority inheres in the office, not the person. This proposition can be played either way, to the advantage of either the superior or the subordinate. It all depends. Richard M. Nixon made good use of the separation of person and office to secure his reelection to the presidency, but he was then signally unsuccessful in convincing his detractors that in protecting the office of the presidency, he was not merely trying to save himself.

Relation: Credibility

Credibility is closely tied to competence, and both are linked to sapiential authority, which is the right to be heard by virtue of knowledge or expertise. Sapiential authority is not limited to formal vertical relations and usually, in fact, cuts right across the organization chart. Both technical competence (know-how) and actual operating experience confer an authority of competence. When people possess authority they have the ability to produce reasons for their orders, if challenged, or at least they are believed to have this capacity. In fact, they are rarely challenged when they possess competence or sapiential authority.

THE AUTHORITY PROCESS

For too long now, the main tradition in regard to authority has been structural in its broad assumptions: People ought to do what they are told to do, particularly if told to do so by their lawful superiors; if they disagree, they should do what they are told and complain afterward. Such structural mandates are incompatible with our moral attitudes and with the actual processes involved in the exercise of authority. A crucial task of organizational behavior students is to explore the actual process within which authority is exercised.

To travel the vectors of the moral geometry of authority relations requires a grounding in the social contract theory of Jean Jacques Rousseau and Immanuel Kant. People are born free, and each one has a right to the most extensive basic liberty compatible with a like liberty for others. When authority is exercised, it is exercised in the form of a contract which abridges or constrains this freedom. Both parties should enter freely into that contract. Thus the acceptance and the assumption of authority represent the different ends of a social contract which is integral to the nature of employment relations. This social, and psychological, contract is the agreement on values and norms between A and B in Figure 14–4 which constitutes legitimate authority.

But even within such a framework, managers have intuitively developed practical and pragmatic processes for the exercise of authority. Three different terms, describing different aspects of this process, are currently in use—consensus formation, risk syndication, and working within the subordinate's zone of indifference. They all involve participation.

Consensus formation, risk syndication, zone of indifference

Consensus, the present vogue word among managers, is difficult to define. A few strongly react to the term *consensus management,* but all use it, including the military. Let us start to define this term by saying what it is *not.* It is not decision making by unanimity, nor is it rule by the majority. It is a more subtle matter. In a positive sense, the more powerful clique or minority (usually two or three persons) agrees on a solution which in a negative sense the majority agrees not to oppose or make unworkable. It is not that top management has had a change of heart and become more democratic in spirit; but the reality of the

FIGURE 14–4
Utilitarian, normative, and coercive power

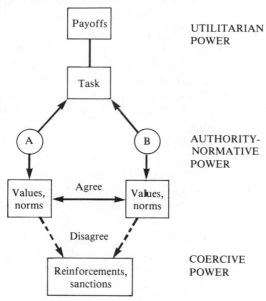

complexity of the modern organization has gotten to them. Those who yesterday were less powerful today derive their power from realities such as the fact that the handful of employees who punch the cards that program the machines can just as easily program their betters.

Reaching the consensus has become a ritual, usually started when top management formulates contingencies over martinis in the executive dining room, followed by a series of task forces which gather data, and then the critical meetings begin. As in the "Aha! experience" so beloved of Gestalt psychologists, the chief executive discerns the emergence of a consensus. The various parties have exercised their rights to be heard, and the emergent decision incorporates their ideas as far as this is possible.

Commitment has been achieved through risk syndication, which represents the sharing not only of the dangers and penalties inherent in the decision but also of the payoffs. The beauty of risk syndication is that recent research on decision making suggests that groups are prepared to make riskier decisions. The people who complain most about the length of such processes (due largely to interminable committee meetings) are those who risk least and stand to gain least, but their commitment is vital.

This is why, in general, it is important to operate within the zone of indifference of subordinates. This describes the area of behavior within which subordinates are prepared to accept direction, and the direction is seen as legitimate.

AUTHORITY VALUES

When authority is being exercised properly in regard to matters of any moment, the several parties involved are usually aware of the gravity of the matter under consideration. They envelop the occasion with a certain sanctity, if not piety, which is compounded in varying amounts from four separate elements: legality (the law requires it), precedent (it is honored by time), legitimacy (it is seen as morally appropriate), and due process (proper and tried procedures have removed all reasonable doubt). These values are supremely functional and serve to allow reason, rationality, and reasonableness their full sway. Time is not a factor; there is an absence of duress; cases are to be argued, and argued persuasively if possible; roles (prosecutor, defendant, devil's advocate, etc.) are institutionalized.

When people are exercising authority properly, they experience an emotion which is, at the lower end of the scale, a peculiar amalgam of warm glow, comfortable smugness, boredom, and moral superiority, and at the upper end a heady mixture of hubris, omniscience, and omnipotence like that which took the United States to Vietnam—a quiet glow of moral rectitude and righteous indignation. Now all this augurs well—for the status quo, at least. The mills of authority grind small and exceedingly slowly. The point is that authority is for stability, the establishment, the established, and, if it is for change at all, for gradual change. Authority is identified in many people's minds, especially young people's, with the forces of repression—hard as this may seem to the established members of our society, many of whom who have fought and worked hard to establish due process, precedent, and legitimacy in place of arbitrary fiat, unappealable decisions, caprice, personal pleasure, and the convenience of the powerful.

But now, a question is being raised not only about the legitimacy of authority but about the very concept itself. Many of the young people of our society see all authority as intrinsically bad. The presumption of societies previous to our own was that authority was built into the very fabric of society. The balancing position between these extremes is that authority relations are consensual—that the several parties to an agreement or contract must agree that in a disagreement there is some civil manner in which the dispute can be resolved (ultimately, by recourse to the courts). When authority is rejected, power relations which are coercive are substituted.

FROM AUTHORITY TO POWER

When authority is exercised (see Figure 14–5), an ambience of legality, precedent, and legitimacy envelops the process. The whole

FIGURE 14–5
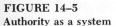
Authority as a system

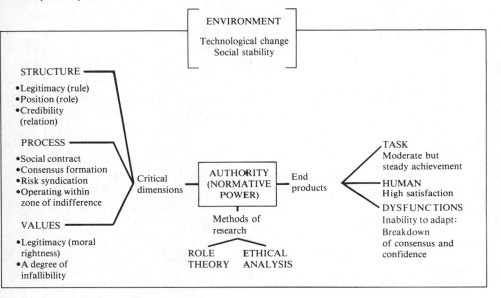

thing is subject to due process (capable of challenge through appeal); basically, this is a recycling process by different persons who test for rationality and reduce caprice. Time is not a constraint, and reason, reasonableness, and persuasion are given their place.

When authority breaks down, as it has in our postindustrial society, the result is power. When the consensus of authority breaks up, power relations emerge which are ultimately coercive—"He made him an offer he could not refuse." What is being challenged in modern times is not the legitimacy of a particular authority system, but the very concept of authority. The crisis of authority—whether exemplified in the Chicago Seven trial, with the defendants tied to chairs while being tried on a conspiracy count, or the helter skelter of Charles Manson and his disciples, or My Lai, or Watergate—makes an understanding of power a sine qua non for the manager of today.

TOPIC 2
Power

Power and authority are in dialectical juxtaposition: power goes beyond legitimate authority; authority is legitimate power. Thus if power represents the interpretation of authority, it shows the same broad characteristics as authority. In structural terms, power is a property of a social relation; power is a function of clout, "can do," knowledge, and competence. In process terms, power presumes prediction and control of behavior through the restructuring of the other person's perceptions. In terms of values, the power ethic is one of coercion, control, and manipulation which challenges and stretches legitimacy.

Continually stretching legitimacy ensures that power has a corrupting element to it. Statesmen and scholars who have shown too much explicit interest in power have been badly treated by history; Machiavelli is the classic example. As the great historian Thomas Macaulay observed, "out of his surname they coined an epithet for a knave, and out of his Christian name a synonym for the devil." This stretching of legitimacy is both a human temptation and an organizational opportunity.

People crave for and play with power in a pathological way that is essential for both personal and organizational effectiveness. But "they" cannot be allowed unbridled power; power must be offset in some way. Hence the need for a balance, not only of power, but also of prudence. An organization run according to authority (moral and pure,

"You know gentlemen, I find it terrifying to realize that we are the powers that be."

Reprinted by permission *The Wall Street Journal*.

freely contracted) degenerates into old-fashioned bureaucracy, bound with red tape and stifling to the imagination. The illegitimate use of power attracts a particular personality who gets a charge out of "pulling a fast one," getting things done, making things happen—all by playing the power game. It is the illegitimacy, the bending of the rules, the squaring of the circle that intrigues the power hungry.

Corporate health or effectiveness is the ability to mobilize the power centers of an organization to maintain flexibility, growth, and adaptation to the turbulence of the environment. Coercive power goes beyond authority and of necessity is somewhat illegitimate and therefore attracts some pathological people. This is the basic dilemma of organizational power. The issue is how organizational health and personal pathology can work together. The answer is, nicely.

STRUCTURAL BASES OF POWER

Power is the ability of people to make others do their will, voluntarily or otherwise. While all American managers exercise power, few are in fact comfortable with power or its dynamics. In fact, we distrust managers who make it obvious that they are seeking power or who who even talk too much about it. This reaction to power has enormously increased in the past decade with the publication of such books as Charles Reich's *The Greening of America*, in which he argues "It is not the misuse of power that is evil; the very existence of power is evil."

Why has the distrust of power become so acute? Amitai Etzioni, in *A Comparative Analysis of Complex Organizations*, identifies three different kinds of power: utilitarian, normative, and coercive. Normative power, which is based on legitimacy, essentially coincides with authority. Utilitarian power is related to the payment of inducements either to join the organization or to do things for it. Coercive power arises when conformity is exacted through the control of rewards or sanctions.

The manager's power base is a function of organizational factors. Explicitly, this means that the exercise of power requires recognition that managers are dependent on others, particularly others they do not directly control. Because managers are so dependent, John P. Kotter points out in "Power, Dependence, and Effective Management," they have become increasingly vulnerable. To operate effectively in this context of dependency, they need to develop skill in managing and using power effectively. Kotter gives an interesting illustration of how this organizational dependency affects the exercise of power:

> After nearly a year of rumors, it was finally announced in May 1974 that the president of ABC Corporation had been elected chairman of the board and that Jim Franklin, the vice president of finance, would replace

him as president. While everyone at ABC was aware that a shift would take place soon, it was not at all clear before the announcement who would be the next president. Most people had guessed it would be Phil Cook, the marketing vice president.

Nine months into his job as chief executive officer, Franklin found that Phil Cook (still the marketing vice president) seemed to be fighting him in small and subtle ways. There was never anything blatant, but Cook just did not cooperate with Franklin as the other vice presidents did. Shortly after being elected, Franklin had tried to bypass what he saw as a potential conflict with Cook by telling him that he would understand if Cook would prefer to move somewhere else where he could be a CEO also. Franklin said that it would be a big loss to the company but that he would be willing to help Cook in a number of ways if he wanted to look for a presidential opportunity elsewhere. Cook had thanked him but had said that family and community commitments would prevent him from relocating and all CEO opportunities were bound to be in a different city.

Since the situation did not improve after the tenth and eleventh months, Franklin seriously considered forcing Cook out. When he thought about the consequences of such a move, Franklin became more and more aware of just how dependent he was on Cook. Marketing and sales were generally the keys to success in their industry, and the company's sales force was one of the best, if not the best, in the industry. Cook had been with the company for 25 years. He had built a strong personal relationship with many of the people in the sales force and was universally popular. A mass exodus just might occur if Cook were fired. The loss of a large number of salesmen, or even a lot of turmoil in the department, could have a serious effect on the company's performance.

After one year as chief executive officer, Franklin found that the situation between Cook and himself had not improved and had become a constant source of frustration.

The characteristics of power

According to Kotter, managers successful at managing power and using it effectively share a number of common characteristics:

1. They are sensitive to what others consider to be legitimate behavior in acquiring and using power.

2. They have good intuitive understanding of the various types of power and methods of influence. They are sensitive to what types of power are easiest to develop with different types of people.

3. They tend to develop all the types of power, to some degree, and they use all the influence methods. Unlike managers who are not very good at influencing people, effective managers usually do not think that only some of the methods are useful or that only some of the methods are moral.

4. They establish career goals and seek our managerial positions that allow them to successfully develop and use power. They look for

jobs, for example, that use their backgrounds and skills to control or manage some critically important problem or environmental contingency that an organization faces.

5. They use all of their resources, formal authority, and power to develop still more power. To borrow Edward Banfield's metaphor, they actually look for ways to "invest" their power where they might secure a high positive return.

6. Effective managers engage in power-oriented behavior in ways that are tempered by maturity and self-control.

7. Finally, they also recognize and accept as legitimate that, in using these methods, they clearly influence other people's behavior and lives.

Thus, speaking in structural terms of the rules, roles, and relations of power:

1. The rule of power is to use all means available to achieve a particular objective and to discount moral considerations to some extent.
2. In role terms, power is basically a personal matter.
3. In relational terms, managers accept the fact that they are dependent on so many other people and they come to terms with their own vulnerability.

THE PROCESS: THE POWER PLAY

In purely structural terms, the ability to exercise power emerges from a personal matrix of organizational clout, can-do, information management, and control of access. To exercise power effectively, a manager must be willing and indeed keen to restructure the perceptions of subordinates. Very often this means treating information as a scarce commodity. Thus, as Henry Mintzberg has pointed out, the manager's behavior tends to be a ad hoc, fragmented, and oriented toward the immediate in terms of information requirements.

Closely allied to the management information capability is the control of personal access to key figures. Former President Richard Nixon allowed his staff to create a palace guard, to build a "Berlin Wall" in the White House which effectively isolated him not only from irritations but from useful alternatives. Another expert in the exercise of power was Howard Hughes, who showed a positive genius for "delegating" decision making so the option of changing his mind always remained with him.

There has been a recent proliferation of books of advice on how to exercise power. For example, Michael Korda's *Power! How to get it, how to use it* offers tips for the young executive, who would do well to receive them with a pinch of salt. Korda recommends that executives should practice the "power gaze" (see Figure 14–6); speak quietly so

FIGURE 14–6
Face-to-face, eyeball-to-eyeball exercise of power

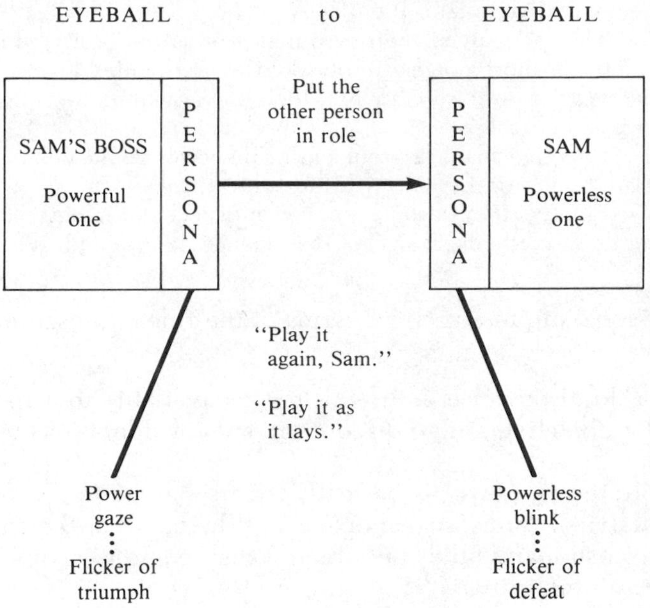

EYEBALL   to   EYEBALL

that others will have to lean forward to hear what they have to say, carry ultimate power symbols such as Swiss watches, and never give up control of, for example, other people's expense accounts. There are other books which teach executives to ignore their altruistic instincts and win through intimidation.

VALUES: THE POWER MOTIVE

David McClelland, studying the effects of alcohol on fantasy, touched on the relationship between power imagery and drinking in alcoholics. In *The Drinking Man,* McClelland points out that the American concept of power is predominantly negative. To deal with this problem, McClelland develops the notion of the two faces of power, power which is personalized and power which is socialized.

McClelland defines the power motive broadly, as the need to have impact, or concern about controlling other people or groups. One interesting finding to emerge from his work is that male college students who scored high in power tried to associate with the prestigious and powerful, owned status-conferring things like expensive cars, read sporty magazines, and engaged in gambling and aggressively male pursuits. The archetype of men with the power motive is Don Juan.

Inevitably in such a context, people, both the powerful and the powerless, fear power. For McClelland the good-bad aspect of power

Box 14–1: A good power drive

A manager's job calls for someone who can influence people rather than for someone who likes doing things. Above all, a good manager, apparently, likes power. David C. McClelland of Harvard University first postulated that if managers are to get to the top of their organizations, they must have a strong need for achievement. Now McClelland is saying that top managers must have a need for power, that is a concern for influencing people. But the power motivation must ultimately be of benefit to the organization as a whole and not of benefit only to the managers personally. Managers therefore must develop socialized power.

McClelland concludes that managers with the right power motivation would share the following characteristics:

1.   They are more organization-minded; that is, they tend to join more organizations and to feel responsible for building up these organizations. Furthermore, they believe strongly in the importance of centralized authority.

2.   They report that they like to work. This finding is particularly interesting, because our research on achievement motivation has led many commentators to argue that achievement motivation promotes the "Protestant work ethic." Almost the precise opposite is true. People who have a high need to achieve like to get out of work by becoming more efficient. They would like to see the same result obtained in less time or with less effort. But managers who have a need for institutional power actually seem to like the discipline of work. It satisfies their need for getting things done in an orderly way.

3.   They seem quite willing to sacrifice some of their own self-interest for the welfare of the organization they serve. For example, they are more willing to make contributions to charities.

4.   They have a keen sense of justice. It is almost as if they feel that if a person works hard and sacrifices for the good of the organization, he should and will get a just reward for his effort.

All managers are not able to benefit from the kind of training McClelland has developed as a means of mobilizing power motivation, however. For example:

. . . Henry Carter managed a sales office for a company which had very low morale (around the 20th percentile) before he went for training. When morale was checked some six months later, it had not improved. Overall sales gain subsequently reflected this fact since it was only 2% above the previous year's figures.

Oddly enough, Henry's problem was that he was so well liked by everybody that he felt little pressure to change. Always the life of the party, he is particularly popular because he supplies other managers with special hard-to-get brands of cigars and wines at a discount. He uses his close ties with everyone to bolster his position in the company, even though it is known that his office does not perform well compared with others.

His great interpersonal skills became evident at the workshop when he did very poorly at one of the business games. When the discussion turned to why he had done so badly and whether he acted that way on the job, two prestigious participants immediately sprang to his defense, explaining away Henry's failure by arguing that the way he did things was often a real help to others and the company. As a result, Henry did not have to cope with such questions at all. He had so successfully developed his role as a likeable, helpful friend to everyone in management that, even though his salesmen performed badly, he did not feel under any pressure to change.

Reference: David C. McClelland and David H. Burnham, "Power Is the Great Motivator", *Harvard Business Review*, March–April 1976.

motivation revolves around the maturity of the individual trying to exercise power. There are four stages to power: Stage I, "It strengthens me"; Stage II, "I strengthen myself"; Stage III, "I have impact on others"; and Stage IV, "It moves me to do my duty (for others)." The argument is moral; individuals ought to strive for personal development so that they can operate at a Stage IV level (see Box 14–1).

Figure 14–7 summarizes power as a system. Inevitably, if you fool around with power too much, you end up as a Machiavellian.

FIGURE 14–7
Power as a system

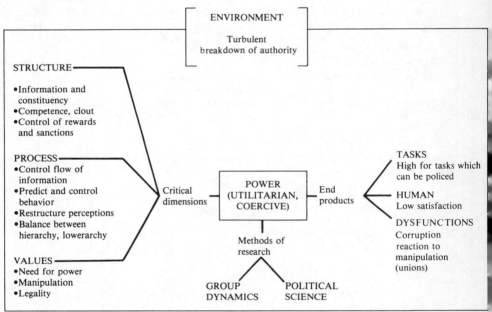

TOPIC 3
The Machiavellian

The original text on manipulation was written in the 15th century by Niccolo Machiavelli, who dedicated *The Prince* to the medieval ruler Lorenzo the Magnificent. *The Prince* is concerned with the reality of politics—how to win power and hold it. For Machiavelli, political expediency is placed above morality, and deceit and craft are permitted, in order to maintain authority. It is part of the paranoia of people in organizations to believe that Machiavellianism is always a factor in management.

Manipulation is also studied by behavioral scientists. Richard

Christie, a social psychologist at Columbia University, has studied Machiavellianism as a personality trait of the con artist or operator who prospers by deceiving others.

MACHIAVELLIANISM: THE EXERCISE OF POWER IN INTERPERSONAL RELATIONS

Modern behavioral scientists have searched for a method to measure Machiavellianism. The basic underlying proposition behind such efforts is the belief that there is no management without Machiavellianism, that every executive act involves a con man or operator. It amounts to the idea that you can't get action without exercising power. According to Christie, in "The Prevalence of Machiavellian Orientations," Machiavellianism is simply the exercise of power in interpersonal relations.

A basic proposition of conspiracy theory (see Chapter 15) is the belief that power has to be exercised to achieve change, to get organizations to move from the top dead-center position of established authority relations. Thus legitimacy has to be broken by illegitimate means. The paranoid personality is pre-occupied with power relations, either as executor or executed, and always as executive. Yet even though Machiavellians may have illusions of grandeur, they are usually not psychotic enough to be hospitalized.

The Machiavellian works with means, not ends

The Machiavellian is preoccupied with means as opposed to ends. Any end will do. What is important is the game, the chase, the action. In this frame of reference, it is both futile and ridiculous to pursue a political purpose by means that are bound to fail. Success means the achievement of a purpose, irrespective of what that purpose may be.

The Machiavellian is cool

The Watergate conspirators, the most prominent example of Machiavellians in recent times, revealed a disregard for conventional morality and, more particularly, an ability to treat people as things. They were basically "cool" in interpersonal relations; once one becomes emotionally involved with another person, it is difficult to treat that person as an object. One of the striking characteristics of both H. R. Haldeman and John D. Ehrlichman was their ability to handle conflict and stress and to put up a cool front in the face of considerable difficulties.

Curiously, many of the Nixon aides in the White House had worked in advertising or public relations. The cri de coeur of Madison Avenue is that man does not live by bread alone, but also by images. People live by their perception of reality, and perceptions can be restructured by playing around with the stimulus, the process, the person, the context, the backdrop, the perspective, or the actual sequencing of events.

The Machiavellian separates work and nonwork

Chuck ("I would walk over my grandmother, if necessary") Colson, the White House aide who found religion after 'Watergate, was described by Douglas Hallett in *The New York Times Magazine* for October 20, 1974, as follows:

> Colson is very attentive to other people's feelings in his personal life. His wife, Patty, is an enormously warm and supportive individual with whom Chuck maintains a honeymoon relationship; they wait on and feed each other, embrace freely and affectionately, and share private sign language and jokes in a manner one rarely finds in a middle-aged couple. At his best, these characteristics carry over into his professional life. At dinner one evening, Chuck's wife started criticizing John Dean. She had hardly begun when Colson pounded his water glass down on the table and shouted, "I won't have it. I won't have that in my house. If we do what we think is right, that's enough. He's doing what he thinks is right and if he's not he has to live with himself."

Machiavellians make a sharp distinction between work and nonwork. Work is a battlefield where "attack is the best defense," and an all-round defense or even paranoia may be absolutely essential.

The Machiavellian is paranoid

Warned that he might have committed a crime, Nixon decided "to put the wagons up around the President on this particular conversation." The White House tape transcripts revealed that on April 25, 1973, the President queried Haldeman from 7:46 to 7:53 P.M. over the telephone about the possibility that John Dean might have secretely taped or written a memorandum about a White House conversation:

H: Yes, sir.

P: Is there any, uh, way that, uh, even surreptitiously or discreetly or otherwise I mean, that, ah, way you could determine whether uh, this matter of whether Dean might have walked in there with a recorder on him? I don't know.

H: No, I don't think there is any way. I think ya gotta, so remote as to be almost beyond possibility. And uh, and if he did (unintelligible).

P: Well we've gotta I mean, it's, it (unintelligible) but the point is that that's ah, that's a real bomb isn't it?

H: Ah, ya.

OUTMANEUVERING THE MACHIAVELLIAN

Why were the Watergate conspirators eventually caught? They took counsel; they formed alliances; they edited, filtered, and even suppressed information; they compromised themselves, the president and the American people; they used negative timing and self-dramatization; they were confident; they were "the boss." They were always cool—manipulative, uninvolved, technique oriented. They refused to give the other guy satisfaction.

In effect, they used behavioral technology. They rehearsed evidence; they wrote Harvard Business School case answers for everything; they "papered files"; they rewrote the news for the president. They could distinguish between the illegal and the "nonlegit but legal"; they used calculated leaks, smear campaigns, lists of enemies, a department of dirty tricks. They structured perceptions and used the psychological distance routines (control access, "put it down on paper," "I shall explain what you mean").

But something went wrong. They were outmaneuvered by a smarter, more genial Machiavellian, who understood how the political side of management works.

This man was Senator Sam ("I have a Harvard law degree but don't hold it against me") Ervin, who understood the game perfectly. As chairman of the Senate committee investigating the Watergate affair, Ervin gave lessons on the Constitution. And since the Constitution does not authorize burglaries or the employment of government officials to harass citizens, executive privilege emerged as an inferior neurotic adjustment with zero functional characteristics. Ervin's disingenuous and disarming manner turned the committee into a successful fishing expedition which brought forth the climactic admission that everything at the White House had been taped.

Ervin went fishing by giving lessons in English. For example, Ehrlichman and Haldeman had equipped themselves with a tough old lawyer called John Wilson, who earned his place in history by calling the senator from Hawaii "a dirty little Jap." One of the more memorable exchanges between Ervin and Wilson went like this:

WILSON: How do you know that, Mr. Chairman?
ERVIN: Because I can understand the English language. It is my mother tongue.

When Ervin asked if people knew what the word *eleemosynary* meant, he gave a giant clue to what the game was to be. Eleemosynary is an adjective describing or pertaining to alms, charity, or charitable donations. It can also mean charitable. When big contributors give to political candidates they try to make the gifts appear as eleemosynary as possible. Thus Ervin showed what could be done with a good word which had been kept out of circulation.

The looking-glass war

Ervin turned the committee into a real-life drama which was always better than the soap operas it preempted on television. Ervin, who looks like a genial Humpty-Dumpty, cast himself as Alice in Wonderland. The beauty of the drama was that Ervin, with his Southern drawl, conducted himself with a certain old world charm and integrity. So honest and decent was Sam that one senator said he would trust him with his wife's dentures.

Like Lewis Carroll's crocodile, Ervin went about his business calmly and with self-assurance:

> How cheerfully he seems to grin
> How neatly spreads his claws,
> And welcomes little fishes in
>   With gently smiling jaws!

The big fish in Ervin's expedition was that collective Humpty-Dumpty, the Nixon administration.

Ervin soon had witnesses running through Humpty-Dumpty's lines, as when Ehrlichman tried to distinguish between *literal* and *actual.* He got them to look in the looking glass of the TV and say in a rather scornful tone, "When I use a word it means just what I choose it to mean—neither more nor less."

It was true theater. No matter how hard the villains tried, they couldn't win. No matter how often used such soporific bromides as "at that point in time," the game was up. And even though "The Queen was in a furious passion and went stamping about, and shouting 'Off with his head!' about once in a minute," the drama wound its way forward to its inglorious end. The key issue is: How was this trick pulled off? How do you impose your script on others? How do you get them to abandon their craziness for yours?

When the Nixonites came on with their "team players" who were expert at "containment" and proficient at "downfield blocking," Ervin met them with elegant English—and led them through the mysteries of *Alice in Wonderland.* He won the looking-glass war because he fought it in the political arena where his opponents were least skilled. His craziness was stronger than theirs.

TOPIC 4
What every manager should know about organizational politics

The first thing every manager should know about the political process in organizations is how to distinguish between authority and power. Authority is appropriate when the task is routine, relations are legitimate, and you are acting out of your office. Power is appropriate when the situation is changing dramatically, the legitimacy is not clear, and you are acting from strength (you control resources, information, payoffs, or hit men).

Authority works through consensus formation, risk syndication, working within the zone of indifference of subordinates, and delegation. Making a power play is quite different, because the object of this exercise is to manipulate other people's perceptions and behavior. Thus, authority relations are always consensual; power relations are ultimately coercive.

POLITICKING

Politicking aims to get other people to do what you want them to. It is achieved mainly by putting the actors in the right roles, in the right sets, in the right place, with the right scripts.

The classical management of roles follows certain rules.

1. Define the impossible—objectives.
2. Keep the other guy in role.
3. Use managerial language.
4. Insist on getting everything in writing.
5. Require subordinates to repeat what you say.
6. Wear conservative clothes.
7. Ration time carefully.

Authority: From black and white to delicate shades of gray

The structural optic of authority looks at the executive role through the prism of legality and legitimacy. The rule with authority is legitimacy, which presumes a shared value base between superiors and subordinates, so that when instructions are given to subordinates their critical faculties are suspended and they fall in line. In this visual world of black and white, officers and men, an executive goes through the managerial ritual and things happen. But when the rule of law and order begins to break down, so does the relation of credibility. Credibility is closely tied to competence, and both are linked in the idea of sapiential authority.

The whole apparatus of authority, with its ideas of total responsibility, can come tumbling down. The business of writing role descriptions with an introductory paragraph, list of functions, decisions, and review mechanisms, and drawing up organization charts, has been largely discarded. Not even the process of management by authority described in Topic 1, with its ideas of consensus formation, risk syndication, and working within the zone of indifference of subordinates, is likely to save it.

We are moving out of optical space, which is essentially made up of clearly defined fields with sharp black-and-white outlines where things such as roles are as separate as the spaces between buildings. When this traditional classical organization theory is followed, managerial space can be focused in lines of type; you do this and I do that. Instructions go down the line through a series of magnifying lenses which show up more small print at each level, and reports flow up the line through a series of condensers which remove small print and leave only headlines. The system moves from here to there, and both the manager and the managed view them as separate in time as well as in space.

Acoustical space is different; here there are all sorts of delicate shades of gray. In this twilight of authority, there is an intimacy in which it is not clear who is doing what to whom. Interaction fills the void separating one role from another. Existential myths and magic homogenize corporate space, unifying and joining together roles that in the classical, visual world of black and white would fly apart.

Defeating Machiavellianism

Machiavellians can be defeated by bigger and better Machiavellians. To win a victory against a more powerful adversary in a system, it may be necessary to use a most sophisticated Machiavellian strategy. To find such a strategy it is useful to read biographies of great men and women, follow controversies such as the Watergate saga on TV, and, above all, examine your own organizational experiences. The goal is to figure out exactly the rules of the game in town, this week.

Managing political behavior

To manage the political system effectively, a manager ought to understand that in the battle between the superiors and the subordinates, the hierarchs and the lowerarchs, no matter how devious the latter are, the former usually win. The main reason is that bureaucratic organizations, by their very nature, are structured so that they can be used as power instruments by top management. A critical question every executive ought to ask about any plan is whether the dysfunctions exceed the eufunctions. In other words, if the bad outcomes are greater than the good outcomes, the manager ought to think again and look for a more realistic and reasonable strategy.

REVIEW AND RESEARCH

1. Compare and contrast authority and power, using the following headings: source, behavioral relations (cognitive, affective, and action patterns), process, norms, share of the payoffs.

2. What has caused the breakdown in legitimacy between the student, the faculty, and the administration in universities?

3. What is risk syndication? How is it achieved in a management group?

4. Discuss the concept *zone of indifference*. Subordinates have different levels of indifference. Why? How should a manager adjust strategy to cope with these different levels?

5. At various times a manager can act (*a*) with authority, (*b*) in an authoritarian way, and (*c*) in an authoritative way. Compare and contrast these different styles according to (*i*) the task, (*ii*) position power, (*iii*) leader-member relations.

6. Describe a situation where either you had power over somebody or somebody had power over you. What was the source of power? How did it affect the relation, your perception of the other party, and the distribution of the payoffs?

7. In international politics, experts no longer discuss the balance of power they refer instead to the balance of prudence. What do you think might be the differences between these two approaches?

8. What is power equalization? How did students try to achieve it in the universities? Did they succeed? If not, why not?

9. Why haven't work councils worked in the United States, although they have had a limited success in Europe?

10. How can you train executives to develop their skills in exercising power? Relate your answer to game theory and Fiedler's contingency theory.

GLOSSARY OF TERMS

Authority. Legitimate or normative power, flowing from an "author" (person, document, law) whose influence is accepted. Legitimacy—which implies a social contract based on consensus formation, risk syndication, and subordinate compliance—is the chief distinction between authority and other forms of power; authority cannot exist except in this moral climate.

Coercive power. Power which operates in a context of legality rather than legitimacy and functions chiefly through the use of rewards and sanctions, compelling behavior rather than seeking consensus and compliance. Coercion is usually overt and more visible than other forms of power; it emerges when a system of legitimate authority breaks down.

Consensus formation. The process through which authority gains the compliance of subordinates or group members in general, though it is not necessarily unanimity or even majority rule; a powerful minority may agree on a course of action which the majority agrees not to oppose.

Crisis of authority. The breakdown of legitimacy which gives rise to challenge, conformation, and coercion.

Power. The source of the influence needed in organizations to direct, control, make decisions, and secure cooperation in achieving the organization's goals. Power has three major aspects (see definitions): authority, coercive power, and utilitarian power.

Power motive. The need to have impact or the desire to control other people or groups.

Risk syndication. The process of getting the parties who are involved to participate in making a decision and thus share in both the accountability for the decision and the distribution of the payoffs.

Sapiential authority. The right to be heard by virtue of knowledge or expertise.

Utilitarian power. The pragmatic influence exerted on organization members by their desire to accomplish tasks and receive task rewards; a form of power implicit in organization structure and goal orientation and thus more static (less dynamic) than authority or coercion.

Zone of indifference. The area of behavior within which a subordinate is prepared to accept direction or influence; in general, he must see an instruction as within his jurisdiction and competence, and within the law and his value system, or he may be mobilized to oppose and reject it.

DEBATE: The Machiavellians versus the humanists

The dominant metaphor of the political theory of the firm sees the organization as a great bureaucratic arena in which executives and their hangers-on are players in the game of organizational realpolitik. The supreme advantage of the metaphor of game playing is that by reducing personal responsibility, it frees individuals to make decisions. But, of course, the metaphor of the game, like the use of any other organizational model, can lead to disastrous consequences.

In *The Best and the Brightest,* Pulitzer Prize winner David Halberstam reveals the devastating consequences of how the corporate game, with its idea of players moving off and on the board, helped to get the United States into the messiest war of its history. In Halberstam's presentation, the "good guys," the humanists, accepted North Vietnamese nationalism, feared the military-industrial complex more than communism, and worried about world poverty. The "bad guys," the rationalists, the Machiavellians, believed that the real threat to the free world was communism, an international conspiracy which understood only one thing—force

In the ensuing corporate struggle, the rationalists outfought, outmaneuvered, and outlasted the humanists. The chief rationalist was Robert McNamara, described by Halberstam as "a ferocious infighter; statistics and force ratios came pouring out of him like a great uncapped faucet," and when he didn't have the data, he invented them.

Questions
1. Are you a Machiavellian or a humanist?
2. Must people be manipulated to get things done?

ISSUE

The Bakke case moves to the factory

In 1974, the Kaiser aluminum plant located in Gramercy, Lousiana, set up, in conjunction with the United Steel Workers Union, a program to train skilled craftsmen. As part of the affirmative action program, one black was admitted for every white. Brian Weber, who had worked in the plant for ten years, was left out. He therefore sued both the company and the union, charging reverse discrimination.

Weber won his case in the lower courts, and the company and the union were forced to revise the training program to make no racial discrimination in selecting applicants. The Supreme Court agreed to hear Kaiser's and the union's appeal, and its decision against Weber may profoundly affect how applicants are selected for training programs.

The dilemma facing the Supreme Court had its origins in the Civil Rights Act of 1964, which made it illegal to discriminate on the basis of race. Subsequently the federal government issued an executive order requiring all government contractors to institute affirmative action programs to bring about a better balance of minority workers. Generally the federal courts have supported affirmative action programs. But the Supreme Court, in deciding the landmark Bakke case, set some limits on the extent of these programs. In the Bakke case what was being challenged was a strict quota for minority students in a California medical school.

The basic question for American businesses is how to execute affirmative action programs without leaving themselves open to the charge of reverse discrimination.

Question

How should companies solve this problem?

DIAGRAM SUMMARY OF CHAPTER 15

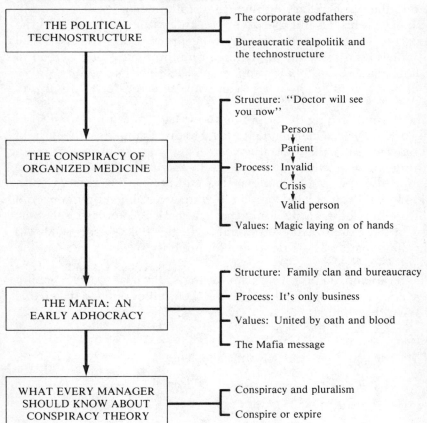

15

The conspiracy theory:
Its godfathers, capos,
and capers

ORGANIZATIONAL POLITICS IN ACTION

J. Edgar Hoover's management of the FBI has provided some exceedingly interesting insights into organizational politics. Hoover, who is seen by some as a shrewd bureaucratic genius, cared less about crime than maintaining his crime-busting image. He realized from the outset that he could obscure the bureau's failures by magnifying its sometime successes.

We can learn much from Hoover's political savvy about how to exercise power in an organizational setting. Throughout much of his career, Hoover relayed sensitive information about important political figures, compiled by his agents, to various presidents so that he could build up political support for the bureau. Thus Hoover's behavior embraced the first principle of organizational realpolitik—control of sensitive, restricted, or valuable information.

Control of subordinates

To control subordinates Hoover constructed an archaic set of rules of personal behavior. He also developed so many specific procedures for conducting investigations that he bred deep cynicism in FBI agents, who set out to find ways of breaking the rules, without being caught.

Of course, when power is exercised excessively, subordinates behave sycophantically. They lose their independence, and their judgment, and they often act irrationally.

In this paranoiac atmosphere, stenographers were encouraged to report violations, anonymously, if they wished. Defaulters would be sent to "Siberia," such as Butte Montana, Okalahoma City, or New Orleans.

So powerful was the autocratic control system Hoover developed that a whole new organizational language was created to describe it. For example, the Washington headquarters of the FBI was referred to in internal memos as the seat of government (SOG). The inspectors who operated out of this office to check on procedural violations were called goons, and they were said to be looking for subs, shorthand for substantial violations of the manuals.

All organizations operate to a greater or lesser extent like the FBI. Fear and anxiety have to be mobilized to ensure, at least to a degree, compliance with controls. In the FBI, when a SAC (special agent in charge) heard there was a "contract" out for him, he would tremble in his boots and try to get the system back on line. Many of his subordinates believed that Hoover had diabolically designed the rules to provide a justification for firing anybody, at any time.

Hoover's rules about dress were even more finicky than IBM's. Agents were expected to wear white shirts and dark ties, to wear jackets in the office, and to keep their hair short.

Hoover's written communications were known as "blue gems" because they were written in blue ink in a cryptic style. For example, Hoover wrote on one agent's file: "Give this man what he deserves." The agent was given both a letter of censure and a transfer to a post he wanted.

The only person who seems to have fazed Hoover was Robert Kennedy. As attorney general, Kennedy once summoned Hoover to his office and threw darts throughout the conversation. What really maddened Hoover was that Kennedy often missed and ripped the wall; for Hoover, this was "desecration of government property."

Accomplishments

What Hoover's managerial style tells us about organizational politics can be summarized in the following suggestions:

1. Concentrate on what is visible and viable rather than what is valuable.
2. Make sure your upward link to your superior is secure.
3. Use rules as a substitute for supervision.
4. Get the "goods" on other powerful people in competing departments.
5. Employ selective information leaks to enhance your position.
6. Endow yourself with charisma by inserting a communication buffer between yourself and subordinates.

However history may judge Hoover, he did manage to build up an extremely efficient élite corps of investigators who were incorruptible and who felt they belonged to a crack organization. The basic question remains: Was J. Edgar Hoover master or victim of the conspiracy theory?

THE ULTIMATE MACHIAVELLIANISM

The conspiracy theory, the ultimate Machiavellianism, is the belief that a few people are secretly conspiring together to accomplish a particular goal, usually the perpetration of an unlawful or wrongful act or the use of such methods to accomplish a particular purpose. The most natural way to approach the conspiracy theory is through the eyes of the chief honchos in the FBI, the NKVD, the American Secret Service, MI5, or France's Deuxieme Bureau. They have contingency plans for everything, and these plans make an ordinary citizen's sense of persecution seem almost benign.

For example, when President John F. Kennedy was assassinated in Dallas, the Secret Service put into operation two major and several minor contingency plans which made them kings for a brief period. One contingency was based on the idea that an "unknown" foreign power was putting into operation a plan to execute the president and all his successors (hence Johnson could not be sworn in quickly because he was too busy lying on the floor like a gangster under "an open contract"), and the other assumed that "they" were going to knock off all the Kennedys. This paranoia led to doctors being beaten up, a priest arriving with a relic of the cross, doctors pronouncing Kennedy

Box 15–1: A plethora of conspiracy theories

When the House Assassinations Committee issued its report in 1978 it noted that "Scientific accoustical evidence establishes a high probability that two gunmen fired at President John F. Kennedy. . . . [He] was probably assassinated as a result of a conspiracy."

What is puzzling about the committee's report is the insertion of the idea of a *probable* conspiracy. Was there indeed an incredible coincidence, or was there in fact a conspiracy. Apparently both the committee and the general public have a tremendous need to explain these tragedies and make them meaningful.

As a *New York Times* editorial of January 7, 1979, points out:

Implicitly, the report dilutes the word "conspiracy." But one should not have to be a close or sophisticated reader to understand that. It is not hard to find language that suggests, say, "two maniacs" rather than "massive plot." Considering how open the subject is to suspicion and exploitation, we wish the committee had found it.

Conspirators breed conspiracies.

alive though he was DOA, and the fear of an assassination attempt being made at the airport near Air Force One from a black limousine screaming across the field, which turned out to be Lady Bird rejoining her husband. Even the House Assassinations Committee has seriously considered conspiracies (see Box 15–1).

TOPIC 1
The political technostructure

THE CORPORATE GODFATHERS

The corporate godfathers who run the world's multinational corporations (MNCs) are the first in history to have the know-how, the adhocracies, the hardware, the finance, and the finagling fanaticism to make a credible go at acting as a sort of international Cosa Nostra in managing global affairs. Alexander the Great wept for lack of places to conquer; Napoleon met his Waterloo; Churchill presided over the dissolution of the British Empire, and the Pax Americana has had its hand bitten off by ingrates. But where they failed, today's executives may well succeed, for the sun never sets on a true MNC.

The MNCs include such companies as Xerox, IBM, ITT, Volkswagen, Fiat, Shell, 3M, General Motors, and Ford. By virtue of their size at least $100 million in annual sales), economic power, technological excellence, and international connections (operate in at least six countries, and foreign subsidiaries account for 20 percent of total assets, sales, or labor force), they have tremendous influence on the political and economic policies of host and parent countries alike.

Working through the great corporations that straddle the world, that know no boundaries and speak all tongues, but mainly the common language of capitalism, affluence, and influence, these international corporate godfathers are producing a cultural and organizational revolution. In 1971 General Motors, one of these giants, had gross annual sales of $28 billion, which exceeded the GNP of all but 14 or 15 countries. (Switzerland's GNP, for example, was $26 billion.) The top men in these corporations not only make governments tremble, but by their decisions they determine the life-styles of generations of people everywhere. In the process, Plato's idea of the nation-state has been knocked sideways.

Carl A. Gerstacker, chairman of the Dow Chemical Company, has been dreaming since 1972 of finding a neutral off-shore island, owned by no government, for his family headquarters. And as Leonard Woodstock, president of the UAW would say, "Mr. Gerstacker has put us on notice."

BUREAUCRATIC REALPOLITIK AND
THE TECHNOSTRUCTURE

The paradox par excellence is the "failure of success" thesis by which capitalism produces growth, but only at a tremendous social cost. Too many interstate highways and autos; too much booze and tobacco; too many kinds of dog food; too much cholesterol—and not enough fresh air, water, or ideas; health care; decent housing; or safe streets. How did it all come about?

Such poisons flow from the fact that the technostructure, made up of corporate oligarchs who run the bureaucracies, are now the game players in the realpolitik of the nation. The technostructure runs its organizations, public and private, neither in response to the market nor in obedience to social need, but in accordance with the rules of bureaucratic politics. For the technopoliticians, lawyers, accountants, PR men, economists, and behavioral scientists, their first loyalty is to the team. And what is good for General Motors may not necessarily be good for the country.

The "Manhattan argument" for the big corporation, which brought us the atomic bomb and got us to the moon on order and at short notice, is that the imperatives of technology require organizations large and powerful enough to plan the future, to control suppliers, and to create and manipulate markets. The argument is that, dangerous as it may be, the large corporation is the sine qua non of the postindustrial society.

But the educated public is becoming wary of thesis, which leaves large corporations free to prey on the people. The extraordinary advantages enjoyed by the IBMs, ITTs, and AT&Ts, through their control over technology, territories, tasks, finance, and minds, enables them to operate like monolithic city-states which can defy governments at their whim. The conspiracies by which they operate give them virtually untouchable power.

As Adam Smith, the economist for all seasons, pointed out in 1776 in *Wealth of Nations:* "People of the same trade seldom meet together, even for merriment and diversion, but the conversation ends in a conspiracy against the public, or in some contrivance to raise prices." Galbraith has carried Smith's line of argument into modern times to show how planning of prices, production, and preferences is built into the mature corporation's psyche, forcing it into illicit relations with all sorts of strange economic bedfellows.

Galbraith has shrewdly demonstrated, in *Economics and the Public Purpose,* how the top executives of the great corporations develop their own particular purposes which they impose on others. Predictably, production for private affluence not only has resulted in public squalor but has brought about the ruination of classical economic theory in the process.

Almost 50 years ago Harvard economist Joseph A. Schumpeter pronounced large firms to be more innovative than small firms. In *The Theory of Economic Development* Schumpeter argued that profits are the juices behind the corporate process of dynamic innovation and suggested that some degree of monopoly is an inevitable consequence of modern technology and mass production. But John M. Blair's *Economic Concentration,* based on his scholarly study of noncompetition in United States extracted from 44 volumes of Senate Anti-Trust Subcommittee hearings, argues against the simplistic notion that the large-scale enterprise is more efficient and more innovative. As often as not, large corporations seem to have a positive genius for killing innovation. The motives behind this stifling of invention can be understood through the study of corporate realpolitik.

Corporate officials are concerned with one thing only—the success of corporate officials. Their potential enemies include stockholders, regulatory commissions, tax collectors, creditors, labor unions, and customers. With such a formidable list of enemies, corporate officials do not try to maximize profits but merely to satisfice—to provide something (not too much) for everybody, just enough to keep stockholders and directors happy without bringing down the wrath of the regulatory agencies, consumer groups, or business competition upon them. They have a passion for secrecy and make a gigantic effort to protect their books and bailiwicks from the prying eyes of outsiders (a category which includes the firm's "owners," the stockholders). They know that controlling information is the key to exercising power.

The primary affirmative purpose of the corporate officials comprising the technostructure, is the growth of the firm. In fact, growth is the sine qua non of capitalism. This hunger for growth has produced an accumulation of power whereby a few hundred firms exploit the world's economy for their own purposes. Large multinational firms produce about $450 billion of the gross world product (estimated at $3 trillion) and are growing at the rate of 10 percent a year. The net result of all this economic concentration and consequent noncompetition is to make a mockery of economics theory which follows the conventional wisdom that the customer is sovereign and the corporation is subject to the state. For example, as a firm saturates a market or comes under restrictive legislation, it broadens its horizons and seeks new markets in other countries.

The mature corporations which, to use Galbraith's phrase, "completed the euthanasia of stockholder power" are very difficult for governments and economists to deal with because they can plan and operate on a global scale. This capability has undercut the U.S. (and destroyed the British) government's ability to control fiscal events.

The growth of the technostructure has had important implications for the economic system. The well-documented separation of ownership and management in many large corporations has led to the development of motivations in officials which are quite different from those of the entrepreneur. In many cases the iron law of oligarchy (see Box 15–2) is brought to bear, and there is an increasing concentration of power in the hands of a few administrators.

Box 15–2: The iron law of oligarchy

Robert Michels points out in his classic thesis, *Political Parties,* that "who says organization says oligarchy." Michels thus suggests that as organizations grow and develop, an oligarchy takes control. This organizational transformational thesis applies not only to autocratic but also to democratic organizations. It applies as much to unions as to business.

Basically the argument runs something like this: As the number of members in an organization increases, there is an inevitable increase in the number of administrators. Ultimately the effect is to concentrate power in the hands of a few people at the top of the organization.

There is abundant evidence to support the idea that the iron law of oligarchy applies also to voluntary organizations and cults. Both Jim Jones and Charles Manson, for example, managed groups in an oligarchic manner. The same oligarchical changes have been noted in the management of the social services. As social service agencies became larger and more structured they became subject to what Daniel Moynihan has called "the professionalization of reform." The hard-headed professionals are taking over from the soft-hearted amateurs, mainly because they know more about how to organize.

TOPIC 2
The conspiracy of organized medicine

A beautiful example of how organizations operate is the way the medical profession has sorted itself out. In the process of doing this, organized medicine has occasionally made its clients more ill than they need be. The phenomenon of how organized medicine functions and malfunctions has a great deal to say about organizations.

STRUCTURE: "DOCTOR WILL SEE YOU NOW"

The medical profession understands the sacred mumbojumbo of roles better than any other occupational group. In fact, the medical form of the conspiracy theory of organizations is brilliantly revealed in the medical relationship where you play patient so he or she can play doctor. Doctors take the Hippocratic oath, become shamans of a sort, and use their juju to work cures and protect people from evil and obnoxious influences.

Of course, the principal actor needs conspirators to make the magic work. A nurse says to you in the waiting room, prompting you in your role, "Doctor will see you now." Not "A doctor", not "The doctor", but "Doctor". Not the indefinite article, but the generic idea of doctor itself. It is not a doctor with whom you are meeting but the *idea* of doctor, the charismatic embodiment of the role. Only this perception of the role can declare you in-valid, dead, or even alive. So overwhelming is this charismatic role concept that even the "gods" themselves, in their conventions, are puzzling over how and when they can practice euthenasia.

Thus, doctors' work is replete with role prescriptions and proscripcope around the neck, engages in magical practices, sings incantations, induces trances, engages in exhaustive dances, and makes people practice self-torture. An elaborate and esoteric language is used which has been unconsciously designed to bamboozle the patient: cardiac infarction, coronary thrombosis, hebephrenic schizophrenia, appendectomy. Prescriptions are written in a language of ancient scientific formulas which only the pharmacist, a partner in the conspiracy, can decipher.

Thus, doctors work is replete with role prescriptions and proscriptions (dos and don'ts) which enable them to pursue the dramatic ritual of their lives. They have a full supporting cast of players, including nurses, pharmacists, specialists, and patients, who know their place and sanctify the doctors' actions (see Figure 15–1).

FIGURE 15–1
Structure of the medical profession interaction

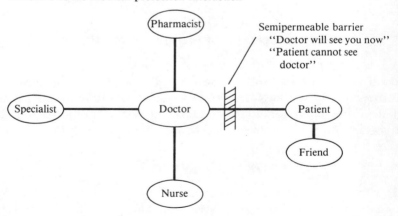

This medical conspiracy intuitively exploits the therapeutic effect of drama, which creates an image and an ambience that can objectify reality and resolve human conflicts. Any number of people can play patient at the medical center and come away exhilarated, relieved—improved by the therapy of real-life drama.

So complete is the doctor-patient conspiracy that people are beginning to wonder just how many of the so-called diseases can be organized within the categories of psychosomatic (all in the head), iatrogenic (induced by the physician), and fatal (irreversible anyway).

PROCESS: MAKING PEOPLE IN-VALID AND VALID

In the hospital a dramatic and traumatic transformation of the patient is achieved by the process of socialization. The process is so dramatic that a kind of amnesia is induced which blots out what really happened (see Figure 15–2).

FIGURE 15–2
Sequence of the
medical process

Waiting
↓
Documentation
↓
Giving samples
↓
Stripping
↓
Examination
↓
Diagnosis
↓
Visiting pharmacist
↓
Receiving medication
↓
Spontaneous cure

The dynamics of socialization, as spelled out by Edgar H. Schein of MIT, involves three steps: unfreezing, changing, and refreezing. This is what frequently happens in the hospital. The unfreezing process is facilitated by turning the person into a patient or an individual who is temporarily in-valid and therefore, subject to the sapiential authority of the physician. The patient, whose VANE now is in a state of flux, is treated. When the change process is sufficiently complete, the doctor decides that the patient is well on the way to recovery. The process of refreezing or rehabilitation is often completed elsewhere. When the doctor is satisfied, for whatever reason, the patient is discharged. The process is now complete. This process used to be eufunctional for most cases but is now increasingly dysfunctional.

Thus the physicians of our society have created elaborate, convoluted, complex organizations called hospitals which certify our diseases, usually on the basis of multiphasic screening, and prescribe cures which are often worse than the diseases. Ivan Illich, in *Medical*

Nemesis: The Expropriation of Health, has described how medical organization has turned existence into a form of organizational madness which dehumanizes people. As Illich points out:

> . . . Health care is turned into a standardized item, a staple; when all suffering is "hospitalized" and homes become inhospitable to birth, sickness and death; when the language in which people could experience their bodies is turned into bureaucratic gobbledegook; or when suffering, mourning and healing outside the patient role are labeled a form of deviance.

VALUES: THE MAGIC LAYING ON OF HANDS

In "the good old days" of medicine, 50 years ago, the presumption was not unreasonable that X dollars allocated to medicine would produce Y units of health. What happened within this framework was that patients were conditioned to reach out for more medicine than they could cope with. The truth is that modern medicine has not been particularly incrementally effective; life expectancy beyond infancy has not improved significantly in the past 100 years. What Illich is arguing for is a review and a change in the medical institutions of our society.

Organized medicine provides a good model of how organizations develop systems which serve the needs of the "powerful better" rather than the common person. The same kind of analysis and argument can be made about institutions in other domains. You can, no doubt, think of similar examples in the military, higher education, business, religious communities, and even in communes. The central truth about organizations is that they exist to support and sustain organizations. It's all a question of conspiracies. Or is it?

TOPIC 3
The Mafia: An early adhocracy

The conspiracy theory of organizations maintains that a small group of people, usually some kind of elite has gotten together to plot the destiny of the organization (and perhaps of the nation, if not the world). The Watergate transcripts provided abundant evidence that the Office of the President was organized like a fortress under a state of siege, with lists of enemies, a department of dirty tricks, intelligence units, and countersurveillance experts.

Executives found Watergate fascinating because it reminded them so much of what was going on in their own organizations. To numerous executives, organizations are groups of cliques and cabals concerned with technopolitical intrigues and conspiracies of various magnitudes. Tom Burns, a sociologist from Edinburgh University, has described how cliques and cabals emerge in industrial organizations. In "The Reference of Conduct in Small Groups: Cliques and Cabals in Occupational Milieux," Burns describes how in one firm he studied cabals drew their recruits from the Young Turks who were preoccupied with moving up the hierarchy, who were concerned with power, patronage, and prestige, and who tried to capture the support of more powerful corporate oligarchs. Cliques, on the other hand, were made up of older men who had been passed over; the "oldies" tended to select comics who could ridicule the antics of the Young Turks.

Thus organizations intuitively invent their own system of checks-

"The toughest part of this job is keeping Dad convinced that nepotism is OK."

Reprinted by permission *The Wall Street Journal*.

and-balances to keep conspiracies within limits. These Mafia-like families rarely engage in out-and-out war but prefer to settle their conflicts by the use of side payments. This avoidance of internecine (between the nephews) conflict is not always possible, or even indeed desirable. The Mafia is the best model in modern times of how organizational internecine conflicts are regulated where the costs are low and the prices are high.

THE STRUCTURE: FAMILY CLAN AND BUREAUCRACY

The Mafia, with its structure of godfather, capos, consiglieres, buttonmen, and soldiers organized into families, seems a cross between a military bureaucracy and a Highland clan (see Figure 15–3). But, in

FIGURE 15–3
Organization table for the Cosa Nostra

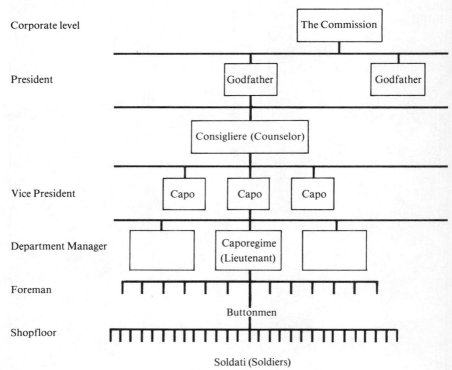

fact, it is more of an example of an early adhocracy, in which there is a small number of key posts with tenure, but the capability to call up "soldiers" as a kind of militia when the going gets rough. For example, the Gambino family in New York is said to have 900 members; the Genovese family, headed by Frank "Funzi" Tieri, is believed to have 600 members.

The family don, who is something more than a company president but less than a ruling monarch, runs a tight, businesslike shop controlled by careful accountancy procedures. But it is an organization which would be the envy of the military with a low tail-to-teeth ratio. The don has one single staff officer, the consigliere, who passes on the instructions for action and acts as an information buffer to isolate him from "the others." And, of course, the Mafia answer to "buy or make" is to subcontract out.

Putting out "the contract" gives a good insight into how the organization socializes its new members by requiring them to earn their "bones" by knocking off an enemy of the family. Such killings are, of course, a mark of inefficiency and reveal a failure to use the regular channels of the organization. With their well-defined areas of jurisdiction (you might think rivers and railways were invented as markers for the Mafia), these channels specify lines of command and built-in appeal systems. With a supportive value system, they maintain good order and discipline.

La Cosa Nostra (Our Affair), the core of organized crime, is made up of approximately 5,000 people throughout the United States who are organized in 24 families, each headed by a godfather who organizes his gang along military lines. To control competition among families, the Mafia has set up a loose confederation under a board of directors called the Commission. But the Mafia employs other ethnic groups. In many respects, according to Ralph Salerno, who was the New York City Police Department's chief Mafia expert until his retirement in 1967, the leadership has always been a "happy marriage of Italians and Jews." In an article in *Time* magazine (August 22, 1969), Salerno was quoted as saying: "It's the three M's—moxie, muscle, and money. The Jews provide the moxie, the Italians provide the muscle, and they both provide the money."

The same article in *Time* describes the size of the Mafia graphically:

> In money terms, the organization is the world's largest business. The best estimate of its revenue, a rough projection based on admittedly inexact information of federal agencies, is well over $30 billion a year. Even using a conservative figure, its annual profits are at least in the $7 billion to $10 billion range. Though he meant it as a boast, Meyer Lansky, the gang's leading financial wizard, was actually being overly modest when he chortled in 1966: "We're bigger than US Steel." Measured in terms of profits, Cosa Nostra and affiliates are as big as US Steel, the American Telephone and Telegraph Company, General Motors, Standard Oil of New Jersey, General Electric, Ford Motor Company, IBM, Chrysler and RCA put together.

THE PROCESS: IT'S ONLY BUSINESS

Francis Ford Coppola made a brilliant movie out of Mario Puzo's *The Godfather,* an intriguing saga of intrigue and violence in the Corleone family, a Mafia gang, set in postwar New York. *The Godfather* was such an attractive proposition for TV that NBC realized $6.2 million in advertising income from the first showing. Don Corleone, masterfully played by Marlon Brando, exercises power ("I'll make him an offer he can't refuse") with great distinction and discretion through his consigliere, who in turn passes the information on to the caporegime (capo), a kind of criminal vice president. (See Figure 15–4 for a brief outline of the Mafia scenario.)

FIGURE 15–4
The Mafia scenario

AIM	METHOD
Phase I—entrepreneurial	
Determine which business you are in—drugs, gambling, prostitution, numbers, unions, protection.	Buy over or corrupt local "pols" and put police on the take.
Select a pilot area for new product.	Show power by removing local gangs. Select someone big and "make him an offer he can't refuse".
Introduce new product on a larger scale.	Give local agents a good discount; stress advantages of high volume business.
Phase II—dealing with the competition	
Dig in and consolidate.	Call up buttonmen and soldiers to meet the competition.
Eliminate the "odd" godfather and a few capos of the competing family.	Bring into action some hidden force, such as a legal cop no one expects, involving clever use of deception.
Go into a state of siege.	Take to "the mattresses" and fight it out.
Phase III—signing the peace treaty	
Get the other godfather to sue for peace.	Do something really vicious, like execute his son or take him hostage.
Sign the peace.	Call the commission together to regulate the dispute and swear on *your* honor.
Phase IV	
Exploit the market.	Introduce strict budgetary control, production planning and control, proper bookkeeping.
Phase V	
Diversify into legal businesses—wholesale foods, entertainment, hotels, etc.	Buy hotels in Vegas or Florida.

Everything is done in a businesslike way; business school professors allege that the families send their bright sons to graduate school to get MBAs. And in *The Godfather* Michael, played by Al Pacino, is a decorated officer in the Marines, who has just come back from the Pacific.

VALUES: UNITED BY OATH AND BLOOD

It is the organization's code of conduct which sets it apart in a behavioral sense. Whatever outsiders may think, the Mafia people live by a code of manliness, honor, and willingness to keep secrets which is valid for them. It is the code of an ethnic trade union which is legitimate for its constituency because the members cannot get legal justice. It is a code which has never changed, and the penalty for violation is death.

FIGURE 15–5
Structure, process, and values of the Mafia

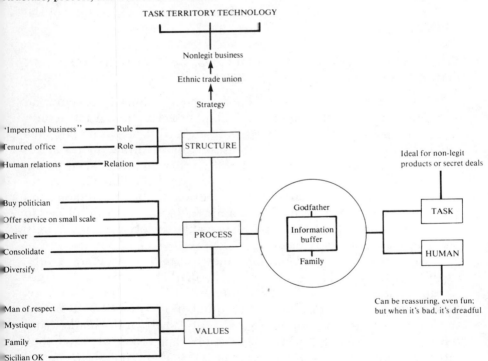

When a recruit joins the Mafia he is put through an elaborate Masonic-like ritual to socialize him to the family. The *Time* article cited above describes this ritual:

Flanked by the boss and his lieutenants, the initiate and his sponsor may stand in front of a table on which are placed a gun and, on occasion, a knife. The boss picks up the gun and intones in the Sicilian dialect: *"Niatri representam La Cosa Nostra. Sta famigglia è La Cosa Nostra* (We represent La Cosa Nostra. This family is Our Thing)." The sponsor then pricks his trigger finger and the trigger finger of the new member, holding both together to symbolize the mixing of blood. After swearing to hold the family above his religion, his country, and his wife and children, the inductee finishes the ritual. A picture of a saint or a religious card is placed in his cupped hands and ignited. As the paper burns, the inductee, together with his sponsor, proclaims: "If I ever violate this oath, may I burn as this paper."

Mafia trials do not make use of a judge or a jury but are democratic in general principle. After hearing both the prosecution and the defense, each family member present is given two pieces of paper, one marked with an *M* for morte(death) and the other with an *N* for no. After the vote is taken the sentence is either carried out forthwith, or there are handshakes all round.

Figure 15–5 summarizes the structure, process, and values of the Mafia organization.

THE MAFIA MESSAGE: EXPLOITING A WEAKNESS TO FORM A STRATEGY AND A STRUCTURE

What can the executive learn from the Mafia? Primarily, recognition of the need to think through the relation between strategy, structure, and effectiveness. The Mafia starts from an acceptance of its people's social disadvantage; a Wasp society is unlikely to allow poor, uneducated immigrants from Sicily any significant part in the legal corporate system. But such ethnic exclusion has pushed Sicilian families together, encouraging them to develop cohesion, mobilize paranoia, and keep their values distinct. Such an ethnic trade union is well placed to provide the illicit services that a respectable society cannot publicly provide but so earnestly desires.

Once they decide what business they are in, the structure is relatively easy to define. In macro terms, the market is structured according to territory, task (drugs, sex, numbers, booze), and technology. Economically a kind of oligopolist's quiet life is pursued; to be too successful in terms of profitability, visibility, share of the market, and return on investment could be extremely dangerous. In brief they satisfice, taking just a little more than they need, enough to pay off investors (godfathers, government officials, police, political parties, etc.), but not the maximum, which would bring down the wrath of the government.

In micro terms, the structure is a small adhocracy with a small number of tenured people but with a large number of available reservists. The structure is an odd but effective mixture of family and military organization. The rule (loyalty), the role (office tenure for life), and the relation (human relations—family) together achieve a dialectical fusion of opposites which can be best understood in terms of its values.

The process involves people and things. The Mafia rivals the Marines in the effort it devotes to recruitment, selection, socialization, and separation. Conflict revolution is clearly defined with a built-in appeals system.

The values emphasize machismo, family honor, mystery, paternalism, and "business is impersonal". But legitimacy (a sense of being right) is maintained.

TOPIC 4
What every manager should know about conspiracy theory

CONSPIRACY AND PLURALISM

Figure 15–6 is the contingency model of the political organization as a system. In summarizing the conspiracy theory as it applies to organizations, it is necessary first to distinguish between conspiracy theory and pluralism (see Figure 15–7).

In *conspiracy theory:*

1. The organizational world is controlled by a few people who move in the same world, use the same clubs, live in the same suburbs, went to the same private schools, and so on.
2. They exercise diabolical, Machiavellian power. They pull strings and people jump, or their heads fall off.
3. The world can be divided into godfathers, dons, and capos, territories, tasks, and technologies.

In *pluralism:*

1. The world is not monolithic. A number of institutions exist that interact, cooperate, and come into conflict. One institution can control (or fool) all of the people some of the time and some people all of the time, but not all of the people all of the time.
2. Events are not completely predictable.
3. Different institutions come on top at different times. For example, the unions may be on top at one time, but this situation changes.
4. The communications media (TV, the newspapers) can upset the balance of power.

FIGURE 15–6
The political organization as a system

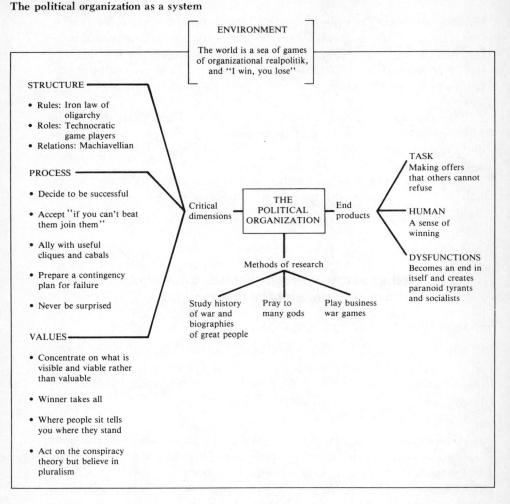

ENVIRONMENT

The world is a sea of games
of organizational realpolitik,
and "I win, you lose"

STRUCTURE

• Rules: Iron law of
    oligarchy
• Roles: Technocratic
    game players
• Relations: Machiavellian

PROCESS

• Decide to be successful

• Accept "if you can't beat
    them join them"

• Ally with useful
    cliques and cabals

• Prepare a contingency
    plan for failure

• Never be surprised

VALUES

• Concentrate on what is
    visible and viable rather
    than valuable

• Winner takes all

• Where people sit tells
    you where they stand

• Act on the conspiracy
    theory but believe in
    pluralism

Critical dimensions

THE
POLITICAL
ORGANIZATION

End products

TASK
Making offers
that others cannot
refuse

HUMAN
A sense of
winning

DYSFUNCTIONS
Becomes an end in
itself and creates
paranoid tyrants
and socialists

Methods of research

Study history
of war and
biographies
of great people

Pray to
many gods

Play business
war games

FIGURE 15–7
Comparison of conspiracy theory and pluralism

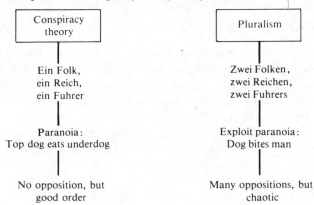

Conspiracy
theory

Ein Folk,
ein Reich,
ein Fuhrer

Paranoia:
Top dog eats underdog

No opposition, but
good order

Pluralism

Zwei Folken,
zwei Reichen,
zwei Fuhrers

Exploit paranoia:
Dog bites man

Many oppositions, but
chaotic

CONSPIRE OR EXPIRE

Why do many managers believe in the conspiracy theory of organizations, equating the real world with *The Manchurian Candidate* or *The Godfather* or *Chinatown?* Part of the answer is that life is like that. There are real companies who plot the downfall of other organizations and institutions by devious means which capture the popular imagination and terrify both sets of managers, friend and foe. The justified paranoia of these managers forces them in their self-interest to act as if things might get worse, which lends the whole thing a quality of self-fulfilling prophecy.

The most famous mindless and irresponsible conspiracy was Watergate, with a plot full of holes (because of incompetence) and glib cynicism. What made Watergate so interesting was its abrasive quality—a mixture of unction, horror, and comedy.

The critical paradox of Watergate was that the conspirators were just ordinary middle-class people who sometimes behaved like thugs and other times like clowns or buffoons. They were mostly just pedestrian poltroons who pulled switches, fixed meetings and expenses, "papered files," and "deep-sixed" documents, but the end effect was that they had to be treated like dangerous madmen.

There comes a time where madness has to be met with madness, craziness with craziness, complexity with complexity, diabólism with diabolism, as was noted in the discussion of Watergate in Chapter 14. People find the conspiracy theory of organizations comforting partly because it makes meaningful a senseless, chaotic, purposeless world. Instead of believing that Adolph Hitler was a rather good artist who loved the movie *Gone with the Wind,* valued respectability, was a brilliant propagandist, tactician, and bluffer, and had a fantastic head for technical data, most people prefer to believe the simple scenario that assigns him the role of the chief madman of the 20th century. All the data on Hitler cannot be fitted together. But assigning him functional paranoia was justified, for it freed us from our guilt and our anxiety and enabled us to meet pathology with pathology, to send our psychopaths against his psychopaths.

War, corporate or international, is too important to be left to the generals or even the godfathers. War of any sort may be only an extension of politics (or politics by any other means), but it is still only an extension. Our job is to recognize the script, figure out the roles, watch the action, and keep the place. Conspire or expire.

REVIEW AND RESEARCH

1. Why is there such a strong and widespread desire to establish that President John F. Kennedy's assassination was the result of a conspiracy?

2. Why do some MNC executives wish to move to some offshore island?
3. Why is Adam Smith an economist for all times?
4. Why does the iron law of oligarchy apply to democratic organizations?
5. Can the conspiracy of organized medicine be broken? How?
6. Why are modern organizations organized like the Mafia?
7. Why do so many people believe in the conspiracy theory?

GLOSSARY OF TERMS

Conspiracy theory. The belief that one person, group, or party controls every-thing. Conspiracy theory is very useful to underdogs because it allows them to license their paranoia.

Iron Law of Oligarchy. Maintains that all organizations end up as dictator-ships, with the top dogs running everything—even if the organization is meant to be democratic (e.g., a trade union or university).

Pluralism. The view that a number of parties or organizations control society. If one party is dominant, it will not be so forever. Pluralism is the pre-ferred belief of top dogs.

Technostructure. The small group of executives who have the necessary technical and analytical skills to manage organizations.

DEBATE: The FBI versus the Mafia

Question: Why can neither side win completely?
Hints:

1. Reread sections in the chapter dealing with the FBI and the Mafia.
2. Would it be wholly desirable for one side to win?
3. Why does the franchise of crime pass from one ethnic group to another?

INCIDENT

Jim Jones and the People's Temple

One of the most puzzling phenomena psychologists have sought to explain is the suicide cult, such as Jim Jones and his People's Temple disciples. At Jones's urging, 913 men, women, and children died by poison in late 1978 to forestall the consequences of an investigation by a U.S. congressman and the media into their experiment in communal living in the Guyana jungle.

A rash of books has tried to tell the inside story of the People's Temple and the massacre in Guyana, but it remains a mystery. Most of these books give an account of Jones's rise from Middle West obscurity to California prominence. He is shown as a master manipulator, a political boss, or a tyrant who bound his subjects to him by confession and blackmail and changed faces to attract different types of followers.

Psychologists have noted that when a cult group finds its belief systems threatened, it may well retreat into the desert in search of isolation. When a group feels that its belief system is no longer generally shared or, at a minimum, respected, dramatic changes begin to happen. In these circumstances the charismatic leader assumes a messianic role.

Comparisons can be made with the cargo cults of New Guinea and Melanesia. In these Pacific societies, when a Christian missionary arrived and persuaded the island's residents that their religion and way of life were inferior to civilized ways, new cults emerged which blended Christianity and native concepts. The most dramatic instances revolved around the notion held by the islanders that God was labeling crates of cargo for delivery from the sky to the Melanesians, but the Europeans were intercepting the shipments. To get ready for the millenium when the cargo would reach its rightful destination, the Melanesians built airfields and warehouses.

In many respects the People's Temple fit into the same category. Like the Melanesian cargo cults, Jones's cult came to prominence in the upheavals of the 1970s when people were experiencing economic and social disintegration. Many of its members, the old, the poor, and the black, felt powerless and alienated in modern America. Jones developed a leadership style which combined Bible Belt preaching with revolutionary rhetoric.

Questions

1. How was the People's Temple organized?
2. Do you know of other institutions organized along similar lines?

DIAGRAM SUMMARY OF CHAPTER 16

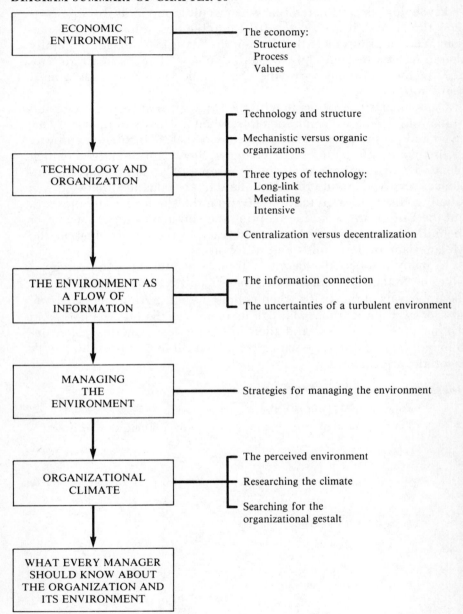

ECONOMIC
ENVIRONMENT

The economy:
  Structure
  Process
  Values

TECHNOLOGY AND
ORGANIZATION

Technology and structure

Mechanistic versus organic
organizations

Three types of technology:
  Long-link
  Mediating
  Intensive

Centralization versus decentralization

THE ENVIRONMENT AS
A FLOW OF
INFORMATION

The information connection

The uncertainties of a turbulent environment

MANAGING
THE
ENVIRONMENT

Strategies for managing the environment

ORGANIZATIONAL
CLIMATE

The perceived environment

Researching the climate

Searching for the
organizational gestalt

WHAT EVERY MANAGER
SHOULD KNOW ABOUT
THE ORGANIZATION AND
ITS ENVIRONMENT

16

The organization and its environment

WINNING AND LOSING: TEXAS INSTRUMENTS

An excellent example of a company struggling with growing pains is Texas Instruments, which has been to the electronics industry what General Motors is to the automobile market. While TI rules the market in pocket calculators and digital watches, however, it has fumbled in minicomputers and microprocessors.

Peter Schuyter described the firm's organizational history in "Winning and Losing at Texas Instruments":

> "T.I. is like a beautiful woman who is past her prime," says a competitor, W. J. Sanders 3d, chairman of Advanced Micro Devices Inc. And Thomas H. Mack, an analyst who follows the semiconductor industry for Paine Webber, Mitchell, Hutchins says: "Texas Instruments is a structured, systematic organization, but it often lacks the insight to react to fast-changing market conditions. They run well in a straight line, but they are not so good on the curves."
>
> T.I. understandably, sees things differently. "We do stub our toe occasionally," says chief executive J. Fred Bucy, "But we are quick to recover."
>
> Much of the company's considerable success to date stems from unrelenting attention to productivity, using such devises as robot arms and computerized assembly systems to crank out its products at lower and lower cost. Its dedication to automation has enabled Texas Instruments to gain market share by driving down prices to levels its competitors cannot match.
>
> A visitor to the company is likely to come away thinking he has spent a hitch aboard a spit-and-polish battleship. The desks are bare and the floors polished linoleum. From one low-slung glass-and-concrete facility

to another, whether in Dallas, Lubbock, Austin, or Nice, France, T.I.'s buildings look the same. The workers, from Fred Bucy on down, usually wear conservative, white shirts, with security passes clipped to their pockets—a striking contrast to the informal, low-key world of the high technology companies that populate California's "Silicon Valley." Then, too, managers talk with evangelistic zeal about the company's O.S.T. (for objectives, strategy and tactics) system, T.I.'s version of management by objective.

DEFINING THE ENVIRONMENT

To understand what is happening to Texas Instruments, we have to embark on an escalation in our study of organizational behavior. We have looked at the individual, hopefully grasped something of the complexities of personality, and puzzled over the mysteries of motivation theory. We have considered the working group as a web of structure, process, and values that is a microcosm on its own. But we have found that there are worlds of groups outside the working group, and the way the intra- and intergroup realpolitik is managed is the essence of the organizational approach to leadership.

Now all of these escalations, from the individual to the working group and from the group to the organization as a group of groups, serve mainly as stepping stones for the final escalation. To take this last step, it is necessary to accept that there is something outside the organization called the environment; that the organization and the environment interact; and that the environment is made up of other organizations.

Organizations are open systems which trade with their environments—importing materials, energy, information, and people; transforming them; and exporting them into the environment with value added. But unless we can relate such a statement to the tough, complex realities, unless we can get a handle on the environmental forces—political, economic, legal, technological, and ecological—that impinge on an organization, then something vital will have been left out of the analysis.

The characteristics of the environment

A major theoretical exercise—a somewhat baffling one—in organizational behavior is to find a category system to define the characteristics of the environment. It is usual to begin this analysis by differentiating between the internal and external environments, as shown in Figure 16–1. The internal environment is determined by the organization's programming, technical, and personnel forces affecting decision making. The external environment has two elements, the immediate and

FIGURE 16–1
The organization's internal and external environments

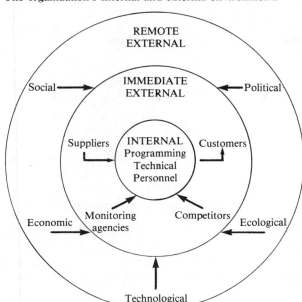

the remote. The immediate element consists of forces arising from interactions with customers, suppliers (material, equipment, cash, capital, energy, people, and information), competitors, and monitoring agencies (trade unions, professional associations, trade associations, consumer groups, political and religious groups, government agencies, the Mafia, and so on). The remote element, which may be the more important, consists of the social, economic, political, technological, and ecological forces that affect or may affect the organization.

From research we know a good deal about how organizations work in terms of the management of groups as cliques, cabals, and coalitions. We know how they work by rules of satisficing—taking just a little more than they need, enough to keep stockholders and boards of directors happy, but not the maximum, which would bring down the wrath of the government and consumers. We know how side payments are arranged for the groups that lose out ("you never know, you might need them again"). We know something (not as much as we would like) about how internecine strife is regulated. But what is rather unclear is how the organization manages its environment. To get into this subject, we will look at the economic environment.

What role do profits play? Traditional economic theory has it that profits are the carrots that induce enterpreneurs to endure uncertainty and engage in dynamic innovation—new products, new marketing concepts, and new technology. Tradition also says that competition should keep corporate gains like International Business Machines, Xerox, and General Motors from monopolizing the market. But the modern approach, as expounded by John Kenneth Galbraith, sees economics as a branch of politics—the "dismal science" is nothing less than the study of corporate realpolitik. The great corporations develop their own peculiar purposes, which they impose on lesser corporations. But being too successful in terms of profitability, share of the market, and return on investment can be extremely dangerous. Most large American corporations have learned this lesson and have shown a strong desire for the monopolist's or oligopolist's "quiet life."

TOPIC 1
The economic environment

While other economic systems (socialist and communist) may be of interest, for North Americans the economic environment is the modified capitalism which has developed and evolved on our continent. We will consider this environment in terms of its structure, process, and value elements.

THE ECONOMY

The "failure of success" paradox in the Western economic environment, whereby the capitalist system produces growth, but only at a tremendous price, was noted in Chapter 15. As Galbraith pointed out in *The Affluent Society*, it was growth via production for private affluence that brought public squalor. To pursue the question of how the parochial interests of the technostructure took precedence over the interests of most North Americans (more so in Canada than in the United States, because of the branch plant economy mentality), it is necessary to examine the changes in the structure of the economy, its processes, and the values by which it is governed.

Structure

The structure of the American economy consists of a relatively small number of extremely large organizations and a very large number of extremely small ones. The large firms account for a disproportionate share of employment, output, and investment; in many industries one or a few large firms completely dominate. In 1968, the 200 biggest held 60 percent of manufacturing assets, up from 45 percent at the end of World War II.

Process

Economists like Galbraith, and the general public, have largely rejected the argument that advanced technology requires mammoth corporations powerful enough to control production, finance, markets, and minds. Usually, in fact, the multinational corporation can operate through influence in government rather than directly through the marketplace; such corporations function like governments. To understand this point better, it is necessary to look further into the subject of economics.

Economics comes in two sizes, macro and micro. Macroeconomics is concerned with national income, investment, savings, and interest rate changes, and it should be able to make predictions about the size of the gross national product and its component elements. As often as not such predictions are seriously in error, however, because microeconomics, which is concerned with how firms fix prices and make a buck, has little to do with the dismal science of economics, but everything to do with politics and the psychology of power.

Classical economics emphasized the manner in which competition allocated resources in an objective and efficient manner. Free enterprise has been a mainstay of our social and economic thought, and much political and economic exhortation has been delivered against any interference with free competition. However, unfettered competition led to such violent fluctuations in business activity that the ability of the firm to carry out technological development was seriously impaired, as was the reputation of the capitalist system. This led to an acceptance of planning as a valid alternative to the free play of short-term market forces. In different countries macroeconomic planning is carried out with varying levels of governmental participation and influence. Although in the United States, government planning is still not consciously accepted, its development and the development of private corporate planning has reached a very high stage. It is curious—and unfortunate—that this fact has largely escaped general notice, so that a greal deal of rhetoric is still couched in archaic free-enterprise terms. The economic literacy of vast numbers of Americans remains at the lemonade-stand level in the midst of space-age technology.

Galbraith describes the main function of planning as the replacement of unreliable market forces. This can involve vertical integration to assure the supply of customers, control over the market by virtue of relative size, and long-term contracts, and the use of advertising and marketing policies to ensure suitable levels of demand. Essential to this approach is the use of a pricing policy which, unlike classical ones, is concerned not with profit maximization but with long-term stability and growth. A. D. Kaplan and others lend support to the theory that pricing is based more on a firm's cost structure and production goals than on market forces. Prices should be low enough to attract new customers but high enough to generate reasonable profits. Stability, discouragement of competitors, and social acceptability are also important factors. While it is true that the market is an information system registering customers' tastes and ability to spend, it is also an open system into which the firm can make inputs that will significantly affect the outcomes.

Values

The separation of ownership and management has led to significant changes in the motives of business leaders. The drive for maximum profits has diminished as salary payment has become the major means of compensating management. The relative affluence enjoyed by most workers has to some extent reduced the significance of pay as a motivation for work; and, as the level of sophistication of the technostructure has increased and the variety of job opportunities has gone up, the effectiveness of compulsion as a motivating force has diminished.

The corporation has ceased to be the rapacious exploiter of both its employees and the public that it has previously been considered to be. On the other hand, we have only begun to assess the "prices" that both corporate growth and affluent consumption have exacted in ecological pollution, dwindling natural resources, and similar areas. The current interest in issues like overpopulation conservation signals at least an examination of values such as "growth is always good." With the darkening clouds of a visible energy crisis, our economic values may well have to change from those of children turned loose in a candy store.

The technostructure has diffused power and lent new importance to the utilization of each individual's abilities. This has required adaptation of corporate goals to identify with those of its individual members as well as that of society in general. The concern for efficiency has made it an article of faith to permit the expert to do a job with a minimum of interference. In Jean-Jacques Servan-Schreiber's words, "this wager on man is the origin of America's new dynamism." In *The American Challenge,* he contrasts the American willingness to trust human nature with the French fear of delegation and remarks on the debilitating effect on economic effort of his country's centralized controls.

The desire of managers in the technostructure to do their jobs to the best of their ability without interference affects the economic goals which are set. Stable and growing profits are sought to avoid confrontations with shareholders, while restraint in pricing is practised to avoid public conflict and the threat of government interference.

TOPIC 2
Technology and organization

The rapid rate of technological change has left most people in the new industrial state more than a little breathless. For most people, technology has become a threat rather than a challenge. Just as many people have stereotypes about foreigners, in thinking about organizations many managers talk about structure as if all organizations were arranged the same way. For many, the model they carry around in their heads is a composite made up partly of the organization of an infantry division and partly of what General Motors looked like in the 1930s. In fact, as modern research has shown, technology and structure are very closely interlocked.

How can technology be defined? Joan Woodward, of the Imperial College of Science and Technology in London, notes in "Industrial Behaviour—Is There a Science?":

> One variable which it is possible to isolate, and which may prove to be the most important single determinant of industrial behavior, is technology. Technology has been defined by some American sociologists, in particular Dubin, by dividing it into two major phases—firstly, the tools, instruments, machines, plant or technical formula basic to the performance of the work, and secondly, the body of ideas which express the goals of the work, its functional importance and the rationale of the methods employed.

TECHNOLOGY AND STRUCTURE:
THE WOODWARD STUDIES

A central problem in the development of a comprehensive organization theory is to determine in what ways particular types of technology constrain organizational structures. As a first step in this direction it is necessary to produce a classification of technology. Woodward tackled this problem in an extensive study of 100 industrial firms in the south of England. She divided the firms surveyed into three categories according to their technology. The three main groups were (1) firms that produced units or small batches, generally to the customers' individual orders; (2) large-batch and mass-production firms; and (3) firms producing on a continuous process basis. Using the data collected in this brilliant research, Woodward and her research associates were able to demonstrate a clear relation between level of technology and a number of organization factors, as described in "Industrial Behaviour—Is There a Science?":

> Among the organizational characteristics showing a direct relationship with technical advance were: the length of the line of command; the

span of control of the chief executive; the percentage of total turnover allocated to the payment of wages and salaries, and the ratios of managers to total personnel, of clerical and administrative staff to manual workers, of direct to indirect labour, and of graduate to non-graduate supervision in production departments. . . .

My own work in south Essex demonstrated the closeness of the link between technology and industrial behavior at both management and operator levels. It showed, too, that the most intractable problems of organization and industrial relations seemed to occur in two types of production—batch production and line production based on the assembly of components. It also suggested that organizational and behavioural patterns are as much more consistent at what might be called the extremes of the technical scale, in unit production and process industry, than they are in these middle ranges. Variations in behaviour observed in the batch production area appeared to be related to the procedures used to rationalize production and to predict results.

For example, the number of levels of management in direct production departments increased with technical advance, process plants having the longest lines. Woodward's empirical analysis of the actual number of hierarchical levels in an industrial organization makes the claim of management theorists that there are n levels (usually five), and only n levels, in the ideal organization look naive.

The span-of-control concept did not stand up any better to rigorous investigation. Technical factors also seemed to explain the wide variations in the span of control of chief executives, the people responsible to the policy-forming body for the conduct of their firm's business. In unit production firms the number of people directly responsible to the chief executive ranged from 2 to 9, the median being 4; in large-batch and mass-production firms the range was from 4 to 13, the median being 7; and in process production firms the range was from 5 to 19, the median being 10.

MECHANISTIC VERSUS ORGANIC ORGANIZATIONS

Contrary to the views of early theorists, it is not possible to establish universal structures and laws which are valid irrespective of matters of technology. The classicists, such as Max Weber and Lyndall Urwick, drawing heavily on their experience of early 20th-century technology and organization and taking intellectual sustenance from Frederick W. Taylor's notions of scientific management—recommended that work be divided according to function (for example, sales, production, maintenance, personnel). For them the central issues were the span of control, unity of command, and the need for a sharp division between line and staff.

In modern terms such organizations would be described as mechanistic, following the well-known classification system developed by Tom Burns and G. M. Stalker in *The Management of Innovation.* They identify two systems of management operation: the mechanistic, which is appropriate to relatively stable conditions and has all the characteristics of the classical pattern; and the organic, which is more appropriate to an environment of dynamic change and innovation such as is found in science-based industries like electronics, and aerospace. (see Figure 16–2.)

In a careful study of Scottish firms which were interested in entering the electronics field, Burns and Stalker were able to illuminate the problems of switching from a mechanistic to an organic system of management. The unstructured and highly dynamic environment of the organic system often created widespread anxiety and insecurity

FIGURE 16–2
The mechanistic versus the organic organization

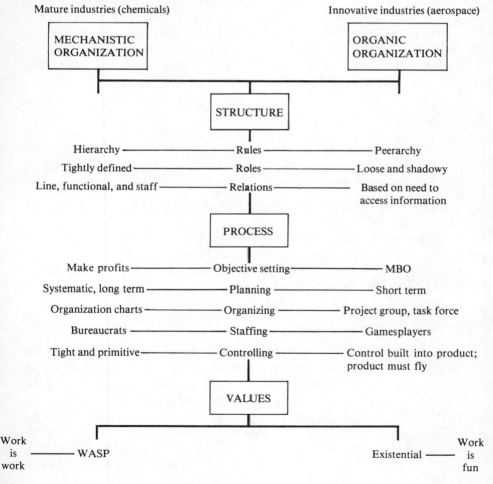

among the "rear mirror driving" old-style managers, whose whole political and status system was threatened. In just such circumstances, the high ground for power is the control of some scarce resource, which in this case turned out to be technical information. And thus organizational fire fights broke out between laboratory groups (research, development design) and production and sales groups.

The organic system, which is much more market oriented, recruits development engineers for sales liaison, avoids jurisdictional disputes (both by not having rigid product divisions and by appointing liaison managers who can bridge departmental boundaries), and above all regards the market as a source of design idea.

THREE TYPES OF TECHNOLOGY

Changing technology and structure have increased the need for most business firms to operate as open systems, interacting with their environment and modifying their strategies and structure to fit particular needs. One function of the managerial technostructure is to plan for orderly growth of the organization by reducing uncertainty.

James Thompson, in *Organizations in Action,* identifies three types of technology:

1. *Long link.* Involves a series of interdependent actions, as in an automobile assembly line.
2. *Mediating.* Links clients who wish to become interdependent, like the savers and borrowers in a bank.
3. *Intensive.* Selects, combines, and applies techniques based on feedback from the object itself; for example, a hospital.

Each type of organization tries to reduce the uncertainty in its environment by different means.

Firms with a long-link technology will attempt vertical integration to ensure that the supplies and markets required by the core technology are available. Steel mills, aluminum companies, and auto makers offer examples of this type of activity.

Vertical integration

A good example of vertical integration is provided in a study of the petroleum industry in the United States, which is dominated by 18 large firms (the "majors") which produce about 70 percent of the domestic crude oil, control some 80 percent of the refinery capacity, and market about 72 percent of the gasoline sold in the United States. Vertical integration, which is standard for the majors, means that the company operates in every phase of the business, including exploration and production, transportation, refining, distribution, and marketing. Not content with the gigantic advantage of vertical integration, most of the majors work hand in glove with one another—where one is marginal in one function (say refining crude) or one area, another major will carry the function for a favor elsewhere. The fuel shortage beginning in late 1973 may well have been engineered by the majors before the Organization of Petroleum Exporting Countries (OPEC) got into the act. The suspicion of the Federal Trade Commission is that some of the majors did conspire to maintain and reinforce a noncompetitive market structure in the refining of crude oil into petroleum products.

Thompson notes that there are limits to integration based on the extent to which the factors surrounding the main mission fan out. The producer of a widely used raw material (such as steel or many basic chemicals) cannot capture a significant part of the market and put it under its control. The use of long-term sales contracts is a method for dealing with such uncertainties.

Horizontal integration

Firms with a mediating technology try to reduce uncertainty by increasing the population they serve. The enormous growth in chain stores and bank branches indicates the widespread desire of the competing firms to ensure that they will not run into difficulties by being overly dependent on one section of the market. McDonald's, a good example of mediating technology, has shown the way forward in market penetration in the fast-food industry.

Firms with intensive technology will try to incorporate the object worked on into their domain. Perhaps the most typical example of this is the military-industrial complex in the United States, where the lines between supplier and customer become very blurred.

CENTRALIZATION VERSUS DECENTRALIZATION

Companies also try to reduce uncertainty by less legitimate means. Certain methods of market control such as price fixing or collusion are not acceptable, even if they do not result in higher markups than would be achieved in other, less unruly competitive environments, by quieter methods.

At the heart of such industrywide efforts are the issues of centralization and decentralization in organizational structure. Growth and diversification provide financial strength to withstand unexpected problems and stabilize earnings by increasing the range of markets served. They also provide an outlet for increases in capacity or technological capability resulting from changes in the environment for the firm's basic activity. A. D. Chandler describes how the growth of DuPont into a chemical giant was to a considerable extent the result of a desire to use surplus plant capacity or to apply research discoveries made in an unrelated field.

The growth of business enterprise and the increasing variety of activities undertaken by some firms has increased interest in the study of appropriate organizational structures and technologies.

Companies with highly interdependent parts operating unified technologies find the centralized organization structure to be most appropriate. Vertical integration leads to units whose operations are different in many respects but touch at those points where the outputs of one unit become the inputs of the other. Such firms can decentralize management, but each unit must adhere carefully to a plan which integrates all of the input-output variables. Those companies whose technologies are highly diversified and independent of one another have a problem maintaining a valid basis of organizational control, which accounts for some waning in the enthusiasm for conglomerates. It is obvious that central management in such firms cannot assume the passive role thrust upon most shareholders today, since the rationale for the existence of the organization would then be more questionable. The development of task teams of specialists to provide expertise to the different parts of the organization may be a way of utilizing the resources of the larger organization.

The growing complexity of the organization structure, the need for frequent interaction with many levels of the environment, the continuous need for technical innovation, and the sophistication and high educational level of the technostructure are creating a need for administrative procedures that are different from the old standardized bureaucracy. Information—its collection, processing, distribution, and suppression—lies behind these new procedures and is becoming a critically important aspect of the successful operation of business organizations.

TOPIC 3
The environment as a flow of information

All organizations are open to environmental influences, though obviously some are more open than others. And, of course, some degree of closedness in terms of boundary maintenance (usually maintained by gatekeepers, who are agents of the system's power structure) is necessary to maintain the system's identity. While early theorists treated organizations as closed systems, where the prime problem was the transformation of inputs into outputs, the modern approach is to treat the organization as an open system which interacts with its environment. An excellent example of this approach is the Lawrence and Lorsch contingency theory of organization described below, in which environmental uncertainty is the major independent variable. In such a model, the understanding and control of information is the principal means to reduce uncertainty.

The open systems theorist conceptualizes the environment in informational terms and sees it as a source of both threats and opportunities arising from other organizations. This interconnectedness is what F. E. Emery and E. L. Trist call the "causal texture of organizational environment," which almost invariably turns out to be enormously complex. This discussion treats the environment as a flow of information. Since the environment contains a surfeit of information, the organization's objective is seen as to search for, collect, process, and disseminate only as much of it as it needs to maintain its viability.

Organizations, of necessity, evoke elaborate, complex, complicated informational strategies for bringing the data about their environments under control. Elaborate intelligence apparatuses are created to engage not only in such systematic "rifle" techniques as market research, technological forecasting, analysis of government action, and evaluation of competitors' performance, but also in such "shotgun" techniques as reading newspapers, journals, and competitors' advertising; attending conventions; and even on occasion indulging in a little industrial espionage.

The curious aspect of this intelligence operation is that the effectiveness of the total process is only as good as the top executives are in evaluating what is presented to them. Thus the critical limitation is not the timeliness, reliability, and validity of the intelligence collected but the sophistication, relevance, and accessibility of the minds of the executives. What top management allows itself to believe is the decisive factor.

THE INFORMATION CONNECTION: LAWRENCE AND LORSCH

Paul R. Lawrence and Jay W. Lorsch, who are among the leading theoreticians in this field, have aligned their concepts with Thompson's ideas described briefly above. Early in the history of industrial organizations it was perceived that the variety of tasks to be performed demanded a segmentation of functions into major task areas, each dealing with a particular subenvironment of the firm such as the market or the technoeconomic or scientific structures. Lawrence and Lorsch identify degrees of certainty and uncertainty in each subenvironment by measuring three major dimensions of information:

1. Rate at which information changes.
2. Time span of feedback.
3. Certainty of information at any one time.

Box 16–1: Contingency design

Jay Galbraith has presented an interesting analytical framework for looking at organizational design. In designing complex organizations, Galbraith has proposed a contingency theory which is based on two fundamental, well-established propositions:

1.   There is no one best way to organize.
2.   Any way of organizing is not always equally effective.

Galbraith reaches this conclusion after reviewing Burns and Stalker's work on mechanistic and organic organizations, Woodward's studies on the relationship between structure and effectiveness, and Chandler's comparative historical analysis of 70 of America's largest industrial firms. Following Lawrence and Lorsch, Galbraith argues that there are two considerations in organizational design, differentiation (how to organize subtasks in a manner which facilitates effective performance) and integration (how the differentiated subtasks are put together). His conclusion is that the best way to organize is contingent on the uncertainty and diversity of the basic tasks being performed by the organizational unit.

The organization is viewed as an information-processing network. As the degree of uncertainty increases, the organization must evolve a strategy to process greater units of information. In order to achieve coordination, the firm must develop rules, programs, and procedures. It must also develop some kind of hierarchy of authority and reward power so that decisions can be referred to the proper person. As task uncertainty increases, the volume of information referred upward also increases, leading to an overload. To combat this overload the amount of discretion exercises at lower levels is increased. Galbraith describes this process as targeting or goal setting.

As the number of exceptions increases, the hierarchy is further overloaded. One way of reducing the number of sections is simply to reduce the required level of performance. Typically, this is achieved in organizations by increasing the amount of time available for a job, the support staff, or the expenses. In all of these cases more resources, called slack resources, will be consumed.

It is possible for a firm to enjoy a high degree of certainty in one subenvironment while facing great uncertainty in another. The extent to which the different parts of the environment are similar determines whether the total environment is diverse or homogenous. The greater the diversity, the greater the need for differentiation of the organization into different units dealing with various parts of the environment. Box 16–1 provides an explanation of how information factors are integrated into organizational design.

THE UNCERTAINTIES OF A TURBULENT ENVIRONMENT

Emery and Trist have provided an extremely useful concept in "The Causal Texture of Organizational Environments," describing

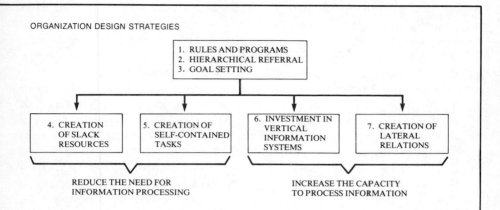

ORGANIZATION DESIGN STRATEGIES

1. RULES AND PROGRAMS
2. HIERARCHICAL REFERRAL
3. GOAL SETTING

4. CREATION OF SLACK RESOURCES

5. CREATION OF SELF-CONTAINED TASKS

6. INVESTMENT IN VERTICAL INFORMATION SYSTEMS

7. CREATION OF LATERAL RELATIONS

REDUCE THE NEED FOR INFORMATION PROCESSING

INCREASE THE CAPACITY TO PROCESS INFORMATION

Another way of reducing the amount of information processed is to change the organizational design so that each group has all the resources it needs to perform its own tasks. For example, a production unit might have allocated to it programming, engineering, and personnel managers so that it becomes self-sufficient in these three respects. The creation of slack resources and the development of self-contained tasks reduce the need for information processing.

Investment in vertical information systems is another way of coping with uncertainty. Such a strategy would require, for example, the development of a new plan rather than making incremental changes in the old one. Creation of lateral relations is another way of coping with uncertainty. This arises when integrating roles or units between subdepartments are at the same level.

The object in organizational design is to choose a strategy which is least expensive in its environmental context.

environment as a causal texture which can be classified as (1) placid, random; (2) placid, clustered; (3) disturbed-reactive; or (4) turbulent. The turbulent environment, which affects most organizations, is highly complex and characterized by dynamic processes.

A business enterprise is not a physical object which interacts only to a slight extent with its environment but a complex of processes and interactions embedded in a cultural environment which places a system of constraints or limits on its development. The traffic of effects between organizations and society is a two-way affair; no organization can be isolated from its cultural background. Further, a business organization may develop its own peculiar culture or organizational climate—patterns of communication and behavior developed within the context of the larger culture pattern. Certain cultural factors are relevant in the study of organizations: historical, economic, technological, and theoretical forces are of major importance.

An important question is how organizations cope with the uncertainties of the turbulent environment of our time. Emery and Trist point out that in the turbulent environment the dynamic processes arise from the field itself. Turbulence is characterized by complexity, which is largely generated by interactions of other organizations which may not directly interact with the organization most disturbed.

The operation of a turbulent environment is illustrated by Emery and Trist with the example of a company which for many years had maintained a steady 65 percent share of the market for its principal product, a canned vegetable. The company had made a massive investment in automated plants to can this product, but in the postwar era it was faced with changes in government controls which facilitated the manufacture of cheaper cans, the availability of alternative products, quick-freeze technology, and the emergence of supermarkets, which placed bulk orders with small firms to can the product under supermarket brand names and offered a wider range of similar products to consumers, who were widening their area of choice as affluence grew. In brief, governmental, technological, and marketing forces impinged on this company's operation, and these environmental forces to some extent were at least one step removed from the immediate environment of the firm.

The firm in this example—like far too many firms—paid insufficient attention to interorganizational relations. Typically, such firms think and act in terms of the simple input-transformation-out-put model shown in Figure 16–3, dealing only with interactions among processes

FIGURE 16–3
Closed system with simple environmental effects

within the organization and exchanges between the organization and its environment. The model has fixed system boundaries (solid lines) which are permeable (broken lines) only at the input and output points. The management of the canned vegetable company treated the firm as this kind of relatively closed system instead of realizing that it was in fact part of a turbulent environment (see Figure 16–4), affected by changes in the social context brought about by the enterdependencies of the parts of the environment.

The fact is that almost no firm, in these complex times, is an island; organizational environments are such that externally induced changes are going to be more significant than internally induced changes for virtually every organization. The critical issue, then, is how an organi-

FIGURE 16-4
Model of firms in a turbulent environment

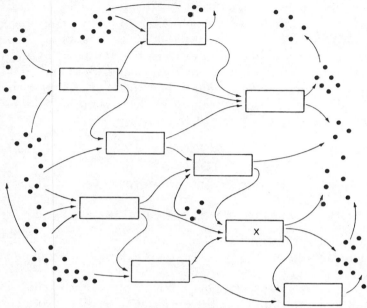

Source: Shirley Terreberry, "The Evolution of Organizational Environments,"
Administrative Science Quarterly, vol. 12 (March 1968), pp. 590–613.

zation can deal with such changes. The levels of complexity and uncertainty induced by the accelerating rate of change make long-range
predictions of the future, based on extrapolation from a noncomparable
past, subject to considerable error. Given the emergence of turbulent
environments, organizations can only cope with change by developing
a pragmatic flexibility, where the emphasis is on the process of short-
run adaptive reaction.

A useful lead for dealing with this problem has been suggested by
William Evan, who has put forward the idea that the organization
should be treated as a social actor and the idea that the organization set
(similar in structure to R. K. Merton's role set) should be utilized as a
means of studying relations between the organization and a turbulent
environment.

This discussion of the turbulence of contemporary environments
points up the difficulty of making predictions, which in turn compels
management to proceed by satisficing rather than optimizing, to accept
bounded rationality, to keep some of its options open by allowing a
plurality of coalitions with various objectives within its system, to review continuously the spectrum of goals, to seek regulated competition, to favor bargaining, co-optation, and coalition strategies—and

above all to recognize that organizational survival and growth is a function of the ability of the system to learn and perform according to changes in the environment. To achieve this level of adaptation, organizations are required to devote more effort to information processing than to production and maintenance activities. The development of such information strategies has been greatly facilitated by the rapid improvement of the information-processing capacities of computers. It also has led to the transformation of the subject of organizational behavior, with systematic efforts being made to write out definitions, concepts, and findings in information and transactional terms.

TOPIC 4
Managing the environment

STRATEGIES FOR MANAGING THE ENVIRONMENT

Essentially, organizations manage their environments and make them more munificent by managing their external dependencies. To achieve the measure of certainty necessary for survival, organizations attempt a number of strategies, including co-optation and cooperation, the use of long-term contracts, the exploitation of illegal collaboration (price-fixing cartels and conspiracies), lobbying the various levels of government, and merger and acquisition activity.

Co-optation, for example, is widely used by government agencies, universities, banks, business and religious organizations, hospitals, prisons, and many other organizations as an accommodating mechanism. This process of selective alliances allows representatives of powerful groups in the environment a say in setting goals and selecting means, in return for information of what their parent organizations are going to do. Co-optation, which essentially involves exploitation of the "old boy" net, is somewhat hazardous. The wrong external groups or group representatives may be selected, or the structure of representation may not reflect the realities of the environment; or the conflict of interests involved may impair the judgments of the parties involved, who are unable to navigate the shoals marked "collusion" and "conspiracy" by the mapmakers from government antitrust agencies.

Cooperation through interlocking directorates

One way businesses cooperate is through the use of interlocking directorates. In 1978 the Senate Committee on Intergovernmental Affairs indicated that virtually all U.S. companies are interlocked directly or indirectly because the same men or women sit on different corporate boards. Business leaders vigorously defend the principle on the basis that a firm is an economic entity which must interact with its environment; it must understand and control the information flow. To their minds, proximity does not necessarily produce conflict of interest.

Thirteen of the largest companies in the United States—the American Telephone and Telegraph Company, BankAmerica Corporation, Chase Manhattan Corporation, Citicorp, Exxon Corporation, Ford Motor Company, General Motors Corporation, Manufacturers Hanover Corporation, Metropolitan Life Insurance Company, Mobil Corporation, J. P. Morgan and Company, Prudential Insurance Company of America, and Texaco Inc.,—account for 240 direct and 5,547 indirect interlocks. While AT&T directors, for example, cannot sit on the boards of competitors, the company is linked indirectly with its closest rival, IBM, through joint membership on 22 boards.

In 1913 Louis Brandeis said, "The practice of interlocking directorates is the root of many evils. If offends laws human and divine." Nevertheless, businesses need to cooperate to cooperate. But the mix of cooperation and competition remains an open and vital question.

Presentation and infiltration

To ensure a market for their products or services, many companies make extensive use of political and presentation skills. An interesting example of this kind of salesmanship is the effort CPA firms make to market their services.

Like other professionals, accountants have traditionally regarded aggressive advertising of their services as inappropriate behavior. But this has now changed, as top executives of the major CPA firms in the United States have begun making special efforts to present their services in the best possible way to important potential clients. These presentations typically include audiovisual aids and flip charts. Accounting services for a large firm may bring in as much as $1 million in revenue, and the cost of presentation may run as high as $100,000. Accounting firms try to figure out what the client's auditing needs are and respond accordingly.

Accounting firms urge their people to join the right civic groups, country clubs and religious organizations. As Deborah Rankin points out in "How C.P.A.'s Sell Themselves":

> The Los Angeles office of Peat, Marwick seems to have developed the art of stalking potential clients to an extremely advanced state. The office charts the memberships of decision makers at sought-after companies and then compares these memberships with those of its own partners. Not only does the office check out the country clubs and other organizations the officers of target companies belong to but also it checks out the memberships of those officials' bankers and insurance brokers, the

schools the executives' children attend and the religious organizations their families are affiliated with.

An organized approach to getting new business is certainly not unique, however. Ernst & Ernst draws up a "personal assignment calendar" for all its top employees. It lists the names of influential persons (such as investment bankers or Securities and Exchange Commission staff members) whom employees are expected to contact within a given period.

Twice a month Ernst & Ernst employs fill out "contact reports" that indicate what key individuals they have met with. Only person-to-

Box 16–2: Dealing with multiple dependencies

Executives are having their authority and autonomy whittled away by forces over which they have little or no control. It seems the manager has lost control of his or her own destiny, as turbulent changes in the external environment create multiple dependencies.

Warren Bennis, president of the University of Cincinnati since 1971, points out in "Leadership: A Beleaguered Species?":

> In an analysis of my own time allocation, a research analyst determined that "50 percent of the university president's contacts were with external people, 43 percent with internal constituents, 4 percent with trustees, and 3 percent with personal or undetermined contacts. Sixty-seven percent of phone calls, 43.7 percent of mail, and 38.9 percent of meetings were with external groups."

Bennis claims there are over 500 organized pressure groups on the campus. He says:

> These pressure groups are intentionally fragmented. Going their separate and often conflicting ways, they say: "No, we don't want to be part of the mainstream of America—we just want to be us," whether they're blacks, Chicanos, women, the third sex, or Menominee Indians seizing an empty Catholic monastery. They tell us that the old dream of "the melting pot," of assimilation, does not work. They have never been "*beyond* the melting pot" (as Glazer and Moynishan put it) . . .

And the members of these groups are becoming increasingly litigious. Bennis found he was being made the victim of an amorphous, unintentional conspiracy to prevent changes in the university's status quo. To overcome these difficulties, Bennis quotes Schumacher's *Small Is Beautiful:*

—We are poor, not demigods.
—We have plenty to be sorrowful about, and are not emerging into a golden age.
—We need a gentle approach, a nonviolent spirit, and small is beautiful. . . .

Bennis argues that the leader is more than a judge, more than a manager, more than a negotiator. The leader must be something of a politician.

> . . . "Politics" might do it, if we think of the term as the arrangement of human life, relationships, and organizations in comfortable and rational modes. The leader engaged in such politics will need all the skills—of vision, conceptualization, issue definition, social architecture, and more—necessary to clarify and arrange the conduct of organized human endeavor.

Reference: Warren Bennis, "Leadership: A Beleagured Species?" *Organizational Dynamics*, vol. 5, no. 1 (1976), pp. 3–16.

person contacts consisting of "more than a brief casual encounter" may be reported, according to an internal cover sheet explaining the firm's program to employees.

In a sharply competitive environment, accounting firms, like many other organizations, are forced to cast their political nets quite wide to land new clients. The CPA firm is heavily involved in political processes not only within the organization but also with members of other organizations. To meet these political challenges auditors are trying to develop appropriate political organizational skills which will enable them to get new clients by rubbing shoulders with other influential people. They have to deal with multiple dependencies (see Box 16–2); the climate has changed.

TOPIC 5
Organizational climate

THE PERCEIVED ENVIRONMENT

Every organization has a corporate zeitgeist or general climate and is characterized by a particular, distinctive ambience. How this ambience is perceived—how this bundle of "vibes" is organized into a gestalt—is termed *organizational climate.* Climate is usually easy to recognize. In many organizations, it hits you as you walk through the front door. The House of Commons reeks of pomp, persuasion, and power. The U.S. Marine Corps has can-do written all over it, in crew cuts, ramrod backs, and machismo. The hippie commune smells of permissiveness, passion, pot, and patter. The question is not whether climate exists, but how to get a handle on it.

One way is to pick up the contingency model for the study of organizational behavior, and model the organizational climate, as in Figure 16–5. Climate may be thought of as the perception of the characteristics of an organization. Since the actual environment is well described by Emery and Trist's classifications, and we have opted for the idea that the turbulent environment is the one most firms must deal with, the model in Figure 16–5 deals with these perceptions. The structure, process, and value dimensions and other system elements are the aspects of organizations that can be considered in assessing their distinctive climates. These aspects have to do with both the internal environment and the way the organization deals with external environments.

Structurally, organizations can be judged in terms of complexity and such constraints as roles, regulations, and red tape. Is there an official organization chart, and how slavishly do people stick to channels? Organizational climate, like air conditioning, can be switched

FIGURE 16–5
The perceived environment as a system

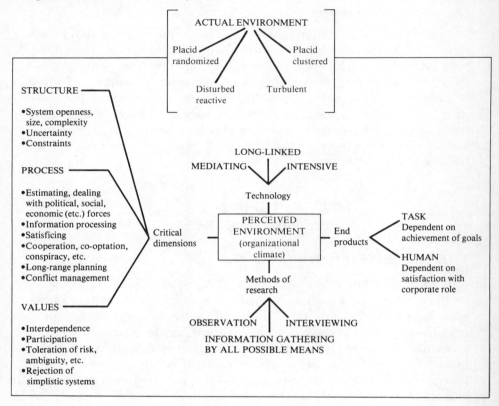

not only on and off but also up and down. "Getting into role" is normally preceded by a standard set of signals. Size and structure are closely linked. Usually bigness is associated with more impersonal relations, centralization, more absenteeism, lower morale. Technology and structure also are closely related. The atmosphere of the automobile assembly line is alienating better educated and less complaint workers. Weariness of spirit, which has hit the auto plants hardest, is related to job boredom—which in turn is generating both poor workmanship and absenteeism. To meet this problem Chrysler Corporation, for example, has asked plant managements to consult the workers and to keep four principles in mind:

1. Fix responsibility as far down the line as possible.
2. Give enough authority to go with it.
3. Make workers aware of the concrete results of their suggestions.
4. Create a climate which encourages change.

Such proposals adknowledge that it is not sufficient to change specific job characteristics such as wages, schedules, and job designs; it is vital to establish a different climate.

Organizational climate is concerned with the perception not only of structure but also of organization processes. The handling of information is a critical factor determining climate. Information can be communicated internally in an autocratic, benevolent, consultative, or par-

Reprinted by permission *The Wall Street Journal.*

ticipative climate. External and overall information management includes the researching and gathering of all possible data and the evaluation of all the impinging social forces. Management of conflict is another process factor. The extent to which conflict is perceived as being confronted and not suppressed varies widely from organization to organization. Ultimately, climate is concerned with the reading of other people's minds and the unscrambling of their motivations and values.

RESEARCHING THE CLIMATE

Much of the organizational literature uses the term *climate* as interchangeable with the term *environment* and, as we have been doing, seeks to identify the perceived characteristics that make up the climate. Researchers have identified (often through the use of questionnaires and rating scales) many significant areas of organizational members' perceptions, including:

1. Structure: perception of constraints such as rules, regulations, red tape, closeness of supervision and direction, tightness of budgets. "You've got to recite the history of the alphabet here before you can get a pencil out of the storeroom."
2. Autonomy: feelings of setting one's own pace, running one's own show. "You're on your own here as long as you produce. Nobody breathes down your neck every time you turn around."
3. Reward structure: share of the payoffs, psychic and financial; promotion-and-achievement, profit-and-sales orientations. "You get a fair shake around here if you can deliver the goods."
4. Warmth, support, consideration: an ambience of good fellowship and helpfulness. "They're nearly all good eggs."
5. Tolerance of conflict: the extent to which conflict is confronted and not suppressed. "They like everything, and I mean everything, right out in the open."
6. Need for innovation: technological and managerial rate of change. "If something has been operational here for 24 months and hasn't been declared obsolescent for 23, somebody's slipping."

Since climate represents the perceived environment, it is a bridging concept between people and the organizations in which they work (see Box 16–3). Climate is thus an individual's perception of the environment's structure, processes, and values as they relate to his task achievement and human satisfaction in the particular organization to which he belongs. For example, it has been found that there is a relationship between job satisfaction and climate. G. Litwin and R. Stringer found that satisfaction was highest in "affiliation-induced" climates, relatively high in "achievement-induced" climates, and low in "power-induced" climates.

Box 16-3: Climate surveys—a productive way to vent employee gripes

Climate surveys provide a means of not only getting employees' opinions out in the open but of forcing managers to face up to and handle difficult situations. These surveys zero in on particular departments with questions such as: "Does your boss make assignments clear?" and "Do you get recognition for a job well done?"

The survey provides for a no-holds-barred, two-way feedback process and develops an interpersonal exchange between managers and subordinates. The aim is to explain away unwarranted employee gripes and resolve legitimate ones. At the feedback sessions, employees get together with managers to propose changes designed to overcome particular difficulties.

Numerous companies, including General Electric, American Can, Westinghouse, and Gulf, are making extensive use of climate surveys. The major problem they have uncovered is that employees are unhappy with the available information on opportunities for advancement. To solve this problem, companies are asking senior executives to make presentations on company career opportunities and are trying to ensure that job openings are properly advertised within the company. Climate surveys also have a kind of Hawthorne effect; any time a company survey is done, employees' expectations go up.

SEARCHING FOR THE ORGANIZATIONAL GESTALT: LIKERT'S SYSTEMS

Sophisticated executives seek a gestalt or configuration or frame of reference which will enable them to synthesize the multitude of concepts and findings constantly emerging from research and practice. Useful theories have the same obsolescence characteristics as jet fighters and date themselves as they emerge from the drawing boards of organization theorists. Such theories should be judged in terms of both validity and utility.

FIGURE 16-6
Likert's model of changes in organizational climate

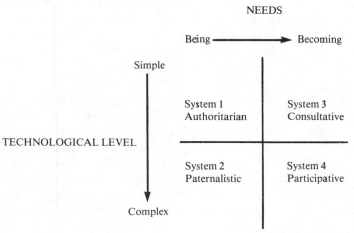

FIGURE 16–7

PLANT	TECH-NOLOGY	NEEDS	CLIMATE
Small knitting factory in the West of Ireland	Simple	Being (survival)	Authoritarian-paternalistic
Quaker chocolate factory in England	Moderately complex	Being to becoming	Paternalistic-consultative
Car plant in Detroit	Complex	Being to becoming	Paternalistic-consultative
Apollo space project	Highly complex	Becoming (self-actualizing)	Participative

One of the most significant reasons why theories cannot keep up with events is that events won't stand still. A useful model for getting a reading on this rapid rate of organizational change has been provided by the seminal work of Rensis Likert, who has proposed the model of changes in organizational climate shown in Figure 16–6. The model illustrates that as the technological mandate changes, human needs expand and different organizational climates emerge. Examples of organizations and their places in such a spectrum are given in Figure 16–7. In a complex, technologically advanced industry, System 4 is most appropriate.

CONCLUSIONS

In summary, climate is a variable which describes how people perceive organizations (essentially, how they see the elements of the contingency model—structure, process, and so on). But climate after a while achieves a somewhat separate existence, a kind of functional autonomy. What life-style does for the individual and morale for the group, climate does for the organization. Now climate, culture, ideology, mythology, call it what you may, is not a completely rational thing. It inevitably contains elements that cannot be reconciled. Establishing the right climate is a vital executive activity and an area where behavioral scientists can play, a significant part, even though the instruments they use are imperfect. (See Box 16–4.)

Three points should be stressed. First, climate is an atmosphere, an ambience, an *esprit de corps*, a corporate zeitgeist. Second, while climate may be difficult to measure, people are usually immediately alerted to it; it comes on as a corporate aura, odor, echo, flavor. It can be intoxicating, soporific, aphrodisiac, enervating, apathy inducing, stimulating, hysteria producing. Third—and above all—climate affects

Box 16–4: How executives perceive their organizations

In order to manage businesses properly, executives must find out what the managers really think about the company. For years Sears, Roebuck and Company has been successfully carrying out surveys of the attitudes of its hourly rated employees. In 1971, to take this idea to its logical conclusion, it set out to find out how managers perceived the company by means of such a survey.

The executive survey focused on a number of problems in several critical and sensitive areas. The questionnaire included a group of attitude scales that had been employed to measure job satisfaction at the hourly employee level. Also included were wide-ranging questions that captured perceptions of the organizational climate. Inevitably the questionnaires were long; on the average they took three hours to complete. Nevertheless, some 18,000 people completed the questionnaires in 1971.

SOME FINDINGS OF THE STUDIES

One set of survey results concerned the company's transfer policies, which affected several thousand executives each year. A major finding was that these frequent moves were somewhat resented by the executives, who expressed the conviction that valuable training experience could be obtained otherwise. Many respondents also pointed out these moves could be financially exacting. In view of these findings company policies were changed to provide adequate financial protection for those who had to move. In addition, the custom of frequently moving people was reconsidered and the career planning system was reorganized to allow people to rotate cross jobs in one store or unit, or at least within a city.

A second major result emerging from the survey was related to the matter of executive compensation. Previously each executive, in addition to salary, had received a yearly bonus based on the profits of the corporation. The survey revealed a growing feeling that the bonuses developed a negative motivation. Since the bonuses were tied to overall profits, they were highest when profits were relatively easy to obtain, and in bad years, which required more effort, they often decreased. To overcome these problems the bonus was incorporated into managers' regular salaries. But to ensure productivity, managers holding key jobs which clearly influenced profits were rewarded with a more direct bonus system.

The survey also turned up some data on leadership at Sears, Roebuck. One interesting point brought out was a need for closer interchange between managers and subordinates. As Frank J. Smith and Lyman W. Porter pointed out,

> In a number of cases, pointing out the extent and nature of this problem to managers resulted in corrective action. One senior executive, for example, actually rearranged his schedule and administrative practices in order to make regularly scheduled field trips with his junior assistants. This not only gave him a first hand view of their needs and problems, but also of their abilities to cope with situations in the field. While this senior executive had risen from their ranks, he had not held a junior staff position in his present department. These visits, therefore, gave him a much better understanding of how the department functioned as well as helping cement his relationships with his people.
>
> A very practical by-product of his action was a noticeable improvement in the quality of performance reviews with his subordinates. Because of his firsthand observations, he was able to be highly specific both in acknowledging good performance and in coaching subordinates in dealing with problems.
>
> In addition, his direct dealing with junior staff members freed some of his senior assistants and allowed them to take on greater responsibilities for department programs and facilitated their own growth and development.

Reference: Frank J. Smith and Lyman W. Porter, "What Do Executives Really Think about Their Organizations?" *Organizational Dynamics,* vol. 6, no. 6 (1977).

judgment, which is what Watergate told us about the 1972 presidential campaign. The climate of can-do, total delegation by (and isolation of) the president, business (not political) efficiency, complete loyalty, football symbolism, and the paranoia of black-and-white issues led to poor judgment and bad decision making.

TOPIC 6
What every manager should know about
the organization and its environment

The most important thing a manager should know about the organization's environment is that an organization must adjust its internal dynamics to the turbulence of the external environment if it wishes to survive. The environment is made up of economic, technological, and informational elements.

THE ECONOMIC ENVIRONMENT

The economic environment for the firm consists of a relatively small number of extremely large organizations and an extremely large number of small organizations. These firms compete (cooperate and conflict) with each other to make good things happen. All these firms have created a need for managers who have the necessary technical and managerial skills. Collectively such managers are known as the technostructure—they manage the technology.

THE TECHNOLOGICAL ENVIRONMENT

The behavioral scientists at Britain's Tavistock Institute of Human Relations have developed the idea of treating organizations as sociotechnical systems which focus attention on the transactions between the organization and its environment. In the sociotechnical approach management is concerned with managing both the internal system and the external environment. To be effective, it must also control the boundary conditions.

One of the most important findings to emerge from Tavistock seems very obvious now but revolutionized management theory. This is the fact that technology is a major determinant not only of behavior and attitudes at work but of how the work itself is organized.

The early research work in this area was carried out by Woodward, who showed that firms are organized in different ways according to their technology. For example, a plant set up to manufacture sulphuric acid is organized in quite a different way from an electronics firm producing sophisticated guidance systems for missiles. Burns and Stalker labeled the first kind of organization mechanistic. This means that the firm has well-established policies and procedures and clearly defined roles which can be set out on an organization chart. They labeled organizations such as electronics firms, where the organization grows up around the point of innovation, organic. This type of firm is made up of project teams which cut across hierarchical ranks, and it operates in quite a different manner.

The Tavistock social scientists built on the work of Burns and Stalker to develop the idea of the organization as a sociotechnical system which interacts with its environment. Thus in the systems approach, executives are concerned with the management of both the internal system and the external environment.

In the United States, meanwhile, James Thompson was defining different forms of interdependence among units in the organization according to their technology. Thompson noted, for example, that an assembly line is organized very differently from a bank, and both are organized rather differently from a hospital. As a result of Thompson's research, organizational design began to develop very rapidly in the United States. Lawrence and Lorsch, both from the Harvard School of Business, came up with all sorts of interesting findings. For example, they showed that participative management in routine structured situations could be counterproductive.

THE INFORMATIONAL ENVIRONMENT

The Lawrence and Lorsch view stresses the organization as a system of information flows. The exchange of information, the transmission of meaning, and the orientation of decision-making processes to changing environments represent the very essence of organizational life. Essentially, this means that every organization is a communications system, and thus every organization is in the communications business. Universities, publishing houses, television companies, and newspapers obviously are in the communication business—that is, they acquire information, process it, and transmit it. But it is possible to think of any organization as being in this business.

This new approach treats the organization as a system of energy/information transformations. The idea is that the organization is a sort of social organism which, like the amoeba, interacts with environment, swallowing up such inputs as energy, information, and people, transforming them, and transporting them to the environment with value added.

This view of the organization as a giant amoeba stresses the environmental context in which the organization finds itself. The interaction between the environment and the organization is complicated and complex, but fortunately Trist and Emery have come up with a neat analysis of different kinds of environment which has proved to be extremely helpful to practicing managers.

Four different kinds of environment have been identified. The first two (placid, random and placid, clustered) are mainly of interest to students of biology. The third and fourth are of more interest to students of management. The third, a disturbed-reactive environment, is the kind where one organization of a set makes a move and causes waves to ripple through the other organizations, which in turn react to this disturbance.

A good example of a disturbed-reactive environment is the automobile industry in the United States. From the early sixties to the early seventies, it reacted not only to ecological and governmental regulatory organizations but also to external threats from Japanese and European car manufacturing companies. Because they were unable to disengage from this constantly increasing stress, they could not pursue an untrammeled trajectory.

U.S. automobile manufacturing companies of the eighties are very different social animals from their 1970 counterparts. They have become much more complex and convoluted, and much less self-confident. In the process they are becoming much more useful members of American society, as they are forced to produce more economical, less lethal, more comfortable, and more attractive cars for the American people. The U.S. automobile industry, which has had to face an increasingly turbulent environment, is changing environments.

MANAGING THE ENVIRONMENT

Organizations manage their environments to make them more munificent. Basically this means cooperation as well as competition. Sometimes the process is illegal, but more often organizations interact through careful market planning and analysis where the cooperation is implicit and tacit. This makes it important to belong to the right "old boy" net.

REVIEW AND RESEARCH

1. Explain the concept of satisficing. Why don't General Motors and Ford combine to knock out Chrysler and American Motors?
2. Define the internal and external environments of a firm with which you are familiar.
3. What are the organizational arguments that favor the survival of capitalism?
4. Explain how aerospace firms cope with the uncertainties of the environment.
5. List the factors of organizational climate. Assess your business school or organization on these factors.

6. List some of the factors that make environments turbulent.

7. Consider a change in the environment such as the invention of a relatively inexpensive domestic appliance combining computer, copying machine, television, and videotape recording functions. How would the introduction of such a machine affect work and leisure?

GLOSSARY OF TERMS

Climate. Often used interchangeably with *environment*, but more usefully thought of as the environment as it is perceived; a corporate ambience or aura typifying an organization's style.

Environment. All of the surrounding elements and factors with which an organization interacts and trades. The organization's internal environment consists of programming, technical, and personnel factors; its immediate external environment includes suppliers, competitors, customers, and monitoring agencies; its remote external environment includes all of the political, social, economic, technological, and ecological factors which impinge on its activities.

Likert's systems. Describes organizational style or internal environment as an evolution through four systems along axes of changing human needs and technological levels: System 1, authoritarian; System 2, paternalistic; System 3, consultative; and System 4, participative. System 4 is most appropriate in a complex, technologically advanced industry; it fulfills human needs for industrial democracy.

Mechanistic organization. A management system in stable conditions where the emphasis is on (1) coordination of different functions by hierarchical control; (2) vertical communications through a well-structured authority system with responsibilities clearly defined; and (3) insistence on loyalty to the organization.

Organic organization. A management system appropriate to a rapidly changing technological and social environment where (1) the emphasis is on expertise as opposed to structural authority; (2) roles are loosely defined and successful innovation is the focus for a temporary structure with which to carry out the project; (3) organizational omniscience is rejected; (4) horizontal communications are the order of the day and take the form of information and advice rather than instructions; and (5) loyalty is to the ethos of technological excellence rather than the organization.

Sociotechnical system. An industrial production organization with high technical and social interrelations, interacting with its environment (an open system).

Technology. A crucial variable in organizational behavior, it can be defined in two ways—as tools, instruments, machines, plants, or technical know-how, and as a corpus of knowledge derived from applied science (social and physical) for transforming particular problems in aerospace, the military, and so on. Thompson has identified three types: long-linked technology (automated automobile assembly line), mediating technology (telephone exchange system), and intensive technology (research laboratory).

DEBATE: Democracy works, versus autocracy is better

PRO: Workers in the executive suite

In the United States, participative management has been financed not by the government but by private philanthropy, notably the Ford Foundation. The forms of participative management vary widely. A. H. Raskin, in an article entitled, "The Workers in the Executive Suite," has given three interesting examples of how participative management can be used to improve the quality of work and to enrich jobs:

> At the Rushton Mining Company in central Pennsylvania autonomous work teams rotate jobs and dig coal unsupervised. The foreman puts his energies into improved safety, and the accident rate has dropped to record lows. Every miner gets top pay; yet the costs run a third lower for the self-directed crews than for those using standard methods.

> At the Harman auto mirror factory in Bolivar, Tenn., a union-management committee developed an earned idle time concept that enables workers to go home or to take adult education courses inside the plant if they complete their production quotas in less than eight hours. A sharing plan on cost savings kept the plant from closing last year when the market for auto mirrors plummeted.

> In the Tennessee Valley Authority, a joint committee reorganized the work structure for 400 engineers who plan placement of transmission lines through all the giant utility's region. A new branch dealing solely with environmental affairs was set up at the group's suggestion. Management is so pleased that the job enrichment experiment will be extended this year to other authority divisions.

CON: Stonewalling plant democracy

In the early 1970s General Foods Corporation opened a dog-food plant in Topeka, Kansas, designed to run with minimum supervision. In this experiment workers were allowed to make job assignments, schedule coffee breaks, interview prospective employees, and even decide on pay raises.

The experiment was widely heralded as a model for the future. While at first General Foods described it as very successful, it is now discouraging publicity about the Topeka plant. An article in *Business Week* (March 28, 1977) reported employee's attitudes toward the experiment:

> "The system went to hell. It didn't work," says one former manager. Adds another ex-employee: "It was a mixed bag. Economically it was a success, but it became a power struggle. It was too threatening to too many people." He predicts that the plant will eventually switch to a traditional factory system. In fact, he says, the transition has already begun.

In effect, the team system, which is the basis of the experiment, came squarely up against the GF bureaucracy. The Topeka system was designed by a GF task force assisted by Richard G. Walton, a professor of business administration at Harvard University. The system eliminated a number of levels of management; team members worked under the direction of a "coach" rather than a foreman and rotated between dreary and meaningful jobs. The system was a great success at least at Topeka, but creating a system is very different from maintaining it. Basically the system flew in the face of corporate policies.

The *Business Week* article argued that Topeka managers suffered because of their involvement with this experimental system. A number of managers who developed the system have left the company. As one executive points out: "They saw we had created something the company couldn't handle, so they put their boys in. By being involved, I ruined my career at General Foods."

The demand for participative management

How does the young American executive view the management of the system? An increasing number expect to play a larger part in the critical decision making that affects the environment in which they work.

What they are looking for is participative management. Many young managers are sure they know how to run the business better than the managers at the top, and even the unions are feeling this demand for participation. As one young shop-floor worker put it, "Participation means more than being permitted to drive the beer truck to the local's annual picnic."

A growing number of companies in the United States and western Europe are offering workers a chance to participate in management. In the United States this upsurge of interest in participative management is due to employers' worries about high absenteeism, low productivity, and slowdowns in production lines. These evidences of employee malaise have become so general that they have earned a diagnostic label—the Lordstown syndrome. This title was invented to describe the terrible things that happened during a three-week wildcat strike in 1972 at General Motors's superefficient Vega plant at Lordstown, Ohio.

Question

How can participation be developed in management in the United States?

CHAPTER 17 —— ORGANIZATIONAL DECISION MAKING ——⌐ Rational decision making
    ⊢ Creative decision making
    ∟ Group decision making

CHAPTER 18 —— CONFLICT IN ORGANIZATIONS ——⌐ Structure of conflict
    ⊢ Process of conflict
    ∟ Values of conflict

CHAPTER 19 —— ORGANIZING DEVELOPMENT ——⌐ The T group
    ⊢ Change strategies
    ∟ Critical review

part V

THE ORGANIZATION: DECISION, CONFLICT, AND DEVELOPMENT

DIAGRAM SUMMARY OF CHAPTER 17

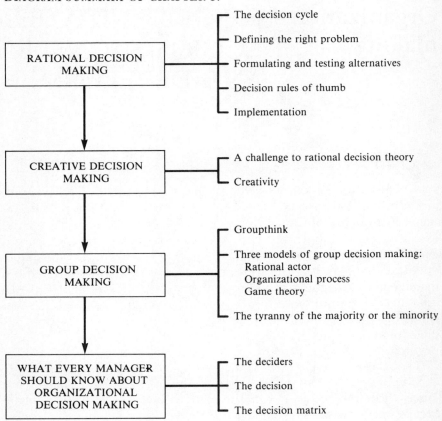

17

Organizational decision making

DECISION MAKING: THE PRESIDENT IN SNEAKERS

A penetrating look at how executives in fact make decisions is provided in the film *After Mr. Sam,* made in the early 1970s by the National Film Board of Canada. It depicts how Sam Steinberg, the chief executive of Steinberg Limited, a Canadian supermarket chain, engaged the help of top management in finding his successor. The movie opens at company headquarters in Montreal, where Mr. Sam and top management are going through an exercise in organizational development to determine the most important problem the company is facing at the time. This management group, which is made up of two main elements, family and nonfamily, concludes that the principal problem is who is to succeed Mr. Sam (see Figure 17–1).

The chairman of the conference is Harry Suffrin, the director of OD at Steinberg, who has presented to the group the notion that its first job is to define the company's overall objectives. A violent debate breaks out between Mr. Sam, who is arguing for definition of objectives, and Jack Levine, who is arguing that the important point is to define the organizational structure. Eventually Mr. Sam agrees that structure is important, and the meeting concludes when he reads a short statement of the company's objectives.

Following this meeting in Montreal, the group reassembles in the company's training center, a resort motel located in the Laurentiens north of the city. The same actors are now costumed quite differently. Business suits are set aside, and the players are disguised in their fun clothes. Amidst much shuffling around, courtesy exchanges, and meals consumed, the discussion goes on about the struggle over structure.

FIGURE 17–1
Three stages in Steinberg's decisions regarding succession to the presidency

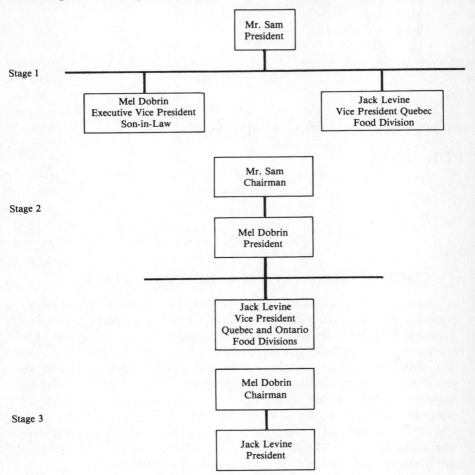

Jack Levine is head of the antifamily group (if such a term is appropriate in a family business where there is much goodwill and bonhomie). At the time the movie was made he was the vice president in charge of the Quebec Food Division. He sets out to fight, not for the presidency, which undoubtedly will go to someone in the family, but rather to achieve a reorganization in which he will come out as a group vice president in charge of all Steinberg's food divisions.

Thus we have the basic ingredients for an interesting game of managerial decision making. There is a scenario, a plot, prizes, players, and options. At first sight it looks like the classical conflict situation (hawks versus doves) in the form of family versus nonfamily.

But in this polarized debate there emerges a bridging force in the form of the company's legal counsel. He seems to be in neither camp and advances this argument to Mr. Sam:

> Look, there is really no reason from a legal point of view why you should consult us. You are perfectly entitled to make the appointment yourself. But I am pretty sure, knowing you, that you will want to consult other members of your family. And by the same token you will probably want to consult your top management group too. Nevertheless, the decision will be yours and yours alone.

The OD exercise is concluded on a fairly pleasant note when Mr. Sam indicates that he appreciates the guidance and direction he has received. He advises the meeting that he will make the decision in the next few months.

After the movie was made Steinberg made his decision: He would become chairman of the board, and his son-in-law, Mel Dobrin, would be president of the company. Levine achieved the group vice presidency he sought in the organizational structure. After Steinberg's death in 1978, Dobrin was made the chairman and Levine the president of Steinberg Limited.

The movie provides an excellent opportunity to see managers in action. It also demonstrates how OD can be used to provide a public agenda within which many private agendas can be tested out. By bringing in the National Film Board to film this decision as it was made, both some glamour and some constraints were injected into the corporate body politic. The exercise reveals how decision making usually begins in a metaphysical context, then moves to a more operational level where the nitty-gritty of the organization chart is defined. It also reveals the virtues of postponing decisions and the actualities of the process of optimization.

UNDERSTANDING DECISION MAKING

To the modern executive like those in the Steinberg OD exercise, life is a process of continuous decision making, an excruciating process of deciding what to do today, what can be safely postponed. Decisions are needed as to whether to buy or sell, whether to fire a troublesome subordinate or remonstrate with her or him, whether to send a memo increasing controls or call a conference to talk the problem out, whether to order a new computer system or get the current one sorted out. Traditionally, executives have solved the endless multitude of problems coming their way by intuition. A cardinal principle of decision theory, however, is that intuition alone is not sufficient to meet the complexities of modern life.

Decision theory presumes that executive decision makers cannot master all the information available. Therefore they must calculate the odds in favor or against, not in terms of mathematical probabilities but rather in terms of their will to win. It presumes that executives operate under bounded rationality, trying to accommodate the elusive facts of value and utility within a framework of probability. To get the best out of decision theory, they must understand the decision process and grasp the difference between two basically different types of organizational decisions: programmable and nonprogrammable (see Figure 17–2).

FIGURE 17–2
Basic types of decisions

DECISION TYPE	PROCESS	GROUP METHOD
Programmable	Routine; computable by algorithm	Factory meeting to schedule production
Nonprogrammable:		
1. Creative	Limited heuristic	Technological forecasting group to select new product
2. Negotiated	Noncomputable; conflict technology	Management–labor union bargaining

Decision makers must also be able to categorize the environment as to whether outcomes can be specified in terms of certainty, risk, or uncertainty. All decisions have varying degrees of risk and uncertainty, depending on the environment in which the decision maker operates. To resolve questions of uncertainty, it is important to grasp how information-processing systems function.

Decision making and problem solving are interlocked, in the sense that thinking and action are intermeshed. Two types of decision theory, descriptive and normative (see Figure 17–3), have been developed to explain this relation and how the decision-making process works.

FIGURE 17–3
Kinds of decision theory

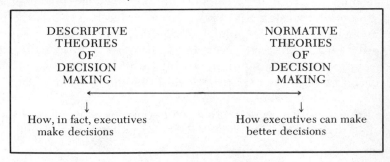

DESCRIPTIVE THEORIES OF DECISION MAKING	NORMATIVE THEORIES OF DECISION MAKING
How, in fact, executives make decisions	How executives can make better decisions

TOPIC 1
Rational decision making

Herbert A. Simon has suggested that organizations are made up of three layers: an underlying system of physical processes, a layer of programmed decision processes, and a top layer of nonprogrammed decision processes. Top management makes the critical decisions which middle management absorbs into its plans, which in turn monitor the physical processes at the bottom layer.

The decision-making process, according to Simon, consists of three steps:

1. The sensor subsystem searches the environment for conditions calling for a decision. This is essentially an intelligence activity. The aim of this two-way process is to capture data about events impinging on the organization and its immediate environment.
2. The data processing subsystem manipulates and is manipulated by these data.
3. The decision-making subsystem enables a particular course of action to be selected.

The modern approach to decision making in organizations treats the organization as a coalition of individuals or groups who formulate goals through formal and informal bargaining, coupled with a search of the environment for suitable opportunistic problems to solve.

R. M. Cyert and J. G. March, in *A Behavioral Theory of the Firm*, have identified five major goals for modern organizations: production, sales, inventory, market share, and profit. Organizations also usually have a certain amount of organizational slack, which constitutes a kind of reserve which by effective management can be committed to new battles. Organizational slack arises when the rewards (financial or psychic) exceed the amount needed to obtain members' contributions. (For example, organizational slack would presumably be taken up if a decision by a consultant to fire 20 percent of the personnel were im-

FIGURE 17–4
How coalitions bargain to achieve goals

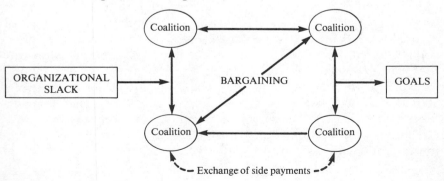

plemented.) Figure 17–4 illustrates how coalitions within the organization employ organizational slack in a bargaining process whose aim is the satisfaction of some varying combination of the five major goals.

THE DECISION CYCLE

Organizational members are continuously searching the environment to find means of meeting goals better or to uncover solvable problems that will induce new goals for the organization. Figure 17–5 shows how a decision cycle might then begin to operate.

FIGURE 17–5
A decision cycle

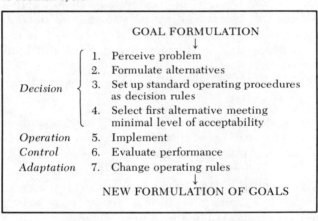

The quality, quantity, reliability, relevance, and presentation of information gathered which results in the members' perception of the problem is a function of their satisfactions and the amount of organizational slack available. Choice arises as a response to a perceived problem. A typical decision cycle begins with a search of the environment to select a suitable problem which is tested for relevance against organizational goals (present or future). (see Box 17–1). Then standard operating procedures (rules of thumb) are applied to solve the problem. In the process various alternatives are formulated and evaluated. Normally the first alternative which meets the minimum level of acceptability on the complete range of standards is selected. Afterward the strategy selected is evaluated, and in this process organizational learning takes place. Adaptation is based on past performance evaluated against both expectations and the performance of other comparable organizations. It focuses the perceptions of members on salient elements of the environment. Thus the search process produces information which is biased in particular ways.

Box 17–1: Identifying the problem

Traditional managers are seldom criticized on the grounds that they cannot solve problems. This they can do. But it is charged that they solve the wrong problems. In effect, the suggestion is that managers are better at finding the right answers than at asking themselves the right questions. The real problem in management is that executives are likely to come up with the right answer to the wrong question.

To try to avoid the main pitfalls in problem identification, Charles Kepner and Benjamin Tregoe, two management consultants, have invented a model which may prevent managers from jumping to conclusions in problem solving. The K-T model requires managers to test their explanations of events vigorously to determine whether or not they have hit on real causes. It provides a way of being sure that decisions are not based on false notions of what produces problems.

Kepner and Tregoe argue, essentially, that the scientific method, especially the idea that hypotheses must be exposed to evidence that can refute them, can be applied to the problem-solving process. To apply the K-T model it is necessary to follow these steps:

1. State the goal of the system.
2. State the actual performance.
3. Identify the difference between the desired and actual performance.
4. State the general nature of the problem.
5. Break down the general problem into a set of manageable subproblems.

Reference: Charles H. Kepner and Benjamin B. Tregoe, *The Rational Manager* (New York: McGraw-Hill Book Co., 1965).

The amount of data provided by organizational members is a function of their level in the organization, their area of operations, what their superiors desire, what will get them favorable decisions, how easy the data are to collect, and what they will be held accountable for collecting later. Inevitably, considerable bias is introduced in the process.

DEFINING THE RIGHT PROBLEM

The decision cycle represents a systems approach to decision making. If decision making is remedial (putting out fires), fragmented (deals with one problem partially at a time), and serial, then the system is bound to get unbalanced. But this imbalance is exactly what a system is designed to cope with. As one subsystem gets out of balance the other subsystems push and pull to bring the whole system back into line somewhat further forward. It operates by a process of one step forward, two steps back.

Decision making is more likely to go wrong because the wrong problem is selected than because of faulty analysis of the problem. Figure 17–6 illustrates two problems, the first easily solvable according to the algorithmic process and the second difficult to solve in any way. Problem P_1 may be easy to define and capable of efficient solu-

FIGURE 17–6
Decision making in two types of problems

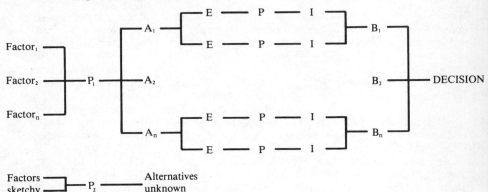

Factors ──┐
          ├─P₂ ─── Alternatives
sketchy ──┘   unknown

tion, but P_2 may be the more important problem. As Peter Drucker puts it, "Efficiency is doing things right; effectiveness is doing the right thing." Ideally a manager does the right things right.

What it amounts to is that if you take any problem too seriously you have to pay elsewhere. For example, when Allied planners in World War II became convinced that if the convoy battle against the U-boat was lost in the North Atlantic we would lose the war—an essentially correct conclusion—there was a distinct danger of so overkilling the U-boat problem in the North Atlantic that the U-boats would decide to go somewhere else, like the Caribbean or the Indian Ocean, and screw up Allied efforts there. Thus the principle of suboptimization was born. If you overkill on production, maintenance and quality will suffer. If you are too thorough on quality, little or nothing will get out the gate.

FORMULATING AND TESTING ALTERNATIVES

Managers, like good physicians, begin the process of decision making by making a diagnosis of the problem to be solved. The diagnosis:

1. Identifies the problem.
2. Specifies the causes.
3. Defines the effects.
4. Helps to clarify the goal to be achieved.

Following the diagnosis, they set out to find possible solutions to the problem. Rarely do they hit on one perfect way to solve it. Instead, as shown in Figure 17–7, they frequently list the alternatives available to solve the problem and evaluate each against a set of criteria which tests the appropriateness of each solution. If none is completely satis-

FIGURE 17–7
Considering alternatives

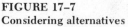
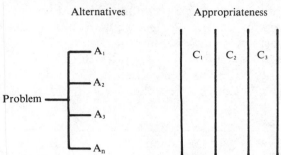

factory, they look for further alternatives, hoping to find a better solution. To find other alternatives, they can either draw on their own experience or find out what other executives or companies have done in similar circumstances.

In the past, experience has usually turned out to be a good guide to finding solutions to problems, provided allowances are made for changed circumstances. This is increasingly not the case in present

FIGURE 17–8
Extending cigarette manufacturers' options

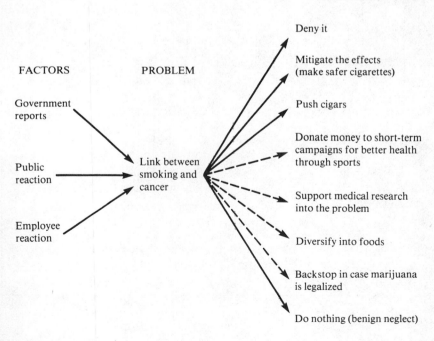

circumstances, however, and novel solutions to novel problems have to be evolved. In the new industrial state—with the emergence of the consumer, rapidly changing technology, increasing government regulation, rising competition, and new value systems—the conservative solutions of yesterday are less relevant to today's problems.

U.S. automobile manufacturers, under the gun from foreign competition and beset by the difficulties of designing cars which are safe to ride in, give acceptable miles per gallon of gasoline consump-

"Ed, you're the only person I know who *always* makes money in the Stock Market. What's your secret?"

tion, and keep the pollution of exhaust emission down to a safe level, can no longer rely on past experience as a guide to solving their current problems. They are jammed into an entirely new set of problems, which cannot be solved by styling changes. Automobile owners are looking for safety, reliability, and a car they can afford to keep on driving. What is needed is fresh, imaginative, and distinctive thinking to develop models which are relevant to contemporary needs.

Effective decision making is facilitated by refusing to accept the spectrum of alternatives that appears at first sight. Figure 17–8 illustrates both the readily apparent (solid lines) alternatives that cigarette manufacturers may have come up with when their industry was charged with contributing to lung cancer and a few of the less obvious ones (broken lines) that might be developed with further thought, synectics sessions, asking for suggestions, and so forth.

DECISION RULES OF THUMB

Two types of decision theory, normative and descriptive, were defined above (see Figure 17–3). Normative theory specifies courses of action that conform to the manager's belief and values. Descriptive theory deals with how managers in fact manage the probabilities of uncertain events. Basically managers tend to act in a conservative manner.

It is naturally difficult for managers to engage in rational decision making. Basically, this is because their capacity for information processing is significantly limited. Managers tend to follow what is called the law of small numbers, whereby even small samples are viewed as representative of the population from which they are drawn, and they are likely to underestimate the errors and unreliability inherent in such small samples. They are also subject to the availability fallacy, whereby they are led to draw conclusions on the evidence that they have because it is available rather than because it is relevant. There is abundant evidence that managers overestimate their own abilities and suffer from the illusion of control. One way a manager obtains confidence about a decision is by structuring the thesis.

There are several decision rules which can help managers make decisions more effectively. The first proposition suggests application of the principle of divide and conquer. The problem must be broken into structurally related parts. Research suggests that decomposing problems improves judgment.

Managers also can be provided with assistance in assessing problems. Generally, advice should be given in interview form rather than through computer techniques for assessing probabilities. Managers can develop this skill by making probability forecasts about particular events and later comparing the assessed probability to the "truth." Contrary to what a lot of decision theorists would like, executives make little use of sophisticated operations or research techniques.

Many analysts use an approach developed by Harvard Business School and Stanford Research Institute. In facing a new problem a manager lists the alternatives, constructs a model of interrelations, assesses the problem of relative contingencies, finds out what the boss wants, and finally assesses the possible alternatives. Usually the alternatives are presented in the form of a decision tree which makes it easier to determine the one to be implemented.

IMPLEMENTATION: THE CONSEQUENCES OF POSTPONING A DECISION

Tremendous problems can develop in an organization if the chief executive is not willing to bite the bullet or to defuse a potentially explosive situation which is about to blow up. An example of this refusal to bite the bullet was the Firestone Tire and Rubber Company's hydra-headed controversy over the safety of its Firestone 500 steel-belted radial tires. In October 1978, the Department of Transportation, arguing that the 23.6 million 500 radials produced could be unsafe, ordered their recall. It had evidence of more than 14,000 tire failures, 29 deaths, and more than 50 injuries involving these tires.

Firestone could have forestalled the recall if it had made up its mind to bite the bullet and deal with the problem beforehand, because its own studies had revealed radial defects as early as 1975. The company was heavily criticized for not facing up to this problem, and as pressures escalated its stock dipped and there was a loss of market share.

This particular problem arises when the steel belts which rest between the tread and the carcass of the tire begin to develop adhesion problems. As heat builds up it changes the chemical makeup of the adhesives binding the tire components together. In a crisis of this nature the company should have made a radical decision in the early stages. Postponing the decision was fatal.

TOPIC 2
Creative decision making

A CHALLENGE TO RATIONAL DECISION THEORY

Rational decision theory is undergoing a major transformation, mainly because many managers have found the theory irrelevant. The argument is that rational decision theory excludes many important variables and is unable to make accurate predictions about organizational outcomes. Herbert Simon, who was recently awarded the Nobel Prize for his work in applied economics, has made the most succinct statement of the basic problem of rational decision making. Simon assumes that humans have a limited capacity to process information. Further, they are capable of learning and can develop rules of thumb to help them in decision making. Executives make short-term decisions that come up with satisficing rather than optimizing solutions.

Chris Argyris has challenged the argument that rationality is the basis of most executive decision making and instead has suggested that the importance of intuition has been underestimated. Simon's argument is that Gresham's law applies to decision making, that is, programmed activity drives out nonprogrammed activity. Indeed, Simon is optimistic that the rules governing nonprogrammed decision making will soon be understood. Argyris's argument is that the concept of satisficing explains the naturalness of low-level aspiration and the bungling of bureaucrats who have allowed themselves to settle for something less than the best solution. The answer for Argyris is to create an organizational environment where trust, openness and individuality dominate.

Moving beyond analysis

Thus, an increasing number of managers and behavioral scientists are becoming disenchanted with the idea of a hard-nosed, more numerate, classical-type manager who solves problems through the use of analytical techniques such as operations research, corporate planning, and the development of management information systems. This backlash against the quantitative analysis approach is derived to a significant extent from the failure of such techniques to come up with answers to modern corporate problems. A major critic of analytical managers is Harold J. Leavitt, who characterizes the analytical style as a preference for the language of numbers, a capacity for breaking a problem into its components, and a search for operational decision rules.

Analytical managers tend to employ a cognitive style which is convergent: that is, like engineers, they work toward the answer at "the back of the book." The classical analytical manager is seen as being tough-minded, as using logic and analytical techniques rather than intuitive synthetic ones. The example cited by Leavitt as the analytical manager par excellence is Robert McNamara, who has shown a brilliant analytical skill not only as secretary of defense but also as president of the Ford Motor Company.

The classical analytical manager uses a method which places a heavy weight on established facts, quantitative data, and verifiable conclusions. Many of the most respected academics follow "the method," and it can be truly effective in getting out research and certainly in getting it published in academic journals.

But "the method" needs to be supplemented for application in organizations, mainly because managers have become very efficient at solving the wrong problems. If they are going to be effective, the first step must be to find the right problem. In "Beyond the Analytic Manager," Leavitt divides the problem-solving process into three stages: problem finding, problem solving, and solution implementation. He sets out to rectify the matters of problem identification and implementation.

Unfortunately, management education has little to say about the problem-finding process, Such questions as "Is this a crisis?" or "What do we truly want to do?" are typically not raised in courses on decision making. To get the problem-finding process going is not only difficult but can end in disaster. Executives who attend meetings and sit as mute witnesses to the dissection of trivial problems are often puzzled by their own inability to get the group going on the right problem.

How can this situation be corrected? Basically, managers must stop thinking like scientists (see Figure 17–9) and become more creative. Some behavioral scientists have suggested that what executives need

FIGURE 17–9
How managers and scientists think

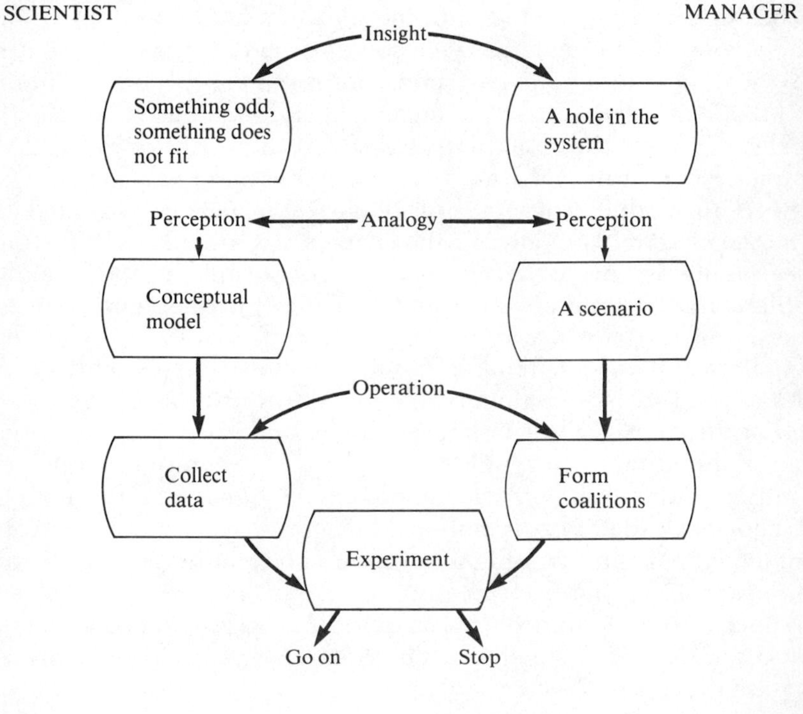

are courses in consciousness raising, ranging from Zen to TM, to improve their creativity.

What is creativity? P. E. Vernon argues in *Creativity* that it "involves novel combinations or unusual associations of ideas which must have theoretical or social value or make an emotional impact on other people." Surprisingly little systematic study has been given to the creative process. Figure 17–10 defines it as a three-stage process and suggests appropriate behaviors for each stage.

FIGURE 17–10
Stages in the creative process

STAGE	TYPE	BEHAVIORS
Preparation	Conscious	*Saturation.* Investigating the problem in all directions to become fully familiar with it, its setting, causes, and effects. *Deliberation.* Mulling over these ideas, analyzing and challenging them, viewing them from different optics.
Latent period	Unconscious	*Incubation.* Relaxing, switching off, and turning the problem over to the unconscious mind. *Illumination.* Emerging with possible answers–dramatic, perhaps off beat, but fresh and new.
Presentation	Conscious	*Verification.* Clarifying and fleshing out the idea, testing it against the criteria of appropriateness. *Accommodation.* Trying the solution out on other people and other problems.

Psychological research has shown that creative people are less anxious and more autonomous, dynamic, and integrated; they see themselves as being different from less creative people. They are less authoritarian, more achievement oriented, and more accepting of their inner impulses. They appear to have better psychological well-being. A technique for improving creativity which recognizes these traits is synectics.

Synectics

Synectics, a creative problem-solving technique developed by William J. J. Gordon, means different things to different people. One view emphasizes the idea of bringing together people with different perspectives, skills, and information and locking them in a room until they come up with a novel solution to a problem. The word *synectics,* like many popular organization words, is derived from the Greek and means fitting together different and irrelevant elements. This is what synectics sets out to do: provide a venue and a vehicle for integrating apparently different and irrelevant elements of a situation to formulate new solutions to problems.

The idea behind synectics is that the creative process can be taught. The synectics paradigm involves two paradoxical steps: making the strange familiar, and making the familiar strange.

Because creative individuals seem to respond well to a moderate level of conflict, they apparently can cope better with their own wild fantasies, which they somehow channel toward solving problems. The aim in synectics is to facilitate the process of "letting go" so that the participants' imagination can run riot.

Reconciling opposites

Creative executives have an ability to resolve the tension between opposites productively. They are able to engage in Janusian thinking, which takes its name from the Roman god of doorways and beginnings, whose two faces look in opposite directions. In Janusian thinking, an executive is able to look at and reconcile two opposites or antitheses simultaneously. For example, a creative executive can see a development problem from the point of view of both research ("We need further time to prepare the process') and production ("We want to begin manufacturing on Monday").

And like poetry which describes moments of great emotion recollected in moments of tranquillity, creative things apparently come to executives out of the blue, away from the office.

The creative cognitive style

People perceive their environment by an active porcess of transaction, rather than being passive recipients of the sense data with which environment bombards them. People receive information in characteristic ways, interpret it idiosyncratically, and store it in the filing subsystem of their memory banks. As A. J. Cropley puts it in "Creativity":

> Hence, the cognitive approach to creativity asks about the extent to which highly creative people are prepared to take risks in their thinking, about their willingness to take in large quantities of the information the environment has to offer (rather than to restrict themselves to a narrow, but safe, segment of it), about their capacity for quickly changing their point of view, and so on. . . .

Box 17–2: How creative are you?*

N.B. Time yourself while doing this test.

1. Complete the doodle.

2. The Inuit rely on seals for survival, but the animals are difficult to hunt. They can be captured when they come up for air at holes in the ice, but their hearing is so sensitive that they will not come up to a hole if they hear footsteps above them. How can the Inuit overcome this?

3. A farmer keeps six pigs in pens of equal size, which he has constructed of 13 gates. An emergency requires that he take one gate to another place on the farm. How can he build six pens of equal size with only 12 gates?

4. Change the amount shown into six by adding one line.   IX

5. Using a checkerboard and eight checkers, place the checkers on any of the 64 squares so that no two checkers are on the same vertical, horizontal, or diagonal line.

6. Punctuate the following words to form a meaningful sentence.
John where Jim had had had had had had had

7. Place six coins in two rows, to form a cross, as shown. By moving only one coin change the pattern into two rows of four coins.

8. In a room with no windows, no trapdoors, and the door locked from the inside, there is a man, hanging by a rope around his neck, three feet off the floor. There are no tables, chairs or other objects; the room is completely empty. The walls are out of reach of the man's arms. That's all there is — empty room, dangling corpse and a puddle of water. How did the man die?

* Answers are on p. 516.
Source: *The Canadian Gazette*, June 30/July 1, 1978.

Thus, those people whose cognitive style involves the least censoring of the information in the external world are most likely to be creative thinkers.

. . . the fact [is] that the highly creative thinker is, to put it plainly, prepared to think boldly. . . .

The creative thinker is, above all, flexible and adaptable in his intellectual functioning.

Box 17–2 provides an interesting test by which you can measure your own creativity.

TOPIC 3
Group decision making

There is abundant evidence to support the proposition that groups make riskier decisions than individuals do. There are four possible reasons. First, risk takers are persuasive in getting more cautious companions to shift their positions. Second, as members of a group familiarize themselves with the issues and arguments they seem to feel more confident about taking risks. Third, responsibility for decision making can be diffused across members of the group. Fourth, there is the suggestion that in our culture people do not like to appear cautious in a public context.

GROUPTHINK

Examination of two decisions made by President John F. Kennedy's administration provides a good insight into the processes of group decision making. The first was the Bay of Pigs decision, which ended in a disaster. The second, related to the Cuban missile crisis, was widely regarded as brilliant.

The Bay of Pigs decision

In giving their full approval to the Bay of Pigs intervention President Kennedy, Dean Rusk, Robert McNamara, and other Cabinet members assumed that a brigade of Cuban exiles could invade Cuba (at the Bay of Pigs) and topple Castro, without jeopardizing the U.S. government. The actual military operation was a fiasco. The ammunition ships failed to show up on schedule; the brigade of exiled Cubans was surrounded, and 1,200 members were captured and ignominiously held.

Irving L. Janis notes in *Victims of Groupthink* the vivid picture of the president's reactions as given in Theodore Sorensen's *Kennedy:*

> . . . When the first news reports revealed how wrong his expectations had been, President Kennedy was stunned. As the news grew worse during the next three days, he became angry and sick at heart. He realized that the plan he thought he had approved had little in common with the one he had in fact approved. "How could I have been so stupid to let them go ahead?" he asked. Sorensen wrote, "His anguish was doubly deepened by the knowledge that the rest of the world was asking the same question."

Answers to Box 17–2

Answers:

1. Any doodle that goes outside the confines of the box is a creative one and scores 5 points.

2. Two Inuit walk one behind the other, carefully synchronizing their footsteps. The seals hear only one set of steps. One Inuk stops at a hole while the other walks on to a nearby hole. The seals avoid the second hole and the first Inuk becomes the successful hunter. Score 5.

3. Score 5.   4. Score 5. SIX

5. Score 5 for this or any other correct solution, there are several.

6. John, where Jim had had "had," had had "had had." Score 5.

7. Score 5 if you moved one coin on top of the centre coin, thus:

8. The man hanged himself by stepping off a three-foot-high block of ice that he took into the room with him and that had melted by the time he was found. Score 5.

SCORING: Total your scores. If you completed all the items in 10 minutes or less, award yourself a bonus of 10 points. A maximum score of 50 (including bonus points) ranks as brilliant, 40 as highly creative. A 30-35 indicates strong flashes of creativity but not a consistently creative personality. At 20-25 you aren't letting your mind off the leash enough. Below 20 you may be (and very probably are) reliable, tolerant, predictable and many other sterling things, but creative isn't one of them.

Sources for quiz: A. Kowalski, K. Weber, and Dr D. Barrett of Management Concepts Limited, Toronto.

Others' reactions are also noted by Janis:

> Arthur Schlesinger, Jr., in his authoritative history of the Kennedy administration, recalled that "Kennedy would sometimes refer incredulously to the Bay of Pigs, wondering how a rational and responsible government could ever have become involved in so ill-starred an adventure." The policy advisers who participated in the deliberations felt much the same way, if not worse. Allen Dulles, for example, was "still troubled and haggard" several days later and offered to resign as chief of the CIA. Secretary of Defense McNamara, when he left the government seven years later, publicly stated that he still felt personally responsible for having misadvised President Kennedy on the Bay of Pigs. All who participated in the Bay of Pigs decision were perturbed about the dangerous gap between their expectations and the realities they should have anticipated, which resulted, as Sorensen put it, in "a shocking number of errors in the whole decision-making process."

In retrospect, it is difficult to understand how men of such intellectual brilliance, who could mobilize so much analytical ability collectively, could fail to detect the serious flaws in the invasion plan.

The Cuban missile crisis decision

Within a year or so after the Bay of Pigs fiasco, the Soviet Union worked out an arrangement to set up missiles with atomic warheads in Cuba. For five days starting on October 16, 1962, the U.S. Executive Committee met continually to formulate a plan of action. They considered a wide range of options, including threats of a massive air strike or a naval blockade. As Janis describes it:

> The crisis continued for another eight days, and the same group continued to meet daily until the crisis was finally resolved by Khrushchev's offer to withdraw the missiles. On October 22, President Kennedy gave his dramatic speech revealing to the world the hitherto secret evidence of the offensive missile sites in Cuba and announcing the United States government's decision to quarantine Cuba. Khrushchev promptly denounced the blockade as "piracy." Eighteen Soviet ships—some of them almost certainly carrying nuclear armaments—continued relentlessly on their course toward the quarantine zone. During the next few suspenseful days the United States repeated its threat to board Soviet ships, forced several Soviet submarines to surface near the quarantine zone, and actually did board a Lebanese vessel chartered by the Soviet Union. These actions were calculated to postpone a direct military confrontation while demonstrating the firm resolve of the United States government to counteract the missile build-up in Cuba. Then, on October 24 and 25, shortly before reaching the quarantine zone, most of the Soviet cargo ships (including all those with large hatches, presumed to be carrying nuclear missiles) turned around and headed back toward Russian ports.

The Executive Committee handled the decision-making process with distinction and very effectively. Contingency plans were evolved which gave the president real choices, laid out in the form of graduated steps. But perhaps more important than the formulation of these alternatives was the way the committee handled the actual decision-making process. For example, at one point it decided that an additional warning message, not a formal ultimatum, should be sent to the Soviet leaders, asking them to remove the missiles. The crisis was resolved on October 26 when the Soviets removed the missiles in exchange for assurance that the United States would not invade Cuba.

The Executive Committee, led mainly by Robert Kennedy and Robert McNamara, was able to function in a very effective way because problems were analyzed rationally and the process of decision making allowed members to argue against specific proposals. And indeed it was a polarization which took place in this committee that produced the phrase "hawks versus doves." It must not be forgotten that the Executive Committee, in formulating its decision, had the capability of both options.

The Bay of Pigs decision had catastrophic consequences for both the invading force and the United States. But a year later the same group made a extremely effective decision. It had developed considerable skill in its ability to make good group decisions.

THREE MODELS OF GROUP DECISION MAKING

Graham T. Allison, in *Essence of Decision,* quotes J. F. Kennedy on the mysteries of decision making: *"The essence of ultimate decision remains impenetrable to the observer—often, indeed, to the decider himself. . . . There will always be the dark and tangled stretches in the decision-making process—mysterious even to those who may be most intimately involved."*

President Kennedy may well have been talking about the problems he faced in resolving the Cuban missile crisis. Allison gives a vivid account of the crucial decisions surrounding the crisis which represents a breakthrough in the application of organizational and political theories to events.

Allison proposes three basic conceptual models that can be used to explain and predict the behavior of decision makers. They range from the rational actor to the organizational process to the mechanics of game theory.

Model I.   The rational actor or classical model

When confronted by a puzzling problem, the rational actor considers certain basic questions, which include the following:

1. What is the problem?
2. What are the alternatives?
3. What are the costs and benefits associated with each alternative?

The rational actor essentially tries to create a scenario or war game for looking at the problem. One of the advantages of the rational actor model is that it encourages the analyst to think what he would do if he were in the opponent's shoes.

The basic concepts of the model include: (1) goals and objectives, (2) alternatives, (3) consequences, and (4) choice. The underlying value is rationality. The power of the model derives from its rigor.

Model II.   The organizational process approach to decision making

In this model, decisions do not emerge from rational analysis and deliberate choices but rather as an output of larger organizations which apply standard operating procedures to the problem. Organizations are said to have repertoire programs and standing orders which lead to automative responses to the problem.

The best example of Model II in action are the ideas developed by H. A. Simon, such as satisficing, bounded rationality, and organizational slack. The object of the exercise is to avoid uncertainties and to use rules of thumb to find minimal solutions to problems.

Model III.   The game theory approach

Model III of organizational choice is based on the notion that organizations are made up of groups of game players involved in a central competitive game. The name of the game is politics, and bargaining is the main activity. The apparatus of an organization has as its center a political leader who is encompassed by a circle of central players.

These game players share power but in a context where one group temporarily triumphs over other groups. At any given time in any organization a large number of games are in process. Some of the questions suggested by Model III include:

1. What are the existing action channels for making things happen on the problem?
2. Which players are central?
3. What guidance can be derived in regard to outcomes by studying the styles and stances of these players?
4. What are the deadlines?
5. What foul-ups are likely?

Applying Allison's Model III to business organizations, the basic point is that presidential power is the power to persuade. Underneath the image of the "president in boots" is one of the "president in sneakers," moving from department to department trying to persuade other executives to climb on the band wagon. The president cannot issue instructions to cover every contingency but has to bargain with other executives and cliques to derive power.

In this context, business is a more or less complex arena for internal bargaining among executives and cliques. This palace perspective gives organizations a much more realistic backdrop. Bargaining becomes the hidden hand in organizations, and executives are forced to develop a bureaucratic policy framework to predict what is going to happen. Policy making becomes a process involving a series of concentric circles.

As Allison points out:

> RFK and Sorensen were the engineers of consensus. According to RFK's published recollection of the ExCom deliberations, "There was no rank, and, in fact, we did not even have a chairman." But the others recall that Robert Kennedy "soon emerged as the discussion leader." RFK recalled that "the conversations were completely uninhibited and unrestricted." Sorensen remarks on the "sense of complete equality." Nevertheless, he allows that in "shaping our deliberations when the President was absent, the best performer . . . was the Attorney General. McNamara has affirmed that it was Robert Kennedy "acting with his brother's consent, who did so much to organize the effort, monitor the results and assure the completion of work on which recommendations to the President were based." Stevenson compared the Attorney General to "a bull in a china shop." In another participant's words, "Bobby made Christians of us. We all knew little brother was watching; and keeping a little list of where everyone stood." In any case, the group moved toward consensus.
>
> Acheson, the leader of the air-strike advocates, attacked the Attorney General sharply on Wednesday. He received an invitation to visit the White House on Thursday. The President listened to his argument, but Acheson left with no question in his mind about where the buck stopped. That evening Kennedy informed the entire group of his decision in favor of the blockade. Friday was to have been the day of consensus, culminating in a formal decision that would be announced to the nation on Sunday evening.

In this game theory approach to decision making, where you stand on an issue depends on where you sit. Rarely do two sets of eyes see the problem from the same optic or perspective. Styles of play are very important (see Box 17–3).

Allison gives a good example of how the game players saw the game differently depending on their positions in the Cuban missile crisis. Kennedy turned the problem over to his 14-member Executive Com-

Box 17–3: A group portrait

In David Halberstam's words, those brilliant executives who brought us the Bay of Pigs, the Cuban missile crisis, Vietnam, and the trip to the moon were "the best and the brightest." They grew up during the Great Depression and reached manhood in World War II. They took control of our destiny in the 1960s and nearly turned us upside down in the 1970s. Many of them had outstanding careers as statesmen, politicians, entrepreneurs, and best-selling authors. In their lives there is a surprising amount of what Freud called the psychopathology of everyday life.

How do we know all this? Our reporter is George E. Vaillant, who is in charge of a study of a sample of men from a "higher competitive college" which is not named but is unmistakably Harvard. In his latest book *Adaptation to Life,* Vaillant, a 43-year-old psychiatrist, reports a study of 95 men from the classes of 1942, 1943, and 1944. These men, now in their fifties, constitute an elite of white males (80 percent Protestant, 10 percent Catholics, and 10 percent Jewish).

Vaillant's book tells much about the strategies of coping, how the individual's ego develops ingenious ways to deal with the patterns of success and failure. Vaillant began his research when he was 33 and his subjects were 46. After a quick glimpse of them at their college reunion, he exclaimed to his 54-year-old department chairman, "I don't want to grow up!" His initial impression was that these men were leading lives of quiet desperation.

In his interviews, Vaillant found that the men who at 19 had radiated charm were now bland examples of the grey-flannel-suit type. In college many of them had exhibited the traits associated with successful adult adaptation. In actual fact, however, these traits showed little correlation to midlife outcomes. Vaillant comes up with much evidence supporting the thesis that alcoholism, sadomasochistic marriages, depression, and psychosomatic ailments accompany overachievement and self-defeat. When asked to review their lives at forty-seven, many either forgot or denied the role model or ideals they had acknowledged as important at 19.

The pain of the late forties is, of course, associated with the midlife crisis, which in turn is connected with the fear of death. The argument is that if men in their forties are depressed, it is because they are confronted with the reality of their instincts and acknowledge their own pain. One major finding in this study was the fact that the men with the best marriages had the richest friendships and became the company presidents.

One of the most interesting findings was that people confronted with conflict engage in unconscious but often creative behavior. They utilize a variety of ego defense methods, including projection, repression, and sublimation, to keep stress within reasonable limits and to restore emotional balance. The aim is to obtain "time out" to master changes in self-image and to handle unresolved conflicts. What it amounts to is that the human ego grows in adversity as well as in prosperity.

Vaillant seems to be telling executives they have to be ready to cope, not only with problems, but also with personal disasters. Their ability to recover from pain can be an intense learning experience. In short, life is difficult for everyone. To put it another way, if you look hard enough at your enemies you can in fact come to love them.

Apparently, the men who took part in this study were not lacking in empathy or enjoyment in their personal lives. In fact, the best adapted men displayed more of both qualities. According to *Psychology Today* (September 1977), J. F. Kennedy was very likely an original member of the Vaillant study. Most of the members of "the best and the brightest" have lived through the terrifying experiences of our time and have come to terms with them by adapting their egos to make the apparently meaningless events of life meaningful.

Reference: George E. Vaillant, *Adaptation to Life* (Boston: Little, Brown & Co., 1977).

mittee which included the secretary of defense, Robert McNamara; the special assistant for national security affairs, McGeorge Bundy; and the attorney general, Robert Kennedy. The committee split itself into two polarized factions, the hawks and the doves. Kennedy's absence from many meetings turned out to be extremely advantageous. It allowed his brother, Bobby, a freer hand at testing out different ideas.

Allison points out how difficult it is to understand exactly how decisions emerge from the web of bureaucratic infighting. As many executives know, the process of crisis management is obscure and terribly risky. In the light of this analysis, it is easy to understand how top management frequently flies into a flap when a crisis explodes.

In conclusion, it is plausible to argue that management theorists, who write about organizations without taking part, are inclined to look for general causes as the explanation of events. Managers who cope with daily crises, however, imagine that everything is attributable to particular incidents or personalities and their own skill in pulling wires. As Alexis Tocqueville pointed out, "it is presumed that both are equally deceived."

Nevertheless, examining organizational crises through the conceptual lenses provided by Allison can provide insights into the unstated categories and assumptions that channel our thinking and influence our choices. Muddling through organizational choices can be facilitated to some extent by examining Allison's book, to get some clues as to how to handle the tyranny of the majority.

THE TYRANNY OF THE MAJORITY AND/OR THE MINORITY

One of the problems of pluralistic societies is the menace of fanatic factions. But if a pluralistic society is to survive, cliques and pressure groups must be allowed to have their say. In an organizational setting the same argument applies, but to a limited extent. The problem in an organization is to avoid the tyranny of the majority. It requires real managerial skills to encourage the expression of minority opinions so that factions are not pushed around by any overbearing majority.

But another major problem from a managerial point of view is the possible tyranny of the minority, who argue for rights and privileges recognizing their unique circumstances. To overcome this type of problem, managers have to seek insight into what a minority is trying to achieve.

In organizations, when too many decision makers and too many groups try to exercise vetos over decisions, organizational paralysis can result.

TOPIC 4
What every manager should know about organizational decision making

THE DECIDERS

In making decisions, managers seem to hold particular assumptions about the process. These assumptions include:

1. They will make limited use of information.
2. Their own utility function is unclear, subjective, and subject to variation.
3. They will work under conditions of bounded rationality.
4. They will use simplified models.
5. The system will sort itself out.

THE DECISION: THE BASIC PROCESS

In rational decision-making theory, management begins its review of decision making by listing the important decisions required by the organization. The relations between these decisions are specified and flow charted. Decision-flow analysis facilitates both understanding what decisions are being made by default and deciding how the structure of responsibilities and performance measurement can be linked. In the first instance, the decision analysis is carried through in broad

FIGURE 17–11
Environment types and decision modality

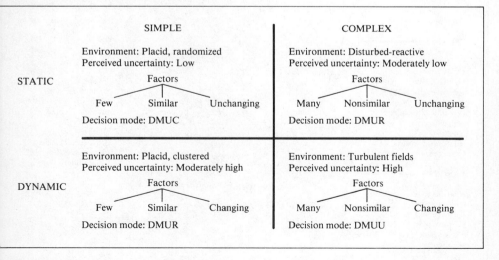

sweeps, with somewhat coarse analysis, if need be, to ensure that the whole system is reviewed.

In designing the organizational structure, decisions with the same or overlapping informational requirements are grouped in a particular manager's role specification. The decision-making system is not perfect, and the deficiencies must be identified and managed. Three groups—the information systems specialists, the operations research men, and the line managers—must work together.

The particular decision-making mode or method used depends on the environment of the organization. Figure 17–11 links the four environments identified by F. E. Emery and E. L. Trist (see Chapter 16) to the conditions of decision making under certainty (DMUC), under risk (DMUR), and under uncertainty (DMUU).

THE DECISION MATRIX: DECISION MAKING AS A SYSTEM

The contingency model of decision making as a system is shown in Figure 17–12. Using this model as a guide will help draw together the key concepts of this chapter into a format the executive can follow when deciding to decide.

FIGURE 17–12
Decision making as a system

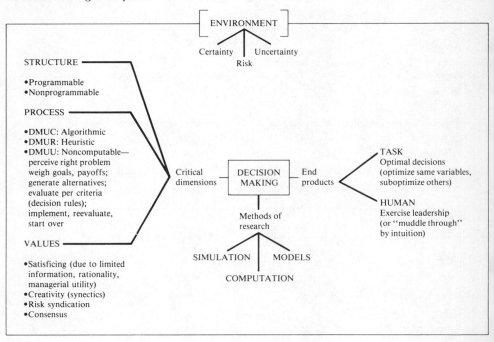

Programmable decisions, under certainty or near-certainty, are generally computable and straightforward. Heuristics can be applied to nonprogrammable decisions. The states of risk and uncertainty present the executive with increasing complexity. The problem must be chosen for its importance rather than its ease of solution. The executive must get used to thinking in terms of suboptimization, where scoring on one critical decision variable must be paid for by suboptimizing other variables. He must decide what is important to him, that is, assign values to particular outcomes in view of ultimate goals. He must not surrender his freedom of choice to the computer, which is only an adjunct of human intelligence. And he must accept that decision making is nearly always sporadic, fragmented, and rarely a matter of solving a complete problem in one continuous effort.

In terms of structure, the executive must decide whether the decision is programmable or nonprogrammable. This involves distinguishing among the states of certainty, risk, and uncertainty, and thus it points to the kinds of processes to be used.

To make all this operational, the executive must recognize that effective management involves a blend of risk syndication, consensus management, and operating within the zone of indifference of subordinates: Different situations require different executive styles. Thus the executive carefully selects *his* issues. An effective leader relies on an accurate, up-to-date information backup and is content to have the choice of structuring the sequence of decisions. Individual decisions can be made by consensus as long as he has the significant say in how the series of decisions is sequenced. In other words, other events decide individual events, not the "decision makers" for that particular event.

Thus the executive must seek to understand what is happening in the environment—not only the interactions between the organization and its inputs and outputs, but also the interactions between other organizations whose fusions and fissions may dramatically change the course of history of the organization. The rates of externally induced change will inevitably make internally induced change into a side show, with the players locked in roles and scripts of yesteryear while the rest of the global village speculates about their impending demise. The turbulent environment of modern times refuses to stand still. Consideration of this existential complexity is a necessity if we are to avoid the catastrophes predicted by the computer Cassandras of modern times.

REVIEW AND RESEARCH

1. You have been offered an appointment in a large metropolitan city outside your own state as a personal assistant in charge of corporate planning to

the president in a *Fortune* 500 company. (Select a company in the nearest large city outside your state.) Define the conditions (financial, intrinsic to the role), prospects, and other factors which would:

a. Take you to the new job.

b. Keep you in your present position.

Use the decision process sequence to make your decision to quit or stay.

2. Consider a decision (e.g., selection of a person, project, product, etc.) which was recently made in any organization with which you are familiar. List the other decisions that impinged on the focal decision. Identify the spectrum of choice, critical decision rules, quality and quantity of data collected, processes employed. Plot the decision on a yes-no decision tree. How could the quality of the decision be improved?

3. Identify the spectrum of choice, critical decision rules, information collected, processes employed, etc., for one of the following:

a. The U.S. National Security Council during the Cuban missile crisis.

b. President Nixon's decision to fire Special Prosecutor Archibald Cox in the Watergate case.

4. What is the most important organizational decision in which you have participated? List the search processes employed. Identify the filters in the information process. Construct a process flowchart of the actual decision.

5. Describe the personalities, life-styles, and operating procedures of three risk takers you know. Develop a composite portrait.

6. List the rules for creative group decision making. Use these rules either (a) to design a new urban rapid transit system, or (b) to select teams of students to find full-time jobs as a team after the team graduates.

7. What have you learned about executives as deciders from actual experience? Why *don't* executives follow the book and use the standard decision processes?

8. How is decision making affected by organizational climate? Use Rensis Likert's System 1, 2, 3, and 4 (see Chapter 16) to help you formulate your answer.

GLOSSARY OF TERMS

Certainty. State of knowledge in which the decision maker knows before the event the specific outcomes that will result from each course of action.

Creative decision-making process. Decision making under nonprogrammable circumstances, involving three basic stages: preparation, latent period, presentation. The preparation stage is conscious and includes the processes of saturation and deliberation; the latent period involves the subconscious processes of incubation and illumination; the presentation stage (conscious) includes the processes of verification and accommodation (see Figure 17–10).

Decision process. Subject to the limitations of risk and uncertainty, the decision process follows the basic steps of (1) setting goals and evaluating utilities, (2) perceiving the correct problem, (3) formulating alternatives, (4) setting up standard operating procedures as decision rules, (5) selecting the first alternative which meets a minimal level of acceptability, (6) implementing that alternative, (7) evaluating performance, and, if necessary, (8) changing the operating procedure and formulating new goals (starting the process again).

Organizational decisions. Organizational choices, which may be (1) programmable, (2) nonprogrammable—creative, or (3) nonprogrammable—negotiated, corresponding to conditions of relative certainty, risk, and uncertainty, respectively. Programmable decisions presume agreed-upon goals, computational (algorithmic) processes, and predictable outcomes, and are characteristic of classical theory. Nonprogrammable decisions assume conditions of risk or uncertainty in regard to outcomes, demand creative and heuristic processes, are not computable, and are usually sporadic rather than continuous.

Iterative process. A trial-and-error approach to solving problems. It involves making a trial decision and evaluating the outcome of this decision with respect to a desired objective. If the objective has been reached, the process stops; if not, another decision is made and the process is continued until the objective has been reached.

Risk. A state of knowledge in which the decision maker can specify outcomes to each alternative course of action and assign probabilities to the likelihood of each outcome; measurable uncertainty.

Synectics. A group problem-solving technique developed by Gordon in which various elements are fitted together to produce novel and creative alternatives with a view to reaching group consensus.

Uncertainty. A state of knowledge in which the decision maker may be able to specify the outcomes for each particular course of action but is unable to assign probabilities.

DEBATE: Does participation always improve effectiveness?

Theorists such as Rensis Likert and Chris Argyris have assumed that the participative form of structure is most conducive to effectiveness. This view is also supported by Alfred D. Chandler, who argued from his study of General Motors that decentralization improves profitability.

Against this view Mauk Mulder has argued, in "Power Equalization through Participation," that the participation of the less powerful in decision making may in fact lead to a widening of the power differences between the powerful and the less powerful.

It is impossible to reach a generalized conclusion regarding the relationship between decentralization and participation on the one hand and effectiveness on the other.

Question
How can participation be used to reach effective decisions?

DIAGRAM SUMMARY OF CHAPTER 18

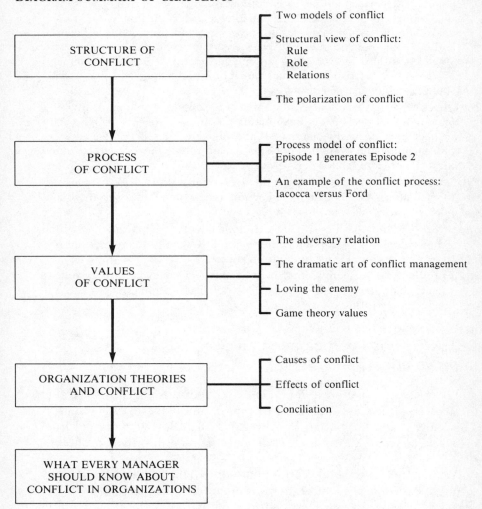

18

Conflict in organizations

A CONFLICT DRAMA: "YOU'RE BRILLIANT, BUT BORED. I'M BRILLIANT, AND YOU'RE FIRED"

The scene is a room in an expensive hotel in Boston. The noises of an expense-account cocktail party going on next door are percolating in. The president is standing with his back to the window; he has a full tumbler of scotch in his hand. Facing him, with his back to the door, is an executive holding a nearly empty glass.

PRESIDENT: I wanted to have a chance to talk to you, John.

EXECUTIVE: Yes, sir.

PRESIDENT: You're brilliant, but bored. I'm brilliant, and you're fired.

EXECUTIVE: What do you mean?

PRESIDENT: I mean you have too high an IQ for this assignment, and therefore I'm letting you go.

EXECUTIVE: Just like that.

PRESIDENT: I'm giving you three months' salary in lieu of notice.

EXECUTIVE: You mean I'm off payroll as of now.

PRESIDENT: In effect, yes. I want to you fly back tomorrow morning to New York to clean out your desk. I have already hired your replacement.

EXECUTIVE: Why can't I stay on in Boston over the weekend and clean out my desk on Monday morning? (The argument shifts from the focus of firing to cleaning out desks and continues for some time.)

PRESIDENT: OK, Monday's all right by me.

EXECUTIVE: I appreciate that, sir.

PRESIDENT: Can I ask you a question? About your feelings?

EXECUTIVE: Sure, go ahead.

PRESIDENT: What are you planning to do tonight? I suppose once you have called your wife, you might get a few drinks under your belt.

EXECUTIVE: The thought had crossed my mind.

PRESIDENT: I wonder if you would be offended if I offered you this bottle of Chivas Regal—for old time's sake.

EXECUTIVE: Oh, I don't mind.

PRESIDENT: I want you to do one last thing for me.

EXECUTIVE: Such as?

PRESIDENT: Go next door. Say good-bye to your personal assistant and the company treasurer. He has an envelope for you with your check in it.

EXECUTIVE: Right now?

PRESIDENT (nods): Gook luck—and good-bye.

The president shakes hands with the executive, who leaves. No sooner has the executive put down the phone after calling his wife than he receives a call from his former assistant, who offers to spend the evening commiserating with him over the gift bottle of scotch.

ON COOLING OUT THE MARK

What the assistant is doing is cooling the mark out. The victim of a firing must suddenly adapt to a new state. He or she faces an identity crisis. In the language of the underworld, the mark, the victim, the sucker, the fall guy—the person who is done in—has to be cooled off.

Erving Goffman, a brilliant sociologist whose methods of exposition appear to owe as much to the cinema as to the behavioral sciences, paints a penetrating picture of the process in "On Cooling the Mark Out." Goffman analyzes the confidence game—the con, as practitioners call it—and comes up with a description of the dramatic process which reveals the structure (the actors), the process (the actual steps), and the values (underlying beliefs).

Goffman's description of the con applies not only to the fired executive but can also be easily adapted to fit the process of finding and fitting in a new manager. There are executive search consultants who find the "victim" who is sold the organization. Eventually, he is "sold the dummy" (makes his big mistake), and he has to go. Now sometimes the mark, the failed executive, is not willing to go quietly. The mark has to be cooled out.

Corporate life is, in fact, a succession of dramas similar in structure, processes, and values to the theme Goffman has addressed. Such themes cannot be fully understood in logical terms. Corporate life, with its capers, caprices, and coronaries, cannot be understood in simple behavioral science terms but can be grasped in terms of drama and existentialism.

TOPIC 1
Structure of conflict

TWO MODELS OF CONFLICT

In our turbulent environment, where conflict is the order of the day, it is small wonder that many corporate executives are bewildered by the forces of organizational change. Old concepts of human relations, including the notion that conflict per se is harmful and should be avoided at all cost, do not square with the facts any longer. Indeed, the new approach is that conflict, if properly handled, can lead to more effective and appropriate arrangements.

Contrary to conventional wisdom, the most important single thing about conflict is that it is good for you. While this is not a scientific statement of fact, it reflects a basic and unprecedented shift of emphasis—a move away from the human relations point of view which saw all conflict as bad.

We can say that an organizational revolution has been taking place, characterized by an acceleration of healthy subversive tendencies which gathered force and speed in the 1960s in protest against the iron law of corporate oligarchy. This is a protest against the presumption that, in organizations, policies and instructions flow down the hierarchy and reports flow up. It is a protest against the cozy paternalistic world of classical management theory where top management carries total responsibility. It is a protest exemplified by the success of Lawrence Peter and Raymond Hull's *The Peter Principle*, which was on the best-seller lists for many months. It is increasingly a middle-class protest by executives and professionals and decreasingly a protest from a diminishing shop floor. It is a protest with its own particular diabolism; some of the games played in executive suites make Edward Albee's "Get the Guests" and "Bring up the Baby," as portrayed in *Who's Afraid of Virginia Woolf?* seem like nursery pastimes.

In this new frontier environment, conflict is the order of the day. The change is so radical that managers may wonder just how it came about.

Realistic reassessment

The emerging view of conflict, as shown in Figure 18–1, reverses many of the cozy nostrums of human relations management which had its intellectual origins in the Hawthorne studies of the 1920s. As noted in Chapter 3, these studies "proved" the then startling proposition that interpersonal relations count more for productivity than the quality of the physical environment, such as the level of illumination. An entire school of management grew up around the notion that if people were

FIGURE 18–1
Human relations and realistic models of conflict

HUMAN RELATIONS MODEL (old view)	REALISTIC MODEL (new look)
Conflict is by definition avoidable	Conflict is inevitable
Conflict is caused by troublemakers, boat rockers, and prima donnas	Conflict is determined by structural factors such as the physical shape of a building, the design of a career structure, or the nature of a class system
Legalistic forms of authority such as going through channels or sticking to the book are emphasized	Conflict is integral to the nature of change
Scapegoats are accepted as inevitable	A minimal level of conflict is optimal

well treated, they would produce. Conflict, by definition, was harmful and should be avoided. Those who generated conflict were troublemakers and were bad for the organization.

The new view is that perfect organizational health is not freedom from conflict. On the contrary, if properly handled, conflict can lead to more effective and more appropriate adjustments.

STRUCTURAL VIEW OF CONFLICT

The structural view of conflict presupposes that the conflict arises from the shape of the system or from the anatomy of the organization. Conflict arises from the fact of two structures, two sets of rules, roles, and relations, which cannot be fitted together, cannot be brought face to face. The rules are unclear, inchoate, and ill defined; the roles create demarcation disputes; and the relations are confused because managers and subordinates send the wrong signals.

Rule-oriented conflict

Much of this structural conflict has its origins in the development and interpretation of rules. For example, project managers often report that one source of conflict is rule definition, mainly concerning priorities and procedures, selection of technical opinions, and recruitment of staff.

FIGURE 18–2
The appeal system in action

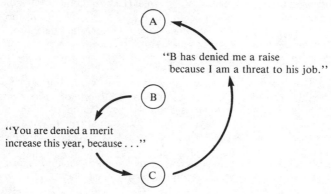

"B has denied me a raise
because I am a threat to his job."

"You are denied a merit
increase this year, because . . ."

Traditionally, organizations have resolved such structural conflicts by the development of formal appeal mechanisms. In this way conflict that cannot be resolved at one level can always be referred to a superior (see Figure 18–2). Perhaps a more commonly used means of structural conflict resolution is to eliminate the weaker party. More typically, however, these conflicts are not individual issues but involve infighting between coalitions who have organized themselves into groups (see Box 18–1).

Role-oriented conflict

Structural conflict also arises in the vertical dimension because hierarchy imposes a necessary strain between the top and lower levels of the hierarchy. The occupants of the roles in the lower levels are not lesser people but only further down the totem. This produces a top

Box 18–1: Organizing conflict

Conflict has to be organized in groups, as Ralph Dahrendorf points out:

First, for effective conflict regulation to be possible, both parties to a conflict have to recognize the necessity and reality of the conflict situation and, in this sense, the fundamental justice of the cause of the opponent. . . . A second prerequisite of effective conflict regulation is the organization of interest groups. So long as conflicting forces are diffuse, incoherent aggregates, regulation is virtually impossible. . . . Thirdly, in order for effective regulation to be possible, the opposing parties in social conflicts have to agree on certain formal rules of the game that provide the framework of their relations.

Source: Ralf Dahrendorf, *Class and Class Conflict in Industrial Society.* Stanford, Cal.: Stanford University Press, 1959.

Box 18-2: The fate of the fired executive

To find out what it feels like to be a once-successful executive who becomes unemployed as the result of being fired, *The New York Times* conducted interviews of executives who had been let go and who lived in the affluent North Shore suburbs of Chicago. The survey revealed a world of frustration, disappointment, and other psychological problems. All the executives interviewed were college graduates who had been employed for at least ten years, whose salaries had ranged from $25,000 to $40,000, and who were from 30 to 50 years old.

Not unexpectedly, being fired was a traumatic experience. But apparently executives can make it back from this kind of experience—they all found jobs again at salaries the same or nearly the same as before. In terms of the timespan of the layoff, the rule seems to be one week for every $1,000 of salary, according to management consultants. Thus an executive who had been earning $26,000 could expect a six-month or 26-week interval before finding a comfortable appointment.

Executives often are taken by surprise when they are fired. Most firms have no systematic means of seriously reviewing a manager's performance, but a particular routine is usually used to terminate an executive. In many ways it is like an old French execution; the superiors try to rush the victim, take him by surprise, guillotine him, and dispose of the body in one swift act. For example, the *Times* article reported the reaction of a 44-year-old Harvard business graduate who had been a vice president for a food processing concern:

> "I thought I was doing a good job. I had never been let go before. I never thought I would. I had been with my firm 13 years, and then I was called back from a business trip one day and told to report to my boss immediately. It was a Friday. I remember that look on my boss's face. He told me the company didn't need me any longer. I was given my final paycheck. I cleaned out my desk picked up my briefcase and walked out."

How did unemployment affect the executives surveyed? A 47-year-old marketing vice president said: "The whole thing was devastation to my personality. I got angry at myself at first, and then I was constantly on edge. It was very hard."

"I was used to such an active day, and then there was this sudden emptiness," a division sales manager for an electronics company explained. Getting out of bed in the morning becomes a chore, and wide swings in moods are noted. Jack, employed or unemployed, is greatly dependent on his wife Jill for support.

Many advertisements must be answered and interviews taken before a job offer is produced. The survey found:

> A 38-year-old plant manager from Northbrook, a Chicago suburb, said he answered 103 newspaper ads before he got three responses and two of them were form letters. A $35,000-a-year Chicago advertising executive said he had 30 interviews during a two-month period, but no job offer resulted. Another man had 75 interviews in five months. He had two job offers, but neither were ones he felt he could accept. A Glencoe manufacturing executive said that, despite hundreds of contacts with companies where someone had put in a good word for him, he had only 10 interviews and one offer.

In my experience, shifting an executive (either out of the company or out of a particular slot) requires a dramatic effort, involving a conspiracy of the superior and colleagues (and occasionally subordinates) who do the actual firing. First the victim has to be placed in an ambivalent context, which mobilizes his guilt feelings to argue that he is not OK. Next he is sent on vacation or to take a course so that the final arrangements can be made in his absence. When he returns he has to be taken by storm and gotten out physically.

Reference: *The New York Times,* October 20, 1974.

dog–underdog syndrome in organizations. The problem is that top–dogs, especially chief executive officers (CEOs), are articulate, aggressive, and persuasive, and they love creating win-lose competition among the underdogs. This aggressive strutting behavior causes problems involving perceptions, emotions, and behaviors (see Figure 18–3).

FIGURE 18–3
Conflict between top dog and underdog involves perceptions, emotions, and behaviors

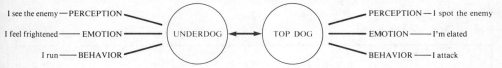

As Chris Argyris has pointed out, CEOs are not unaware of the amount of hassle they thereby created for "their people." What they do is to creatively exploit it. These dog fights are dominated by executives who have a strong sense of the jugular and who must dominate their turf or territory. But it would be a gross oversimplification to imagine that such conflicts are relatively easy to deal with. The reality of the matter is quite different. Structural conflict is often expressed in (subtle and elusive ways that defy simple and logical explanations. (Box 18–2 suggests what it feels like to be fired.)

Relation-oriented conflict

Effective managers seem to gravitate naturally to a gamesman style which allows them to play the executive game with great dramatic skill and for high stakes. The method owes more to poker than to chess. The essential ingredient in both management and poker is conflict, but the conflict always involves bluffing. Experienced executives develop considerable skill in playing out the dramatic roles with great speed and with great force. The art of conflict management, like good poker, fosters the development of a style which is both complex and captivating.

THE POLARIZATION OF CONFLICT

Aggression at the level of destructive behavior may well represent a serious social danger. An aggressive state may precipitate certain perceptual changes. For example, an individual suffering from aggression may develop tunnel vision, focusing on an enemy or the object of danger to the exclusion other perceptual cues. Polarization may develop to such an extent that the individual is unable or unwilling to recognize delicate shades of grey and sees every problem in black and white.

Else Frenkel-Brunswik has argued that such phenomena as tunnel vision and perceptual polarization represent specific examples of a more generic phenomenon called intolerance of ambiguity—the very fundamental need that individuals have to impose meaning and structure on unstructured, inchoate, ill-defined situations. This ability to structure one's perception almost certainly has survival value for the individual in the sense that it makes it possible to test whether the

Box 18–3: A conflict model

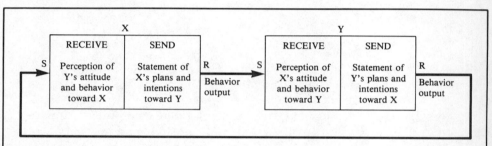

An extremely valuable and widely used model for understanding conflict uses stimulus-response technology:

This model has the following advantages:

1. It has very wide generality. It can be used to analyze conflict between countries, organizations, groups, or individuals. For example, if X = America and Y = Russia, a very useful model is available for discussing international conflict.
2. It exploits the systems approach and underscores the fact that conflict is frequently cyclical and self-locking (a vicious circle).
3. It combines two basic behavioral science paradigms:
   a. Stimulus + Attitudes = Perception
   b. Stimulus → Response

In this model, X's perception of Y's behavior leads to X's response, which is then interpreted by Y according to his attitudes toward X; this structures Y's response. So the vicious circle is maintained.

This model can be used very successfully to collect data about X's perception of Y and vice versa. The next stage in the exercise is the confrontation of stereotypes. This procedure has been used to research stereotypes in both management-labor contexts and American-Russian confrontations. It has the practical advantage of providing the action-oriented researcher with a source of hard data about stereotypes which, when presented to the parties to a dispute, frequently induces a sense of cognitive dissonance which may in turn lead to the breaking up of well-established and "frozen" prejudices. In other words, this model emphasizes that perceptions play an important part in shaping and maintaining conflict positions; and further, that factually defining perceptions allows the conflict system to be explicated and may facilitate attitude changes. Stereotype confrontation can change stereotypes.

environment is threatening or not. There is apparently a variance between those who can tolerate a high level of ambiguity and conflict and those who can tolerate only a low level.

Conflict situations inevitably are made up of at least two individuals who hold polarized points of view, who are somewhat intolerant of ambiguities, who ignore delicate shades of grey, and who are quick to jump to conclusions. Given a frozen situation like this, it is extremely difficult to deal with conflict. The important cognitive problem is to introduce dissonance into the system. Basically this is achieved by providing intelligence that the opposition has characteristics or displays behavior similar to one's own. Such intelligence helps to break up both hostility and hardened images and offers the possibility of restructuring at a more favorable level (see Box 18–3).

TOPIC 2
Process of conflict

THE PROCESS MODEL OF CONFLICT

Conflict is a fascinating but frequently misunderstood subject which generates considerable ambivalence because of its ability either to do great harm or, if exploited, to do great good. A more sensible approach to conflict is developed through the process model of dyadic conflict. The presumption of dyadic conflict is that conflict occurs between two social units. Conflict is a process which begins when one party sees the other as frustrating or about to frustrate some interest of his or hers.

Kenneth Thomas, in "Conflict and Conflict Management," proposes the process model as an explanation of conflict which is based on the idea (see Figure 18–4). For example, the Allies imposed such a harsh settlement on Germany at the Treaty of Versailles in 1919 that World War II became an inevitable consequence. Putting it in Thomas's language, the German nation experienced the frustration of economic ruin, developed the conceptualization that they were being victimized by Bolsheviks and the international Jewry. They developed the behavior of rearming, which led to the outcome of occupying or reoccupying the Rhineland, Austria, Czechoslovakia, and Poland. When Episode 1, German expansion, was complete, Episode 2, World War II, began. Thus Thomas gives central importance to the ideas that episodes are interlocked, and each episode follows a sequence of frustration, conceptualization, behavior, and outcome.

Thomas also has developed a model to illustrate the different types of solutions to conflict. Five conflict-handling orientations are shown in Figure 18–5.

FIGURE 18–4
Process model of dyadic conflict

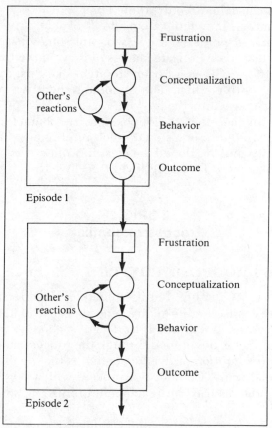

Frustration

Conceptualization

Other's
reactions

Behavior

Outcome

Episode 1

Frustration

Conceptualization

Other's
reactions

Behavior

Outcome

Episode 2

Source: Adapted from Kenneth Thomas, "Conflict and
Conflict Management," in *Handbook of Industrial and Organizational Psychology*, M. D. Dunnette, ed., Copyright ©
1976 by Rand McNally College Publishing Company, Figure
1, p. 895.

AN EXAMPLE OF THE CONFLICT PROCESS: IACOCCA
VERSUS FORD

In July 1978, Lee Iacocca became the third Ford Motor Company
president in 11 years to be fired, and the second in a row to be removed abruptly and virtually without explanation. As the (Montreal)
Gazette reported July 17:

"He (Ford) just said it was one of those things and he hated to do it
but he had to do it," Iacocca said . . .

Iacocca then noted that other top Ford executives—including Ernest
Breech, who retired early as Ford chairman in 1960 after rebuilding the
company after the Second World War—had met similar fates.

FIGURE 18–5
Five conflict-handling orientations, plotted
according to a person's desire to satisfy his or her
own and the other person's concern

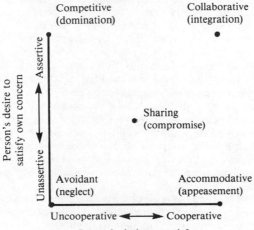

Source: Adapted from Kenneth Thomas, "Conflict and
Conflict Management", in *Handbook of Industrial and
Organizational Psychology*, M. D. Dunnette, ed., Copyright © 1976 by Rand McNally College Publishing Company, Figure 4, p. 901.

"You just surmise that the Breeches of the world got too big, too soon,
and he doesn't want strong guys around," Iacocca said. "You know, he
wants to diffuse and bureaucratize the company as he gets to be 61.

"I guess that's the only thing I can come up with because I really
don't have a good, sound answer myself."

Whatever the cause of his dismissal, Iacocca probably sealed his
fate several years previously by putting himself at odds with Bunkie
Knudsen, who was also dismissed somewhat summarily (see Chapter
6). Ironically, Knudsen was continuing a family tradition: William
("Big Bill") Knudsen had been fired by Henry Ford, Henry Ford II's
grandfather. (See Box 18–4 for further details.)

Probably no one really knows why Ford fired Iacocca. A widely
held view is that Iacocca got too strong and too near the top. Iacocca
was regarded by his subordinates as an intense, dynamic man who
could be euphoric in success and a terror when things went awry.

Iacocca professed to be bewildered by his dismissal. As *The New
York Times* expressed it July 16, 1978, Iacocca's question to Ford was:
"What did I do wrong?"

When executives disagree with Henry Ford 2d, he likes to remind
them whose name is on the front of the building where they all work.
Last week this matter of nomenclature was brought to Lee A. Iacocca's

Box 18–4: The principles of executive war

In 1943, when Henry Ford II, sometimes described as the last tycoon, fought for control of the Ford Motor Company, he was 26. Excluding Japan, Ford is the No. 1 producer of cars worldwide. (General Motors is the largest in the United States.) To survive in this harshly competitive world, Henry Ford II had to exercise power, sometimes ruthless power.

Part of this ruthlessness was forced on him by the experience of trying to recapture the Ford Motor Company (FMC) from Harry Bennett, a crony of Henry Ford Sr. Bennett's ruthlessness was demonstrated, for example, in his efforts to maintain discipline at the Rouge plant. To get Bennett out of the chair at FMC became absolutely necessary; between 1931 and 1941 company profits totaled out to zero.

Bennett literally established gangland rule at the Ford Motor Company. For example, while GM recognized the United Auto Workers (UAW) in February 1937, Henry Ford's response was an all-out battle against the union, with Bennett in charge. One result was the infamous "battle of the overpass." In this bit of street fighting UAW men led by Walter Reuther, who were distributing leaflets and newspapers, were attacked by Ford labor goons. To get Bennett (a former naval officer who always had guns on his desk) out involved the risk of force.

Henry Ford II ran Bennett off the premises, but only after a tremendous struggle. Ford was made president in September 1945. In trouble and lacking competent executives, Ford hired the so-called "Whiz Kids" who had been working together during World War II on operations research problems. One was Robert McNamara, who became president of Ford; another was Arjay Miller, who subsequently became the dean of the Stanford Business School but who also served as president of Ford.

Miller was appointed president of the company in 1963 and was eased out of the way in 1968 to make way for Semon E. (Bunkie) Knudsen, an executive vice president of General Motors. But "things did not work out for Bunkie," mainly because he could not mobilize the support of Lee Iacocca, who took over the top spot himself.

In a management shake-up in April 1978, Henry Ford II announced the formation of a triumvirate to run the company. Iacocca, who had invented the Mustang and had been

attention in particularly dramatic fashion when he was ousted as president of the Ford Motor Company.

The shakeup at the highly competitive automobile industry's No. 2 company came as the culmination of a growing dispute between the outsider and the company's chairman, a member of its founding family. Their differences began years ago, company sources said, and became sharper in recent months.

"I've been with the company for 32 years," Mr. Iacocca is said to have told Mr. Ford. "What did I do wrong?" Mr. Ford's reply, according to a person familiar with the situation, was: "I just don't like you."

In terms of the dynamics of organization the point seems to be that in family-dominated businesses it is dangerous to be too successful, too visible, and too vulnerable at the same time. Lee Iacocca was on two timetables, his own and Henry Ford II's. By his own little black president since 1970, was included, but no one person was strong enough to run the show. Robert McNamara, who could have filled the bill, had left. Three months later, Iacocca was summarily dismissed.

HENRY FORD AND CONFLICT MANAGEMENT

While Henry Ford II's style has veered toward the autocratic, he did save the company. But how can the succession problem be resolved? What can the student of organizational behavior learn about conflict management from watching Henry Ford II in action? He wanted the ultimate power, and the cabinet or triumvirate of executives ensured control for him and lack of control for them. What would you do if you were Henry Ford II?

In formulating your answer keep in mind the American Oedipus myth: hard-riding "cowboy" son comes home to claim his inheritance; the bad guys have moved in; they are moved out. Henry Ford II solved his riddle of the Sphinx and found his identity. But what does his management style tell us about conflict management? Some suggested lessons include:

1. There is always a physical basis to power.
2. People (particularly subordinates) love a winner.
3. Winners attract other winners.
4. Everybody cannot end up winners.
5. Informal power cannot be transferred.
6. When in doubt, divide and conquer.
7. Keep people guessing; be unpredictable.
8. For the owner-manager, the managerial revolution never took place.
9. Winning is everything.
10. As Henry Ford II puts it, "Never explain; never complain."

In short, two principles: Keep it in the family, and father knows best.

book, Iacocca was right on schedule if not a little ahead; by Henry Ford II's little black book, he was too far ahead.

Many in the company thought Iacocca operated like a Medici prince who had created his own city-state within the company. When Bunkie Knudsen was taken down, Iacocca played a critical part. But after the night with the long knives, the knight with the knife has to be eventually removed. In technical terms, conflict Episode 1 (Bunkie Knudsen's firing) led to conflict Episode 2 (Lee Iacocca's firing).

There is a certain Monty Python aspect to the conflict process; in some respects executive life is like a black comedy. Even when managers are avowed antagonists, they can observe the social niceties and continue to function together. It's all a matter of conflict values.

TOPIC 3
Values of conflict

THE ADVERSARY RELATION

Everyone is familiar with the adversary relation between lawyers in famous legal trials. This adversary relation is also basic to the settlement of disputes between management and labor; the "us versus them" relation is an integral element of industrial life. But it is perhaps not recognized that the adversary relation is also an integral part of the executive system.

But before adversaries can adverse, they must converse. Or, put another way, conflict implies cooperation. The courts cannot function without a structure of actors playing judge, jury, prosecution, and defendant; a process or a web of appealable procedures; and a value set that ordains decorum, decency, and precedent. The executive system requires a similar system, but it is a much more informal one.

How this system works is often a source of consternation to the inexperienced. Many plaintiffs in court are surprised that the prosecuting and defending counsels can meet socially, although they exchange fireworks and sly digs in the courtroom.

The same kind of decorum obtains in business conflicts, and for good reason. Both parties must not only arrange the social niceties that allow these conflicts to run their courses, they must also be ready in other circumstances to be on the same side of some other struggle between coalitions.

This apparent genius for being two-faced about corporate matters may confound some women executives: "How can men do such things, and put such a pleasant face on it?" Many explanations have been offered for such differing perceptions. Men have been exposed more often not only to the rough and tumble of team games but also to the formation of a guard of honor to applaud the winning team off the field. Another explanation is that male executives hold many meetings informally, off the record.

One way or another, both men and women can learn the dramatic art of conflict management.

THE DRAMATIC ART OF CONFLICT MANAGEMENT

Conflict management is an example of a black art for transforming inputs into outputs with value added. The transformational aspect of putting two and two together to get five (or more frequently, fixing things so that one's opponents or competitors get three for their answer) represents the core of the matter. But the results cannot be achieved by direct statement; they always involve some inversion, some negation, some deception, some sleight of hand—in essence, there is a defiance of logic. How else could 2 plus 2 equal 5?

To understand management, then, we can think of it as a form of drama. Drama, like management, gives expression to subtle and elusive forces that defy logical explanation. When properly exercised, conflict management is always dramatic and induces an imaginative response which is at once startling, vivid, and exciting for the participants.

Conflict is an essential ingredient of both management and drama. The conflict may take several forms—an enemy to be defeated, a moral dilemma to be resolved, a woman or a man to be won, a contract to be signed, a production quota to be beaten—all these involve the manager in facing choices and making decisions, that is, taking action.

Getting into management means getting a slice of the action. The action may involve negotiation, hiring or firing people, or even just making supportive noises. In such action lines must be spoken, but lines that get somewhere, that help to resolve the conflict. Ineffective managers may be seen as being good at "shooting a line" but are not expected to follow through with action. For effective managers, talk by itself is not enough; it must advance the action.

When conflict management is viewed as a dramatic form, the function of managers is not to make verbal statements (this is left to organization theorists) but to induce imaginative responses. The other actors receive not an answer to a question, but an experience. The art of conflict management allows the manager to develop a life-style or ambience which is at once both complex and captivating, which defies logical definition, but which nevertheless makes it possible to advance the action and get somewhere. This executive style creates an image of action, of force, of probabilities controlled. The image sets the scene, fixes the action, and significantly determines the choices of the other actors.

An executive play progresses from the beginning, through the middle to the end (or, if you like, from exploitation, through complication, to resolution or denouement). The case of the fired executive presented at the beginning involves a widely used routine or ritual. It has to be as highly structured and carried out with as much gusto as the confidence game perpetrated in the movie *The Sting*.

THE STING AND THE HIT MEN

An executive can learn a lot about the perverse process called firing (letting go, making redundant, separation, the shake out—a variety of labels are used) from reading or seeing *The Sting*. Even a quick glance at the chapter headings of the novel or the sequence titles of the movie suggests the different stages of the process: the setup, the hook, the take, the shutout, the sting. *The Sting* deals with the settling of a score, making a play for Lonnegan, a "numbers king" played by Robert Shaw in the film. There are many similar cons in business which are nearly as elaborate and certainly as dramatic.

In the film Hooker, a young con artist played by Robert Redford, has seen his sidekick and mentor, a black named Luther, killed off by Lonnegan. Hooker asks for help "to cheat the cheaters for fun and profit—with a little revenge to sweeten the take". He appeals to Gondorff, a top con man played by Paul Newman, who is on the lam, holed up in a whorehouse when he makes his first appearance in the movie. *The Sting* shows blow for blow how to take the other guy, take him for all he's worth, for his shirt.

My point is that most successful managers know this. But the victim has to love the victor. This strange phenomenon is known as the Stockholm syndrome, so called because in a bank holdup in Stockholm which turned into a hostage incident, two of the female tellers subsequently married bank robbers.

LOVING THE ENEMY

Loving the enemy is integral to conflict management. Exhibiting the Stockholm syndrome, many victims of hijackings seem to come to love the hijackers and speak of their captors in glowing terms. According to a psychiatrist, David G. Hubbard, director of the Aberrant Behavior Center in Dallas, hijackers are cashing in on a widespread hostility to authority. Once passengers believe they are not going to be killed, they come to regard the hijackers as desperados lashing out against the system.

The powerful in organizations also build admiration through sheer menace. In order to survive, subordinates learn to identify with their aggressor. This survival technique, as Chris Argyris has pointed out, is widely practised by subordinates of CEOs. Threat analysis shows that victims identify with and learn to love those who have them overwhelmingly in their grasp. They overcome their anxieties and love the master.

There is also abundant sociological evidence from researchers such as Albert J. Reiss, Jr., that the police operate in a manner which reflects a sharing of the values of the criminal groups with whom they have to interact. What it amounts to is that, contrary to the popular view that there are only a few "rotten apples" in a police force, a significant proportion of the police observed (some 20 percent) were in criminal violation of the law.

What is causing these violations? According to Reiss the policeman finds himself used as an instrument of the law, but a law interpreted by district attorneys (with their plea bargaining sessions), judges (who have high-handed ways with cops), juries (often pro criminal as ordinary citizens). Some officers, who feel they have been picked as the fall guy by the system, retire into their own version of legitimacy. This outlook meets their needs by establishing a system of values, norms, reinforcements, and sanctions which lets them cope with law and order on the boundary between two different worlds, one above board and the other under the table.

To understand what is happening in any system, we have to look at the legal and the illegitimate, the formal and the informal mores. Now we have a fairly clear idea of such distinctions on the shop floor, between the formal organization and the workers, and we have a glimmering of the relation between "informal" shop stewards and the formal union apparatus. There is also abundant evidence of how labor leaders can take that step beyond heavy-handed bureaucracy to establish personal fiefdoms. A few unions employ gangster techniques, and from time to time beyond the unions we catch occasional glimpses of the Mafia, the ultimate ethnic trade union. But to understand such love-hate relations more fully, it is necessary to turn to the game theory.

GAME THEORY VALUES

One of the most interesting developments in modern thought that is of great interest to managers is game theory. Much of early conflict management theorizing was based on a physical science model. Game theory makes it clear to managers that it is necessary to develop models that truly reflect conflict behavior.

The basic premise of the theory of games, developed by John von Neumann and Oskar Morgenstern, is that in the vast majority of human encounters a decision maker faces, one or more other decision makers who can make choices that will either help or hinder are involved. Business, in other words, can be compared to a game of poker.

To many game theorists, poker is the most skillful of all card games. Von Neumann got interested in the study of poker at an early age and published his first paper on the game in 1928, when he ws 23. This paper caused a sensation among mathematicians. Von Neumann recognized that each player's winnings or losses depended not only on his own moves but on the moves of others. What von Neumann did was to set out a winning strategy on paper, regardless of what the opponent did.

Game theory makes five basic assumptions about human behavior.

1. Each player knows what he or she wants.
2. Everybody knows everybody else's preferences.
3. The situation is completely knowable.

4. The situation can be mapped out in terms of outcomes.
5. The players are presumed to be rational in desiring to maximize their respective utilities.

In *The Theory of Games and Economic Behavior*, Von Neumann and Morgenstern included an interesting example which dealt with the interaction of two competing actors. The theory of games is applied to Sir Arthur Conan Doyle's tale of how Sherlock Holmes outwitted the diabolical Professor Moriarty. In Doyle's story, the final problem occurs when Holmes, seeking to escape the murderous Moriarty, races to a railway station in London and boards a train for Dover to get to the Continent. As the train leaves the station, Holmes sees Moriarty on the platform, and Moriarty sees him. Moriarty, left behind, charters a train and renews the pursuit. Holmes realizes that Moriarty is rich enough to hire a train. There is one stop between London and Dover, at the town of Canterbury. The strategic choice is whether Holmes should get off at Canterbury, but there is a probability that Moriarty will guess that Holmes will do this, and he will act likewise.

Von Neumann and Morgenstern demonstrated that all this he-thinks-I-think-he-thinks kind of reasoning is superfluous. In its place, they developed a matrix with specific payoffs which spells out the optimal strategy for Holmes; Holmes gets off at Canterbury, and Moriarty's train rolls on to Dover. Von Neumann introduced this minimax theory, which showed how to minimize one's maximum loss, in 1928. If Moriarty had used this strategy, Holmes would have been 48 percent dead, from a probable point of view, when his train left the station in London.

Good strategy requires the use of the minimax principle. But a good poker player, or a good executive, for that matter, recognizes that it is necessary to obscure the specific pattern of play by randomizing the strategy with chance plays.

TOPIC 4
Organization theories and conflict

CAUSES OF CONFLICT

We have considered conflict from the conceptual point of view of structure, process, and values. The structural aspect focuses on the factors of rules, rules, and relations which shape conflict behavior in an organization. Focusing on structure is meant to make managers aware that the shape of the system determines interaction and communication and therefore what is likely to happen. The process aspect focuses on the sequence of events and is meant to draw managers' attention to the historical deterministic aspects of the situation, so they will be able to ride the coattails of their organizations' history. The values aspect focuses on the mind-sets of the protagonists and is meant to help managers put a stop to self-fulfilling prophecies.

Thus the causes of conflict are related to the framework in which the organization functions, or the organization theory which determines its structure, process, and values. Figure 18–6 relates the causes of conflict to the classical, human relations, systems, and existential theories and suggests ways in which conflict is managed in each type of organization.

FIGURE 18–6
Organization theory, causes, and coping procedures

ORGANI-ZATION THEORY	CAUSE OF CONFLICT	MAIN-LINE APPROACH TO COPING WITH CONFLICT	DISPOSAL OF RESIDUE OF CONFLICT
Classical	Poor structural definitions or personal factors	Structure communications, define positions	Appeals system and complaint sessions
Human relations	Overrigid structural definitions	Catharsis in work situation through allowing subordinates to express themselves to "considerate" superiors	T-group training
Systems	Faulty informational structures and processes	Structure information flow in correct chunks: ·Use spindles ·Use buffers	Transcendental meditation
Existential	Bad faith	Refusal to act unfree, meeting of minds	Retire to commune, drop out

EFFECTS OF CONFLICT

Conflict, like stress, is good in small doses for the adrenalin. This after-shave effect of conflict is quite bracing, and its absence is a major criticism of the human relations school. A minimal level of conflict or arousal fits with modern theories of motivation, which argue not for tension reduction per se but for the maintenance of an optional level of stimulation. Conflict is seen as part of the process of testing and assessing oneself. As such, it may be highly enjoyable, as it makes it possible to experience the pleasure of full and active use of one's capacities.

Conflict is also a function of both intragroup and intergroup forces. Conflict in groups helps to surface far-out but useful views which would otherwise be suppressed.

Group dynamics recognizes the need for both selective support and conflict. If conflict is diagnosed properly, systemic problems can be properly defined.

The consequences of conflict are neither intrinsically good nor bad. The conciliation of conflict is concerned to make conflicts productive, creative, and useful.

CONCILIATION

Conflict is the central problem of organizational life. The techniques of operations research make it possible to quantify measures of end products and to police performance to such an extent that organizations inevitably come under a considerable degree of control, usually achieved by the removal of organizational slack. Such structuring of behavior often serves to increase the amount of conflict and tension within the organization.

The general techniques for the alleviation of conflict can be described under the heading of conciliation. The major techniques of conciliation are negotiation, mediation, and arbitration.

Negotiation

Many organizational conflicts get balked at the level of negotiation. Negotiation is the process whereby the parties to a dispute come together with a view to determining the terms of a contractual exchange which will be acceptable to both parties. Intellectually, negotiation consists of defining the quid pro quo which is acceptable to either party; emotionally, negotiation consists of defining and testing the power situation between the parties; behaviorally, negotiation is usually the process of bringing the parties together in a face-to-face situation where the terms of the bargain can be worked over.

Mediation

In the process of mediation, a third party is invited to try to resolve the difficulties facing disputing parties. Mediation is especially important because frequently the power displayed at the phase of negotiation produces such a sharp polarization of behavior and sentiment that the parties become isolated from one another. In such circumstances the mediator frequently is able to maintain some degree of contact and communication between the parties, who may well be located in different places far away from the conference room.

Arbitration

If mediation fails, disputes sometimes go to arbitration, the process whereby the dispute is referred to a third party who is given the power to formulate a settlement binding on both parties. Compulsory arbitration occurs when the parties are compelled (e.g., by law) to accept arbitration; voluntary arbitration is agreed to by the parties without such compulsion.

The basic value: Conflict is good for you

The first step in the process of conciliation is the recognition by the parties in dispute that conflict is not only universal but a necessary prerequisite of organizational change. Basic to this approach is the belief that conflict contributes to functional effectiveness. The function of conflict is to save the system from ossification.

A second major difficulty in trying to establish conciliation arises from man's need for attitudinal consistency. Attitudinal consistency, or cognitive consonance as it sometimes is called, refers to the need people have to ensure that their beliefs do not contain elements which are mutually contradictory. This "it is a question of principle" attitude is a major stumbling block to effective conciliation. A significant difficulty of the conciliator in a dispute is to break down the frozen but antithetical attitudes of the disputants; the problem is the need to introduce inconsistency to the minds of both parties, which frequently have snapped closed. Once both parties have admitted the possibility of inconsistency in their beliefs, even in a limited context, the way has been opened for further development.

Figure 18–7 relates the causes and cures of conflict as expressed in the value systems of the four organization theories.

FIGURE 18–7
Causes and cures of conflict related to organization theory value systems

ORGANIZA- TION THEORY	CAUSE	CURE
Classical	"Too many malcontents."	"Shoot a few peasants."
Human relations	"It's because she's insecure."	"Talk to her like a Dutch uncle."
Systems	"Nobody knows who wants what, where, when, why."	"It's all a question of information privileges."
Existential	"It's all due to male chauvinism."	"We need to get our heads together. . . ."

TOPIC 5
What every manager should know about conflict in organizations

THE DRAMA THEORY OF CONFLICT

In the structural view, conflict arises from the shape of the organization. It results when there are two structures—two sets of rules, roles, and relations—which cannot be reconciled. The rules are not clear, the roles overlap, and the relations are confused because the wrong signals are being sent.

Organizations are the corporate theaters of action, where people act out their roles, speak their scripts, say their piece, and earn their bread. But you can't play your part if you don't know your lines. And you can't know your lines unless you know the play. And you can't get the best out of your part unless you know where to stand on the stage, what your cues are, how to project your voice, how to hide your bad side, where the prompter is, and so on. This is what the drama of executive conflict is all about—the stagecraft of the corporate theater of action, where games players encounter other games players.

The underlying proposition behind such efforts is the belief that there is no management without drama, that every executive act involves an imposition of meaning—your meaning. What it amounts to is that you can't get action without imposing your meaning on a situation.

Managing the meaning is simply exercising the power of persuasion in interpersonal relations. But a basic proposition of the drama theory of management is the belief that the power has to be exercised in a meaningful way to get change, to get organizations to move from the dead-center position of established authority relations. Legitimacy may have to be broken by nonlegitimate means.

The process is essentially concerned with the sequencing of events, the plot of acts, scenes, and lines which has its own pattern of momentum. A story, even a prosaic corporate operation, must have a beginning, a middle, and an end. In more dramatic terms, there must be an overture, openers, rising action, a climax, falling action, a conclusion, and a denouement. All these events are interlocked, so that Episode 1 generates Episode 2.

The most important thing a manager should know about the political dramas of conflict is that they are important, interesting, and ubiquitous. It is important to learn to love the game of real politik, which means developing not only a successful style but a commitment to surefire and visible success. The manager on the way to the top must develop a high ability to project the right image, to move into high-profile success, to act with distinction and great force. There is considerable evidence that managers with a dramatic sense of the moment produce superior performance and morale.

This sense can be developed. Basically, it is a capacity to grasp, develop, and impose meaning on relatively unstructured situations. To manage meaning effectively a manager must take part in the *structure*, assume a place in the *process*, and have what it takes in terms of *values*.

Game rules

There are certain guidelines which can help managers apply the drama theory of conflict. In the exploitation of conflict, the objective must always be to achieve a creative, acceptable, and realistic resolution.

One of the most effective means of formulating game rules for executive conflict is to consider the three roles an executive might play in a conflict situation: the initiator, the defendant, or the conciliator. At one time or another, most executives are called on to play each of these roles.

The executive who is the initiator of conflict should:

1. Start at a low level and advance on a narrow front on one or two related issues, following a well-documented route.
2. Maintain second-strike capability.
3. Pick the terrain with care; where and when the case is heard is vital.
4. Be prepared to escalate, either to a higher level in the organization or to a meeting of peers.
5. Make it objective, private, and routine; above all, keep it formal.
6. Search for reaction and remember that it may be necessary to settle for token conformity in the first instance.
7. Reinforce success and abandon failure.

When the role is that of defendant, the executive should:

1. Not overreact; keep cool; let the initiator state the case; listen carefully and neutrally.
2. Ascertain the scale of the strike; try to build a decision tree with "go–no go" decision rules.
3. Ask for the name of the game. If it is the game of courtroom, for example, ask for the counsel for the defense.
4. Ask not only for an exact definition of the "charge," but also for the evidence with, if possible, identification of the sources.
5. If it is a "minor crime," be prepared to plead guilty.
6. Ascertain the various lines of appeal.

7. Consider the option of keeping a waiting brief and be prepared to reserve the defense; take notes; above all, let the initiator score somewhere—and then try for informality.

The executive who is the conciliator should:

1. Get the parties to the dispute to realize that conflict is not only universal but a necessary requisite of change.
2. Break down the attitudinal consistency of each disputant (the belief that one's attitudes do not contain contradictory elements).
3. After breaking down frozen but antithetical attitudes of the disputants, minimize the individual loss of face.
4. Break the conflict into fractional, workable components.
5. Consider common-enemy, high-interaction, shared subordinate goal strategies.
6. Remember that nobody loves a go-between.

CONFLICT AS A SYSTEM

The systems concept as shown in Figure 18–8 always supposes an interlocking network in which, if one element is changed, some or all

FIGURE 18–8
Conflict as a system

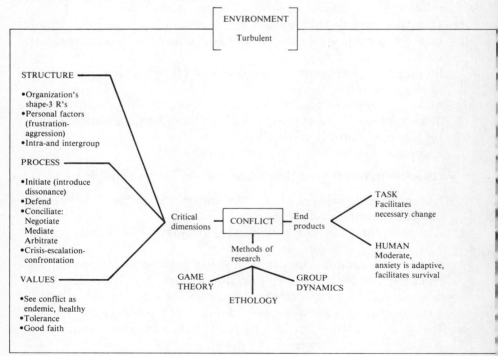

of the other elements will be affected. Thus part of the structure of conflict relates to the personal factor of aggression and frustration. Zoos drive apes psycho; the corporate zoo drives men anomic. Another structural factor is the structure of the organization; the systems concept of interacting change elements is one of the things that produces conflict.

A realistic model of conflict recognizes that the environment of the modern organization is turbulent. In this state of social turbulence, the rate of change in the environment inevitably outstrips the rate of change in the organization, leaving it in a maladapted state. Less powerful members of the organization have a vested interest in recognizing this lag, and more powerful members have an interest in denying it; hence the powerful must be alert if they are not to lose control of the situation.

While conflict may be the unintended result of poor coordination, the deliberate initiation of conflict can also be important. It can compel the organization to define goals, change processes, and reallocate resources. But conflict is only likely to produce constructive change when there is a rough balance of power between the parties to the dispute.

Predictability of the model

Conflict usually follows a particular pattern and is frequently quite predictable. For example, the pattern of wage negotiations is well established, although a change in economic conditions, such as the government's fiscal policy defining its reaction to inflation, can affect the ritual.

Most organizations have evolved procedures that deal with such contingencies, but not all. University administrators in the late 1960s discovered to their horror that they had no procedures for dealing with conflict, and no properly constituted lines of appeal. In fact, even a cursory examination of the student revolution of the sixties emphasizes that the pattern was predictable: (1) *crisis* (the establishment commits a "crime"), (2) *escalation* (occupation of administrative offices), (3) *confrontation* (showdown with officials), and (4) *further crisis* (challenging the legitimacy of the committee appointed to investigate the original charge). When the immediate fight is over, the organization is left to build not only a new hierarchy and an appeals system, but also a new code of ethics.

The need for managers to familiarize themselves with the structures, processes, and values of conflict is becoming more pressing. How to make conflict work for you is going to be an increasingly crucial management issue in our rapidly changing society.

REVIEW AND RESEARCH

1. Why is conflict good for you? Under what conditions? Why has there been a radical change in viewing organizational conflict?
2. What did university students teach administrators about the conflict process in the sixties?
3. Critically evaluate the two models of conflict.
4. How can conflict within a group be controlled? Illustrate your answers by considering a group such as a football team, a platoon, a work group, or a fraternity committee.
5. How can conflict be mitigated between a production work group and a marketing group in a particular industry? Select an industry with which you are familiar.
6. Develop a plan of action to regulate the conflict between an automobile manufacturer and its franchised dealers.
7. Develop a model using the "prisoner's dilemma" game as a means of gaming a situation where two companies are in collusion and are the only bidders for a building with a city administration.
8. Develop a theory of conflict to cover the matrix:

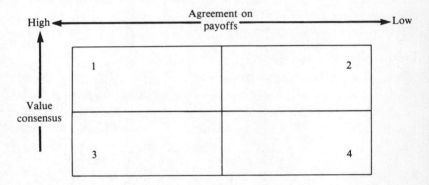

What circumstances would generate cells 1, 2, 3 and 4? What should be the best strategies for handling each contingency?
9. Define the roles of the initiator, the defendant, and the conciliator. Select an example from your own experience and describe the attitudes, behaviors, and strategies of each party in the conflict.
10. How can you make conflict work for you?
11. Compare and contrast the relative merits and disadvantages of using confrontation versus mediation in a conflict situation.

GLOSSARY OF TERMS

Arbitration. The process whereby a dispute is referred to a third party acceptable to both disputing parties, who ask the third party to formulate a settlement which will be binding. Arbitration may be voluntary (entered into freely by the two parties) or compulsory (forced upon the disputants by some outside power, such as government).

Cognitive consonance. Attitudinal consistency; the need people have to ensure that their beliefs do not contain contradictory elements.

Conciliation. The process of bringing into harmony, or effecting a settlement between, conflicting parties. The major techniques of conciliation are (see definitions) negotiation, mediation, and arbitration.

Conflict. Opposition or dispute between persons, groups, or ideas, which may be discussed according to two models:

Human relations model. The more classical view that conflict is unhealthy and should be avoided; this "old look" assumes that every society is a well-integrated, relatively persisting configuration of elements which contribute to its functioning through a fundamental consensus, and that conflict is caused by malfunction or by troublemakers.

Realistic model. The "new look" at conflict sees it as endemic, inevitable, and healthy, and looks at the management of conflict as the central problem for organizational analysts. This model assumes that change and conflict are ubiquitous and that society rests on constraint of some of its members by others. The value of conflict lies in its facilitation of needed change and, because its proper management emphasizes the need for common interests and values, eventual social cohesion.

Frustration-aggression hypothesis. The theory that frustration (persistent blockage of goal-directed behavior) leads to aggression (attack on the perceived blockage), and that aggressive behavior presupposes frustration.

Game theory. The set of mathematical operations through which game players learn to evaluate and predict reactions and potential moves (their own and other players'), bargain, and evolve tactics and an optimal strategy; the development of models which define outcomes in terms of utilities and probabilities; a model of conflict among several people in which the principal modes of resolution are collusion and conciliation.

Intolerance of ambiguity. The fundamental need of people to impose meaning and structure on inchoate, ill-defined situations. This ability to structure a perceptual environment has survival value for the individual; however, when change and conflict are seen as necessary, the individual must also learn some degree of tolerance for ambiguity to survive.

Mediation. The process whereby a third party is invited to try to resolve the difficulties facing the parties to a dispute, often by acting as a go-between.

Negotiation. The process whereby the parties to a dispute come together to bargain over terms which will be acceptable to both parties.

Tacit bargaining. Element of game theory which assumes a degree of interdependence between disputing parties, so that, even without complete communication, both parties accept that cooperation and mutual constraint will be necessary to resolve their conflict.

Zero-sum game. A game in which whatever one player loses, the other wins; the plus and minus balance is always zero. Nonzero sum games are those in which conflicting parties can achieve pluses in excess of their minuses (or the reverse).

DEBATE: And what do *you* do?

The scene is a class reunion, five years after graduation.

CHARLIE: I'm in computers . . . do you, uh, do anything?

MARILYN: I'm in personnel.

CHARLIE: You mean . . . you drive the welcome wagon for new employees?

MARILYN: No, I don't. What I . . .

CHARLIE: I know, you're into human relations. You write the Ann Landers agony column during working hours.

MARILYN: No. If you would stop vibrating with masculine omniscience for a moment, I could. . . .

CHARLIE: OK. OK. I'm getting the picture.

MARILYN: Look. What I do is, I'm an organizational analyst.

CHARLIE: Ha! You psychoanalyze organizations!

MARILYN: You're more right than you realize. But I'm not a psychiatrist. I'm a behavioral scientist in business—I'm in personnel.

CHARLIE: Good! Let me tell you about my dreams.

Questions

1. In how many ways does Charlie "hate" Marilyn?
2. In how many ways does Marilyn "hate" Charlie?
3. What makes them different?
4. Will Charlie ever get the message?

EXERCISE

Diagnosing and managing your conflict style

Answer the following questions with a YES or a NO.

1. Most trouble in business arises from shop stewards, radicals, or prima donnas.
   Yes_____   No_____
2. Most work problems would vanish if people just followed exactly their job descriptions.
   Yes_____   No_____
3. Managers have abdicated their leader role.
   Yes_____   No_____
4. Conflict is basically bad, injurious to mental health, and counter-productive.
   Yes_____   No_____
5. Conflict is caused by poor communications.
   Yes_____   No_____

6. Conflict is spread by stereotyping (e.g., He is an Uncle Tom, a Captain Quigg, a troublemaker, an SOB, etc.)
Yes_____   No_____

7. When people start talking *to* each other instead of *at* each other, problems will start to go away.
Yes_____   No_____

8. What more people need is a week in an encounter group (or T group or EST group or Gestalt therapy group, etc.)
Yes_____   No_____

9. At the bottom of every problem you will find the wrong information in the wrong hands at the wrong time.
Yes_____   No_____

10. When the workers can read printouts on production, marketing, and finance, everything is going to be OK.
Yes_____   No_____

11. There is an instital information gap between sales and production. What we need is a SOLD (sales organization liaison department).
Yes_____   No_____

12. To get good government in the United States. What we need is a set of telex machines in the basement of the Oval office to copy everything going into the Pentagon, State Department, CIA, and FBI.
Yes_____   No_____

13. Conflict is good for you.
Yes_____   No_____

14. Most conflicts arise from the powerful trying to screw the poor, the weak, the ethnics, the less powerful out of their rights.
Yes_____   No_____

15. What we need is a true meeting of minds. Then we can avoid zero-sum compromises (you win, I lose).

16. Small is beautiful.
Yes_____   No_____

Answers: A yes to Questions 1 through 4 indicates a classical orientation to conflict; a yes to Questions 5 through 8 suggests a basic human relations view of conflict; a yes to Questions 9 through 12 reveals a preoccupation with the information aspects of systems; a yes to questions 13 through 16 reveals a true existential spirit.

How did you score? What is the correct position? The answer is the old contingency one, "It all depends. . . . "

DIAGRAM SUMMARY OF CHAPTER 19

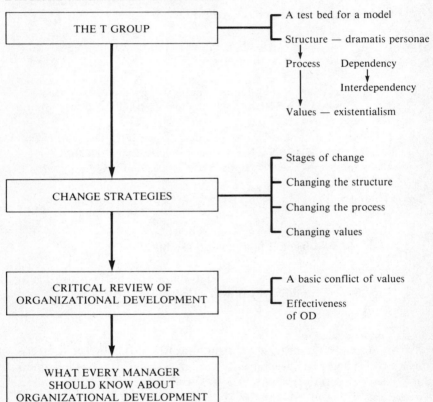

19

Organizational development

ORGANIZATIONS AS PHROG FARMS*

By Jerry B. Harvey

A short time ago I received a telephone call from a friend of mine who was employed as an OD specialist in a large corporation.

"Jerry, I've just been fired," he said.

"Fired? You mean you are out of a job completely?"

"Well, not completely," he replied. "I'm just no longer an OD specialist. In fact, the whole function has been wiped out. They have given me a make-work job in salary administration. It's a nothing job, though. I hate it. I was really interested in doing OD. All I'm doing now is scutt work and drawing a paycheck."

"Why were you fired, Hank?"

"I'm not really sure. I've never heard the reason directly. My boss's boss was the one who really did the firing. He told my boss to do it."

"Why did he tell your boss he wanted you fired?"

"My boss was vague about it. He just said his boss had said I wasn't powerful enough to do the job."

"What did your boss's boss say to you when you asked him about it?"

"I haven't talked with him."

"Why not?"

* Reprinted, by permission of the publisher, from *Organizational Dynamics*, Spring 1977, Copyright © 1977 by AMACOM, a division of American Management Associations. All rights reserved.

"That would be violating the chain of command. You don't do that around here."

"Why not?"

"You can get fired for that."

"But Hank," I said, "You *have* been fired."

"Oh!"

And then, perhaps because I had recently read my children the fable of *The Princess and the Frog*, I said, "Hank, your boss's boss is correct. You aren't powerful enough to do the job. In fact, for all intents and purposes, he has turned you into a phrog. I can almost see you in a big phrog pond with your boss's boss sitting on a willow stump saying to himself, 'I think I'll turn ol' Hank into a phrog.' And then he waves a magic wand, mutters some mystical-sounding incantation, and concludes with, 'Hank, you are a phrog,' and suddenly you have web feet. Hank, you are now a phrog."

The silence at the other end of the line was seemingly interminable.

Finally, out came the poignant, one-word reply that echoed down the line, "Ribbit."

ORGANIZATIONAL "CULTURE"

To grasp why Hank turned into a phrog, it is necessary to understand what organizational development is all about. Organizational development (OD), a major growth activity in organizations, is an attempt to achieve corporate excellence by integrating executives' need for growth with organizational goals. It is concerned with changing posture, perspective, and process, but it is a value change in a systems context which is appropriate to the contemporary turbulent environment with all its built-in uncertainties.

To get to the heart of what is involved in this kind of change, it is necessary to think of an organization as a giant protein-like molecule with lots of small radicals stuck on and with roles for atoms. Traditionally, these giant molecules have achieved their success by virtue of specifying authority, defining lines of communication, setting out areas of delegation, and generally operating in a relatively placid, fairly well-defined environment with a fair measure of control. This earlier approach to organizations is substantially structural in character. What is neglected in this structural optic is the notion of organizational culture.

Organizational culture includes the rules, policies, rituals, folkways, rubrics, and all the various subroutines which form the corporate subconscious. An OD consultant like Hank, to act properly as a change agent, must be a sort of corporate Freud who helps a business group in the systematic exploration and management of this culture. The consultant assists the group in identifying its corporate philosophy, strategy, and operating tactics by examining these cultural beliefs, many of which are buried in the minds and behaviors of the executives. A complete cultural renaissance is needed if the corporation is to escape from the conventions of red tape and moribund procedures which can inhibit effective decision making. But to achieve such changes, the OD specialist has to exercise power. Hank was not powerful enough.

If the model of the organization is perceived as a giant molecule with roles for atoms, it is possible to think of the structural forces as the bonds which link the various roles in the system, specifying who can speak to whom, who can initiate contacts, and who can spend what. It is possible to think of the culture as the electrostatic field—silent, pervasive, lying below the surface—which holds all these various roles in position and helps to define and reinforce the forces flowing along the bonds. In terms of organizational development, if it is possible to change the cultural frame of reference (that is, the value system), then all the various structural relations will be correspondingly affected. Training the system to facilitate this cultural reformation is the essence of OD. Hank was not powerful enough to train the system. Hank had not learned enough in the T group.

TOPIC 1
The T group

A TEST BED FOR A MODEL

The structure, process, values contingency model for the study of organizational behavior can be applied at a variety of levels, including the individual, the group, and the organization, and to a variety of problems, including conflict management, decision making, and organizational development. To show how the model operates, I have selected the T group because of its theatrical quality and the ease with which the structure (the actors), the process (acts and scenes), and values can be documented. In addition, the T groups brevity and completeness make for illustrative simplicity, and the T-group style provides a major clue to how OD developed.

Some executives can be compared to walking T groups, but with a difference. They have experienced T groups and know about sensitivity training, catharsis, feedback, and Johari window, dyads, group dynamics, and games executive play, but now they are into more complex management-theatrical productions where information science and advance technologies predominate. The more perceptive among them will easily recognize that the model presented here has left out two critical variables, technology and the ecology.

T groups are social islands in the sun where a bunch of people meet in seclusion to rediscover the wheel of group dynamics. In the T group the heady expectation is that the heavy will be seen as heavy, the hostile as counterproductive, and so on. When T groups work, they work very well. A quick glance at the T group reveals the structure of the dramatic personae, the process of events, and the values in terms of myths, mysteries, and manners. Figure 19–1 models the T group as a system.

FIGURE 19–1
T-group systems model

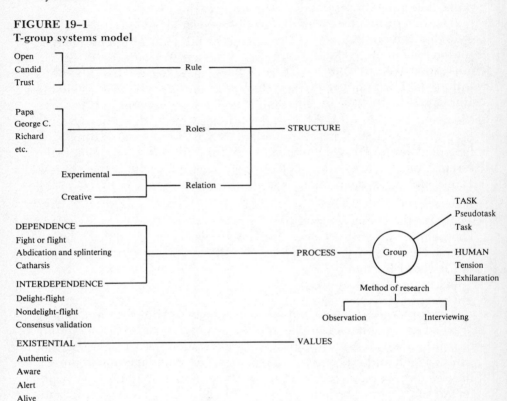

In terms of structure it is possible to cast T groups in a variety of ways. One scientific and useful structural outlook encompasses the task specialist (who zeros in on the problem: "Let's move out," "OK, OK, OK"), human relations specialist ("Let Bill have his say," "I don't think you are being fair to yourself," "I like your style"), the eccentric "You've really got something going for you—Me. How's that grab you?"), the father figure ("I appreciate your seeking my confirmation"), the scapegoat ("I'm fed up being on the receiving end"), the isolate ("No comment at this time"), and the observer ("I'm here to observe, therefore I can't say how I feel").

Such scientific snapshots of the cast who emerge in a group can be useful and are in fact widely used. But another set of stereotypes also can be useful. Groups can work quite well when the roles are supplied from the movies or TV. Participants in the script for a T group described in this section said they were reasonably comfortable with the roles of celebrities and other stereotypes. The rules favor openness, trust, spontaneity, and risk betting. The roles are apparently up for grabs. The relations are meant to favor credibility and creativity.

In terms of process, what the participants are looking for is a lifestyle that is more loving if not intimate, creative if not zany, joyful but not too exuberant, trusting but not credulous, open but not too accessful, responsive but not too reactive, but above all integrated, complete, and alive. The whole idea in terms of values is to let the existential hiding inside you out for a holiday.

THE STRUCTURE: THE DRAMATIS PERSONAE

The cast in the T-group drama to be described in this section is a composite photograph in my mind built out of the scores of groups I have worked with. I have given aliases to the participants to help you recognize the characters and put what they have to say in perspective. The people you will encounter in this group might be identified with Ernest Hemingway, Truman Capote, George C. Scott, Papa Freud, and Richard Burton.

The names of the players indicate easily recognizable types, not real people. Of necessity the descriptions are composed almost entirely of stereotypes. It would not be productive to apply such labels in a real-life situation, and you should not expect to encounter similar caricatures. Nevertheless, recognizing the exaggerated characteristics will lend meaning to the T-group experience described here.

"Ernest": Caucasian male, age 45, crew cut, ramrod back. Engineering graduate, builds radar stations in the Pacific. He has just returned from Guam after finishing a contract. Ex-enlisted man USMC, married to a French girl he met in Vietnam. Direct, trustworthy, efficient. Likes watching football on TV. Favorite question for him, "Did you ever kill anyone over there?" His answer, "One of ours or one of theirs?" Basically OK; people respect him even if they don't love him.

"Papa Freud": 39, Jewish, from Boston. Undergraduate work at Harvard because of the local-boy break. MBA at Harvard Business School. Lived in Shaker Heights, Cleveland, while working as a sales manager for a hat manufacturer. Working for Ph.D. in clinical psychology. Separated from wife, who put him through grad

school, and three kids. His favorite comment, "I'm conflicted." He hums a lot to himself, muttering "Must keep calm, calm, Calm, CALM."

"Truman": 28, Born in Trinidad of Indian-Negro parents. He has an unexpected squeaky voice and wears far-out clothes. He is in advertising and people like working with him because he is so nice and nonthreatening. He has rabbit teeth which jump out at you when he talks. His favorite question is, "Why do people talk down to me? Especially when I am on the up and up." Surprisingly, he was decorated as a helicopter warrant officer pilot in Vietnam. His favorite aphorism is, "The U.S. has three things going for it—God, guts and get-up-and-go. The last's my option."

"George C.": Born in LA, athletic scholarship to UCLA, MBA. Tough, testy, nondrinker. Age 40, Afro hair style, mod clothes. Fast talker; joins full stops to capital letters to exclude interruptions. Thinks everybody else talks funny. Favorite aphorism for citizens in their fifties: "Just think what I'll have achieved when I'm 50. This world is full of meatheads." In spite of his flamboyance, people warm up to him. He secretly believes he is going to drop dead before he is 45.

"Richard": 55, played football at school, served in the Navy during World War II, law degree from Yale. Worked for a time as a model. Big dreamer. Worked as a tax attorney most of his life in D.C.; lived in Richmond, Virginia. Divorced and remarried a young woman who is a radical feminist. Favorite sayings, "I get on better with young people," "There are no problems, only thinking makes it seem so."

"T" (the trainer): Age indeterminate, friendly, worried look. Wears turtles, slacks and Addidas. Has degree in industrial engineering and doctorate in clinical psychology. Smiles too much. Favorite phrases, "Don't you agree?" "Please feel free to criticize me. No holy cows here." But he gets very tense when criticized. Tries too hard to present a zany look.

THE PROCESS

Act 1.   Dependence

Fight or flight. The group goes through several stages of development as it grows, the first of which is called fight or flight. The most striking characteristic of the first period is anxiety—a general defensive feeling that things are not OK. Free-floating anxiety seeks a focus, as members try to reassure each other. The most common manifestation is a desire to achieve structure either by demanding that the trainer either take up a more directive role or produce an explicit statement of goals. The participants surreptitiously study the trainer to see how she or he is taking things. Participants take their reference from their past. At this stage, typically one of the participants will try to leave. Pairing is very common as a defense.

Overture

T: . . . we have an excellent group.

ERNEST: How do you know we are excellent?

T: You look like a nice bunch of guys.

ERNEST: What are you—some kind of fag?

T: I didn't mean to . . .

TRUMAN: Hang on a minute, Ernest. Let's see what T can do. We've paid our money.

RICHARD: I want to hear how T is going to change us. That's a mighty big threat.

T: I have a little model here.

ERNEST: A model T.

T: Ha. Ha. Yeh. It's a three-stroke model—unfreezing, change, refreezing . . .

RICHARD: So you're building up the tension deliberately. Isn't that manipulation?

Abdication and splintering.   The next phase is a period of abdication and splintering. The trainer exhibits a paradox of omnipotence and powerlessness. The members treat the trainer as a god—and, of course, gods should be in absentia. Typically two or more subgroups emerge who try to fill the power gap left by the leader's abdication. Usually some kind of incident is created. Examples include the investigation of why somebody left the group; a debate on how many subgroups should be formed; the charge of manipulation against the trainer; and demands for the appearance of the president of the company to explain the score.

Whatever happens, the group seizes on an incident and gets to work. The detailed sequence includes: incident, investigation, escalation crisis, confrontations, evaluation, and replay.

Fleeing

ERNEST: What would you say if I just got up and walked out of this room and never came back?

T: I would wonder why, but you're free to go.

ERNEST: Can you guys hack this?

GEORGE C: I've been in worse. At least it gets you out of the house, away from the wife and kids.

T: Would you like to tell us why you want to quit?

ERNEST: Oh, forget it.

Conflict management

ERNEST: I don't like the way you're handling this group. You're pulling it on us.

T: I don't understand.

RICHARD: You want us to spell it out for you? Go for God's sake, Ernest, go. Get the hell out of here.

PAPA: I think they are trying to tell you something, T. We need a little time on our own.

T: If I leave, how can I stay in touch?

PAPA: We'll call you back when we need you.

GEORGE C.: Just a minute, Papa Freud. You're going too quickly. I would like T to stay.

T (walks to the board takes the chalk in his hand): What is the problem here? Let's start with me. What's the score there? (T begins writing on the board. After 30 minutes he has headings: trainer's personality; group rules, roles, relations; conflict management; manipulation; machismo.)

PAPA: You've fixed us good, T. You created the problem. You escalated. You deescalated. I say, "Out, and with you your 30 pieces of silver."

Catharsis.   The next phase is catharsis, or purging of the soul. The group is getting itself together, developing complexity, logistics, and an infrastructure of supportive rules, roles, and relations. This state of catharsis is achieved only if the group successfully solves its crisis, real or imaginary.

At this time the group usually dispenses with the leader. Members talk about finally having made it: "I really got into the action. Before I was spectating. I knew we weren't going to make it unless I moved out and got into things."

Interdepencence

To the bemused T-group trainer the episode evokes a sense of déjà vu: Here is the brooding Richard, still haggard from a decade of corporate brawling with his boss, George C., gushing like a schoolboy over his new relations with George C. Even though George C. has just explained why he could never really love Richard, Richard has the floor.

RICHARD: I'm over the moon, fantastically happy. You respect me, George C. I know you don't love me. But you respect me.

GEORGE C.: Yes. I respect you.

RICHARD: George C., You have a very fierce temper and go into some ugly moods. But you are beautiful.

GEORGE C.: You know, T. I've said everything I ever wanted to say to this group. It has been quite an extraordinary experience.

T: Thank you, George C.

RICHARD: I appreciate your candor, George C. I didn't realize how much you depended upon me. . . .

Act 2. Interdependence

Delight-flight. In the next stage, delight-flight, the group experiences a happy sense of belonging, a sense of being part of something which is bigger and better than any one of them. This good gestalt ("I am really getting a charge out of this thing—now all the warfare is over") is fairly short lived.

PAPA: We're working well together now. We're having a ball. Balling the Jack. At least I am. How about you Richard? How are you making out?

ERNEST: Good for you, Papa. But I am zonked out. We should be working together, but we ain't. All we are doing is breaking into subgroups—the headshrinkers versus the straights.

PAPA: You always were a loser. A born loser.

ERNEST: Do me a favor. Drop dead.

PAPA: But you said . . .

ERNEST: Bull.

Nondelight-flight. The group now moves into nondelight-flight. This period is marked by a war between subgroups, in this case, between the head-shrinkers, led by Papa, and the straights, led by Ernest. The headshrinkers want more intimacy (meetings in the swimming pool), more joy, more let it all hang out, more awareness, less structure, less substantive material—in two words, more love. The straights have gone as far as they are prepared to go. In their view the strategy of "You tell me what it is wrong with me and I'll tell you what is wrong with me" is not only dangerous but also boring, which is even worse.

GEORGE C: You know, Truman, what's wrong with you is that you won't accept the idea that a manager is an adult in TA terms, a responsible information-processing reality-centered role in the apparatus.

RICHARD: Let me answer for you, Truman. George C., you are a primal horde father—the big paramount chief. If you would stop playing father knows best we might get somewhere. You talk down to people, even when you have something sensible to say.

GEORGE C.: You know what's wrong with you, Richard? You play Child—Naughty little boy. You make everything chaotic. It's a defense.

Consensus validation. In the last phase, consensus validation, the two subgroups come together in the subroutine of evaluation, which is typically a somewhat threatening experience which produces hostility all round. The reality of termination (the logistics of getting the curtain down, the actors off stage, and the critics calmed down) and evaluations (confirmation or disconfirmation of one's assessment) cannot be denied. This is tricky work which has to be handled with care and discretion. The straights regard the evaluation as an unproductive invasion of privacy, and the headshrinkers fear discrimination, particularly the opportunity afforded for paying off old scores.

GEORGE C.: What we should do with evaluation is use a set of scales and complete them anonymously. I don't want to make any judgments until I've had time to reflect.

TRUMAN: I hope everybody is going to exercise some Christian charity in reviewing themselves and others. I know. . . .

ERNEST: I want to get an early plane. Let's get this over with by turning it into a confessional job. OK with you, T?

Then the group settles down to the serious business of evaluating the experience and themselves. If the trainer handles the sequencing of speakers right and controls the intensity and amplitude of responses, this session can be the capstone of the exercise.

Finale

T: . . . go round the group and get some reactions. Papa, would you start the ball rolling?

PAPA: I've had a ball. But I'm a walking T group; I've been in therapy since I was five. You know, I've got a Jewish mama for a wife and Portnoy's father for a son—real good stuff.

ERNEST: I don't know. I really don't know. I need time. The meeting was a real think piece.

GEORGE C.: Yes. You need a good shake-up periodically. Gets rid of the cobwebs.

At the end of the session the T-group trainer should explain the dramatic and existential aspects of the experience.

TOPIC 2
Change strategies

Modern change strategies, such as T group, owe much to the young Karl Marx, who asserted that the point is to change the world and not merely to interpret it. OD consultants intuitively accept and act on a dialectical or critical conception of knowledge and truth. A description of the status quo is only a necessary preliminary to changing it.

OD consultants need a dialectical imagination which can comprehend the organizational world, not only as it is but as it could be. "Is" and "ought" are dialectically interlocked in an imperative for change. Research is defined as a form of action; action and knowledge are inextricable. The change agent gets involved in the actual change. In this transactional paradigm, participation is both a prerequisite and a prerogative, and people discover both their potential and power: their potential for growth and self-actualization and their power to break boundaries, laws, and promises without perishing in the process. Participation, potential, and power make a shambles of the traditional means-ends schema.

This is a value-loaded science of change which pays scant heed to the value-free world of traditional behavioral science—the ever-decreasing microcosm of "All I want is the facts." In organizations there are no "facts" that are sterile, clean, pure, untouched by the human hand. Everything is contaminated by human values. Rather than resenting this, the effective OD consultant develops a dialectical imagination by seeking to combine action and thought in trying to change organizations in a systematic way.

STAGES OF CHANGE

The principal stages of change are organizational diagnosis, implementation, and evaluation. As shown in Figure 19–2, each stage has

FIGURE 19–2
Stages of change

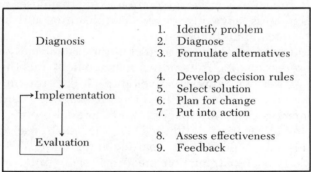

critical steps. Diagnosis involves, first, searching for and *identifying* significant organizational problems. From a general analysis, the OD consultant should be able to isolate specific problems, assess the magnitude and direction of each problem identified, and attach to each problem a measure of relative importance. Second, the OD consultant must *diagnose* the nature of the problem and its significant dimensions through a sound, methodical approach, and bring to bear the important aspects of relevant disciplines. Third, the OD consultant should *formulate alternatives*, devising a reasonably comprehensive set of viable solutions.

The stage of implementation involves *developing decision rules* to judge the relevance and appropriateness of a particular solution. The OD consultant must be competent to choose and justify the set of criteria used. He or she then *selects* an optimum solution consistent with the criteria. Working out the implications of this decision, the OD consultant *plans* the change and then *puts it into action.*

The final stage is evaluation of the change. This involves *assessing* the effectiveness of the program in achieving objectives. *Feedback* is essential to evaluation and is used to make necessary adaptations in the further implementation of the change process.

These stages need fleshing out with consideration of techniques, processes, and possible pitfalls, as outlined in the following sections.

Diagnosis

Organizational diagnosis is essentially concerned with the identification, delineation, and definition of the specific problems (issues, challenges, opportunities), their causes, consequences, and likely effect on the organization's viability. Most executives are so closely integrated with the corporate tissue that they find it difficult, if not impossible, to come up with answers that group symptoms into meaningful patterns. In fact executives given to making diagnoses are seen by their colleagues as engaging in special pleading and are usually thrown into states of guilt and anxiety.

A fantastic variety of diagnostic techniques is currently in use, including observation (e.g., attending management meetings), interviewing (e.g., ask two representatives of each department, "How do you feel about the present crisis in your department?"), and examination of documents (e.g., newspaper reports, annual reports, policy papers, minutes of meetings). While O.D. specialists use all of these methods, most have a penchant for particular techniques such as questionnaires, surveys, confrontation meetings, or T groups. The questionnaire survey—using scales like those used by Rensis Likert, which scale organizations on several dimensions like authority, communication, and leadership—is widely used to pigeon-hole the organization as to whether it corresponds to Likert's System 1, 2, 3 or 4.

Diagnosis is essentially concerned with establishing a bank of reliable and reasonably valid data about the state of the organization which reflects a variety of sources, levels, and optics.

Implementation

Increasingly, corporate executives are making a conscious, deliberate, and collaborative effort to introduce change. Basically such executives are trying to link organization theory into strategic planning, operational handling, and tactical activities. In terms of strategy, goals or objectives have to be defined; operationally, a well-defined line of approach must be worked out; and tactically, a sequence of detailed steps will have to be invented to facilitate progress along operational vectors.

This plan for change must fit the organizational diagnosis. For instance, if the basic problem appears to be one of destructive conflict among students, faculty, and administrators arising out of three separate socio-occupational systems that are out of contact, it is hardly sufficient to set a general goal of "increased communication." Likewise "sending people on courses" in unlikely to be successful. What are needed are new structures of government; different processes of consultation, decision, and appeal; and new, overlapping value sets. It is unlikely that the changes in structure, process, and values can be kept in balance, so inevitably resistance will be encountered. Only careful tactical planning will overcome such resistance.

The most important thing to know about the planning of change is that it is not so much a programme as a process. Change is a process where diagnosis, formulation of alternatives, implementation, and evaluation succeed and interact with each other without reaching a full stop. The process is both iterative and participative.

Planning, to be participative, must allow "the people being planned" to input their ideas into the body of planning. This kind of *planification*, as the French term it, calls for continuous dialogue, *animation sociale*, negotiation, and bargaining among interest groups. Planning is both a technical and a political process. As a political process, change advocates have to know what it takes to make a planning decision legitimate, who can vote, how polling is to take place, what counts as a mandate for (or veto against) action, who has to be paid off or allowed to mislead himself. Rarely, of course, does planning for change involve actual voting—but many are polled in some form of consultation. Planning for change is a collaborative, democratic, and iterative process; it establishes a basis of legitimacy for modes of action that facilitate the mobilization of the power centres of an organization to maintain its viability and adaptability to changes in the environment.

Plans must be implemented to be meaningful. The plan must clearly state who, what, where, when, how, and how much. Getting into action with a plan for change can be a real hassle, especially if the top brass have not been properly sold on the problem, perspective, and prospects. Top management is unlikely to introduce large-scale changes unless they feel themselves under intense pressure. Given this level of tension, the change advocate will have to show real human relations skill in helping his senior colleagues to handle their tensions and anxieties.

Evaluation

When change agents are allocating resources to the three major stages of change, they should budget a little extra for the follow-up. Once the change is underway, there is a real danger of slacking off in terms of effort. Did the plan work out? To what extent were the objectives reached? What dysfunctions were generated? Assessment may require the employment of fairly sophisticated statistical experimental designs with control groups to ascertain if a real change took place. At least the opinions of participants should be polled.

Changing is a way of life in organizations, and trying to answer a question usually generates more questions than answers. All questions concerned with evaluation turn around the basic issue, "What are managers trying to achieve by planned change?"

CHANGING THE STRUCTURE

Organizational design

Organizational design is the conscious effort to develop a structure that will achieve the objectives and plans of the firm. Organizational design is defined in *The Management of Organization Design* (Ralph H. Kilmann, Louis R. Pondy, and Dennis P. Selvin, ed.), as "the arrangement, and the process of arranging, the organization's structural characteristics to attain or improve the efficiency, effectiveness, and adaptability of the organization."

The aim of organizational design is to come up with some kind of responsive organization that can achieve the firm's task with some effectiveness and efficiency. This means that people have to be put into groups and that each group must be given some kind of assignment. Then these groups and their assignments have to be organized in a way that enables the firm to achieve its goals and so the several groups do not get in each others' hair (see Box 19–1).

Organizational designs traditionally developed around the classical concepts of organizational charts, role description, and centralization and decentralization. During the 1950s new concepts emerging from personality theory and group dynamics facilitated the development of human relations type designs. In the 1970s, the growing belief that organizations do not operate in a vacuum, isolated from other organizations, led to greater emphasis on systems design, based on the information revolution.

The information revolution

The information age is upon us in the sense that we have the technological resources to provide a fantastic range of telecommunication

Box 19–1: GE: Synergy and SBUs

One of the best managed companies in the world is the General Electric Company. After World War II it pioneered decentralization and then recentralized through a system of corporate controls, held in position by a strategic planning system which exploits synergy (combined operation). This system uses strategic business units (SBUs), which are more than product lines. It provides GE with a new corporate ritual which makes good things happen.

GE, an $18 billion enterprise in the first ten of the *Fortune* 500 for sales, net income, assets, number of employees and shareholders, is the largest diversified company in the world. It is more an agglomerate (organic growth gave them their diversity) than a conglomerate like ITT.

Thirty years ago the top management of GE was a one-man operation led by "Electric Charlie" Wilson, but today direction is provided by a group of managers who make more use of management techniques than they exploit the results of scientific research. This calls for strategic planning, and SBUs have been superimposed over the organizational structure as a means of pulling critical groups together. This task-force approach to strategic planning works, if profitability is any guide.

functions both in the home and in the office. The long predicted marriage of computers and communication is at hand. The three giants of the communication, computer, and office machine industries—AT&T, IBM, and Xerox—have proposed establishing specialized business data communication networks.

New developments in communication technology include the use of satellites, the conversion of telephone switching equipment from analog to digital processing, and the growth of two-way cable systems. This technology allows employees to stop talking about the offices of the future and start working in them. With these new data communication networks offices are able to move data around the country electronically, and, as the price of facsimile and terminal equipment drop, economically.

Box 19–2 outlines six stages in the growth of data processing. To make all these changes possible there have been astonishing advances in microcircuitry. In the 1950s it took a $200,000 computer that weighed 3 tons, had 2,000 vacuum tubes, and required 10 tons of air conditioning equipment to perform the same functions that a three-chip, nine-ounce programmable calculator which costs less than $300 can handle in the 1980s.

So great are these technological developments that companies like Xerox are suggesting in their ads that informaton management does not threaten the work ethic. Their argument is that information management is not a way of sidestepping hard work, but a way of making it more productive.

Box 19–2: Managing changes in data processing

As companies grow and develop, so do the various management functions. Many companies are experiencing real problems with managing changes in data processing, for example. Richard L. Nolan has identified six stages in the development of the data processing function.

SIX STAGES OF DATA PROCESSING GROWTH

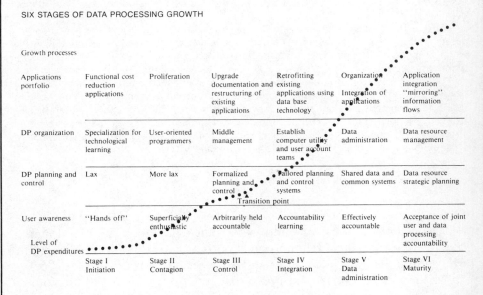

Growth processes						
Applications portfolio	Functional cost reduction applications	Proliferation	Upgrade documentation and restructuring of existing applications	Retrofitting existing applications using data base technology	Organization Integration of applications	Application integration "mirroring" information flows
DP organization	Specialization for technological learning	User-oriented programmers	Middle management	Establish computer utility and user account teams	Data administration	Data resource management
DP planning and control	Lax	More lax	Formalized planning and control	Tailored planning and control systems	Shared data and common systems	Data resource strategic planning
			Transition point			
User awareness	"Hands off"	Superficially enthusiastic	Arbitrarily held accountable	Accountability learning	Effectively accountable	Acceptance of joint user and data processing accountability
Level of DP expenditures						
	Stage I Initiation	Stage II Contagion	Stage III Control	Stage IV Integration	Stage V Data administration	Stage VI Maturity

As the data processing function moves from stage to stage there is a shift in the relationship between computer staff and line managers. In Stage 1 accounting procedures are typically automated. In Stage 2, given the success of Stage 1, data processing people experience low control and high slack. By Stage 3 there is recognition in the company that the managers need to regain control of data processing.

To assume effective data processing, the firm first has to recognize which stage it is in. Then it must choose a data processing strategy and develop a data processing growth plan.

Reference: Richard L. Nolan, Managing the Crisis in Data Processing, *Harvard Business Review*, March–April, 1979.

CHANGING THE PROCESS

Process consultation

Process consultation is a new modus operandi used by OD consultants who have graduated beyond T groups. Process consultants such as Edgar Schein and Chris Argyis see themselves as sociotherapists who work, through the concepts of diagnosis and helpful intervention, with healthy organizations. "Alive" organizations can achieve growth

FIGURE 19–3
Process consultation sequence

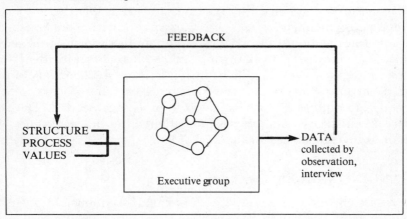

through process consultation, both in economic and interpersonal terms (see Figure 19–3).

The organization being helped plays a key part in the process. As Schein points out in *Process Consultation:*

> The job of the process consultant is to help the organization to solve its own problems by making it *aware of organizational processes,* of the consequences of these processes, and of the mechanisms by which they can be changed. The process consultant helps the organization to learn from self-diagnosis and self-intervention. The ultimate concern of the process consultant is the organization's capacity to do for itself what he has done for it. Where the standard consultant is more concerned about passing on his knowledge, the process consultant is concerned about passing on his skills and values.

Process consultancy, right from the first, involves the client with the consultant in the process of joint diagnosis. The consultant enters the organization without a clear mission in terms of structure but with a set of process concepts which can help the client identify problems. Schein has defined process consultation as follows:

> P-C is a set of activities on the part of the consultant which help the client to perceive, understand, and act upon process events which occur in the client's environment.

Intervention strategy

The intervention strategy requires the behavioral scientist to go right into the organization and confront the executives with the actualities of their business. The method, in effect, requires the interventionist to be a T-group apparatus.

The basic assumption of intervention strategy is that there is something wrong with organizations—they are suffering from organizational dry rot. Interventionists work in a rather similar way to radical students. Once they get into an organization and create an incident, they insist on the incident being investigated fairly and objectively; a process is set up to investigate the incident. Then the process is challenged, and a process to investigate the process is needed. Thus the interventionist invents a process to challenge the process which was meant to investigate the incident.

CHANGING VALUES

Process change is concerned with the actual sequence of organizational events. The seminal conception emerged from the three-step model proposed by Kurt Lewin: unfreezing, changing, refreezing. Integral to this model is the notion that behavioral and attitudinal changes follow a basic sequence and that this change process changes values. Figure 19–4 models this basic sequence.

FIGURE 19–4
How the change process changes values

	UNFREEZING	CHANGING	REFREEZING
Goal	Inappropriate	Generalized	Specific
Social relations	Break-up	New and tenuous	New, reinforced
Self-esteem	Anxiety, tension	Growth	New integration
Motive for change	External	External/internal	Internal

Unfreezing must be understood as a process of mobilizing frustration, increasing tension, and fostering disintegration and dependency. Change is thus made possible by the disintegration of old and inappropriate group relations, behavior patterns, and life-styles.

The crux of the changing phase is facilitating the group formulation of new goals, strategies, and processes relevant to its needs and aspirations. These processes maximize participation, enhance authenticity, and improve communication flow.

The refreezing phase is essentially concerned with the reintegration of system forces through the formulation of a new set of rules, roles, and relations. In the refreezing phase, a new set of values, norms, reinforcements, and sanctions is confirmed and internalized.

Before this paradigm of change can be invoked and operationalized it is necessary for a considerable level of tension to exist in the system.

The OD consultant

The OD consultant must be a competent executive or professional who has the necessary experience and power-manipulation skills to facilitate the change. Typically when change programs are being introduced, it is optimal to begin at the top and then (counting on top management's support) set about changing middle and lower management.

In brief, there is considerable evidence to support the proposition that there is a link between prestige and influence. Research work in clinical psychology suggests that even brief contacts with a prestigious psychiatrist can have therapeutic effects for patients. Presumably this "hail and farewell" effect has a correlate in process consultancy, where important organizational clients are prepared to pay large fees to have a distinguished consultant pay infrequent and brief visits to their organizations. Figure 19–5 indicates how a consultant or change agent establishes a successful pattern.

FIGURE 19–5
Success pattern of changer–changee relation

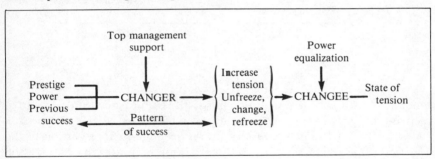

As Lewin once observed: If you want to understand some social system, try to change it. Thus it frequently happens that management's feel for new organizational structure, process, or values only emerges after the start of an intensive change strategy.

The managerial grid: A design for changing managerial styles and values

A method of conceptualizing managerial style in order to apply behavioral science insights to organizational change efforts is the managerial grid developed by Robert R. Blake and Jane A. Mouton. In this concept it is assumed that all executive styles can be plotted on a grid with two dimensions, concern for production and concern for people. As shown in Figure 19–6, a manager's style is plotted by ratings of

FIGURE 19–6
The managerial grid

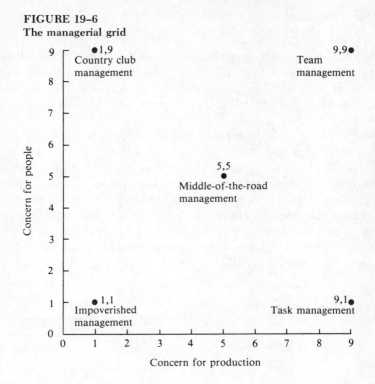

from 1 to 9 on each of the dimensions. Blake and Mouton recognize five principal styles, as plotted in Figure 16–6.

A rating of 1,1 indicates *impoverished management:* exertion of the minimum effort to get the required work done to maintain organization membership.

A rating of 9,1 indicates *task management:* the manager is high in task efficiency but low in concern for human satisfaction. Men are regarded as just another commodity—another instrument of production.

A rating of 1,9 indicates *country club management:* high human satisfaction but low work tempo. Production is incidental to the elimination of conflict and the establishment o good fellowship.

A rating of 5,5 indicates *middle of the road management:* adequate task performance while maintaining morale at a satisfactory level. A certain amount of production push is necessary—but not flat out. Fairness and firmness are in order.

A rating of 9,9 indicates *team management:* high task achievement from committed people who have a common stake in the firm's purposes, with good relationships of trust and respect.

TOPIC 3
Critical review of organizational development

Organizational development has been widely criticized because it presents itself as a science, but when you come in contact with it it turns out to be a religion. Organizational development as a science is seen as a method of technology for improving effectiveness; as a religion its aim is to "humanize" organizations.

A BASIC CONFLICT OF VALUES

Thus organizational development faces a basic conflict of values. According to Frank Friedlander, the underlying values of organizational development are as shown in Figure 19–7. Thus OD consultants

FIGURE 19–7
Values of organizational development

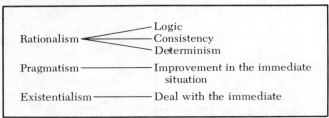

frequently find themselves conflicted. Further, it has been argued that organizational development has been largely unsuccessful because the values being propagated are at variance with the values of our politico-economic system.

Nevertheless, organizational development continues to be widely used to solve the problems of business organizations and to address the special problems of multinational corporations. A wide variety of OD techniques now being used include the grid, team building, survey feedback, and a variety of structural approaches. Increasingly researchers are spending more time developing a series of measures that might be used to describe and evaluate OD interventions.

George Strauss has criticized the fundamental character of the concept in "Organizational Development":

> For my taste, OD has been plagued by too much evangelical hucksterism. Though considerable thought has been given to professional ethics, there are as yet no generally accepted codes of behavior. OD techniques have been subjected to some scientific research, but it is a bit premature to conclude that OD is truly a scientific method or the

"science-based" approach. And it is downright misleading to suggest that OD's utility has been proven scientifically valid. . . OD is a fad, and American companies are suckers for gimmicks.

THE EFFECTIVENESS OF ORGANIZATIONAL DEVELOPMENT

How effective is organizational development? Figure 19–8 suggests some criteria for effective OD efforts. While OD specialists might say

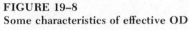

FIGURE 19–8
Some characteristics of effective OD

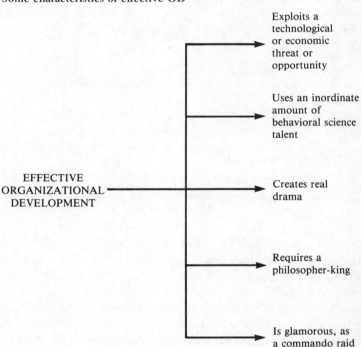

they work well, most managers have serious doubts. They believe that the significant changes in organizations come from outside (see Figure 19–9), from social, economic, and technological developments such as computers, copiers, the pill, and so on.

For example, in the United States great changes in work design have been necessary because women are entering the work force in greater numbers and are seeking better paid, more challenging jobs. Further, federal government legislation against discrimination has compelled large organizations, both public and private, to change the

Figure 19–9
Dynamics of successful organization change

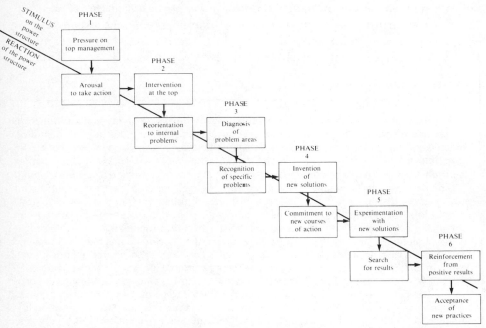

Source: Adapted from Larry E. Greiner, "Patterns of Organizational Change," *Harvard Business Review*, May–June, 1967.

ground rules to help women take their rightful place at work. Dramatic changes are favoring a more androgynous managerial style.

OD can play a critical part in developing these styles. Many of the technologies that are utilized in OD have been borrowed from trainers who specialize in consciousness-raising groups.

OD has also been criticized for its lack of precise meaning. When attempts are made to assess its validity, the research usually concludes that the participants enjoyed the experience, but they need time to think it over and assess its relevance to the back-home work situation. Little or no systematic efforts have been made to assess effectiveness in terms of improving productivity and profitability.

My personal experience with organizational development has been largely limited to three different companies. In the first, at the Glacier Metal Company in England, the attempt to change the culture of a factory reported by Elliott Jacques was a considerable success at the beginning. But later, as the company came under pressure from the stop-go British economy, things did not work out so well. Further, for the project to be a success required an immense investment of behavioral science talent, mainly from the Tavistock Institute of Human Relations (see Box 19–3).

Much the same applies to the famous experiment at the Harwood Manufacturing Company, which manufactures pajamas. My experience from visiting Harwood in Marion, Virginia, is that the experiment, at least in that particular plant, is now essentially over . This is

Box 19–3: The Glacier system of management

By any standards, the Glacier studies must be regarded as a tremendous contribution to management knowledge because of their scope, significance, and design. These studies, which began in 1948, arose largely from the collaboration of two men, Wilfred Brown (one-time chairman of Glacier, who is "an industrial philosopher-king") and Elliott Jaques (a psychiatrist who has fused psychoanalysis and field theory to provide a new orientation).

The Glacier Metal Company, which is probably the most studied, best documented, and most heavily dissected organization, is a successful public company, employing 4,500 people in six locations. It is the largest manufacturer of plain bearings in Europe and occupies a special position in the esteem of those who study organization theory. In scope, length, theoretical significance, and general impact, the Glacier studies merit comparison with the Hawthorne investigations. In fact, the Glacier research started in the human relations period and was at first largely concerned with making committees effective.

In Glacier, the essentially human relations view is in turn giving way to Brown's conception of "task management," whose flavor and economy may be gathered from two propositions, one positive and the other negative. In task management, optimal organization is a function of the work to be done (task) and the resources available to do it (personnel, technical, and economic); personality plays no part.

THE FACTORY IS THE STATE "WRIT SMALL"

The most comprehensive exposition of the Glacier system has been provided by Brown in *Exploration in Management.* In the policy document for the company there are outlined four systems of organization: the legislative system, the executive system, the representative system, and the appeals system.

The function of the legislative system is to make policy for the whole organization. In May, 1949, the managing director introduced a revolutionary change in the Works Council. He proposed that the Council should become a policy-making body for the company so that "every major policy decision would become a matter for consultation with the entire Works Council." The managing director rightly argued that there were two stages in management: policy making and executive action. He further argued that the Works Council should be responsible for policy, and management for executive action.

The executive system represents a network of roles for carrying out the day-to-day work of the company within the framework of the company policy.

From Tavistock, Glacier adopted the following ideas:

1. That the individual's behavior can be explained through the analysis of the complex of forces acting on him. These forces can involve personal, social, and historical factors. Some may be unconscious.
2. Making these forces explicit is the technique of "working through." Inherent in this approach is the optimistic view that chance factors are of minimal significance.
3. When all is known (by working through), then all will be well.
4. The sociotechnical systems approach provides the basis of task management.

Source: Joe J. Kelly, *Is Scientific Management Possible?* (London: Faber & Faber, Ltd., 1968).

another example of the importance of economic and technological factors. The clothing manufacturing industry used to be concentrated in the northeastern United States, where a pool of unskilled labor was readily available. In the forties these industries moved further south to avoid rapidly developing unionization. And in time, the manufacturer of pajamas, shirts, and so on moved to Puerto Rico, Taiwan, or South Korea. Harwood became relatively unimportant.

In the third OD effort in my experience, the Steinberg behavioral science project in Canada, OD has had a significant but limited success. A major reason has been the supermarket and department store chain's ability to move from one behavioral science concept to another. For example, in the midsixties the company was mainly interested in the ideas of Frederick Herzberg and Blake and Mouton, and in the seventies they took up assessment centers.

One way or another, Steinberg has managed to carry out the OD exercise with a great deal of panache and distinction. For example, they managed to get the National Film Board to make movies about their behavioral science innovations. The net effect has been to give Steinberg an upbeat, zippy corporate management style which allows big issues to be discussed under the NFB cameras.

Thus, in general terms, OD can be a success, but often at an inordinate price, and only when the owner or the chief executive can form a liaison with a truly outstanding behavioral scientist. And such philosopher-king dyads are hard to come by.

In short, organizational development can be compared to a commando raid. It is interesting and exciting and good public relations when it is happening, but commando raids do not win wars. Usually, indeed, commando combat tactics are absorbed into the prosaic infantry combat regiment to good effect. Likewise, OD works best when it is used to create verve, drama, and decision in one unit of the organization. Then the structure, process, and values that signal its success can be allowed to percolate into the more prosaic parts of the organization.

TOPIC 4
What every manager should know about organizational development

The most important thing for a manager to know about organizational development is that it is a new, exciting idea in training which seeks to manage the corporate culture collaboratively so that good things can happen in the material and moral sense. Organizational development sets out to change corporate values by getting people to become more creative and to participate in decisions that affect their lives. The object of the exercise in this applied behavioral science effort is to change values, so that the firm's climate is also changed. The client is not the individual, not the group, but the organization itself. The aim is to achieve organizational renewal and revitalization.

Frequently organizational development involves the use of T groups. These modern change structures require OD consultants who have a dialectical imagination. Such consultants can lead the organization through the stages of diagnosis, implementation, and evolution.

Sometimes a change is achieved through structural means, by redrafting organization structure, company policies, and job descriptions, or through a management information system. These structural changes must be achieved with a specific process that facilitates the participation of executives in formulating the actual choices. The change agent, therefore, must develop an effective intervention strategy. As the structure and the process change, so do the values. In effect the organization, in going through the steps of unfreezing, changing, and refreezing, changes its values.

This may make organizational behavior seem more like a religion than a science. Somehow or other, however, the effective OD consultant can put rationalism, pragmatism, and existentialism together to make good things happen.

ORGANIZATIONAL DEVELOPMENT AS A SYSTEM

Organizational development is still in an evolutionary state. Recognizing the limitations this imposes on a contingency model, we can attempt to model it as a system, as in Figure 19–10. Since change in organizations is what OD is all about, this model incorporates methods of change rather than methods of research—although they may amount to the same thing. Organizational literature has a dearth of written-up projects describing the kinds of problems that can be tackled using OD approaches, so the need for research is evident.

It seems unrealistic to believe that OD can solve all corporate problems. Corporate development people and OD consultants have to be sensible about overselling this new training art form, especially in terms of the size and complexity of the problems it can solve. Only corporate managers can solve complex, long-term organizational problems, for only they are ultimately accountable; only they control the real power and resources. Corporate officials are the licensed pilots of our jumbo-jet-like enterprises; they have their hands on the controls and are not about to relinquish them.

OD is a new technique which starts as a method for training the system, for revealing processes, and for changing perspectives and evolving new values—all through creative problem solving. It could become a way of life, a corporate zeitgeist which somehow permeates the mysteries of management, freeing up the executive to make effective decisions in an existential context.

FIGURE 19–10
Organizational development as a system

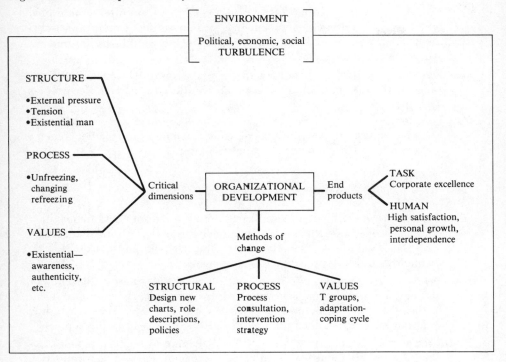

REVIEW AND RESEARCH

1. Develop an outline plan of the changes that have taken place in the airline business since 1920. Make sure your answer includes references to the introduction of jets, jumbo jets, and SSTs, cargo carrying, charters, feeder airlines, airport facilities, passenger attitudes, and the military-industrial complex. Include in your answer a scenario to explain the future decline of the airline business.

2. How can planned change be introduced in organizations? OD is not always a necessity in introducing change. In fact, it may be a positive disadvantage. List the kinds of change where OD would be inappropriate.

3. What are the stages through which a T group goes? If a group member knows about these stages, the roles likely to emerge, and the process itself, does he leave himself open to the charge of manipulating fellow group members if he "plays along" with the group? If the answer is yes, what would you say about the T-group trainer? Can these difficulties be overcome?

4. Critically evaluate process consultation.

5. Discuss: "Life today is just one amusing (boring) T group."

6. What are the objectives of OD? Develop an OD plan for your business school.

7. Critically evaluate the managerial grid. Develop a new three-dimensional grid based on information processing, system sophistication, and traditional versus existential value dimensions. How would you implement this grid?

8. Develop a new plan of training that goes beyond OD and takes cognizance of the effects of the environment. Entitle your paper "Ecosystems Training."

9. Develop a training program to make executives more creative. Make sure that you consider the possibilities of using encounter groups, the women's movement, and "the power of lateral thinking."

GLOSSARY OF TERMS

Intervention strategy. Strategy used by the behavioral scientist or consultant who intervenes directly in organizational life and confronts executives with the actualities of their behavior. The interventionist uses T-group technology to bring process and value change.

Leaderless group. A type of T group in which no official leader is appointed or chosen, but members are asked to work on a problem; the intended result is that the group structures itself in a particular way, roles (including different kinds of leadership) emerge, and people take up these roles.

Managerial grid. A concept developed by Blake and Mouton in which managerial styles are identified by plotting a manager's concern for production and concern for people on a grid which rates each dimension on a scale of 1 to 9. Blake and Mouton identified five principal *management styles* according to their position on the grid: 1,1, impoverished; 9,1, task; 1,9, country club; 5,5, middle of the road; and 9,9, team management.

Organizational development. An attempt to achieve corporate excellence by integrating executives' need for growth with organizational goals. OD is concerned with changing postures, perspectives, and processes, primarily through value changes in a systems context which is appropriate to the contemporary turbulent environment, with its inherent uncertainties.

Power equalization. A model which recognizes that a more stable, appropriate, and adaptive change is possible if the changee has an equal share of power with the changer.

Process change. Change achieved principally through Lewin's unfreezing-changing-refreezing model. Unfreezing involves mobilizing tension and frustration in the system to disintegrate inappropriate behaviors; changing means facilitating the formulation of new goals, strategies, and processes; refreezing is concerned with reinforcing and confirming new values and norms until they become internalized.

Process consultant. An organizational development scientist who helps the organization to solve its problems by making it aware of its processes, the consequences of these processes, and the mechanisms by which they can be changed. The process consultant stresses self-diagnosis and self-intervention. The ultimate concern is to pass on skills and values so the organization can do for itself what the consultant has done for it—in contrast to the structural consultant, who is concerned with passing along knowledge.

Process consultation. A set of activities through which a consultant helps a healthy organization to perceive, understand, and act upon process events which occur in its environment, with a view to changing and improving its processes. Process consultation incorporates value consultation, since value changes are implicit in process changes, and it uses intervention strategy on the part of the consultant. Schein describes seven steps in process consultancy: (1) initial contact; (2) defining the formal and psychological contracts between client and consultant; (3) selecting a setting and a method of work; (4) data gathering and diagnosis; (5) intervention; (6) reducing involvement; and (7) termination.

Reentry problem. The difficulty of putting into effect in the company setting what one has learned in the T group.

Sensitivity training. A method of training which attempts to make people more aware of their personality dynamics, for example motives, defense mechanisms, anxieties, effect on others, and adaptation to group roles. Research indicates that sensitive people are above average in intelligence, tolerance, independence, responsibility, and considerateness; less consistent results indicate that the sensitive are more imaginative, more domineering, and less gregarious than average.

Structural consultation. The traditional approach to helping organizations (usually organizations in more or less trouble) through structural changes—changing organizational charts, guidelines, and procedures; clarifying roles, delegation of responsibility, and line-staff relations; and developing more pervasive control techniques such as production planning and budgetary controls.

T group. Initially an unstructured, leaderless group in which individuals participate in order to learn about themselves (see *Sensitivity training*) and about group dynamics. The desired benefits for participants are: (1) insight into one's own personality dynamics, behavior, and attitudes, and into those of others; (2) increased openness, receptivity, and tolerance of differences; and (3) improved operational skill in interpersonal relations, associated with greater willingness to take risks and try out new relationships.

Value consultation. Consultation which strives to import new values into the system. This is, in actuality, part of process consultation, rather than a separate technique, since the data gathering and feedback used in process consultation are intended to have an impact on the organization's value system (and, incidentally, on its structure if necessary). Many organizations achieve value changes by introducing personnel who have been exposed to different cultures.

DEBATE: Successful versus unsuccessful organizational development

Successful OD: Harwood Manufacturing Company

The Failure of Success, by Alfred J. Marrow, publicized the unusual story of the Harwood Manufacturing Company which began in 1937 when Marrow, then fresh from receiving a doctorate in psychology, was appointed president of the family firm. With his academic background and ownership status, Marrow was in an especially favorable position to apply behavioral science concepts. Working initially with the distinguished German psychologist Kurt Lewin, Harwood rapidly adopted participative management as the major strategy for improving organizational performance.

Shortly before Marrow took over as president, Harwood moved its manufacturing operations from New England to the rural community of Marion, Virginia. The low productivity rates and high turnover of empolyees being experienced at the new plant threatened the very existence of the company and presented the first challenge for the application of behavioral science. After conventional methods failed to unearth the cause of the problem, Marrow invited Lewin to visit the plant.

Lewin quickly identified the cause of the high turnover as fear of failure on the part of apprentice operators who were striving to reach a production rate of 60 units per hour. Many who approached this rate, but despaired of attaining it, left the company. The quitting rate actually increased as the operators' productivity went up, with a rate of 96 percent among operators at the 55-unit-per-hour level. By providing short-range targets in small increments, Lewin was able to give new operators frequent opportunity for achievement; within a year the quitting rate was down by half. The application of behavioral science at Harwood Manufacturing was on its way.

During the association of a number of distinguished academics with Harwood over the years, the main thrust of their program was toward highly practical goals. Marrow and Lewin agreed at the beginning that there should be "no action without research," but they likewise insisted that there should be no research without action. The standards used to measure success in applying participative management were generally economic, for example, unit production cost, production volume, absenteeism, and turnover rate. Although Likert scales were used to measure shifts in workers' attitudes, no project was considered a success simply because employee opinion had shifted in the desired direction. Demonstrable contribution to the profit goals of the company appears to have been the objective more than "happy" employees.

The largest participative management project attempted by the Harwood organization came when the company took over its major competitor, Weldon Manufacturing. Weldon's operations were quite similar to Harwood's, with the important exception that Harwood had much higher productivity and consequently was much more profitable. Management decided that Weldon's authoritarian management style was responsible for its high costs and set out to introduce participative management on a major scale.

The project started with sensitivity training sessions, team-building and problem-solving meetings for all levels, and attempts to delegate influence and authority downward. There was considerable skepticism among employees accustomed to authoritarian methods, and progress was so slow that the company's financial position was threatened. After seven months, the following more drastic measures were adopted:

1. Sensitivity training sessions to work out antagonisms and develop collaboration were held, starting with top management.
2. "Family groups" of employees who worked together were arranged; attendance was compulsory.
3. The sessions were held away from the plant on an intensive basis, lasting two to four days. A psychologist attended each session.

Although the meetings were unstructured in the sense that an agenda was not followed, the pattern that established itself consisted of (1) problem census and discussion, (2) personal relationships, and (3) assessment of the participants' own behavior and desire for change.

The more intensive program produced the desired changes in behavior, and considerable improvement in motivation, coordination, and cooperation was achieved. As the program was spread down to lower levels in the organization over a period of 18 months, the employees began to develop team spirit and morale and to accept responsibility for their own production goals. A dramatic turnaround in profitability and other performance indices also took place.

A research study four and a half years after the intensive program ended indicated that the benefits continued to be realized and that no retrogression to previous managerial patterns was evident. The study concluded that participative management is attractive to employees, who will resist any attempt to reassert authoritarian measures.

Unsuccessful OD: Manchester Manufacturing

What happens when management simultaneously introduces the managerial grid, management by objectives, and participative management to a business firm? Walter R. Nord and Douglas E. Durand, in "Beyond Resistance to Change," argue that radical switches from autocratic to participative management can cause serious trouble. They studied the application of OD techniques to a firm called Manchester Manufacturing, a medium-sized company with three major and several smaller plants located in several midwestern and southern cities. Most of the company's sales came from products manufactured using mass production technology.

Nord and Durand report that at the time of their study, top management consisted of a president and four other men:

> The president, Jim Atkins, was a major stockholder in the firm and spent long hours at the business. A somewhat contemplative personality, he was very popular with his employees, who viewed him with respect and affection and agreed that he displayed a strong concern for their welfare.
>
> In addition to the president, the top-management group included Harold Field, Charles Post, a sales manager, and a young M.B.A. Harold Field, an organizational process consultant, was hired as a member of the top team by the president. His primary duties involved implementing "team management" throughout the organization and maintaining and restructuring previously instituted management programs. Because Field had been hired only six months prior to our study, he played no part in introducing most of the programs described in this article.
>
> Charles Post initially entered the company as an assistant to Atkins. Post was an engineer by training but had developed an intimate knowledge of the applications of recent developments in the behavioral sciences. As he saw it, he was selected to complement Atkins's 1,9 Managerial Grid style. Because of his commanding personality, technical expertise, high energy level, and verbal skills, Post greatly influenced Atkins. He played a key role in the company's change effort.
>
> The sales manager had many years' experience at Manchester Manufacturing; the young M.B.A. had been with the company only three years or so.

Sometime before Nord and Durand carried out their study, Manchester Manufacturing had begun to introduce a participative management system. Every manager had been through a one-week, Phase 1 training program of the managerial grid, and the company made a special effort to institute a management by objectives (MBO) program. Work teams were a major innovation by which top management attempted to increase the participation of lower level managers.

The managers had a general favorable attitude toward the company, as indicated by such statements or "While we have a lot of complaints around here, it's better than any other place to work," and "While we have a lot of bitches, our bitches are at a higher level than elsewhere." But management was criticized because of a lack of ability to follow up on decisions. As one manager put it: "Top management is not action oriented. They shouldn't remove themselves from the thrust of the company's effort as they often have done. They must be involved more totally with things such as customers and conflict within departments." Other managers challenged the proliferation of new management programs. One man said, "In the past, we've had a number of different systems but haven't taken a set of policies and stuck with it. We've had so many changes, it's like "future shock." We tend to jump around from one to another; we change every six months when it really takes two years to see if it would work." Nord and Durand noted other reactions:

> In addition, some individuals suggested that top management used the participative techniques as a way to avoid making decisions or taking action. To the degree that new approaches appeared to delay action, they contributed to the pervasive feeling that the firm was not results-oriented. [According to one worker] "The president doesn't like to direct; he prefers to arbitrate and referree. He can arbitrate a zero-sum situation so that both parties lose. Because he doesn't want to have hard feelings, both parties wind up losing."

Thus, Nord and Durand point out, management finds itself in a double bind: "You're damned if you do and you're damned if you don't."

A criticism of the grid was that employees believed that Post had made a mistake in characterizing the management style as 1,9 before the grid was introduced. Many of the lower level supervisors thought the advice requiring them to be candid was inappropriate because a subordinate cannot tell a boss what he or she thinks: "You just can't pick apart your boss." The MBO system was criticized because it was believed the program conflicted with organizational goals, and it made the managers vulnerable to criticism.

Nord and Durand concluded:

> The ambivalence of top management toward participation and toward change in general is strikingly reflected in the divided perceptions among the managers at Manchester. Precisely 38.8 percent viewed the organization as flexible and willing to change, and by an amazing coincidence, the same number of managers viewed the organization as reluctant to make changes.
>
> Clearly, the lower-level managers were receiving different and contradictory messages from the top. Did this perceptual confusion arise from ambivalence on top management's part, faulty perceptions by some lower-level managers, or a combination of the two? Our data doesn't permit a definitive answer. Certainly, a number of managers seemed to believe that participation for the most part would be restricted to matters of secondary importance and that most decisions of consequence would still be made at the top or not at all.

Questions

1. Why was Harwood a successful OD effort?
2. Why was the Manchester OD effort not successful?

CHAPTER 20 ——— ORGANIZING THE FUTURE

— The economy of the 80s

— Organizational design
  in the future tense

— The new liberated manager

part VI

THE FUTURE

DIAGRAM SUMMARY OF CHAPTER 20

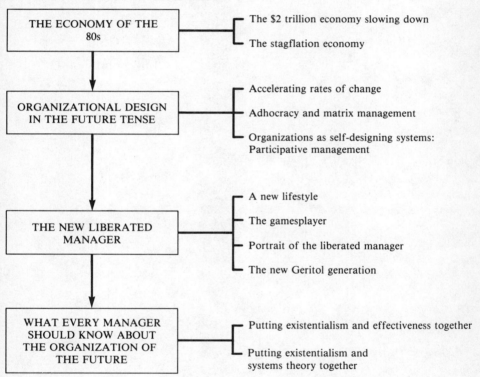

THE ECONOMY OF THE 80s
- The $2 trillion economy slowing down
- The stagflation economy

ORGANIZATIONAL DESIGN IN THE FUTURE TENSE
- Accelerating rates of change
- Adhocracy and matrix management
- Organizations as self-designing systems: Participative management

THE NEW LIBERATED MANAGER
- A new lifestyle
- The gamesplayer
- Portrait of the liberated manager
- The new Geritol generation

WHAT EVERY MANAGER SHOULD KNOW ABOUT THE ORGANIZATION OF THE FUTURE
- Putting existentialism and effectiveness together
- Putting existentialism and systems theory together

20

Organizing the future

ROOTS FOR MOBICENTRIC EXECUTIVES

A glimpse at the manager of the future is afforded by the resistance young executives are offering to the nomadic life which was a job requirement of their executive fathers. For an increasing number of managers offered promotions on the basis of "move up or else," the answer is, "no thanks."

Only a decade ago the refusal rate was no more than 10 percent; now this figure is more like 40 to 50 percent. This represents a fundamental shift in executive values. Instead of marching to the company drumbeat of onward and upward, many are following pop star Billy Joel's suggestion: "If that's movin' up, then I'm moving out."

A *Time* magazine article (June 12, 1978) notes that:

> American executives are becoming increasingly interested in things money cannot buy, notably a stable home life, a safe environment, a wholesome community, sun, fun and culture. For example, Mark Burns, 42, a fast-rising IBM executive in Chicago, turned down three transfers in order to raise his three children in one place. But Burns is aware that his refusals limited his possibilities at IBM, whose initials, many employees joke, stand for I've Been Moved. Hence, Burns came to the conclusion he must switch careers and now is president of a small bank on Chicago's South Side.

Often it isn't only the man's position that determines the decision to stay put. With approximately 40 percent of American women holding jobs, there are two careers and two paychecks to be considered. The Bureau of Labor Statistics estimates that 30.4 million U.S. families

(53 percent of the total) have at least two earners. *Time* magazine (August 21, 1978) notes the emergence of a "powerful and growing subgroup: moneyed, self-indulgent, career-oriented families in which the husbands are in their mid-20s to mid-30s. Of the 11 million families in this age bracket, nearly four million are households where the wife has a full-time job. And many of the multiple-earner families have combined incomes of $30,000—and occasionally much more." But unfortunately, futurologists failed to forecast this massive new trend.

DOES FUTUROLOGY HAVE A FUTURE?

Nevertheless, managers have an intense interest in trying to forecast the future. Indeed, they are so intent on trying to catch a glimpse of what the world will look like by the turn of the century that they are making massive investments in futurology. Futurology has been cynially described by Ambrose Bierce, in *Devil's Dictionary*, as scientific prophecy, or the art and practice of selling one's credibility for future delivery. Indeed, many of the predictions have a distinct science fictional ring. For example, Stephen Rosen, in *Future Facts*, suggests how you will live in just a few short years: You'll take a 21-minute subway ride from New York to Los Angeles, you'll swallow a knowledge pill that teaches you Spanish or any other subject, you'll eat and drink food and beverages that heat and chill themselves in a matter of seconds, you'll control your weight by electric brain stimulation, and enzymes will keep you young indefinitely.

To counter such zany forecasts, managers are turning to think tanks such as the Hudson Institute, Rand Corporation, and the Club of Rome to get a better insight into what the future will look like. Herman Kahn, the dynamic director of the Hudson Institute, offers an exciting scenario of declining population growth but rising levels of affluence in *The Next 200 Years* (coauthored by William Brown and Leon Martel). Kahn seems always conscious of Thomas Malthus looking over his shoulder, forecasting doom. Malthus, a 19th-century clergyman, came up with the unique proposition that food production rises in arithmetical progression, while the world population rises in geometric progression.

The modern Malthusians are the Cassandras of the Club of Rome, who have warned managers that their corporate world, in its bid for affluence, is consuming and polluting itself to death. The sponsors of the Club of Rome commissioned Dennis Meadows of MIT to construct a computer program that would generate equations linking the world's resources, population, and pollution in a mathematical matrix. The odd thing about Meadow's computer was that all answers in all circumstances were written in the calculus of doom.

At one time, futurologists were content to predict what 1984 was going to be like; this was the title of a famous science fiction piece by George Orwell which predicted a world in which bureaucracy had gone mad and Big Brother controlled everything. All that Orwell was doing was adding an appendix to such pessimistic literary works as H. G. Wells's *Mind at the End of its Tether* and Aldous Huxley's *Brave New World*.

To some managers, behavior control technology, which has arrived on their desks from the laboratories of behavioral scientists, represents the future. Many of them are fascinated by films such as *A Clockwork Orange*, which paints a picture of a Pavlovian man triggered by Beethoven's symphonies to commit sadistic crimes. The antihero of *A Clockwork Orange* is apprehended by the authorities and turned over to their psychologists, who recondition him to behave like a zombie.

Executives are puzzled whether their own views are a fair indication of what lies in store for their grandchildren. Indeed, efforts are being made to determine whether, in fact, futurology has a future.

Time magazine, in an essay entitled "Is There Any Future in Futurism?" (May 17, 1976), has this to say about forecasting the future:

> Such perceptions may be glimpses of tomorrow, or they may be magnifications of the present—shadows thrown upon a screen labeled A.D. 2000. They may be accurate, or they may be as invalid as the predictions of almost a century ago that saw city dwellers transported everywhere by that new-fangled invention, the balloon. Forecasters have a habit of extrapolating from their surroundings: the scientist from the laboratory, the statistician from his calculator, the administrator from his think tank. Such predictions rise, in Lewis Mumford's phrase, from a mind "operating with its own conceptual apparatus, in its own restrictive field . . . determined to make the world over in its own oversimplified terms, wilfully rejecting interests and values incompatible with its own assumptions."
>
> Does this mean that prediction has no future? Hardly. The human race can no more stop prophesying than it can stop breathing. Indeed, if anything has a future, it is futurism. The United Nations Institute for Training and Research sponsored an international survey of futures studies. Sweden has a Secretariat for Futures Studies reporting directly to the Prime Minister. The European Communities are now contemplating the establishment of a permanent group, "Europe + 30", to forecast Europe's needs for the next three decades. Last February Ohio's Senator John Glenn conducted a symposium on "Our Third Century." Scores of experts testified, among them Barry Commoner, Alvin Toffler (*Future Shock*), Nelson Rockefeller, B. F. Skinner, and Buckminster Fuller.
>
> In an epoch of uncertainties, the hunger for prediction is rising to the famine level. Never before has speculative fiction been so popular. Thirty-five science fiction books were published in 1945; in 1975, 900 such books were published. Even the pseudo sciences are flourishing. Shrewdly unspecific astrological charts can be found in most major

newspapers (Pisces: Do your work despite passing moments of stress). The *National Enquirer*'s annual contest to gauge readers' psychic ability is among the weekly's most popular features. In fact, it has become impossible to lead a modern life without some form of prophecy. Every stock market letter, every long-range weather report and baseball schedule is a prediction; every garden and every child is an expressed belief in the future. As Toffler observes, "Under conditions of high-speed change, a democracy without the ability to anticipate condemns itself to death."

TOPIC 1
The economy of the eighties

THE $2 TRILLION ECONOMY: SLOWING DOWN

As the United States approached the 1980s, the gross national product was moving above the $2 trillion level. This means that output was approaching $10,000 for every man, woman, and child in the country. This had been achieved at a time with no strikingly new consumer goods; cars were shrinking and fuel bills were increasing. In the first seven years of the seventies, total output of goods and services was growing at a rate of roughly 10 percent a year. Only 3 percent represented real growth, however, with the remaining 6–7 percent representing inflation. If this rate of growth would have continued, the United States would have hit the $3 trillion mark in 1982.

The U.S. growth in GNP declined in 1979, however. Indeed, the rate of productivity growth in the United States had been declining ever since the midsixties. As consequences of this slowdown, U.S. living standards have risen less rapidly, and inflationary pressures have dramatically increased. An economic prerogative seems to be developing that more may not be better, or even possible.

This drop in productivity has been attributed to a decline in the capital-labor ratio and to lower R&D expenditures, among other things. Another factor is that, compared with both Japan and West Germany, the recent leaders in productivity, the United States has been spending too much in the unproductive military sector.

The decline in productivity is coupled with a realization that the world is running out of natural resources like oil, coal, copper, and arable land. The general feeling abroad is that Americans are living beyond their means. Values regarding productivity also are changing as existential man replaces to some extent both the administrative and economic models.

The prospect of continuous economic growth has been described as "the unwritten and unconfessed religion of our times." Some critics have proposed that a moratorium is necessary, not a time of benign neglect. While the insane demand for growth may not be fruitful, innovation is. As Dennis Gabor, winner of the 1971 Nobel Prize in physics for the invention of the holograph (a three-dimensional "picture"), points out in *Innovations: Scientific, Technological, and Social:*

> History must stop, the insane quantitative growth must stop—it must take an entirely new direction. Instead of working blindly toward things bigger and better, it must work toward improving the quality of life rather than increasing its quantity. Innovation must work toward a new harmony, a new equilibrium; otherwise it will only lead to an explosion.

The pressures of inflation, fueled by the cost of energy, and the concomitant decline of the stock market and the dollar have led some economists to predict a worldwide crisis of capitalism. Robert L. Heilbroner describes the psychological history of capitalism as "a tale of alternating euphoria and despair." For our society to achieve a period of even modest growth, Heilbroner argues in *Beyond Boom and Crash*, we will have to make great institutional changes in terms of economic planning which will call for a restructuring of the capitalistic framework.

THE STAGFLATION ECONOMY

The economy of the eighties is most likely to be a period of stagflation, characterized by simultaneous high unemployment and inflation. To try to explain this apparent contradiction, post-Keynesian economics has revised the conventional wisdom of traditional economics. The basic assumptions of post-Keynesian theory include:

1. National economies will go through continual, though uneven, expansion; investment, pricing, and income distribution are interlocked.
2. Credit will be a decisive factor.
3. The interactions of large corporations and trade unions will be vital.
4. The growth of real wages will depend more on technological factors, worker productivity, investment, and the proportion of non-wage income devoted to government spending.
5. For U.S. society to function, some kind of income policy will be required.

The job market

Demographic data suggest that the demand for college graduates in the eighties will be three times greater than for all workers, although many graduates may continue to find it difficult to get jobs they regard as appropriate. Job prospects for college graduates sagged in the 1970s when members of the postwar baby boom reached the labor market, creating a situation where the supply exceeded the demand. As an entirely different cohort—the young men and women born during the period since 1960—reaches 18 and begins looking for work, the number of young people entering the labor market will decline significantly.

Supply and demand of graduates will move more into balance, although an increasing number may be required to enter nontraditional fields. There will be greater interest in career-related majors. Shrewd students will select specializations in engineering, accounting, or management where demand is likely to grow and where they can participate in the design of future organizations.

TOPIC 2
Organizational design in the future tense

Organizational design may be defined as a conscious and deliberate effort to problem solve and plan processes. The emphasis is on rationality, logic, simplicity, and reliability, and the object is to improve the functioning of the organization. Basically, organizational design deals with structural rearrangement and improvements in efficiency or effectiveness. Many future-oriented organization theorists are attempting to develop contingent designs.

This emphasis on design and rationality may create the impression that organizational charts are designed scientifically. Examination of the history of most organizations reveals the existence of many irrational design choices, however. For example, when Henry Ford fired Lee Iacocca, the president of Ford Motor Company, his only explanation was that he did not like the man.

Management theorists are recognizing the need for organizational design to take cognizance of interpersonal factors. Further, organizations do not operate in a vacuum isolated from other organizations, and the stage of implementation is essentially political. Thus organizational design cannot be considered as a purely rational process.

ACCELERATING RATES OF CHANGE

Managers have been so bombarded with the phrase "the accelerating rates of change" that they may have become immune to the seriousness of its implications. Jonas Salk describes the world today as in transition between Curve A and Curve B, which together constitute the biological sigmoid curve (see Figure 20–1).

The lower curve represents the line of exponential growth, the message of which seems to be "grow, expand, increase." In the transition

FIGURE 20–1
The sigmoid curve

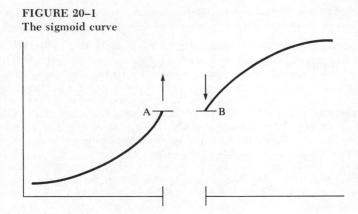

period, feedback becomes confused and ambivalent, and the message is "grow—don't grow." If the organism evolves to Stage B, the transition is completed and stability is achieved.

Organizations in the transition from an industrial to a postindustrial society are caught between Stages A and B. A new society is needed that is appropriate to this kind of uncertainty. In this context, organizations will function better as they develop more autonomous work forces which give employees more participation in plant design and operation (see Box 20–1).

ADHOCRACY AND MATRIX MANAGEMENT

A new type of organization is emerging which is challenging the bureaucracy of organization man. Alvin Toffler, of *Future Shock* fame, has called this new form the adhocracy. The single most salient characteristic of the adhocracy is its short life span. This built-in obsolescence is a direct result of the rapid and unexpected change which is characteristic of the turbulent environment of the 1980s.

These emerging adhocracies demand a radically different perspective and posture. Instead of permanence, the demand is for transience; instead of the organization man, we find the mobicentric (mobile) manager who accepts high mobility between organizations and constant reorganization within them.

What will be the characteristics of the new organizations of the postindustrial society? According to Warren Bennis, the key word will be *temporary*. The organizations that will emerge will be adaptive, rapidly changing, ad hoc structures manned by members of the technostructure who owe allegiance not to the company but to the professional association that is the custodian of their expertise and the

Box 20–1: Organizational design in new plants

When companies such as General Foods, Procter and Gamble, H. J. Heinz, Rockwell, and General Motors make plans for new plants, they are also developing organizational designs that are quite revolutionary. These innovations relate to employee selection, plant design, job design, pay system, organizational structure, and management style.

In terms of selection, applicants for job positions are briefed more fully on what lies ahead, to help them make *valid* decisions. Often new employees participate in the design of the plant, and a major effort is made to design jobs that are challenging, motivating, and satisfying. Typically, everyone starts at the same salary, but a few plants have moved toward profit-sharing or cost-savings-sharing plans.

In terms of organizational structure, the object is to shorten the distance between the general manager and the shop-floor or production worker. This attenuation has been achieved by either eliminating the foreman role or having the foreman report directly to the general manager (eliminating the general foreman and superintendent positions). Such structural changes mean that supervisors, who frequently direct a number of work groups, must adopt a more participative style of leadership.

Many of these new plants have been found to be more effective. For example, the Topeka plant of General Foods reports low absenteeism and turnover, lower production costs, and higher employee satisfaction. But there are problems, including, as Edward E. Lawler III points out, the distinction between permissiveness and participation:

. . . In most new-design plants, workers have raised issues that seemed to the managers concerned to go "too far." For example, in one case employees wanted to install a color television set in a work area. The managers considered this undesirable but had a great deal of difficulty dealing with the issue. They felt that if they said no they would be violating the participative spirit of the plant. They finally did refuse, because they felt that it would harm productivity and that it represented an example of permissive rather than participative management.

Line changes require functional management adaptation. Since shop-floor people are concerned with selection and pay administration, personnel managers must be able to interact with them. There are also conflicts between the head office and the plant managers. At Topeka, for example, when managers at the plant level came into conflict with line and staff managers at the corporate level, they left the corporation. Lawler notes "The generic interface disputes at Topeka were partly caused by the threat these new plants pose to traditional organizations. They are living demonstrations of a different way to operate, and as such they automatically raise the question of whether the rest of the organization needs to change."

Reference: Edward E. Lawler III, "The New Plant Revolution," *Organizational Dynamics,* Winter 1978.

recognized licensing authority which allows them to practise and to go from one assignment to another.

Adhocracy, in the form of matrix management, project management, or the task force, is a relatively recent development which has antecedents in aerospace, computers, and the military. It is an organizational creature with a brief life span, built to cope with tight deadlines and highly exacting specifications which would turn conventional organizations, with their rigid line-staff relations, upside down. Classical bureaucracy may be appropriate for a company which is producing standardized products in high volume, but where considerable innovation is required, the matrix or project forms of management are more effective (see Box 20–2).

Box 20–2: What is a matrix organization?

A concise definition of a matrix organization has been provided by Stanley M. Davis and Paul R. Lawrence:

> The identifying feature of a matrix organization is that some managers report to two bosses rather than to the traditional single boss; there is a dual rather than a single chain of command.
>
> Companies tend to turn to matrix forms:
> 1. When it is absolutely essential that they be highly responsive to two sectors simultaneously, such as markets and technology.
> 2. When they face uncertainties that generate very high information processing requirements.
> 3. When they must deal with strong constraints on financial and/or human resources.
>
> Matrix structures can help provide both flexibility and balanced decision making, but at the price of complexity.
>
> Matrix organization is more than a matrix structure. It must be reinforced by matrix systems such as dual control and evaluation systems, by leaders who operate comfortably with lateral decision making, and by a culture that can negotiate open conflict and a balance of power.
>
> In most matrix organizations there are dual command responsibilities assigned to functional departments (marketing, production, engineering, and so forth) and to product or market departments. The former are oriented to specialized in-house resources while the latter focus on outputs. Other matrices are split between area-based departments and either products or functions.
>
> Every matrix contains three unique and critical roles; the top manager who heads up and balances the dual chains of command, the matrix bosses (functional, product, or area) who share subordinates, and the managers who report to two different matrix bosses. Each of these roles has its special requirements.
>
> Aerospace companies were the first to adopt the matrix form, but now companies in many industries (chemical, banking, insurance, packaged goods, electronics, computer, and so forth) and in different fields (hospitals, government agencies, and professional organizations) are adapting different forms of the matrix.

Source: Stanley M. Davis and Paul R. Lawrence, "Problems of Matrix Organizations," *Harvard Business Review*, May–June 1978.

Problems of matrix management

Matrix management provides a means of bringing a number of specialists together to work on particular problems. As Stanley M. Davis and Paul R. Lawrence point out in "Problems of Matrix Organizations," the matrix design has many benefits, but to reap these benefits management must know how to prevent and treat its problems.

Bechtel, Citibank, Dow Chemical, Shell Oil, Texas Instruments, and TRW have all used the matrix form of organization. It is particularly useful in technological or diversified companies where many complex and conflicting problems have to be balanced.

Davis and Lawrence list the problems to which the matrix is vulnerable, specifying nine pathologies: "tendencies toward anarchy, power struggles, severe groupitis, collapse during economic crunch, excessive overhead, sinking to lower levels, uncontrolled layering, navel gazing, and decision strangulation." Thus the matrix form creates a lot of confusion. Subordinates cannot recognize the boss to whom they are responsible, and, by its inarticulate nature, it encourages power struggles.

Given all these problems, when business declines the matrix is blamed for poor management and the high costs it generates. The basic problem of the matrix is that there is too much democracy and not enough action which represents a response to the marketplace. One remedy for this situation, is for managers to be patient until they have gained a wider experience of where the matrix is appropriate. The organization also must be given sufficient time to travel the learning curve so that some of these pitfalls can be overcome. Early identification of problems is important, and if they cannot be resolved from within the matrix, the conflict ought to be escalated into the upper levels of the hierarchy. Davis and Lawrence believe that in the future "matrix organizations will become almost commonplace and that managers will speak less of the difficulties and pathologies of the matrix than of its advantages and benefits."

ORGANIZATIONS AS SELF-DESIGNING SYSTEMS: PARTICIPATIVE MANAGEMENT

Research has found that the design of an organization ought to be put into the hands of the insiders, the people who actually do the work. While this principle can not be applied to all organizations, many systems should allow some measure of self-design. When employees are not given sufficient autonomy, they may react by taking some form of labor action.

The Apollo 3 astronauts conducted the first daylong sitdown strike in outer space because they felt ground control was treating them like robots. Each day they received about six feet of computer instructions telling them exactly what to do for every part of the day. The astronauts told them, "You have given us too much to do. We're not going to do a thing until you get your act in better order." They asked the flight director to send them shopping lists of tasks which would allow them some control over how to organize their day.

The cause of the trouble was that ground control saw themselves as the planners, with the astronauts as the operators who carried out their plans. Theoretically the astronauts were very highly motivated, but in fact their favorite passtime in space was just staring into it, watching the sun and the earth spin by. Their tight work schedules did not allow much time for stargazing, however, and there was a real problem of how to exercise authority to ensure that the tasks would be completed. Perhaps NASA was overwhelmed by its own rhetoric and came to believe that the astronauts were in fact supermen.

The problems of organizational design that faced the crew of Apollo 3 in December 1973 were described by Karl E. Weick, a professor of psychology at Cornell University, in "Organization Design," Weick's long experience with organizational problems led to the conclusion that Apollo 3 was a kind of sociotechnical system, and all sorts of interesting problems emerged from the sophisticated technology needed to operate the spacecraft. Weick points out that the magnitude of the problem could be inferred from the following description:

> "There were some forty thousand items stashed away in over a hundred cabinets in the space station, and Pogue bitched that none of them was ever stowed where a person might logically expect to find them. Although there were six men and a computer in Houston whose sole purpose was to help the astronauts keep track of items in the space station, the system, which had been breaking down since the beginning of the second mission because of the progressive failure of crews to report where they put things, had now collapsed altogether. To confuse Pogue more, all the cabinets looked alike, and although they were numbered and their contents were sometimes written on the outside, the writing was small and the labels were difficult to read, particularly if Pogue approached them sideways or upside down. He had a stowage list, but he found it useless. 'The stowage list refers to numbers that are not even here!' he griped."

Weick notes that

> . . . The conspicuous issue of designing stowage is visible in this example, but so too is the issue of an intricate interweaving of design and technology and the prospect that self-designing systems may need to rearrange and edit their tools and trappings as well as their time and territory. There is also in this example the hint that prior "designs" restrict freedom of design of subsequent occupants severely.

In sociotechnical terms, design can become too separate from implementation. In self-designed sociotechnical systems, implementation clarifies design, and design clarifies implementation.

For example, Steinberg's, a large supermarket chain in Canada, made a special effort to involve the clerks at the checkout counters in the process of designing not only the actual layout of their stations but also the mode of operation. Such a use of job enrichment as a means of

What workers and managers want

In spite of all the discussion of self-actualization through job enrichment and talks about improving the quality of the working environment, many American production workers would still opt for more money rather than more enrichment. A plan that would appeal to most would be more money, not too much challenge, and a four-day week.

The idea of a shorter working week has been spreading slowly but steadily, not only in factories and offices but also in banks and government agencies. The reason is that the four-day, 40-hour week has been a success for both bosses and employees. A survey by the Bureau Labor of Statistics in 1974 showed that 1.1 million full-time workers (roughly 2 percent of the labor force) were regularly working fewer than five days a week, many of them on a four-day schedule. The compressed work schedules are most popular among young workers who are disenchanted with uninspiring, repetitive work tasks.

Designing a four-day week is an excellent task with which to begin participative management. Redesigning the work week gives management a real chance to show its good faith in developing a new climate for decision making.

At the managerial level, however, there is a major problem in involving lower and middle managers in top-management decision making. Inexperienced managers do not have the organizational savoir faire or the financial, economic, and marketing expertise to contribute to top management decisions. Nevertheless, there is abundant evidence from studies of executives' attitudes that junior and middle-level managers lack confidence in the decision-making skills of their superiors. Thus the big issue is a practical one, How can participative management be made effective, given the lack of knowledge and expertise of junior management? One possible answer lies in developing the new executive, liberated style.

TOPIC 3
The new liberated manager

A NEW LIFE-STYLE

Liberated managers apply the principles of Zen to the art of management (see Box 20–4). They want to stop the world, to ski and surf, to meditate and write poetry, to be themselves, to drop out and get into the existential stream. The liberated manager is the existential executive, the games player. When the liberated manager cleans out his desk and heads for the door, his "superiors" find it hard to accept his departure. He has fired the organization.

What this new executive is trying to do is develop a unique exuber-

Box 20–4: Managing by Zen

Research on Japanese-managed firms in the United States suggests a different approach to management than the cards-on-the-table American style. The American approach to management maximizes mathematics and science and plays down mystique. Traditionally, Japanese management has presumedly been successful because of its participative consensus building, which gets the key people on board.

Japanese executives working in this country behave in a way which is similar to American managers, but with two differences. A survey of American and Japanese companies reported by Richard Tanner Pascale in "Zen and the Art of Management" found that:

1. Three times as much communication was initiated at lower levels of management, then percolated upward.
2. While managers of Japanese companies rated the quality of their decision making the same as did their American counterparts, they perceived the quality of *implementation* of those decisions to be better.

As Pascale points out, the Japanese manager's use of ambiguity is an art, especially in dealing with subordinates:

A Japanese manager conducts the dialogue in circles, widening and narrowing them to correspond to the subordinate's sensitivity to the feedback. He may say, "I'd like you to reflect a bit further on your proposal." Translated into Western thought patterns, this sentence would read, "You're dead wrong and you'd better come up with a better idea." The first approach allows the subordinate to exist with his pride intact.

To watch a skilled manager use ambiguity is to see an art form in action. Carefully selecting his words, constructing a precise tension between the oblique and the specific, he picks his way across difficult terrain. In critiquing a subordinate's work, for example, the executive occasionally finds it desirable to come close enough to the point to ensure that the subordinate gets the message but not so close as to "crowd" him and cause defensiveness.

The idea is to let things flow. An Oriental proverb puts it: Success is going straight—around the circle.

The Japanese distinguish between our notion of organization and their notion of the company. The company may achieve the same tasks as the organization, but it occupies more space and moves, in a spiritual sense, like a regiment. Japanese managers also have a different attitude to the "bottom line":

. . . To the Eastern mind it is "man," not the "bottom line," that is the ultimate measure of all things. He is not the source of all things, as some who view man in total command of his destiny might proclaim. Nor is he the objectified contributor to all things, as some organizations appear to presume in weighing his contributions against their costs.

A Japanese, while concerned with the bottom line, is not single-minded about it as many Westerners are. Rather, he proceeds with a dual awareness—that there is a second ledger in which "success" is debited or credited in terms of his contribution to the quality of relationships that ensue. So the professional manager defines his role not only as one who accomplishes certain organizational tasks but also as an essential intermediary in the social fabric.

Reference: Richard Tanner Pascale, "Zen and the Art of Management," *Harvard Business Review,* March–April 1978.

ant, lyrical life-style to send out a signal identifying himself. This is in contrast to W. H. Whyte's dedicated organization man in the grey flannel suit. The organization man started to make his exit from the executive scene because a new style of organization, more appropriate to the eighties, was emerging.

Liberated managers like to select problems that interest them, utilize their trained capabilities, and give them high visibility. They like to be in on acquisition and merger project management groups, with computer, logistics, and secretarial support. They are motivated by the idea of "get a new job, master it, and move on," and they believe that strengths travel better than weaknesses.

They put loyalty to their career first, and are likely to look for corporate slots with academy companies such as Proctor and Gamble or to accept a spell at a crack university business school. They welcome conflict as a means of clarifying issues.

THE GAMESMAN

The new type of manager who is taking over the leadership of advanced technological companies in the United States has been described as a gamesman, motivated not to build or preside over empires but to lead winning teams. Whyte's *The Organization Man*, published in 1956, epitomized the popular view of the executive which prevailed for two decades. Whyte noted a decline in the Protestant ethic, particularly its emphasis on individuality, which had led to the emergence of a type of manager guided by a corporate social ethic.

As we move into the eighties, a society which has become increasingly dependent on technology has spawned the corporate gamesman. This is an existential figure who likes to cut deals and to gamble—essentially, a flexible, competitive player, a glory seeker.

The portrait of the corporate games player was developed by Michael Maccoby in *The Gamesman*. Maccoby based his research on interviews with 250 managers in different parts of 12 major companies. He had received psychoanalytical training under Erich Fromm and used an interesting research technique. He had completed a study of the impact of technology on culture and personality in a Mexican village, and while discussing his experiences with David Riesman he got the idea of studying the people who create technology for corporations.

Maccoby labels his method of investigation socio-psychoanalytical research. Assuming the role of the corporate anthropologist, he approached large corporations very much in the same way he had approached the Mexican village. A structured interview was used. In some cases wives and secretaries were also interviewed. Data were collected not only on a manager's work but on the relationship between his work and his personality. Further information was collected on his family life and relationships with his wife and children. The manager was also given a Rorschach inkblot test. The interviewer, with the clinical experience of a psychoanalyst, did not pretend to be a detached, objective observer and could deal with resistance.

Four different ideal character types were identified. Most executives are a mixture of two or more.

The craftsman.   Holds traditional values, including the work ethic, respect for people, concern for quality and thrift. When he talks about his work, he shows an interest in the process of making something he enjoys building. He sees others in terms of whether they help or hinder him in doing a craftsmanlike job.

The jungle fighter.   Lusts for power. He experiences life and work as a jungle where one must eat or be eaten, and the winner may destroy the losers. Jungle fighters tend to see their peers as either accomplices or enemies and their subordinates as objects to be used.

There are two types of jungle fighters, lions and foxes. The lions are conquerors who, when successful, may build an empire. The foxes make their nests in the corporate hierarchy and move ahead by stealth and politicking. The most gifted foxes encountered rose rapidly, but in each case they were eventually destroyed by those they had used or betrayed.

The company man.   Part of the protective organization. At his weakest, he is fearful and submissive, seeking security even more than success. At his strongest, he is concerned with the human side of the company, interested in the feelings of the people around him, and committed to maintaining corporate integrity. The most creative company men sustain an atmosphere of cooperation and stimulation, but they tend to lack the daring to lead highly competitive and innovative organizations.

The gamesman.   Sees business life in general, and his career in particular, in terms of options and possibilities, as if he were playing a game. He likes to take calculated risks and is fascinated by techniques and new methods. The contest hypes him up and he communicates his enthusiasm, energizing his peers and subordinates. He competes to gain fame and glory, the exhilaration of victory. His main goal is to be known as a winner, his deepest fear to be labeled a loser.

Maccoby found the gamesman more frequently at the higher levels of the corporation. Sometimes he had some attributes of the company man. His work stimulates and reinforces attitudes essential for intellectual growth (see Box 20–5).

Box 20–5: Jack Wakefield is a gamesman; Ray Shultz is a jungle fighter

Michael Maccoby provides examples of the gamesman and the jungle fighter:

> Jack Wakefield looks like Tom Sawyer grown up. . . . He is extremely likable and seems open, yet one always feels in danger of being tricked or slightly conned. He is very seductive. He seems gregarious, yet when one knows him bitter, he is introverted and a little lonely. . . . Serious on the one hand, he is also boyish and playful, with a twinkle in his eye. Top management of a major multinational corporation saw him, at the age of 32, as one of the young managers with the highest potential, a comer. He brought energy, verve and originality to his work. He was a person who could motivate others to go beyond themselves. Furthermore, he was one of the rare young managers who expressed real social concern, as well as interest in his own self-development. . . . Although he thought his high ideals got in the way of work and he worried about maintaining his integrity, Wakefield was deeply drawn to his work. He was both excited by it and highly rewarded because he did it well. In the end, he defined himself in terms of work. Away from work, he had difficulty connecting, either with his wife or with others who shared his professed ideals. . . . Like the typical gamesman, he is a collection of seeming paradoxes. He is idealistic, yet shrewd and pragmatic; cooperative, yet highly competitive; enthusiastic, yet detached; earnest, yet evasive; graceful, yet restless; energetic, yet itchy.
>
> Ray Schultz . . . is playful, often a joker, but also like a fanatical football coach who has to win. Even more than Wakefield, Schultz cannot stand a situation that is static, where there is no action. He is the one who told us with a straight face that the three people he most admired historically were Vince Lombardi, Jesus Christ and Harry Truman."

Reference: Michael Maccoby, *The Gamesman* (New York: Simon and Schuster, 1976).

PORTRAIT OF THE LIBERATED MANAGER

Change is the secure element in life for the now liberated manager. They become anxious when they stand still. They search for a divergent cognitive style, such as that of a scientist, and have a strong preference for problems with an open-ended spectrum of answers. They consider themselves resource persons, able to input their ideas into a project and welcoming the opportunity to interface with other functional specialists. These functions appear to reduce the visible autocratic elements in the executive role.

Their approach to love and intimate relationships is also exemplified by change; when a relationship stops growing it ends, and they move on. Socially they make sure they are in line with their reference group in regard to choice of car, club, or residence. They are fashion conscious and realize that clothes have status connotations.

What they really want is more joy in their work. They want to live and work more fully and to overcome feelings of personal doom which can make them feel impotent and fearful. They want to be turned on

to their work, to feel potent, alive, even "sexy" in a responsive, creative, experimental, myth-making role.

Many options are usually open to them in making business decisions, but none is absolutely free of risk or disadvantage. They must
make decisions which inevitably only reduce the degree of uncertainty, not eliminate it. In many, if not most, instances it is impossible
to say whether they were right. Thus they opt for the "best decision" in
the hope of securing consensus from superiors and colleagues. The

Box 20–6: Michael C. Bergerac, an existential executive

New managers like to make up their own compensation packages. Their ideal is executives
like Michael C. Bergerac, who left his job as president of ITT-Europe to become chief
executive officer of Revlon, Inc. As incentive he had a contract worth more than $5
million—$1.5 million just for reporting for work on September 16, 1974, and an option of
70,000 shares (already worth $2 million on paper). Described both as the Catfish Hunter of
American business and as the first big corporate bonus baby, Bergerac, who was 42 at the
time of the job switch, was capitalizing on his big asset—the remaining years of his
productive managerial activity.

Bergerac has many characteristics of the existential executive. Born in Biarritz, he
attended the schools of law and political science at the Sorbonne and earned a masters
degree in economics from the University of Paris. After a summer at Cambridge University,
he took a Fulbright scholarship to UCLA to study for an MBA. He fell in love with California,
married an American, and went to work for the Cannon Electric Company in Los Angeles,
which was acquired by ITT in 1963. "I went with the furniture," Bergerac said in an
interview with Marylin Bender in *The New York Times* (May 11, 1975).

Bergerac's mental agility is said to compensate for the lack of product knowledge he
displayed on each new job. All he knew about electronics when he started at Cannon, he
said, was how to turn on a light switch. When ITT sent him to Europe in 1966 as group
manager for industrial products, he said his main distinction was "not to know what they
were." "A certain number of companies, small in size, large in trouble were doing $14
million in sales and losing $4–$5 million. I sold one, closed two, moved another from
Belgium to Germany, had to fire half the people, but some of them are still good friends."
By 1970, sales were at $375 million and after-tax earnings at $25 million. He went on to
ITT-Europe, "knowing very little about its major business, telecommunications."

At Revlon, he acknowledges, "a lot of people are better at products than I and thank
God for that. The problem, then, is to create an environment where they can flourish
instead of having their creativity repressed. On the other side, one must have some minimum discipline so that tremendous creativity doesn't drive you into bankruptcy." Bergerac
admits he's good at motivating people.

One thing the liberated manager likes about Michael Bergerac is that he was not willing
to wait for Harold Geneen, chief executive officer of ITT, to retire. Rather, he moved over to
the top slot at Revlon and made a terrific killing in the process. The big question is whether
ITT will take over Revlon or Revlon will buy a chunk of ITT. Bender noted that "Confronted
with that suggestion, Mr. Bergerac reacted with a wide grin. The luxurious moustache he
grew on his annual big game hunting expedition to Africa last summer twitched. "I have no
such thought," he said.

Reference: Marylin Bender, *The New York Times,* May 11, 1975.

executive act is iterative; approximate solutions are resubstituted in the original equations to improve the accuracy and quality of the decision-making process.

The existential style of the liberated manager is essentially a search for an alternative and a supplement to the analytic style. Analysis is good for problem solving but has nothing to say about either problem finding or solution implementation. The existential executive tries to move laterally in a mental context where intelligence and feel (a compound of hunch, hypotheses, hype, vibes, and experience) count, to find the real problem. In cognitive terms, they are trying to turn on their metaphoric, intuitive and analogic processes, employing the right side of the cerebral hemisphere instead of the left, which is the processor of linear, rational, and digital thought. In seeking an alternative for analytic skills, they hope to see the gestalt of a problem. They try to develop an intuitive-synthetic cognition with an inventive, integrative, and symbolic mode of operation.

The most important goal liberated managers acknowledge is to realize their personal destiny, to find an organization role designed for themselves rather than fitting into a predesigned role. (See Box 20–6 for an explanation of how one existential executive solved this problem.) They accept responsibility for their own actions and their effects; this is their new ethos or moral frame of reference. The existentialist's pathos is the ability to move people emotionally, for they realize that the heart has reasons the head does not understand.

The liberated manager will soon be a member of the new Geritol generation.

THE NEW GERITOL GENERATION

Demographically, the future belongs to the offspring who comprised the postwar baby boom. One in every three Americans is now a member of that part of the population, and this generation will be the most important economic factor of the 1980s. The number of Americans in this 35–44 age group will jump from 28 million to 40 million by 1990. By 1990, their average household income will be close to $30,000 in real terms. They are major users of credit and mortgages and appreciate convenience products. This will have a tremendous effect not only on the market but on how organizations are run.

Ten years ago, the balance of young people in the population brought on the era of the youth cult. Today, it is the age of the middle-aged (see Box 20–7). For this emerging Geritol generation, work is going to have to be organized differently. Not only will the jeans have to be cut wider, but work definitions will have to have more latitude.

This generation wants work in pleasant surroundings which offer a chance for personal growth and development and opportunities for

Box 20–7: Executive age and corporate performance

A widely held myth in our society is that there is a negative relationship between advanced age and executive performance. This myth, usually summed up with the proposition "If you have not made it by forty, you have had it," has finally been put to rest.

Research by Stanley Davis compared the profitability and growth of a number of *Fortune* 500 companies with the ages of the senior officers. Analysis of the data revealed no connection between management age and corporate performance. His argument is that management ought to review the issue of mandatory retirement. He cites the finding of an unpublished General Electric study some years ago that "the company's mature strategic business units (SBUs) performed better when operated by older, more experienced managers, and that the newer, growth-targeted SBUs achieved more favorable results when directed by younger managers who had more current knowledge than experience."

Reference: Stanley M. Davis, "No Connection between Executive Age and Corporate Performance" ("Ideas for Action"), *Harvard Business Review*, March–April 1979.

mingling with nice people. They expect to be paid, but pay is probably less important than the nature of the job itself and a say in deciding work conditions.

Is the work ethic in America declining? One answer is to be found in the fact that most of this new generation are members of two-paycheck families. This permits employees more autonomy at work, and bosses can expect to be challenged on such issues as arbitrary dismissal or unreasonable transfers. There will also be dramatic changes in the work rules, according to Caroline Bird in *The Two-Paycheck Marriage: How Women at Work are Changing Life in America*. Having two paychecks means shifting the power from the employer to the employee.

Inevitably, there is going to be a need for more part-time and flex-time schedules. Jobs will have to be redesigned to make them more attractive to women, students, and workers in semiretirement. Volunteers will be replaced by paid professionals. There will be more choice in jobs, especially for women.

TOPIC 4
What every manager should know about the organization of the future

The most important thing the manager should know is that a new management style is emerging which is quite different from that of the organization man of the fifties. The new liberated managers like problems with challenge that give them high visibility. They are mobile; when they can't change the system, they change systems. They are existentialists who utilize a divergent style of thinking. In cognitive terms they are trying to turn on the right cerebral hemisphere and become more intuitive and creative.

PUTTING EXISTENTIALISM AND EFFECTIVENESS TOGETHER

The alter ego of the liberated manager is Robert Townsend, who wrote *Up the Organization.* But to become like Townsend means changing leadership styles. Chris Argyris has a useful idea that managers carry inside their heads two kinds of theory of action, what they do and what they say they are doing. They need to synchronize the two, but such switches do not come easily. Valid and useful information, power sharing, and the avoidance of defensive behavior are all required.

A good example of the new liberated manager is the gamesman, an essentially existential figure who seems to believe the battle of the boardroom can be won in the seminar rooms of the Harvard Business School. The gamesman is cooperative and playful but is compulsively pushed to win. As anyone knows who has ever taken a course in psychoanalysis, winning is not all it is cracked up to be, and gamesmen need help to handle the anxiety and guilt of winning.

Being a liberated manager is more than just being an existentialist, therefore. One way or another, existentialist managers must overcome their anxieties and deliver the goods in good shape, to the right people, on schedule. This means a union of existentialism and effectiveness. Putting the two big Es together is a tough assignment which can make management not only an exciting challenge but a lot of fun.

The manager of tomorrow can put existentialism and effectiveness together to deliver the goods our society wants; they work, they are safe, they are beautiful. The good guys must learn how to come first.

PUTTING EXISTENTIALISM AND SYSTEMS THEORY TOGETHER

In essence, two great forces are running in opposite directions, on a collision course. One force has its origins in the "mindless, liberal, technocratic, managerial vision" held by system theorists and behavioral engineers like Forrester and Skinner, who believe the answers lie in studying large gestalts (for example, the world). They believe the configuration of these entities can be solved by running equations through data-loaded computers and by treating people as if they were subatomic particles in the atoms of primary groups, which are held together in the molecules of organization, which in turn are part of the complex protein molecule known as a society, which in turn is . . . and so on until the ultimate gestalt is reached.

The other force, sustained by a social form of the principle of uncertainty, is held by existentialists who believe ultimately that all is chaos and anarchy and that all social arrangements are temporary; power based, and thus nonbinding in any real sense. All meaning is a temporary mnemonic somewhat arbitrarily put together to facilitate memory and communication.

As William Irwin Thompson, a professor of humanities at York University, puts it in his provocative book *At the Edge of History,* culture has split into mechanism and mysticism. The mechanists are obsessed with the power of technology. They essentially see humans as information-processing systems whose life-style can be controlled by changing the software, in terms of either the data fed into them or the program or paradigm they are led to install. The mechanists see the high ground of the modern battlefield in terms of who has first access to the computer printout.

There can be no quarrel about seeing the future organization as an information-processing system. In Figure 20–2 we gather some of the heuristics of this chapter into the contingency model framework. No

FIGURE 20–2
The organization of the future as an information-processing system

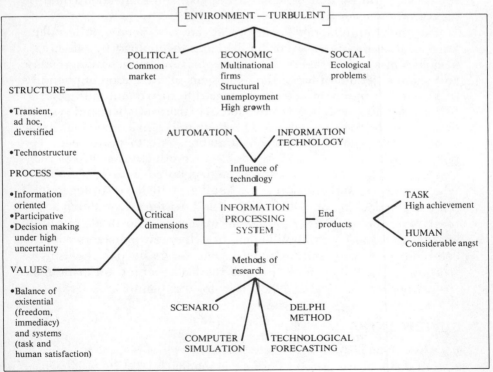

doubt the futility of futurism means that we have overlooked elements that will turn out to be of great importance, but we have included elements as values and end products which can readily be seen as paradoxical.

The information-processing system is task efficient, but it is also inherently antidemocratic. Even though sensitive systems analysts would like the processes to be participative, with all information made available to those whom it affects, it is nearly impossible to achieve this in practice. The powerful control the information-processing function and decide the timing and, more importantly, the sequencing of the releases. The actual sequencing and timing, in Skinnerian terms, are a contingent reinforcement strategy which beckons the uninitiated flies, those in the lower levels of the hierarchy, into the web of the information values of the spiders, those in the upper levels. The new systems of tiered technostructures manned by liberated managers are essentially layers of information strata; each successive layer as you move upward is incapable of being digested by those just below unless it is predigested.

The existentialist, knowing this initially turned to the counterculture and Yoga, Zen, or the human potential movement in search of planetary mysticism. They wanted holiness back in their lives, to make life meaningful, so that personal needs like self-realization could be measured on a sanctified scale.

The more enlightened and sophisticated corporate philosopher-kings realize the necessity of humanizing technology by effecting a marriage of systems theory and existentialism. If alienation, apathy, and anomie get out of hand, the explosions of frustration euphemistically titled "ripping off" can be expected to thrive and multiply.

The crucial issue is how the two forces of existentialism and systems theory, which are heading toward each other like space capsules in the same orbit but going in opposite directions, are to be docked. The postindustrial society—heading for lower productivity, zero population growth, and pollution control, and peopled with existentialists who are aware, authentic, and awakening—will have to negotiate a plan for the docking of systems theory and existentialism. Such a synthesis will not come from traditional managers who think in purely analytical, linear terms; it will come from the new managers who can combine linear and nonlinear logic, who can go beyond themselves, who care. . . . Who can see beyond the facts, behind the paradigms . . ., who dare to be free. Who's next for this hemlock?

REVIEW AND RESEARCH

1. Why is futurology such a rapidly expanding area of research?
2. List the principal methods of studying futurology. Classify each method

under the following headings: suitable problems, kind of data collected, time span, choices highlighted, and cautions.

3. Write a brief outlining a policy controlling multinational companies which the United Nations might adopt.

4. Compare managements in the United States, Europe, and Japan. How do they differ? How are they similar?

5. List the ten most important changes in technology which have taken place in the past ten years. How have they affected management?

6. Guesstimate the ten most important changes in technology, biology, and behavioral technology that will take place in the next ten years. How will these changes affect management?

7. How does a computer modify the structure of an organization? In the future, what effect will the computer have on the structure of an organization? How will it affect middle-rank executives? What plans should be drawn up now to help such executives?

8. What changes should be made in university business schools to take cognizance of developments in (a) technology, (b) behavioral technology, (c) ecology, (d) the counterculture? Devise a curriculum to meet the opportunities of the new society that these forces will create.

9. Effective participation in organizations depends on power equalization. How can this condition be achieved in business?

GLOSSARY OF TERMS

Adhocracy. The ad hoc style of organization, in the form of matrix management, project management, or the task force. Military, aerospace, and computer technologies brought about the emergence of the temporary organization manned by highly mobile members of the technostructure put together to perform a specific task and then disbanded.

Computer simulation. A research technique in which interrelated abstractions or analogies of the real world are modeled by feeding data into computers; used to forecast highly technical system operations.

Counterculture. A separate culture formed in reaction to the established value system; in our times, a value system stressing freedom, immediacy, authenticity, and awareness as opposed to control, manipulation, hypocrisy, etc.

Delphi method. A research technique which attempts to pool the judgments of experts by successive polling, with feedback of their previous answers and reasons for answers between polls.

Multinational firms. International conglomerates with above-average growth and profits, high in technology; firms which operate in several countries, whose foreign subsidiaries account for at least 20 percent of total assets, and whose annual sales are at least $100 million qualify in this class; most are American at present.

Scenario writing. A research technique which requires the formulation of a hypothetical narrative of a possible sequence of events.

Technostructure. J. K. Galbraith's term for the interlocking of large, mature, technologically sophisticated private corporations with government planning and economic policy (particularly in areas such as the military and space programs), necessitating the rethinking of past economic ideologies. An important concomitant of the technostructure is the cooperation of the educational system in producing the needed technocrats.

DEBATE: The "me too" generation, versus the new existentialists who accept responsibility for their actions

As we move into the 1980s a great debate is developing between the hedonists, who take a no-fault attitude toward life and concentrate on love of self, and those who argue that if a society is to survive, individuals must rediscover personal guilt and accept responsibility for their actions, realizing that we are all dependent, one on the other.

PRO

For a special issue of *Life* magazine in December 1979, Tom Wolfe contributed an article entitled "The Sexed-Up, Doped-Up, Hedonistic Heaven of the Boom-Boom Seventies." In this article, Wolfe explains how it came about that marijuana has essentially been decriminalized in the United States. You can now see young people sitting outside their offices in New York and Los Angeles at lunchtime smoking marijuana. This hedonism of the 1970s is derived from the boom of booms, in which the economy kept on expanding with exponential certainty. In such a context Wolfe is able to quote Hemmingway with approval: "Morality is what you feel good after."

CON

Unfortunately, a surprising number of the proponents of the "Me" decade have ended up as burnt-out cases. To avoid such a fate an increasing number of people are turning to new secular religions such as the human potentials movement.

Eugene Kennedy's article "The Looming '80's" in *The New York Times Magazine* for December 2, 1979, argues that there is a crisis of authority. Somehow or other we have to get beyond no-fault insurance for cars and no fault-divorce for battling spouses into a situation where people accept responsibility for their actions. The decade of the seventies began with the *Love Story* idea that love means "Never having to say you're sorry." It ended with the bittersweet truth of the rediscovery of the existential consequences of relationships. As we move into the eighties, people are looking for authority and the legitimacy of established relations.

Question

How can this paradox of narcissims versus authority be resolved in a business context?

Bibliography

ABÉ, KOBO. *The Box Man*, Trans. E. Dale Saunders, New York: Alfred A. Knopf, 1974.

ACKOFF, RUSSELL L. "The Development of Operations Research as a Science." *Journal of Operations Research Society of America*, vol. 4, (June 1956).

––––––. "Management Misinformation Systems." *Management Science*, vol. 14 (December 1967).

ADAMS, J. S. "Inequity in Social Exchanges." In L. Berkowitz (ed.), *Advances in Experimental Social Psychology*. Vol. 2. New York: Academic Press, 1965.

AIKEN, M., and HAGE, J. "Organizational Interdependence and Interorganizational Structure." *American Journal of Sociology*, vol. 33, no. 6 (1968), pp. 912–31.

ALBROOK, ROBERT C. "Why It Is Harder to Keep Good Executives." *Fortune*, November 1968.

ALLAND, ALEXANDER. *The Human Imperative*. New York: Columbia University Press, 1972.

ALLISON, GRAHAM T. *Essence of Decision: Explaining the Cuban Missile Crisis*. Boston: Little, Brown & Co., 1971.

ALLPORT, G. W. *Personality: A Psychological Interpretation*. New York: Holt, Rinehart & Winston, 1937.

––––––. "The Open System in Personality Theory." *Journal of Abnormal and Social Psychology*, vol. 61 (1960), pp. 301–11.

AMERICAN MANAGEMENT ASSOCIATION. *Manager Unions*. New York, June 1972.

ANGELL, R. C. "Sociology of Human Conflict." In E. B. McNeil (ed.), *The Nature of Conflict*. Englewood Cliffs, N.J.: Prentice-Hall, 1965.

623

ANSOFF, H. I. "The Firm of the Future." *Harvard Business Review,* September–October 1965.

ARDRESKI, S. *Social Sciences as Sorcery.* London: André Deutsch, 1972.

ARGYLE, M., and DEAN, J. "Eye-Contact, Distance, and Affiliation." *Sociometry,* vol. 28 (1965), pp. 289–304.

————; GARDNER, G.; and CIOFFI, F. "The Measurement of Supervisory Methods." *Human Relations,* vol. 10 (1957).

ARGYRIS, CHRIS. *The Impact of Budgets on People.* New York: Controllership Institute, 1952.

————. *Personality and Organization.* New York: Harper & Bros., 1957.

————. "Individual Actualization in Complex Organizations." *Mental Hygiene,* vol. 44 (April 1960), pp. 226–337.

————. *Interpersonal Competence and Organizational Effectiveness.* Homewood, Ill.: Richard D. Irwin, 1962.

————. "Some Unintended Consequences of Rigorous Research." *Psychological Bulletin,* vol. 70 (1968), pp. 185–97.

————. *Intervention Theory and Method.* Reading, Mass.: Addison-Wesley Publishing Co., 1970.

————. "Personality vs. Organization." *Organizational Dynamics,* Fall 1974.

ASCH, S. E. "Studies of Independence and Conformity: A Minority of One against a Unanimous Majority." *Psychological Monographs,* vol. 70, no. 9 (1965).

ASHOUR, AHMED S. "The Contingency Model of Leadership Effectiveness: An Evaluation." *Organizational Behavior and Human Performance,* vol. 9 (June 1973).

ATKINSON, J. W. *An Introduction to Motivation.* Princeton, N.J.: D. Van Nostrand Co., 1964.

————, and FEATHERS, N. T. (eds.). *A Theory of Achievement Motivation.* New York: John Wiley & Sons, 1966.

BAGEHOT, W. *The English Constitution.* London: Fontana, 1963.

BALES, R. F. "Some Uniformities of Behavior in Small Social Systems." In S. E. Swanson, T. M. Newcomb, and E. L. Hartley (eds.), *Readings in Social Psychology.* New York: Henry Holt & Co., 1952.

BANDURA, A. *Principles of Behavior Modification.* New York: Holt, Rinehart & Winston, 1969.

BANTON, M. "Role." *New Society,* May 7, 1964.

BARITZ, L. *The Servants of Power: A History of the Use of Social Science in American Industry.* New York: John Wiley & Sons, 1965.

BARNARD, C. I. *The Function of the Executive.* Cambridge, Mass.: Harvard University Press, 1938.

BAVELAS, ALEX. "Communication Patterns in Task-Oriented Groups." In D. Cartwright and A. Zander (eds.), *Group Dynamics.* New York: Harper & Row, 1960.

————, and STRAUSS, G. "Group Dynamics and Intergroup Relations," in W. F. Whyte et al., *Money and Motivation*. New York: Harper & Row, 1955.

BEM, SANDRA LIPSITZ. "Androgyny vs. the Tight Little Lives of Fluffy Women and Chesty Men." *Psychology Today*, September 1975, pp. 58–62.

BENNIS, WARREN G. "Beyond Bureaucracy." *TRANSACTION*, July–August 1965.

————. "Leadership: A Beleaguered Species?" *Organizational Dynamics*, vol. 5, no. 1 (1976), pp. 3–16.

BENSON, HERBERT. "Your Innate Ability for Combatting Stress." *Harvard Business Review*, July–August 1974, pp. 49–60.

BERG, IVAR. *Education and Jobs: The Great Training Robbery*. New York: Frederick A. Praeger, 1972.

BERKOWITZ, N. H., and BENNIS, W. G. "Interaction Patterns in Formal Service-Oriented Organizations." *Administrative Science Quarterly*, vol. 6 (1961–62).

BIERCE, AMBROSE. *Devil's Dictionary*. Owing Mills, Md.: Stemmer House, 1978 (originally published 1906).

BION, W. R. "Experiences in Groups." *Human Relations*, vol. 3 (1950), p. 3.

————. *Experiences in Groups*. London: Tavistock Publications, 1961.

BIRD, CAROLINE. *Social Psychology*. New York: Appleton-Century, 1940.

————. *The Two-Paycheck Marriage: How Women at Work Are Changing Life in America*. New York: Rawson Wade, 1979.

BLAIR, JOHN M. *Economic Concentration*. New York: Harcourt, Brace, & World, 1973.

BLAKE, ROBERT R. "Studying Group Action." In L. P. Bradford, J. R. Gibb, and K. D. Benne (eds.), *T-Group Theory and Laboratory Method*. New York: John Wiley & Sons, 1964.

————, and MOUTON, J. S. *The Managerial Grid*. Houston: Gulf Publishing Co., 1964.

———— and ————. *Corporate Excellence through Grid Organization Development*. Houston: Gulf Publishing Co., 1968.

————; SHEPARD, H. A.; and MOUTON, J. S. *Managing Intergroup Conflict in Industry*. Houston: Gulf Publishing Co., 1964.

———— et al. "Breakthrough in Organization Development." *Harvard Business Review*, November–December 1964.

BLAU, PETER M. *Dynamics of Bureaucracy*. Chicago: University of Chicago Press, 1955.

————, and DUNCAN, O. D. *The American Occupational Structure*. New York: John Wiley & Sons, 1965.

————, and SCOTT, W. R. *Formal Organizations*. London: Routledge & Kegan Paul; San Francisco: Chandler Publishing Co., 1963.

BLAUNER, ROBERT. *Alienation and Freedom*. Chicago: University of Chicago Press, 1964.

BLOOD, MILTON R., and HULIN, CHARLES L. "Alienation, Environmental Characteristics and Worker Responses." *Journal of Applied Psychology*, vol. 53 (June 1967), pp. 284–90.

BLUMENSEN, MARTIN. *The Patton Papers, 1940–1945*. Boston: Houghton Mifflin Co., 1974.

BOTTOMORE, T. B., and RUBEL, M. *Karl Marx: Selected Writings*. London: Penguin, 1963.

BOULDING, KENNETH E. "General Systems Theory—The Skeleton of Science." *Management Science*, vol. 2 (April 1956), pp. 197–208.

BRAY, D. W. "The Identification of Executive Ability." *Business Review*, May 1967, pp. 140–47.

————, and CAMPBELL, R. J. "Selection of Salesmen by Means of an Assessment Center." *Journal of Applied Psychology*, vol. 52, no. 1 (1968), p. 18.

BRAYFIELD, A. H., and CROCKETT, W. H. "Employee Attitudes and Employee Performance." *Psychological Bulletin*, vol. 52, no. 5 (1955), pp. 396–424.

BRECH, E. F. L. *Organization—The Framework of Management*. London: Longmans, 1965.

BROVERMAN, INGE K.; BROVERMAN, DONALD M.; CLARKSON, FRANK E.; ROSENKRANTZ, PAUL S., and VOGEL, SUSAN R. "Sex Role Stereotypes and Clinical Judgments of Mental Health." *Journal of Consulting and Clinical Psychology*, vol. 34 (1970), pp. 1–7.

BROWN, R. *Social Psychology*. New York: Free Press, 1965.

BROWN, WILFRED. *Exploration in Management*. London: Heinemann Educational Books Ltd., 1960.

————, and JAQUES, E. *The Glacier Project Papers*. London: Heinemann Educational Books Ltd., 1965.

BRUNER, J. S. *The Relevance of Education*. New York: W. W. Norton & Co., 1971.

————, and GOODMAN, C. C. "Value and Need as Organizing Factors in Perception." *Journal of Abnormal and Social Psychology*, vol. 42 (1947), pp. 33–44.

BRUNSON, RICHARD W., SR. "Perceptual Skills in the Corporate Jungle." *Personnel Journal*, vol. 51 (January 1972).

BUCHANAN, BRUCE, II. "Building Organizational Commitment: The Socialization of Managers in Work Organizations." *Administrative Science Quarterly*, December 1974.

BUCKLEY, WALTER. *Sociology and Modern Systems Theory*. Englewood Cliffs, N.J.: Prentice-Hall, 1967.

———— (ed.). *Modern Systems Research for the Behavioral Scientist*. Chicago: Aldine Publishing Co., 1968.

BURNS, JAMES MACGREGOR. *Leadership*. New York: Harper & Row, 1978.

BURNS, TOM. "The Directions of Activity and Communications in a Departmental Executive Group." *Human Relations*, vol. 7 (1954), pp. 73–97.

————. "The Reference of Conduct in Small Groups: Cliques and Cabals in Occupational Milieux." *Human Relations*, vol. 8 (1955), pp. 467–86.

————, and STALKER, G. M. *The Management of Innovation.* London: Tavistock Publications Ltd., 1961.

BYHAM, W. C. "Assessment Center for Spotting Future Managers." *Harvard Business Review*, July–August 1970.

CAMPBELL, JOHN P. "Organizational Effectiveness: Theory, Research, Utilization, Introduction." *Organization Administrative Sciences*, vol. 7, no. 1 (1976).

————, and DUNNETTE, M. D. "Effectiveness of T-Group Experiences in Managerial Training and Development." *Psychological Bulletin*, vol. 70 (1968), pp. 73–104.

————; ————; LAWLER, E. E.; and WEICK, K. E. *Managerial Behavior, Performance, and Effectiveness.* New York: McGraw-Hill Book Co., 1970.

CANNON, W. B. *The Wisdom of the Body.* New York: W. W. Norton & Co., 1932.

CAPLAN, R. "Organizational Stress and Individual Strain: A Social Psychological Study of Risk Factors in Coronary Heart Disease among Administrators, Engineers, and Scientists." Unpublished Ph.D. thesis, University of Michigan, 1971.

————, and FRENCH, J. R. P., JR. "Final Report to NASA." Unpublished paper, University of Michigan, 1968.

CAREY, A. "The Hawthorne Studies: A Radical Criticism." *American Sociological Review*, vol. 32 (1967), pp. 403–17.

CARLISLE, ARTHUR ELLIOTT. "MacGregor." *Organizational Dynamics*, Summer 1976.

CARLSON, S. *Executive Behavior.* Stockholm: Strombergs, 1951.

CARNEGIE, DALE. *How to Win Friends and Influence People.* New York: Pocket Books, 1958.

CARSON, IAIN. "How Top Men Make Up Their Minds." *International Management*, April 1971.

CARTER, E. EUGENE. "The Behavioral Theory of the Firm and Top Level Corporate Decision." *Administrative Science Quarterly*, vol. 16 (1971), pp. 413–28.

CARTWRIGHT, DORWIN. "Power: A Neglected Variable in Social Psychology." In W. G. Bennis, K. D. Benne, and R. Chin (eds.), *The Planning Change.* New York: Holt, Rinehart & Winston, 1966.

————, and ZANDER, A. *Group Dynamics.* 2d ed. New York: Harper & Row, 1960.

CATTELL, R. B. *The Scientific Analysis of Personality.* Chicago: Aldine Publishing Co., 1965.

CHAFETZ, JANET SALTZMAN. *Masculine, Feminine or Human? An Overview of the Sociology of the Gender Roles.* 2d ed. Itasca, Ill.: F. E. Peacock, Publishers, 1978.

CHANCE, J. E., and MEADERS, W. "Needs and Interpersonal Perception." *Journal of Personality*, vol. 28 (1960), pp. 200–210.

CHANDLER, A. D., JR. *Strategy and Structure*. Cambridge, Mass.: MIT Press, 1962.

CHASE, STUART. *Men at Work*. New York: Harcourt, Brace & World, 1941.

CHESLER, PHYLLIS. *Women and Madness*. New York: Doubleday, 1972.

CHINOY, ELY. "Manning the Machines—The Assembly Line Worker." In P. C. Berger (ed.), *The Human Shape of Work*. New York: Macmillan Co., 1964.

CHOMSKY, NOAM. *Language and Mind*. New York: Harcourt, Brace, Jovanovich, 1972.

CHRISTIE, R. "The Prevalence of Machiavellian Orientations." Paper presented at a symposium at the annual meeting of the American Psychological Association, Los Angeles, 1964.

CLARK, RUSSELL D., III. "Group-Induced Shift toward Risk: A Critical Appraisal." *Psychological Bulletin*, vol. 76, no. 4 (1971), pp. 251–70.

CLAY, M. J., and WALLEY, B. H. *Performance and Profitability*. New York: Humanities Press, 1965.

COBBS, B. B. *A Report on the Health of Air Traffic Controllers Based on Aero-medical Examination Data*. Published report to the Federal Aviation Agency, University of Michigan, 1972.

COCH, L., and FRENCH, J. R. P. "Overcoming Resistance to Change." *Human Relations*, vol. 1 (1948).

COHEN, MICHAEL D.; MARCH, JAMES G.; and OLSEN, JOHAN P. "A Garbage Can Model of Organizational Choice." *Administrative Science Quarterly*.

COLEMAN, J. C. *Personality Dynamics and Effective Behavior*. Chicago: Scott, Foresman & Co., 1960.

COLEMAN, RICHARD P., and RAINWATER, LEE. *Social Standing in America: New Dimensions of Class*, New York: Basic Books, 1978.

COOLEY, C. H. *Social Organization*. New York: Charles Scribner's Sons, 1909.

————; ANGELL, R. C.; and CARR, L. J. *Introductory Sociology*, New York: Charles Scribner's Sons, 1933.

COOPER, D. "The Anti-Hospital: An Experiment in Psychiatry." *New Society*, vol. 11 (March 1965).

COOPER, G. L. "The Influence of the Trainer on Participant Change in T-Groups." *Human Relations*, vol. 22, no. 6 (1969), pp. 515–30.

COOPER, R., and PAYNE, R. "Extraversion and Some Aspects of Work Behavior." *Personnel Psychology*, vol. 20 (1967), pp. 45–57.

COSER, L. A. *The Functions of Social Conflict*. New York: Free Press of Glencoe, 1955.

CROPLEY, A. J. "Creativity." In P. E. Vernon (ed.), *Creativity*. London: Penguin, 1970, and New York: Humanities Press, Inc.

CROZIER, M. *The Bureaucratic Phenomenon*. Chicago: University of Chicago Press, 1964.

CUBBON, ALLAN. "The Hawthorne Talk in Context." *Occupational Psychology*, vol. 43 (1969), pp. 111–28.

CUMMINGS, L. L.   "Management Effectiveness II: Performance at the Graduate Student Level." *Academy of Management Journal*, vol. 10, no. 2 (June 1967), pp. 145–60.

CYERT, R. M., and MARCH, J. G.   *A Behavioral Theory of the Firm.* Englewood Cliffs, N.J.: Prentice-Hall, 1963.

————; SIMON, H. A.; and TROW, D. B.   "Observation of a Business Decision." *Journal of Business*, vol. 29 (1956).

DAHRENDORF, RALF.   "Towards a Theory of Social Conflict." *Journal of Conflict Resolution*, vol. 2 (June 1958), pp. 170–83.

————.   "Out of Utopia: Toward a Reorientation of Sociological Analysis." *American Journal of Sociology*, vol. 64 (September 1958), pp. 115–27.

————.   *Class and Class Conflict in Industrial Society.* Stanford, Cal.: Stanford University Press, 1959.

DALE, ERNEST.   *The Great Organizers.* New York: McGraw-Hill Book Co., 1960.

————, and URWICK, L. F.   *Staff in Management.* New York: McGraw-Hill Book Co., 1960.

DALTON, MELVILLE.   "The Industrial 'Rate-Buster': A Characterization." *Applied Anthropology*, vol. 7 (Winter 1948), pp. 5–18.

————.   *Men Who Manage.* New York: John Wiley & Sons, 1959.

DANIEL, D. RONALD.   "Management Information Crisis." *Harvard Business Review*, September–October 1961.

DAVIS, STANLEY M.   "No Connection between Executive Age and Corporate Performance." *Harvard Business Review*, March–April 1979.

————, and LAWRENCE, PAUL R.   "Problems of Matrix Organizations." *Harvard Business Review*, May–June 1978.

DECI, E. L., and VROOM, V. H.   "The Stability of Post-Decision Dissonance: A Follow-Up Study of the Job Attitudes of Business School Graduates." *Organizational Behavior and Human Performance*, vol. 6 (1971), pp. 36–49.

DEGAULLE, CHARLES.   *Memoirs of Hope, Renewal and Endeavor.* New York: McGraw-Hill Ryerson, 1972.

DEGREENE, KENYON B. (ed.).   *Systems Psychology.* New York: McGraw-Hill Book Co., 1970.

DELGADO, J. M. R.   *Physical Control of the Mind.* New York: Harper & Row, 1969.

DEMAAGD, GERALD R.   "Matrix Management." *Datamation*, vol. 16, no. 13 (1970), pp. 46–49.

DEVORE, I.   "Primate Behaviour." *International Encyclopedia of the Social Sciences*, vol. 14 (1968), pp. 351–60.

DICHTER, ERNST.   "The World Customer." *Harvard Business Review*, July–August 1962, pp. 113–22.

DIESING, P.   "Noneconomic Decision-Making." *Ethics*, vol. 66, no. 1 (October 1955), pp. 18–35.

DILL, WILLIAM R.   "Environment as an Influence on Managerial Autonomy."
Administrative Science Quarterly, vol. 2 (March 1958), pp. 409–43.

DOLLARD, JOHN, et al.   *Frustration and Aggression*. New Haven, Conn.: Yale
University Press, 1939.

DONNELLEY, JOHN F.   "Participative Management at Work." *Harvard Business Review*, January–February 1977.

DOWLING, WILLIAM F. (ed.).   "Job Redesign on the Assembly Line: Farewell
to Blue-Collar Blues?" *Organizational Dynamics*, vol. 2, no. 2 (1973) pp.
51–67.

―――――.   Interview with Warren Bennis. *Organizational Dynamics*, Winter
1974.

―――――.   "Hawthorne Revisited: The Legend and the Legacy." *Organizational Dynamics*, Winter 1975, pp. 66–80.

DRUCKER, P. F.   "The Employee Society." *American Sociological Review*,
vol. 58 (1952), pp. 358–63.

―――――.   *Managing for Results*. New York: Harper & Row, 1964.

DUBIN, ROBERT.   "Power and Union Management Relations." *Administrative Science Quarterly, vol. 2 (June 1957)*.

―――――.   "Business Behavior Behaviorally Viewed." In G. B. Strother (ed.),
Social Science Approaches to Business Behavior. Homewood, Ill.:
Richard D. Irwin, 1962.

―――――.   *Theory Building*. New York: Free Press, 1969.

―――――.   "Theory Building in Applied Areas." In M. D. Dunnette (ed.),
Handbook of Industrial and Organizational Psychology. Chicago: Rand
McNally College Publishing Co., 1976.

DUBOS, RENE.   *A God Within*. New York: Charles Scribner's Sons, 1972.

DUNCAN, R. B.   "Characteristics of Organizational Environments and Perceived Environmental Uncertainty." *Administrative Science Quarterly*,
vol. 17 (1972), pp. 313–27.

DUNNETTE, MARVIN D.   *Personnel Selection and Placement*. Belmont, Calif.:
Wadsworth Publishing Co., 1966.

―――――.   "The Role of Financial Compensation in Managerial Motivation,"
Organizational Behavior and Human Performance, vol. 2 (1967), pp.
175–216.

―――――.   *Handbook of Industrial and Organizational Psychology*. Chicago:
Rand McNally College Publishing Co., 1976.

EMERY, F. E.   *Characteristics of Socio-Technical Systems*. London: Tavistock Publications, 1959.

―――――.   "Bureaucracy and Beyond." *Organizational Dynamics*, Winter
1974.

―――――, and TRIST, E. L.   "Socio-Technical Systems." In C. W. Churchman
and M. Verhuist (eds.), *Management Science Models and Techniques*. Vol.
2. New York: Pergamon Press, 1960.

―――――, and ―――――.   "The Causal Texture of Organizational Environments." *Human Relations*, vol. 18, no. 1 (1965).

ERIKSON, ERIK. *Childhood and Society.* 2d ed. New York: Norton, 1963.

————. *Identity: Youth and Crisis.* New York: W. W. Norton & Co., 1968.

ETZIONI, AMITAI. *A Comparative Analysis of Complex Organizations.* New York: Free Press, 1961.

EVAN, WILLIAM M. "Indices of the Hierarchical Structure of Industrial Organizations." *Management Science,* vol. 9 (1963), pp. 468–77.

————. "Conflict and Performance in R.&D. Organizations." *Industrial Management Review,* vol. 7 (1965), pp. 37–45.

EWING, D. W. "Tension Can Be an Asset." *Harvard Business Review,* September–October 1964.

EYSENCK, H. J. *The Structure of Human Personality.* London: Methuen & Co., Ltd., 1953.

FAYOL, HENRY. *General and Industrial Management.* London: Sir Isaac Pitman, 1949.

FIEDLER, F. E. "The Leader's Psychological Distance and Group Effectiveness." In D. Cartwright and A. Zander (eds.), *Group Dynamics.* 2d ed. New York: Harper & Row, 1960.

————. "The Contingency Model: A Theory of Leadership Effectiveness." In C. W. Backman and P. F. Secord (eds.), *Problems in Social Psychology.* New York: McGraw-Hill Book Co., 1966.

————. *A Theory of Leadership Effectiveness.* New York: McGraw-Hill Book Co., 1967.

————. "Validation and Extension of the Contingency Model of Leadership Effectiveness: A Review of Empirical Findings," *Psychological Bulletin,* vol. 76, no. 2 (1971), pp. 128–48.

————. "The Leadership Game: Matching the Man to the Situation." *Organizational Dynamics,* Winter 1976.

————; CHEMERS, M. M.; and MAHAR, L. *Improving Leadership Effectiveness: The Leader Match Concept.* New York: John Wiley & Sons, 1976.

FILLEY, A. C., and HOUSE, ROBERT J. *Managerial Process and Organizational Behavior.* Glenview, Ill.: Scott, Foresman & Co., 1969.

FLEISHMAN, E. A. "Leadership Climate, Human Relations Training, and Supervisory Behavior." *Personnel Psychology,* vol. 6 (1953), pp. 205–22.

————, and HARRIS, E. F. "Patterns of Leadership Behavior Related to Employee Grievances and Turnovers." *Personnel Psychology,* vol. 15 (1962), pp. 43–56.

FOREHAND, G., and GILMER, B. "Environmental Variation in Studies of Organizational Behavior." *Psychological Bulletin,* vol. 22 (1964), pp. 361–82.

FORRESTER, JAY W. *Industrial Dynamics.* Cambridge, Mass.: MIT Press, 1961.

FOURAKER, L. E., and STOPFORD, J. M. "Organizational Structures and the Multinational Strategy." *Administrative Science Quarterly,* vol. 13, no. 1 (1968).

FRENCH, J. R. P., JR., and RAVEN, B. "The Bases of Social Power." In D.

Cartwright (ed.), *Studies in Social Power*. Ann Arbor, Mich.: Institute for Social Research, 1959.

FRENKEL-BRUNSWIK, E. "Intolerance of Ambiguity as an Emotional and Perceptual Variable." *Journal of Personality*, vol. 18 (1949), pp. 108–43.

FREUD, SIGMUND. *Introductory Lectures on Psychoanalysis*. London: Allen and Unwin, 1923.

FRICK, F. C., and SUMBY, W. H. "Control Tower Language." *Journal of the Acoustical Society of America*, vol. 24, no. 6 (1952).

FRIEDLANDER, FRANK. "OD Reaches Adolescence: An Exploration of Its Underlying Values." *Journal of Applied Behavioral Science*, vol. 12 (January–February 1976), pp. 51–56.

FROMM, E. *Escape from Freedom*. New York: Farrar & Rinehart, 1941.

―――. *The Sane Society*. London: Routledge and Kegan Paul, 1956.

GABOR, DENNIS. *Innovations: Scientific, Technological, and Social*. Toronto: Oxford University Press, 1972.

GALBRAITH, JAY. *Designing Complex Organizations*. Reading, Mass.: Addison-Wesley Publishing Co., 1973.

―――, and CUMMINGS, L. L. "An Empirical Investigation of the Motivational Determinants of Task Performance: Interactive Effects between Instrumentality-Valence and Motivation-Ability." *Organizational Behavior and Human Performance*, vol. 2 (1967), pp. 237–57.

GALBRAITH, JOHN KENNETH. *The New Industrial State*. Boston: Houghton Mifflin Co., 1967.

―――. *Economics and the Public Purpose*. Boston: Houghton Mifflin Co., 1973.

―――. *The Affluent Society*. 3d ed. Boston: Houghton Mifflin Co., 1976.

GAMSON, W. A. "A Theory of Coalition Formation." *American Sociological Review*, vol. 26 (1961), pp. 565–73.

GEIS, L.; CHRISTIE, R.; and NELSON, C. "On Machiavellianism." Study carried out at Columbia University, New York, 1963.

GELLERMAN, S. W. *Motivation and Productivity*. New York: American Management Association, 1963.

GEORGE, C. S. *The History of Management Thought*. Englewood Cliffs, N.J.: Prentice-Hall, 1968.

GEORGOPOULUS, B. S.; MAHONEY, G. M.; and JONES, N. W. "A Path-Goal Approach to Productivity." *Journal of Applied Psychology*, vol. 41 (1957), pp. 345–53.

GERGEN, K. J. *The Concept of Self*. New York: Holt, Rinehart & Winston, 1970.

GERTH, H. H., and MILLS, C. WRIGHT. *From Max Weber*. New York: Oxford University Press, 1946.

GHISELLI, EDWIN E. "Managerial Talent." *American Psychologist*, vol. 18 (October 1963), p. 635.

―――. "Some Motivational Factors in the Success of Managers." *Personnel Psychology*, vol. 21 (Winter 1968), pp. 431–40.

————, and HAIRE, M.   "The Validation of Selection Tests in the Light of the Dynamic Character of Criteria." *Personnel Psychology*, vol. 13, (Autumn 1960), pp. 225–31.

GIBB, C. A.   "Leadership." In G. Lindzey (ed.), *Handbook of Social Psychology*. Reading, Mass.: Addison-Wesley Publishing Co., 1954.

GOFFMAN, ERVING.   "On Cooling the Mark Out." *Psychiatry*, vol. 15 (November 1952), pp. 351–63.

GOODING, JUDSON.   "The Accelerated Generation Moves into Management," *Fortune*, March 1971.

GOODMAN, NELSON.   *Ways of Worldmaking*. Indianapolis: Hackett Publishing Co., 1978.

GOODMAN, P. S., and FRIEDMAN, A.   "An Examination of Adam's Theory of Inequity." *Administrative Science Quarterly*, vol. 16 (1971), pp. 271–86.

GORDON, T. J.   *Ideas in Conflict*. New York: St. Martin's Press, 1966.

GORDON, WILLIAM J. J.   *Synectics*. London: Collier-Macmillan Ltd., 1961.

GOULDNER, ALVIN W.   *Studies in Leadership*. New York: Harper & Bros., 1950.

————.   "Cosmopolitans and Locals: Toward an Analysis of Latent Social Roles—I," *Administrative Science Quarterly*, vol. 2 (December 1957), pp. 281–306.

————.   "The Norm of Reciprocity: A Preliminary Statement." *American Sociological Review*, vol. 25 (1960), pp. 161–79.

GOWIN, E. B.   *The Executive and His Control of Men*. New York: Macmillan Co., 1915.

GREINER, LARRY E.   "Patterns of Organizational Change." *Harvard Business Review*, May–June, 1967.

————.   "Evolution and Revolution as Organizations Grow." *Harvard Business Review*, July–August 1972, pp. 37–46.

GROSSMAN, B. A.   "The Measurement and Determinants of Interpersonal Sensitivity." Unpublished master's thesis, Michigan State University, 1963.

GRUBER, W. H. and NILES, J. S.   "The Coming of New Management." *Organizational Dynamics*, Spring 1974.

GUEST, R. H.   "Of Time and Foremen." *Personnel*, May 1956.

GUETZKOW, H., and SIMON, H. A.   "The Impact of Certain Communication Nets upon Organization and Performance in Task-Oriented Groups." *Management Science*, vol. 1 (April–July 1955).

GULICK, L.   "Notes on the Theory of Organization." In L. Gulick and L. F. Urwick (eds.), *Papers on the Science of Administration*. New York: Institute of Public Administration, 1937.

————, and URWICK, L. (eds.), *Papers on the Science of Administration*. New York: Institute of Public Administration, 1937.

GUTHRIE, TYRONE.   *On Acting*. London: Studio Vista Publishers, 1971.

GYLLENHAMMAR, PEHR G.   "How Volvo Adapts Work to People." *Harvard Business Review*, July–August 1977.

HACKMAN, J. RICHARD. "The Design of Work in the 1980s." *Organizational Dynamics*, Summer 1975.

————; OLDHAM, GREG; JANSON, ROBERT; and PURDY, KENNETH. "A New Strategy for Job Enrichment." *California Management Review*, vol. 27, no. 4, pp. 57–71.

HAGE, J., and AIKEN, M. *Social Change in Complex Organizations*. New York: Random House, 1970.

HAIRE, M. *Modern Organization Theory*. New York: John Wiley & Sons, 1959.

HALBERSTAM, DAVID. *The Best and the Brightest*. New York: Random House, 1969.

HALL, A. D., and FAGEN, R. E. "Definition of System." In Walter Buckley (ed.), *Modern Systems Research for the Behavioral Scientist*. Chicago: Aldine Publishing Co., 1968.

HALL, CALVIN S.; and LINDZEY, GARDNER. *Theories of Personality*. 2d ed. New York: John Wiley & Sons, 1970.

HALL, E. T. *The Hidden Dimension*. New York: Doubleday & Co., 1966.

HALL, J., and WILLIAMS, M. S. "Group Dynamics Training and Improved Decision Making." *Journal of Applied Behavioral Science*, vol. 6 (1970), pp. 39–68.

HALL, ROGER I. "A System Pathology of an Organization: The Rise and Fall of the Old *Saturday Evening Post*." *Administrative Science Quarterly*, June 1976.

HALLETT, DOUGLAS. *New York Times Magazine*, October 20, 1974.

HAPLIN, A. W. "The Leadership Behavior and Combat Performance of Airplane Commanders." *Journal of Abnormal and Social Psychology*, vol. 49 (1954), pp. 14–22.

————, and WINER, B. J. "A Factorial Study of the Leader Behavior Descriptions." In R. M. Stogdill and A. E. Coons (eds.), *Leader Behavior: Its Description and Measurement*. Bureau of Business Research Monograph 88. Columbus: Ohio State University Press, 1957.

HAMACHEK, D. *Encounters with the Self*. New York: Holt, Rinehart & Winston, 1970.

HAMNER, W. C., and HAMNER, E. P. "Behavior Modification on the Bottom Line." *Organizational Dynamics*, Spring 1976, pp. 2–21.

————, and Organ, D. W. *Organizational Behavior: An Applied Psychological Approach*. Dallas, Tex.: Business Publications, Inc., 1978.

HARE, A. P. *Handbook of Small Group Research*. New York: Free Press, 1962.

HARRIS, THOMAS. *I'm OK—You're OK*. New York: Harper & Bros., 1967.

HAY, E. N. "The Validation of Tests," *Personnel*, vol. 29 (1953), pp. 500–507.

HAYNES, JOHN. "The New Workers: A Report." *New Generation*, vol. 52 (Fall 1972).

HEIDER, F. *The Psychology of Interpersonal Relations*. New York: John Wiley & Sons, 1958.

HEILBRONER, ROBERT L. *Beyond Boom and Crash.* New York: W. W. Norton, 1978.

HELLER, JOSEPH. *Catch-22.* New York: Simon & Schuster, 1961.

————. *Something Happened.* New York: Alfred Knopf, 1974.

HERR, MICHAEL. *Dispatches.* New York: Alfred A. Knopf, 1977.

HERZBERG, FREDERICK. *Work and the Nature of Man.* Cleveland, Ohio: World Publishing Co., 1966.

————; MAUSNER, BERNARD; and SNYDERMAN, BARBARA. *The Motivation to Work.* New York: John Wiley & Sons, 1959.

HICKSON, D. J. "Motives of Work People Who Restrict Their Output." *Occupational Psychology,* vol. 35 (1961), pp. 110–21.

————; PUGH, D. S.; and PHEYSEY, D. C. "Operations Technology and Organization Structure: A Reappraisal." *Administrative Science Quarterly,* vol. 14 (1969), pp. 378–97.

————, et al. "A Strategic Contingencies Theory of Intra-organizational Power." *Administrative Science Quarterly,* vol. 16 (1971), pp. 216–29.

HOLLANDER, E. P. "Conformity, Status and Idiosyncrasy Credit." *Psychological Review,* vol. 65 (1958), pp. 117–27.

HOLLINGSORTH, H. L. *Vocational Psychology and Character Analysis.* New York: Appleton-Century, 1929.

HOLMES, T. H., and RAHE, R. H. "The Social Readjustment Rating Scale." *Journal of Psychosomatic Research,* vol. 2 (1967).

HOMANS, G. C. *The Human Group.* New York: Harcourt, Brace & World, 1950.

HORNER, MATINA. "Sex Differences in Achievement Motivation and Performance in Competitive and Non-Competitive Situations." Doctoral dissertation, University of Michigan, 1968.

HORNEY, K. *Our Inner Conflicts.* New York: W. W. Norton & Co., 1945.

HOSKING, DIAN, and SCHRIESHEIM, CHESTER. "Review of *Improving Leadership Effectiveness: The Leader Match Concept.*" *Administrative Science Quarterly,* vol. 23 (September 1978), p. 504.

HOUSE, ROBERT J. "T-Group Education and Leadership Effectiveness: A Review of the Empirical Literature and a Critical Evaluation." *Personnel Psychology,* vol. 20, no. 1 (1967), pp. 1–32.

————. "A Path-Goal Theory of Leader Effectiveness." *Administrative Science Quarterly,* vol. 16, no. 3 (September 1971), pp. 321–38.

————; FILLEY, A. C.; and KERR, S. "Relation of Leader Consideration and Initiating Structure to R. and D. Subordinate Satisfaction." *Administrative Science Quarterly,* vol. 16 (1971), pp. 19–30.

————, and MITCHELL, TERENCE R. "Path-Goal Theory of Leadership." *Journal of Contemporary Business,* Autumn 1974.

————, with WIGDOR, L. A. "Herzberg's Dual-Factor Theory of Job Satisfaction and Motivation: A Review of the Evidence and a Criticism." *Personnel Psychology,* vol. 20 (Winter 1967), pp. 369–89.

HOUSER, J. D. *What the Employee Thinks.* Cambridge, Mass.: Harvard University Press, 1927.

HOVLAND, C. I., et al. *The Order of Presentation in Persuasion.* New Haven Conn.: Yale University Press, 1957.

HUDSON, LIAM. *Cult of the Fact.* London: Cape, 1972.

HULIN, CHARLES L., and BLOOD, M. R. "Job Enlargement, Individual Differences, and Worker Responses." *Psychological Bulletin,* vol. 69 (January 1968), pp. 41–55.

HUNT, J. G. "Fiedler's Leadership Contingency Model: An Empirical Test in Three Organizations." *Organizational Behavior and Human Performance,* vol. 2 (1967), pp. 290–308.

————, and HILL, J. W. "The New Look in Motivational Theory for Organizational Research." *Human Organization,* vol. 28 (Summer 1969), pp. 100–109.

HUNT, R. G. "Role and Role Conflict." In E. P. Hollander and R. G. Hunt (eds.), *Current Perspectives in Social Psychology.* 2d ed. New York: Oxford University Press, 1967.

HUSTON, TED L., and LEVINGER, GEORGE. "Interpersonal Attraction and Relationships." *Annual Review of Psychology,* vol. 29 (1978).

HUXLEY, ALDOUS L. *Brave New World.* Garden City, N.Y.: Doubleday & Co., 1932.

ILLICH, IVAN. *Medical Nemesis: The Expropriation of Health.* New York: Pantheon Books, 1976.

JAMES, D. CLAYTON. *The Years of MacArthur,* vol. II, *1941–1945.* New York: Houghton Mifflin, 1975. © 1975 by Houghton Mifflin Company.

JAMES, WILLIAMS. *Principles of Psychology.* New York: Henry Holt & Co., 1890.

JANIS, IRVING, L. "Group Identification under Conditions of External Danger." *British Journal of Medical Psychology,* vol. 36 (1963), pp. 227–38.

————. *Victims of Groupthink.* Boston: Houghton Mifflin Co., 1972.

JANOWITZ, M. *Sociology and the Military Establishment.* New York: Russell Sage Foundation, 1959.

JAY, ANTHONY. "How to Run a Meeting." *Harvard Business Review,* March–April 1976.

JENNINGS, EUGENE. "Mobicentric Man." *Psychology Today,* July 1970.

JENNINGS, H. H. "Leadership and Sociometric Choice." In S. E. Swanson, T. M. Newcomb, and E. L. Hartley (eds.), *Readings in Social Psychology.* New York: Henry Holt & Co., 1952.

JOHNSON, RICHARD A.; KAST, FREMONT E.; and ROSENZWEIG, JAMES E. "Systems Theory and Management." *Management Science,* vol. 10 (January 1964), pp. 367–84.

KAHN, HERMAN; BROWN, WILLIAM; and MARTEL, LEON. *The Next 200 Years.* New York: William Morrow & Co., 1976.

————; PFAFF, W.; and WIENER, ANTHONY J. (eds). *Appendix to the Next Thirty-four Years: A Context for Speculation.* Croton-on-Hudson, N.Y.: Hudson Institute, 1966.

————, and WIENER, ANTHONY J. *The Next Thirty-three Years: A Framework for Speculation.* Vol. 2, *Working Papers,* Commission on the Year 2000 of the American Academy of Arts and Sciences. Corton-on-Hudson, N.Y.: Hudson Institute, 1967.

KAHN, R. L., and FRENCH, J. R. P., JR. "Status and Conflict: Two Themes in the Study of Stress." In J. E. McGrath (ed.), *Social and Psychological Factors in Stress.* New York: Holt, Rinehart & Winston, 1970.

————, and KATZ, D. "Leadership Practices in Relation to Productivity and Morale." in D. Cartwright and A. Zander (eds.), *Group Dynamics.* New York: Harper & Row, 1960.

————; WOLFE, D. M.; QUINN, R. P.; SNOEK, J. K., and ROSENTHAL, R. H. *Organizational Stress: Studies in Role Conflict and Ambiguity.* New York: John Wiley & Sons, 1964.

KAPLAN, ABRAHAM. *The Conduct of Inquiry.* San Francisco: Chandler Publishing Co., 1964.

KAPLAN, A. D. H. *Big Enterprises in a Competitive System.* Washington, D.C.: Brookings Institution, 1964.

KAST, F. E., and ROSENZWEIG, JAMES E. *Organization and Management.* New York: McGraw-Hill Book Co., 1970.

KATZ, DANIEL. "The Functional Approach to the Study of Attitudes." *Public Opinion Quarterly,* vol. 24 (1960), pp. 163–77.

————. "The Motivational Basis of Organizational Behaviour." *Behavioural Science,* vol. 9 (1964), pp. 131–46.

————, and KAHN, R. L. *The Social Psychology of Organizations.* New York: John Wiley & Sons, 1966.

KELLER, R. T.; SLOCUM, J. W.; and SUSMAN, G. I. "Management System, Uncertainty, and Continuous Process Technology." Paper presented at 33d meeting of National Academy of Management, Boston, 1973.

KELLY, JOE. "A Study of Leadership in Two Contrasting Groups." *Sociological Review,* November 1963.

————. "The Study of Executive Behavior by Activity Sampling." *Human Relations,* vol. 17, no. 3 (1964).

————. *Is Scientific Management Possible?* London: Faber & Faber, Ltd., 1968.

————. "Make Conflict Work for You." *Harvard Business Review,* July–August 1970.

————. "Organizational Development through Structured Sensitivity Training." *Management International Review,* vol. 13 (1973).

————, and BILEK, D. "White Collar Unions: Does Middle Management Want Them?" *Canadian Business,* June 1973.

KELMAN, H. C. "Compliance, Identification, and Internalization: Three Processes of Attitude Change." *Journal of Conflict Resolution,* vol. 2 (1958).

KEPNER, CHARLES H., and TREEGOE, BENJAMIN V. *The Rational Manager.* New York: McGraw-Hill Book Co., 1965.

KERLINGER, F. N. *Foundations of Behavioral Research.* New York: Holt, Rinehart & Winston, 1964.

KILMANN, RALPH H, PONDY, LOUIS R, and SELVIN, DENNIS P., (eds.). *The Management of Organization Design: Research and Methodology. Vol. 2.,* New York: Elsevier North-Holland, 1976.

KINGDON, DONALD R. *Matrix Organization.* New York: Barnes & Noble Books, 1973.

KLOCKARS, CARL B. *The Professional Fence.* New York: Free Press, 1974.

KOLB, D. A.; RUBIN, I. M., and McINTYRE, J. M. *Organizational Psychology.* 2nd ed. Englewood Cliffs, N.J.: Prentice-Hall, 1974.

KORDA, MICHAEL *Power! How to Get It, How to Use It.* New York: Random House, 1975.

KORMAN, A. K. "Consideration, Initiating Structure, and Organizational Criteria— A Review." *Personnel Psychology,* vol. 19 (1966), pp. 349–62.

KORNHAUSER, ARTHUR. *Mental Health of the Industrial Worker.* New York: John Wiley & Sons, 1965.

KOTTER, JOHN P. "Power, Dependence and Effective Management." *Harvard Business Review,* July–August 1977.

KRISTOL, IRVING. *Two Cheers for Capitalism.* New York: Basic Books, 1978.

KUHN, T. S. *The Structure of Scientific Revolutions.* Chicago: University of Chicago Press, 1952.

LAING, R. D. *The Divided Self.* London: Tavistock Publications., 1965.

LANDSBERGER, H. A. *Hawthorne Revisited.* Ithaca, N.Y.: New York State School of Industrial and Labor Relations, Cornell University, 1958.

———. "The Horizontal Dimension in Bureaucracy." *Administrative Science Quarterly,* vol. 6, no. 1 (1961–62), pp. 299–322.

LAWLER, EDWARD E., III. "Managers' Job Performance and Their Attitudes toward Their Pay." Unpublished doctoral dissertation, University of California at Berkeley, 1964.

———. "Ability as a Moderator of the Relationship between Job Attitudes and Job Performance." *Personal Psychology,* vol. 10 (1966), pp. 153–64.

———. "Attitude Surveys and Job Performance." *Personnel Administration,* September–October 1967, pp. 485–87.

———. "Job Design and Employee Motivation." *Personnel Psychology.* vol. 22 (1969).

———. "Job Attitudes and Employee Motivation: Theory, Research, and Practice." *Personnel Psychology,* vol. 23 (1970), pp. 223–37.

———. *Pay and Organizational Effectiveness: A Psychological View.* New York: McGraw-Hill Book Co., 1971.

———. "Developing a Motivating Work Climate." *Management Review,* July 1977.

———. "The New Plant Revolution." *Organizational Dynamics,* Winter 1978.

————, and PORTER, L. W. "Antecedent Attitudes of Effective Managerial Performance." *Organizational Behavior and Human Performance,* vol. 2 (1967), pp. 122–42.

————, and ————. "The Effect of Performance on Job Satisfaction." In Dennis W. Organ (ed.), *The Applied Psychology of Work Behavior: A Book of Readings.* Dallas, Tex.: Business Publications, Inc., 1978.

LAWRENCE, PAUL R., and LORSCH, J. W. "Differentiation and Integration in Complex Organizations." *Administrative Science Quarterly,* vol. 12 (June 1967), pp. 1–47.

————, and ————. *Organization and Environment: Managing Differentiation and Integration.* Boston: Division of Research, Graduate School of Business Administration, Harvard University, 1967.

LEAVITT, HAROLD J. "Unhuman Organization." *Harvard Business Review,* vol. 40, no. 4 (1962), pp. 90–98.

————. "Applied Organizational Change in Industry: Structural, Technological, and Humanistic Approaches." In James G. March (ed.), *Handbook of Organizations.* Chicago: Rand McNally & Co., 1965.

————. "Beyond the Analytic Manager: Part II." *California Management Review,* Summer 1975.

————, and WHISLER, THOMAS L. "Management in the 1980's." *Harvard Business Review,* November–December 1958.

LEVINSON, ANDREW. *The Working Class Majority.* New York: Coward, McCann & Geoghegan, 1974.

LEVINSON, HARRY. "On Being a Middle-Aged Manager." *Harvard Business Review,* July–August 1969.

————. "Appraisal of *What* Performance?" *Harvard Business Review,* July–August 1976.

LEVITT, THEODORE. "The Managerial Merry-G-Round." *Harvard Business Review,* July–August 1974.

————. "Management and the Post Industrial Society." *The Public Interest,* Summer 1976, p. 73.

LEWIN, KURT. "Defining the Field at a Given Time." *Psychological Review,* vol. 50 (1945).

————. *Field Theory in Social Science.* New York: Harper & Bros., 1951.

————; LIPPITT, R.; and WHITE, R. K. "Patterns of Aggressive Behavior in Experimentally Created Social Climates." *Journal of Social Psychology,* vol. 10 (1939), pp. 271–99.

LICHTMAN, C. M., and HUNT, R. G. "Personality and Organization Theory: A Review of Some Conceptual Literature." *Psychological Bulletin,* vol. 76 (1971), pp. 271–94.

LICKLIDER, J. C. R., and TAYLOR, R. W. "The Computer as a Communication Device." *Science and Technology,* vol. 76 (1968), pp. 21–31.

LIKERT, RENSIS. "Motivational Dimensions of Administration." In R. Walker (ed.), *America's Manpower Crisis.* Chicago: Public Administration Service, 1952.

————. *New Patterns of Management.* New York: McGraw-Hill Book Co., 1961.

————. *The Human Organization.* New York: McGraw-Hill Book Co., 1967.

LINDBLOM, CHARLES E. *Politics and Markets: The World's Political-Economic Systems.* New York: Basic Books, 1977.

LINTON, R. *The Study of Man.* New York: Appleton-Century-Crofts, 1936.

LIPPITT, GORDON L., and SCHMIDT, WARREN H. "Crises in a Developing Organization." *Harvard Business Review*, November–December 1967.

LITWIN, G., and STRINGER, R. "The Influence of Organizational Climate on Human Motivation." Paper presented at Conference on Organizational Climate, Foundation for Research on Human Behavior, Ann Arbor, Michigan, 1966.

————, and ————. *Motivational and Organizational Climate.* Cambridge, Mass.: Harvard University Press, 1968.

LORENZ, KONRAD. *On Aggression.* London: Methuen & Co., 1966.

LORSCH, J. W., and LAWRENCE, PAUL R. *Studies in Organizational Design.* Homewood, Ill.: Richard D. Irwin, 1970.

————, and ————. *Organization Planning: Cases and Concepts.* Homewood, Ill.: Richard D. Irwin, 1972.

LOUIS, ARTHUR M. "Donald Frey Had a Hunger for the Whole Thing." *Fortune*, September 1976.

LUCE, R. D., and RAIFFA, H. *Games and Decisions.* New York: John Wiley & Sons, 1957.

LUCIETTO, LENA L. "Speech Patterns of Administrators." *Administrator's Notebook,* vol. 18, no. 5 (1970).

LUNDBERG, C. C. "On Plotting Individual Change in Human Relations Training." *Training Development Journal*, vol. 22, no. 6 (1968), pp. 50–57.

LUTHANS, F., and WHITE, D. D., JR. "Behavior Modification: Application to Manpower Management." *Personnel Administration*, July–August 1971.

MCCLELLAND, D. C. *The Achieving Society.* Princeton, N.J.: D. Van Nostrand Co., 1961.

————. "That Urge to Achieve." *Think*, vol. 32 (November–December, 1966), pp. 19–23.

MCCLELLAND, DAVID. *The Drinking Man.* New York: Free Press, 1972.

————, and BURNHAM, DAVID H. "Power is the Great Motivator", *Harvard Business Review*, March–April 1976.

MCGRATH, J. E. (ed.). *Social and Psychological Factors in Stress.* New York: Holt, Rinehart & Winston, 1970.

MCGREGOR, D. M. *The Human Side of Enterprise.* New York: McGraw-Hill Book Co., 1960.

MCINTYRE, JOAN. *Mind in the Waters: A Book to Celebrate the Consciousness of Whales and Dolphins.* Toronto: McLelland & Stewart, 1974.

MCLUHAN, MARSHALL. *The Gutenberg Galaxy: The Making of Typographic Man.* Toronto: University of Toronto Press, 1962.

————, and FIORE, Q. *The Medium Is the Message.* New York: Bantam Books, 1967.

McQUADE, WALTER. "What Stress Can Do to You." *Fortune,* January 1972.

MACCOBY, MICHAEL. *The Gamesman.* New York: Simon and Schuster, 1976.

MADDI, SALVATORE R. *Personality Theories: A Comparative Analysis.* 3d ed. Homewood, Ill.: Dorsey Press, 1976.

MAIER, N. R. F. *Frustration: The Study of Behavior without a Goal.* New York: McGraw-Hill Book Co., 1949.

MALONE, ERWIN L. "The Non-Linear Systems Experiment in Participative Management." *Journal of Business.* January 1975, pp. 52–64.

MANCHESTER, WILLIAM R. *The Death of a President.* New York: Harper & Row, 1967.

MANLEY, T. R., and McNICHOLS, C. W. "OD at a Major Government Research Laboratory." *Public Personnel Journal,* vol. 6 (January–February 1977), pp. 51–61.

MANN, F. C. "Studying and Creating Change: A Means to Understanding Social Organization." In *Research in Industrial Human Relations.* New York: Harper & Bros., 1957.

MARCH, JAMES G. *Handbook of Organizations.* Chicago: Rand, McNally & Co., 1965.

————, and SIMON, HERBERT A. *Organizations.* New York: John Wiley & Sons, 1958.

MARROW, ALFRED J. *The Failure of Success.* New York: American Management Association, 1972.

————; BOWERS, DAVID G.; and SEASHORE, STANLEY E. *Management by Participation: Creating a Climate for Personal and Organizational Development.* New York: Harper & Row, 1967.

MARX, KARL. *Economic and Philosophical Manuscripts of 1844.* Trans. Martin Milligan. London: Lawrence & Wishert, 1959.

MASLOW, A. H. *Motivation and Personality.* New York: Harper & Bros., 1954.

MAY, ROLLO. *The Meaning of Anxiety.* New York: Ronald Press Co., 1950.

————. *Psychology and the Human Dilemma.* Princeton, N.J.: D. Van Nostrand Co., 1967.

MAYFIELD, E. C. "The Selection Interview—A Re-evaluation of Published Research." *Personnel Psychology,* vol. 17 (1964), pp. 239–60.

MAYO, ELTON. *The Human Problems of an Industrial Civilization.* New York: Macmillan Co., 1933.

————. *The Social Problems of an Industrial Civilization.* Cambridge, Mass.: Harvard University Press, 1947.

MEADOWS, DENNIS H.; MEADOWS, D. L.; RONDERS, J.; and BEHRENS, W. III. *The Limits to Growth.* New York: Universe Books, 1972.

MECHANIC, DAVID. "Sources of Power of Lower Participants in Complex Organizations." *Administrative Science Quarterly,* vol. 7 (1962), pp. 349–64.

MERTON, R. K.   "Bureaucratic Structure and Personality." *Social Forces*, vol. 18 (1940), pp. 560–68.

————.   *Social Theory and Social Structure*. Glencoe, Ill.: Free Press, 1957.

MEYERSOHN, ROLF.   "The Price of Copylation." *New Society*, vol. 4 (January 1968).

MICHELS, ROBERT.   *Political Parties*. Glencoe, Ill.: Free Press, 1958.

MILES, R. E.   "Human Relations or Human Resources." *Harvard Business Review*, vol. 43, no. 4 (July–August 1963), pp. 148–57.

MILGRAM, STANLEY.   "Some Conditions of Obedience and Disobedience to Authority." *Human Relations*, vol. 18 (1965), pp. 57–75.

MILLER, D. W., and STARR, M. K.   *The Structure of Human Decisions*. Englewood Cliffs, N.J.: Prentice-Hall, 1967.

MILLER, E. J., and RICE, A. K.   *Systems of Organization: The Control of Task and Sentient Boundaries*. London: Tavistock Publications, 1967.

MILLER, GEORGE A.   *Spontaneous Apprentices: Children and Language*. New York: Seabury Press, 1977.

MILLS, TED.   " 'Creeping Corporatism' vs. Rising Entitlements." *Harvard Business Review*, November–December 1976.

MINTZBERG, HENRY.   *The Nature of Managerial Work*. New York: Harper & Row, 1973.

————.   "The Manager's Job: Folklore and Fact." *Harvard Business Review*, July–August 1975.

————.   "Planning on the Left Side and Managing on the Right Side." *Harvard Business Review*, July–August 1976.

MISUMI, J., and SHIRAKASHI, S.   "An Experimental Study of the Effects of Supervisory Behavior on Productivity and Morale in a Hierarchical Organization." *Human Relations*, vol. 19 (1966), pp. 297–307.

MITCHELL, G. DUNCAN.   *A Hundred Years of Sociology*. London: Duckworth, 1968.

MITCHELL, T. R.   "Leader Complexity and Leadership Style." *Journal of Personality and Social Psychology*, vol. 16 (1970), pp. 166–74.

————.   "Organizational Behavior." *Annual Review of Psychology*, 1979.

MITFORD, JESSICA.   *Kind and Usual Punishment*. New York: Random House, 1973.

MONEY, JOHN.   *Man and Woman, Boy and Girl*. Baltimore: Johns Hopkins University Press, 1972.

MOONEY, J. D., and REILEY, A. M.   *Onward Industry*. New York: Harper & Bros., 1931.

————, and ————.   *The Principles of Organization*. New York: Harper & Bros., 1947.

MORENO, J. L.   *Who Shall Survive?* Washington, D.C.: Nervous and Mental Diseases Publishing Co., 1934.

MORSE, J., and LORSCH, J. W.   "Beyond Theory Y." *Harvard Business Review*. May–June 1970, pp. 61–68.

MORSE, NANCY, and REIMER, E. "The Experimental Change of a Major Organizational Variable." *Journal of Abnormal Social Psychology,* vol. 52 (1956), pp. 120–29.

MULDER, MAUK. "Communication Structure, Decision Structure, and Group Performance." *Sociometry,* vol. 23 (1960), pp. 1–14.

————. "Power Equalization through Participation." *Administrative Science Quarterly,* vol. 16 (1972), pp. 31–39.

MUNN, N. L. *Psychology, The Fundamental of Human Adjustment.* London: George G. Harrap Co., 1961.

MYERS, M. SCOTT. "Conditions for Managerial Motivations." *Harvard Business Review,* January–February 1964.

————. "Who Are Your Motivated Workers?" *Harvard Business Review,* January–February 1966.

————. "Every Employee a Manager." *California Management Review,* vol. 10 (1968).

NELSON, GOODMAN. *Ways of Worldmaking.* Indianapolis: Hackett Publishing Co., 1978.

NEUMANN, JOHN VON, and MORGENSTERN, OSKAR. *Theory of Games and Economic Behavior.* Princeton, N.J.: Princeton University Press, 1947.

NOLAN, RICHARD L. "Managing the Crisis in Data Processing." *Harvard Business Review,* March–April 1979.

NORD, WALTER R., and DURAND, DOUGLAS E. "Beyond Resistance to Change." *Organizational Dynamics,* Autumn 1975.

————, and ————. "What's Wrong with the Human Resources Approach to Management." *Organizational Dynamics,* Winter 1978.

OPSAHL, R. L., and DUNNETTE, M. D. "The Role of Financial Compensation in Industrial Motivation." *Psychological Bulletin,* vol. 66 (1966), pp. 94–118.

ORWELL, GEORGE. *Animal Farm.* New York: Harcourt, Brace & World, 1946.

OSGOOD, C. E.; SUCI, G. J.; and TANNENBAUM, P. H. *The Measurement of Meaning.* Urbana: University of Illinois Press, 1957.

PARKINSON, C. NORTHCOTE. *Parkinson's Law.* Boston: Houghton Mifflin Co., 1957.

PARSONS, TALCOTT. "Some Ingredients of a General Theory of Formal Organizations." In A. W. Halpin, *Administrative Theory in Education.* Chicago: Midwest Administration Center, University of Chicago, 1958.

————. *Structure and Process in Modern Societies.* New York: Free Press, 1960.

PASCALE, RICHARD TANNER. "Zen and the Art of Management." *Harvard Business Review,* March–April 1978.

PASSELL, PETER; ROBERTS, MARC; and ROSS, LEONARD. "The Limits to Growth. World Dynamics, and Urban Dynamics." *New York Times Book Review.* April 2, 1972.

PATERSON, T. T. *Authority.* Glasgow: Department of Administration, University of Stratheclyde, 1963.

PERROW, CHARLES. "A Framework for the Comparative Analysis of Organizations." *American Sociological Review,* vol. 32 (April 1967), pp. 190–208.

————. *Organizational Analysis: A Sociological View.* Belmont, Calif.: Wadsworth Publishing Co., 1970.

PETER, LAWRENCE J., and HULL, RAYMOND. *The Peter Principle.* New York: William Morrow & Co., 1969.

PFEFFER, JEFFREY. "Merger as a Response to Organizational Interdependence." *Administrative Science Quarterly,* vol. 17 (1972).

PFIEFFNER, J. M., and SHERWOOD, F. P. *Administrative Organization.* Englewood Cliffs, N.J.: Prentice-Hall, 1960.

PIAGET, JEAN. *The Language and Thought of the Child.* New York: Harcourt, Brace & World, 1926.

PIOTROWSKI, Z. A., and ROCK, M. R. *The Perceptanalytic Executive Scale: A Tool for the Selection of Top Managers.* New York: Grune & Stratton, 1963.

PORTER, ALBERT; MENTON, ARTHUR F.; and HALPERN, SEYMOUR. "Hopkins' Syndrome: A Study of Compulsion to Work." *Business Horizons,* vol. 13 (June 1970).

PORTER, E. H. "The Parable of the Spindle." *Harvard Business Review,* vol. 40 (1962), pp. 58–66.

PORTER, L. W., and LAWLER, E. E. "Properties of Organization Structure in Relation to Job Attitudes and Job Behavior." *Psychological Bulletin,* vol. 64 (1965), pp. 23–51.

————, and ————. *Managerial Attitudes and Performance.* Homewood, Ill.: Richard D. Irwin, 1968.

PRITCHARD, R. D. "Equity Theory: A Review and Critique." *Organizational Behavior and Human Performance,* vol. 4 (1969), pp. 176–211.

PUGH, D. S. "Modern Organizational Theory: A Psychological and Sociological Study." *Psychological Bulletin,* vol. 66 (1966), pp. 235–51.

————; HICKSON, D. J.; HININGS, C. R.; and TURNER, C. "Dimensions of Organizational Structure." *Administrative Science Quarterly,* vol. 13 (1968), pp. 65–105.

————; ————; ————; and ————. "The Context of Organizational Structures." *Administrative Science Quarterly,* vol. 14 (1969); pp. 91–114.

PUZO, MARIO. *The Godfather.* New York: G. P. Putnam's Sons, 1969.

RANK, OTTO. *The Myth of the Birth of the Hero.* New York: Johnson reprint, 1914.

RANKIN, DEBORAH. "How C.P.A.'s Sell Themselves." *The New York Times,* September 25, 1977.

RAPPOPORT, ANATOL. *Fights, Games, and Debates.* Ann Arbor: University of Michigan Press, 1974.

RASKIN, A. H. "The Workers in the Executive Suite." *The New York Times,* January 4, 1976.

————. "Trying the Four-Day Week." *The New York Times*, January 15, 1978.

RASKIN, MARCUS G. *Being and Doing.* New York: Random House, 1971.

RATHER, DAN, and GATES, GARY PAUL. *The Palace Guard.* New York: Harper & Row, 1974.

REDDIN, W. J. *Managerial Effectiveness.* New York: McGraw-Hill Book Co., 1970.

REICH, CHARLES. *The Greening of America.* New York: Random House, 1970.

REISS, ALBERT J., JR. *The Police and the Public.* New Haven, Conn.: Yale University Press, 1971.

RICE, A. K. *Productivity and Social Organization.* London: Tavistock Publications Ltd., 1958.

————. *The Enterprise and Its Environment.* London: Tavistock Publications Ltd., 1963.

RICE, BERKELEY. "Skinner: The Important Influence in Psychology," *New York Times Magazine*, March 17, 1968.

RIDGWAY, W. F. "Dysfunctional Consequences of Performance Measurement." In A. H. Rubenstein and C. J. Haberstroh (eds.), *Some Theories of Organization.* Rev. ed. Homewood, Ill.: Richard D. Irwin, 1966.

RIESMAN, DAVID. *The Lonely Crowd.* New Haven, Conn.: Yale University Press, 1950.

RIM, YESHAYAHU. "Who Are the Risk-Takers in Decision Making?" *Personnel Administration*, March–April 1966.

ROBERTS, EDWARD B. ed., *Managerial Applications of System Dynamics.* Cambridge, Mass.: MIT Press, 1978.

ROCKART, JOHN F. "Chief Executives Define Their Own Data Needs." *Harvard Business Review*, March–April 1979.

ROETHLISBERGER, F. J. *Management and Morale.* Cambridge, Mass.: Harvard University Press, 1943.

————. "The Foreman: Master and Victim of Double Talk." *Harvard Business Review*, vol. 23 (1945), pp. 283–98.

————, and DICKSON, W. J. *Management and the Worker.* Cambridge, Mass.: Harvard University Press, 1959.

ROGERS, C. R., and SKINNER, B. F. "Some Issues Concerning the Control of Human Behavior: A Symposium." *Science*, vol. 124 (1956), pp. 1057–66.

ROMMETVEIT, R. *Social Norms and Roles.* Minneapolis: University of Minnesota Press, 1954.

ROSEN, STEPHEN. *Future Facts.* New York: Simon and Schuster, 1976.

ROSZAK, THEODORE. *The Making of a Counter Culture.* Garden City, N.Y.: Doubleday & Co., 1969.

ROWAN, ROY. "Watch Out for Chemical Reactions at the Top." *Fortune*, September 25, 1978.

————. "Keeping the Clock from Running Out." *Fortune*, November 6, 1978.

ROY, DONALD F. "Quota Restriction and Gold-Bricking in a Machine Shop." *American Journal of Sociology,* vol. 57 (March 1952), pp. 430–37.

―――――. "Banana Time: Job Satisfaction and Informal Interaction." *Human Organization,* vol. 18 (1960), pp. 158–68.

SALANCIK, GERALD R., and PFEFFER, JEFFREY. "An Examination of Need-Satisfaction Models of Job Attitudes." *Administrative Science Quarterly,* vol. 22 (September 1977), p. 453.

SALES, S. M. "Organizational Role as a Risk Factor in Coronary Disease." *Administrative Science Quarterly,* vol. 14 (1969), pp. 325–36.

SANFORD, N. "Will Psychologists Study Human Problems?" *American Psychologist,* vol. 20 (1965), pp. 192–202.

SCHEIN, EDGAR H. "Interpersonal Communication, Group Solidarity, and Social Influence." *Sociometry,* vol. 23 (1960), pp. 148–61.

―――――. "Management Development as a Process of Influence." *Industrial Management Review,* vol. 2 (1961), pp. 59–77.

―――――. *Process Consultation.* Reading, Mass.: Addison-Wesley Publishing Co., 1969.

―――――. *Organizational Psychology.* 2nd ed. Englewood Cliffs, N.J.: Prentice-Hall, 1970.

SCHEIN, VIRGINIA E. "Relationships between Sex Role Stereotypes and Requisite Management Characteristics among Female Managers." *Journal of Applied Psychology,* 1975, pp. 340–44.

SCHELLING, THOMAS C. *Strategy of Conflict.* Cambridge, Mass.: Harvard University Press, 1966.

SCHRANK, ROBERT. *Ten Thousand Working Days.* Cambridge, Mass.: MIT Press, 1978.

SCHUMACHER, ERNST F. *Small Is Beautiful: Economics as if People Mattered.* New York: Harper & Row, 1973.

SCHUMPETER, JOSEPH A. *The Theory of Economic Development.* Trans. Redvers Opie. Cambridge, Mass.: Harvard University Press, 1934.

SCHUYTEN, PETER J. "The Metamorphosis of a Salesman." *The New York Times,* February 25, 1979, Sect. 3, p. 1.

―――――. "Winning and Losing at Texas Instruments." *The New York Times,* May 13, 1979, Sect. 3.

SCOTT, W. C. *The Management of Conflict.* Homewood, Ill.: Richard D. Irwin, 1965.

SEASHORE, STANLEY E. "Administrative Leadership and Organizational Effectiveness." In R. Lickert and S. P. Hayes, Jr. (eds.), *Some Applications of Behavioral Research.* Paris: UNESCO, 1957.

―――――, and YUCHTMAN, E. "Factorial Analysis of Organizational Performance." *Administrative Science Quarterly,* vol. 12 (December 1967), pp. 377–95.

SEEMAN, M. "On the Personal Consequences of Alienation in Work." *American Sociological Review,* vol. 32 (1967).

―――――. "The Urban Alienations: Some Dubious Theses from Marx to Marcuse." *Journal of Personality and Social Psychology,* vol. 19 (1971), pp. 135–43.

SELYE, HANS. *The Stress of Life.* New York: Mc-Graw-Hill Book Co., 1956.

SELZNICK, P. *T.V.A. and Grass Roots.* Berkeley: University of California Press, 1949.

————. *Leadership in Administration.* London: Row Peterson, 1957.

SERVAN-SCHREIBER, JEAN-JACQUES. *The American Challenge.* New York: Atheneum, 1968.

SHANNON, C. E., and WEAVER, W. *A Mathematical Theory of Communication.* Urbana: University of Illinois Press, 1949.

SHEPPARD, HAROLD L., and HERRICK, NEAL. *Where Have All the Robots Gone?* New York: Free Press, 1972.

SHERIF, MUZAFER. "Experiments on Group Conflict and Cooperation." *Scientific American,* vol. 195 (November 1956), pp. 54–58.

SIDNEY, E., and BROWN, M. *The Skills of Interviewing.* London: Tavistock Publications, 1961.

SIEGMAN, J.; BAKER, N. R.; and RUBENSTEIN, A. H. "The Effects of Perceived Needs and Means on the Generation of Ideas for Industrial R&D Projects." *IEEE Transactions on Engineering Management,* December 1967.

SIFFORD, DARRELL. "U.S. School Desegregation: Has It Been a Success?" *The Gazette* (Montreal), Thursday, October 12, 1978.

SIMON, HERBERT A. *Administrative Behavior.* New York: Macmillan Co., 1945.

————. "Recent Advances in Organization Theory." In Stephen K. Bailey et al., *Research Frontiers in Politics and Government: Brookings Lectures, 1955.* Washington, D.C.: Brookings Institution, 1955.

————. *Models of Man.* New York: John Wiley & Sons, 1957.

SIMPSON, R. L. "Vertical and Horizontal Communication in Formal Organizations." *Administrative Science Quarterly,* vol. 4 (September 1959), pp. 188–96.

SINGER, J. D. "The Political Science of Human Conflict." In E. B. McNeil (ed.), *The Nature of Conflict.* Englewood Cliffs, N.J.: Prentice-Hall, 1965.

SKINNER, B. F. *Walden Two.* New York: Macmillan Co., 1948.

————. *Science and Human Behavior.* New York: Macmillan Co., 1953.

————. *Beyond Freedom and Dignity.* New York: Alfred A. Knopf, 1971.

SLOAN, A. P. *My Years with General Motors.* Garden City, N.Y.: Doubleday & Co., 1964.

SMARDON, RAYMOND A. "In Collective Bargaining, The 'Winner' Can Be a Loser." *Harvard Business Review,* July–August 1976, p. 7.

SMITH, ADAM. *The Wealth of Nations: Representative Selections.* Bruce Mazlish, ed. New York: The Bobbs-Merrill Co., 1961.

SMITH, E. E., and KNIGHT, S. S. "Effects of Feedback on Insight and Problem-Solving Efficiency in Training Groups." *Journal of Applied Psychology,* vol. 43 (1959), pp. 209–11.

SMITH, FRANK J., and PORTER, LYMAN W. "What Do Executives Really Think About Their Organizations?" *Organizational Dynamics*, vol. 6, no. 6 (1977), pp. 68–80.

SMITH, LEE. "Executives and the Mid-Life Crisis." *Dun's Review*, June 1965.

SOMMER, R. "Small Group Ecology." *Psychological Bulletin*, vol. 67 (1967). pp. 145–52.

————. *Personal Space*. Englewood Cliffs, N.J.: Prentice-Hall, 1968.

STONER, J. A. F. "Risky and Cautious Shifts in Group Decisions: The Influence of Widely Held Values." *Journal of Experimental Social Psychology*, vol. 4 (1968), pp. 442–59.

STRAUSS, GEORGE. "Some Notes on Power Equalization." In Harold J. Leavitt (ed.), *The Social Science of Organizations*. Englewood Cliffs, N.J.: Prentice-Hall, 1963.

————. "Organizational Development: Credits and Debits." *Organizational Dynamics*, Winter 1973, pp. 2–18.

STROTHER, G. B. *Social Science Approaches to Business Behavior*. Homewood, Ill.: Richard D. Irwin, 1962.

SUPER, DONALD E., and HALL, DOUGLAS T. "Career Development: Exploration and Planning." *Annual Review of Psychology*, vol. 29, 1978.

SYMONDS, CHARLES P. "Uses and Abuse of the Term Flying Stress." In Air Ministry, *Psychological Disorders in Flying Personnel of the RAF Investigated during the War, 1939–45*. London: H.M. Stationery Office, 1947.

TAYLOR, FREDERICK W. *Principles of Scientific Management*. New York: Harper & Bros., 1947.

TERKEL, STUDS. *Working: People Talk about What They Do All Day and How They Feel about What They Do*. New York: Random House, Pantheon Books, 1974.

TERREBERRY, SHIRLEY. "The Organization of Environments." Unpublished doctoral dissertation, University of Michigan, 1968.

————. "The Evolution of Organizational Environments." *Administrative Science Quarterly*, vol. 12 (March 1968), pp. 590–613.

THAYER, LEE. *Communications and Communication Systems*. Homewood, Ill.: Richard D. Irwin, 1968.

THOMAS, E. J., and FINK, C. F. "Effects of Group Size." *Psychological Bulletin*, vol. 60 (1963), pp. 371–84.

THOMAS, KENNETH. "Conflict and Conflict Management." In Marvin D. Dunnette (ed.), *Handbook of Industrial and Organizational Psychology*. Chicago: Rand McNally College Publishing Co., 1976.

THOMPSON, JAMES D. *Organizations in Action*. New York: McGraw-Hill Book Co., 1967.

THOMPSON, WILLIAM IRWIN. *At the Edge of History*. New York: Harper & Row, 1971.

THURSTONE, L. L. "Primary Mental Abilities." *Psychometric Monograph*, No. 1, 1938.

TIGER, LIONEL. *Men in Groups*. London: Nelson, 1969.

TILLES, SEYMOUR. "The Manager's Job: A Systems Approach." *Harvard Business Review*, vol. 41 (January–February 1963), pp. 73–81.

TOFFLER, ALVIN. *Future Shock*. New York: Bantam Books, 1970.

TORRANCE, E. P. "Function of Expressed Disagreement in Small Group Processes." In A. H. Rubenstein and C. J. Haberstroh (eds.), *Some Theories of Organization*. Homewood, Ill.: Richard D. Irwin, 1966.

TOWNSEND, ROBERT. *Up the Organization*. New York: Alfred A. Knopf, Inc., 1970.

TRIST, E. L., and BAMFORTH, K. W. "Some Social and Psychological Consequences of the Long-Wall Method of Coal-Getting." *Human Relations*, vol. 4 (1951).

————, and SOFER, C. *Exploration in Group Relations*. Leicester: Leicester University Press, 1959.

TURNER, A. N., and LAWRENCE, P. R. *Industrial Jobs and the Worker: An Investigation of Response to Task Attributes*. Boston: Harvard University Press, 1965.

TURNER, G. *The Car Makers*. London: Eyre & Spottiswoode, 1963.

URWICK, LYNDALL. *The Elements of Administration*. New York: Harper & Row, 1943.

U.S. DEPARTMENT OF HEALTH, EDUCATION, AND WELFARE. *Work in America*. Washington, D.C.: U.S. Government Printing Office, 1973.

VAILLANT, GEORGE E. *Adaptation to Life*. Boston: Little, Brown & Co., 1977.

VERNON, RAYMOND. *Sovereignty at Bay*. New York: Basic Books, 1971.

VON BERTALANFFY, LUDWIG. "The Theory of Open Systems in Physics and Biology." *Science*, vol. 3 (January 1950), pp. 23–29.

————. *General Systems Theory*. New York: George Braziller, 1968.

VROOM, VICTOR. "Some Personality Determinants of the Effects of Participation." *Journal of Abnormal and Social Psychology*, vol. 59 (November 1959), pp. 322–27.

————. *Work and Motivation*. New York: John Wiley & Sons, 1964.

WALKER, C. R., and GUEST, R. H. *The Man on the Assembly Line*. Cambridge, Mass.: Harvard University Press, 1952.

WALKER, N. *A Short History of Psychotherapy*. London: Routledge and Kegan Paul, 1957.

WALLACH, M. A., and KOGAN, N. "The Roles of Information and Consensus in Group Risk Taking." *Journal of Experimental Social Psychology*, vol. 1 (1965), pp. 1–19.

WALTON, RICHARD E., and DUTTON, JOHN M. "The Management of Interdepartmental Conflict." *Administrative Science Quarterly*, vol. 14 (March 1969).

————, and MCKERZIE, R. B. *A Behavioral Theory of Labor Negotiations: An Analysis of a Social Interaction System*. New York: McGraw-Hill Book Co., 1965.

————, and SCHLESINGER, LEONARD A. "Do Supervisors Thrive in Participative Work Systems?" *Organizational Dynamics,* Winter 1979, pp. 25–38.

WATSON, PETER. *War on the Mind: The Military Uses and Abuses of Power.* New York: Basic Books, 1978.

WEBBER, ROSS A. *Management: Basic Elements of Managing Organizations.* Homewood, Ill.: Richard D. Irwin, 1975.

WEBER, MAX. *The Protestant Ethic and the Spirit of Capitalism.* New York: Charles Scribner's Sons, 1958 (first ed., London: Allen and Unwin, 1930).

————. *From Max Weber* (ed. H. H. Gerth and C. W. Mills). London: Oxford University Press, 1946.

WEICK, KARL E. "Organization Design: Organizations as Self-Designing Systems." *Organizational Dynamics,* Autumn 1977.

WELLS, H. G. *Mind at the End of Its Tether.* New York: Didire, 1946.

WHEELIS, ALLEN. *Quest for Identity.* New York: W. W. Norton & Co., 1966.

WHITEHEAD, R. "The Cybernetic Approach in Business." *Scientific Business,* vol. 3, no. 9 (May 1965).

WHITEHEAD, T. N. *Leadership in a Free Society.* London: Oxford University Press, 1936.

WHITMAN, R. M. "Psychodynamic Principles Underlying T-Group Processes." In L. P. Bradford, J. R. Gibb, and K. D. Benne (eds.), *T-Group Theory and Laboratory Method.* New York: John Wiley & Sons, 1964.

WHITSETT, DAVID A. "Where Are Your Unenriched Jobs?" *Harvard Business Review,* January–February 1975.

————, and WINSLOW, E. K. "At Analysis of Studies Critical of the Motivator-Hygiene Theory." *Personnel Psychology,* vol. 20, (Winter 1967).

WHYTE, W. F. *Street Corner Society, The Social Structure of an Italian Slum.* Chicago: University of Chicago Press, 1943.

————. "The Social Structure of the Restaurant." *American Journal of Sociology,* vol. 54 (1949), pp. 302–10.

WHYTE, W. H., JR. "How Hard Do Executives Work?" *Fortune,* January 1954.

————. *The Organization Man.* New York: Simon & Schuster, 1956.

WIENER, NORBERT. *Cybernetics.* Cambridge, Mass.: MIT Press, and New York: John Wiley & Sons, 1961.

WILENSKY, H. L. *Organizational Intelligence, Knowledge and Policy in Government and Industry.* New York: Basic Books, 1967.

WILLIAMS, JONATHAN. "A Life Spent on One Problem." *The New York Times,* November 26, 1978.

WILSON, EDWARD O. *Sociobiology: The New Synthesis.* Cambridge, Mass.: Belknap Press of Harvard University Press, 1975.

WOLFF, HAROLD. *Stress and Disease.* 2d ed. Springfield, Ill.: C. C Thomas Press, 1968.

WOODWARD, JOAN. "Management and Technology." *Problems and Progress in Industry.* London: H.M. Stationery Office, 1958.

————. "Industrial Behaviour—Is There a Science?" *New Society,* October 1964.

———— (ed.). *Industrial Organization: Theory and Practice.* New York: Oxford University Press, 1965.

———— (ed.). *Industrial Organization: Behaviour and Control.* New York: Oxford University Press, 1970.

WOODWORTH, R. S., and SCHLOSBERG, H. *Experimental Psychology.* Rev. ed. New York: Henry Holt & Co., 1955.

WORTHY, J. C. "Organizational Structure and Employee Morale." *American Sociological Review,* vol. 15 (1950), pp. 169–79.

YANKELOVICH, DANIEL. *The Changing Values on Campus: Political and Personal Attitudes on Campus.* New York: Washington Square Press, 1972.

ZALKIND, SHELDON C., and COSTELLO, T. W. "Perception: Some Recent Research and Implications for Administration." *Administrative Science Quarterly,* September 1962, pp. 218–235.

ZUCKERMANN, S. *The Social Life of Monkeys and Apes.* London: Routledge and Kegan Paul, 1932.

Acknowledgments

In addition to the source references given in the Bibliography and in the credit lines of boxes and figures, the publishers of the following selections have requested that acknowledgment be given as follows:

Selection on pp. 44–45, by F. W. Taylor (pp. 43–46). Copyright, 1911 by Frederick W. Taylor; renewed 1939 by Louise M. S. Taylor. Reprinted by permission of Harper & Row, Publishers.

Selections on pp. 79–80 from "Hawthorne Revisited: The Legend and the Legacy," by William F. Dowling, editor, reprinted by permission of the publisher from *Organizational Dynamics*, Winter 1975, pp. 66–80. © 1975 by AMACOM, a division of the American Management Associations.

Selection on p. 80 from *The Sane Society*, by Eric Fromm. Reprinted by permission of Holt, Rinehart and Winston, Inc., Publishers.

Quotations on pp. 82–83 and 361 from Studs Terkel, *Working: People Talk about What They Do All Day and How They Feel about What They Do*. © 1974 Pantheon Books, a division of Random House, Inc.

Selections on p. 86 from *Social Standing in America*, by Richard P. Coleman and Lee Rainwater. © 1978 by Basic Books, Inc.

Selections on pp. 92–93 from John F. Donnelley, "Participative Management at Work," *Harvard Business Review*, January–February 1977. Copyright © 1976 by the President and Fellows of Harvard College; all rights reserved.

Selection on pp. 93–94 from Pehr G. Gyllenhammar, "How Volvo Adapts Work to People," *Harvard Business Review*, July–August 1977. Copyright © 1977 by the President and Fellows of Harvard College; all rights reserved.

nizational Dynamics, Winter 1973. © 1973 by AMACOM, a division of the American Management Associations.

Selection on p. 254 from *Walden Two* by B. F. Skinner, copyright 1948 by the Macmillan Publishing Co., Inc.

Selections on p. 256 from Peter Watson, *War on the Mind: The Military Uses and Abuses of Psychology*. © 1978 by Peter Watson, Basic Books, Inc., Publishers, New York.

Selection on p. 327 from "Management Tunes in on Employee Gripes," *The New York Times*, Sunday, October 16, 1977. © 1977 by The New York Times Company.

Selections on p. 330 from Lena L. Lucietto, "Speech Patterns of Administrators," *Administrator's Notebook*, vol. 18, no. 5. The *Administrator's Notebook* is published by the Midwest Administration Center of the University of Chicago.

Sections on pp. 333–35 and 346–47 from Anthony Jay, "How to Run a Meeting," *Harvard Business Review*, March–April 1976. Copyright © 1976 by the President and Fellows of Harvard College; all rights reserved.

Selections on pp. 347–48 and 516–17 from *Victims of Groupthink* by Irving L. Janis. Copyright © 1972 by Houghton Mifflin Company. Reprinted by permission of the publisher.

Selections on pp. 387–88 reprinted by permission from *Time*, The Weekly Newsmagazine, June 12, 1978. Copyright Time, Inc., 1978.

Selection on p. 395 from "A Rare Hamburger Headquarters." Reprinted by permission from *Time*, The Weekly Newsmagazine, February 28, 1972. Copyright, Time, Inc., 1972.

Selections on pp. 406 and 605–6 from Karl E. Weick, "Organization Design: Organizations as Self-Designing Systems," *Organizational Dynamics*, Autumn, 1977. © 1977 by AMACOM, a division of American Management Associations.

Selections on p. 412 from Irving Kristol, *Two Cheers for Capitalism*. © 1978 by Basic Books, Inc., Publishers, New York.

Selections on pp. 425–27 from John P. Kotter, "Power, Dependence, and Effective Management," *Harvard Business Review*, July–August 1977. Copyright © 1977 by the President and Fellows of Harvard College; all rights reserved.

Selection on p. 429 from David C. McClelland and David H. Burnham, "Power Is the Great Motivator," *Harvard Business Review*, March–April 1976. Copyright © 1976 by the President and Fellows of Harvard College; all rights reserved.

Selection on pp. 463–64 from *The New York Times*, May 13, 1979, Section 3. © 1979 by The New York Times Company.

Selection on pp. 476–77 from Jay Galbraith, *Designing Complex Organizations*, p. 15. © 1973, Addison-Wesley Publishing Company, Reading, Massachusetts. Reprinted with permission.

Selection on pp. 481–83 from *The New York Times*, Sunday, September 25, 1977. © 1977 by The New York Times Company.

Name index

Subject index

*This book has been set VIP in 10 and 9 point
Caledonia, leaded 2 points. Part and chapter
numbers are Caslon #540 Roman. Part titles
are 20 point Palatino and chapter titles are 18
point Palatino. The size of the type page is 27
by 46½ picas.*